Lecture Notes in Computer Science 8526

Commenced Publication in 1973
Founding and Former Series Editors:
Gerhard Goos, Juris Hartmanis, and Jan van Leeuwen

Foreword

The 16th International Conference on Human–Computer Interaction, HCI International 2014, was held in Heraklion, Crete, Greece, during June 22–27, 2014, incorporating 14 conferences/thematic areas:

Thematic areas:

- Human–Computer Interaction
- Human Interface and the Management of Information

Affiliated conferences:

- 11th International Conference on Engineering Psychology and Cognitive Ergonomics
- 8th International Conference on Universal Access in Human-Computer Interaction
- 6th International Conference on Virtual, Augmented and Mixed Reality
- 6th International Conference on Cross-Cultural Design
- 6th International Conference on Social Computing and Social Media
- 8th International Conference on Augmented Cognition
- 5th International Conference on Digital Human Modeling and Applications in Health, Safety, Ergonomics and Risk Management
- Third International Conference on Design, User Experience and Usability
- Second International Conference on Distributed, Ambient and Pervasive Interactions
- Second International Conference on Human Aspects of Information Security, Privacy and Trust
- First International Conference on HCI in Business
- First International Conference on Learning and Collaboration Technologies

A total of 4,766 individuals from academia, research institutes, industry, and governmental agencies from 78 countries submitted contributions, and 1,476 papers and 225 posters were included in the proceedings. These papers address the latest research and development efforts and highlight the human aspects of design and use of computing systems. The papers thoroughly cover the entire field of human–computer interaction, addressing major advances in knowledge and effective use of computers in a variety of application areas.

This volume, edited by Randall Shumaker and Stephanie Lackey, contains papers focusing on the thematic area of virtual, augmented and mixed reality, addressing the following major topics:

- VAMR in education and cultural heritage
- Games and entertainment

- Medical, health and rehabilitation applications
- Industrial, safety and military applications

The remaining volumes of the HCI International 2014 proceedings are:

- Volume 1, LNCS 8510, Human–Computer Interaction: HCI Theories, Methods and Tools (Part I), edited by Masaaki Kurosu
- Volume 2, LNCS 8511, Human–Computer Interaction: Advanced Interaction Modalities and Techniques (Part II), edited by Masaaki Kurosu
- Volume 3, LNCS 8512, Human–Computer Interaction: Applications and Services (Part III), edited by Masaaki Kurosu
- Volume 4, LNCS 8513, Universal Access in Human–Computer Interaction: Design and Development Methods for Universal Access (Part I), edited by Constantine Stephanidis and Margherita Antona
- Volume 5, LNCS 8514, Universal Access in Human–Computer Interaction: Universal Access to Information and Knowledge (Part II), edited by Constantine Stephanidis and Margherita Antona
- Volume 6, LNCS 8515, Universal Access in Human–Computer Interaction: Aging and Assistive Environments (Part III), edited by Constantine Stephanidis and Margherita Antona
- Volume 7, LNCS 8516, Universal Access in Human–Computer Interaction: Design for All and Accessibility Practice (Part IV), edited by Constantine Stephanidis and Margherita Antona
- Volume 8, LNCS 8517, Design, User Experience, and Usability: Theories, Methods and Tools for Designing the User Experience (Part I), edited by Aaron Marcus
- Volume 9, LNCS 8518, Design, User Experience, and Usability: User Experience Design for Diverse Interaction Platforms and Environments (Part II), edited by Aaron Marcus
- Volume 10, LNCS 8519, Design, User Experience, and Usability: User Experience Design for Everyday Life Applications and Services (Part III), edited by Aaron Marcus
- Volume 11, LNCS 8520, Design, User Experience, and Usability: User Experience Design Practice (Part IV), edited by Aaron Marcus
- Volume 12, LNCS 8521, Human Interface and the Management of Information: Information and Knowledge Design and Evaluation (Part I), edited by Sakae Yamamoto
- Volume 13, LNCS 8522, Human Interface and the Management of Information: Information and Knowledge in Applications and Services (Part II), edited by Sakae Yamamoto
- Volume 14, LNCS 8523, Learning and Collaboration Technologies: Designing and Developing Novel Learning Experiences (Part I), edited by Panayiotis Zaphiris and Andri Ioannou
- Volume 15, LNCS 8524, Learning and Collaboration Technologies: Technology-rich Environments for Learning and Collaboration (Part II), edited by Panayiotis Zaphiris and Andri Ioannou

- Volume 16, LNCS 8525, Virtual, Augmented and Mixed Reality: Designing and Developing Virtual and Augmented Environments (Part I), edited by Randall Shumaker and Stephanie Lackey
- Volume 18, LNCS 8527, HCI in Business, edited by Fiona Fui-Hoon Nah
- Volume 19, LNCS 8528, Cross-Cultural Design, edited by P.L. Patrick Rau
- Volume 20, LNCS 8529, Digital Human Modeling and Applications in Health, Safety, Ergonomics and Risk Management, edited by Vincent G. Duffy
- Volume 21, LNCS 8530, Distributed, Ambient, and Pervasive Interactions, edited by Norbert Streitz and Panos Markopoulos
- Volume 22, LNCS 8531, Social Computing and Social Media, edited by Gabriele Meiselwitz
- Volume 23, LNAI 8532, Engineering Psychology and Cognitive Ergonomics, edited by Don Harris
- Volume 24, LNCS 8533, Human Aspects of Information Security, Privacy and Trust, edited by Theo Tryfonas and Ioannis Askoxylakis
- Volume 25, LNAI 8534, Foundations of Augmented Cognition, edited by Dylan D. Schmorrow and Cali M. Fidopiastis
- Volume 26, CCIS 434, HCI International 2014 Posters Proceedings (Part I), edited by Constantine Stephanidis
- Volume 27, CCIS 435, HCI International 2014 Posters Proceedings (Part II), edited by Constantine Stephanidis

I would like to thank the Program Chairs and the members of the Program Boards of all affiliated conferences and thematic areas, listed below, for their contribution to the highest scientific quality and the overall success of the HCI International 2014 Conference.

This conference could not have been possible without the continuous support and advice of the founding chair and conference scientific advisor, Prof. Gavriel Salvendy, as well as the dedicated work and outstanding efforts of the communications chair and editor of *HCI International News*, Dr. Abbas Moallem.

I would also like to thank for their contribution towards the smooth organization of the HCI International 2014 Conference the members of the Human–Computer Interaction Laboratory of ICS-FORTH, and in particular George Paparoulis, Maria Pitsoulaki, Maria Bouhli, and George Kapnas.

April 2014   Constantine Stephanidis
                                    General Chair, HCI International 2014

Organization

Human–Computer Interaction

Program Chair: Masaaki Kurosu, Japan

Jose Abdelnour-Nocera, UK
Sebastiano Bagnara, Italy
Simone Barbosa, Brazil
Adriana Betiol, Brazil
Simone Borsci, UK
Henry Duh, Australia
Xiaowen Fang, USA
Vicki Hanson, UK
Wonil Hwang, Korea
Minna Isomursu, Finland
Yong Gu Ji, Korea
Anirudha Joshi, India
Esther Jun, USA
Kyungdoh Kim, Korea

Heidi Krömker, Germany
Chen Ling, USA
Chang S. Nam, USA
Naoko Okuizumi, Japan
Philippe Palanque, France
Ling Rothrock, USA
Naoki Sakakibara, Japan
Dominique Scapin, France
Guangfeng Song, USA
Sanjay Tripathi, India
Chui Yin Wong, Malaysia
Toshiki Yamaoka, Japan
Kazuhiko Yamazaki, Japan
Ryoji Yoshitake, Japan

Human Interface and the Management of Information

Program Chair: Sakae Yamamoto, Japan

Alan Chan, Hong Kong
Denis A. Coelho, Portugal
Linda Elliott, USA
Shin'ichi Fukuzumi, Japan
Michitaka Hirose, Japan
Makoto Itoh, Japan
Yen-Yu Kang, Taiwan
Koji Kimita, Japan
Daiji Kobayashi, Japan

Hiroyuki Miki, Japan
Hirohiko Mori, Japan
Shogo Nishida, Japan
Robert Proctor, USA
Youngho Rhee, Korea
Ryosuke Saga, Japan
Katsunori Shimohara, Japan
Kim-Phuong Vu, USA
Tomio Watanabe, Japan

Engineering Psychology and Cognitive Ergonomics

Program Chair: Don Harris, UK

Guy Andre Boy, USA
Shan Fu, P.R. China
Hung-Sying Jing, Taiwan
Wen-Chin Li, Taiwan
Mark Neerincx, The Netherlands
Jan Noyes, UK
Paul Salmon, Australia

Axel Schulte, Germany
Siraj Shaikh, UK
Sarah Sharples, UK
Anthony Smoker, UK
Neville Stanton, UK
Alex Stedmon, UK
Andrew Thatcher, South Africa

Universal Access in Human–Computer Interaction

**Program Chairs: Constantine Stephanidis, Greece,
and Margherita Antona, Greece**

Julio Abascal, Spain
Gisela Susanne Bahr, USA
João Barroso, Portugal
Margrit Betke, USA
Anthony Brooks, Denmark
Christian Bühler, Germany
Stefan Carmien, Spain
Hua Dong, P.R. China
Carlos Duarte, Portugal
Pier Luigi Emiliani, Italy
Qin Gao, P.R. China
Andrina Granić, Croatia
Andreas Holzinger, Austria
Josette Jones, USA
Simeon Keates, UK

Georgios Kouroupetroglou, Greece
Patrick Langdon, UK
Barbara Leporini, Italy
Eugene Loos, The Netherlands
Ana Isabel Paraguay, Brazil
Helen Petrie, UK
Michael Pieper, Germany
Enrico Pontelli, USA
Jaime Sanchez, Chile
Alberto Sanna, Italy
Anthony Savidis, Greece
Christian Stary, Austria
Hirotada Ueda, Japan
Gerhard Weber, Germany
Harald Weber, Germany

Virtual, Augmented and Mixed Reality

**Program Chairs: Randall Shumaker, USA,
and Stephanie Lackey, USA**

Roland Blach, Germany
Sheryl Brahnam, USA
Juan Cendan, USA
Jessie Chen, USA
Panagiotis D. Kaklis, UK

Hirokazu Kato, Japan
Denis Laurendeau, Canada
Fotis Liarokapis, UK
Michael Macedonia, USA
Gordon Mair, UK

Jose San Martin, Spain
Tabitha Peck, USA
Christian Sandor, Australia

Christopher Stapleton, USA
Gregory Welch, USA

Cross-Cultural Design

Program Chair: P.L. Patrick Rau, P.R. China

Yee-Yin Choong, USA
Paul Fu, USA
Zhiyong Fu, P.R. China
Pin-Chao Liao, P.R. China
Dyi-Yih Michael Lin, Taiwan
Rungtai Lin, Taiwan
Ta-Ping (Robert) Lu, Taiwan
Liang Ma, P.R. China
Alexander Mädche, Germany

Sheau-Farn Max Liang, Taiwan
Katsuhiko Ogawa, Japan
Tom Plocher, USA
Huatong Sun, USA
Emil Tso, P.R. China
Hsiu-Ping Yueh, Taiwan
Liang (Leon) Zeng, USA
Jia Zhou, P.R. China

Online Communities and Social Media

Program Chair: Gabriele Meiselwitz, USA

Leonelo Almeida, Brazil
Chee Siang Ang, UK
Aneesha Bakharia, Australia
Ania Bobrowicz, UK
James Braman, USA
Farzin Deravi, UK
Carsten Kleiner, Germany
Niki Lambropoulos, Greece
Soo Ling Lim, UK

Anthony Norcio, USA
Portia Pusey, USA
Panote Siriaraya, UK
Stefan Stieglitz, Germany
Giovanni Vincenti, USA
Yuanqiong (Kathy) Wang, USA
June Wei, USA
Brian Wentz, USA

Augmented Cognition

**Program Chairs: Dylan D. Schmorrow, USA,
and Cali M. Fidopiastis, USA**

Ahmed Abdelkhalek, USA
Robert Atkinson, USA
Monique Beaudoin, USA
John Blitch, USA
Alenka Brown, USA

Rosario Cannavò, Italy
Joseph Cohn, USA
Andrew J. Cowell, USA
Martha Crosby, USA
Wai-Tat Fu, USA

Rodolphe Gentili, USA
Frederick Gregory, USA
Michael W. Hail, USA
Monte Hancock, USA
Fei Hu, USA
Ion Juvina, USA
Joe Keebler, USA
Philip Mangos, USA
Rao Mannepalli, USA
David Martinez, USA
Yvonne R. Masakowski, USA
Santosh Mathan, USA
Ranjeev Mittu, USA

Keith Niall, USA
Tatana Olson, USA
Debra Patton, USA
June Pilcher, USA
Robinson Pino, USA
Tiffany Poeppelman, USA
Victoria Romero, USA
Amela Sadagic, USA
Anna Skinner, USA
Ann Speed, USA
Robert Sottilare, USA
Peter Walker, USA

Digital Human Modeling and Applications in Health, Safety, Ergonomics and Risk Management

Program Chair: Vincent G. Duffy, USA

Giuseppe Andreoni, Italy
Daniel Carruth, USA
Elsbeth De Korte, The Netherlands
Afzal A. Godil, USA
Ravindra Goonetilleke, Hong Kong
Noriaki Kuwahara, Japan
Kang Li, USA
Zhizhong Li, P.R. China

Tim Marler, USA
Jianwei Niu, P.R. China
Michelle Robertson, USA
Matthias Rötting, Germany
Mao-Jiun Wang, Taiwan
Xuguang Wang, France
James Yang, USA

Design, User Experience, and Usability

Program Chair: Aaron Marcus, USA

Sisira Adikari, Australia
Claire Ancient, USA
Arne Berger, Germany
Jamie Blustein, Canada
Ana Boa-Ventura, USA
Jan Brejcha, Czech Republic
Lorenzo Cantoni, Switzerland
Marc Fabri, UK
Luciane Maria Fadel, Brazil
Tricia Flanagan, Hong Kong
Jorge Frascara, Mexico

Federico Gobbo, Italy
Emilie Gould, USA
Rüdiger Heimgärtner, Germany
Brigitte Herrmann, Germany
Steffen Hess, Germany
Nouf Khashman, Canada
Fabiola Guillermina Noël, Mexico
Francisco Rebelo, Portugal
Kerem Rızvanoğlu, Turkey
Marcelo Soares, Brazil
Carla Spinillo, Brazil

Distributed, Ambient and Pervasive Interactions

Program Chairs: Norbert Streitz, Germany,
and Panos Markopoulos, The Netherlands

Juan Carlos Augusto, UK
Jose Bravo, Spain
Adrian Cheok, UK
Boris de Ruyter, The Netherlands
Anind Dey, USA
Dimitris Grammenos, Greece
Nuno Guimaraes, Portugal
Achilles Kameas, Greece
Javed Vassilis Khan, The Netherlands
Shin'ichi Konomi, Japan
Carsten Magerkurth, Switzerland

Ingrid Mulder, The Netherlands
Anton Nijholt, The Netherlands
Fabio Paternó, Italy
Carsten Röcker, Germany
Teresa Romao, Portugal
Albert Ali Salah, Turkey
Manfred Tscheligi, Austria
Reiner Wichert, Germany
Woontack Woo, Korea
Xenophon Zabulis, Greece

Human Aspects of Information Security, Privacy and Trust

Program Chairs: Theo Tryfonas, UK,
and Ioannis Askoxylakis, Greece

Claudio Agostino Ardagna, Italy
Zinaida Benenson, Germany
Daniele Catteddu, Italy
Raoul Chiesa, Italy
Bryan Cline, USA
Sadie Creese, UK
Jorge Cuellar, Germany
Marc Dacier, USA
Dieter Gollmann, Germany
Kirstie Hawkey, Canada
Jaap-Henk Hoepman, The Netherlands
Cagatay Karabat, Turkey
Angelos Keromytis, USA
Ayako Komatsu, Japan
Ronald Leenes, The Netherlands
Javier Lopez, Spain
Steve Marsh, Canada

Gregorio Martinez, Spain
Emilio Mordini, Italy
Yuko Murayama, Japan
Masakatsu Nishigaki, Japan
Aljosa Pasic, Spain
Milan Petković, The Netherlands
Joachim Posegga, Germany
Jean-Jacques Quisquater, Belgium
Damien Sauveron, France
George Spanoudakis, UK
Kerry-Lynn Thomson, South Africa
Julien Touzeau, France
Theo Tryfonas, UK
João Vilela, Portugal
Claire Vishik, UK
Melanie Volkamer, Germany

HCI in Business

Program Chair: Fiona Fui-Hoon Nah, USA

Andreas Auinger, Austria
Michel Avital, Denmark
Traci Carte, USA
Hock Chuan Chan, Singapore
Constantinos Coursaris, USA
Soussan Djamasbi, USA
Brenda Eschenbrenner, USA
Nobuyuki Fukawa, USA
Khaled Hassanein, Canada
Milena Head, Canada
Susanna (Shuk Ying) Ho, Australia
Jack Zhenhui Jiang, Singapore
Jinwoo Kim, Korea
Zoonky Lee, Korea
Honglei Li, UK
Nicholas Lockwood, USA
Eleanor T. Loiacono, USA
Mei Lu, USA

Scott McCoy, USA
Brian Mennecke, USA
Robin Poston, USA
Lingyun Qiu, P.R. China
Rene Riedl, Austria
Matti Rossi, Finland
April Savoy, USA
Shu Schiller, USA
Hong Sheng, USA
Choon Ling Sia, Hong Kong
Chee-Wee Tan, Denmark
Chuan Hoo Tan, Hong Kong
Noam Tractinsky, Israel
Horst Treiblmaier, Austria
Virpi Tuunainen, Finland
Dezhi Wu, USA
I-Chin Wu, Taiwan

Learning and Collaboration Technologies

Program Chairs: Panayiotis Zaphiris, Cyprus, and Andri Ioannou, Cyprus

Ruthi Aladjem, Israel
Abdulaziz Aldaej, UK
John M. Carroll, USA
Maka Eradze, Estonia
Mikhail Fominykh, Norway
Denis Gillet, Switzerland
Mustafa Murat Inceoglu, Turkey
Pernilla Josefsson, Sweden
Marie Joubert, UK
Sauli Kiviranta, Finland
Tomaž Klobučar, Slovenia
Elena Kyza, Cyprus
Maarten de Laat, The Netherlands
David Lamas, Estonia

Edmund Laugasson, Estonia
Ana Loureiro, Portugal
Katherine Maillet, France
Nadia Pantidi, UK
Antigoni Parmaxi, Cyprus
Borzoo Pourabdollahian, Italy
Janet C. Read, UK
Christophe Reffay, France
Nicos Souleles, Cyprus
Ana Luísa Torres, Portugal
Stefan Trausan-Matu, Romania
Aimilia Tzanavari, Cyprus
Johnny Yuen, Hong Kong
Carmen Zahn, Switzerland

External Reviewers

Ilia Adami, Greece
Iosif Klironomos, Greece
Maria Korozi, Greece
Vassilis Kouroumalis, Greece

Asterios Leonidis, Greece
George Margetis, Greece
Stavroula Ntoa, Greece
Nikolaos Partarakis, Greece

HCI International 2015

The 15th International Conference on Human–Computer Interaction, HCI International 2015, will be held jointly with the affiliated conferences in Los Angeles, CA, USA, in the Westin Bonaventure Hotel, August 2–7, 2015. It will cover a broad spectrum of themes related to HCI, including theoretical issues, methods, tools, processes, and case studies in HCI design, as well as novel interaction techniques, interfaces, and applications. The proceedings will be published by Springer. More information will be available on the conference website: http://www.hcii2015.org/

General Chair
Professor Constantine Stephanidis
University of Crete and ICS-FORTH
Heraklion, Crete, Greece
E-mail: cs@ics.forth.gr

Table of Contents – Part II

VAMR in Education and Cultural Heritage

Games and Entertainment

Medical, Health and Rehabilitation Applications

Industrial, Safety and Military Applications

Table of Contents – Part I

Interaction Devices, Displays and Techniques in VAMR

Designing Virtual and Augmented Environments

Avatars and Virtual Characters

Developing Virtual and Augmented Environments

VAMR in Education
and Cultural Heritage

Touching the Past: Haptic Augmented Reality for Museum Artefacts

Mariza Dima[1], Linda Hurcombe[2], and Mark Wright[3]

[1]University of Edinburgh, Edinburgh, UK
mdima@exseed.ed.ac.uk
[2]University of Exeter, Exeter, UK
L.M.Hurcombe@exeter.ac.uk
[3]Liverpool John Moore University, Liverpool, UK
M.W.Wright@ljmu.ac.uk

Abstract. In this paper we propose a novel interaction technique that creates the illusion of tactile exploration of museum artefacts which are otherwise impossible to touch. The technique meets the contextual necessity, often requested by museum curators, to background technology and to direct the focus of the museum visitor's experience to the artefact itself. Our approach relies on the combination of haptic interaction and the adaptation of a well-known illusion that enables museum visitors to make sense of the actual physical non-touchable artefact in an embodied way, using their sensory and motor skills. We call this technique Haptic Augmented Reality.

Keywords: Museum, haptics, touch, authenticity, haptic augmented reality.

1   Introduction

Touch is part of a larger complex of senses which interrelates mental and bodily processes, the haptic sense. Haptic exploration is a fundamental experience that assists people in perceiving and making sense of the physical world around them. The sensory information of the museum exhibits, particularly surface texture and material, is particularly important for museum visitors since the artefacts themselves are the center of the social, educative and entertaining experience of a museum visit. Whilst the value of touch experiences can be debated there is a growing literature on sensory engagement in museums which seeks to redress the imbalance which has traditionally allowed the visual sense to dominate [10] [14].

The emphasis on touch experiences in heritage settings and museums has emerged as a distinctive trend from this exploration [6] [24] alongside discussions of sensory perceptions of materiality as social constructs within both past societies and our own with the two not necessarily coinciding [15]. The value of touch has thus received nuanced debate within museums studies and has been explored as a related set of sensory concepts [23]. A feature of the role of touch has been the emotional connections of objects and people and the charisma of objects where it is possible to see

R. Shumaker and S. Lackey (Eds.): VAMR 2014, Part II, LNCS 8526, pp. 3–14, 2014.

ancient artefacts displayed in museums as having an extended object biography bringing them into our contemporary cultural context [10] [16].

Within digital technologies and computer applications a number of views and directions have emerged but the heritage sector in general is seeing a range of developments in the applications of haptic and virtual presentations of objects within museums [11] [5] [8]. In the networking cluster described more fully below the concerns of heritage sector curators, exhibitions officers and conservators was not so much on the value of adding touch experiences to the museum experience but on how to balance curating the objects whilst providing touch experiences. The charisma of objects and the desire of people to touch them were acknowledged. Well-known objects were seen as particularly problematic. That is why the focus of the installations discussed here was one of the Lewis chess pieces as these objects are amongst the most popular artefacts in the whole of the collections within the National Museums Scotland.

2   Design Process

Virtual handling of museum artefacts lies within a complex context of different professional practices, technological development and end-user needs. As part of the Science and Heritage programme funded by EPSRC-AHRC, Linda Hurcombe led an international project bringing researchers from different disciplines into a networking cluster focused on 'Touching the Untouchable: increasing access to archaeological artefacts by virtual handling'.

It was therefore appropriate to adopt a design led user-centred approach that would bring the many experts involved in a creative dialogue. The interaction technique we present in this paper was one of the outcomes of two design-led workshops that took place for two days each over the period of six months. Many of the key-issues that are related to curatorial practice and technological development were described and discussed in the first workshop, and prototype ideas were developed and presented in a second workshop six months later. From the first meeting of this group it was evident that there were multiple issues faced by the heritage sector and many potential ideas for solutions.

The workshops involved 26 participants from 19 institutions and 6 countries. Disciplines included archaeology, conservation and curation together with art and interaction design, computer science and haptic human-computer interfaces. Representatives from small and national museum collections, artifact specialists, the National Trust, Historic Palaces, the Royal National Institute for the Blind attended and all presented different points of emphasis offering a richly textured insight into professional practices. The transdisciplinary nature of the first workshop allowed key issues to be raised and discussed from a plethora of perspectives, while design sessions involved participants in collaborative hands-on work and cultivated a number of ideas that were developed as first prototypes and evaluated in the second workshop.

On the first day participants gave short position presentations on their work and the key issues as they saw them. There were also demonstrations of museum specimens and haptic technology. The second day consisted of a plenary session where stakeholders discussed a broad range of themes and opportunities arising from the previous day. Topics included haptic device capabilities, archaeology research agendas, curation and end users and the potential benefits of virtual handling.

Key issues that were raised included:

- Haptic installations may deflect interest away from the ancient items on show both physically and conceptually.
- The technology for virtual touch needs not to overwhelm its physical setting e.g. a museum gallery and must be able to cope with the visitor numbers (i.e. size of machine, noise, ease of use)
- Can haptic experiences get away from the computer desktop?
- Products and solutions could be expected to be diverse according to the kind of user and their setting. Rapid-prototyping could be explored for its practical issues and scope.
- Financial mechanisms for public display varied and virtual technologies need to be assessed against the robustness of device and costs to set up and expertise to maintain them.

The focus of the present paper is on two of many more prototypes which were developed in response to these key issues and which were presented in the second workshop for testing and evaluation. They were well received by the stakeholders and after some corrections were made, they were deployed and evaluated in two museums: the National Museum of Scotland in Edinburgh and the Orkney Museum in Kirkwall. These evaluations and prototypes flowed from the first networking grant which pursued them to proof of concept stage. More recent work was undertaken as part of a second grant also led by Hurcombe within the Science and Heritage programme which allowed them along with some of the other ideas to be given more extensive public trials and development. The full range of installations developed is covered elsewhere [17] but here the focus is on one famous object presented in two contrasting ways.

3   The Prototypes

The museum exhibit that was used is an iconic 12th century Scottish artefact known as the Lewis Queen chess. The artefact is displayed in the National Museum of Scotland behind a glass case. Both prototypes use the same visual illusion but employ different media, one digital and one non-digital. The visual illusion is borrowed from the theatre tradition and is called Pepper's Ghost. A large sheet of glass is placed between the audience and the stage. A ghostly image of an actor below the stage is then projected onto the glass giving the illusion that a ghost is on stage with the actors. Using the Pepper's Ghost illusion we employed two different media, a 3-D printed replica of the chess piece and a haptic device. Both used the glass of the museum case itself as a reflective surface thus ensuring that the focus was the real object or the haptic experience.

The replica was created by laser scanning the original artefact, mirroring it to the original (i.e. lateral inversion of the scan data before printing) so that the user's experience would match the object in the case. The need to present mirror images as part of virtual reality and co-location interfaces is part of virtual reality issues [3] [18]. The replica was then painted black so that it would absorb light thereby reducing its reflection in the glass case. The replica is placed facing the chess piece at an equal distance from the display glass (Fig.1). When a user places her hands on the replica and concentrates her gaze at the original piece behind the glass, she can see her hands reflected in the glass apparently touching the real artefact in the display case (Fig.2). Because she sees the actual artefact (and her hands) and touches the replica she experiences the sensation that she is actually touching the artefact itself. The illusion is further strengthened by placing a cover over the replica to shield it from the user's direct gaze. This cover also contains a light to illuminate the user's hands so that their reflection is brighter.

Fig. 1. The Lewis Chess piece behind the glass and the mirrored 3-D printed replica

The second prototype uses the same illusion but employs a Sensable™ Omni 6DoF haptic device instead of the user's hands. The haptic device is placed outside the display case and positioned towards the left of where the replica was so that the reflection of the pen-like stylus of the haptic device is positioned close to the artefact in the display glass. Instead of a replica, a haptic model created from the laser scan of the artefact is algorithmically positioned into the haptic device's workspace at an equal distance from the display case (Fig.3). The haptic version is invisible but the model can be traced and felt in the physical space by moving the stylus using the same combined visual and haptic feedback as with the replica prototype.

Fig. 2. Visitor interaction with the replica. Her gaze is concentrated at the original artefact behind the glass

This is a novel way of using a haptic device for immersing museum visitors into a deep understanding of the museum exhibits. In [19] museum visitors explore the surface of a digital daguerreotype case from the collection of the Natural History Museum of Los Angeles County. Similarly, the Haptic Museum, developed in the University of Southern California, is a haptic interface that allows museum visitors to examine virtual museum artefacts with a haptic device [21]. The 'Museum of Pure Form' is a virtual reality system that allows the user to interact with virtual models of 3-D art forms and sculptures using haptic devices and small-scale haptic exoskeletons [1,2]. The Senses in Touch II, which was installed in the Hunterian Museum in Glasgow, was designed to allow blind and partially-sighted museum visitors, particularly children, to feel virtual objects in the collection via a PC and Wingman haptic mouse [13]. The projects described above have used detailed virtual models of the museum artefacts and allowed the visitor to explore them with the haptic technology. Our goal was to diverge from the computer screen, and use the haptic technology in a way that evokes direct haptic interaction with the physical artefact without actually touching it providing the illusion of doing so.

Equally, the Pepper's ghost technique has been used in the Virtual Showcase, a mirror-based interface for viewing real artefacts augmented with virtual geometry [3]. In Virtual Showcase no touch is used as the focus is on adding additional virtual objects and other elements onto the real object. ARToolkit-based optical tracking is used for tracking the user's head movement in real time to ensure collocation with the virtual components. Head tracking was important in the Virtual Showcase because of the virtual geometry. In our prototype no tracking of the head is required. As long as the

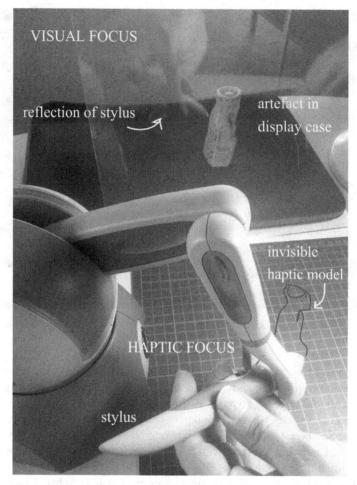

Fig. 3. The haptic device prototype

replica or the invisible haptic model are placed in exactly the same orientation and same distance from the surface of the glass case, the illusion of co-location is preserved under all translations and rotations of the viewing angle which preserve a direct line of sight from the viewpoint through the case wall to the real artefact.

3.1   Embodiment and Sense-Making

Our interaction with the world around us is embodied and multi-modal and we make sense of the world by enacting in it. Enactive knowledge is direct, in the sense that it is natural and intuitive, based on the perceptual array of motor acts. The goal of both prototypes was to create an embodied and immersive experience for the visitors in order to provide a sense of authenticity for the ancient artifact. Embodiment and situated cognition places interaction at the center of meaning making and extends the concept of mind to include the body and environment [25], [7], [22].

The illusion of manipulation that the presented interaction technique creates can be explained as directly analogous to a classic experiment in situated cognition and perceptual plasticity [20]. A subject places their hand on a table hidden behind a partition. On the other side of the partition they can see a dummy hand. Their real hand and dummy hand are touched by fingers of a researcher which are synchronized to touch in the same place at the same time but the subject can only see the finger that touches the dummy hand not the one that touches their real hand. After a short time the subject perceives the dummy hand to be their own. In the two prototypes, the visual stimulus of the researchers visible finger is replaced by the reflection of the users own hands or haptic probe. The synchronized haptic stimulus is provided by the subjects' fingers touching the replica or felt through the haptic device when it collides with the invisible virtual 3d model of the artefact. The haptic device enables haptic exploration and sense-making through multi-modal motor action which makes them an enactive interface [12]. The combination of haptic and visual feedback in both prototypes enriches the array of senses during the interactive experience and creates more dimensions of embodiment than having only visual cues.

4   Evaluation

The replica based prototype is created using digital technology of laser scanning, 3D modelling and rapid prototyping but is itself a non-digital tangible interface. It offers a simple, robust and apparently technology free interaction backgrounding technology entirely. The haptic device is a digital interface and uses the same laser scan to build its virtual haptic model. Our intention is to compare these two prototypes in a real museum setting.

It is a challenge to evaluate user experience that is closely related to embodied, tacit understandings, such as in this case. The evaluation goals concern subjective opinions of visitor focus, degree of engagement and phenomenological experience. As these goals are subjective and not easily mapped to any objective quantifiable factor our evaluation was a combination of gathering feedback, verbal or written, and close observation of the way the visitors used the interface, their gestural motions as well as the social interaction among them during their experience.

We were present at all time next to the exhibits and were interacting with the visitors, observing their interaction with the artefact through both interfaces, having informal discussions about their experience, often using probing questions, and triggering their reflection when something would break their experience. The visitors were then asked if they would like to fill in a qualitative questionnaire. They were then asked to rate with a 5 point Likert Scale (from strongly disagree, disagree, neutral, agree or strongly agree) the following statements:

1. It is important to engage more senses than the visual as part of the museum experience.
2. The installation/replica gave a sense of how the ancient object would feel.
3. The installation/replica was straightforward to use.

4. Because of the installation/replica there was a better understanding of the ancient objects.
5. Overall, the installation/replica enhanced the museum experience.

They were also prompted to write any more detailed comments.

Both prototypes attracted a number of visitors most of whom were eager to discuss with the researchers and learn more about the project as well as its technical details. A large number of visitors would stay for a considerable time and explore the possibilities of the interface, giving us verbal feedback and discussing details of its use. As only one person at a time could use each prototype, visitors would gather around and watch, conversing with one another and with the researchers until it was their turn. Children were particularly drawn to the installations and they were the ones to stay longer and explore it. This shows that both interfaces can enable playful engagement.

There were 60 questionnaire responses over the two days installation at the National Museum of Scotland and the two days at the Orkney Archaeological Museum. The initial empirical results demonstrated the potential of both prototypes to provide a novel embodied experience of untouchable artefacts. Visitors' comments were very positive for both prototypes but particularly for the replica.

The rapid prototype installation successfully produced the sense of haptic exploration of the chess piece in a natural and simple way. The setup synchronised the visitors' visual and haptic cues, and consequently, their interaction with the replica was directly translated as interaction with the real statue. One visitor commented 'As I felt it, I felt like I was touching the one in the reflection and not the replica'. Another one said that it 'feels real and that you feel more connected to its history'.

One drawback of the replica installation was the double image of the hands on the glass created by the refraction of the light on the perplex glass. A few visitors found this a bit distracting, though not detrimental to the whole experience. The double image can be corrected in future versions by calculating optical parameters based on a specific position where the visitor will be standing. Another interesting comment made by three visitors was that the texture of the replica should be improved to match as much as possible the material of the original piece. This would improve the perception of the exhibited piece and will be taken forward in future designs.

The main drawback of the haptic interface that was reported from the discussions and written comments was that the haptic device could not provide a detailed outline of the statue. Most visitors could not easily perceive the fine details of the statue with the stylus. One reason for this was the size and detail of the exhibit. The installation could work very well for larger objects or small objects with little details. The lack of precision can be slightly improved by developing a more sensitive collision detection system between the haptic device controller and the haptic geometry which allows for more detailed tracing of the carved details. One of the future tests is to use an artefact with few details and compare user responses, both verbal and bodily, with those received in this study. The aim will be to investigate the extent to which the interface conveys sufficient realism starting from relatively simple objects. The lack of detailed information was also attributed to the single-point contact of the device compared to the multi finger touch of the hands.

5   Discussion

The visitors agreed unanimously that the combination of visual and haptic cues gave a much better sense of the object, and increased the sense of authenticity in comparison to just viewing it in its case. Because of the size of the chess piece, some visitors commented that a seated position would bring the piece on their eye height and reduce the fatigue from standing up and using the interface.

The comparison between the haptic device and the replica showed that the multi-finger tactile interaction with the replica produced considerably richer information than the single-point contact of the haptic device. The surface texture and material of an artefact plays a significant role when exploring haptically an object and the Phantom haptic device cannot provide this level of haptic rendering at sufficient quality. The authors acknowledge that a single contact point is relatively little information compared to the amount of haptic sensations that a finger can give by touching a texture or a complex surface. The key issue is whether small additions to the museum experience are worthwhile.

The two different installations allow comparative assessments on such issues which add to the current literature on heritage applications of haptic and virtual experiences with objects. Our research juxtaposed two different experiences to the same object allowing for direct comparisons. The relative costs, maintenance issues, and ease of use, as well as the visitor feedback and comments all pointed in favour of the computer mediated but physical replica compared to the active haptic device. Yet without the trial this was not a predictable outcome as the readiness of visitors to engage with the virtual reflection and the coalignment of visual hand image with touch experience was one of the key trial results. In contrast, the haptic pen could have been handled by visitors in much the same way as a simple wooden stick could be drawn across the face of a textured object to probe aspects of its morphology and textures.

The trial results certainly relate to cognitive perception but they also relate back to the clear directive of the end-users: to hide the technology and for it not to overwhelm the visitors. Visitors were clearly more comfortable aligning real touch of a hidden replica co-located with a virtual reflection than working an obvious computer-related largely unfamiliar device. Though the design of the pen was fairly robust and easy to use as a device once shown, not many visitors knew about haptic pens and the device by its nature could not be hidden. These are important aspects in the willingness of visitors to engage with unfamiliar technologies versus their desire to interact with objects within glass cases. Such results have been highlighted in other research [5] [11] reinforcing our conclusion that the familiarity of the touch experience at the level of embodied practice can affect visitor perceptions but that as haptic devices are developed and become more mainstream experiences they can more easily be applied. Still, these statements are based on observing the visitors' readiness to engage with the installations and from some visitor comments about preferences between the two. It is more difficult to attribute this to familiarity versus immediacy which the replica presents stronger than the haptic pen whether produced by 3D printing or other means.

Finally, the 3D print technologies are reducing in price and are now not so expensive. Compared to using a PHANToM, the 3D printed replica is a lower cost solution.

6   Further Developments

Further innovations have been explored within the project to give better textures and tactile qualities such as weight and more personal interactions but these raise many other issues which require fuller discussion elsewhere [17].

The results from the comparison between the two interfaces indicated that the haptic device prototype provides a less complex sensation of the artefact. However, there is ample scope for the use of haptic devices within this setup if the interaction mechanism is enriched with dynamic elements and other modalities, for example with sound feedback, extra touchable geometry, explanations, and texture all of which can be dynamic, personalized information. While this can be equally possible with the replica (e.g. by using depth cameras to calculate the hands position), the implementation through a haptic device is much easier and cost-effective.

Another development that is particularly for the haptic device prototype is to use the interface with museum artefacts that have missing parts as the device can be used to feel the invisible missing piece. In addition, a draw function can be implemented through which users can draw extra geometry. In [9] an early research on this process is presented, and the Virtual Showcase [3] that was mentioned in the literature review also allows the presentation of stereoscopic images overlaid on top of real objects. We envisage that this study will have numerous applications in museum research as well as learning.

7   Conclusion

We have presented a novel haptic interaction paradigm which gives the impression of direct haptic interaction with museum artefacts in their display cases. The prototypes solve the problem of technology taking focus from the artefact as attention is not on a graphic display or replica but the real artefact itself. The approach was tested in a real Museum environment and was found to provide enhanced engagement with a real precious artefact. Compared to the digital prototype, the non-digital conveyed richer sensory information about the artefact during interaction. However, the digital interface offers the opportunity for easily adding extra interactive elements that can enhance immersion. While much remains to be done, our work shows that the technique we developed has the potential of becoming a useful way of evoking multimodal embodied exploration of intangible artefacts, with significant educative and economic advantages for museums and similar exhibition and learning spaces.

Acknowledgements. The research reported here was part of the Science and Heritage programme and used funding from EPSRC-AHRC as part of for a network cluster grant *Touching the Untouchable* and an AHRC development grant on *Touching the Past* both led by Linda Hurcombe; Mark Wright was CI on the latter. The research could not have happened without the substantial commitment and support shown by Dr Alison Sheridan (Principal Curator of Early Prehistory) of National Museums Scotland who came to the first workshop, hosted the second and who was involved in all the trials reported here. She facilitated access to the Lewis chess pieces case, arranged permissions and dealt with numerous practical and conceptual issues. The Orkney Museum staff also hosted the trial and we particularly thank Sheila Wilson, and Janette Park as curators as well as project researchers Lynda Aiano and Penny Cunningham. Dr Ian Summers (Physics, Exeter) particularly developed the idea of using pepper's ghost alongside the authors listed here and used them in another project installation. He, together with his former research student Dr Matt Philpott contributed to the success of the public trials of all of the installations.

References

1. Bergamasco, M., Frisoli, A., Barbagli, F.: Haptics technologies and cultural heritage applications. In: Proceedings of Computer Animation, pp. 25–32 (2002)
2. Bergamasco, M., Avizzano, C., Di Pietro, G., Borbogli, F., Frisoli, A.: The museum of pure form: System architecture. In: Proceedings of 10th IEEE International Workshop on Robot and Human Interactive Communication, pp. 112–117 (2001)
3. Bimber, O., Fröhlich, B., Schmalstieg, D., Encarnação, L.M.: The Virtual Showcase. IEEE Computer Graphics & Applications 21(6), 48–55 (2001)
4. Botvinick, C.J.: Rubber hands 'feel' touch that the eyes see. Nature 391, 756 (1998)
5. Brewster, S.A.: The impact of haptic 'touching' technology on cultural applications. In: Digital Applications for Cultural Heritage Institutions, pp. 273–284 (2005)
6. Chatterjee, C., Helen, J. (eds.): Touch in Museums: policy and practice in object handling. Berg, Oxford (2008)
7. Clark, A.: Being There: Putting brain, body and world together again. MIT Press (1998)
8. Contreras, F., Farjas, M., Melero, F.J.: Fusion of Cultures. In: Proceedings of the 38th Annual Conference on Computer Applications and Quantitative Methods in Archaeology, Granada, Oxford. BAR International Series 2494 (2010)
9. Dima, M., Arvind, D.K., Lee, J., Wright, M.: Haptically extended augmented prototyping. In: Proceedings of 7th IEEE/ACM International Symposium on Mixed and Augmented Reality, pp. 169–170 (2008)
10. Dudley, S. (ed.): Museum Materialities: Objects, Engagements and Materialities. Routledge, London (2009)
11. Figueroa, P., Coral, M., Boulanger, P., Borda, J., Londono, E., Vega, F., Prieto, F., Restrepo, D.: Multi-modal exploration of small artifacts: An exhibition at the Gold Museum in Bogota. In: Proceedings of the 16th ACM Symposium on Virtual Reality Software and Technology. ACM (2009)
12. Froese, T., McGann, M., Bigge, W., Spiers, A., Seth, A.K.: The enactive torch: A new tool for the science of perception. IEEE Transactions on Haptics 5(4), 365–375 (2012)
13. Gibson, E., Penfold-Ward, J., Tasker, S., Williamson, J., Wood, C.: Senses in touch II. University of Glasgow, Third-year project report (2001)
14. Gosden, C., Phillips, R., Edwards, E. (eds.): Sensible Objects: Colonialism, Museums and Material Culture. Berg, Oxford (2007)
15. Hurcombe, L.: A sense of materials and sensory perception in concepts of materiality. World Archaeology 39, 532–545 (2007)

16. Hurcombe, L.: Archaeological Artefacts as material Culture. Routledge, London (2008)
17. Hurcombe, L., Sheridan, A., Summers, I., Wright, M., Dima, M., Philpott, M.: Touching the Past (in preparation)
18. Jang, J.S., Jung, G.S., Lee, T.H., Jung, S.K.: Two phase calibration for a mirror metaphor augmented reality system. In: Proccedings of IEEEE, vol. 102(2) (2014)
19. Lazzari, M., McLaughlin, M.L., Jaskowiak, J., Wong, W., Akbarian, M.: A Haptic Exhibition of Daguerreotype Cases for USCs Fisher Gallery. Prentice Hall (2002)
20. Matthew, B., Cohen, J.: Rubber hands 'feel' touch that eyes see. Nature 391 (1998)
21. McLaughlin, M.L., Sukhatme, G., Hespanha, J., Shahabi, C., Ortega, A., Medioni, G.: The haptic museum. In: Proceedings of the EVA 2000 Conference on Electronic Imaging and the Visual Arts, Florence, Italy (2000)
22. Noe, A.: Action in perception. MIT Press (2006)
23. Patterson, M.: The Senses of Touch. Berg, Oxford (2007)
24. Pye, E. (ed.): The Power of Touch: Handling objects in museums and heritage contexts Left Coast Press (2008)
25. Varela, F.: The Embodied Mind. MIT Press (1992)

Augmented and Geo-Located Information in an Architectural Education Framework

Ernest Redondo[1], Janina Puig[1], David Fonseca[2], Sergi Villagrasa[2], and Isidro Navarro[2]

[1] Universidad Politécnica de Cataluña-Barcelona Tech. Barcelona, Spain
ernesto.redondo@upc.edu, janinapuig@hotmail.com
[2] Architecture School - La Salle, Universitat Ramon Llull. Barcelona, Spain
{fonsi,sergiv,inavarro}@salle.url.edu

Abstract. This work aims to design an academic experience involving the implementation of an augmented reality tool in architecture education practices to improve the motivation and final marks of the student. We worked under different platforms for mobile devices to create virtual information channels through a database associated with 3D virtual models and any other type of media content, which are geo-located in their real position. The basis of our proposal is the spatial skills improvement that students can achieve using their innate affinity with user-friendly digital media such as smartphones or tablets, which allow them to visualize educational exercises in real geo-located environments and to share and evaluate students' own-generated proposals on site. The proposed method aims to improve the access to multimedia content on mobile devices, allowing access to be adapted to all types of users and contents. The students were divided into various groups, control and experimental, in respect of the function of the devices and activities to perform. The goal they were given was to display 3D architectural geo-referenced content using SketchUp and ArMedia for iOS and a custom platform or Android environment.

Keywords: Augmented reality, e-learning, geo-e-learning, urban planning, educational research.

1 Introduction

The implementation of new technology in the teaching field has been largely extended to all types of levels and educational frameworks. However, these innovations require approval, validation and evaluation by the final users, the students. A second step of the proposal (that will be generated in the first semester of 2014) will be to discuss the advantages and disadvantages of applying mixed evaluation technology in a case study of the use of interactive and collaborative tools for the visualization of 3D architectonic models. We will use a mixed-method of evaluation based on quantitative and qualitative approaches to measure the level of motivation and satisfaction with this type of technology and to obtain adequate feedback that allows for the optimization of this type of experiment in future iterations.

R. Shumaker and S. Lackey (Eds.): VAMR 2014, Part II, LNCS 8526, pp. 15–26, 2014.

The current paper is based on three main pillars: The first pillar focuses on teaching innovations within the university framework that cultivate higher motivation and satisfaction in students. The second pillar concerns how to implement such an innovation; we propose the utilization of determinate tools (AR) of so-called Information Technologies (IT), so that students, as "digital natives," will be more comfortable in the learning experience. Finally, the study will employ a mixed analysis method to concretely obtain the most relevant aspects of the experience that should be improved both in future interactions and in any new technological implementations within a teaching framework.

2   Background

Augmented reality (AR) technology is based on overlapping virtual information in real space. AR technology makes it possible to mix virtual objects generated by computers with a real environment, generating a mixed environment that can be viewed through any technological device in real time. The main characteristics of an augmented reality system are [1]:

- Real-time interactivity
- Use of 3D virtual elements
- Mix of virtual elements with real elements

Augmented reality has emerged from research in virtual reality. Virtual reality environments make possible total immersion in an artificial three-dimensional (3D) world. The involvement of virtual reality (VR) techniques in the development of educational applications brings new perspectives to engineering and architectural degrees. For example, through interaction with 3D models of the environment, the whole construction sequence in time and space of a deck can be simulated for students' better understanding [2]. We can also explore hidden structure through ghosted views within the real-world scenes [3] or find several examples of AR and VR applied to monitoring the maintenance of new buildings and to preserve cultural heritage [4-6].

Evaluating the use of VR or AR applications in an industrial setting is a complex task, but some statistics suggest performance improvements of up to 30%, with involved employees reporting higher levels of engagement [7]. Applications of AR that support technicians in the field have the potential to reduce costs by up to 25% through quicker maintenance or component substitution, identification and setup of new connections, solution of faults and misconfigurations, with less burden on back-end personnel and system resources.

2.1   Recent Improvements in Mobile Learning

Between 2008 and 2009, new platforms and paradigms emerged to propel AR development in smartphones, such as Junaio, Layar and Wikitude. All of these companies embraced a new concept that consisted in creating an augmented reality browser with

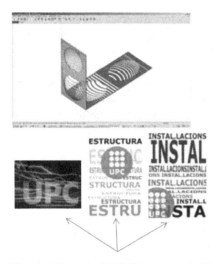

Fig. 1. AR at the UPC University. A 3D model visualized through a mobile device screen thanks to the camera detection of a regular shape or code.

a number of features that allowed developers to produce AR content according to a specific set of rules, and, finally, enabled end-users to view computer generated elements superimposed on the live camera view of common smartphones. These AR browsers are compatible with most mobile operating systems, such as Android, the iPhone OS, or the Symbian.

A framework in which this technology could potentially be used in more interesting ways is the representation and management of territory, because real scenes could be "completed" with virtual information. This method would facilitate a greater awareness and better understanding of the environment, especially if used in the educational framework. Last year research at universities worldwide focused on the development of AR applications (AGeRA[1], GIS2R[8], ManAR[9]), tools (GTracer for libGlass[10]), educational platforms (TLA[11]), or open resources and contents (ISEGINOVA AR Project[12]) such as 3D architectural models (3D ETSAB AR[13-14]).

2.2 GIS Limitations

Real-time performance and qualitative modeling remain highly challenging, and in situ 3D modeling has become increasingly prominent in current AR research, particularly for mobile scenarios [15]. The main problem of all these applications seems to be the location or geographical information, because a Geographic Information System (GIS) is needed to provide, manage and filter public queries with different levels of accuracy and upgradeable information. In short, we need to link a 3D model to a database that contains all the necessary information associated with it. Furthermore, the introduction of new learning methods using collaborative technologies offers new opportunities to provide educational multimedia content.

While GPS (Global Positioning System) has satisfactory accuracy and performance in open spaces, its quality deteriorates significantly in urban environments. Both the accuracy and the availability of GPS position estimates are reduced by shadowing from buildings and signal reflections. Mobile AR applications for outdoor applications largely rely on the smartphone GPS. Also, GPS provides the user position based on triangulation of signals captured from at least 3 or 4 visible satellites by a GPS receiver. Standard GPS systems have 5m to 30m accuracy due to limitations such as [16]:

- Being unavailable (or slow in obtaining position) when satellite signals are absent (such as underground), and when meteorological conditions block transmission, and
- Satellites can provide erroneous information about their own position.

Already well known applications are Wikitude, Nokia City Lens, Google Goggles and Metaio Junaio. Today's sensors' capabilities in stability and precision have noticeably improved. For example, GPS accuracy is increased with differential GPS or DGPS, which brings the accuracy of readings to within 1–3 meters of the object, as compared to the 5–30 meters of normal GPS. DGPS works using a network of stationary GPS receivers [17]. The difference between their predefined position and the position as calculated by the signals from satellites gives the error factor. This error component is then transmitted as an FM signal for the local GPS receivers, enabling them to apply the necessary correction to their readings.

2.3   TICS at University

Recently, experiences of the implementation of TIC in university degrees concluded that "digital natives" with a periodical activity on networks and chats are better students [18]. The use of VR technologies on practical courses for graduate and undergraduate student's aims to develop personal skills [19] introduced in the European Educational Space (EEES), such as a methodical approach to practical engineering problems, teamwork, working in interdisciplinary groups and time management.

In previous publications [20-21] we explained the impact of mobile learning AR technologies introduced in engineering degrees on the academic results of our students, having found that they increased their motivation and satisfaction in classroom.

3   Case of Study

This item presents a teaching methodology for a practical course in architectural degree where the students improve AR and VR technologies through their own mobile devices. The course design follows previous examples [23] of moodle-based evaluation systems for the actual requirements within EEES on new skills for professional technicians such as spatial vision, orientation or teamwork.

At the same time, to test the accuracy and satisfaction of GPS systems only available in smartphones and iOS devices, we developed an Android tool (RA3) based on

Fig. 2. On the left is an iOS screen displaying options with ArPlayer of Armedia. On the right is the application RA3 developed for Android devices.

markers as location encoders (i.e. markers with regular shapes, such as QR code-like markers) associated with specific points of the environment or objects.

3.1   Methodology

The proposed course focused on two points:

- On the one hand, the structure that defines the acquisition of knowledge is an inverted pyramid: students cannot perform an activity without having completed and assimilated the activity before. Therefore, only students who have built a 3D model will be able to insert it into a landscape or photograph according to its geometrical space or perspective. Similarly, only smartphone owners are able to play AR applications for iOS platforms. To separate mobile device users from the rest of the class, all students completed a pre-test that defined two main groups; a control and experimental group.
- On the other hand, the work of the students with the proposed methodology, not only helps them to improve their spatial skills (to be able to compare their 3D proposals located and displayed in its location, allowing understand and correct common design errors in particular focused on the size of the models) but this work also improves the educational proposal identifying strengths and weaknesses from the usability of the method.

During the designed course at the Architecture University of Barcelona (ETSAB-UPC), four main exercises were developed in order to evaluate particular skills linked to architectural and engineering careers, such as spatial perception, orientation or occlusion. These kinds of abilities can also be introduced with specific AR experiences [24].

3.2   Contents

The first activity of the course was to generate a database of 3D sculptures of Andreu Alfaro. These virtual sculptures, in the second part of the course, then had to be integrated in a nineteenth-century square through a photographic refund. The third exercise was the virtual representation of the chosen architectural environment, one of the few arcaded squares of Barcelona, the Plaza Masadas. Finally, every student promoted their own urban intervention according to the regulation and urban plans.

Fig. 3. Two examples of photographic proposals of 3D sculptures in the middle Plaza Masadas, Barcelona

In the photographic proposals of the object or piece in the middle of a square, the realism of the image can be diminished if the ambient occlusion or point of view of both images (the real square and the 3D sculpture) is in contradiction. Lighting, for example, is an element of realism that is dynamic and produces shadows that, when missing; break the realistic effect of AR. To avoid ambient occlusion contradictions, the students were required to select several properties such as color, reflection or material, and use tools that introduced the latitude and light-time during the render process of 3D models in Artlantis, V-ray or 3DStudioMax to offer more interactive real environment [25]. Then, Photomatch options of SketchUp were used to match the 3D model in the chosen square's photography according to its point of view.

The third part of the practical course introduced teamwork abilities into the previously evaluated skills of geometric performing, spatial visualization or orientation and ambient occlusion. Different segments of the existing arcaded buildings around the square had to be developed in two partner groups separately according the urban plans that expected the reconstruction of one corner of this place. The more or less extensive adjustments undertaken to connect every segment with the entire compilation determined the

Fig. 4. 3D model of the section of an arcaded square in Barcelona

first mark of the group, with the second mark coming from the result of a controlled exam in which every student had to represent a part of a similar arcaded square in 3D.

The fourth exercise implemented physical and urban properties in the main 3D model. A personal approach was required that discussed material, color, landscaping and urban furniture in the proposed space. The grade for this project was obtained from two perspectives rendered in a human point of view.

Before the final exercise an experimental group composed of students who had passed the "digital natives" pre-test, have worked using AR with two location strategies for 3D models, marker-based and GPS location. Evaluating the academic results obtained finally by the students, it became clear this experience enabled an improvement in their spatial abilities, as intended. The two main platforms for mobile devices, Android and iOS (ArPlayer and RA3) determined the location strategy for each user in order to integrate their own project on its real environment. Placing the 3D model in its real environment, the application displays different options of interaction such as rotation, scale and light-orientation. Playing with application choices, the student should obtain a final scene with his device in order to compare it with his previous virtual representations and exercises.

Fig. 5. Rendering of two projects in a human point of view

4   Conclusions

The teaching methodology explained in connection with this item is thought to introduce our grade students to virtual and hand-held augmented reality (HHAR) to superimpose virtual models on real scenes. Having previously developed test methods to confirm the motivation of our students to work with VR and AR technologies, our next point will be to determine the best resources and systems to introduce these techniques in the educational community.

In later papers the implementation of this methodology in a practical course at the Architecture University of Barcelona (ETSAB) will give us information about advances and users' results about different issues:

- VR software and rendering
- AR applications
- GIS (geographical information) systems on mobile devices

Computer graphics have become much more sophisticated, becoming more realistic. In the near future, researchers plan to display graphics on TV screens or computer displays and integrate them into real-world settings. Therefore, geometrical formulation of 3D architecture for virtual representation is now possible with 3D SketchUp, Rhinoceros or Autocad due their compatibilities in DBX or DWG files to generate a database.

In the field of architecture, virtual reality rendering requires several options for ambient occlusion such as color, reflection or material, using tools and files allowing the introduction of the latitude and light-time. Based on these premises we will work with Artlantis, V-ray or 3DStudioMax to offer more interactivity with real-world environment.

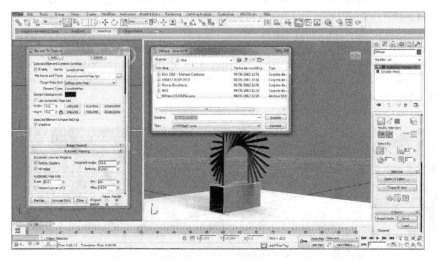

Fig. 6. Geographic information channel linked on a 3D model

The implementation of AR can be explored in various areas of knowledge, contributing significantly in education. It provides great potential in the creation of interactive books, allowing intuitive and easy to learn interaction. Developing on our previous experiences using AR applications we decided to use ArMedia (iOS) and to develop a new application for Android, RA3. The major difference between the two platforms that display AR services is the GIS (geographical information system): iOS works with GPS and Android needs a marker based on regular shapes (i.e. QR codes) as location encoders. GPS systems are not currently accurate enough to aid in the teaching of architecture. Therefore, in case of urban planning it is recommended to replace the GPS for location based on shapes or QR codes.

Fig. 7. Comparison of composed images of different students from the experimental group and the process to adapt the proposal in a correct size

Fig. 8. Student proposals with compositions more similar using AR

Analyzing the experience, and accepting that we are in the first feasibility study phase of the methodology to be implemented, the first conclusion of the exercise is that the students detect the correct point of view after placing the 3D geometry in the scene from its photo-composition. In other words, they are not capable of interpreting the information from the EXIF file, a situation that can lead to a great disparity of data because of the lack of homogeneity in the sensors. With this procedure, the angle of vision of a flat monocular image is reduced (with a relatively closed field ranging between 40–45°), very differently from the panoramic field that has a human user. For this reason, the proposed sculptures are smaller, as it has happened with the students that carried out the experiment, it will be necessary to adjust them in the final step using the RA. In relative terms, the increase in the size of the sculptures has been around 25%, once the students were located in situ and they were able to see the size of the square firsthand. This adjustment has been similar in both the iOS devices and Android, and whether their screens were 4 or 7 inches, which means that the size of the screen it is not significant.

Regarding the use of markers, six works were delivered: two were with markers and four geo-referenced. All students described some relative difficulties for fine adjustment of the models, although these were not insurmountable. On the other hand, the initial location of the object was considered easier using the mark, after which the students proceeded to move, rotate and scale the model on its final location. The only disadvantage is that it must always be visible in the scene.

For the students who used geo-referencing, the most difficult initial step was to locate the object in the square given the lack of accuracy of the mobile phones GPS, which forced them to move through the square in addition to adjusting the height in relation to the observer. The best way to facilitate this first approach is to use a QR code on the location to download the model.

To conclude, we can affirm that the experiment is viable and, if we can corroborate these results in the future with a big sample of users, we will be able to affirm that these experiments are the proof of the suitability of the method to solve these types of problems of urban design. Similarly, initially we can affirm that the students felt comfortable and were very motivated with this type of experiment in comparison with traditional classes, involving themselves for more hours than expected, which generated quality work and consequently an increase in their qualifications that are currently being evaluated.

Acknowledgements. Project funded by the VI National Plan for Scientific Research, Development and Technological Innovation, 2008-2011, Government of Spain. No EDU-2012-37247/EDUC.

References

1. Dionisio Correa, A.G., Tahira, A., Ribeir, J.B., Kitamura, R.K., Inoue, T.Y., Karaguilla Ficheman, I.: Development of an interactive book with Augmented Reality for mobile learning. In: 2013 8th Iberian Conference on Information Systems and Technologies (CISTI), June 19-22, pp. 1–7 (2013)

2. Zita Sampaio, A., Viana, L.: Virtual Reality used as a learning technology: Visual simulation of the construction of a bridge deck. In: 2013 8th Iberian Conference on Information Systems and Technologies (CISTI), June 19-22, pp. 1–5 (2013)
3. Kalkofen, D., Veas, E., Zollmann, S., Steinberger, M., Schmalstieg, D.: Adaptive ghosted views for Augmented Reality. In: 2013 IEEE International Symposium on Mixed and Augmented Reality (ISMAR), October 1-4, pp.1–9 (2013) doi:10.1109/ISMAR. 2013.6671758
4. Zita Sampaio, A., Rosario, D.P.: Maintenance planning of building walls supported on Virtual Reality technology. In: 2013 8th Iberian Conference on Information Systems and Technologies (CISTI), June 19-22, pp. 1–7 (2013)
5. Redondo, E., Sánchez Riera, A., Puig, J.: Gironella tower in Gerunda, teaching roman architecture, using 3D modeling and augmented reality: A case study. In: S.A.V.E. Heritage - International Forum S.A.V.E. Heritage Safeguard of Architectural, Visual, Environmental Heritage, Capri, pp. 102-1–102-9 (2011)
6. Perrone, F.R., Heidrich, F.E., Gomes, H.M., Almeida da Silva, A.B.: Desenvolvimento de Aplicativo para Visualização de Patrimônio Histórico-Arquitetônico em Realidade Aumentada. In: SIGRADI 2012, vol. 1, pp. 366–368 (2012)
7. Terenzi, G., Basile, G.: Smart Maintenance. An Augmented Reality Platform for Training and Field Operations in the Manufacturing Industry. ARMedia, 2nd White Paper of Inglobe Technologies Srl (2013).
8. Dias, L., Coelho, A., Rodrigues, A., Rebelo, C., Cardoso, A.: GIS2R — Augmented reality and 360° panoramas framework for geomarketing. In: 2013 8th Iberian Conference on Information Systems and Technologies (CISTI), June 19-22, pp. 1–5 (2013)
9. Ramirez, H., Mendivil, E.G., Flores, P.R., Gonzalez, M.C.: Authoring Software for Augmented Reality applications for the use of maintenance and training process. In: 2013 International Conference on Virtual and Augmented Reality in Education, vol. 25, pp. 189–193 (2013)
10. de Paiva Guimaraes, M., Farinazzo Martins, V., Colombo Dias, D., Contri, L.F., Barberi Gnecco, B.: Development and debugging of distributed virtual reality applications. In: 2013 8th Iberian Conference on Information Systems and Technologies (CISTI), June 19-22, pp. 1–6 (2013)
11. Regan, D.A.: Training and Learning Architecture: Infrastructure for the Future of Learning. In: Invited Keynote International Symposium on Information Technology and Communication in Education (SINTICE), Madrid, Spain (2013)
12. Vieira Cardoso, P., de Castro Neto, M.: ISEGI-NOVA AR project Augmented Reality applied to the Universidade Nova de Lisboa. In: 2013 8th Iberian Conference on Information Systems and Technologies (CISTI), June 19-22, pp. 1–6 (2013)
13. Redondo, E., Sánchez Riera, A., Fonseca, D., Peredo, A.: Architectural Geo-E-Learning. Geolocated Teaching in urban environments through mobile devices: A case study and work in process. In: Shumaker, R. (ed.) VAMR/HCII 2013, Part II. LNCS, vol. 8022, pp. 188–197. Springer, Heidelberg (2013)
14. Redondo, E., Fonseca, D., Sánchez, A., Navarro, I.: Aplicaciones para el aprendizaje móvil en educación superior. Universities and Knowledge Society Journal 11(1), 152–174 (2014)
15. Nguyen, T., Grasset, R., Schmalstieg, D., Reitmayr, G.: Interactive Syntactic Modeling With a Single-Point Laser Range Finder and Camera. In: 2013 IEEE International Symposium on Mixed and Augmented Reality, ISMAR (2013)
16. Perey, C., Terenzi, G.: AR-Assisted 3D Visualization for Urban Professional Users. ARmedia First White Paper of Inglobe Technologies Srl (October 2013)

17. Cirulis, A., Brigmanis, K.B.: 3D Outdoor Augmented Reality for Architecture and Urban Planning. In: 2013 International Conference on Virtual and Augmented Reality in Education Procedia Computer Science, vol. 25, pp. 71–79 (2013)
18. Gómez-Aguilar, D.A., García-Peñalvo, F.J., Therón, R.: Visual assessment of the relationships among students participation and their outcomes on eLearning environments. In: 13th IEEE International Conference on Advanced Learning Technologies, ICALT (2013) (July 13, 2013)
19. Häfner, P., Häfner, V., Ovtcharova, J.: Teaching Methodology for Virtual Reality Practical Course in Engineering Education. In: 2013 International Conference on Virtual and Augmented Reality in Education, Procedia Computer Science, vol. 25, pp. 251–260 (2013)
20. Fonseca, D., Martí, N., Redondo, E., Navarro, I., Sánchez, A.: Relationship between student profile, tool use, participation, and academic performance with the use of Augmented Reality technology for visualized architecture models. Computers in Human Behavior 31, 434–445 (2014), doi:10.1016/j.chb.2013.03.006
21. Sánchez, A., Redondo, E., Fonseca, D., Navarro, I.: Construction processes using mobile augmented reality. A study case in Building Engineering degree. Advances in Information Systems and Technologies 206, 1053–1062 (2013), doi:10.1007/978-3-642-36981-0_100
22. Vaca, J.M., Agudo, J.E., Rico, M.: Evaluating competences in engineering: a Moodle-based eportfolio. In: XV Simposio Internacional de Tecnologías de la Información y las Comunicaciones en la Educación, Madrid, Spain, pp. 67–74 (September 2013)
23. Roca-González, C., Martín-Gutiérrez, J., García-Domínguez, M., Hernan-Pérez, A.S., Mato-Carrodeguas, C.: Improving Spatial Skills: An Orienteering Experience in Real and Virtual Environments With First Year Engineering Students. In: 2013 International Conference on Virtual and Augmented Reality in Education, Procedia Computer Science, vol. 25, pp. 428–435 (2013)
24. Imbert, N., Vignat, F., Kaewrat, C., Boonbrahm, P.: Adding Physical Properties to 3D Models in Augmented Reality for Realistic Interactions Experiments. In: 2013 International Conference on Virtual and Augmented Reality in Education, Procedia Computer Science, vol. 25, pp. 364–369 (2013)

The Didactical Design of Virtual Reality Based Learning Environments for Maintenance Technicians

Tina Haase[1], Nathalie Weisenburger[3], Wilhelm Termath[2],
Ulrike Frosch[3], Dana Bergmann[3], and Michael Dick[3]

[1] Fraunhofer Institute for Factory Operation and Automation IFF[1], Sandtorstr. 22, 39106
Magdeburg, Germany
Tina.Haase@iff.fraunhofer.de
[2] Berufsforschungs- und Beratungsinstitut für interdisziplinäre Technikgestaltung e.V.,
Max-Greve-Straße 30, 44791 Bochum, Germany
[3] Otto-von-Guericke Universität Magdeburg, Lehrstuhl für Betriebspädagogik, 39104
Magdeburg, Germany

Abstract. The paper at hand describes the necessity of developing didactically designed Virtual Reality (VR) based learning environments. Changing industrial processes triggered by the fourth industrial revolution will influence working and learning conditions. VR based learning environments have the potential to improve the understanding of complex machine behavior. The paper describes possibilities for the investigation and documentation of expert knowledge as a crucial source for developing VR scenarios. The consideration of learning objectives and the current state of the learners know how are essential for designing an effective learning environment. The basic theoretical approaches of didactics and their application to virtual learning environments will be presented with an example for the maintenance of a high voltage circuit breaker. Finally experiences from the practical use will be reflected and next steps on the way to a user specific learning environment will be discussed.

Keywords: Virtual Reality, Maintenance, Expert knowledge, learning theory, learning objectives.

1 Motivation

German industry is on the threshold of the fourth industrial revolution, also called "Industry 4.0". It is driven by the increasing integration of internet technologies with traditional industries such as manufacturing. That will lead to a more and more autonomous production process.

The core of the revolution is the complete penetration of the industry, its products and its services with software while products and services are connected via the internet and other networks. This change leads to new products and services that change the life and work of all people. [1]

---

[1] Under the direction of Prof. Dr.-Ing. habil. Prof. E. h. Dr. h. c. mult. Michael Schenk.

R. Shumaker and S. Lackey (Eds.): VAMR 2014, Part II, LNCS 8526, pp. 27–38, 2014.
© Springer International Publishing Switzerland 2014

The technological changes are accompanied by the demographic development. [2] Experienced expert workers will retire while there are not enough well qualified young people. The challenge of companies is the integration of the experiential knowledge with the latest knowledge and information of the young professionals. A main part of experiential knowledge is tacit knowledge [3], which means that people are not aware of their experience and have difficulty verbalizing it. The first section of the paper at hand will give a short overview of how this knowledge can be investigated.

Changing industrial processes will also change the maintenance process. Maintenance technicians will take a responsible role within production with the objective of minimizing downtimes of the machine and by planning procedures under the aspect of resource and energy efficiency.

The vocational training of maintenance technicians involves facing the challenge that many machines are not available for training, cannot be used because of dangerous processes or are hardly comprehensible. Other challenges arise due to insufficient visibility of important assembly groups or the increase of invisible network processes. The understanding of processes and the resulting confidence is a prerequisite for safe and efficient maintenance procedures. [4]

Technology based learning environments that are based on virtual 3D models can overcome the restrictions of today's learning methods. For planning and arranging technology based learning environments in a target-oriented way, didactical designs are essential. Didactics describes a system of conditions and interdependent decisions which demonstrate all factors of teaching and learning in a target-oriented practice. In this context didactics refers to the following criteria: identification of learning objectives, the content of learning, application of methods, media and the pedagogical field and where teaching and learning is situated. All points interdepend and have to be considered in the respective context. [5-6]

The paper at hand will describe the conceptual design of such a learning environment under the aspect of didactics. The above mentioned didactical aspects and their application to the learning environment will be presented. An example of the maintenance of a high voltage circuit breaker serves as a descriptive example.

2   The Role of Expert Knowledge for Maintenance Processes

There are many tasks in the production process that cannot solely be taught in classroom trainings as these tasks are very complex and require the ability of decision making. This kind of problem solving competence can only be gained within the working process and goes along with experiential knowledge. In the maintenance process you will find comparatively easy tasks that follow a defined checklist and don't require special know how. On the other hand there are very complex tasks, e.g. the failure analysis and the ability of reflecting and comparing the current situation with similar experiences in the work life. [7]

"A main part of this experiential knowledge is the so called tacit knowledge. Technicians are often not aware of this special knowledge what becomes noticeable when they can't verbalize their knowledge. So, tacit knowledge is more than just the systematically received knowledge within vocational education, it is the result of the workers technical handling in their everyday work life. [8-9]" [10]

For the design of VR based learning environments it is therefore relevant to take experiential knowledge into account and to offer technicians opportunities to make experiences in the virtual world.

The challenge of bringing experiences to VR is to investigate the tacit knowledge as it is related to persons and situations. Narrative methods have revealed the potential to receive valuable knowledge from experts by telling stories. One method that is applied by the authors is the so called triad interview [11].

"It is characterized by a locally and timely defined dialogue about an agreed topic where three persons with very specific roles take part:

- The narrator as the technical expert for the topic is responsible for the validity of the knowledge.
- The listener as the novice technician who wants to learn from the expert is responsible for the usefulness of the knowledge.
- The technical layperson who is the methodical expert and moderator and who is responsible for the comprehensibility. " [10]

So far triad interviews were documented in texts which are not optimal for its application within the organization due to the limited connectivity of novice technicians to written texts. Virtual Reality has the potential to keep the narrative structure of stories and is therefore very well suited to transfer experiential knowledge whereby allowing an easy access for novice users.

3   Theoretical Basis for Learning in Virtual Worlds

We already emphasized the importance of making tacit knowledge of experts explicit and to make use of the potential of VR for its documentation. In this section we start by identifying basic learning theories for a suitable didactic design of virtual learning environments. Learning environments should provide certainty of action, especially in dangerous situations and activities which require a high level of competence. If a proper prototype does not yet exist, a qualification is already possible in the process of developing.

VR based learning environments can be classified to Leontjevs activity theory [12]. Following this theory from 1977, knowledge of employees is not only represented in their heads, but also in their working activities. In 1987 Engeström [13] extended this theory with aspects of learning and development processes. It results in the so called activity system (Fig. 1) which contains the subject (e.g. the acting technician), the object (e.g. a maintenance task) and the integration to a community of practice (e.g. a group of experts for the maintenance of a special device). Furthermore it is embedded to an organization with its rules and values that influence the handling and decision making of employees. All parameters of the activity system influence the outcome.

The quality of the outcome can be improved by assigning a well-designed didactical learning setting that is represented in the triangle of subject, object and mediating artifacts.

The paper at hand focuses on this triangle of the activity system, describes basic didactic theories from vocational education and puts them in relation to learning theories with respect to their application in VR based learning environments.

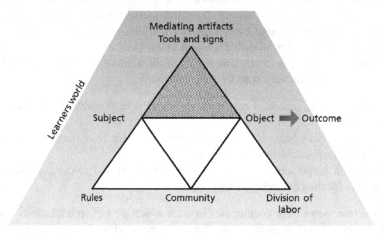

Fig. 1. "Activity- and learning theory" according to Engeström 1987 [13]

Based on the current state of the learner's knowledge, the learning objectives are defined. Therefore the following aspects have to be taken into account: learner, types of knowledge, learning objectives, the learning content and organizational structures within the company.

3.1   The Learner in the Context of a Community

According to Dreyfus and Dreyfus [14] becoming an expert in a domain is highly dependent upon a developmental progression from novice to advanced beginner to expertise.

The authors identify "(…) five stages of competence development and the four corresponding developmental learning areas". (They) "have a hypothetical function for the identification of thresholds and stages in the development of occupational competence and identity" [15]. Though, they also have a didactic function in the development of work-related and structurally oriented vocational courses.

When considering a person whose skills are developing from deficient to competent Lave and Wenger [16] state that the quality of their learning situation becomes crucial to the learning outcome. [15]. The authors point out that learning as a path from inability to ability is accomplished as a process of integration into the community of practice of those who already demonstrate expertise. [15]

3.2   Knowledge Types

There are many different terminologies to differentiate between types of knowledge. Anderson et al. [17] identify in their taxonomy of learning outcomes four major categories of knowledge relevant across all disciplines:

1. Factual knowledge,
2. Conceptual knowledge,
3. Procedural knowledge and
4. Metacognitive knowledge.

Factual knowledge consists of the basic elements. It includes knowledge of specific facts and terminology (bits of information). Conceptual knowledge refers to more general concepts and is based on the interrelation of basic elements within a larger structure that enable them to function together. It includes knowledge of categories, principles and models. [17]

Both, factual and conceptual knowledge constitute knowledge of "what". The two other types – procedural and metacognitive knowledge – constitute knowledge of "how to" [18]. Procedural knowledge ranges from completing routine exercises to solve new problems and includes methods of enquiring information, knowing procedures and criteria for using skills, algorithms, techniques and methods. Metacognitive knowledge implies "knowledge of cognition in general as well as awareness and knowledge of one's own cognition" [17]. It includes knowledge of general strategies, that might be used for different tasks, within diverse conditions, and the knowledge of the extent to which the strategies are effective [19]. From Anderson's [17] perspective all these types of knowledge play complementary roles in processes of problem solving. A further definition in this context is the work process knowledge. It describes a type of knowledge that guides practical work and, as contextualized knowledge, goes far beyond non-contextual theoretical knowledge. [cf. Eraut et al., 1998 at [15]]   A characteristic of practical work process knowledge is the mastery of unpredictable work tasks, fundamentally incomplete knowledge (knowledge gap) in relation to non-transparent, non-deterministic work situations. This is a special feature of vocational work. Meta-competence can be created, namely the ability to cope with the knowledge gap while solving unpredictable tasks and problems in vocational work [15].

3.3   Learning Objectives

A learning objective describes intended behavior as well as special knowledge, skills and attitudes of the learner, which are caused by educational activities. The newly developed behavior has to be observable and verifiable. Learning objectives refer to three domains: cognitive (knowledge), affective (attitude or self) and psychomotoric (skills).

In 1956 Benjamin Bloom created the taxonomy of learning domains, a classification system for learning objectives in order to promote higher forms of thinking in education. The cognitive domain includes knowledge and the development of intellectual abilities. [20]

Bloom`s taxonomy involves six major categories, which are demonstrated in the following illustration, ranging from the simplest behavior to the most complex one:

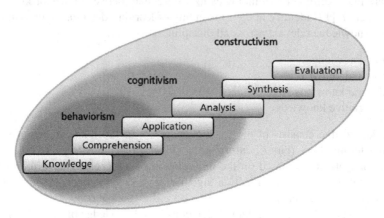

Fig. 2. Allocation of Blooms learning taxonomy to the main learning theories

The application of the learning taxonomy itself does not ensure the didactical implementation. First of all it describes the cognitive process of gaining knowledge. Together with the existing knowledge about learning theories and the analysis of learning environments the taxonomy is essential for a professional didactical design of technology based learning environments. [21] The following section describes the characteristics of the learning theories behaviorism, cognitivism and constructivism and their relation to Blooms taxonomy.

Behaviorism. Behaviorist-oriented forms of learning are suitable for simple learning processes that trigger a stimulus-response connection, which leads to permanent change in behavior. [22] This learning theory can be assigned to the lower levels of Blooms learning taxonomy, e.g. for learning facts or hand grips.

Table 1. Behaviorism – Pros and Restrictions

Behaviorism	
Pro	Restrictions
This approach is suitable only for the trigger associations for simple forms of learning. (e.g. learning vocabulary, factual knowledge)	Situations that require a lot of knowledge and are complex cannot be conveyed with this approach.
Example: Facts about the technical equipment (e.g. facts, parameters, …)	

Cognitivism. The cognitive approach focuses on the mental processing of information to knowledge. Every learning process is an active construction of knowledge.

The interaction between external information supply and the mental processes of recognition requires the learner to incorporate prior knowledge with new one. [23]

Table 2. Cognitivism – Pros and Restrictions

Cognitivism	
Pro	Restrictions
This approach is suitable for integrating information in a goal-oriented process in order to develop cognitive maps. Learning content can be adjusted automatically to the user's skills. (e.g. model learning, training videos, …).	This approach gives no ability to reflect or proof the learning context and it doesn't consider the social aspect of learning
Example: Visualization of best-practice solutions for a maintenance task.	

Constructivism. Constructivism is an epistemology founded on the assumption that, by reflecting our experiences, we construct an individual understanding of the world we live in. Each of us generates own "rules" and "mental models," which are used to make sense of ones experiences." In essence, a constructive learning environment provides real-world or problem-based learning situations that are focused on authentic learning [24]. The theory of situated learning is a partial aspect of constructivism; it claims that every idea and human action is a generalization, adapted to the ongoing environment. From this perspective learning situations are characterized by complex, multi-perspective and problem-containing requirements.

Table 3. Constructivism – Pros and Restrictions

Constructivism	
Pro	Restrictions
VR reveals the potential for the implementation of 'learning by doing' due to its interactive characteristic. This allows users to make experiences in a safe environment, independently from the availability of the real machine.	The application needs to be designed carefully with respect of the user's level of knowledge: the high degree of freedom might be challenging for novice users as they can feel lost in the application. In this case user-specific assistance is required.
Example: Interactive exploration of the virtual learning environment including the functionality and components of the technical device.	

4   Example: Maintenance Training for a High Voltage Circuit Breaker

The following section describes a learning application that was developed for the maintenance of a high voltage circuit breaker [25]. Using the learning environment, technicians shall be prepared for acting safely and confidently in their future working environment. In this regard being able to internalize how to handle dangerous and complex processes is essential. This knowledge forms the basis for safe handling in the real working environment. [7]

Consequently the first learning module deals with the *exploration of the high voltage circuit breaker* and its two main components: three pole columns and the operating mechanism.

So far 2D-drawings (e.g. exploded view drawings) were widely used within technical trainings and are well known from user manuals. Assigning the assembly parts and their denomination using these drawings is a behavioristic learning strategy that might be suitable for easy assembly structures. In case of the operating mechanism that contains many single parts, the use of a 2D-drawing (Fig. 3a) is limited because it shows only one predefined perspective and exactly one state of the device. For the transfer to other states of the operating mechanism a higher capability of abstraction is required.

The virtual learning environment introduces a constructivist approach that connects the well-known 2D drawing with an interactive model (Fig. 3b) of the operating mechanism. Users can explore the device individually according to their demands. Used in classroom training, the mechanical behavior is no longer only presented in a teacher-centered approach. Users can now explore the components and the functionality by interactively using the virtual model on a laptop or an immersive VR system. It can be summarized that factual knowledge can be designed in a behavioristic manner in case of comparatively easy models (e.g. easy assignment tasks). For more complex systems it is recommended to extend the approach to a constructive one.

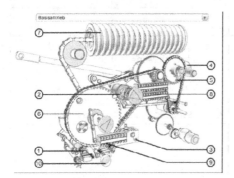

Fig. 3. (a) 2D drawing and (b) virtual model of the operating mechanism

In the second learning module technicians can make themselves familiar with best-practice solutions of chosen maintenance tasks. The visualized tasks were chosen because of their relevance and their complexity. Together with the technical experts the working processes were discussed, whereas it could be recognized that the discussion that is accompanied by a visual tool is much more intensive than just talking about a process. Before using VR based environments the work process was explained by using written manuals, checklists and videos. The use of a video is a mainly cognitivistic approach where the learner observes another person handling a situation and transfers the knowledge gained to their own task. In many situations videos are well suited, e.g. to have it available on mobile devices and to remember single working steps.

For more complex tasks a feedback from the system and the opportunity of interacting and getting further information is necessary. In the virtual learning environment a work step is described by a set of predefined animations and actions that were developed together with the technical experts, enhanced by additional information that can be accessed from the virtual scene or from a checklist. This design is following a constructive approach.

Fig. 4. Best practice solution combining animations, a checklist and different media

The learning modules are suitable for learning groups of different levels of expertise. For the learning application presented, the taxonomy of Bloom can be interpreted as follows:

1. *Knowledge:* The learner can assign the parts and assembly groups of the pole column and the operating mechanism of one type of high voltage circuit breaker, knows how SF_6 – the isolating gas within the pole column – behaves in case of compression and in which order working steps have to be executed.
2. *Comprehension:* The learner explains the functional processes of the operating mechanism, the pole column and the coupling between as well as the changes of gas and electricity during runtime.
3. *Application:* The learner can apply the knowledge to other types of high voltage circuit breakers.

4. *Analysis:* The learner can divide a real task into subtasks and can use his/her knowledge for problem-solving. Factual knowledge and process knowledge are used for understanding, analyzing and solving the problem.
5. *Synthesis:* Learners can solve problems that were not part of their qualification. Because of their knowledge and experience they can recognize relations and develop new solutions.
6. *Evaluation:* The learner has a far-reaching overview from technical as well as from the economical point of view. This gives him the ability to distinguish between different solutions following the companies' interests. The learner is also able to transfer his/her knowledge to colleagues in a suitable manner.

5   Experiences From Practical Use

"In order to evaluate the VR learning application a quasi-experimental pretest-posttest-follow-up control group design was chosen, with a group of trainees being taught traditionally by a trainer as the control group (TT) and a second equally sized group of trainees using the virtual reality application as the experimental group (VR). Hence, the trainees were assigned randomly to two groups of 10 persons each. In each training session participated 5 trainees and each one took 8 hours of work. This applies for both conditions, the TT training and VR training as well." [10] The evaluation has revealed a very high acceptance of the learning environment among users. The acceptance was rated even higher from the more experienced workers as they could imagine situations in which the use of the virtual environment would have had improved their understanding of processes and therefore their performance in the job.

The learning environment was easy-to-use for the whole peer group although it was recognized that the learning environment should be defined with respect to the user group. The design as well as the presentation of the content needs to be adapted for older users, e.g. by referring to experiences they made in their work life before.

6   Summary and Outlook

The paper at hand has presented the necessity of considering basic approaches of the didactical design when developing VR based learning environments. Based on the activity theory of Engeström the outcome of the learning system can be influenced by considering the learner, the learning object as well as media that is used for learning. Due to the technical domain that is focused in this paper, especially the field of maintenance, Virtual Reality reveals a high potential for designing learning applications as it allows the very clear and understandable visualization of complex technical processes. Learning in the real working environment is often limited because the equipment is not available or the handling is very dangerous. Learning in VR therefore contains no risk. Beside this the use of Virtual Reality allows learners to interactively solve learning tasks under the aspect of situated learning and the constructive approach of learning.

Future work will focus on the visualization of experiential knowledge. As experiential knowledge is mainly tacit knowledge, narrative methods for its investigation, as described in the paper at hand, need to be developed and applied. They can be improved by using VR-based applications that allow the documentation of stories already within the interview process and can keep the narrative structure. This ensures a better transfer process. Furthermore the access and the presentation of knowledge will be designed adaptively by means of the user characteristics (age, pre-existing knowledge).

References

1. Sendler, U. (ed.): ndustrie 4.0. Beherrschung der industriellen Komplexität mit SysLM. Morgan Kaufmann, Heidelberg (2013)
2. Schenk, M., Wirth, S., Müller, E.: Fabrikplanung und Fabrikbetrieb. Methoden für die wandlungsfähige, vernetzte und ressourceneffiziente Fabrik. vollst. überarb. u. erw. Aufl., 2nd edn. Springer, Berlin (2013)
3. Polanyi, M.: The Tacit Dimension. Doubleday, Garden City (1966)
4. Blümel, E., Jenewein, K., Schenk, M.: Virtuelle Realitäten als Lernräume: Zum Einsatz von VR-Technologien im beruflichen Lernen In: Lernen & lehren, vol. 25(97), pp. 6–13. Heckner Druck- und Verlagsgesellschaft mbH & Co. KG, Wolfenbüttel (2010)
5. Klafki, W.: Neue Studien zur Bildungstheorie und Didaktik: zeitgemäße Allgemeinbildung und kritisch-konstruktive Didaktik, 4th edn. Aufl. Beltz Verlag, Weinheim/Basel (1994)
6. Speth, H., Berner, S.: Theorie und Praxis des Wirtschaftlehreunterrichts, Eine Fachdidaktik, 10th edn. Aufl. Merkur Verlag, Rinteln (2011)
7. Schenk, M.: Instandhaltung technischer Systeme. Methoden und Werkzeuge zur Gewährleistung eines sicheren und wirtschaftlichen Anlagenbetriebs. In: Instandhaltung Technischer Systeme (2010)
8. Neuweg, G.H.: Könnerschaft und implizites Wissen – Zur lehr-lerntheoretischen Bedeutung der Erkenntnis- und Wissenstheorie Michael Polanyis, 3rd edn. Aufl., Münster (2004)
9. Schilcher, C.: Implizite Dimensionen des Wissens und ihre Bedeutung für betriebliches Wissensmanagement. Darmstadt (2006)
10. Haase, T., Termath, W., Martsch, M.: How to Save Expert Knowledge for the Organization: Methods for Collecting and Documenting Expert Knowledge Using Virtual Reality based Learning Environments. In: Procedia Computer Science, vol. 25, pp. 236–246 (2013), doi:10.1016/j.procs.2013.11.029
11. Dick, M., Braun, M., Eggers, I., Hildebrandt, N.: Wissenstransfer per Triadengespräch: eine Methode für Praktiker. In: zfo – Zeitschrift Führung + Organisation, vol. 79, pp. 375–383 (July 2010)
12. Leontjew, A.N.: Tätigkeit, Bewußtsein, Persönlichkeit. Ernst Klett Verlag, Stuttgart (1977)
13. Engeström, Y.: Learning by Expanding - An Activity-Theoretical Approach to Developmental Research. University of Helsinki Press, Helsinki (1987)
14. Dreyfus, H.L., Dreyfus, S.E.: Künstliche Intelligenz: Von den Grenzen der Denkmaschine und dem Wert der Intuition. Dt. Erstausg., 14-16. Tsd. Reinbek bei Hamburg, Rowohlt (1991)
15. Rauner, F.: Practical knowledge and occupational competence. European Journal of Vocational Training 4, 57–72 (2007)
16. Lave, J., Wenger, E.: Situated Learning, Legitimate Peripheral Participation. Cambridge University Press, Cambridge/ New York (1991)

17. Anderson, L.W., Krathwohl, D.R., Airasian, P.W., Cruikshank, K.A., Mayer, R.E., Pintrich, P.R., Raths, J., Wittrock, M.C.: A taxonomy for learning, teaching, and addressing: A revision of Bloom's taxonomy of educational objectives. Longman, New York (2001)
18. Mayer, R.E.: A taxonomy for computer-based assessment of problem solving. Computers in Human Behavior 18, 623–632 (2002)
19. Pintrich, P.R.: The role of metacognitive knowledge in learning, teaching, and assessing. Theory into Practice 41(4), 219–225 (2002)
20. Bloom, B.S.: Taxonomie von Lernzielen im kognitiven Bereich, 5th edn. Aufl. Beltz Verlag, Weinheim und Basel (1976)
21. Reinmann, G.: Blended Learning in der Lehrerbildung: Grundlagen für die Konzeption innovativer Lernumgebungen. Pabst, Lengerich (2005)
22. Baumgart, F. (ed.): Entwicklungs- und Lerntheorien. Klinkhardt, Bad Heilbronn (1998)
23. Göhlich, M., Zirfas, J.: Lernen: Ein pädagogischer Grundbegriff. Kohlhammer, Stuttgart (2007)
24. Jonassen, D.: Thinking technology: Towards a constructivist design model. Educational Technology 34(4), 34–37 (1994)
25. Haase, T., Termath-Bechstein, W., Martsch, M.: Virtual Reality-based training for the maintenance of high voltage equipment. In: Urban, B. (ed.) eLearning Baltics 2012. Proceedings of the 5th International eLBa Science Conference in Rostock, Germany, June 21-22, Fraunhofer Verl, Stuttgart (2012)

Bridging the Gap between Students
and Laboratory Experiments

Max Hoffmann, Katharina Schuster, Daniel Schilberg, and Sabina Jeschke

Institute for Information Management in Mechanical Engineering
Center for Knowledge Management
RWTH Aachen University, Aachen, Germany
max.hoffmann@ima.rwth-aachen.de

Abstract. After having finished studies, graduates need to apply their knowledge to a new environment. In order to professionally prepare students for new situations, virtual reality (VR) simulators can be utilized. During our research, such a simulator is applied in order to enable the visit of remote laboratories, which are designed through advanced computer graphics in order to create simulated representations of real world environments. That way, it is our aim to facilitate the access to practical engineering laboratories.

Our goal is to enable a secure visit of elusive or dangerous places for students of technical studies. The first step towards the virtualization of engineering environments, e.g. a nuclear power plant, consists in the development of demonstrators. In the present paper, we describe the elaboration of an industry relevant demonstrator for the advanced teaching of engineering students. Within our approach, we use a virtual reality simulator that is called the "Virtual Theatre".

Keywords: Virtual Reality, Virtual Theatre, Remote Laboratories, Immersion.

1 Introduction

In terms of modern teaching methods within engineering classes, various different approaches can be utilized to impart knowledge to students. There are traditional teaching techniques, which are still suitable for most of the knowledge transfer. These methods are carried out by the use of written texts or the spoken word. However, due to the increasing number of study paths as well as the specialization of particularly technical oriented classes, there is a need for the integration of new media into the curriculum of most students [1]. Thus, the visualization of educational content in order to explain theory more concrete and tangible has gained in importance. Not least because of the progress in computer science and graphical visualization, the capabilities of visualizing objects of interest within an artificially designed context have grown to an exhaustive amount. However, not only the visualization techniques have emerged, the way of distributing knowledge through teaching media has also grown. One major improvement in reaching students independently to their location are E-Learning Platforms [2]. These technical possibilities of sharing and representing contents open up new opportunities in teaching and learning for students.

R. Shumaker and S. Lackey (Eds.): VAMR 2014, Part II, LNCS 8526, pp. 39–50, 2014.
© Springer International Publishing Switzerland 2014

Thus, in nearly all courses of studies, new media have gained a high significance in the past decade. These new media are continuously replacing conventional media or in other words traditional, static teaching approaches using books and lecture notes. The new media are mostly based on methods of digital visualization [3], e.g. presentation applications like PowerPoint [4]. This switch from the traditional lecture speech to graphical representations have been performed, because this form of presentation enables focusing on the main points of educational content using illustrative representations and pictorial summaries [5]. Despite the positive [6], but also critical discussion about an overwhelming usage of PowerPoint [7–9] as primary teaching tool [10], the usage of presentation software in the classroom has grown constantly [11].

Applications like PowerPoint may be a far reaching advancement for most courses within university. However, even these IT-based teaching supports are limited to a certain kind of knowledge transfer. Especially practically oriented study paths like engineering courses have an urgent need for interaction possibilities. In these highly technical focused studies, the teaching personnel are facing more and more obstacles in imparting their knowledge tangible. Due to the advanced and complex technology level of the relevant applications [12], progressive methods have to be applied to fulfill the desired teaching goals. In order to make the problem based learning methodologies available [13], novel visualization techniques have to be carried out.

Studies of astronautics or nuclear research can serve as an incisive example for the need of innovative visualization capabilities. During astronomy studies, the teaching personnel will face insurmountable obstacles, if they want to impart practical knowledge about aerospace travelling to the students using theoretical approaches. In order to gain deep, experienced knowledge about real situations an astronaut has to face, realistic scenarios have to be carried out. This can for instance be performed by setting up expensive real-world demonstrators that facilitate practical experiences within aerospace travelling events, e.g. by making use of actual acceleration.

However, there is also a need for a visual representation of the situation. In order to fulfill the requirements of a holistic experience, these visualization techniques need to perform an immersive representation of the virtual world scenario. In this connection, the term immersion is defined according to Murray [14] as follow: "Immersion is a metaphorical term derived from the physical experience of being submerged in water. We seek the same feeling from a psychologically immersive experience that we do from a plunge in the ocean or swimming pool: the sensation of being surrounded by a completely other reality, as different as water is from air that takes over all of our attention, our whole perceptual apparatus."

It is obvious that experience can only be impressive enough to impart experienced knowledge, if the simulation of a virtual situation has an immersive effect on the perception of the user. Our latest research on creating virtual world scenarios has shown that immersion has got a high impact on the learning behavior of students [15]. Following the idea of facilitating the study circumstances for students of astronautics, our first demonstrator was carried out in terms of a Mars scenario [16]. Using novel visualization techniques in connection with realistic physics engines, we have carried out a realistic representation of a plateau located on the red planet.

In our next research phase, we want to go further to increase the interaction capabilities with the virtual environment the user is experiencing. In terms of the Mars representation, there were already few interaction possibilities like triggering of object movements or the navigation of vehicles [16]. However, this sort of interaction is based on rather artificial commands than on natural movements with realistic consequences in the representation of the virtual world scenario.

Hence, in the present paper, we want to introduce a more grounded scenario, which is based on the aforementioned idea of enabling the visit of elusive or dangerous places like an atomic plant. Accordingly, our first step in realizing an overall scenario of a detailed environment like a power plant consists in the development of single laboratory environments. In this context, our aim is to focus especially on the interaction capabilities within this demonstrator.

This target is pursued by carrying out a virtual prototype of an actual laboratory environment, which can be accessed virtually and in real-time by a user in a virtual reality simulator. The realization of these demonstrators is also known as the creation of "remote laboratories". In the present paper, we describe the development, optimization and testing of such a remote laboratory. After a brief introduction into the state-of-the-art of this comparatively new research field in chapter 2, our special Virtual Reality simulator, which is used to simulate virtual environments in an immersive way, is described in chapter 3. In chapter 4, the technical design of the remote laboratory including its information and communication infrastructure is presented. In the Conclusion and Outlook, the next steps in realizing the overall goal of a virtual representation of an engineering environment like an atomic plant are pointed out.

2   State of the Art

In the introduction, we concluded that innovative teaching methodologies have to be adopted to be capable of imparting experienced knowledge to students. Thus, virtual reality teaching and learning approaches will be examined in the following.

Nowadays, an exhaustive number of applications can be found that make use of immersive elements within real-world scenarios. However, the immersive character of all these applications is based on two characteristics of the simulation: The first one is the quality of the three-dimensional representation; the second one is the user's identification with the avatar within the virtual world scenario.

The modeling quality of the three-dimensional representation of a virtual scenario is very important in order to be surrounded by a virtual reality that is realistic or even immersive. However, a high-quality graphical representation of the simulation is not sufficient for an intensive experience. Thus, according to Wolf and Perron [17], the following conditions have to be fulfilled in order to enable an immersive user experience within the scenario: "Three conditions create a sense of immersion in a virtual reality or 3-D computer game: The user's expectation of the game or environment must match the environment's conventions fairly closely. The user's actions must have a non-trivial impact on the environment. The conventions of the world must be consistent, even if they don't match those of the 'metaspace'."

The user's identification with virtual scenario is rather independent from the modeling of the environment. It is also depending on the user's empathy with the "avatar". Generally, an avatar is supposed to represent the user in a game or a virtual scenario. However, to fulfill its purposes according to the user's empathy, the avatar has to supply further characteristics. Accordingly, Bartle defines an avatar as follows: "An avatar is a player's representative in a world. [...] It does as it's told, it reports what happens to it, and it acts as a general conduit for the player and the world to interact. It may or may not have some graphical representation, it may or may not have a name. It refers to itself as a separate entity and communicates with the player."

There are already many technical solutions that are primarily focused on the creation of high-quality and complex three-dimensional environments, which are accurate to real-world scenarios in every detail. Flight Simulators, for example, provide vehicle tracking [18]. Thus, the flight virtual reality simulator is capable of tracking the locomotion of a flying vehicle within the virtual world, but does not take into account the head position of the user. Another VR simulator is the Omnimax Theater, which provides a large angle of view [19], but does not enable any tracking capabilities whatsoever. Head-tracked monitors were introduced by Codella et al. [20] and by Deering [21]. These special monitors provide an overall tracking system, but provide a rather limited angle of view [18]. The first attempt to create virtual reality in terms of a complete adjustment of the simulation to the user's position and head movements was introduced with the Boom Mounted Display by McDowall et al. [22]. However, these displays provided only poor resolutions and thus were not capable of a detailed graphical representation of the virtual environment [23].

In order to enable an extensive representation of the aimed remote laboratories, we are looking for representative scenarios that fit to immersive requirements using both a detailed graphical modeling as well as a realistic experience within the simulation. In this context, one highly advanced visualization technology was realized through the development of the Cave in 1991. In this context, the recursive acronym CAVE stands for Cave Automatic Virtual Environment [18] and was first mentioned in 1992 by Cruz-Neira [24]. Interestingly, the naming of the Cave is also inspired by Plato's Republic [25]. In this book, he "discusses inferring reality (ideal forms) form shadows (projections) on the cave wall" [18] within "The Smile of the Cave".

By making use of complex projection techniques combined with various projectors as well as six projection walls arranged in form of a cube, the developers of the Cave have redefined the standards in visualizing virtual reality scenarios. The Cave enables visualization techniques, which provide multi-screen stereo vision while reducing the effect of common tracking and system latency errors. Hence, in terms of resolution, color and flicker-free stereo vision the founders of the Cave have created a new level of immersion and virtual reality.

The Cave, which serves the ideal graphical representation of a virtual world, brings us further towards true Virtual Reality, which – according to Rheingold [26] – is described as an experience, in which a person is "surrounded by a three-dimensional computer-generated representation, and is able to move around in the virtual world and see it from different angles, to reach into it, grab it and reshape it." This enables various educational, but also industrial and technical applications. Hence, in the past the research already focused on the power of visualization in technical applications, e.g. for data visualizations purposes [27] or for the exploration and prototyping of complex systems like the visualization of air traffic simulation systems [28]. Furthermore, the Cave has also been used within medical or for other applications, which require annotations and labeling of objects, e.g. in teaching scenarios [29].

The founders of the Cave choose an even more specific definition of virtual reality: "A virtual reality system is one which provides real-time viewer-centered head-tracking perspective with a large angle of view, interactive control, and binocular display." [18] Cruz-Neira also mentions that – according to Bishop and Fuchs [30] – the competing term "virtual environment (VE)" has a "somewhat grander definition which also correctly encompasses touch, smell and sound." Hence, in order to gain a holistic VR experience, more interaction within the virtual environment is needed.

Though, it is our aim to turn Virtual Reality into a complete representation of a virtual environment by extending the needed interaction capabilities, which are, together with the according hardware, necessary to guarantee the immersion of the user into the virtual reality [31]. However, even the Cave has got restricted interaction capabilities as the user can only interact within the currently demonstrated perspectives. Furthermore, natural movement is very limited, as locomotion through the virtual environment is usually restricted to the currently shown spot of the scenario. Yet, natural movements including walking, running or even jumping through virtual reality are decisive for a highly immersive experience within the virtual environment.

This gap of limited interaction has to be filled by advanced technical devices without losing high-quality graphical representations of the virtual environment. Hence, within this publication, we introduce the Virtual Theatre, which combines the visualization and interaction technique mentioned before. The technical setup and the application of the Virtual Theatre in virtual scenarios are described in the next chapter.

3   The Virtual Theatre – Enabling Virtual Reality in Action

The Virtual Theatre was developed by the MSEAB Weibull Company [32] and was originally carried out for military training purposes. However, as discovered by Ewert et al. [33], the usage of the Virtual Theatre can also be enhanced to meet educational requirements for teaching purposes of engineering students. It consists of four basic elements: The centerpiece, which is referred to as the omnidirectional treadmill, represents the Virtual Theatre's unique characteristics. Besides this moving floor, the Virtual Theatre also consists of a Head Mounted Display, a tracking system and a cyber glove. The interaction of these various technical devices composes a virtual reality simulator that combines the advantages of all conventional attempts to create virtual reality in one setup. This setup will be described in the following.

The Head Mounted Display (HMD) represents the visual perception part of the Virtual Theatre. This technical device consists of two screens that are located in a sort of helmet and enable stereo vision. These two screens – one for each eye of the user – enable a three-dimensional representation of the virtual environment in the perception of the user. HMDs were first mentioned in Fisher [34] and Teitel [35] as devices that use motion in order to create VR. Hence, the characteristic of the HMD consists in the fact that it has a perpendicular aligned to the user and thus adjusts the representation of the virtual environment to him. Each display of the HMD provides a 70° stereoscopic field with an SXGA resolution in order to create a gapless graphical representation of the virtualized scenario [33]. For our specific setup, we are using the Head Mounted Display from zSight [36]. An internal sound system in the HMD enables an acoustic accompaniment for the visualization to complete the immersive scenario.

As already mentioned, the ground part of the Virtual Theatre is the omnidirectional treadmill. This omnidirectional floor represents the navigation component of the Virtual Theatre. The moving floor consists of rigid rollers with increasing circumferences and a common origo [33]. The rotation direction of the rollers is oriented to the middle point of the floor, where a circular static area is located. The rollers are driven by a belt drive system, which is connected to all polygons of the treadmill through a system of coupled shafts and thus ensures the kinematic synchronization of all parts of the moving floor. The omnidirectional treadmill is depicted in figure 1.

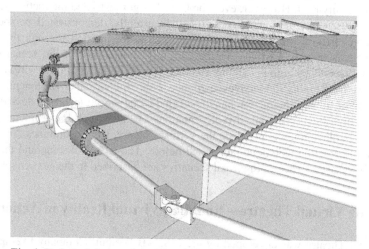

Fig. 1. Technical design of the Virtual Theatre's omnidirectional treadmill

On the central area that is shown in the upper right corner of figure 1, the user is able to stand without moving. As soon as he steps outside of this area, the rollers start moving and accelerate according to the distance of his position to the middle part. If the user returns to the middle area, the rotation of the rollers stops.

The tracking system of the Virtual Theatre is equipped with ten infrared cameras that are evenly distributed around the treadmill in 3 m above the floor. By recording the position of designated infrared markers attached to the HMD and the hand of the user, the system is capable of tracking the user's movements [33]. Due to the unsymmetrical arrangement of the infrared markers the tracking system is not only capable of calculating the position of the user, but is also capable of determining looking directions. That way, the three-dimensional representation of the virtual scenario can be adjusted according to the user's current head position and orientation. Furthermore, the infrared tracking system is used in order to adjust the rotation speed of the rollers no only according to the user's distance from the middle point, but also according to the difference of these distances within a discrete time interval. Using these enhanced tracking techniques, the system can deal with situations, in which the user stands without moving while not being located in the middle of the omnidirectional floor.

The cyber glove ensures the tactile interaction capabilities. This special hand glove is equipped with 22 sensors, as indicated above, which are capable of determining the user's hand position and gestures [33]. This enables the triggering of gesture based events like the grasping of objects. Additionally, special programmable gestures can be utilized in order to implement specific interaction commands.

After setting up the required hardware of the Virtual Theatre, the user can plunge into different scenarios and can be immersed by virtual reality. After the development of learning and interaction scenarios as described in [16], our main interest here is focused on the development of remote laboratories, which represent the first step towards the realization of a virtual factory. The development, testing and evaluation of our first "Remote Lab" are described in the next chapter.

4   Development of Remote Laboratories in the Virtual Theatre

The described setup of the Virtual Theatre can be used to immerse the user into a virtual reality scenario not only for demonstration purposes, but especially for the application of scenarios, in which a distinctive interaction between the user and the simulation is required. One of these applications consists in the realization of remote laboratories, which represent the first step towards the creation of real-world demonstrators like a factory or an atomic plant into virtual reality.

Fig. 2. Two cooperating ABB IRB 120 six-axis robots

The virtual remote laboratory described in this paper consists in a virtual representation of two cooperating robot arms that are setup within our laboratory environment (see figure 2). These robots are located on a table in such a way that they can perform tasks by executing collaborative actions. For our information and communication infrastructure setup, it doesn't matter, if the robots are located in the same laboratory as our Virtual Theatre or in a distant respectively remote laboratory. In this context, our aim was to virtualize a virtual representation of the actual robot movements in the first step. In a second step, we want to control and to navigate the robots.

In order to visualize the movements of the robot arms in virtual reality, first, we had to design the three-dimensional models of the robots. The robot arms, which are installed within our laboratory setup are ABB IRB 120 six-axis robotic arms [37]. For the modeling purposes of the robots, we are using the 3-D optimization and rendering software Blender [38]. After modeling the single sections of the robot, which are connected by the joints of the six rotation axes, the full robot arm model had to be merged together using a bone structure. Using PhysX engine, the resulting mesh is capable of moving its joints in connection with the according bones in the same fashion as a real robot arm. This realistic modeling principally enables movements of the six-axis robot model in virtual reality according to the movements of the real robot. The virtual environment that contains the embedded robot arms is designed using the WorldViz Vizard Framework [39], a toolkit for setting up virtual reality scenarios.

After the creation of the virtual representation of the robots, an information and communication infrastructure had to be set up in order to enable the exchange of information between the real laboratory and the simulation. The concept of the intercommunication as well as its practical realization is depicted in figure 3.

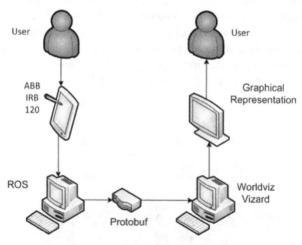

Fig. 3. Information and Communication Infrastructure of the remote laboratory setup

As shown in the figure, the hardware of the remote laboratory setup is connected through an internal network. On the left side of the figure, a user is demonstrated, who operates the movements of the real robot arms manually through a control interface of the ABB IRB 120 robots. This data is processed by a computer using Linux with embedded Robot Operating System (ROS). The interconnection between the real laboratory and the virtual remote laboratory demonstrator is realized using the Protocol Buffers (Protobuf) serialization method for structured data. This interface description language, which was developed by Google [40], is capable of exchanging data between different applications in a structured form.

After the robots' position data is sent through the network interface, the information is interpreted by the WorldViz Vizard engine to visualize the movements of the actual robots in virtual reality. After first test phases and a technical optimization of the network configuration, the offset time between the robot arm motion in reality and in virtual reality could be reduced to 0.2 seconds. Due to the communication design of the network infrastructure in terms of internet-based communication methods, this value would not increase significantly, if the remote laboratory would be located in a distant place, for example in another city or on the other side of the globe.

The second user, which is depicted in the right upper part of figure 3 and who is located in the Virtual Theatre, is immersed by the virtual reality scenario and can observe the positions and motions of the real robots in the virtual environment. In figure 4, the full setup of the real and the remote laboratory is illustrated.

Fig. 4. Manual control of the robots and visual representation in the Virtual Theatre

In the foreground of the figure, two users are controlling the movements of the actual robots in the real laboratory using manual control panels. In the background on the right side of the picture, the virtual representation of the two ABB IRB 120 robot arms is depicted. The picture on the right side of the wall is generated using two digital projectors, which are capable of creating a 3-D realistic picture by overlapping the pictures of both projections. The picture depicted on top of the robot arms table is a representation of the picture the user in the VR simulator is actually seeing during the simulation. It was artificially inserted into figure 4 for demonstration purposes.

This virtual remote laboratory demonstrator shows impressively that it is already possible to create an interconnection between the real world and virtual reality.

5   Evaluation

The results of first evaluations within the test mode of our virtual remote laboratory demonstrator have shown that the immersive character of the virtual reality simulation has got a major impact on the learning behavior and especially on the motivation of the users. Within our test design, students were first encouraged to implemented specific movements of an ABB IRB 120 robot using the Python programming language. After this practical phase the students were divided into two groups.

The first group had the chance to watch a demonstration of the six axis robots carrying out a task using "LEGO" bricks. After seeing the actual movements of the robots within our laboratories, the students were fairly motivated to understand the way of automating the intelligent behavior of the two collaborating robots.

The second group of students had the possibility to take part in a remote laboratory experiment within the Virtual Theatre. After experiencing the robot movements in the simulated virtual environment performing the same task as the real world demonstrator, the students could observe the laboratory experiment they were just experiencing in the Virtual Theatre recorded on video. Their reaction on the video has shown that the immersion was more impressive than the observation of the actual robot's movements performed by the other group. Accordingly, the students of the second comparison group were even more motivated after their walk through the virtual laboratory. The students of the second group were actually aiming at staying in the laboratory until they finished automating the same robot tasks they just saw in virtual reality.

6   Conclusion and Outlook

In this paper, we have described the development of a virtual reality demonstrator for the visualization of remote laboratories. Through the demonstrated visualization techniques in the Virtual Theatre, we have shown that it is possible to impart experienced knowledge to any student independent of his current location. This enables new possibilities of experience-based and problem-based learning. As one major goal of our research project "ELLI – Exzellentes Lehren und Lernen in den Ingenieurwissenschaften (Excellent Teaching and Learning within engineering science)", which addresses this type of problem-based learning [13], the implemented demonstrator contributes to our aim of establishing advanced teaching methodologies. The visualization of real-world systems in virtual reality enables the training of problem-solving strategies within a virtual environment as well as on real objects at the same time.

The next steps of our research consist in advancing the existing demonstrator in terms of a bidirectional communication between the Virtual Theatre demonstrator and the remote laboratory. Through this bidirectional communication we want to enable a direct control of the real laboratory from the remote virtual reality demonstrator. First results in the testing phase of this bidirectional communication show that such a remote control will be realized in the near future. In order to enable a secure remote control of the remote laboratory, collision avoidance and other security systems for cooperating robots will be carried out and tested in the laboratory environment.

As the overall goal of our project consists in the development of virtual factories in order to enable the visit of an atomic plant or other elusive places, our research efforts will finally focus on the development of a detailed demonstrator for the realistic representation of an industrial environment.

Acknowledgment. This work was supported by the project ELLI (Excellent Teaching and Learning within engineering science) as part of the excellence initiative at RWTH Aachen University.

References

1. Kerres, M.: Mediendidaktik. Konzeption und Entwicklung mediengestützer Lernangebote. München (2012)
2. Handke, J., Schäfer, A.M.: E-Learning, E-Teaching and E-Assessment in der Hochschullehre. Eine Anleitung, München (2012)
3. Craig, R.J., Amernic, J.H.: PowerPoint Presentation Technology and the Dynamics of Teaching. Innovative Higher Education 31(3), 147–160 (2006)
4. Szabo, A., Hastings, N.: Using IT in the undergraduate classroom. Should we replace the blackboard with PowerPoint? Computer and Education 35 (2000)
5. Köhler, T., Kahnwald, N., Reitmaier, M.: Lehren und Lernen mit Multimedia und Internet. In: Batinic, B., Appel, M. (Hrsg.), Medienpsychologie, Heidelberg (2008)
6. Bartsch, R.A., Cobern, K.M.: Effectiveness of PowerPoint presentation in lectures. Computer and Education 41, 77–86 (2003)
7. Creed, T.: PowerPoint, No! Cyberspace, Yes. The Nat. Teach. & Learn. F. 6(4) (1997)
8. Cyphert, D.: The problems of PowerPoint. Visual aid or visual rhetoric? Business Communication Quarterly 67, 80–83 (2004)
9. Norvig, P.: PowerPoint: Shot with its own bullets. The Lancet 362, 343–344 (2003)
10. Simons, T.: Does PowerPoint make you stupid? Presentations 18(3) (2005)
11. Jones, A.M.: The use and abuse of PowerPoint in teaching and learning in the life sciences: A personal view. In: BEE-j 2 (2003)
12. André, E.: Was ist eigentlich Multimodale Mensch-Technik Interaktion? Anpassungen an den Faktor Mensch. In: Forschung und Lehre 21(01/2014) (2014)
13. Steffen, M., May, D., Deuse, J.: The Industrial Engineering Laboratory. Problem Based Learning in Industrial Eng. Education at TU Dortmund University. In: EDUCON (2012)
14. Murray, J.H.: Hamlet on the Holodeck: The Future of Narrative in Cyberspace, Cambridge (Mass.) (1997)
15. Schuster, K., Ewert, D., Johansson, D., Bach, U., Vossen, R., Jeschke, S.: Verbesserung der Lernerfahrung durch die Integration des Virtual Theatres in die Ingenieurausbildung. In: Tekkaya, A. E.; Jeschke, S.; Petermann, M.; May, D.; Friese, N.; Ernst, C.; Lenz, S.; Müller, K.; Schuster, K (Hrsg.). TeachING-LearnING.EU discussions. Aachen (2013)
16. Hoffmann, M., Schuster, K., Schilberg, D., Jeschke, S.: Next-Generation Teaching and Learning using the Virtual Theatre. In: 4th Global Conference on Experiential Learning in Virtual Worlds in print, Prague, Czech Republic (2014)
17. Wolf, M.J.P., Perron, B.: The video game theory reader, NY, London (2003)
18. Cruz-Neira, C., Sandin, D.J., DeFanti, T.A.: Surround-Screen Projection-based Virtual Reality. The Design and Implementation of the CAVE. In: SIGGRAPH 1993 Proceedings of the 20th Annual Conference on Computer Graphics and Interactive Techniques, pp. 135–142. ACM, New York (1993)
19. Max, N.: SIGGRAPH 1984 Call for Omnimax Films. Computer Graphics 16(4), 208–214 (1982)
20. Codella, C., Jalili, R., Koved, L., Lewis, B., Ling, D.T., Lipscomb, J.S., Rabenhorst, D., Wang, C.P., Norton, A., Sweeny, P., Turk, G.: Interactive simulation in a multi-person virtual world. In: ACM - Human Fact. in Comp. Syst. CHI 1992 Conf., pp. 329–334 (1992)

21. Deering, M.: High Resolution Virtual Reality. Com. Graph. 26(2), 195–201 (1992)
22. McDowall, I.E., Bolas, M., Pieper, S., Fisher, S.S., Humphries, J.: Implementation and Integration of a Counterbalanced CRT-based Stereoscopic Display for Interactive Viewpoint Control in Virtual Environment Applications. In: Proc. SPIE, vol. 1256(16) (1990)
23. Ellis, S.R.: What are virtual environments? IEEE Computer Graphics and Applications 14(1), 17–22 (1994)
24. Cruz-Neira, C., Sandin, D.J., DeFanti, T.A., Kenyon, R.V., Hart, J.C.: The CAVE: Audio Visual Experience Automatic Virtual Environment. Communications of the ACM 35(6), 64–72 (1992)
25. Plato: The Republic. Athens (375 B.C.)
26. Rheingold, H.: Virtual reality. New York (1991)
27. Nowke, C., Schmidt, M., van Albada, S.J., Eppler, J.M., Bakker, R., Diesrnann, M., Hentschel, B., Kuhlen, T.: VisNEST – Interactive analysis of neural activity data. In: 2013 IEEE Symposium on Biological Data Visualization (BioVis), pp. 65–72 (2013)
28. Pick, S., Wefers, F., Hentschel, B., Kuhlen, T.: Virtual air traffic system simulation – Aiding the communication of air traffic effects. In: 2013 IEEE on Virtual Reality (VR), pp. 133–134 (2013)
29. Pick, S., Hentschel, B., Wolter, M., Tedjo-Palczynski, I., Kuhlen, T.: Automated Positioning of Annotations in Immersive Virtual Environments. In: Proc. of the Joint Virtual Reality Conference of EuroVR - EGVE - VEC, pp. 1–8 (2010)
30. Bishop, G., Fuchs, H., et al.: Rsearch Directions in Virtual Environments. Computer Graphics 26(3), 153–177 (1992)
31. Johansson, D.: Convergence in Mixed Reality-Virtuality Environments: Facilitating Natural User Behavio, Schweden (2012)
32. MSEAB Weibull: http://www.mseab.se/The-Virtual-Theatre.htm
33. Ewert, D., Schuster, K., Johansson, D., Schilberg, D., Jeschke, S.: Intensifying learner's experience by incorporating the virtual theatre into engineering education. In: Proceedings of the 2013 IEEE Global Engineering Education Conference, EDUCON (2013)
34. Fisher, S.: The AMES Virtual Environment Workstation (VIEW). In: SIGGRAPH 1989 Course #29 Notes (1989)
35. Teitel, M.A.: The Eyephone: A Head-Mounted Stereo Display. In: Proc. SPIE, vol. 1256(20), pp. 168–171 (1990)
36. http://sensics.com/products/head-mounted-displays/zsight-integrated-sxga-hmd/specifications/
37. ABB, http://new.abb.com/products/robotics/industrial-robots/irb-120 (last checked: January 27, 2014)
38. Blender, http://www.blender.org/ (last checked: January 27, 2014)
39. WorldViz, http://www.worldviz.com/products/vizard (last checked: January 27, 2014)
40. Google, http://code.google.com/p/protobuf/wiki/ThirdPartyAddOns (last checked: January 27, 2014)

Applying Saliency-Based Region of Interest Detection in Developing a Collaborative Active Learning System with Augmented Reality

Trung-Nghia Le[1,2], Yen-Thanh Le[1], and Minh-Triet Tran[1]

[1] University of Science, VNU-HCM, Ho Chi Minh city, Vietnam
[2] John von Neumann Institute, VNU-HCM, Ho Chi Minh city, Vietnam
nghia.le.ict@jvn.edu.vn, lythanh@apcs.vn,
tmtriet@fit.hcmus.edu.vn

Abstract. Learning activities are not necessary to be only in traditional physical classrooms but can also be set up in virtual environment. Therefore the authors propose a novel augmented reality system to organize a class supporting real-time collaboration and active interaction between educators and learners. A pre-processing phase is integrated into a visual search engine, the heart of our system, to recognize printed materials with low computational cost and high accuracy. The authors also propose a simple yet efficient visual saliency estimation technique based on regional contrast is developed to quickly filter out low informative regions in printed materials. This technique not only reduces unnecessary computational cost of keypoint descriptors but also increases robustness and accuracy of visual object recognition. Our experimental results show that the whole visual object recognition process can be speed up 19 times and the accuracy can increase up to 22%. Furthermore, this pre-processing stage is independent of the choice of features and matching model in a general process. Therefore it can be used to boost the performance of existing systems into real-time manner.

Keywords: Smart Education, Active Learning, Visual Search, Saliency Image, Human-Computer Interaction.

1 Introduction

Skills for the 21st century require active learning which focuses on the responsibility of learning on learners [1] by stimulating the enthusiasm and involvement of learners in various activities. As learning activities are no longer limited in traditional physical classrooms but can be realized in virtual environment [2], we propose a new system with interaction via Augmented Reality (AR) to enhance the attractiveness and collaboration for learners and educators in virtual environment. To develop a novel AR system for education, we focus on the following two criteria as the main guidelines to design our proposed system, including real-time collaboration and interaction, and naturalness of user experience.

R. Shumaker and S. Lackey (Eds.): VAMR 2014, Part II, LNCS 8526, pp. 51–62, 2014.
© Springer International Publishing Switzerland 2014

The first property emphasizes real-time collaboration and active interaction between educators and learners via augmented multimedia and social media. Just looking through a mobile device or AR glasses, an educator can monitor the progress of learners or groups via their interactions with augmented content in lectures. The educator also gets feedbacks from learners on the content and activities designed and linked to a specific page in a lecture note or a textbook to improve the quality of lecture design. Learners can create comments, feedback, or other types of social media targeting a section of a lecture note or a page of a textbook for other learners or the educator. A learner can also be notified and know social content created by other team members during the progress of teamwork.

The second property of the system is the naturalness of user experience as the system can aware of the context, i.e. which section of a page in a lecture note or a textbook is being read, by natural images, not artificial markers. Users can also interact with related augmented content with their bare hands. This helps users enhance their experience on both analog aesthetic emotions and immersive digital multisensory feedback by additional multimedia information.

The core component to develop an AR education environment is to recognize certain areas of printed materials, such as books or lecture handouts. As a learner is easily attracted by figures or charts in books and lecture notes, we encourage educators to exploit learners' visual sensitivity to graphical areas and embed augmented content to such areas, not text regions, in printed materials to attract learners. Therefore in our proposed system, we do not use optical character recognition but visual content recognition to determine the context of readers in reading printed materials.

In practice, graphical regions of interest that mostly attract readers in a page do not fully cover a whole page. There are other regions that do not provide much useful information for visual recognition, such as small decorations or small texts. Therefore, we propose the novel method based on saliency metric to quickly eliminate unimportant or noisy regions in printed lecture notes or textbooks and speed up the visual context recognition process on mobile devices or AR glasses. Our experimental results show that the whole visual object recognition process can be speed up 19 times and the accuracy can increase up to 22%.

This paper is structured as follows. In Section 2, the authors briefly present and analyze the related work. The proposed system is presented in Section 3. In Section 4, we present the core component of our system – the visual search engine. The experiments and evaluations are showed in Section 5. Then we discuss potential use of the system in Section 6. Finally, Section 7 presents conclusion and ideas for future work.

2   Related Work

2.1   Smart Educational Environment

Active learning methods focus on the responsibility of learning on learners [1]. To create an environment for leaners to study efficiently with active learning methods, educators should prepare and design various activities to attract learners. The educators also keep track of the progress for each member in team-work, and simulate the enthusiasm and collaboration of all learners in projects.

Learning activities are not necessarily to be in traditional physical classrooms but virtual environment as well [3]. An educator is required to use various techniques to attract learners' interest and attention to deliver knowledge impressively to them. Augmented Reality (AR) is an emerging technology that enables learners to explore the world of knowledge through the manipulation of virtual objects in real world.

AR has been applied in education to attract learners to study new concepts easily. With handheld displays, users can see virtual objects appearing on the pages of MagicBook [4] from their own viewpoint. After the work was published, several implementations of AR books were created for education, storytelling, simulation, game, and artwork purposes such as AR Vulcano Kiosk and S.O.L.A.R system [5].

AR has also shown great potential in developing and creating an interactive and a more interesting learning environment for the learners. Therefore, useful methods such as interactive study, collaboration study are proposed to enhance this. The classroom environment can be implemented in many ways: collaborative augmented multi user interaction [2] and mixed reality learning spaces [3].

However, these systems still have some limitations. First of all, they do not explicitly describe mechanism and processes for educators and learners to interact and collaborate efficiently in virtual environment with AR. Second, the educators may not have the feedbacks from learners to redesign or organize augmented data and content that are linked to sections in a printed material to improve the quality of education activities. Third, although AR system permits different users to get augmented information corresponding to different external contexts, all users receive the same content when looking at the same page of the book. And the last limitation is that these systems usually give unnatural feeling due to using artificial markers.

The mentioned problems motivate us to propose our smart education environment with AR and personalized interaction to enhance the attractiveness and immersive experience for educators and learners in virtual environment to improve efficiency in teaching and learning. In our proposed system, educators can receive explicit and implicit feedbacks from learners on the content and activities that are designed and linked to a specific lecture in a printed material.

2.2 Visual Sensitivity of Human Perception

A conventional approach to evaluate the attraction of objects in an image is based on textural information. In this direction, regional structural analysis algorithms based on gradient are used to detect features. However, saliency is considered better to reflect sensitivity of human vision to certain areas on an image thus benefits context awareness systems [6]. Visual saliency [7], human perceptual quality indicating the prominence of an object, person, or pixel to its neighbors thus capture our attention, is investigated by multiple disciplines including cognitive psychology, neurobiology, and computer vision. Salient maps are topographical maps of the visually salient parts of scenes without prior knowledge of their contents and thus remains an important step in many computer vision tasks.

Saliency measures are factors attracting eye movements and attention such as color, brightness, and sharpness, etc. [8]. Self-saliency is a feature that expresses the inner region complexity, which includes color saturation, brightness, texture, edginess, etc. Whereas, relative saliency indicates differences bet1een a region and its surrounding regions such as color contrast, sharpness, location, etc. Saliency measures can be combined with different weights to determine important regions more efficiently.

Most of saliency object detection techniques can be characterized as bottom-up saliency analysis, which is data-driven [9], or top-down approach, which is task-driven [6]. We focus on pre-attentive bottom-up saliency detection techniques. These methods are extensions of expert-driven human saliency that tends to use cognitive psychological knowledge of the human visual system and to find image patches on edges and junctions as salient using local contrast or global unique frequencies. Local contrast methods are based on investigating rarity of an image region with respect to local neighborhoods [8]. Whereas, global contrast based methods evaluate saliency of an image region using its contrast with respect to the entire image [10].

In this paper, the authors propose an efficient based human vision computation method to detect automatically high informative regions based on regional contrast in order to determine which region contains meaningful keypoint candidates. This reduces redundant candidates for further processing steps.

3   Overview of Proposed System

3.1   Motivations: Advantages of Smart Environment

The main objective of our system is to create a smart interactive education environment to support real-time collaboration and active interaction between educators and learners. Via special prisms, i.e. mobile devices or AR glasses, both educators and learners are linked to the virtual learning environment with real-time communication and interactions. Our proposed system has the following main characteristics:

1. *Interactivity*: Learners and educators can interact with augmented content, including multimedia and social media, or interact with others via augmented activities, such as exercises or discussion.
2. *Personalization*: Augmented content and activities can be adapted to each learner to provide the learner with the most appropriate, individualized learning paradigm. The adaptation can be in active or passive modes. In active mode, each learner can customize which types of augmented content and activities that he or she wants to explore or participate. In passive mode, an educator can individualize teaching materials to meet the progress, knowledge level, personal skills and attitudes of each learner.
3. *Feedback*: Interactive feedbacks from learners can be used to help an educator redesign existing teaching materials or design future teaching activities. Besides, feedbacks of a learner can also be used to analyze his or her personal interests, knowledge level, personal skills and attitudes toward certain types of activities in learning.
4. *Tracking*: The progress of a learner or a group of learners can be monitored so that an educator can keep track of the performance of each individual or a group.

3.2   Typical Scenarios of Usage for an Educator

The proposed system provides an educator with the following main functions:

1. Design augmented content and activities for lectures
2. Personalize or customize augmented content and activities for each learner or a group of learners
3. Monitor feedbacks and progress of each learner or a group of learners

The first step to create an AR-supported lecture is to design augmented content and activities for lectures. Lecture documents in each course include textbooks, reference books, and other printed materials. An educator can now freely design lectures with attached augmented materials (including multimedia, social media, or activities) that can be revised and updated over terms/semesters, specialized for different classes in different programs such as regular or honors program, and adapted to different languages. Because of wide variety of attached augmented media and activities, an educator can customize a curriculum and teaching strategies to deliver a lecture.

An educator uses our system to design augmented content (including multimedia objects or activities) for a lecture and assigns such content to link with a specific region in a printed page of a lecture note/textbook (c.f. Figure 1). Augmented media are not only traditional multimedia contents, such as images, 3D models, videos, and audios, but also social media contents or activities, such as different types of exercises, an URL to a reference document, or a discussion thread in an online forum, etc.

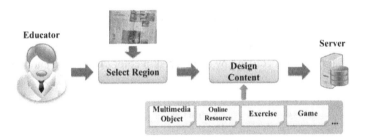

Fig. 1. Design augmented content for printed lecture notes and textbooks

For a specific page, an educator first selects a graphical region that can visually attract learners' attention, and links it to augmented contents, either resources or activities. The system automatically learns features to recognize the selected graphical region together with embedded resources to a remote server. An educator can also design different sets of augmented contents for the same printed teaching materials for different groups of learners in the same class, or for classes in classes in different programs, to utilize various teaching strategies and learning paradigms.

After designing AR-supported teaching materials, an educator can interact with learners via augmented activities during a course. Useful information on learners' activities and interactions are delivered to an educator so that the educator can keep track of the progress of a learner or a group of learners, update and customize augmented resources or activities to meet learners' expectation or level of knowledge, and redesign the teaching materials for future classes.

3.3   Typical Scenarios of Usage for a Learner

A learner can use a mobile device or smart glasses to see pages in a textbook, a reference book, or a printed lecture handout. Upon receiving the visual information that a learner is looking at, the server finds the best match (c.f. Section 4). Then the system transforms the reality in front of the learner's eyes into an augmented world with linked media or activities. Dynamic augmented contents that match a learner's personal profile and preferences are downloaded from the server and displayed on the learner's mobile device screen or glasses(c.f. Figure 2)..

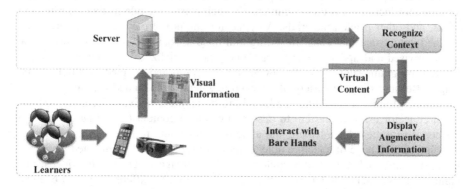

Fig. 2. Learners use the proposed system

Learners can interact with these virtual objects with their bare hands. Skin detection algorithm is used to enable learners use their bare hands to interact with virtual objects appearing in front of their eyes. An event corresponding to a virtual object is generated if that object is occluded by a human skin color object long enough.

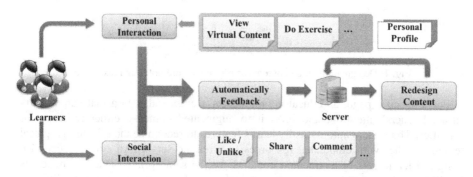

Fig. 3. Interaction and feedback

Learners can add a new virtual note or comment to a specific part of a printed lecture and share with others. They can also do exercises embedded virtually as an augmented content linked to printed lecture notes. When learners use this system, their behaviors are captured as implicit feedbacks to the educator (c.f. Figure 3). An educator can now analyze learners' behaviors and intention to adjust teaching materials to well adapt to each learner of a group. With collaborative filtering methods, the system can recommend to educators which types of augmented content are appropriate for a specific learner based on learners' profiles.

4   Visual Search Optimization with Saliency Based Metric

4.1   Overview

For mobile visual search (MVS) applications, most of existing methods use all keypoints detected from a given image, including those in unimportant regions such as small decoration or text areas. Different from state-of-the-art methods, our approach reduces the number of local features instead of reducing the size of each descriptor. Only keypoints with meaningful information are considered. As our method is independent of the choice of features, the combination of our idea with compact visual descriptors will give more efficiency.

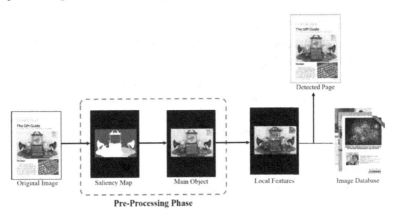

Fig. 4. Our approach to detect a page in a printed lecture note or textbook

We propose the idea to utilize the saliency map of an image to quickly discard keypoints in unimportant or insensitive regions of a template image as well as a query image (c.f. Figure 4). The visual sensitivity of each region is evaluated to determine keypoints to be preserved and those to be removed. This helps to reduce computational cost in local feature extraction of an image. As keypoints in unimportant regions can be removed, the accuracy of visual object recognition can also be improved.

Figure 5 shows our proposed method with two main steps. First, an arbitrary image is decomposed into perceptually homogeneous elements. Then, saliency maps are derived based on the contrast of those elements. The proposed saliency detection algorithm is inspired by the works in object segmentation with image saliency [10]. In our approach, regions of interest can be discrete and there is no need of merging.

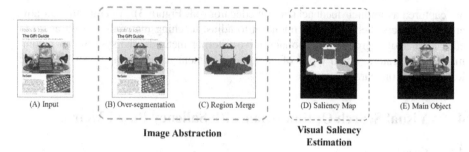

(A) Input   (B) Over-segmentation   (C) Region Merge   (D) Saliency Map   (E) Main Object

Image Abstraction   **Visual Saliency Estimation**

Fig. 5. Pre-processing phase

4.2   Image Abstraction

To simplify illustrations from color images, visual contents are abstracted by region based segmentation algorithms. A region grows by adding similar neighboring pixels according to certain homogeneity criteria, increasing size of region gradually. The proposed algorithm for this phase includes two steps: Over-Segmentation (c.f. Figure 5.B) and Region Growing (c.f. Figure 5.C).

Over-Segmentation: An image is over-segmentation by the watershed-like method. The regions are merged on the basis of a similarity color criterion afterwards: $\left\| \left| c_i - c_j \right| \right\|_2 \leq \theta$ where c_i and c_j are pixels in the same region.

Region Growing: Neighboring segments are merged based on their sizes, which are the number of pixels of each region. If a region whose size is below a threshold, it is merged to its nearest region, in terms of average Lab color distance. To speed up, we use Prim's algorithm [11] to optimize merging regions.

4.3   Visual Saliency Estimation

An image captured from a camera is intentionally focused on meaningful regions by human vision which reacts to regions with features such as unique colors, high contrast, or different orientation. Therefore, to estimate the attractiveness, the contrast metric is usually used to evaluate sensitivity of elements in image.

A region with high level of contrast with surrounding regions can attract human attention and is perceptually more important. Instead of evaluating the contrast difference between regions in an original image, the authors only calculate the contrast metric based on Lab color between regions in the corresponding segmented image. As the number of regions in the original image is much more than the number of regions in its corresponding segmented image, our approach not only simplifies the calculation cost but also exploits the meaningful regions in the captured image efficiently. The contrast C_i of a region $\mathcal{R}_i$ is calculated as the difference between Lab color of R_i and its surrounding regions:

$$C_i = \frac{\sum_{j=1}^{n} \omega(\mathcal{R}_j) \left\| \left| c_i - c_j \right| \right\|_2}{\sum_{j=1}^{n} \omega(\mathcal{R}_j)} \tag{1}$$

where c_j and c_i are Lab colors of regions $\mathcal{R}_j$ and $\mathcal{R}_i$ respectively, and $\omega(\mathcal{R}_j)$ is the number of pixels in region $\mathcal{R}_i$. Regions with more pixels contribute higher local-contrast weights than those containing only a few pixels. Finally, C_i is normalized to the range $[0,1]$. Figure 6 shows that our method can provide better results than existing saliency calculation techniques.

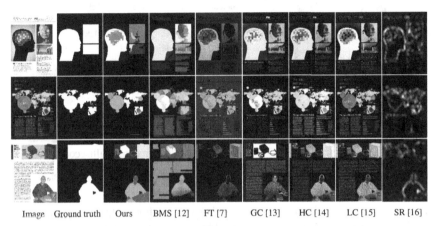

Image   Ground truth   Ours   BMS [12]   FT [7]   GC [13]   HC [14]   LC [15]   SR [16]

Fig. 6. Visual comparison between the proposed method and other state-of-the-art methods

5   Experiments and Evaluation

5.1   Page Detection Evaluation

We conduct the experiment to evaluate the efficiency of our proposed method by matching local features extracted from images in the dataset to compare the accuracy and performance of the proposed process with the original method which does not filter out keypoints and the other state-of-the-art saliency detection methods. Since the proposed process is independent of the keypoint extraction and recognition algorithms, experiments are conducted to evaluate our approach using four popular local features: BRIEF [17], BRISK [18], SIFT [19], and SURF [20].

Experiment is conducted in a system using CPU Core i3 3.3 GHz (with 4GB RAM). Our dataset consists of 200 pages (with resolution 566×750) of reference materials for students in Computer Science, including MSDN Magazine, ACM Transaction Magazine, and IEEE Transaction Magazine. Each typical page includes three types of regions: background, text region, and image.

All local features are extracted in two scenarios: extracting all keypoints and extracting only keypoints in important regions. Image matching is then performed with each pair of images. The accuracy of matching is computed as proportion of correctly matched pairs of images over the number of image pairs. The result of this experiment is shown in Figure 7(a).

On average, the proposed method outperforms conventional methods up to 7%. Especially, when using SIFT feature, the accuracy is boosted approximately 22%. Moreover, our saliency detection module is replaced by different existing state-of-the-art

methods such as BMS [12], FT [7], GC [13], HC [14], LC [15], and SR [16] to evaluate efficiency of our approach. In most cases, our process can provide better results
than others. Incorporating our pre-process stage can not only preserve the robustness of
conventional methods but also boost up the accuracy.

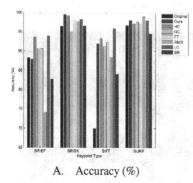

Saliency	Local Features			
Methods	BRIEF	BRISK	SIFT	SURF
Ours	**90.42**	**4.02**	**21.33**	**44.34**
FT	93.48	6.12	26.80	46.76
SR	444.35	43.83	35.17	263.76
HC	261.04	23.09	37.60	180.75
BMS	193.48	14.44	41.50	79.55
GC	328.97	43.87	88.19	220.26
LC	717.25	56.92	104.62	465.71
Original	1000.48	78.00	218.66	661.12

A.   Accuracy (%)   B.   Performance (millisecond)

Fig. 7. Accuracy and performance of page detection of printed reference materials

In addition, the experiments also show that our method outperforms other algorithms with all common local features (c.f. Figure 7.B). On average, using SIFT, our
method is 10.3 times faster than conventional method with no filtering out keypoints.
Similarly, using BRIEF and SURF, our method is 11 and 15 times faster, and especially that of using BRISK features is more than 19.4 times.

Overall, our approach does not only boost up the running time up 19.4 times but
also increases the accuracy of recognizing magazines to 22%. This is the crucial criteria for real-time AR system for magazines, books, and newspapers.

6   Potential Usage of Proposed System

For each course in a specific teaching environment, it is necessary to identify which
types of augmented contents are required by end-users, i.e. educators and learners.
Therefore, we conduct surveys to evaluate the practical need for our system in enhancing the enthusiasm and attractiveness for learners, including high school students
and undergraduate students.

In the meeting with high school teachers and students in enhancing learning experience in Chemistry, we identify the first two main requirements for our system. The
first is 3D visualization of chemical elements, substances, atoms, molecules, and stoi-
chiometry. The second is to assist teachers in the visualization and simulation for
chemical reactions. Although no activities have been set up for students, it is a new
teaching activity with the assistance of our smart educational environment via AR.

In the meeting with instructors of the two courses on Introduction to Information
Technology 1 and 2, we identify more interesting augmented contents including mul-
timedia/social media data and augmented activities that can be established via our
system. These two courses aim to provide the overview on different aspects in Information Technology for freshmen as a preparation and guidance for students following

the teaching strategy of Conceive - Design - Implementation - Operation (CDIO). With the assistance of our system, we can deploy the trial teaching environment for freshmen volunteers to join the active learning activities with AR interactions. The volunteers use the proposed system in the two courses. Students are assigned to read printed materials with AR media, to discuss and do exercises with others via our system. We collect useful feedbacks from participants to evaluate the usefulness and convenience of our system as well as the satisfaction of volunteers with the system and favorite functions. Based on the qualitative interviews in this study, most students find that our system can provide a more interesting and attractive way to study than traditional approaches do. Moreover, the features of collaboration in our system successfully attract students' interest and trigger their motivation in reading documents.

7   Conclusion and Future Work

The authors propose a new method for organizing a collaborative class using AR and interaction. Via our proposed system, learners and educators can actively interact with others. Learners can do exercises embedded virtually as augmented contents linked to a printed lecture note. They can add a new virtual note or comment to a specific part of a printed lecture and share with others as well. Besides, educators get feedbacks from learners on the content and activities designed and linked to a specific page in a lecture note or textbook to improve the quality of lecture designs. Educators can also keep track of the learning progress of each individual or each group of learners.

In our proposed system, we focus on providing the natural means of interactions for users. The system can recognize the context, i.e. which section of a page in a lecture note or a textbook is being read, by natural images, not artificial markers. Users can also interact with related augmented contents with their bare hands.

We also propose a new method based on saliency metric to quickly eliminate irrelevant regions in a page of a book or printed material to enhance the accuracy and performance of the context aware process on mobile devices or AR glasses. Furthermore, our method works independently of the training and detecting stage. It is compatible to most well-known local features. Therefore, this stage can be incorporated into any existed system for printed material detection and recognition.

There are more saliency metrics for implementation in our visual search engine, thus requires further experiments. In addition, the authors are interested in applying psychology and neuroscience knowledge of human vision in further research. To enhance the system, we are doing classification by Neuron network algorithm to analysis the profiles and learn their behaviors in order to utilize better.

References

[1] Bonwell, C.C., Eison, J.A.: Active learning: Creating excitement in the classroom. School of Education and Human Development, George Washington University, Washington, DC, USA (1991)

[2] Kaufmann, H., Schmalstieg, D., Wagner, M.: Construct3D: A Virtual Reality Application for Mathematics and Geometry Education. Education and Information Technologies 5(4), 163–276 (2000)

[3] Winkler, T., Kritzenberger, H., Herczeg, M.: Mixed Reality Environments as Collaborative and Constructive Learning Spaces for Elementary School Children. In: The World Conference on Educational Multimedia, Hypermedia and Telecommunications (2002)

[4] Billinghurst, M., Kato, H., Poupyrev, I.: The MagicBook - Moving Seamlessly between Reality and Virtuality. IEEE Computer Graphics and Applications 21(3), 6–8 (2001)

[5] Woods, E., et al.: Augmenting the science centre and museum experience. In: The 2nd International Conference on Computer Graphics and Interactive Techniques in Australasia and South East Asia (2004)

[6] Goferman, S., Zelnik-Manor, L., Tal, A.: Context-Aware Saliency Detection. IEEE Transactions on Pattern Analysis and Machine Intelligence 34(10), 1915–1926 (2012)

[7] Achanta, R., Hemami, S., Estrada, F., Susstrunk, S.: Frequency-tuned salient region detection. In: 22nd IEEE Computer Society on Computer Vision and Pattern Recognition, pp. 1597–1604 (2009)

[8] Ma, Y.-F., Zhang, H.-J.: Contrast-based image attention analysis by using fuzzy growing. In: 11th ACM International Conference on Multimedia, pp. 374–381 (2003)

[9] Siva, P., Russell, C., Xiang, T., Agapito, L.: Looking Beyond the Image: Unsupervised Learning for Object Saliency and Detection. In: 26th IEEE Conference on Computer Vision and Pattern Recognition (2013)

[10] Qiong, Y., Xu, L., Shi, J., Jia, J.: Hierarchical Saliency Detection. In: 26th IEEE Conference on Computer Vision and Pattern Recognition (2013)

[11] Prim, R.C.: Shortest connection networks and some generalizations. Bell System Technical Journal 36(6), 1389–1401 (1957)

[12] Zhang, J., Sclaroff, S.: Saliency detection: A boolean map approach. In: The IEEE International Conference on Computer Vision, ICCV (2013)

[13] Cheng, M.-M., et al.: Efficient Salient Region Detection with Soft Image Abstraction. In: IEEE International Conference on Computer Vision (2013)

[14] Cheng, M.-M., Zhang, G.-X., Mitra, N.J., Huang, X., Hu, S.-M.: Global contrast based salient region detection. In: 24th IEEE Conference on Computer Vision and Pattern Recognition, pp. 409–416 (2011)

[15] Zhai, Y., Shah, M.: Visual Attention Detection in Video Sequences Using Spatiotemporal Cues. In: The 14th Annual ACM International Conference on Multimedia, pp. 815–824 (2006)

[16] Hou, X., Zhang, L.: Saliency Detection: A Spectral Residual Approach. In: 20th IEEE Computer Society Conference on Computer Vision and Pattern Recognition (2007)

[17] Calonder, M., Lepetit, V., Strecha, C., Fua, P.: BRIEF: Binary robust independent elementary features. In: 11th European Conference on Computer Vision, pp. 778–792 (2010)

[18] Leutenegger, S., Chli, M., Siegwart, R.Y.: BRISK: Binary Robust Invariant Scalable Keypoints. In: 13th IEEE International Conference on Computer Vision (ICCV), pp. 2548–2555 (2011)

[19] Lowe, D.: Distinctive Image Features from Scale Invariant Keypoints. International Journal of Computer Vision 20(2), 91–110 (2004)

[20] Bay, H., Ess, A., Tuytelaars, T., Gool, L.V.: SURF: Speeded Up Robust Features. In: 9th European Conference on Computer Vision, pp. 404–417 (2006)

A 3D Virtual Learning System for STEM Education

Tao Ma, Xinhua Xiao, William Wee, Chia Yung Han, and Xuefu Zhou

Department of Electrical Engineering and Computing Systems,
University of Cincinnati, USA
mata@mail.uc.edu, xinhuaxiao@gmail.com,
{han,zhoxu}@ucmail.uc.edu

Abstract. A recent boom has been seen in 3D virtual worlds for entertainment, and this in turn has led to a surge of interest in their educational applications. Although booming development has been seen, most of them only strengthen the traditional teaching methods using a new platform without changing the nature of how to teach and learn. Modern computer science technology should be applied in STEM education for the purpose of rising learning efficiency and interests. In this paper, we focus on the reasoning, design, and implementation of a 3D virtual learning system that merges STEM experiments into virtual laboratory and brings entertainment to knowledge learning. An advanced hand gesture interface was introduced to enable flexible manipulation on virtual objects with two hands. The recognition ability of single hand grasping-moving-rotating activity (SH-GMR) allows single hand to move and rotate a virtual object at the same time. We implemented several virtual experiments in the VR environment to demonstrate to the public that the proposed system is a powerful tool for STEM education. The benefits of this system are evaluated followed by two virtual experiments in STEM field.

Keywords: 3D virtual learning, Human machine interface (HCI), hand gesture interaction, single hand grasping-moving-rotating (SH-GMR), STEM education.

1   Introduction

Digital virtual worlds have been used in education for a number of years, as the common use of which, the issues of providing effective support for teaching and learning arouse continuing discussions. Considerable limitation exists in the modern pedagogies and their practices. According to Mohan, "students are presented with the final results of knowledge but not with data and experience to think about" [1]. Many current educational tools, instead of enhancing the notions of interaction and student-centered learning, only strengthen the traditional teaching methods using a new platform without changing the nature of how to teach and learn. The functions of computers in online learning environments and the existing interactive systems are far from what is desirable. Examination based teaching assessment, although widely being used, always has difficulty in revealing teaching effect and instructing the succeeding action of teachers and students [2]. If technology can give timely feedback to

R. Shumaker and S. Lackey (Eds.): VAMR 2014, Part II, LNCS 8526, pp. 63–72, 2014.

players in the process of learning activity, learners would timely adjust their understanding, behaviors, and implementation. Computer games are much attractive to young people, which provide a possible breakthrough to push forward new instructive technologies. Playing games in virtual worlds with educational purposes, students are not only able to learn knowledge, but also explore new experiments on their own [3]. The fast development of Internet-based communication technologies, e.g. online video chat, portable devices, mobile platforms and cloud computation, allows instructors and learners to be connected and get access to knowledge anytime and anywhere such that they can have "face-to-face" talk and "hands-on" educations even if they are not in the same classroom.

A recent boom has been seen in 3D virtual worlds for entertainment, and this in turn has led to a surge of interest in their educational applications. We will focus on the reasoning and the design of a 3D virtual learning system that merges real experiments in virtual laboratory and brings entertainment to knowledge learning. The design of the system aims at improving teaching and learning efficiency and interest by introducing advanced human machine interface and VR interactive teaching software into classroom and online learning. We will discuss the benefits of applying hand gesture interface and VR environment into e-learning and also give a design of the system with two examples.

2   Benefit Analysis of 3D Virtual Learning

Our advanced hand gesture interaction and the VR environment described above perfectly meet the demand of the purpose of the online virtual learning and training. The benefits of the system are:

Empowerment. Pan [4] stated that VR is an empowerment technique that opens many new path for learning. VR-based learning provides a paradigm shift from old pedagogies since it provides interaction with all human sense, such as vision, sound, and even touches, taste and smell [5]. The VR interactive teaching system focuses on students, their learning motivation and learning practice. Instead of receiving input from teachers all the time, students are able to control their own learning by manipulating learning materials and practicing in or out of classroom. Even though student-centered teaching has been advocated for ages, the fact is many teachers find it hard to shift and transfer their power to students, not to say there are teachers who are not aware of their current roles. One of the reasons for the hard shift is the lack of creative and friendly learning environments, in which activity and practice play an indispensable role.

Learning by Doing. We all know that when learning new and abstract concepts, e.g. global warming, sound transmission, magnet, etc. we find it is hard to understand without connecting to a concrete example. Things could be different when students have something that they can see and manipulate in front of them because it helps them connect abstract concepts with concrete experiences. Furthermore, they are provided with more practice and knowledge through the exploration in a 3D interactive system. For instance, in the study of heat transformation, students are not only able to understand the concept of it, but also able to get to know under what circumstances and structure and through what types of objects that heat can be transferred.

Sustaining the Learning Interest. One of the benefits of game-like educational technology is to motivate learners and sustain their learning interest by letting learners control their world of knowledge/game, interact, explore and experience it. The interaction with the system is a key for learners to build more on their previous knowledge, though they might go through many trials of failure before they can move on to the next step. In the process of practicing, learners can modify their solutions to achieve the best performance required for the law in STEM areas.

Better Teaching Performance. Teaching and learning are mutual process [6]. The introduction and application of 3D interactive system is not to decrease the significance of teachers but to help teachers better their teaching by using technology into classroom. Compared to words, visual products such as videos and animation carry much more information. Therefore, a combination of words and animations could enhance the amount of output of information and knowledge. More importantly, teachers are able to explain topics by connecting concrete concepts as with real world, by motivating students and sustain their interests.

Materializing Abstract Knowledge. There are many abstract concepts, models, processes, methods existing in STEM field need to be showed dynamically and sur-realistically. Illustrating only by descriptive characters and figures may not be enough to give students whole pictures of them. An application aiming at explaining the concept of food chain, asks players to initialize the quality of grass, rabbit, and fox. Running this game, the qualitative relationship among these creatures shows on the screen in a dynamic way, forcing the players to consider the environment in an equilibrious way to achieve ecological balance. The system can also display invisible matter in a visible way, such as energy and force.

Real Time Assessment. The traditional classroom teaching is not able to give immediate feedback information about the learning and performance of students because teachers are not able to stay around students watching all the time. Formative assessments, summative assessments, and official assessments are three typical techniques used for classroom assessments [7]. But these methods do not provide specific and timely information about student learning. They are always slow respond, biased, and limited by test writers. The paper-and-pencil test that is the most common use assessment is more the enhancement of lower level cognitive behavior rather than that of higher level cognitive behavior, according to Bloom's Taxonomy classification. This problem is improved by adding an intelligent assessment agent module in the system. Running as a background agent, it monitors learners operation in real time and makes assessment about whether instructive objectives are reached.

Improved Online Communication and Cooperation Experience by Cloud Computing. The most advantage of cloud computing is that information and services can be accessed anytime and anywhere by different platforms. Users are always able to get access to educational applications, personal information, performance assessments and real time communication from instructors or others. These will greatly lower the learning cost and boost the flexibility, which is very suitable for online learning. Students' learning process, special needs, assessment, etc, can be stored in cloud and then checked by instructors. Moreover, cloud computing provides a platform for convenient communication, collaboration, team-building and group-centered project.

3   Design of the Hand Gesture Interface

According to the need of e-learning and e-business, we design an efficient and low-cost human computer interaction interface. Our proposed hand gesture interface is designed to recognize two hands movements, hand poses (open hand and closed hand), and single hand rotations. There is no need to extract individual finger movements in this case. Also, we properly allocate the stereo camera to prevent it from dealing with complex situations. Moreover, we carefully design the gestures of applications so that hand overlapping is not necessary.

As shown in Figure 1(a), the stereo camera is placed on top of the computer screen and tilts down to capture the hands that are placed right above the table. This arrangement prevents from capturing human heads in the view. Also, the reflection of ambient light on hand is mostly uniform, which reduces the recognition error caused by shadow changes. In addition, it is suitable for long time operation because users' hands are well supported by the table. Users' hands are free to move in horizontal (x), vertical (y) and depth (z) direction, and rotate in yaw, pitch and roll.

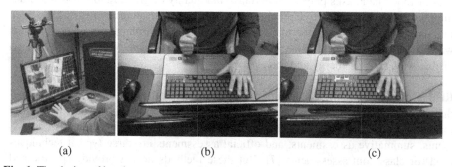

(a)   (b)   (c)

Fig. 1. The design of hand gesture interaction. (a) hardware configuration, (b) left camera view, (c) right camera view.

One of our contributions to hand gesture interaction is that the system is capable of recognizing single hand grasping-moving-rotating (SH-GMR) activity. Compared with traditional two hand "steering wheel" [8] gesture for rotating a virtual object, a hand gesture interface with single hand rotation integrated is able to fully control an object [9, 10]. Figure 2 illustrates the SH-GMR activity by an example. SH-GMR contains three major actions: preparing, grasping, and moving and rotating.

A human hand changes its shape from open-handed status (a hand with fingers stretched) to a grasping posture such that an object is captured and fully controlled. Moving and rotating action may occur simultaneously or independently. Keeping the same grasping gesture, the hand shifts or rotates so that the virtual object is shifted and rotated correspondingly. The hand changes its shape back to the open-handed posture, thus releasing the virtual object from being controlled. Compared with the traditional "steering wheel" gestures for object rotating, this method naturally maps hand gestures in the real world to the 3D virtual space.

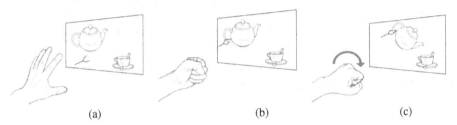

(a)   (b)   (c)

Fig. 2. Illustration of the SH-GMR activity, (a) initial posture, (b) grasping action, (c) moving and rotating actions

In our design, all of the icons, objects, and shapes are treated as physical objects and can be interacted with very natural hand gestures. Users manipulate objects by common sense, not by memorizing a bunch of hand gestures. Only two poses (open and closed) are needed to be discriminated, which allows a wide tolerance range for users' real postures.

Figure 3 shows the diagram of the whole system that we design. The input sensor is the calibrated stereo camera. Hand parameters, including positions, status, rotation angles, etc, are extracted from the hand gesture interface module for each frame. The VR environment in the e-learning module reacts to the gesture input with dynamic information.

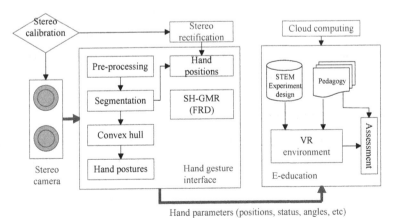

Fig. 3. The system diagram of the e-learning and e-business using the proposed hand gesture interface

4   Implementation of the 3D Virtual Learning System

4.1   Stereo Camera

Considering that the two applications are e-learning and e-business, mature and low-cost stereo imaging technology should be used. Webcams are chosen to be the image sensors for our system. Two high quality webcams with VGA resolution and 30fps frame rate are physically aligned and fixed on a metal base. They can be easily mounted on computer screens or tripods. The physical alignment makes the optic axis of the two cameras parallel and pointing to the same direction. Due to the manufacturing defects and the imperfect alignment, the output images should be undistorted and rectified before they are used to extract depth information.

4.2   Camera Calibration and Rectification

Single camera checkerboard calibrations are implemented for both left and right cameras. We use Heikkila and Silven's [11] camera model that takes focal points and principal points as the camera intrinsic parameters. Lens distortion, including radial distortion and tangential distortion, are described by 5 parameters. 16 different checkerboard images are taken to guarantee a robust estimation of the camera parameters. Then, the stereo calibration estimates the translation vector T and rotation vector R characterizing the relative position of the right camera with respect to the left camera (reference camera).

   With the intrinsic parameters, an undistortion process [11] is applied on each camera in each frame to suppress tangential and radial distortion. To simplify the computation of pixel correspondence, two image planes need to be rectified first. A. Fusiello et al. [12] proposed a rectification procedure that includes image plane rotation, principal point adjustment and focal length adjustment. Let $m = \begin{bmatrix} u & v & 1 \end{bmatrix}^T$ be the homogeneous coordinates of pixels on the right camera's image plane. The transformation of the right camera's image plane are $m^{new} = (K_{ave}R_n)(K_oR_o)^{-1}m^{old}$, where m^{old} and m^{new} are the homogeneous coordinates of pixels on the right camera's image plane before and after rectification, R_n is an identity matrix, and R_o is the rotation matrix of the camera before the rotation.

4.3   Hand Gesture Recognition

For the purpose of generating skin color statistics, luminance and chrominance need to be separated. We convert the image sequence from RGB color space to YCbCr [13] by:

$$\begin{cases} Y = 0.299R + 0.587G + 0.114B \\ C_r = R - Y \\ C_b = B - Y \end{cases}$$

, (1)

where, Y is the luminance component, and Cb and Cr are the chrominance components. This color space conversion has to be done on both left and right cameras.

Color-based segmentation is used to discriminate hands from their background. S. L. Phung and et al. [14] proved that Bayesian classifier performs better compared to linear classifier and Gaussian single and mixture models. Whether a pixel is considered as a skin pixel is decided by a threshold τ:

$$\frac{p(X \mid \omega_0)}{p(X \mid \omega_1)} > \tau \tag{2}$$

where ω_0 and ω_1 denote skin color and non-skin color, $p(X \mid \omega_0)$ and $p(X \mid \omega_1)$ are the conditional probability density functions of skin and non-skin colors. A color calibration procedure is needed when users first use the system. Users are asked to wave their hands in the camera view so that the training data of the skin color can be acquired. With this, the system is able to adaptively learn users' skin color as well as lighting conditions.

We want to discriminate hand in open and closed poses by learning the geometrical features extracted from hands. A contour retrieving algorithm is applied to topologically extract all possible contours in the segmented images. We empirically use the two largest segmented areas as hand segmentations because normally two hands are the largest skin color areas in the view. A convex hull and its vertex set are computed [15]. The number of vertex after a polygon approximation procedure should be in the range of 8 to 15 considering both computational cost and accuracy. Several features can be extracted from the convexity: the distance between the starting point A and the ending point B of each defect, and the distance between depth points C and the farthest points on hand D. Distance l_{AB} and l_{CD} fully describe the situation of two adjacent fingers.

To help determine the open hand and closed hand poses, we train a classifier using the Cambridge Hand Gesture Dataset [16]. The reason is that the image in the dataset has the similar camera position with ours, and the dataset provides sequences of hand actions that are suitable for learning hand dynamics. We select 182 images from the dataset and manually label them with w_0 (open hand) and w_1 (closed hand). For each image, we extract l_{AB} and l_{CD} distance from all convexity defects of the hand. The training vector is described as {L, ω_i}, where L is the set of l_{AB} and l_{CD} distance in a hand. A support vector machine is trained on the resulting 14-dimensional descriptor vectors. Radial basis function is used as the kernel function to nonlinearly map the vectors to higher dimension so that linear hyper plane can be decided.

Since there is no need to track single finger movements, positions of hands on both camera views are decided by two coordinates: (x_L, y_L) and (x_R, y_R). The coordinate of one hand on each camera view is calculated by the center of gravity of the hand segment. This will smooth the vibration caused by the segmentation. After the image rectification, we have $y_L = y_R$. The disparity along x direction is computed by $d = x_L - x_R$. The depth z of the point is given by:

$$z = \frac{fT}{d}$$

(3)

where f is the focal length, T is the baseline of the stereo camera. Note that the unit in equation (3) is in pixel.

Existing hand interaction is highly limited by the current two-hand rotation gesture due to the lack of the research on hand fist kinematics. A single fist rotation detector (FRD) is crucial to implement the SH-GMR activity that makes possible control of different objects by two hands simultaneously. With this concern, a feature-based FRD was proposed to extract robust and accurate fist rotation angle [9]. The features we find on fists are called "fist lines" which are 3 clearly dark lines between index, middle, ring and pinky fingers.

The FRD is a three-step approach. The first step is fist shape segmentation locating single fist in a search window. A clustering process is used to decide the fist position along human arms. The second step finds rough rotation angles with histograms of feature gradients using Laplacian of Gaussian (LOG), and then refines the angles to higher accuracy within $(-90°, 90°)$ with constrained multiple linear regression. The third step decides the angle within $(-360°, 360°)$ by making use of the distribution of other edge features on the fist.

5   Benefit Evaluation with two Examples

We implemented two simple virtual science experiments to demonstrate the improvement. Figure 4(a) shows an analog circuit experiment that help students learn how to measure electrical quantities with a multimeter. In the virtual environment, a student is able to turn on the multimeter and twist the dial plate to a right setting with single hand operation. Then, the student drags both probes to connect to the resistor with two hands operation. If the setting and the connection is correct, the resistance value can be read from the screen of the multimeter. In the circuit experiment, all electronic components are listed in a virtual toolbox. Students are allowed to take out demanded objects from the toolbox, and make circuits in the space.

Figure 4(b) shows a virtual environment for implementing chemical experiments. Kinds of experiment equipments are placed on the table in the space, including beakers, test tubes, flasks, alcohol lamps, etc. Different chemicals can be found in virtual containers. The text descriptions of the chemical compositions are popped out if users put hands on them. The figure shows a user is holding a flask containing certain chemical liquid on his right hand and a breaker containing another chemical power on the left hand. He is pouring the liquid from the flask to the breaker to trigger certain chemical reaction. The shifting and moving of an object is fully controlled by one hand. The chemical reaction can be displayed in the form of color changes, animations, sound effects, etc, to give the user the feedback of his operations.

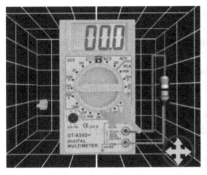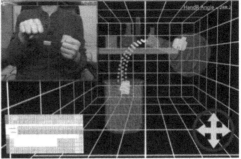

Fig. 4. Simple applications of the virtual learning systems. (a)   Multimeter (b) chemical experiment.

6   Conclusion

The objective of this paper is to boost online teaching and learning efficiency as well as interests with modern computer science technologies, a 3D virtual learning system for STEM education. In the proposed system, students are able to carry out virtual STEM experiments with advanced hand gesture interface and VR environment. The theoretical reasoning and two examples above illustrate the improvement from current e-learning paradigms. Fully functioned online education systems that aim at particular grades and disciplines are urgently needed. Future research should focus on the usability study of the more applications for a better understanding of their benefits.

References

1. Mohan, B.: Language and content, reading, p. 146. Addison-Wesley, MA (1986)
2. Gibbs, G., Simpson, C.: Conditions under which assessment supports students' learning. Learning and Teaching in Higher Education 1(1), 3–31 (2004)
3. Mansureh, K., Atsusi, H.: Examining the Pedagogical Foundations of Modern Educational Computer Games. Computers & Education 51(4), 1729–1743 (2008)
4. Pantelidis, V.S.: Virtual Reality in the Classroom. Educational Technology 3(4), 23–27 (1993)
5. Psotka, J.: Immersive Training Systems: Virtual Reality and Education and Training. Instructional Science 23(5-6), 405–431 (1995)
6. Gibbs, G., Simpson, C.: Conditions Under Which Assessment Supports Students' Learning. Learning and Teaching in Higher Education 1(1), 3–31 (2004)
7. Peter, W.: Airasian, Classroom Assessment. McGraw-Hill, Inc., (1991)
8. Hinckley, K., Pausch, R., Proffitt, D., Kassell, N.F.: Two-Handed Virtual Manipulation. In: ACM Trans. Computer-Human Interaction, pp. 260–302 (1998)
9. Ma, T., Wee, W., Han, C., Zhou, X.: A Method for Single Hand Fist Gesture Input to Enhance Human Computer Interaction. In: Intl. Conf. on HCI, vol. 5, pp. 291–300 (2013)

10. Ma, T., Wee, W., Han, C., Zhou, X.: A Study of Hand Fist Kinematics and Its Detection Method That Enhances Human-Machine Interaction. In: In Proceeding of International Conference on Multimedia and Human Computer Interaction (MHCI), Toronto, Canada (July 2013)
11. Heikkila, J., Silven, O.: A four-step camera calibration procedure with implicit image correction. In: Proceedings of the Conference on Computer Vision and Pattern Recognition, pp. 1106–1112 (1997)
12. Fusiello, A., Trucco, E., Verri, A., Verri, R.: A Compact Algorithm for Rectification of Stereo Pairs. Journal Machine Vision and Applications 12(1), 16–22 (2000)
13. Charles, P.: Digital Video and HDTV, ch. 24, pp. 291–292. Morgan Kaufmann (2003)
14. Phung, S.L., Bouzerdoum, A., Chai, D.: Skin segmentation using color pixel classification: analysis and comparison. IEEE Transactions on Pattern Analysis and Machine Intelligence 27(1), 148–154 (2005)
15. Bradski, G., Kaehler, A.: Learning OpenCV. O'Reilly Media (2008)
16. Kim, T.K., Wong, S.F., Cipolla, R.: Tensor Canonical Correlation Analysis for Action Classification. In: IEEE Conference of Computer Vision and Pattern Recognition, pp. 1–8 (2007)
17. Haralick, R., Shapiro, L.: Computer and Robot Vision, vol. 1, pp. 346–351. Addison-Wesley Publishing Company (1992)

Visible Breadboard: System for Dynamic, Programmable, and Tangible Circuit Prototyping with Visible Electricity

Yoichi Ochiai[1,2]

[1] The University of Tokyo
Graduate School of Interdisciplinary Information Studies
7-3-1 Hongo, Bunkyo-ku, Tokyo, 113-0033 Japan
ochyai@me.com
[2] Japan Society for the Promotion of Science,
6 Ichiban-cho, Chiyoda-ku, Tokyo, 102-8471 Japan

Abstract. This paper reports a new system for prototyping circuits called the Visible Breadboard. The Visible Breadboard is a solderless breadboard that allows users to make or erase physical wirings with tangible input by hand and to see the voltage level of each hole at all times by a colored LED light.

The Visible Breadboard has 60 solid-state relays set in parallel crosses and controlled by a micro-controller. These relays connect the 36 holes on the system surface. The connected holes work as wirings in the circuit into which users can insert electronic materials. Each hole has an AD converter function working as a voltmeter and a full-color LED. The voltage of each hole can be visualized by these full-colored LEDs. Users can operate this system by touching the surface with their fingertips. Users can also connect the Visible Breadboard to a PC. When the Visible Breadboard is connected to the PC, it functions as a new kind of interface for developing and sharing circuits.

Our experimental results showed that this device enables users to build circuits faster and more easily than an ordinary solderless breadboard.

Keywords: Rapid Prototyping, Physical Computing, HCI.

1   Introduction

Nowadays there is great interest in hobby electronics and DIY. Open source programming languages and IDEs such as Arduino [1] and Processing [2], are in widespread use. With the use of a solderless breadboard, soldering is no longer required to build electronic circuits for these purpose. The hobby electronics and DIY environments have become easy and accessible by spreading of instruction on web. Moreover, there are many communities and people interested in DIY and hobby electronics on the internet and their communications are seen on SNS.

Learning electronics and having a knowledge of electronic circuits help people understand what energy and system are. When we make a circuit, it is very easy to

R. Shumaker and S. Lackey (Eds.): VAMR 2014, Part II, LNCS 8526, pp. 73–84, 2014.

understand power consumption, for example, comparing an actuator that is very large to an LED that is small.

Many articles and tips regarding DIY and hobby electronics are available on the web. In these communities, it is easy to share schematic diagrams and pictures of circuits, but very difficult to share actual circuits.

Furthermore, although a great deal of information about hobby electronics and DIY is available, it is still difficult to understand what happens in the actual circuits and to share these circuits. IDEs have become more workable, but building a circuit is still manual work and difficult for a beginner. In the real world, we cannot see voltages in the circuit and are not able to "UNDO" our actions.

When we want to know the voltage in a circuit, we use a voltmeter. It shows us the voltage by analog meter or LCD display, but does not visualize the voltage on the circuit. It is also difficult to measure multi-points in the circuit at the same time. Moreover, when we teach electronics in the classroom or workshop, it is difficult to share a circuit. There are often mistakes made copying a circuit.

To address these problems, we have developed a new system, which we named the Visible Breadboard (Fig. 1). The Visible Breadboard has dynamic circuit connections for each hole using solid state relays and visualizes the voltage on the surface with a colored light.

From the viewpoint of programming materials [3], circuits made of solid state relays can be defined as "real programming material" that change physical characteristics through programming and using electricity.

This research paper will first cite some of the related researches and discuss the reason our research is relevant in section 2. Secondly, it will explain the implementation and function of device in section 3 (hardware), 4 (middleware), and 5 (software). Thirdly, it will show some of the conducted experiments in section 6. After that it will discuss the limitations and experimental results in section 7. Lastly, we will conclude with possible future work in section 8.

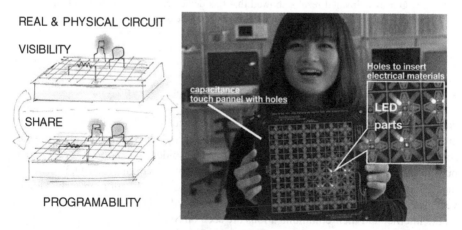

Fig. 1. (left) concept picture shows "real circuit", "visible voltage", "circuit programability", and "share" for prototyping purpose. (right)system overview

2   Related Work

2.1   Tangible Prototyping Tools

Many tangible devices for prototyping have been developed, such as the Algoblock, a development of Suzuki and Kato [4]. Algoblock is a tangible programming language, an advanced research, aimed at collaboration and visualization. It is good for collaborative learning and programing but it is not aimed at prototyping a circuit.

There are tangible prototyping tools for electronics, such as react3D Electricity [5] and Denshi blocks [6]. react3D Electricity is a tangible [7] circuit simulator but users cannot use real electronic materials. A Denshi block is a physical block that contains an electronic component. Users can make a circuit with these blocks but it is difficult to add other electronic materials, which are not included in the Denshi block package.

Research has been done on visualization of power consumption such as Flo [8]. As a visualization tool, however, it does not target hobby electronics or DIY. It is a tool for monitoring electricity in the home.

While there has been significant advanced research on prototyping tools, there is no research on tangible prototyping tools using real electronic materials.

2.2   Position of Study

Here we show the position of this study in Table 1. This study focused on the user experience with "real circuit", "visualization of voltage", and "circuit programability".

Table 1. Position of this study

		Circuit Programability	
		Available	Not available
Circuit	Real	This Research* Denshi Block [6](nondigital)	Ordinary Solderless Breadboard
	Virtual	react3D electricity* [5]	

*Visibility on electricity

3   Hardware Implementation

This section describes the composition of our system in 3.1. Following which we describe each modules by processing order.

3.1   Visible Breadboard System Prototype

The Visible Breadboard Prototype system is composed of two sub-systems. The first is a device that functions as a solderless breadboard. In this paper, we call this the

Visible Breadboard Device. The second is the software for a personal computer. We call this the Visible Breadboard Software. We describe the Visible Breadboard Software in Software section 5.

3.2   Visible Breadboard Device

From a functional viewpoint, the Visible Breadboard Device is separated into four modules: sensor board with holes, solid state relay board, voltage sensing board, and full color LED board. The connections for each module are shown in Fig. 2. These four modules are assembled into three physical layers.

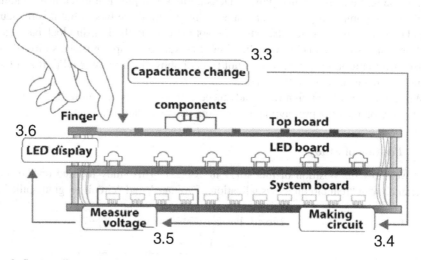

Fig. 2. System diagram and the connection for each four modules.(side view). Visible Breadboard device has the structure of three layers: Sensor board, LED board, and system board.

The Visible Breadboard Device is controlled by a single micro-controller (Arduino MEGA with ATMEGA 1280)

3.3   Sensor Board with Hole

This module detects a user's finger position on the surface by sensing a capacitance change (like SmartSkin [9]). A finger touch changes the capacitance of the metal pads, which are set on the surface of the top board. This module enables users to input by finger touching and tracing the surface. Four pads seen around the hole are connected horizontally and vertically, enabling the system to detect a coordinate position of the finger, as shown by the arrows in Fig. 3. This module looks for a capacitance change by cross-sensing: vertical and horizontal position sensing. Each hole on this board is connected to both the solid state relay and voltage sensing module.

3.4   Solid State Relay Board

The Solid State Relay Board is placed in the bottom physical layer of the Visible Breadboard Device (Fig. 2). This module (Fig. 4) has 60 solid state relays placed between the 36 holes connected to the Sensor Board. By switching these solid state relays ON / OFF, the connection status of the holes is changed dynamically. Active solid state relays form the wiring between the holes and complete a circuit with the electronic materials inserted into the Sensor Board.

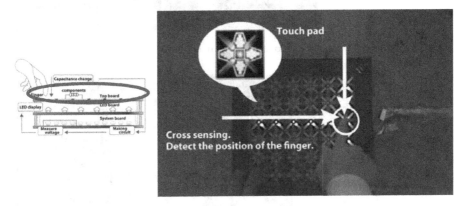

Fig. 3. Top view of Visible Breadboard device

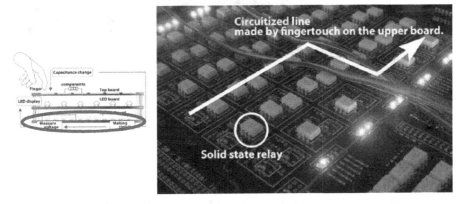

Fig. 4. SSR board on bottom layer of Visible Breadboard device

These solid state relays are controlled by eight shift registers. The shift registers are controlled by a micro controller with serial connections.

3.5   Drive Sensing Voltage of Each Hole

This module (Fig. 5) measures the voltage value of the 36 points. The drive control of the solid state relays enables switching the connection of the micro-controller AD converter

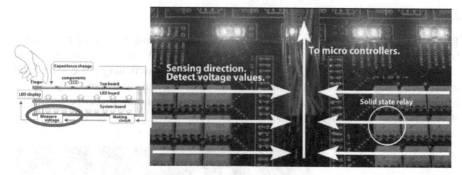

Fig. 5. Drive sensing module by SSR in bottom layer. (close-up)

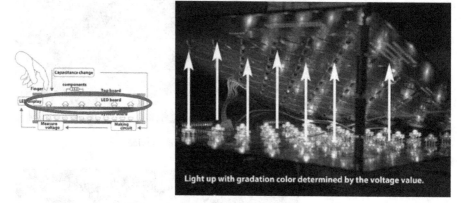

Fig. 6. LED displaying modules (with opening top board)

and the holes of the Sensor Board into which the users inserts the electronic materials. Though this module can measure only six points at once, we think that it is sufficient for this device because the full-color LED system (showing the voltage in color) in this device is lighted by the drive control system (six LEDs at once).

3.6   Displaying The Voltage

User can choose the "start voltage color" and the "end voltage color" in the configuration mode. This module (Fig. 6) changes its LED color by gradation corresponding to the voltage value (Fig. 7). The color is determined by Equation (1).

$$C = v\left(\frac{Re - Rs}{L}, \frac{Ge - Gs}{L}, \frac{Be - Bs}{L}\right)$$

C = color of full color LED, v = voltage   (1)

(Rs,Gs,Bs):start color (Re,Ge,Be):end color

L = ADConverter' s maximum value

3.7   Hardware Specification of the Visible Breadboard Device

The hardware specification of the Visible Breadboard Device is shown in Table 2. We developed four Visible Breadboard Devices. They can be connected to each other to make 144 holes available. There is a resistance value between the holes because this device uses Solid State Relays for the wiring. However, this is an allowable margin error for the circuits that can be built on this hardware. The distance between two holes is approximately 12 times larger than found on an ordinary solderless breadboard. This is large, but allows users to use extensions (Fig.7) for small electronic materials or IC chips.

Table 2. Hardware Specification

weight	1200g
size	24.2cm (W) 24.2cm (L) 6cm (H)
number of holes	36holes
distance between 2holes	3.2cm
voltage sampling frequency	30Hz
AD Converter	1024 steps (0- 5V)
LED Color steps	RGB Color 8096 steps
Micro-controler	Atmega1028 (ArduinoMEGA)
Clock	16MHz
Input Voltage	0-5V with Optional OPAMP max voltage 48V
Resistance value between holes	2Ω

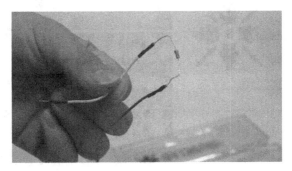

Fig. 7. Parts extension for Visible Breadboard device (wire with socket)

4   Middleware Implementation

The Visible Breadboard Device has several features for interaction with users. The following sections describe basic wiring and visualization, checking the connection function, UNDO/REDO, and digital color mode.

4.1   Basic Wiring and Visualization

Users can control the Visible Breadboard Device by touching the pads on the surface. This section describes the connection algorithm. If users touch one hole (Fig. 8 (left).1) and then another next to it (Fig. 8 (left).2), these two holes are connected or cut (Fig. 8 (left).3). If a hole is connected to others, the LED for the voltage visualization (placed below the sensor board) turns on. For example, users can make the circuit shown in Fig. 8 (right).

Example 1: Fig. 8 (right-up) is a circuit with resistors, an LED, and a capacitor. The RED light shows that the voltage is Vcc (5 V) and the BLUE light shows that the voltage is GND (0 V). In Fig. 10, LED (A) is on because there is an electric current in the circuit.

Example 2: Fig. 8 (right-bottom) is a circuit with resistors only. The RED light shows that the voltage is GND (0 V) and the BLUE light shows that the voltage is Vcc (5 V). In Fig. 11, the holes on each side of interval (A) have different colors because there is no connection (left hole shows GND and right hole shows Vcc).

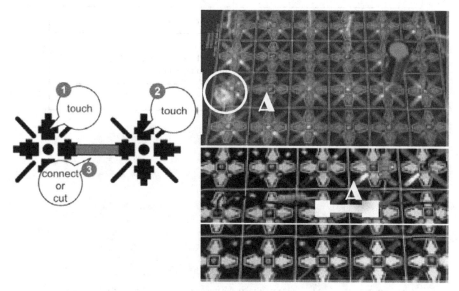

Fig. 8. (left) Connection Algorithm (right-up) Example 1: RED is V+, BLUE is GND (right-bottom) Example 2: RED is GND, BLUE is V+

4.2   "Checking the Connection" Function

The Visible Breadboard Device has an indicator for voltage visualization but there is no indicator for the connection of the holes. To compensate for this, the Visible Breadboard Device has a "checking the connection" function. When users press the button on the right side of the sensor board, the voltage visualization LEDs blink in sequence to show the connection of each hole.

4.3   UNDO/REDO

The Visible Breadboard Device has a wiring UNDO and REDO function. Using this, users can erase and remake a connection easily. Furthermore, if the users push the UNDO and REDO button repeatedly, the wiring in the circuit repeats the cutting and connecting rapidly. Users can make a high-speed voltage change. This is useful to view the waves on the breadboard.

Additionally, if the users push the REDO button slowly, they can see, slowly and in order, what happens in the circuit when the connection is made.

4.4   Digital Color Mode

The Visible Breadboard Device has two visualization modes. The first is a basic visualization using gradation of the LED color, like thermography. The second is a "digital color mode". In this mode, the LED shows a different color for every 1V step. It is helpful for checking and understanding what happens in the digital circuit.

4.5   Other Features

The Visible Breadboard Device has some other features: "Sound", "Auto Save", and "Color palette for the voltage". The Sound system gives users visual and sound feedback. The Auto Save system enables users to emulate an ordinary solderless breadboard. With an ordinary solderless breadboard, the circuit remains connected without electricity. With the Visible Breadboard, the circuit that users develop disappears if the power is turned off. The Auto Save features compensates for this shortcoming. With Color palette for the voltage, users can set their preferred color configuration.

5   Software Implementation on PC

The Visible Breadboard Software, which runs on the PC, has several utilities for the Visible Breadboard Device. This section describes the "Voltage visualization on the PC" and "Copy the data from device" functions.

5.1   Voltage Visualization on PC

The Visible Breadboard Software has a voltage visualization feature (Fig. 9). When the Visible Breadboard Device is connected to a PC via a USB cable, data from the

AD Converter are sent to the PC. The software captures the voltage data of the 36 holes on the Visible Breadboard Device and shows them as a 3D bar graph. The colors on the bar graph change corresponding to the color settings of the Visible Breadboard Device's voltage visualization.

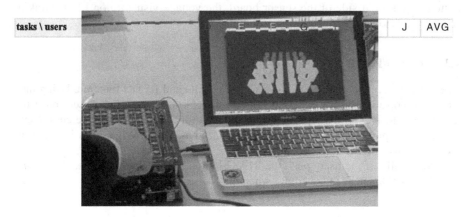

Fig. 9. Voltage visualization on PC. Also user can share the circuit built with this device via internet.

5.2   Circuit Share

The Visible Breadboard Software can capture all the data (connection data of holes, visualization data, and settings) from the Visible Breadboard Device. This software can import and export these data as files. It enables users to copy and share the actual physical circuit via internet or email.

6   Evaluation

6.1   Experimental Design and Participants

We ran a task-oriented   circuit-building test with ten users, nine male and one female, with average age 20.8.

Before starting the test, we explained, for two minutes, how to use an ordinary solderless breadboard and the Visible Breadboard. We let the participants practice for a few minutes on each. Then all participants knew how to use both systems.

For the first test, users made 25 connections on the Visible Breadboard. This was to verify the capacitance sensor and resistance of the participant's finger skin.

6.2   Questionare

After the wiring test, there were eight tasks relating to making a circuit. We tested four kinds of circuit ((a), (b), (c), and (d)) and users made these on both the ordinary solderless breadboard and the Visible Breadboard. For (a) and (b), we showed the participants a picture of the correct circuits and the users made the circuits from the picture. In experiments (c) and (d), we showed the participants a schematic. They then made the circuits on both the ordinary solderless breadboard and the Visible Breadboard.

Table 3. Experimental Result of 10 users on wiring task (unit: second)

Make Wiring on Visible Breadboard	12	16	14	12	15	10	11	10.8	30	10.9	14.17
(a) Breadboard	74	214	112	71	152	84	53	155	98	51	106.4
(a) Visible Breadboard	50	60	49	29	49	57	23	36	51	24	42.8
(b) Breadboard	102	221	157	129	137	106	89	183	150	45	131.9
(b) Visible Breadboard	30	45	36	35	43	65	22	66	95	57	49.4
(c) Breadboard	115	154	101	39	62	87	26	63	77	55	77.9
(c) Visible Breadboard	37	42	37	26	32	60	15	26	31	85	39.1
(d) Breadboard	81	119	189	94	83	30	32	116	38	51	83.3
(d) Visible Breadboard	37	58	52	49	30	45	27	77	52	63	49

6.3 Results

The results of the user experiments are shown in Table 2. There were ten participants, A to J. It is seen in the average column that for every circuit tested in this experiment, the Visible Breadboard was faster than the ordinary solderless breadboard.

After the wiring experiment, we tested the voltage visualization effect of this device. All of the people who took part in this experiment answered the question: "Where is the GND or Vcc?", correctly. It was easy for people to distinguish the Vcc from the GND with the Visible Breadboard.

7 Discussion

The difference of the speed between the ordinary solderless breadboard and the Visible Breadboard depended on the complexity of the circuit. When people used many bread wires to develop the circuit on the ordinary solderless breadboard, the difference of the speed increased quickly.

The Visible Breadboard accelerates building the circuit, enables users to share the circuit, and visualize the voltage in the circuit. It is useful for the first circuits that beginners make or children make in the school.

We presented this system in many places including SIGGRAPH [10]. People suggested that the full-color LED display should be replaced by an LCD display because the drive control makes the LED display blink. We think this will be better when the LCD displays become lighter.

8   Conclusion and Future work

We would like to make this system a   product and gather additional data for future research. This paper introduced a new kind of system for prototyping and sharing circuits. It makes building circuits easier and faster. Moreover, the ability to visual the voltage was certainly very effective for people using the device.

Acknowledgement. This work has been partially supported by the Exploratory IT Human Resources Project 2009, IPA Japan (Mitoh Youth). Our appreciation goes out to Prof. Junichi ISOYA, Prof. Teiichi NISHIOKA, Yohei SUMITOMO, and Yoshihiko OZAKI at the University of Tsukuba. Our appreciation also goes out to Shutaro ISHII and Junichi SATO at the University of Tokyo. We also would like to thank Masaya TSURUTA and Keisuke TOYOSHIMA in jiseCHI.co.ltd.

Appendix

Visible Breadboard Instruction Movie   (Video on YouTube).

```
http://www.youtube.com/watch?v=nsL8t_pgPjs
```

References

1. Arduino, `http://arduino.cc`
2. Processing, `http://processing.org/`
3. Coelho, M.: Programming the Material World: A Proposition for the Application and Design of Transitive Materials. In: The 9th International Conference on Ubiquitous Computing (Ubicomp 2007), Innsbruck, Austria (2007)
4. Suzuki, H., Kato, H.: AlgoBlock: A Tangible Programming Language, a Tool for Collaborative Learning. In: Proceedings of 4th European Logo Conference, Athens, Greece, pp. 297–303 (August 1993)
5. Uhling, F.: react3D Electricity - Tangible users Interface, video on YouTube (February 04, 2008), `http://www.youtube.com/watch?v=6qTTQKWfV8Q` (access March 31, 2010)
6. Denshi Block, `http://www.denshiblock.co.jp/`
7. Ishii, H., Ullmer, B.: Tangible bits: towards seamless interfaces between people, bits and atoms. In: Proc. CHI 1997, pp. 234–241. ACM Press (1997)
8. Shrubsole, P., Lavrysen, T., Janse, M., Weda, H.: Flo: Raising Family Awareness about Electricity Use. In: Proc. CHI 2011, Vancouver, Canada, May 7-12 (2011)
9. Rekimoto, J.: SmartSkin: An Infrastructure for Freehand Manipulation on Interactive Surfaces. In: Proc. CHI 2002, Minneapolis, Minnesota, USA, April 20-25 (2002)
10. Ochiai, Y.: The Visible Electricity Device: Visible Breadboard. In: Proc. ACM SIGGRAPH 2010, Los Angeles, California, USA (July 2010)

The Application of Augmented Reality for Reanimating Cultural Heritage

Sasithorn Rattanarungrot, Martin White, Zeeshan Patoli, and Tudor Pascu

Interactive Systems Group, Department of Informatics, University of Sussex,
Brighton, United Kingdom, BN1 9QJ
{s.rattanarungrot,m.white,m.z.patoli,t.pascu}@sussex.ac.uk

Abstract. This paper presents the design of a service-oriented architecture to support dynamic cultural content acquisition on a mobile augmented reality system for reanimating cultural heritage. The reanimating cultural heritage system provides several domain interfaces (Web, Web3D, Mobile and Augmented Reality) for presenting cultural objects accessed from an aggregated RCH data repository via web services. This paper largely focuses on the augmented reality system, but discusses the Web, Web3D and Mobile domains to set the paper in context. The mobile augmented reality system performs multiple objects tracking to augment digital media contents on real world cultural object scenes. The proposed mobile augmented reality system is composed of a mobile interface (smartphone, tablet), middleware including the augmented reality SDK and supporting software modules for the augmented reality application, and a web service framework.

Keywords: service-oriented architecture, multiple object tracking, web service framework, augmented reality.

1 Introduction

Reanimating Cultural Heritage: Reanimating cultural heritage is a Beyond Text Large Project [1][2][3] funded by the UK Arts and Humanities Research Council. The resource can be viewed live at www.sierraleoneheritage.org and it currently holds some 3,000 plus digital cultural objects. The project's full title is 'Reanimating Cultural Heritage: Digital Repatriation, Knowledge Networks and Civil Society Strengthening in Post-Conflict Sierra Leone'. The Reanimating Cultural Heritage (RCH) project is a "multidisciplinary project concerned with innovating digital curatorship in relation to Sierra Leonean collections dispersed in the global museumscape" [1]. The project is mainly concerned with establishing a digital repository and primary web interface that allows Sierra Leonean diaspora to access their heritage (cultural objects) digitally while also allowing the diaspora to contribute, through a social media context, their knowledge [3]. illustrates the Home page (with a two randomly selected media objects: in this case a video illustrating aluminium pot making, and a cultural object displayed in the 'From the collection' interface) and shows the Browse

R. Shumaker and S. Lackey (Eds.): VAMR 2014, Part II, LNCS 8526, pp. 85–95, 2014.
© Springer International Publishing Switzerland 2014

interface for the digital resource, which lists all the participating museums' collections in a gallery interface.

If the user clicks on an object in the Browse gallery interface they are taken to that objects results page, also they can do a Quick search for an object or select a more comprehensive search from the home page 'Search collections' tab, ether way the eventually arrive at the cultural object's results page.

Fig. 1. Home page   **Fig. 2.** Browse page

Fig. 3. Result page showing a Test 2D Image of a Wicker Basketillustrates the standard web view displaying a Test 3D Wicker Basket. Note the Facebook social media interface, which allows the diaspora to input their knowledge to the collections, and the ability to display related objects in a 'Related Objects' gallery [3]. While the current live version of the RCH resource does not support 3D media objects it is relatively easy to add this functionality using an abstraction of WebGL, such as X3DOM. To illustrate this we have inserted a temporary test object (Test 3D Wicker Basket Object) into the database and included a 3D interface utilizing X3DOM, see.

In addition to the 2D and 3D interface we have developed a mobile version of the RCH resource, see. Further, by clicking on the AR tab (see) when browsing on a mobile (tablet or smartphone) device, it is possible to switch to an augmented reality view whereby the cultural object of interest can be used to trigger access to media contents, such as the description, metadata, videos, images, etc., or if a 3D object exists, this can also be displayed along with other media contents. This is discussed further in Section 5.

The RCH resource has been developed using a model, view controller design pattern, which enables us to connect different views (web, mobile, 3D, AR interfaces) to the same data repository. Connection to the data repository is achieved via a set of web services discussed in section 2.

The main focus of this paper is to discuss the application of augmented reality for Reanimating Cultural Heritage utilising a new service-oriented architecture

Fig. 3. Result page showing a Test 2D Image of a Wicker Basket

Fig. 4. 3D Model of the Test Wicker Basket

(web services) for accessing media contents and the ability to track multiple objects to trigger data access from the RCH database (via a web service) within the AR scene. This architecture also offers us advantages in creating a better personalisation approach. For example, in scenarios where a user can take images of a museum's object and submit these to a photogrammetry web service to generate a 3D model. That 3D model can then be displayed in the user's home environment along with download data from the RCH repository's result page for that object to re-create an AR based museum experience.

Augmented Reality and Mobile Services: Augmented reality (AR) has become a widely beneficial technique for users' to experience a different of perception of cultural objects represented with computer-generated media contents such as 3D models, labels, text, images, videos, etc. on real environments [4][5]. One of the current challenges for AR technology is to implement effective AR on mobile platforms. Mobile AR has become a most recent development in location based services and interactive graphic applications that allow users to experience visualization and interaction with 3D models or media contents on mobile devices. Currently, mobile AR has also been implemented efficiently in various innovative applications such as gaming, shopping guides, advertising, edutainment, travel guides, museum guides and medical visualization [6]. Adapting the visualization (e.g. better integration with different view domains), tracking (better multiple object tracking), recognition, interaction (user stories), displays and user interface techniques with real world scenes and virtual environments can greatly enhance these varied applications [7][8].

Most mobile indoor AR applications nowadays are based on stand-alone or closed platforms and provide users with limited amounts of data or contents on top of real world scenes. In addition, there is no communication channel for the AR application in order to download or obtain dynamic contents from other third party data sources in real-time [9]. Another limitation for mobile graphic applications, and application in general, that require virtual models is that the models have to be created and designed on desktop computers and then transferred to mobile devices for running or rendering in games or interactive media. Although new generation mobile devices can generate good performance 3D graphics contents, some complicated rendering tasks still require more processing power such as digital cultural heritage scenes, 3D virtual cities

Fig. 5. Example screen shots from the RCH mobile interface showing the Search, Browse and a Cultural Object result along with information Related to that Cultural Object

or complicated 3D models. Therefore, processing image-based reconstruction or 3D photogrammetry tasks by multiple image matching and 3D model building cannot be completely done on mobile devices because of the limited resources.

Nowadays, there are some tools that enable mobile users to create and publish their own AR contents for indoor and outdoor environments such as Junaio, Layar and Aurasma. These applications enable mobile users to create AR environments and save them into their channels on the cloud server. Moreover, the channels can be accessed through an application programming interface (API) on mobile applications, which some application also support it such as Junaio. This technique is useful because it allows general mobile users who don't want to or who can't develop mobile AR applications to have their own AR environments. However, these AR applications still have some restrictions because they are implemented on closed platforms such that a user's AR environment can only be retrieved via the commercial application, i.e. you cannot reuse a Junaio environment in an Aurasma environment. Moreover, most commercial mobile indoor AR applications provide users with limited amounts of data or contents for augmenting real world scenes. There is no communication channel for current AR applications (e.g. Junaio, Layar, Aurasma or specific research application like an AR game, etc.) that allows them to download or obtain dynamic contents from other third party data sources in real-time.

This paper offers a solution that proposes a service oriented architecture for mobile AR system that exploits an AR SDK, multiple object tracking, AR supporting application and web service framework to perform basic AR tasks and dynamic content acquisition by accessing the photogrammetry service or open content providers over mobile/wireless network. In addition, there are some beneficial AR supporting modules that enable mobile users to utilize and manipulate acquired AR media contents on AR preference environments. We then look at the service-orientation of the mobile augmented realty part of the architecture.

2   Architectural Requirements

Several key architectural requirements are proposed to enable construction of the novel service orientation on mobile AR platform including:

Service Orientation on a Mobile AR Platform: The service-oriented architecture (SOA) entirely supports a client-server scheme over mobile/wireless network. To obtain more associated valuable contents and significantly increase the usability and functionality of the proposed mobile AR application, service orientation will be applied on the mobile AR platform, which basically integrates a web service framework into a mobile AR client [12][13]. This feature could be extensively implemented in indoor or outdoor AR scenarios, which AR browser is an application on web service framework to show media contents on real environment. Examples of web services, which developers can easily access to generate platform independent digital contents including: Web Map Services, mash-up services, geospatial and social network data, 3D models, and the Reanimating Cultural Heritage data, etc. The designed mobile AR client should offer advantages from being deployed on a service oriented architecture, which mainly provides third party open services from digital content providers that are currently available to clients on any platform [10][11].

Multiple Object Tracking: One of the basic AR tasks is object tracking used to track and recognize targeted reference objects. Associated contents can then be revealed on the real scene. In the mobile AR client, the tracking module is designed to perform markerless tracking, which require 3D object tracking so that the system can recognize more than one reference object in parallel. Moreover, the system can augment various contents of one reference object at the same time — this will lead to a richer AR environment in terms of media objects associated with the reference objects. That is, multiple objects tracking greatly enhances the interpretation of mobile AR scenarios and their environments where mobile users can obviously view the variety of media contents from multiple reference objects on the screen at the same time. Mobile AR applications can also offer some features for the users to manage and utilize those revealed contents, e.g. saving an AR scenario for future use.

Middleware System and Web Service Provider: The middleware or the back-end system basically is the design of supporting functions working behind the mobile interface and AR SDK. The middleware and web service provider are generally designed to be versatile and open platform respectively so that they can be efficiently implemented in many mobile AR scenarios, which will want to obtain and utilize dynamic digital contents from the web service provider and allow mobile users to create their preferences on AR environments. The middleware system is generally composed of a web service framework and AR supporting modules that concurrently work with AR SDK in order to support the usability and adaptability of acquired AR contents. Moreover, some modules are designed to create connections and request for dynamic contents from the web service provider through a web service framework.

3   Service Oriented Mobile Augmented Reality Architecture

Service oriented mobile AR architecture (SOMARA) is mainly designed to support content and service acquisition on a mobile AR platform. SOMARA is composed of 3 components including:

Mobile Client: The mobile client mostly is an application on a mobile platform (currently iPhone and iPad) that exploits a web service framework and service interfaces from a web service provider into its framework. Thus, the mobile application becomes a component in the SOA. In SOMARA, the mobile client is developed on iOS and native development platform. The mobile AR client utilizes a high quality embedded camera and touch screen user interface to accomplish AR and additional supporting tasks. shows the structure of the mobile client and the components inside.

Mobile interface is a front-end component in the mobile client for mainly support interaction between mobile users and the AR application and AR environments as well as supporting interaction between mobile users and displaying contents via a touch screen. In the SOMARA, the mobile AR client is developed on a mobile platform basis, there is a touch screen user interface, which is focused on AR tasks and features for mobile users to view and interrelate with digital contents being visualized on the screen.

Augmented Reality SDK is open source software on native or hybrid platform designed for mobile AR application development. At the moment, there are existing AR SDKs available to potential AR application developers e.g. ARToolkit, Qualcomm and Metaio SDK. AR SDKs basically provide basic libraries to perform general AR tasks such as object tracking, rendering and visualization. In SOMARA, Metaio native SDK has been exploited in the mobile AR client and native framework. The Metaio native SDK will fully work with the AR application in order to track reference objects, create geometry, load AR contents and their features onto a real world scene depending on each reference object, environments and scenarios that the system is designed to be implemented on. Note we have adapted the tracking module to perform multiple object tracking.

Augmented Reality application is a component of the mobile AR client in the middleware layer designed to largely work with the Metaio native SDK to process some AR tasks, e.g. building geometries, visualizing contents, etc. Moreover, the AR application is also combined with the web service framework for efficiently requesting services and receiving responses, which are dynamic contents or final outcomes from the web service provider. In addition, some modules in the application will work with Global Positioning Systems (GPS) in order to process location base AR contents, personalization and outdoor AR tasks. The following sections explain each module in the application, which is designed to support the proposed features.

Web Service Framework: The web service framework implemented with web service APIs such as SOAP or REST is composed of client and server side service code. The web service framework simultaneously works with the AR application as a middleware layer for creating web service connections, sending requests and receiving responses between the mobile client and web service provider. In the web service framework, there is a XML Parser and XML serialization module to process XML data representing the final outcome of the web service provider. The outcome will then be transferred to the AR application. At the moment we are utilizing XMLHttpRrequest for server side response, but we plan to consider JSON as an alternative to XML for transferring data from the server.

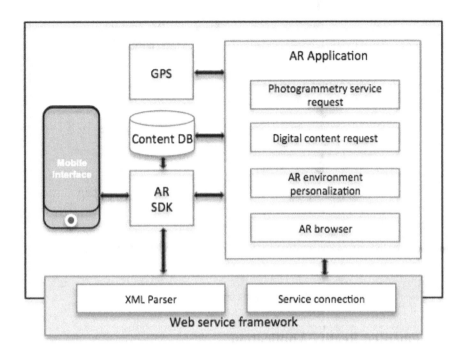

Fig. 6. Mobile augmented reality client

Web Service Provider: The web service provider on an open server side platform is composed of the web service framework and open digital content service providers, which are included into the web service provider. The web service framework offers service interfaces to the mobile AR client and the service connection module is used to communicate with integrated open service providers for processing and dynamic media contents. The web service provider in SOMARA designed to supply a digital content service, a photogrammetry service and other services, which could be third party content providers or any providers that their contents will be beneficially applied into the potential scenarios. Note the RCH Cultural Objects service.

Multiple Object Tracking: Typical AR applications are able to track and recognize only one object. In addition, the applications will present only single content on top of the real scene. In this architecture, the mobile AR client will perform multiple 3D object tracking and visualize associated contents such as 3D models, billboards, images, videos, etc. on reference objects at the same time. presents the process of multiple objects tracking and associated content configuration.

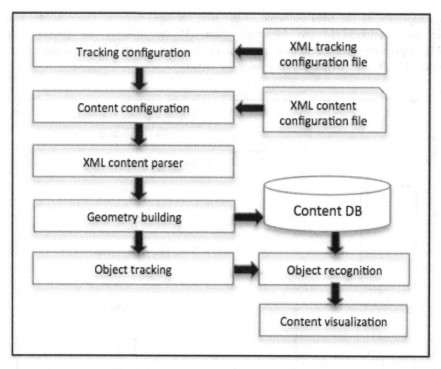

Fig. 7. Multiple objects tracking configuration

4   Augmented Reality Application

The AR application is a middleware system in the mobile client that contains important supporting modules for extensively work with the web service framework, AR
SDK and mobile interface. The designed modules in the AR application are the photogrammetry, digital content (e.g. the RCH cultural objects), personalization and AR
browser request services.

Photogrammetry Service Request: The photogrammetry service enriches the
functionality of the mobile AR client by enabling mobile users to request for image-
based reconstruction services. The photogrammetry service request module handles
connections between the AR application and a web service provider for requesting
photogrammetry services and receiving responses (i.e. a 3D model of a cultural
object). The AR application will capture photos of an intended object and then transfer them via the web service framework to the provider. When a final model is completely done, it will be sent back to the mobile client via the same web service. The
final model will then be visualized and manipulated on the working scene. Note, this
requires existing photogrammetry services, such as Autodesk 123D to adopt a web
services approach.

Digital Content Request: The digital content request module is required when mobile users want to search for other relevant contents from the web service provider. Such digital contents are sent back to the mobile client to allow users to utilize them in the AR environment. These content providers could be the third party or existing open service providers that will be able to provide various kinds of digital contents so that mobile users can put them on their preferred environments, which can also be viewed on the AR browser in other conditions.

Augmented Reality Environment Personalization: The AR environment personalization enables mobile users to create their own interactive AR preferences on the working scene by selecting; manipulating and placing preferred contents and also locations of reference objects or real world scenes on AR environments. This module also allows mobile users to save created AR environments in the XML/JSON formats, including 3D contents provided by the museum or photogrammetry service.

Augmented Reality Browser: The AR browser presents AR preferences, which are saved in the user's profile in standard representation formats including XML and JSON. The AR browser will require object tracking and a GPS module in order to reveal a user's preferences on the AR browser. The browser extensively supports indoor and outdoor uses by tracking proposed objects or user's location so that the application can then provide a saved AR environment. illustrates the Test Wicker Basket Object with associated media contents in an AR scene using the iPhone 5 as the mobile AR interface. Here you can see a video showing how to make wicker baskets, the object label, a test description and a series of related objects.

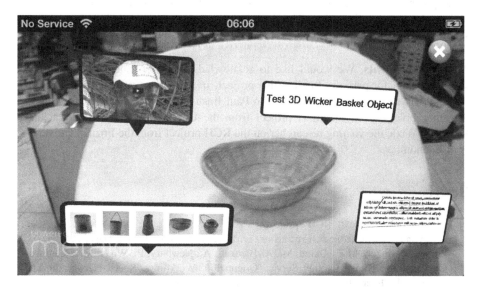

Fig. 8. iPhone 5 AR presentation of a Test Wicker Basket Object

5   Conclusions

The SOA for multiple objects tracking AR system supports dynamic content acquisition over a wireless or mobile network. The mobile client is composed of featured modules to access open services through a web service framework. Planned services include a photogrammetry service based on existing services, such as Autodesk 123D, that enables mobile users to obtain virtual models from image-based reconstruction so that the users are able to design what they want to visualize on the screen. Another aim of this architecture is to support open content utilization so that acquired contents can be freely selected and placed on AR environments together with other perspective contents, e.g. location, geographic or social media data. User preference AR environments can then be view in other situation by augmenting reference 3D objects, markers or markerless such as 2D images. The system is illustrated using a Reanimating Cultural heritage web services that access digital cultural objects from the RCH repository — note we use a Test Wicker Basket Object and associated 3D to illustrate. It is instructive to note that even large collections of cultural 3D objects are not yet mainstream in museum interactive environments, and the use of AR in this context is also rare. We feel that exploring the notion of what is effectively 'user generated 3D contents' in this context is worthy of further exploration.

Future Work. Future work will include the notion of 'crowd sourcing' the generation of high quality 3D to associate with a digital heritage repository, such as RCH, so that eventually over time all objects on display in a museum's gallery (virtual museum) could potentially have a 3D presentation online gathered through an AR application such as discussed in this paper. This will, however, require a 'mind shift' from a museum's perspective; they tend not to allow visitors to take photographs in the museum!

Acknowledgements. We would like to acknowledge the Arts and Humanities Research Council for partially funding this project. In particular, we would also like to acknowledge the input to this work from Paul Basu and Johanna Zetterstrom-Sharp, the anthropologists on the RCH project from the University College London, and Wojciech Wiza, the visiting researcher on the RCH project from the Poznan University of Economics.

References

1. AHRC Beyond Text RCH project, http://projects.beyondtext.ac.uk/reanimatingculturalheritage/index.php (last visited February 7, 2013)
2. Zhang, W., Patoli, M.Z., Gkion, M., Al-Barakati, A., Newbury, P., White, M.: Reanimating Cultural Heritage through Service Orientation, Workflows, Social Networking and Mashups. In: International Conference on CyberWorlds, pp. 177–184 (2009)
3. White, M., Patoli, Z., Pascu, T.: Knowledge Networking through Social Media for a Digital Heritage Resource. In: Digital Heriatge 2013, Marseille (October 2013)

4. Genc, Y., et al.: Marker-less tracking for AR: a learning-based approach. In: Proceedings International Symposium on Mixed and Augmented Reality, pp. 295–304. IEEE Comput. Soc. (2002)
5. Damiani, E., et al.: Augmented reality technologies, systems and applications. Multimedia Tools and Applications 51(1), 341–377 (2011)
6. Papagiannakis, G., Singh, G., Magnenat-Thalmann, N.: A survey of mobile and wireless technologies for augmented reality systems. Comput. Animat. Virtual Worlds 19(1), 3–22 (2008)
7. Zhou, F.Z.F., Duh, H.B.-L., Billinghurst, M.: Trends in augmented reality tracking, interaction and display: A review of ten years of ISMAR. In: 2008 7th IEEE/ACM International Symposium on Mixed and Augmented Reality (2008)
8. Perey, C., Engelke, T., Reed, C.: Current Status of Standards for Augmented Reality, pp. 21–38. Springer, New York (2011)
9. Luo, X.L.X.: From Augmented Reality to Augmented Computing: A Look at Cloud-Mobile Convergence. In: 2009 International Symposium on Ubiquitous Virtual Reality (2009)
10. Lee, R., et al.: Interoperable augmented web browsing for exploring virtual media in real space. In: Wilde, E., et al. (eds.) Proceedings of the 2nd International Workshop on Location and the Web LOCWEB 2009, pp. 1–4 (2009)
11. Selonen, P., et al.: Mixed reality web service platform. Multimedia Systems 18(3), 215–230 (2012)
12. Bellimpasakis, P., Selonen, P., You, Y.: A Web Service Platform for Building Interoperable Augmented Reality Solutions. In: International Augmented Reality Workshop, pp. 1–6 (2010)
13. Wang, R.W.R., Wang, X.W.X.: Applying Service-Oriented Architecture into an Augmented Reality E-business System. In: 2008 IEEE International Conference on e-Business Engineering (2008)

Training to Improve Spatial Orientation in Engineering Students Using Virtual Environments

Cristina Roca-Gonzalez[1], Jorge Martín-Gutiérrez[2],
Cristina Mato Corredeguas[3], and Melchor García-Domínguez[1]

[1] Dpto. Cartografia y Expresión Gráfica en la Ingeniería,
Universidad de Las Palmas de Gran Canarias, Spain
{croca,melchor}@dcegi.ulpgc.es
[2] Dpto. Técnicas y Proyectos en Arquitectura e Ingeniería, Universidad de La Laguna, Spain
jmargu@ull.edu.es
[3] Dpto. Didácticas Especiales, Universidad de Las Palmas de Gran Canarias, Spain
mmato@dde.ulpgc.es

Abstract. This work present the results obtained from a experience performed with freshmen students of the Industrial Engineering degree at Las Palmas de Gran Canaria University aiming for improvement of their spatial abilities. The work linked to spatial abilities show a great lack of uniformity according to the adopted terminology as a consequence of different approaches, researchers' field of study and the research's scale. But all research agree on the relationship between a high level of spatial ability and the possibility of success in certain professional careers and university degrees such as engineering which is our actual case. The pilot study described in this paper, aims to improve the Spatial Orientation component of spatial abilities and for this we conducted two experiences or trainings based on orienteering sports: one was performed in a real environment meanwhile the other took place in a virtual environment. The results show that this component can be trained and improved in both environments without finding any significant difference between both types of training.

Keywords: Spatial abilities, Spatial orientation, Environmental scale, Orienteering, Virtual worlds.

1 Introduction

Most part of our sensations, anything that we experience or learn is acquired through the visual system. Our world could not be understood without the graphic sketches, which have been drawn since prehistory, and now used for designing every product and service demanded by an ever increasing technological society.

The spatial vision is understood as the ability to visualize and manipulate objects in our minds. It's not just an important skill widely recognized in the engineering field, but it's also highly regarded in many other fields. So, van der Geer points out that the spatial vision is important for succeeding in fields such as Biology, Chemistry, Mathematics and Natural Science [1].

R. Shumaker and S. Lackey (Eds.): VAMR 2014, Part II, LNCS 8526, pp. 96–104, 2014.
© Springer International Publishing Switzerland 2014

For predicting the success in university studies, some universities commonly consider academic records and physics or mathematics grades when the case belongs to engineering degrees. Some studies have revealed an existing correlation between ability and success in other engineering fields.

One of the problems found while revising references about spatial abilities is the contradiction about its definition. We may found the same term for identical components or even different terms with the same descriptions. Besides, there is no common agreement about the number of components of that ability, varying between two and ten depending on the authors. Despite the lack of agreement about the definition of this concept, we may outline the one belonging to Linn & Petersen [2] as the "skill in representing, transforming, generating, and recalling symbolic, non-linguistic information".

The structure of the components belonging to the spatial ability has been subject to study since the 40s. Commonly, the spatial ability has been considered to be composed by three components. In Linn & Petersen [2] as well as Lohman's [3] works, the three components are: spatial perception, orientation or spatial rotation and finally, the spatial visualization. Spatial perception measures a person`s ability to sense horizontally or vertically, spatial rotation indicates the ability to quickly rotate any two dimensions figures as well as three dimensions objects through imagination and spatial visualization assesses the ability to manipulate the spatial information belonging to simple objects through complex operations.

Other researchers such as McGee [4] y Maier [5] propose five main components: spatial relations, spatial perception, spatial visualization, mental rotation and spatial orientation. In this classification, we may observe the difference while considering mental rotation and spatial orientation.

We found a couple of issues during the bibliographic revision of the spatial abilities' concept. In first place, the studies don't provide similar results; meanwhile many studies identify the spatial orientation inside their rankings [4-6], others don't [7] and even among those which didn't include them, there is no common agreement according to its definition. Besides, these studies don't pay attention to the dynamic and environmental components, which are considered as quite important factors among the spatial abilities field [8].

Another factor which should be considered is the environmental scale where spatial abilities should be tested [9,10]. Montbello [11] proposes that due to the fact that the human motor and perceptual system interacts in a different way with space depending on scale, there are many psychological systems involved in processing that information in different scales. In a large scale, we don't have any chance to obtain all spatial information referring to any natural and artificial elements which belong to the individual's personal environment. This kind of abilities is very important in movements and navigation. In this sense, we find another taxonomy which regards both dynamic and spatial components proposed by Gary L. Allen[12], sorting the spatial components across three functional families. The first one should answer the 'What is this?' question gathering anything referring to the identification and manipulation of small still objects such as what happens when a written paper test is being solved. The second question is 'Where is it?' including situations where the individual and/or the object may be moving or motionless such as when a ball's trajectory is being calculated. The third question should answer to 'Where am I?' referring to an individual moving across a big scale environment full of still objects such as buildings or vegetation.

2   Aim

Our aim is performing trainings for improving the freshmen's spatial orientation component of spatial abilities enrolled in the engineering graphics subjects on engineering degrees taught at the Civil and Industrial engineering school from Las Palmas de Gran Canaria University. If this training is successful, it will help students easing any studying issues while obtaining better academic results on this subject.

3   Hypothesis

Until now, just a few studies have attempted to relate spatial abilities at different scales, ie, whether the results obtained by measuring spatial skills with psychometric test paper, can predict success on large scale task [13, 14]. Regardless of any correlation, in this work we may assume the spatial orientation as a component of spatial ability so we will try to improve it through specific training designed for this experience. Therefore, the spatial orientation will improve which will help the student towards a better understanding of the Graphic Design subject on engineering.

The training was chosen having in mind that we may focus on tests performed over large environments, so we opted for an orienteering race. Besides, we wanted to evaluate the results performing those tests over two kinds of environments: a real one and a virtual one. Our hypothesis is that performance of that training may improve the spatial orientation of the students.

4   Participants

The participants were 79 freshmen students from the Las Palmas de Gran Canaria University belonging to the Industrial Engineering degree. The average age and standard deviation (SD) was 18.8 (1.3) between 18 and 24 years old for men meanwhile value was 18.8 (1.2) between 18 and 24 years old for women. They were split in two homogeneous groups for performing training as 30 of them undertook training in a real environment meanwhile 33 of them did it on a virtual one.

The experiences were performed in the first week of the first semester during the 2012-2013 academic course, so no student had attended classes of any kind from any Graphic Design subject on engineering before undertaking training. None of them had ever taken part on any orienteering races either. The orientation values were measured using a reliable measurement tool before performing the experience and after its completion: the Perspective Taking/ Spatial Orientation Test developed at the Santa Barbara University by Mary Hegarty et al. [15,16]

5   Experience 1: Real World Orienteering

Thirty participants took part in this experience (10 women and 20 men). The mean value and standard deviation (SD) was 18.7 (1.1) between 18 and 24 years. None of them declared having any previous experience in orienteering sports. For encouraging participation, the three top performers with best times will enjoy an upgrade on their marks as long as it's 4.5 or higher.

The experiment consisted of two phases, first of them 45 minutes long and in the classroom, an expert at orienteering explained the basis for this practice with emphasis on the use of the compass. There were some relevant changes respecting the usual orienteering race. During the race there weren't any geographic elements as well as any building or vegetation which could be used as a reference. Only distances or relative angles were available so they were shown on spot how to measure distances through steps on the plane's scale. Besides, as this wasn't any physical test, they were instructed not to run as celerity relied on the ability to orientate and not on swift movement.

Fig. 1. Left. Expert giving instructions. Right. Students measuring distances through steps.

While using maps, the orienteering method will depend on the ability to interpret them – spatial relations will be established over symbols- and the ability to connect the map with the field and vice versa.

We also considered some common actions from this sport:

- Bringing the map and other race material (compass, card and control's description).
- Map orientation
- Map reading
- Choosing the right path.
- Deciding the most suitable technique

In our experience we omitted some actions for strengthening the desired meaning for the race. The experience took place in a football field where there were only architectonic elements available for setting spatial relations. But given the simplicity of a football field and how the orientation sense was meant to be trained, we omitted the architectonic elements by providing the students with a 'blind map' where the only display belonged to the relative layout of the beacons according to their angle and distance as well as the geographic north.

 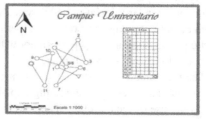

Fig. 2. Left. Football field's map including beacons. Right 'blind map" provided to the participant.

For the second phase, the proper 'orientation race' indeed, there were two tracks designed with a similar length. The students were told that both paths were different, to avoid them following each other. So, they didn't know which path was being followed by the student who previously got into the field. Each student completed both paths, so the results obtained doesn't rely on pure luck.

For performing this test we used the Sportident system. This system is based on the SPORTident-Card, similar to a pen drive. During the race, the system compiles times and numeric codes from the control points. The output offers individual registry values for both intermediate and total times.

Fig. 3. Totals and records partial results

6   Experience 2: Virtual Orienteering

In this experience there were 33 students taking part in it, including 12 women and 21 men. The average age and standard deviation were 18.8 (1.4) between 18 and 24 years old. Like in previous case, no participant had any experience in orienteering sports and involvement was also encouraged with a marks' upgrade in the same conditions of the previous experience.

The first phase of this experience took around 90 minutes and consisted once again on a classroom explanation of the orienteering sport's basics as well as the compass' use and further guidance about use of the given software.

The demo version of the Catching Features program was used and despite being freeware, it included every single feature we needed:

http://www.catchingfeatures.com/

Catching Features is an orientation game where one or several players get immersed in a virtual environment. Players take part in several races using a topographic map with their key and compass as a real race.

Fig. 4. Catching features settings

The game also offers the chance to play on a single player mode or multiplayer against other participants. In the full version there are also online games available.

The settings are quite realistic as the player can move and have points of view across every single direction. Every beacon can be found using the key and compass until the itinerary is complete.

In our experience we ask the students to complete a minimum of six races. They had one week to finish them and they performed them at their own homes through their own computers downloading the game's free trial version.

Catching Features provides several start formats with results obtained in different races. So, a file with the full results was requested to the students for evaluating the experience's performance and applying the incentives.

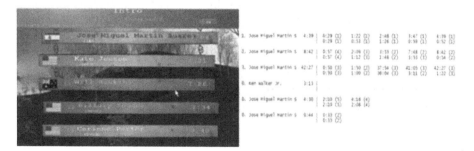

Fig. 5. Student results

7   Measures and Results

In table 1 we find the results obtained by the students in the Perspective Taking Test before and after training for the three groups: Real Orienteering, Virtual Orienteering and Control Group. Mean values prior to training are quite similar in all three groups.

Table 1. Values Pre/Post Test and Gain Scores

	Pre-Test	Post-Test	Gain
Real Orienteering Group	42.33	18.75	23.58
Virtual Orienteering Group	54.77	24.00	30.77
Control Group	54.29	45.65	8.64

An analysis of variance (ANOVA) was carried out with all data obtained from the three groups in the Perspective Taking and Spatial Orientation Test, showing there is no statistical difference between groups prior to this training. So the three groups were statistically equivalent about spatial orientation at the beginning of this study.

We compared the mean values obtained in the pre and post test using the t-Student paired series test and data for the real orienteering group were t=8.08, p-value=0.00; for the virtual orienteering group t=11.90, p-value=0.00 and finally the control group obtained a p-value=0.27.

The groups performing these trainings showed a statistical improvement in their spatial orientation levels. The p-values are below 5% statistical significance which means that any student who performs one of both trainings has a chance over 95% of improving their spatial orientation levels. Besides, the results show there is no improvement in the spatial orientation levels for the control group.

For comparing and checking out if there is any difference between both groups, we carried out the Sefflé contrast over multiples choices.

Table 2. Groups comparison

(I) group	(J) group	Difference between mean values (I-J)	Typical error	Sig.	Confidence interval at 95% Upper limit	Lower limit
1	2	-7.18848	3.49433	.128	-15.9131	1.5361
	3	18.52125(*)	4.28814	.000	7.8146	29.2279
2	1	7.18848	3.49433	.128	-1.5361	15.9131
	3	25.70973(*)	4.21981	.000	15.1738	36.2457
3	1	-18.52125(*)	4.28815	.000	-29.2279	-7.8146
	2	-25.70973(*)	4.21981	.000	-36.2457	-15.1738

*Difference between mean values is significant at .05 level.
1(Real Orienteering),2(Virtual Orienteering), 3(Control Group)

The results show there is no significant difference between the control group and those groups performing the training. Besides, there is no difference between the groups undertaking training in both the real and virtual environments. This means that improvement in spatial orientation is similar performing any of both trainings.

8   Conclusions

Even obtaining the results described in previous section, where we saw that students improved their spatial orientation in any of both trainings, we must consider certain questions while we approach the new experience in subsequent academic courses. Despite how precise and realistic the environment's simulation is, we must consider the fact that people is used to move through a real environment. Despite the visual information available, the field of view in the real world is much wider than in the virtual one, so the spatial information output is much lower in the virtual environment and the update of our body's location may come not only from the visual system but the kinesic one as well. Besides, while in a real environment we need an auto-directed movement from our body, in the virtual one the experience is far more passive.

From the teacher's point of view, it was easier to prepare and perform the virtual experience. Aside from the fact of learning the orienteering race basics and handling the Catching Features app, there was no other relevant issue. However, the preparation of the experience in a real environment held at a football field required not only a great organizational capabilities but also putting together services and staff from the Las Palmas de Gran Canaria University.

From the student's point of view, we received positive feedback; both tests were attractive for them and they performed them enthusiastically and willingly although as we previously mentioned, they were encouraged with a mark's upgrade if they reached the top three. We were surprised by the positive welcome and assessment that the real field test, the orienteering race, had. The interaction component and interpersonal competition got students so involved that they wanted to perform similar tests and showed great interest about the spatial abilities in their curriculums.

Acknowledgements. We wanted to express our most sincere gratitude to Mr. Ulises Ortiz for his support whilst designing the orientation race and making the Sportident system available for acquiring all data from the test. His vast experience in this sport eased the design of the experience in the real field helping to perform it efficiently. We also would like to mention all students taking part in this experience as they showed great enthusiasm and collaboration during the whole test.

References

1. Allen, G.L.: Functional families of spatial abilities: Poor relations and rich prospects. International Journal of Testing 3, 251–262 (2003)
2. Linn, M.C., Petersen, A.C.: Emergence and characterization of sex differences in spatial ability: A meta-analysis. Child. Dev., 1479-1498 (1985)

3. Lohman, D.F.: Spatial abilities as traits, processes, and knowledge (1988)
4. McGee, M.G.: Human spatial abilities: Psychometric studies and environmental, genetic, hormonal, and neurological influences. Psychol. Bull. 86, 889–918 (1979)
5. Maier, P.H.: Spatial geometry and spatial ability–How to make solid geometry solid, pp. 63–75 (1996)
6. Mafalda, R.: Efeitos do uso de diferentes métodos de representaçao gráfica no desenvolvimento da habilidade de visualizaçao espacial, Sao Paulo (2000)
7. Carroll, J.B.: Human cognitive abilities. Cambridge University Press, Cambridge (1993)
8. Hegarty, M., Waller, D.: Individual differences in spatial abilities. The Cambridge handbook of visuospatial thinking, pp. 121–169 (2005)
9. Golledge, R.G.: Spatial Behavoir: A Geographical Perspective. Guilford Press (1997)
10. Hegarty, M., Richardson, A.E., Montello, D.R., Lovelace, K., Subbiah, I.: Development of a self-report measure of environmental spatial ability. Intelligence 30, 425–447 (2002)
11. Montello, D.R.: Scale and multiple psychologies of space. In: Campari, I., Frank, A.U. (eds.) COSIT 1993. LNCS, vol. 716, pp. 312–321. Springer, Heidelberg (1993)
12. Allen, G.L.: Functional families of spatial abilities: Poor relations and rich prospects. International Journal of Testing 3, 251–262 (2003)
13. Allen, G.L., Kirasic, K.C., Dobson, S.H., Long, R.G., Beck, S.: Predicting environmental learning from spatial abilities: An indirect route. Intelligence 22, 327–355 (1996)
14. Montello, D.R., Lovelace, K.L., Golledge, R.G., Self, C.M.: Sex Related Differences and Similarities in Geographic and Environmental Spatial Abilities. Ann. Assoc. Am. Geogr. 89, 515–534 (1999)
15. Kozhevnikov, M., Hegarty, M.: A dissociation between object manipulation spatial ability and spatial orientation ability. Mem. Cognit. 29, 745–756 (2001)
16. Hegarty, M., Waller, D.: A dissociation between mental rotation and perspective-taking spatial abilities. Intelligence 32, 175–191 (2004)

Staging Choreographies for Team Training in Multiple Virtual Worlds Based on Ontologies and Alignments

Emanuel Silva[1,2], Nuno Silva[2], and Leonel Morgado[3]

[1] University of Trás-os-Montes e Alto Douro, Vila Real, Portugal
[2] School of Engineering, Polytechnic of Porto, Porto, Portugal
{ecs,nps}@isep.ipp.pt
[3] INESC TEC (formerly INESC Porto) / Universidade Aberta, Lisbon, Portugal
leonel.morgado@uab.pt

Abstract. In this paper we present an approach that makes possible the staging of choreographies for education and training purposes in potentially any virtual world platform. A choreography is seen here as the description of a set of actions that must or may be executed by a group of participants, including the goals to be achieved and any restrictions that may exist. We present a system-architecture and the formalization of a set of processes that are able to transform a choreography from a platform-independent representation into a specific virtual world platform's representation. We adopt an ontology-based approach with distinct levels of abstraction for capturing and representing multi-actors and multi-domain choreographies to be staged in virtual world platforms with distinct characteristics. Ontologies are characterized according to two complementary dimensions – choreography's domain (independent and dependent) and virtual world platform (independent and dependent) – giving rise to four ontologies. Ontology mappings between these ontologies enable the automatic generation of a choreography for virtually any target virtual world platform, thus reducing the time and effort of the choreography development.

Keywords: virtual worlds, training, choreography, multi-user, model-driven, ontology, mapping.

1   Introduction

Virtual worlds have achieved significant levels of interest for supporting teaching and learning activities [1], [2] since they provide the creation of immersive environments where multiple elements of a team sharing a common virtual space can develop competencies in a simulated context [3], [4]. Choreographies of virtual actors are a specific type of content that represent the set of actions that can be performed simultaneously by human-users and virtual computer-controlled actors thus enabling human trainees/students to play roles as part of teams or within a simulated social context. In this sense, a choreography is the description of a set of actions that must or may be executed by a group of participants, including the goals to be achieved and any restrictions that may exist.

R. Shumaker and S. Lackey (Eds.): VAMR 2014, Part II, LNCS 8526, pp. 105–115, 2014.

Because designing a choreography is a resource-intensive effort, it would be desirable for the result not to be hostage to a specific virtual world platform (VWP) but rather deployable in any VWP. However, as virtual platforms are very heterogeneous in terms of (e.g.) functionalities, data models, execution engines and programing/scripting languages or APIs, deploying a platform-based choreography into another VWP is difficult and time-consuming [5]–[8].

We believe that the approach presented in this paper provides a contribution that facilitates the development, sharing and adaptation of choreographies aimed to be staged in different virtual platforms. For this, we suggest an approach where the conceptual representation model of the choreography is captured in the form of ontologies, and its adaptation to a particular virtual world follows a set of models transformation processes, similar to that suggested by the Model Driven Architecture (MDA) paradigm [9]. The proposed ontology-based definition of choreographies can capture not only the physical aspects as objects but more complex content such as procedures, consisting of sets of actions and conditions in which the actors can perform them.

Thus, this paper presents an approach that deals with the design and representation of platform-independent multi-user choreographies, and their deployment to different VWPs with minimal effort and time using a set of transformation processes based on ontologies and alignments. The rest of the paper comprehends four more sections. In section 2 we present the proposed approach and the description of the system architecture. Section 3 describes the developed experiments. Section 4 compares the related work with the proposed ideas. Finally, Section 5 summarizes the proposal and suggests future directions.

2   Proposed Approach

To deal with VWP with different characteristics, we argue that choreographies should be clearly separated from the technical characteristics of the execution in the VWP.

To this end, the core of the proposal is a "generic high-level ontology" that captures the choreography in a conceptual and abstract fashion, so it is independent from the staging/deployment VWP. Thus, the data model of every virtual world must be captured/represented by the so-called "platform-specific ontology", and a mapping between the generic high-level ontology and the platform-specific ontology must be defined. The mapping will provide the means to transform the platform-independent choreography into a platform-dependent choreography.

To address this the MDA software-development paradigm [9] is adopted and adapted. MDA specifies three default models of a system corresponding to different layers of abstraction: a Computation Independent Model (CIM) the most abstract, which represents the view of the system without any computational complexities; a Platform Independent Model (PIM) that describes the behavior and structure of the system, but without technological details, and a Platform Specific Model (PSM) that combines the specifications in PIM with the specific details of a specific platform.

Based on the concept of model independence and model transformation of MDA, we adopt an approach based on two first-class citizen dimensions: the VWP dimension and the choreography's domain dimension. In fact, unlike in MDA, in our approach the model is not only independent from the VWP but also independent from the (choreography's) domain. Fig. 1 depicts the MDA one-dimensional approach (Fig.1 a) in comparison with the two-dimensional envisaged approach (Fig. 1 b).

The nomenclature O_{PxDx} refers to Ontology, Platform and Domain, with "x" assuming "d" and "i" values for "dependent" and "independent", respectively. E.g. O_{PiDd} stands for "Ontology, Platform-independent, Domain-dependent".

Taking into account the characteristics of ontologies, and considering they are the best way to represent conceptual information in order to bring the intelligent systems

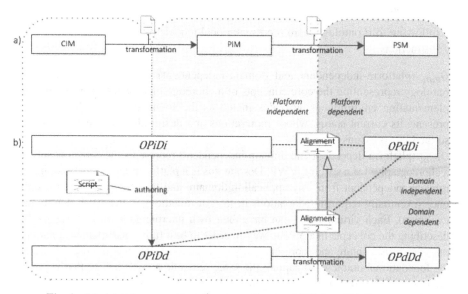

Fig. 1. Model-Driven representation according to: a) MDA and b) Our approach

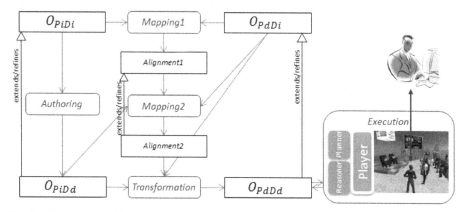

Fig. 2. The system architecture with the processes of authoring, mappings, transformation and execution

closer to the human conceptual level [10], we claim that ontologies are then the adequate knowledge representation model for bridging the gap between the human requirements and the computational requirements [10]–[13], thus able to play the role of both Computation-Independent Model (CIM) and Platform-Independent Model (PIM). Following MDA, the ontology-based choreography representations are successively transformed through a set of processes until the final, platform-specific choreography (O_{PdDd}) that is executed in the specific VWP. The proposed architecture is depicted in Fig. 2, and comprehends four ontologies and five processes.

2.1   Ontologies

The following four ontologies are representational models of the different choreography abstractions:

- O_{PiDi} (platform-independent and domain-independent) is the generic high-level ontology representing the core concepts of a choreography independent of any implementation environment, also designated as the foundational ontology. Fig. 3 presents its current status, whose motivations and design decisions have been described in a previous paper [14].
- O_{PdDi} (platform-dependent and domain-independent) represents the core concepts of a choreography for a specific VWP. Despite this is a platform-dependent ontology, it remains independent from any application domain, and therefore is developed only once (eventually requiring adaptations in face of mutations in the VWP due to any evolution). Each virtual world can have their own interpretation of a choreography describing the concepts in a private way in order to best fit its characteristics, but this ontology must capture and represent every concept corresponding to those defined in the foundational ontology to capture the same semantic knowledge, so that is possible to establish semantic relations between them. Thus, we consider that in order to apply this approach, it is necessary to develop, for each target VWP, an ontology to represent that virtual world platform's particular interpretation of the fundamental ontology. Moreover, this ontology can incorporate additional concepts considering the specific characteristics of that virtual world and using its own terminology.

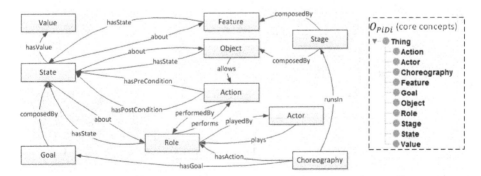

Fig. 3. The Foundational Choreography Ontology (O_{PiDi}): representation of concepts, properties and relations between concepts

- O_{PiDd} (platform independent and domain dependent) is a choreography resulting from the authorship of O_{PiDi}. It captures the representation of a complete choreography for a specific application domain, without any concern about the technical specificities of any platform.
- O_{PdDd} (platform dependent and domain dependent) is a choreography represented in/for a specific VWP. This is the choreography that is intended to serve as a reference for the staging in the virtual world.

2.2   Processes

In the proposed architecture we apply five processes to conduct a successive transformation of models representing the various abstractions of a choreography to adapt its specification to a particular virtual world.

To illustrate the explanation, we will consider a generic Instant Messaging platform for which a choreography will be adapted. This is a very simple platform (developed by the authors for testing purposes, cf. Fig. 7) where there is only the representation of an action called write.

Authoring. Authoring is a user-based process in which the choreographer authors a domain dependent choreography in the form of an ontology. This process is typically performed by an expert that manually builds the ontology. But cnd-user tools can also be developed to allow people without knowledge or training in ontologies to specify the choreography through simple and intuitive interfaces. That is, end-user tools can in a transparent manner, build ontologies instead of human users directly, facilitating the authoring process.

The foundation ontology (O_{PiDi}) is extended and refined semantically to describe the choreography entities specific to an application domain, giving rise to O_{PiDd}. The authoring process must ensure the set of changes applied does not change the semantics defined in O_{PiDi}. For that, the following assumptions must be guaranteed:

- No axioms defined in O_{PiDi} can be removed;
- No contradictions can be added, i.e., O_{PiDd} must be logically consistent;
- No new root elements are allowed. I.e. new entities (classes and properties) are defined as sub entities of those existing in O_{PiDi} and should not create new root elements.

Fig. 4 depicts an excerpt of the ontology resulting from authorship (O_{PiDd}), and more formally its representation using Description Logics (DL) syntax.

New concepts are added as well as restrictions that will define boundaries to the ability of actions execution by the actors. The restrictions are based on the definition of associations between roles (that actors can play) and actions. Commonly, the following two types of restrictions are defined:

1. To constrain the actors allowed to perform an action based on the user's role, i.e. to perform an action, the actor must have a specific role previously defined. The relation between the concepts referenced by the action and role is defined by the property *performedBy*;

2. To assign the role(s) of an actor based on the action(s) s/he performs. Thus, the roles are dynamically assigned during the choreography according to the actions performed by the actor. This association can be seen in a dual perspective. Using a small example: on the one hand, if an actor plays the role Role1 and performs actions Action1 and Action2, s/he shall automatically plays the role Role2 thereafter. On the other hand, to play the role Role2 it is a necessary condition that the actor plays the role Role1 and performs the actions Action1 and Action2.

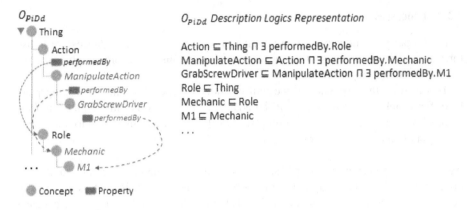

O_{PiDd} Description Logics Representation

Action $\sqsubseteq$ Thing $\sqcap$ $\exists$ performedBy.Role
ManipulateAction $\sqsubseteq$ Action $\sqcap$ $\exists$ performedBy.Mechanic
GrabScrewDriver $\sqsubseteq$ ManipulateAction $\sqcap$ $\exists$ performedBy.M1
Role $\sqsubseteq$ Thing
Mechanic $\sqsubseteq$ Role
M1 $\sqsubseteq$ Mechanic
. . .

Fig. 4. An excerpt of the (O_{PiDd}) Ontology resulting from the authoring process

During the authoring process, the author can take advantage of all the semantic expressiveness of the DL language to elaborate more complex choreographies. For example, if an actor during the choreography cannot play two roles, one can specify using DL that these two roles are disjoint.

Mapping1. Mapping1 is the process that establishes correspondences between the representations of the two choreographies abstractions represented by $O_{P_iD_i}$ and $O_{P_dD_i}$ (Alignment1).

An alignment is a set of correspondences (semantic bridges in this paper). A semantic bridge is a set of information elements describing what entities from both source and target ontology are semantically related, and what conditions must hold in order to be considered [15]. Two types of semantic bridges are considered:

1. Concept Bridge (CB), used to describe the semantic relations between (source and target) concepts;
2. Property Bridge (PB), used to specify the semantic relations between (source and target) properties, either relations or attributes.

In this process all the core concepts (concepts that are direct subclasses of the Thing concept, depicted in Fig. 3) of the foundational ontology (O_{PiDi}) should be mapped to concepts of the platform specific ontology (O_{PdDi}) to ensure that there is full correspondences between both ontologies. Correspondences between properties are defined between properties of two mapped concepts. In order to facilitate understanding, a relation is established between the concept-concept correspondence and the property-property correspondence (Fig. 5).

Mapping2. Mapping2 is the process that establishes correspondences between the domain choreography (O_{PiDd}) and a VWP ontology (O_{PdDi}), i.e. Alignment2. Alignment2 profits from (and extends) Alignment1, thus promoting reuse and reducing efforts (Fig. 5).

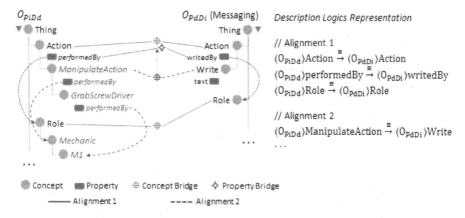

Fig. 5. A partial view of the alignments resulting from Mapping1 and Mapping2

Transformation. Transformation is the process that creates the VWP choreography (O_{PdDd}) from O_{PiDd} and O_{PdDi} and according to the Alignment2.

This is a fully automatic process that "copies" the O_{PiDd} classes and constraints (Fig. 4) to the O_{PdDd} (Fig. 6).

Despite this being an automatic process, choreographers can intervene and edit the resulting O_{PdDd} ontology for additional adjustments. Thus, the O_{PdDd} ontology may be further finely tuned to better fit the implementation platform.

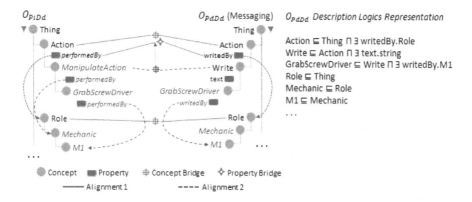

Fig. 6. An extract of O_{PdDd} ontology

Execution. Execution is the process that stages the choreography in a VWP through a Player (computer program) compatible with the VWP who has the ability to schedule actions according to the choreography and control its execution by virtual characters. Further, it monitors the human-user performance by comparing the executed actions with those described by the choreography, and reacts accordingly. This process uses a reasoner mechanism to evaluate whether it is possible to perform the actions, verifying if all necessary conditions are met. When virtual-users are present, a planner is used to calculate a plan of actions for them.

3   Experiments

For the evaluation of our approach we deployed several real-world choreographies that were staged in two different multiuser platforms with very distinct characteristics with human-users only. We used the VWP OpenSimulator[1] (OpenSim) to create a realistic multiuser 3D environment; as a counterpart system, we developed for testing purposes the aforementioned messaging platform. It is a simplified version of text-based virtual worlds of the Multi-User Dungeons era, following Morgado's definition [16]. This messaging platform has very different characteristics from the OpenSim, since it does not allow the representation of scene objects, but enables the development of a team's choreography nonetheless. Its interface provides the actions of the choreography in the form of buttons, the interaction is done by pressing buttons, and when an action is performed successfully by each team member, it is communicated to all other team members by means of a text log (Fig. 7).

Authoring is obviously the most time-consuming and creative process, while semi-automatic Mapping1 and Mapping2 processes require reduced time and effort. Once these processes are done, the transformation and execution processes are fully automatic.

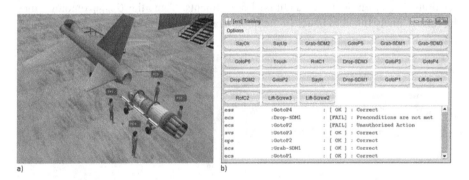

Fig. 7. Staging the choreography in a) OpenSim and b) messaging platform

---

[1]   opensimulator.org/

4   Related Work

There is prior relevant related work addressing the description of plans to represent training procedures to be staged by a single actor as well as by teams with several elements and how actions are distributed among them. But, most approaches design a choreography aiming it to be staged on a particular VWP. This creates strong dependencies with this VWP, making it difficult or even impossible to apply to other virtual worlds. Thus, related work can be categorized according to three dimensions: modeling independence, VWP independence and number and type of the actors.

Some approaches use separate models to represent the specification of procedures and scene [7], [17], [18]. They address team training scenarios but they are strongly dependent on the characteristics of the VWP. Some other approaches attempt to bridge the gap between the representation of procedures and its execution in distinct VWP. However, such approaches are only focused on a single user not allowing the representation of teamwork [19]–[21].

Instead, our approach is capable of representing teamwork choreographies involving multi-users played either by human and virtual-characters. Also, the actions and scene are captured conceptually using a unique choreography model that is converted to potentially any VWP.

5   Conclusions and Future Work

In this paper we propose an approach that allows the development of choreographies and its adaptation and staging in potentially any VWP. For that, based on the concept of MDA and the assumption that the use of ontologies is the best way to represent the conceptual information to approximate the intelligent systems to the human conceptual level, we propose an ontology to capture the semantics of a generic choreography independent of any application domain and VWP. Further, for each VWP is adopted an ontology representing its specific terminology and functionalities, and is mapped with the generic one.

Using a set of alignments between the ontologies we describe a complete sequence of processes that allow adapting a choreography of a specific domain (but independent of any VWP) into a choreography suitable and capable of being staged into a specific virtual world. We also describe the execution process that monitors, manages the staging of the choreography, and uses reasoning engines to aid in the evaluation and validation of actions.

Moreover, ontologies allow the integration in the same model all the modeling information related to the choreography, i.e. the definition of procedures related to teamwork and the information about the scene.

Using alignments between ontologies enables the automation of adaptation of the generic ontology to the specific target ontology, hence contributing to reduce development time and resources.

In future work the Mapping1 and Mapping2 processes can be refined to incorporate automatic matching mechanisms. So, it would be possible to increase the ability to automate these processes while at the same time it reduces the need for user intervention.

Acknowledgments. This work is supported by FEDER Funds through the "Programa Operacional Factores de Competitividade - COMPETE" program and by National Funds through FCT "Fundação para a Ciência e Tecnologia" under the project AAL4ALL (QREN13852).

References

1. De Freitas, S.: Serious virtual worlds, Scoping Guide JISC E-Learn. Programme Jt. Inf. Syst. Comm. JISC UK (2008)
2. Morgado, L., Varajão, J., Coelho, D., Rodrigues, C., Sancin, C., Castello, V.: The attributes and advantages of virtual worlds for real world training. J. Virtual Worlds Educ. 1(1) (2010)
3. Kapahnke, P., Liedtke, P., Nesbigall, S., Warwas, S., Klusch, M.: ISReal: An Open Platform for Semantic-Based 3D Simulations in the 3D Internet. In: Patel-Schneider, P.F., Pan, Y., Hitzler, P., Mika, P., Zhang, L., Pan, J.Z., Horrocks, I., Glimm, B. (eds.) ISWC 2010, Part II. LNCS, vol. 6497, pp. 161–176. Springer, Heidelberg (2010)
4. Pinheiro, A., Fernandes, P., Maia, A., Cruz, G., Pedrosa, D., Fonseca, B., Paredes, H., Martins, P., Morgado, L., Rafael, J.: Development of a Mechanical Maintenance Training Simulator in OpenSimulator for F-16 Aircraft Engines. Procedia Comput. Sci. 15, 248–255 (2012)
5. Media Grid: Open File Formats Technology Working Group (OFF.TWG) Charter, http://mediagrid.org/groups/technology/OFF.TWG/ (accessed: October 14, 2013)
6. Mollet, N., Arnaldi, B.: Storytelling in Virtual Reality for Training. In: Pan, Z., Aylett, R., Diener, H., Jin, X., Göbel, S., Li, L. (eds.) Edutainment 2006. LNCS, vol. 3942, pp. 334–347. Springer, Heidelberg (2006)
7. Gerbaud, S., Mollet, N., Ganier, F., Arnaldi, B., Tisseau, J.: GVT: A platform to create virtual environments for procedural training. In: IEEE Virtual Reality Conference, VR 2008, pp. 225–232 (2008)
8. Vernieri, T.M.: A web services approach to generating and using plans in configurable execution environments (2006)
9. Alhir, S.: Methods & Tools - Understanding the Model Driven Architecture (MDA). Martinig & Associates, fall (2003)
10. Obrst, L., Liu, H., Wray, R.: Ontologies for Corporate Web Applications. AI. Mag. 24(3), 49 (2003)
11. Gruber, T.R.: A translation approach to portable ontology specifications. Knowl. Acquis. 5(2), 199–220 (1993)
12. Fensel, D.: Ontologies: A silver bullet for knowledge management and electronic commerce. Springer, Heidelberg (2004)
13. Gruninger, M., Lee, J.: Ontology Applications and Design-Introduction. Commun. ACM 45(2), 39–41 (2002)
14. Silva, E., Silva, N., Paredes, H., Martins, P., Fonseca, B., Morgado, L.: Development of platform-independent multi-user choreographies for virtual worlds based on ontology combination and mapping. In: 2012 IEEE Symposium on Visual Languages and Human-Centric Computing (VL/HCC), pp. 149–152 (2012)
15. Silva, N., Rocha, J.: MAFRA–an ontology MApping FRAmework for the semantic web. In: Proceedings of the 6th International Conference on Business information Systems (2003)

16. Morgado, L.: Technology Challenges of Virtual Worlds in Education and Training - Research Directions. In: 2013 5th International Conference on Games and Virtual Worlds for Serious Applications (VS-GAMES), pp. 1–5 (2013)
17. Edward, L., Lourdeaux, D., Lenne, D., Barthes, J., Burkhardt, J.M.: Modelling autonomous virtual agent behaviours in a virtual environment for risk. IJVR Int. J. Virtual Real. 7(3), 13–22 (2008)
18. Lopes, A., Pires, B., Cardoso, M., Santos, A., Peixinho, F., Sequeira, P., Morgado, L.: System for Defining and Reproducing Handball Strategies in Second Life On-Demand for Handball Coaches' Education
19. Young, R.M., Riedl, M.O., Branly, M., Jhala, A., Martin, R.J., Saretto, C.J.: An architecture for integrating plan-based behavior generation with interactive game environments. J. Game Dev. 1(1), 1–29 (2004)
20. Young, R.M., Thomas, J., Bevan, C., Cassell, B.A.: Zócalo: A Service-Oriented Architecture Facilitating Sharing of Computational Resources in Interactive Narrative Research (2011)
21. Cash, S.P., Young, R.M.: Bowyer: A Planning Tool for Bridging the gap between Declarative and Procedural Domains. Artif. Intel., 14–19 (2009)

"Make Your Own Planet": Workshop for Digital Expression and Physical Creation

Hiroshi Suzuki, Hisashi Sato, and Haruo Hayami

Kanagawa institute of technology Faculty information Technology
1030 shimoogino Atsugi Kanagawa, Japan
hsuzuki@Kanagawa-it.ac.jp

Abstract. We propose the "Make Your Own Planet" workshop, which combines handicraft and digital representation tools (3DCG effects). In this workshop, a child uses a USB camera to select textures freely in the process of making an original 3DCG planet. All 3DCG planets are then placed in a simulated universe for public viewing. By watching this universe, viewers can appreciate the planet of each child. Further, the texture of each 3DCG planet is translated to a polyhedron template and printed out as a paper-craft template. In this process, children employ computers to transform their planets into physical objects that they can bring home. We first describe the workshop concept and then the method by which it was implemented. Finally, we evaluate the workshop.

Keywords: Digital workshop, 3DCG, Unity, I/O device.

1   Introduction

Workshops are currently viewed as opportunities for experimental learning. As such, various workshops are held every weekend at educational facilities, such as museums and universities. In Japan, workshops have attracted attention as places of learning.

CANVAS [1] is unique in that it promotes activities that link technology to the expression of children. A non-profit organization (NPO) holds a "Workshop Collection" every March at Keio University's Hiyoshi Campus. In Japan, CANVAS develops and hosts workshops for children at various educational facilities. This expo, now in its ninth year, has grown into a big event, attracting about 100,000 parents and children over two days. Not all the workshops in the Workshop Collection use digital technology, but the number of those that do is increasing.

Most of the systems used in these workshops, require operations, such those provided by keyboards and digital mice. For the reasons described above, older elementary school children are targeted in these workshops.

2   The Concept of Digital Workshop

2.1   The Trend of the Digital Workshop

Typical examples of workshops that use technology are those for creating handmade crafts through computer-aided activities. Many universities research and develop

R. Shumaker and S. Lackey (Eds.): VAMR 2014, Part II, LNCS 8526, pp. 116–123, 2014.

systems that support handmade work, such as paper crafts [2], stencil designs [3], and pop-up cards [4]. They then hold workshops to disseminate the results of their research in society. An important purpose of these workshops is to have participants and children experience the "joy of creation" by making their own works.

In these creative workshops, computers support creative activities by providing specialized knowledge, augmenting skills, and reducing and simplifying tasks. In other words, computers serve as specialists or professionals. Here, the relationship between children and computers is vertically structured. However, we attempt to provide structures and devices that enable the active involvement of children in creative activities by using computers; thus, they can experience the "joy of creation."

In this paper, we report the on "Make Your Own Planet" workshop, which combines handicraft and digital representation tools (3DCG effects). In this workshop, a child uses a USB camera to select textures freely in the process of making an original 3DCG planet. All 3DCG planets are then placed in a simulated universe for public viewing. By watching this universe, viewers can appreciate the planet of each child. Further, the texture of each 3DCG planet is translated to a polyhedron template and printed out as a paper-craft template. In this process, children employ computers to transform their planets into physical objects that they can bring home.

2.2   Rerated Work

Workshops that use computers as tools for handmade activities are quite common. Broadly speaking they, can be divided into "programming learning systems," "support systems," "expression tool systems." The planet maker proposed in this paper is an expression tool system.

A programing learning system is the most general example of a workshop that employs computers [5]. Workshop programs that design robots and determine their movements are being implemented all over the world. The purpose of these workshops is to understand the features of sensor devices and programming languages. An understanding of algorithms and complex operations are necessary; thus, they are not appropriate for younger children.

A computer that provides knowledge and offers support system can reduce the difficulty of shaping activities. Therefore, it is possible to produce complex handwork, even with children and beginners. In recent years, support systems for paper crafts [6], pop-up-cards [7], have been developed.

An expression tool system provides to user with expressive activities on a computer. These systems can be seen especially in media art. With "Minimal Drawing" [8], one can draw pictures on a simulated canvas, which is rotated. "Body paint" [9] allows users to draw on walls and experience their own bodies as brushes.

"I /O Brush" [10] is a system relevant to our system. It presents a heightened effect to children by ink drawing that takes pictures as real world objects, thus encouraging youthful creativity. The difference between it and our system is that the latter permits children to create a piece of a three-dimensional entity. Children are able to watch the work of other children at the public viewing. In our system, we liken a three-dimensional planet to drawing. A child's planet is on public view as a 3DCG animation that simulates the universe. Moreover, the system can print on the spot.

3   System Development

The planet maker consists of three modules: the "Paint Module," the "Space Display Module" and the "Mapping module." In this section, we describe each method to develop a module and each module's functions. Figure 1 shows an overview of the system.

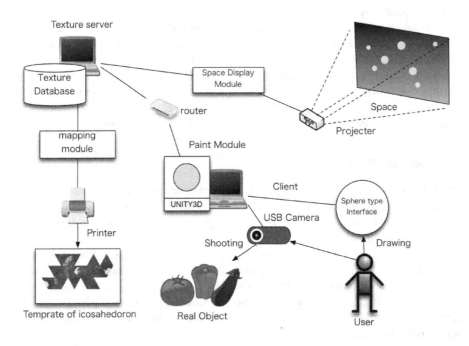

Fig. 1. Overview of the system

3.1   Paint Module

Children can paint the own planets with the Paint Module. This module can paint a 3DCG spherical object using an image captured with a USB camera as ink. Figure 2 shows the principle drawing method.

Spherical Interface
We developed an original tangible interface so that children could paint texture easily on a sphere. This interface consisted of Arduino and Potentiometer. There are a number of buttons on the sphere interface. One performs screen transitions, another is a shutter release button on the USB camera, and a third adjusts volume to alter texture.

These mechanisms are controlled by Arduino, an I / O device. Figure 2 shows the Paint Module GUI and the Spherical interface.

At first, a user takes a picture of an object to use as ink. Next, it is painted with the texture 3DCG display, by specifying the location of any of the spherical interfaces. Paint locations on the sphere are specified by touching the guide above along the longitude. A sphere type interface allows rotation with central axis; thus the user can draw as with a brush.

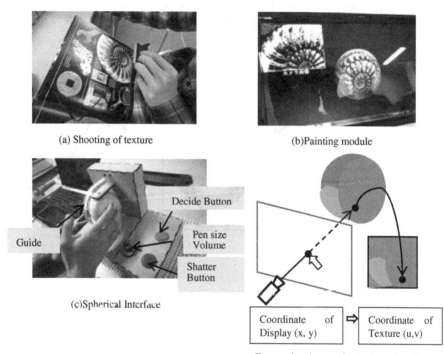

(a) Shooting of texture   (b)Painting module

(c)Spherical Interface

Processing image for texture drawing

Fig. 2. Paint Module and Spherical Type Interface

3.2   Space Display Module

Space display module is a public viewing module that display all planets designed by the children. The texture of the planet made by the paint module is registered to a texture database. The space display module displays each planet with the texture data newly added to the database. By watching this space, children can appreciate the planet of each child.

3.3   Mapping Module

The texture of each 3DCG planet is translated into a polyhedron template with a mapping module and printed out as a paper-craft template. In this process, children are able to transform the planets that they made with computers into physical objects that they can bring home. In other words, children can make digital as well as physical works.

3.4   Planet Sheet

In a workshop, the name of the producer is described on a sheet, and a portion of a named planet is acquired as a picture with a USB camera.

This picture appears as a label on the preview screen of the planet in a space display module. Figure 3 shows the Paint Module GUI and Sphere Interface. Figure 3 shows the flow of making paper craft template.

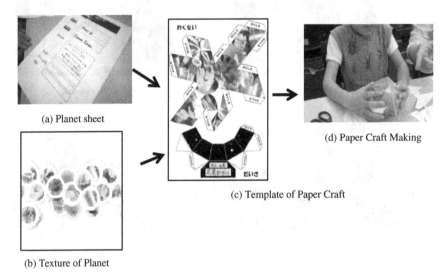

(a) Planet sheet

(b) Texture of Planet

(c) Template of Paper Craft

(d) Paper Craft Making

Fig. 3. Flow of Making a Paper Craft Template

4   Make Your Own Planet Workshop

In order to evaluate our design, we conducted a workshop at the Workshop Correction 9 in Hiyoshi Yokohama. The target age range was six years or older, and the time allowed to experience the workshop was about 60 minutes for each participant.

The workshop was conducted by preparing four client terminals. A total of five instructors were assigned as facilitators to move the workshop forward. After the workshop, a survey was carried out in order to obtain evaluations of the workshop.

5   Discussion

We conducted a survey with five kinds of questionnaires evaluation of the interface, degree of work sharing, satisfaction with one's work, and motivation for future work. Another questionnaire contains questions about the attractive elements of "Make your own Planet."

We obtained the results of the survey of 261 children at the workshop. Table 1 shows the questionnaire and items. Figure 4 shows the result of the questionnaires 1-4.

Table 1. Qestionnaire and Items

Q1	Making the planet a camera and sphere-shaped controller What was easy?
Q2	Did you make any refer to the planet of friends when you make a planet?
Q3	Did you are satisfied with the planet which I made myself?
Q4	If you have a chance, do you want to make a planet in this workshop?

	Answer 1	Answer 2	Answer 3	Answer 4	Answer 5
Q1	Very easy,	Easy	Becoming easy	Difficult	
Q2	referred	Often referred	Not to refer at all		
Q3	Very satify	Satify	Soso	Dissatisfaction	Very dissatisfaction
Q4	Very much	If there is time	A little	Not at all	

	Please choice the order that you thought it was fun in this Wakushop.
	A.Drawing the pattern of the planet sphere-shaped controller.
	B.You can choice of design your own image.
Q5	C.The planet of your come out to the universe of public viewing.
	D.That it is possible to see the planet of many friends
	E.You are able to make papercraft of their own planet.

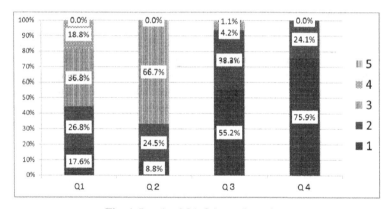

Fig. 4. Result of Q1-Q4 questionnaires

Concerning the usability of the system, 44.4% stated that it was "very easy" or "easy" to use. If "becoming easy with use" is included, the positive opinion was 88.2%. For "work share," "most children stated that they did not "refer at all" to the creations of others. Nearly 70% of the children created an original planet, without referencing those of other participants. An overwhelming 93.2% answered that they "very satisfied" and "satisfied" with their planets. As far as motivation for future work, 75.9% of the children wished to repeat the experience. Since there were no negative opinions, it is clear that the satisfaction with the workshop and the motivation were high. This workshop thus appealed to the children.

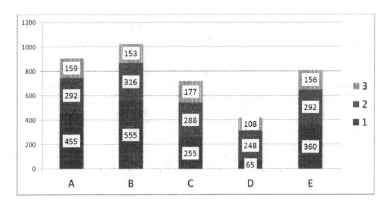

Fig. 5. Answers of Q5 questionnaire

Figure 5 shows the results of the other questionnaire, in which the children ranked activities. The found the ability to choose a pattern freely the most interesting aspect. They had a great interest in employing the planet's spherical controller. Creating a paper planet received third place. From these results, it is clear that making physical objects as paper crafts increased the children's motivation for creative activity.

The proportion of children who created by referring to the works of others was about 30%. The question on the appreciation of the work of a friend had a score lower than those of other items. The children had, however, a positive feeling that their works were shown in a public place.

The space module was received positively, but it did not efficiently function as a tool to stimulate the ideas of children when comparing their works. However, although children liked their own creations, they also expressed a strong desire to view the planets of their peers. The operation of the spherical interface required some practice, but we succeeded in providing an environment in which children employed computers. Thus, we designed and put into operation a fully functioning digital workshop that offered a special creative activity.

6   Future work

For the future, the following two points should be kept in mind. The first is the necessity of improving the spherical interface. The children found it hard to paint part of the pole area of the sphere. The pole area is narrower, since a mounting surface joint is part of the interface base and the sphere. This feature made it difficult to draw. Therefore, we will improve spherical interface, as shown in Figure 6. The second point is the need to improve the space display module used in public viewing. We found that children found it difficult the view the works. To correct this fault, we are currently developing a system that allows a planet to be viewed at the WEB.

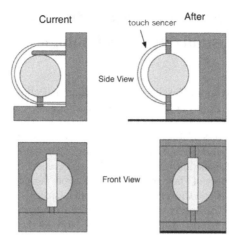

Fig. 6. Image of Improved Spherical Interface

References

1. CANVAS: Workshop Correction, http://www.wsc.or.jp
2. Mitani, J., Suzuki, H.: Making Papercraft Toys from Meshes using Strip-based Approximate Unfolding. ACM Transactions on Graphics (Proceeding of SIGGRAPH 2004) 23(3), 259–263 (2004)
3. Igarashi, Y., Igarashi, T.: Holly: A Drawing Editor for Designing Stencils. IEEE Computer Graphics and Applications 30(4), 8–14 (2010)
4. Mori, Y., Igarashi, T.: An Interactive Design System for Plush Toys. ACM Transactions on Graphics and Applications 30(4), 8–14 (2010)
5. Seymour, A.: Papert: Mindstorms: Children, Computers, and Powerful Ideas. Basic Books (1994)
6. Tama Software: Pepacra Desginer, http://www.tamasoft.co.jp/pepakura/
7. Li, X.-Y., Shen, C.-H., Huang, S.-S., Ju, T., Hu, S.-M.: Popup: Automatic paper architectures from 3D models. In: SIGGRAPH 10 ACM SIGGRAPH, papers: Article No. 111 (2010)
8. Kusachi, E., Junji, W.: Minimal Drawing: Drawing Experience with both User's Intension and Accidental Strokes. Journal of the Virtual Reality Society of Japan 12(3), 389–392 (2007)
9. Mehment Kten.: Body Paint, http://www.memo.tv/bodypaint/
10. Ryokai, K., Marti, S., Ishii, H.: Designing the World as Your Palette. In: Proceedings of Conference on Human Factors in Computing Systems (2005)

Usability Evaluation of Virtual Museums' Interfaces Visualization Technologies

Stella Sylaiou, Vassilis Killintzis, Ioannis Paliokas,
Katerina Mania, and Petros Patias

School of Social Sciences, Hellenic Open University
Lab or Medical Informatics, Aristotle University of Thessaloniki, Greece
Democritus University of Thrace, Greece
Laboratory of Photogrammetry and Remote Sensing,
Aristotle University of Thessaloniki, Greece
sylaiou@gmail.com, billyk@auth.gr,
ipalioka@eled.duth.gr, k.mania@ced.tuc.gr

Abstract. This paper reports on a user-centered formative usability evaluation of diverse visualization technologies used in Virtual Museums. It initially presents the selection criteria and the five museum websites involved in the analysis. Then, it describes the evaluation process, in which a group of subjects explored the museums' on-line resources and answered in two usability questions concerning overall reaction to the website and the subjective satisfaction of the users. After user testing, quantitative and qualitative data have been collected and statistically analysed. However, much research remains to be done on future research in terms of larger sample, different methodologies and varied contexts.

Keywords: history and culture, digital humanitis, cultural informatics.

1   Introduction

The London Charter encourages virtual museums to promote rigorous design of digital heritage visualization however; it suggests that virtual museums should ensure that embedded visualization paradigms follow a human-centric design so that they promote the study and interpretation of cultural heritage assets. The Principle 2 of the London Charter states that computer-based visual media should be employed when they provide added value for the study of cultural assets compared to other methods. It stresses that in order to determine the suitability of each technologically-driven visualization method, a systematic evaluation of such methods should be carried out based on specific evaluation criteria. Relevant research sources utilized should be identified and evaluated in a structured and documented way taking into account best practice within communities of practice. The London Charter's main goal is to encourage dissemination of computer-based visualization so that significant relationships between cultural elements can be determined by visitors. Such dissemination should target to strengthen the study, interpretation and preservation of cultural heritage.

R. Shumaker and S. Lackey (Eds.): VAMR 2014, Part II, LNCS 8526, pp. 124–133, 2014.
© Springer International Publishing Switzerland 2014

Various researches have evaluated museum websites using design patterns [1], usability of virtual museum websites [2,3], utilizing both empirical and expert-based methods combining quantitative and qualitative research methods [4, 5], explored the relationship between the sense of Presence, previous user experience and enjoyment [6], the effect of various visualisation technologies to the sense of Presence [7], have developed guidelines concerning issues ranging from design considerations to project philosophies [8], exploring requirements for online art exhibitions [9]. The main goal of this paper is to explore the usability parameters that can be used as reference for evaluating virtual museums, which often incorporate varied technological elements. After a short introduction to virtual museums and the selected cases for the purposes of research and the usability evaluation, the participants, the experimental procedure and the methods used for the statistical analysis are presented. In the last section of the paper, the research results are analysed and discussed.

2   Virtual Museums

A virtual museum [10] is a complex environment that according to the choices of the design team, determines the visitors' final experience and subsequent attitudes towards the use of digital media in museums. In order to cluster the wide range of existing museum websites into specific representative categories, a team of four scientists experienced in interactive design and the use of Information and Communication Technologies in culture and education, was assembled. Museum online resources were divided according to the presentation method employed for their visualization and grouped/ classified according to that in five technologically-oriented categories of museum sites mainly including: Panoramic images (QTVR), (2) Scalable images with text, (3) Searchable databases, (4) 3D environments, (5) Videos.

The experts shared a preselected pool of museum websites and worked independently to extract within these categories the factors that may influence the user's experience according to their personal understanding and recent research literature on evaluation strategies for virtual museums. Subsequently, the factors were merged into a set of five qualities or capacities: imageability, interactivity, navigability, virtual spatiality and narration as explained in Table 1. Of the five representative cases of virtual museums as presented below, four serve as extensions to existing physical museums, while one is totally imaginary.

Imageability: Panoramic Images. Imageability is defined as the "quality in a physical object that gives it a high probability of evoking a strong image in any given observer. It is shape, colour, or arrangement, which facilitate making of vividly identified, powerfully structured, highly useful mental images of the environment" [11, p. 9]. In VEs of high imageability, users can experience the real museum space through panoramic images that can be manipulated thanks to a set of interactive tools, such as rotate and pan, zoom in and out, and even navigate. The case selected for this study, labeled as M1, is the "Virtual Exhibition Tours" (http://www.nga.gov/onlinetours/index.shtm) of the National Gallery of Art in Washington. In this online environment, visitors can select specific works of art for larger image views, close-up details, streaming audio commentary, and information about the object (Figure 1).

Table 1. Qualities of museum online resources.

Quality	Definition
1. Imageability	Perceptual quality of a VE that makes it memorable
2. Interactivity	The HCI functionality that makes a VE able to communicate with its visitors
3. Navigability	The degree to which navigation capabilities are perceived from structural elements of the VE
4. Virtual Spatiality	The extension of physical museum space and the metaphors of architecture to virtual space
5. Narration	Narration via a collection of videos that engages the virtual visitors providing them the opportunity to investigate a theme in a variety of ways and construct their own meaning

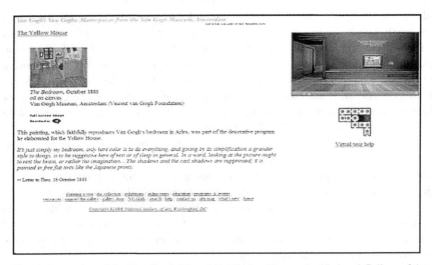

Fig. 1. Screenshot of the Van Gogh Virtual Exhibition Tour at the National Gallery of Art

Interactivity with Scalable Images and Texts. Image scalability provides the opportunity to examine museum artifacts or parts of them in detail by applying zoom tools over high resolution images. These zoom-on-demand features allow viewing aspects of photos that are not visible to the naked eye because of their small size or because of the museums' spatial proximity restrictions. Image exploration tools make VEs highly interactive and enhance museum experience [6]. The selected case for this study, labeled as M2, is the Metropolitan Museum of New York (http://www. metmuseum.org/) (Figure 2).

Fig. 2. Snapshot of an object contained in the section of Greek and Roman Art of the Metropolitan Museum of Art

Navigability: Searching Utility for Images and Texts. This type of online museum environments offers multiple search options and enhanced image manipulation. Searchable databases typically contain 2D representations in the form of photos and flat scans of objects along with their corresponding metadata, which are uploaded to the museum's online database. The hallmark of these sites is a search engine, which allows searching by content, concept, or metadata, thanks to an entry point usually consisting of a text area in which visitors enter search criteria based on keywords. The case selected for this study, labeled as M3, is the Museum of Modern Art (http://www.moma.org/explore/collection/index). Through its database, visitors can navigate the various thematic areas of the museum, and search its collections by artist, work or keyword. It also has an advanced search that allows adding refinement criteria such as period or object management status (Figure 3).

Fig. 3. The advanced search engine of the Museum of Modern Art online database

Virtual Spaciality: Simulation of a 3D Reconstructed Museum Space. Since place and space have been inseparable in our experience of the real world until now, when we experience the Web's placeness, we assume that it must also have the usual attributes of spatiality [Weinberger 2002, p. 56 after 12]. In this type of online re-source allows 'free' and interactive real-time navigation in a 3D space that reproduces more or less realistically the museum galleries. This kind of online resources usually seeks to reproduce as realistically as possible the experience of the visit, with the added value of the multimedia information, the hypertext/spatial navigation, and the possibility to manipulate (zooming, rotation) objects. The case selected for this study, labeled as M4, is the Van Gogh Virtual Museum (http://www.vangoghmuseum.nl/), which constitutes of a typical example of a 3D reconstruction of a museum setting using computer-aided design tools and gaming technologies (figure 4).

Fig. 4. Snapshot of the Van Gogh Virtual Museum

Narrative Videos. The last category corresponds to Virtual Museum websites containing narrative embedded videos. The selected case for this study, labeled as M5, is the Virtual Silver Screen of the Library and Archives Canada (http://www.collectionscanada.ca/silverscreen/). The website uses Flash technologies to present different Canadian films of the early 20th century, which are perceived as historic documents organized by themes that the user can select for visualization (Figure 5).

Fig. 5. Snapshot of the Home page of the Virtual Screen Silver

3   Usability Evaluation

According to ISO-9241 describing the 'Ergonomic requirements for office work with visual display terminals' (ISO, 1998) standard, usability of a system is defined as the ability to function effectively and efficiently, while providing subjective satisfaction to its users. Usability of an interface is usually associated with five parameters (ISO, 1998; Nielsen, 1993), derived directly from this definition: An interface (a) is easy to learn, (b) is efficient to use, (c) is easy to remember, (d) produces few errors, (e) is pleasant to use.

The QUIS (Questionnaire for User Interaction Satisfaction) questionnaire (Schneiderman and Plaisant, 2005) assessed museum participants' contentment, while interacting with the virtual museums. This questionnaire was used as the main instrument recording their subjective assessments. The QUIS questionnaire consists of 7 parts. Part 1 concerning the general experience with ICT (Information and Communication Technologies) is often omitted. Part 2 assesses the overall user reactions as regards to the evaluated system, Part 3 concerns the windows layout of the system, Part 4 the terminology used, Part 5 the learnability of the interface (how easy it is to learn) and Part 6 the system capabilities. For this research needs we have selected the parts of the questionnaire that concern the overall reaction to the website and the subjective satisfaction of the users.

4   Materials and Methods

Due to technical restrictions not all Virtual Museum websites were able to run on tablets, smartphones and other portable media. Thus, the experiment have been conducted in a HP workstation with two 2.4GHz Xeon processors, 2048 MB memory and 19' inches screen to secure the same testing conditions for all.

4.1   Participants

A total of one-hundred sixty-four (164) volunteers (males and females, aged 19-37), mainly undergraduate and postgraduate students from the Aristotle University of Thessaloniki, Greece, participated in the experiment. Virtual visits for academic or professional research are considered the most demanding kind of visits in a virtual museum because they are targeted, have defined learning requirements and time constraints. Random or unintended visits could contribute less to this study. Also, returning (physical and virtual) visitors would have been inconsistent because of their previous experience and knowledge.

All participants reported to have at least basic knowledge of computers and good knowledge of the English language. All students selected had never visited the virtual museum websites before. Participants in all conditions were naive as to the purpose of the experiment.

4.2   Experimental Procedure

The premise of the proposed research is that different visualisation methods -with their specific associated capacities- serve different aims, connected with usability, presence, motivation and learning outcomes. The evaluation methodology proposed is based on questionnaires assessing such aspects of the virtual museum experience, administered after navigating the selected virtual museums presented in Section 3. The results will be used for a comparable evaluation of various approaches regarding the presentation and interaction methods used for museum artefacts. The evaluation and the interviews took place at the laboratory of Photogrammetry and Remote Sensing of the Aristotle University of Thessaloniki, Greece. The interviews have taken place in laboratory-like conditions, where no visitors were allowed, so as the users can be concentrated to the completion of the questionnaires. The evaluation involved only one participant at a time and assistants instructed the end-users if they needed help. Tracking of user errors while navigating as well as the time needed to complete the tasks were not recorded, because it was not our intention to test the users' performance, but the websites' performance. The evaluation used cued testing, which involves explaining to the users the purpose of the project and asking them to perform specific tasks or to answer questions. Four steps were undertaken:

1. Goal setting: users start with a plan of the tasks to be accomplished.
2. Exploration: users explore the interface and discover useful actions.
3. Selection: users select the most appropriate actions for accomplishing their task.
4. Assessment: users interpret the system's responses and assess its progression).

The participants were allowed to select the virtual exhibitions and exhibits they preferred in order to feel they had the control over their own learning. The same procedure was repeated for each of the five museums with only one participant at a time. Each participant experienced all websites and the order of the websites was established randomly. The questionnaires were completed directly after the exploration of the Virtual Museums websites.

4.3   Statistical Analysis

The questions administered were subsequently subject to statistical analysis, which was divided in two parts. An initial prediction stipulated that the Virtual Museum M4 would be the most suitable for learning. According to previously aforementioned researches on constructivistic learning/serious games, the reason would be that it simulates a real visit (emotional component) and allows self-controlled navigation in a reconstructed space as well as interaction with objects. The first part of the analysis sought to verify whether the Virtual Museum (M4) provided the most efficient and engaging experience. The answers to the virtual museum questions were tested for normality before performing the analyses using the Shapiro-Wilk test and the one-sample Kolmogorov–Smirnov test. We proceed with non parametric test Kruskal-Wallis for each question to reject the null hypothesis that all scores are similar for all museums. The hypothesis is rejected on sig. (P)<0.05.

We examined which museums provided statistically significant differences in relation to all aspects investigated highlighted by the Kruskal-Wallis test using the non parametric test Mann-Whitney U Test. Finally, we adjusted p values for multiple comparisons by multiplying p value with number of comparisons (e.g. not adjusted p=0.011 *10 => adjusted p=0.11). A significance level of 0.05 was maintained (p must be <0.05 to be significant). p<0.1 may indicate a trend meaning that if we had more samples possibly it would have been significant.

5   Results and Discussion

Based on the Shapiro-Wilk non-parametric test for normality only few questions in few museums follow normal distribution. We proceed with the non parametric test Kruskal-Wallis for each question to reject the null hypothesis that all scores are similar for all museums. The hypothesis is rejected on sig(P)<0.05. We examine which museums present difference for the questions highlighted by K-W Test using Mann-Whitney Test. We adjust p values for multiple comparisons by multiplying p value with number of comparisons (5 museums in pairs=10). (e.g. not adjusted p=0.011 *10 => adjusted p=0.11). Based on the above the statistically significant differences are:

In the question that concerns the overall reaction of the user to the virtual museum webpage there was statistical difference between:

- The interactive virtual museum with the scalable images and texts (M2) scored better (MDN=5,IQR(6,5-5)) that has scored better than the virtual museum with the panoramic images (M1) (MDN=5,IQR(6-5)) with adjusted p=0.00. Novel interactive technologies that permit the close inspection of virtual museum objects and provide the opportunity to the users have to observe the details of museum objects on a screen are more attracting and engaging for the virtual visitors than the panoramic images that do not provide enough context information about the exhibits and partially distort the museum interior they present.
- The virtual museum that simulated a 3D reconstructed museum space (M4) (MDN=6,IQR=(7-5)) that has scored –as expected- better than the virtual museum with the panoramic images (M1)(MDN=5,IQR=(6-5)) with adjusted p=0.00. In the simulated 3D virtual museum environment the virtual visitor can freely navigate, select and obtain information about the exhibits, whereas in the panoramic images the functions of the virtual museum and the opportunities for navigation and exploration provided to the virtual visitors are limited.
- The interactive virtual museum with the scalable images and texts (M2) (MDN=6,IQR(6,5-5)) that has scored –as expected- better than the virtual museum with the searching utility for images and texts (M3) (MDN=5,IQR(4-6)) with adjusted p=0.00.
- The virtual museum that simulated a 3D reconstructed museum space (M4) (MDN=6,IQR=(7-5)) that has scored –as expected- better than the virtual museum with the searching utility for images and texts (M3) (MDN=5,IQR(4-6)) with adjusted p=0.00. The result is influenced by the phenomenon of disconnectedness, in which the virtual visitors jump from page to page [13, after 14] rather than

following a progressive path in a simulated 3D virtual museum environment that provides a clearer perception of its exhibits.

In the question that concerns the subjective satisfaction:

- The interactive virtual museum with the scalable images and texts (M2) (MDN=6,IQR(7-5)) and the virtual museum that simulated a 3D reconstructed museum space (M4) (MDN=6,IQR(7-5)) have scored better than the virtual museum with the searching utility for images and texts (M3) (MDN=5,IQR(6-4)) with adjusted p=0.03.

The virtual museum with the searching utility for images and texts has received low scores and this can be explained by the fact that it can be useful for people, such as students and experts that search for specific information, but it does not have the ability to connect the virtual museum exhibits with their context and the virtual museum space, to make a deep impression and convey a virtual museum experience that can be accompanied by the sense of entertainment, joy, and learning.

Acknowledgments. The authors would like to thank the participants that take part in the experiment.

References

1. Van Welie, M., Klaasse, B.: Evaluating Museum Websites using Design Patterns, Technical report number: IR-IMSE-001, http://www.welie.com/papers/IR-IMSE-001-museum-sites.pdf (December 2004)
2. Avouris, N., Tselios, N., Fidas, C., Papachristos, E.: Website evaluation: A usability-based perspective. In: Manolopoulos, Y., Evripidou, S., Kakas, A.C. (eds.) PCI 2001. LNCS, vol. 2563, pp. 217–231. Springer, Heidelberg (2003)
3. Karoulis, A., Sylaiou, S., White, M.: Combinatory Usability Evaluation of an Educational Virtual Museum Interface. In: 6th IEEE International Conference on Advanced Learning Technologies (ICALT 2006), Kerkrade, The Netherlands, pp. 340–342 (2006)
4. Sylaiou, S., Almosawi, A., Mania, K., White, M.: Preliminary Evaluation of the Augmented Representation of Cultural Objects System. In: The Proceedings of the 10th International Conference on Virtual Systems and Multimedia, Hybrid Realities-Digital Partners, Explorations in Art, Heritage, Science and the Human Factor, VSMM Conference, Softopia, Ogaki City, Japan, November 17-19, pp. 426–431 (2004)
5. Sylaiou, S., Economou, M., Karoulis, A., White, M.: The evaluation of ARCO: A lesson in curatorial competence and intuition with new technology. ACM Theoretical and Practical Computer Applications in Entertainment 6(2) (April/June 2008), doi:10.1145/1371216.1371226, ISSN: 1544-3574; Impact Factor: 0.033
6. Sylaiou, S., Mania, K., Karoulis, A., White, M.: Presence-centred Usability Evaluation of a Virtual Museum: Exploring the Relationship between Presence, Previous User Experience and Enjoyment. International Journal of Human-Computer Studies (IJHCS) 68(5), 243–253 (2010)

7. Sylaiou, S., Mania, K., Paliokas, Y., Killintzis, V., Liarokapis, F., Patias, P.: Exploring the effect of diverse technologies incorporated in virtual museums on visitors' perceived sense of presence. In: Museums and Intelligent Environments (MasIE), Workshop co-located with the 9th International Conference on Intelligent Environments - IE 2013, Organized by IEEE, National Technical University of Athens, University of Thessaly. IOS Press, Hellenic Open University (2013)
8. Sargent, R.: Building Cybercabinets: Guidelines for Online Access to Digital Natural History Collections. In: Proctor, N., Cherry, R. (eds.) Museums and the Web 2013. Museums and the Web, Silver Spring (2013) (Consulted December 24, 2013), http://mw2013.museumsandtheweb.com/paper/building-cybercabinets-guidelines-for-online-access-to-digital-natural-history-collections/
9. Lopatovska, I., Bierlein, I., Lember, H., Meyer, E.: Exploring Requirements for Online Art Collections. To be Published in the Proceedings of the 76th Annual Meeting of the American Society for Information Science and Technology, Montreal, Canada, November 1-6 (2013), http://www.asis.org/asist2013/proceedings/submissions/posters/38poster.pdf
10. Sylaiou, S., Liarokapis, F., Kotsakis, K., Patias, P.: Virtual museums, a survey and some issues for consideration. Journal of Cultural Heritage 10(4), 520–528 (2009)
11. Lynch, K.: The Image of the City. MIT Press, Cambridge (1960)
12. Pietrykowski, B., Faber, J.: Developing the Virtual Museum: Current Models and Future Directions, http://www.tensionsofeurope.eu/www/en/files/get/Proposal_EM_Virtual_Museum_Pietrykowski.pdf
13. Cody, S.A.: Historical Museums on the World Wide Web: An Exploration and Critical Analysis. The Public Historian 19(4), 40 (1997)
14. McDonald, M.: The Museum and the Web: Three Case Studies, http://xroads.virginia.edu/~ma05/macdonald/museums/all.pdf

Manasek AR: A Location-Based Augmented Reality Application for Hajj and Umrah

Mounira Taileb, Elham Al-Ghamdi, Nusaibah Al-Ghanmi, Abeer Al-Mutari,
Khadija Al-Jadani, Mona Al-Ghamdi, and Alanood Al-Mutari

Faculty of Computing and Information Technology Information Technology department,
King Abdulaziz University P.O Box 42808, Jeddah 21551, Saudi Arabia
mtaileb@kau.edu.sa

Abstract. In this paper a location-based augmented reality application is presented. It is a mobile application whose goal is to facilitate the journey of millions of pilgrims when performing Hajj and Umrah and overcome the difficulties they face. Using the Augmented Reality, the application displays different types of information about the pilgrims surroundings in a mobile camera view. The usability testing of the proposed application ended successfully with a very high rate of positive feedback from users.

Keywords: Location-based Augmented Reality, GPS, compass, accelometer.

1   Introduction

Millions of pilgrims come every year to Mecca[1] to perform Hajj[2] during the days of Hajj or to perform Umrah[3] at any time during the year. Statistics about the number of pilgrims who came to perform Hajj in the last five years are given in table1 [1]. Pilgrims need all the necessary information to accomplish their spiritual journey such as what rituals they must do, what places they must visit, where these places are located and how far are these places. They can get this information from several sources such as: their campaign, ask volunteers, use conventional maps or following the signs. But there are problems when using these sources; some of them are not available all the time like the lack of volunteer, also joining a campaign force the pilgrim to stay all the time with them which prevent him from moving freely. Some of sources do not give the pilgrim accurate and adequate information such as street signs, so they are not enough to guide him. Also, it is not practical to carry manuals all the time, also manuals are not trusted because any one can print and publish them. Some of pilgrims cannot read maps. In addition, many foreign pilgrims are visiting Mecca once in their lifetime and during their presence in the country they would like to learn more about these holy places.

---

[1]   The holy city in kingdom of Saudi Arabia and it contains the holy places of Islam.
[2]   Means literally "to set out for a place". For a Muslim, that place is the Holy City of Mecca.
[3]   Visit of the holy places and perform Tawaf around the Kaaba and Sa'i between Al-Safa and Al-Marwah, after assuming Ihram (a sacred state).

R. Shumaker and S. Lackey (Eds.): VAMR 2014, Part II, LNCS 8526, pp. 134–143, 2014.
© Springer International Publishing Switzerland 2014

Table 1. Distribution of Pilgrims per year

Year	Total number of Pilgrims
2009	2,313,278
2010	2,789,399
2011	2,927,717
2012	3,161,573
2013	1,980,249

To address this issue, this paper presents a mobile application based on Augmented Reality (AR) which aims to facilitate Hajj and Umrah journey for pilgrims through the use of their mobile phones. The proposed application, called Manasek AR, displays all the needed information about the pilgrim's surroundings in a mobile camera view.

The rest of the paper is organized as follows. In section 2, a brief overview of related work is given, followed by the description of the proposed software application in section 3. In section 4, results of the usability testing are discussed. Finally, the section 5 concludes the paper.

2 Related Work

Augmented reality (AR) is considered as variation of Virtual reality (VR). In AR, the user can see the real world, with virtual objects superimposed upon or composited with the real world [2]. In other words, a typical AR environment has digital information transposed onto a real-world view. While in VR, the user is totally immersed in a virtual or synthetic world. Therefore, AR supplements reality, rather than completely replacing it. In [3], an AR system is defined as the user interaction with the real world through supplementing the real world with 3D virtual objects.

Several papers have been written on augmented reality [2], [3],[4] and many application areas use this technology, such as in medical [5] [6] [7] [8], military [9], manufacturing [10] [11], entertainment [12].

Augmented Reality is now emerging as an important technology for many commercial applications in different fields. In tourism, for example, many AR phone applications have been developed such as Wikitude [13], in 2008, and Layar [14].

3 Methodology

Manasek AR utilizes the local-based augmented reality to improve the Hajj and Umrah experience for pilgrims and overcome the difficulties they face. It provides a complete guidance for pilgrims by giving them all the needed information about Hajj and Umrah places in a completely different way that engage them with their immediate surroundings.

Manasek AR locates the place on the mobile screen tracked by the mobile camera of the pilgrim. The position of the place is calculated using the pilgrim's position with GPS, the direction of the device is calculated using the compass and accelerometer. When the object is located, the augmented reality takes place by giving description about the object on the mobile screen. Internet connection is not required for this service because when a place is located, their related information are retrieved from a database, these database contains all the information about the saved places. The architecture of application is given in figure 1.

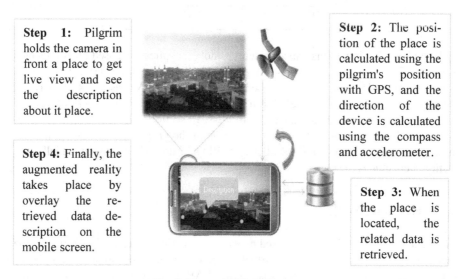

Step 1: Pilgrim holds the camera in front a place to get live view and see the description about it place.

Step 2: The position of the place is calculated using the pilgrim's position with GPS, and the direction of the device is calculated using the compass and accelerometer.

Step 4: Finally, the augmented reality takes place by overlay the retrieved data description on the mobile screen.

Step 3: When the place is located, the related data is retrieved.

Fig. 1. Manasek AR Architecture

The application allows pilgrims to choose the type of information; either locations of Hajj and Umrah places (how far are they from those places), historical information about the places or guidance information of how to perform rituals related to a particular place (Manasek information). Also allows pilgrims to add their campaign place, view maps, and get the recent news of Hajj circumstances through the official account of the Ministry of Hajj and Umrah on twitter.

3.1   Application Features

The features or functions provided by the proposed application are presented and explained in the following.

AR Function and Information Types. This function allows pilgrims to choose the type of information; either locations of Hajj and Umrah places, historical information about these places or guidance information of how to perform rituals related to a particular place (Manasek information). In figure 2, location information about King Abdulaziz gate are displayed. The location information are the distance between the pilgrim and the gate (130m) and also the position of the gate in the holy mosque. Manasek information about Kaaba[4] are given in figure 3, the information are the rituals that should be performed in this place. And in figure 4, historical information about Kaaba are displayed. User can swap the top bar to select a specific information type.

Fig. 2. Location Information

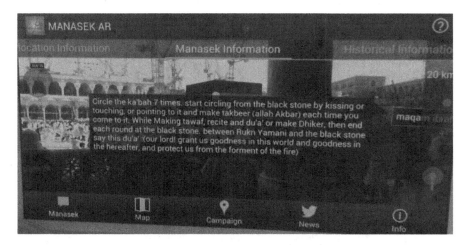

Fig. 3. Manasek Information

---

[4]   Cuboid building at the centre of the holy Mosque in Mecca.

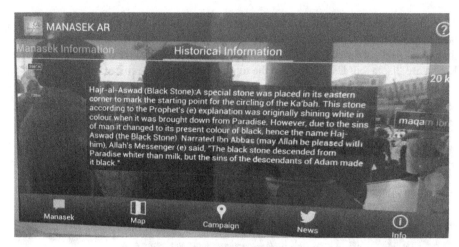

Fig. 4. Historical Information

Help Function. To explain to the user how to use the application properly, developers come up with a new idea that explains the whole interfaces and the functions to the users in an easy and stunning way that fit and suit the nature of smart phones. The following steps show how to use this function:

1. The user has to touch the help button (question mark button according to Android list of legal button) in the top right of each interface screen, as shown in figure 5.
2. A semi-transparent panel will be displayed above the original interface, it includes arrows and brief descriptions of how to deal with the interface component.
3. To remove the instruction panel, the user has to touch the help button again.

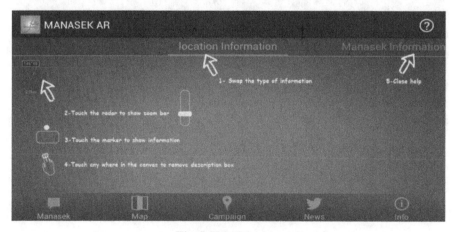

Fig. 5. Help Function

Radar View Function. The radar is used to display the icons for objects outside the user's field of view by some range. It also acts like compass as it illustrates the coordination to the user whenever he/she moves its device. The objects on the radar indicating the existence of places around the user will be moved in and out of the view as the user moves and rotates. The radar view is shown at the top left corner in the tab "Manasek" as illustrated in figure 6.

Fig. 6. Radar View Function

Zoom Bar Function. As mentioned previously, the radar view uses some range to display objects around the user and to allow the user to gain control of this range as he/she want. Developers give the user the possibility to set the radius of data collection from 0m to 20,000m (20 km). To display the zoom bar to the user, he/she has to touch the radar view in the tab "Manasek", and the zoom bar will be immediately displayed in the right side of the screen.

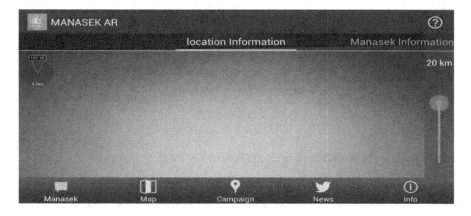

Fig. 7. Zoom Bar Function

Add Campaign. When the user clicks on the campaign tab the camera view will show up. The user should be in the same location of the campaign to add the camping marker because the marker depends on the user location. This procedure is illustrated in figure 8.

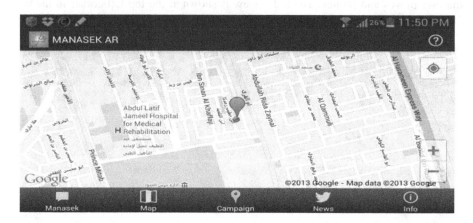

Fig. 8. Add Camping Function

Delete Marker from the Map. When the user add a marker via Add Campaign function, the marker will appear on the map. To delete this marker for any reason, the user should follow these steps:

- Long click on the marker.
- Alter dialog will show up, as shown in figure 9.
- Yes, to delete the marker.
- No, to keep the marker and cancel the operation.

Fig. 9. Delete Marker – View Map Function

News. When the user clicks on the " News " tab for the first time, a blank page is displayed. After that, the user pulls the page to get the recent news from twitter. Finally , the news are returned from twitter and presented as a list, as shown in figure 10. The user can pull the page when he/she wants to see the recent news from twitter .

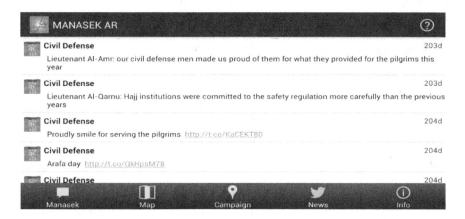

Fig. 10. News Function

The proposed application is similar to the AR software Wikitude [13]. We present in the following the differences between Masasek AR and Wikitude:

- Manasek AR's database content is static and updated under the supervision of developers. Unlike Wikitude, it is mostly user generated.
- Manasek AR is customized only for Hajj and Umrah places and covers them with details. While Wikitude is a world browser.
- Manasek AR provides different types of information for users. It allows pilgrims to choose the type of information; either locations of Hajj and Umrah places, historical information of these places or guidance information of how to perform rituals related to a particular place. Besides, other services are available to help pilgrims in Hajj and Umrah.
- Internet connection is not required for most of the services of Manasek AR. This is because of the static database that contains all the information about the saved places.

4   Usability Testing Results

This testing process involves several users outside developers team , and those who have no idea about the application, and give them a set of tasks that cover all interface functionalities. Tasks are given in the table 2. During usability testing, testers observe the users' attitude. The results of this testing are excellent and most of users perform the tasks without confusion.

Table 2. Usability Testing Results

Task	Comment
View help	Done correctly
Hide help	Done correctly
View map	Done correctly
Show the location information	Done correctly
Show the manasek information	Done correctly
Show historical information	Done correctly
Hide the information box	Done correctly
Show the zoom bar	Done correctly
Hide the zoom bar	Done correctly
Add campaign	Done correctly
Delete campaign	There is some late . Developer solved this problem.
View info	Done correctly
View Twitter timeline	Done correctly

The system testing was performed in the holy Mosque in Mecca. The system recognizes all the places contained in the database, gives the right direction, and displays the correct information according to the selected type of information.

In the usability testing, 35 users outside the developers team were involved. They performed tasks that cover all the interface components. Very good results are obtained and most of users perform the tasks without confusion and give positive feedbacks.

5   Conclusion and Future Work

Manasek AR is classified as a location-based augmented reality application which provides a complete guidance for pilgrims. It displays all the needed information about the pilgrim's surroundings in a mobile camera view. Also it allows pilgrims to add their campaign place, view maps, and get the recent news of Hajj circumstances through the official account of the Ministry of Hajj and Umrah in twitter. Manasek AR's goal is to grasp the opportunity of utilizing AR technologies to improve the Hajj and Umrah experience for pilgrims and overcome the difficulties they face. An evaluation was done to examine its ability to display places' information regarding these places in Mecca correctly. The evaluation ended successfully with a very high rate of positive outcomes. As a future work, the system can be extended to cover different cities and places in Saudi Arabia.

References

1. Ministry of Hajj, Kingdom of Saudi Arabia, http://www.hajinformation.com
2. Azuma, R.: A Survey of Augmented Reality. Presence: Teleoperators and Virtual Environments 6(4), 355–385 (1997)
3. Azuma, R., Baillot, Y., Behringer, R., Feiner, S., Julier, S., MacIntyre, B.: Recent advances in augmented reality. IEEE Comput. Graph 21(6), 34–47 (2001)
4. Rolland, J.P., Davis, L.D., Baillot, Y.: A Survey of Tracking Technologies for Virtual Environments. In: Barfield, W., Caudell, T. (eds.) Fundamentals of Wearable Computers and Augmented Reality, pp. 67–112. Lawrence Erlbaum, Mahwah (2001)
5. Grimson, W.E.L., Ettinger, G.J., White, S.J., Gleason, P.L., Lozano-Pérez, T., Wells III, W.M., Kikinis, R.: Evaluating and Validating an Automated Registration System for Enhanced Reality Visualization in Surgery. In: Ayache, N. (ed.) CVRMed 1995. LNCS, vol. 905, pp. 3–12. Springer, Heidelberg (1995)
6. Mellor, J.P.: Realtime Camera Calibration for Enhanced RealityVisualization. In: Ayache, N. (ed.) CVRMed 1995. LNCS, vol. 905, pp. 471–475. Springer, Heidelberg (1995)
7. Betting, F., Feldmar, J., Ayache, N., Devernay, F.: A New Framework for Fusing Stereo Images with Volumetric Medical Images. In: Ayache, N. (ed.) CVRMed 1995. LNCS, vol. 905, pp. 30–39. Springer, Heidelberg (1995)
8. Edwards, P.J., Hill, D.L.G., Hawkes, D.J., Spink, R., Colchester, A.C.F., Strong, A., Gleeson, M.: Neurosurgical Guidance Using the Stereo Microscope. In: Ayache, N. (ed.) CVRMed 1995. LNCS, vol. 905, pp. 555–564. Springer, Heidelberg (1995)
9. Wanstall, B. H.: on the Head for Combat Pilots. Interavia, 334–338. (A89-39227)
10. Feiner, S., MacIntyre, B., Seligmann, D.: Knowledge-based Augmented Reality. Communications of the ACM 36 7, 52–62 (1993)
11. Tuceryan, M., Greer, D.S., Whitaker, R.T., Breen, D., Crampton, C., Rose, E., Ahlers, K.H.: Calibration Requirements and Procedures for Augmented Reality. IEEE Transactions on Visualization and Computer Graphics 1(3), 255–273 (1995)
12. Maes, P.: Artificial Life Meets Entertainment: Lifelike Autonomous Agents. CACM 38 38(11), 108–114 (1995)
13. Wikitude GmbH. Homepage of Wikitude, http://www.wikitude.com
14. Layar, B.V.: Homepage of Layar, http://www.layar.com

Support of Temporal Change Observation Using Augmented Reality for Learning

Takafumi Taketomi, Angie Chen, Goshiro Yamamoto, and Hirokazu Kato

Nara Institute of Science and Technology, Japan
8916-5 Takayama, Ikoma, Nara, Japan
{takafumi-t,chen-a,goshiro,kato}@is.naist.jp

Abstract. An augmented reality (AR) technology enables to show an additional information by superimposing virtual objects onto the real world. The AR technology is gradually used in the learning environment for observing unseeable objects. Observation is the important process of inspecting a target object with significant details. It forms the basic of all scientific knowledge in education. However, there are only few AR applications which can visualize the temporal changes of the objects. In addition, the effect of this temporal change visualization by AR is not investigated from a scientific aspect. In this study, in order to clarify the effect of temporal change visualization by AR, we have compared the AR-based temporal change visualization method with the conventional temporal change visualization methods in the experiment. Especially, we set an observation of the plant growth as a practical scenario. Through the experiment, we have confirmed that superimpose the past appearance onto the user's viewpoint is effective for temporal change observation scenario.

Keywords: Augmented Reality, Temporal Change Visualization, Leaning Support.

1 Introduction

Augmented Reality (AR) is a technology that integrates virtual elements into real environment that user can interact in real time. By the definition in the literature [1], AR has three characteristics: combines real and virtual, interactive in real time, and registered in 3-D. Due to the interaction, visualization and annotation features provided by AR, many fields, such as entertainment, training, commercial, and education have been successfully implemented and explored. Especially, in the past decades, many AR applications for education have been developed and the usefulness of these applications were explored. However, the effectiveness of AR in the learning process is yet to be explored and evaluated based on learning theories. Furthermore, only a few existing AR prototype systems are created based on the theories to provide Augmented Reality Learning Experiences (ARLEs).

Experiential learning theory [4] proposed learning as a four-stage cycle and emphasizes the importance of experiences in the learning circle. Contextual learning, a curriculum design philosophy, concurs with the importance of experiential learning. It points out that learning only takes place when students process new information with

R. Shumaker and S. Lackey (Eds.): VAMR 2014, Part II, LNCS 8526, pp. 144–155, 2014.
© Springer International Publishing Switzerland 2014

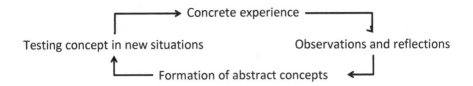

Fig. 1. The Experiential Learning Theory

their personal experiences [3]. The cycle of experiential learning theory (Figure 1) usually starts with having a concrete experience, followed by data collection from observation. Then, collected data is analyzed to make abstractions and generalizations, which are then tested on new situations. This testing stage starts the cycle again which gives the student another set of concrete experiences. In the traditional classroom learning, abstractions and formula are taught by teachers and textbooks. The stages of concrete experience and observations and reflections are limited. These two stages are usually carried out from field trips and experiments which can only be done in limited time and they cannot be repeated or accessed easily. On the other hand, AR can provide learning experiences to the user anytime with more flexible. This research focuses on observation not only because AR has the character as an display technology which is able to perform various visualization methods, but also because it is measurable. We can quantify the observation by evaluate how much information has been collected and if these information are better than information collected using non-AR method. We also noticed there are difficult scenarios in observation that observer needs assistance. We classify these difficult scenarios into three: limitation of senses, occlusion, and temporal changes. In these scenarios, the observation under temporal changes is less explored, and has less related works of supporting visual comparison. Overall, the goal of this research is to develop a prototype system that support observation under temporal changes in the classroom learning and evaluate the temporal change visualization methods.

2   Observation Support by AR

In the observation process, the observer collects data and information about an experience. However, there are several difficult observation scenarios in classroom learning. For example, to observe solar system planets or cells, to observe human organs and to observe physics collision. In this section, we briefly review the literatures related observation support by AR. These literatures can be classified into three groups by the aim of the applications: limitation of senses, occlusion, and temporal changes.

2.1   Limitation of Senses

Human has sense organs that are complicated structures which provides perception and sensation to the environment. However there are things which cannot be sensed due to the limitation of our senses. In many cases we can increase our sensory capabilities by using physical measuring devices. AR technology, with the characteristic of combines real and virtual and as a display technology, has been implemented to support visual difficulties or enhance vision. In recent years, it has been used as a tool to reduce the limitation by visualize subjects that are invisible to the naked eye.

The Real-time Visualization System [6] is an AR education tool combine traditional experiment and computer simulation. In traditional experiment, iron sand is used but it is time-consuming and impossible to deal with complicated models. Although these models can be handled by computer simulations, they are difficult for novice users, and provides little or no interactions. The Real-time Visualization System overcome these disadvantages which allows students to observe magnetic fields and move objects to change the field in real-time. Another example of such system [5] is used to teach organic chemistry by visualizing electron activity and dipole moment. In the traditional teaching, printed materials (e.g. graphics on paper or in books) or molecular models are used. The printed materials have various variety images but are limited to 2D pictures while molecular models have less variety but are display as a 3D structure. By using the system, students can chose elements from a booklet and the system will generate three-dimensional (3D) molecular models.

These systems support the observation under limitations of human senses and using AR to visualize the subjects and allow students to achieve observation in a approachable way. However, as we mentioned previously, these systems are not designed based on learning theories and did not conduct user experiments to evaluate the usefulness and effectiveness of their systems.

2.2   Occlusion

When the occlusion occurred, we need to physically obviate the blocking in order to make an observation. For example, in order to see the underground sewage system, we need to physically break the ground to see the actual pipes that are buried. AR technology as a display technology has been implemented to visualize the occlusion without the need to remove or obviate the blocking.

The miracle [10] visuals the CT dataset for anatomy education. Using the system, the user can see the inside of the human anatomy without dissection courses that are often difficult to take place and requires a lot of effort. XRay-AR is a visualization method implemented in AR applications that shows a see-through affect [8]. Similar to the difficult scenario of limitation of senses in observation, the miracle system used AR to visualize subjects that are hidden. By using the system, complicate experiment and troublesome process can be omit. However, they have the same drawbacks as well. The miracle is not designed based on learning theories and no experiments were conducted; and XRay-AR have not been officially implemented to a particular educational AR prototype system.. Therefore, we cannot determine how learning is effected by the system or this technology.

2.3   Temporal Changes

Temporal changes mean that the changes of the subject happen over time. For example, the changes of height and wight of human being and the changes of colors of leaves according to seasons. To observe temporal changes, the observer needs to pay attention to the subjects carefully to notice the differences between statuses. Observe temporal changes is difficult to achieve because of the time factor. We are not able to see multiple statuses at the same time and compare the differences between statuses to know the changes. One of the most common methods of observing temporal changes is by visual comparison. Forsell *et al.* said "Visual comparison tasks take a central role in visual data exploration and analysis." [2] . In this paper, the authors also describe three phases of comparison:

1. Selection of pieces of information to be compared,
2. Arrangement of the pieces to suit the comparison, and
3. Carrying out the actual comparison.

By using AR, the first two phases are achieve automatically by the system. The Virtual Vouchers [7] is an example how AR assists visual comparison in non-classroom learning. In the field, when botanists need to identify a collected specimen or verify the existence of a new species, they initially consult their own personal knowledge and a paper field guide. In this case, the paper field guide might not contain full specimen collection or species samples, and it is difficult to use. However, the Virtual Vouchers system allows the user to access and view large amount of data and display the data side-by-side with physical specimens.

The CityViewAR [1] is an other example for non-classroom learning of observing temporal changes using visual comparison. This system shows the street view before the 2011 earthquake in Christchurch onto the real buildings which are remained. In this case, students can compare the before and after scenes. The Campus Butterfly Ecology Learning System [11] presented a system that allows students to observer the virtual butterfly simulated and augmented in campus view. Different to the aforementioned systems which are field trip learning, the Campus Butterfly Ecology Learning System is used with the regular classes. However, this system only provides simulation but not visual comparison.

In this research, we focus on supporting temporal changes with the following reasons. First, this category is less explored, and has less related works of supporting visual comparison for temporal changes in classroom learning. Second, to support the observation of temporal changes, not only subjects and states are important but also how to "control" time needed to be taking care of. We propose that observation of temporal changes can benefit from AR technology and an pioneer evaluation is necessary to determine the effective in learning.

3   Visualization of Temporal Changes by AR

In this study, in order to visualize temporal changes of the object, we propose the view-morphing based superimposition that displays the pass appearance of the object. Generally, in AR, superimposed objects are represented by 3D models. However, it is difficult to make a 3D model of the target object by novice users. Especially, in the learning environment, where the typical users may be children. In order to avoid making 3D model

---

[1] www.hitlabnz.org/cityviewar

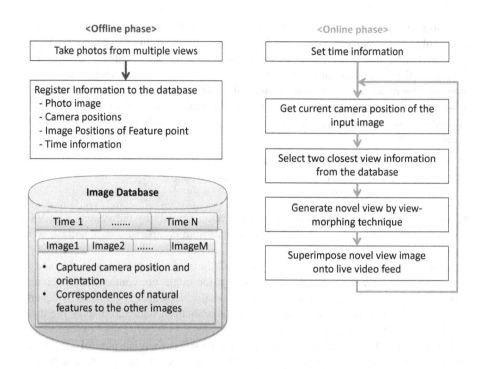

Fig. 2. The flow diagram of the proposed system

of the target object, we employ the view-morphing method [9] to generate synthesized image. The view-morphing method can virtually generate arbitrary view image from a image pair. In order to realize the view-morphing based superimposition, the proposed method is composed of an offline image database construction process and an online novel view image generated and superimposition process as shown in Figure 2. In our method, we assume the environment, which fiducial markers are arranged around the target object and the relative position between the target object and fiducial markers is fixed. In this section, we describe the details of these processes.

3.1 Construction of Image Database

In the offline phase, the user is requested to take multiple photos of the target object from different camera positions and angles with temporal data of time t. The camera pose C_i of the captured image i is calculated using fiducial markers. In addition, feature points are extracted from the captured image, and then corresponding pairs of feature points between the captured image and images in the database are searched. Finally, for each photo, the camera pose C_i, image data, and corresponding information of natural features are registered to the database. In the registered image data, background information is removed by the simple background subtraction method using known background color information.

3.2 Visualization of Temporal Change by Novel View Generation

In the online phase, firstly, the user manually select the target time for comparison, and then AR images are generated iteratively. In the AR view generation process, an image pair for novel view image generation is selected from the database with the following process.

1. Registered images are filtered to become candidate images based on the angels of optical axes and saved camera view direction.
2. Filter the candidate images using the distances between current camera position and registered positions.
3. Select two nearest camera positions that are located on the the left and right hand side of the current camera position.

After finishing the image selection process, the view-morphing process is executed. The original view-morphing method [9] is composed of pre-warping the image pairs, morphing the pre-warped images, and post-warping the morphed image. This method assumes to generate a novel view image without intrinsic and extrinsic camera parameters. From this assumption, the original method needs two image warping processes. On the other hand, in our implementation, camera poses and intrinsic camera parameters of the image pairs are known, and the camera pose and intrinsic camera parameters of the input image from live video feed are also known. By using these known information, we can simplify the original view-morphing method. In our method, the post-warping process is removed by generating the morphing image at the camera position of the input image as shown in Figure 3. The concrete view morphing process is follows.

1. Get the plane π through three points: C_0, C_1, and C_s.
2. Derive the line $\overline{PC_s}$ which is the intersection between two planes: plane π and plane $x = 0$.
3. Get points n_{0i} and n_{1i} $(i = 0, 1)$ that are corresponding points of the end points of the epipolar lines (projected by on line $\overline{PC_s}$) on I_0 and I_1.
4. Calculate the intersection range of n_{0i} and n_{1i} and the average point m of this range.
5. Get point C_0' which is on the line-plane intersection of line $\overline{mC_0}$ and plane $z = 0$, and point C_1' on the intersection of line of $\overline{mC_1}$ and plane $z = 0$.
6. Project images I_0 and I_1 from C_0 and C_1 to C_0' and C_1'.

C_0, C_1, and C_s represents the camera positions of database image 0, database image 1, and input image, respectively. Finally, the generated novel view image is superimposed onto the input image as shown in Figure 4.

4 Experiment

We compared the effectiveness of our proposed visualization method for observation under temporal changes with other visualization methods through the use study. In this experiment, we set an observation of the plant growth as a practical scenario.

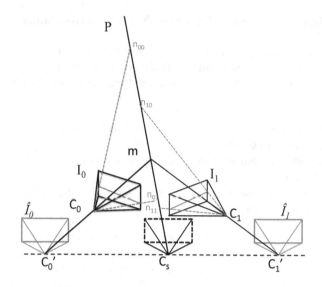

Fig. 3. View-morphing in the proposed method

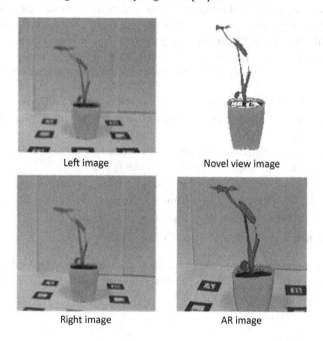

Left image   Novel view image

Right image   AR image

Fig. 4. Example of input and generated images

4.1   Experimental Conditions

Different types of visualization methods are suitable for different difficult scenarios of observation. Forsell *et al.* studied three approaches, side by side, shine-through, and fold, inspired by natural behaviors of printed paper [2]. In this experiment, different with paper-based comparison, we are not about to achieve the method of folding if we want to compare a physical 3-Dimension object. However, side by side and shine-through are possible to accomplish by traditional methods as well as Augmented Reality technology. In this experiment, we carried out seven visualization methods under the category of side by side and shine-through (overlay) for observation and comparison as shown in Figure 5. Characteristics of each visualization method are described as followings.

1. **Side by Side Based Visualization**

   Printed images (Method A): Compare the images that were printed on papers with the subject by putting the papers beside the subject. Participants need to flip to the images that they wants to use for comparison.

   Displayed images (Method B): Participants achieve comparison by locating the subject beside the computer screen where the images are displayed. Images displayed on computer screen are controlled using up and down arrows on the keyboard.

   Displayed limited images on camera image (Method C): The system shows one of the registered images beside the orientation of the subject . In this condition, the system is without the view morphing function.. Participants may turn the subject around to observe from different angles.

   Displayed novel view images on camera image (Method D): Participants are using the system with view morphing function for comparison. The system will generate in-between images based on the saved information and the current camera position.

2. **Overlay Based Visualization**

   Printed transparent pictures (Method E): Compare images printed on transparency with the subject by putting the transparencies in the front of the subject. Comparison are carried out the subject and one image which is rendered besides it using AR system

   AR with limited pictures (Method F): Compare the subject and the image rendered overlay on it using AR system.

   AR with free viewpoint (Method G): Compare the subject and the novel view image generated by view-morphing overlay on it using AR system (the proposed system).

   In the experiment, seven targets are provided to participants alternatively. 48 images were taken in 360 degrees around the target object with 7.5 degrees intervals were taken several days prior to the experiment and saved in database to represent the past status. The participants are required to use those images to conduct observation and comparison.

Fig. 5. Seven different visualization methods

4.2   Design of the User Experiment

In the experiment, the participant is required to observe the subject (plant), find the changes, and rank all seven methods based on the ease of observation and comparison after all the trials.. In each trial, the participant will received a set of images performed in different visualization methods and are requested to use these images to conduct observation and comparison.

The measurements include the quantity of information and the accuracy of information. The quantity is measured by how many changes can the participant notice. How many correct and incorrect identified changes are used for measuring the accuracy of the information. We also require the participant to answer about the advantages and disadvantages of each visualization method. The changes of these plants include new buds, leaves fallen, and changes of angles for outer leaves.

The procedure of the experiment is as follow. First of all, a brief interview with participants to gather basic information. This includes gender, age, any prior experience with AR applications. Secondly, explanations of the experiment, including the purpose of the experiment, the tasks for the participant, how the systems work, are provided. When the participant is ready, s/he can start to observe and compare using the target plant and provided visualization method. During the observation and comparison, the participants are required to mark the changes s/he found marking sheets. At the end of each visualization session, a short questioner which includes five self-report questions and section for comments of advantages and disadvantages about the visualization method. After all seven trials, the participants are required to rank all the visualization methods based on ease of observation and comparison. Lastly, the participants are asked to write the comments regarding to the visualization methods and the experiment. Overall, the experiment took about one and half hours including the post-experiment questionnaires. Five self-reported questions in the questionnaire of each visualization method trial session are listed below. $Q1 \sim Q5$ represent first to fifth questions.

Q1. I think it is easy to notice the changes with this visualization method.
Q2. I think I found all the changes.
Q3. I think it is easy to see the changes of color.
Q4. I think it is easy to see the changes of height.
Q5. I think it is easy to see the changes of angle.

Answers of each question were given on a Liker Scale from 1 (Strongly disagree) to 5 (Strongly agree). The ranking scores of seven visualization methods are given from 7 (the best) to 1 (the worst).

4.3   Result of the User Experiment

The experiment involved 11 participants, 3 female and 8 male, with average age 29. Six of the participants do not have Augmented Reality (AR) development experience but participated AR-related experiments before. Meanwhile, the other five participants have AR development experiences. Each visualization method session took up to 6 minutes long and the whole experiment has a average duration of 90 minutes including the post-experiment questionnaire.

Table 1 shows the mean scores of questionnaires for each visualization method. For question 1, visualization method F has the highest mean score (3.73) and Method A has the lowest mean score of 1.91. Method C and method G share the highest mean score (3.00) in question 2. Methods C, F, G have the highest score for the ease of notice the changes of color, height, angle, respectively. In the mean score of ranking, visualization Method C (Side by side with non-view morphing) has the highest score (5.27), followed by visualization Method D (Side by side with view morphing AR application) with mean score 4.73. Visualization Method A (Side by side with printed images on papers) and B (Side by side with displayed images on computer screen) share the lowest mean score (2.91).

4.4   Discussion

Table 1 shows that detecting color is easier using visualization Methods C and D while is more difficult using Method A and E. The methods that were scored higher for noticing the changes of height are Method F and C and Method B and E are scored lower.

Table 1. The mean scores of questionnaires and the mean scores of ranking for each visualization method. Bold font indicates the highest scores in each question.

	Q1	Q2	Q3	Q4	Q5	Score of Ranking
Method A	1.91	2.18	2.09	2.36	2.55	2.91
Method B	2.45	2.45	2.73	1.91	2.82	2.91
Method C	3.18	**3.00**	**3.55**	3.45	3.18	**5.27**
Method D	2.91	2.55	2.91	3.00	3.00	4.73
Method E	2.27	2.09	1.36	1.91	2.82	3.82
Method F	**3.73**	2.91	2.18	**3.55**	3.55	3.91
Method G	3.27	3.00	2.73	3.36	**4.00**	4.45

The methods that are easier for noticing the changes of angle were Methods C, F and G where the more difficult ones were Method A, B and E. According to the experiment user ranking results, Method C, D and G were scored higher and Method A and B scored the lowest. These scores were reflected in the scores of ease of observation (Q1) for each methods. Method C, F G also scored the highest where Method A and B scored the lowest. Combining these two results we have confirmed that users chose AR methods (C, D, F and G) over non-AR methods (A, B, E) for the ease of observation.

Table 2 shows the mean of detection accuracy of each method. Considering the accuracy of changes detection of each method, Method A has the highest accuracy of changes detection while Method E has the lowest accuracy rate. Even though Method A has the best accuracy, participants did not think it was easy to use for observation and comparison. The reason for this outcome might be that we are familiar to manipulate and compare paper materials in our daily life. However when compared to other visualization methods, it is considerably more time consuming, difficult to manipulate and requires the user to do everything manually. In addition, we can see that Method F has higher detection error than Method G. We conjecture that the result might be caused by the occlusion. Four of participants reported that while using method F for observation and comparison, the occlusion occurs and interrupted their comparison process. We think the occlusion effect is suppressed by the view morphing in Method G.

Throughout the experiment and results, we have noticed that systems with and without view morphing yielded very similar results. We believe this is because the participants were able to access as many as 48 images (every 7.5 degrees around the target object). These images did not differ much to the images created from view morphing since the change of angle was very small. However, the result of detection error of the system with view morphing shows the possibility of improvement of the observation.

5   Conclusion

In this research, we are able to identify the most effective visualization method for observation under temporal changes. The result of our experiment shown that all camera image based visualization methods which includes the AR-based visualization method have higher score than methods without camera images. In the future, the quality of the synthesized images and resolution of camera needed to be improved. The differences between the systems which has view morphing and without view morphing yielded similar results. This might caused by the amount of images that were provided to the participants which is more than usual cases. As the result the selected images may not

Table 2. The mean accuracy of changes detection of each method

	Method A	Method B	Method C	Method D	Method E	Method F	Method G
Accuracy of changes detection	**0.85**	0.84	0.77	0.84	0.67	0.77	0.76
Number of detection error	13	12	12	8	12	**19**	12

differ very much to the view morphing images. We need to conduct additional experiment with reduced number of registered images for non-view morphing system which is more similar to actual comparison and further verify our assumption.

References

1. Azuma, R.T.: A survey of augmented reality. Presence 6(4), 355–385 (1997)
2. Forsell, C., Tominski, C., Johansson, J.: Interaction support for visual comparison inspired by natural behavior. IEEE Transactions on Visualization and Computer Graphics 18, 2719–2728 (2012)
3. What is contextual learning?, http://www.cord.org/contextuallearning-definition/ (accessed October 2012)
4. Kolb, D.A.: Experiential learning: Experience as the source of learning and development, vol. 1. Prentice-Hall, Inc., Englewood Cliffs (1984)
5. Winterthaler, L., Voegtli, B., Fjeld, M., Hobi, D., Juchli, P.: Teaching electronegativity and dipole moment in a tui. In: Proceedings of IEEE International Conference on Advanced Learning Technologies, pp. 792–794. IEEE (2004)
6. Noguchi, S., Matsutomo, S., Miyauchi, T., Yamashita, H.: Real-time visualization system of magnetic field utilizing augmented reality technology for education. IEEE Transactions on Magnetics 48, 531–534 (2012)
7. Feiner, S., White, S., Kopylec, J.: Virtual vouchers: Prototyping a mobile augmented reality user interface for botanical species identification. In: Proceedings of 3DUI 2006 (IEEE Symp. on 3D User Interfaces), pp. 119–126 (2006)
8. Sandor, C., Cunningham, A., Dey, A., Mattila, V.-V.: An augmented reality x-ray system based on visual saliency. In: Proceedings of IEEE International Symposium on Mixed and Augmented Reality, Seoul, Korea, pp. 27–36 (October 2010)
9. Seitz, S.M., Dyer, C.R.: View morphing. In: Proceedings of the 23rd Annual Conference on Computer Graphics and Interactive Techniques, SIGGRAPH 1996, pp. 21–30. ACM, New York (1996)
10. Bichlmeier, C., Blum, T., Kleeberger, V., Navab, N.: mirracle: An augmented reality magic mirror system for anatomy education. In: Coquillart, S., Feiner, S., Kiyokawa, K. (eds.) Proceedings of IEEE Virtual Reality, pp. 115–116. IEEE (2012)
11. Tarng, W., Ou, K.L.: A study of campus butterfly ecology learning system based on augmented reality and mobile learning. In: Proceedings of IEEE Seventh International Conference on Wireless, Mobile and Ubiquitous Technology in Education, pp. 62–66. IEEE (2012)

Augmented Reality Workshops for Art Students

Marcin Wichrowski, Ewa Satalecka, and Alicja Wieczorkowska

Polish-Japanese Institute of Information Technology, Warsaw, Poland
mati@pjwstk.edu.pl, ewasatalecka@ewasatalecka.a4.pl,
alicja@poljap.edu.pl

Abstract. In this paper, we describe the program of our AR workshops dedicated to art students. Our observations regarding supervising such lab courses and students' works are presented. We would like to present a methodology for AR training when the students are not experienced in computer programming. We hope this will encourage other art and IT teachers to join efforts and incorporate AR into curriculum as a very promising concept of merging technology with visual communication. The potential of AR is very high and, therefore, it is important to introduce students to AR and the process of creating their own working projects.

Keywords: Augmented Reality, education, AR workshops, art projects, mobile AR.

1   Introduction

Augmented Reality (AR) applications and services are becoming very popular nowadays, mainly due to expansion of powerful mobile devices and new concepts such as Project Glass by Google[1]. AR projects are no longer just laboratory concepts but existing solutions supporting a constantly growing number of complex tasks, navigation systems, education, entertainment etc. Therefore AR is very close to becoming a household term and is visible in audio-visual media like games, TV, e-learning etc. According to the 2013 Horizon Report[2], the use of wearable technology will increase which will accelerate the expansion of such technologies as augmented reality in the consumer market and educational sector.

In 2013, we began to hold AR workshops for international groups of art students (Poland – Academy of Fine Arts in Katowice, Belgium – Antwerp Royal Academy of Art[3], Finland – Aalto University). Our experience gained during these classes showed that teaching both IT tools and visual communication design was very beneficial to students. Merging knowledge and passion of lecturers from two different faculties, IT (Marcin Wichrowski, Alicja Wieczorkowska) and New Media Art (Ewa Satalecka), shows that such collaboration can yield very interesting projects.

---

[1] http://www.google.com/glass/start/
[2] http://www.nmc.org/publications/2013-horizon-report-higher-ed
[3] http://grafischevormgevers.be/projecten?locale=en_US&wppa-
     album=1&wppa-photo=1&wppa-cover=0&wppa-occur=1

R. Shumaker and S. Lackey (Eds.): VAMR 2014, Part II, LNCS 8526, pp. 156–166, 2014.
© Springer International Publishing Switzerland 2014

2   Related Works

The methodology of teaching AR at universities [1], including previous authors' papers [2], and the attempt to improve the techniques applied so far serves as the motivation for this work. The importance of AR in education is presented in many sources [5], [6], [7]. We propose a methodology based on the findings of [1] and [2], and on our experience from the workshops we conducted for art students.

3   What Is AR?

When we look at the taxonomy of Mixed Reality (Fig. 1) we can observe that AR is a form of Mixed Reality, quite close to Real Environment. In contrast to VR which completely immerses a user in a computer generated world, AR enriches the real world by computer generated content. It could be 2D and 3D objects, audio or video files, textual information, avatar, interactive interfaces etc. The user can interact with these digital virtual objects superimposed upon or seamlessly mixed with the real world. AR supplements reality rather than completely replacing world around the user. It allows real and virtual elements to coexist at the same time and space.

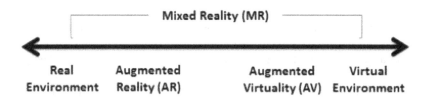

Fig. 1. Mixed Reality [3]

Definition given by Azuma [4] and Kaufmann [5] specifies the implementation of AR by three elements:

- mix of real-world and computer-generated virtual elements,
- interaction is provided in real-time,
- elements are registered in 3D.

We can experience AR using a desktop computer, a mobile device or a special Head-Mounted Display (HMD) (Fig. 2). Because of high availability and rapid development of handheld devices capable of delivering AR content, we decided to focus our workshops only on mobile solutions.

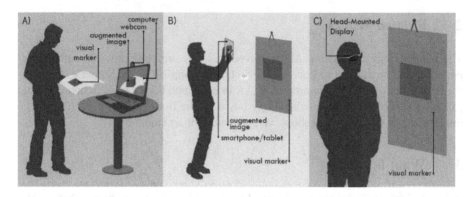

Fig. 2. AR experience on a) a computer, b) a mobile device, c) a Head-Mounted Display

4   Combining Artist's and IT Perspective in Supervising AR Projects

The idea of interdisciplinary workshops combining artistic and IT approaches emerged during joint supervision of final works of students of New Media Art Department at Polish-Japanese Institute of Information Technology. During the cycles of workshops which we held for international groups of students in Poland and later in Belgium and Finland, we tried to observe how the participants use this technology in graphic design. First we gave them a topic – usually quite an open one like "a love poem" or "a message from Finland," then we introduced the processing theory and presented the tools. We began teaching with a group discussion; next we divided responsibilities – an artist lecturer for graphic design quality and an IT specialist lecturer for the quality of engine and ease of perfect delivery. Working as a team of tutors we had the opportunity to discuss parallel design and IT aspects of each project individually. It seemed to be a comfortable situation both for us and for students. The final results were satisfying and made us realize how these workshops triggered inventive and creative works of the participants of our classes. All of the projects presented were done over four–five days of workshops with participants of various levels of technical advancement. Mixed-level groups were even more progressive, well-working and self-supporting classes. We realised that this methodology could be recommended for workshops as a very effective method of skills development and stimulation for the youngest participants. Age differences, various level of abilities and different topics of projects encourage participants to exchange their knowledge and experience.

From the IT point of view, the main challenge behind these workshops was finding a balance between the complexity of tasks given and the level of students' experience in understanding multimedia creation dedicated to AR projects. From our observations most of art students are good at preparing raster/vector graphic and animation forms mainly using Adobe products like Photoshop, Illustrator and After Effects.

Some of them specialize also in 3D computer graphic and 3D modeling. Programming skills are rare. However, our experience shows that aesthetic and well-designed AR project even with basic interaction could be also engaging for most users.

5 Teaching Methodology in Detail

The methodology we propose for AR workshops for art students is based on 5 days training, 7 hours a day, for groups of up to 16 students. The main part is a typical IT workshop, using computers, but students may bring drawings, paper mock-ups etc. Technical requirements for workshops concern installing desktop and mobile applications, providing access to smartphones/tablets (Android/iOS) with Internet connection, webcams, digital photo cameras and a color printer. After completing the workshop, students should acquire the following competences:

- Knowledge of using AR technology, including its pros and cons.
- Understanding technical requirements and available solutions for building AR projects.
- Preparing one's own AR project for mobile devices using automated AR editors.
- Documenting final work in the form of a poster with the description of results.

Having in mind such short time for presenting the main concepts of AR, teaching new applications, preparing final working project and documenting it, it is important to carefully select proper tools and solutions which are adequate to the skill level of usually diverse group of students in terms of technical advancement. Moreover, working with art students differs significantly from teaching IT students. They require much more attention and individual approach, because most of them have little knowledge about concepts behind AR workflow and programming [2].

5.1 Introductory Lecture

The 1st day of the workshop begins with a 2-hour lecture concerning artistic and IT aspects of AR usage.

The artistic part focuses on the observation that we are living in the times of easy access to large amounts of information and sources of knowledge. In the rapid stream of data coming from everywhere we need to survive and safeguard our brains against overload. By designing visual communication we may grade levels of information complexity, and help users make decisions on how much they wish to get in one portion. Visual communications could be used as a form of package for complex information ordered in smaller, graded portions visible with AR.

The IT part of the lecture presents how AR technically works and shows worldwide examples and demos of successful AR projects. Presented works were chosen carefully to show the broad spectrum of possible applications in various fields of life: advertising, marketing, shopping, entertainment, education, supporting complex tasks, navigation/sightseeing, architecture, military, medical etc. Special attention is paid to usage of AR in the art field by presenting projects of installations, objects, books etc.

enriched by this technology. Many of them are works prepared by students during previous workshops, or AR regular classes held by Marcin Wichrowski at Polish-Japanese Institute of Information Technology [2]. Efforts are made to present the best working examples which could be tested by students even during the lecture. This allows bringing a lot of interest and inspiration, especially among persons who did not have a chance to test this technology personally before or are not convinced about the quality and reliability of modern tracking technologies.

The lecture is followed by a one-hour brainstorming session to stimulate imagination of students and discuss pros and cons of this technology. Students decide what task they wish to undertake and in a small seminar they report the aims, the users and the methodology of their projects. They discuss how much AR could help them in problem-solving during the design process. Decisions result in rough sketches and initial projects to be presented on the class forum, and are again discussed and questioned by all of the participants. It helps improve the weak points and sometimes gives a new perspective and inspires changes. Observations made by students during these discussions are very important also from the IT point of view, and allow better understanding what is technically possible to achieve during 5 working days. Each student is supervised individually and has an opportunity to ask questions regarding artistic and IT scopes of planned AR project.

5.2   Basic AR Tools and First Introductory Task

The rest of the 1st day is dedicated to preparing working environment for developing AR projects based on carefully prepared tutorials and with the help of an IT lecturer. Because of the usually low level of programming experience we decided to use Metaio applications, which serve as simple introduction to build and experience AR scenes in a very short time. Metaio offers an integrated environment which consists of:

- Creator (Windows/MacOS)[4] – an automated AR authoring tool dedicated to creating AR scenes for desktops and mobile devices,
- Junaio AR Browser (Android/iOS)[5] – a free mobile AR browser for loading AR channels created with Metaio tools,
- Metaio Cloud[6] - an online host service for storing users' projects.

Thanks to easy configuration and simple workflow, this solution allows creating first working scenes in a really short time. It gives the possibility to use three tracking technologies: image, object and environment based. Creator allows embedding different types of objects such as images, text, videos/animations with alpha channel, animated 3D models, sounds, calendar events, links to websites, buttons for integrating with social networks and 360° panoramas. Students are also taught how to programme interaction in AR scenes.

---

[4] http://www.metaio.com/creator/
[5] http://www.junaio.com/
[6] http://www.metaio.com/Cloud/

Students using image based tutorials develop and test an introductory task "3D photo" in the form of an AR scene under precise supervision of IT lecturer. Standard photograph is divided into several plans that are stored in separate PNG files using Adobe Photoshop. Then the AR scene is created in Metaio Creator by placing these files on the z-axis at varying distances from each other. Background of the photo is recognized as a visual marker and triggers remaining elements on it. This allows creating the impression of 3D look while observing from a different angle using a mobile device (Fig. 3). The presented task guarantees good understanding of proposed AR software and encourage students to test different scenarios.

Fig. 3. Introductory AR scene - "3D photo"

5.3   Experimenting with More Advanced Tools and Basic Programming

During the 2nd day students experiment with various more advanced AR solutions like object and environment tracking, creating 360° panorama or building and placing 3D objects in the surrounding space. We have worked with:

- Metaio Toolbox for object and environment tracking[7],
- Microsoft Photosynth for creating 360° panorama photos[8],
- Autodesk 123D Catch for creating 3D models from photos[9],
- typical applications for image, video and 3D editing, like Adobe Photoshop, Adobe After Effects, and Blender.

These applications were carefully picked from available solutions to guarantee the best compatibility and provide seamless and easy to follow workflow. For programming basic interaction an Augmented Reality Experience Language (AREL) was used. Metaio Creator offers simple built-in code editor for AREL. In most cases interaction involves adding touch events and interfaces to control objects on a screen.

---

[7] https://dev.metaio.com/sdk/toolbox/
[8] http://photosynth.net/
[9] http://www.123dapp.com/catch

5.4   Prototyping and Developing Final Project

The 3rd and 4th days are mainly dedicated to individual technical prototyping supervised by the IT lecturer. The work done during days 3 and 4 is essential for acquiring the skills and finishing the projects on time. Students continue working with concepts proposed during the brainstorming session and after having their idea accepted by lecturers they start to prepare working prototypes. It is the most creative and important part of the workshop, which requires a lot of support from both the artistic and the technical supervisor. Problems that arise in projects are solved individually with the lecturers. It often happens that the proposed idea turns out to be impossible to be finished at a specified time or because of restrictions associated with the selected authoring tool. This is a great lesson showing the real issues that may happen during the implementation of AR projects and ways of dealing with them. Experimenting with prototypes also encourages students to look for the optimal solutions that can work in various conditions. The next step after solving the most significant problems in prototypes is the development of the final projects.

5.5   Final Presentation

The last day is devoted to polishing projects and documenting them in the form of posters, presented later in a dedicated university public space (Fig. 4). Prepared projects may be used to load AR scenes by viewers using free Junaio AR Browser. The final exhibitions got a positive reception from the visitors, and many participants were interested in taking part in the AR experience. This contributes to the popularization of the AR technology among both students and other teachers, who are often interested in the technical details and the possibility of using AR in their projects.

Fig. 4. The final exhibition (The Royal Academy of Fine Arts, Antwerp)

6   Students' Works

Students quickly recognize the potential of AR and they use it in a smart way, usually for adding hidden messages and actions enriching visual communication. Thanks to the technology they were able to use a regular coffee cup (Fig. 5), a spread of a book, a post card, a toy (Fig. 6), a cinema ticket or even a facade of a building as markers – which play the role of keys to get the hidden information or encourage users to interact with image/object using mobile devices. This can evolve into different scenarios - one can read a moving poem even while waiting for a friend in a café, as the poem is visible on a lid of a coffee cup. When reading a picture book for kids, one is able to bring the main characters to life, and have them act their roles on the screens of tablets or phones for educational purposes. A simple stamp on a postcard could be turned into a 3D object presenting architecture, a short video commercial, or any other information we wish to send from our holidays.

Fig. 5. Coffee cup with video projection

Fig. 6. Toy with animated 3D objects

Also a building's facade (Fig. 7) may be read as a marker and deliver a short or long story about itself – the history of the building or some info-graphic which gives us additional visual or verbal information.

Fig. 7. Building's facade with additional typography

One of the projects presents how the same landscape changes with the seasons. Another use of AR is to present a possible interactive game based on a real-life 3D object, whose interior is filled with interactive virtual characters. Traditional drawings set on a cube surface can deliver a nice animation, kind of a moving comic (Fig. 8). Even the real space of a corridor may be mapped to an AR project and changed into a battlefield against an interactive, virtual monster. An ordinary corner or a selected part of the wall is able to produce a sound composed by a student. A traditional art print illustrating a national saga changes into a funny animation, not hurting the book at all.

Users do not need any heavy, big objects to read or watch in order to participate in multimedia artistic experience. The mobile phone is enough to get a really complex message. And this additional information is realized only on request. We are not attacked by its obsessive presence.

7   Summary and Conclusions

Our experience shows that students without any prior knowledge of AR can prepare working projects in less than a week. The most important issue is to select proper AR solutions which are easy enough to encourage students to think about functionality they want to achieve. AR supports delivering complex information ordered and packaged in visual "containers", which could give completely new opportunities for art projects. It helps to organize and to deliver information visually and verbally, and students use it in dynamic and static context, as part of their visual communication projects. They apply AR to books or objects, as "real artefacts": additional messages like instructions, info-graphics, oral or visual information, motion images, translations, etc. They put effort to build visual aspects of their works and it sometimes takes even the form of installations and specially crafted objects which are triggers for AR experience. Students are very inventive in using these forms – for example they create board games based on real or mocked objects mixed with AR characters, add voice messages to objects designed for the visually impaired, use it in children education design, and for entertainment, as part of music and video performances, and many more.

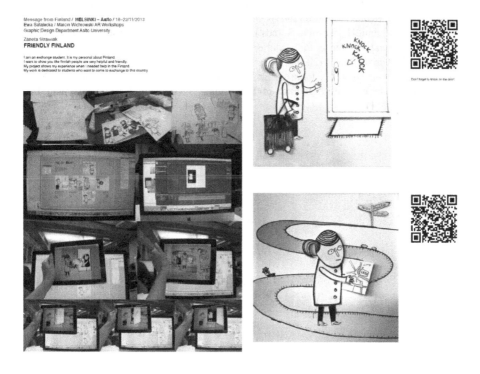

Fig. 8. Poster documenting final work with QR codes for testing AR scene in Junaio

These prototypes herald the development of AR in visual communication design, and show that the possibilities are endless and depend only on creativity of designers and the software used. The popularity of new mobile devices and truly user-friendly AR creation tools continues to grow. For these reasons it pays to join efforts of art and IT teachers, and try to incorporate AR into curriculum as a very promising concept of merging technology with visual communication.

References

1. Waechter, C., Artinger, E., Duschl, M., Klinker, G.: Creating Passion for Augmented Reality Applications – A Teaching Concept for a Lab Course. In: Bebis, G., et al. (eds.) ISVC 2010, Part II. LNCS, vol. 6454, pp. 429–438. Springer, Heidelberg (2010)

2. Wichrowski, M.: Teaching augmented reality in practice: Tools, workshops and students' projects. In: MIDI 2013: Proceedings of the International Conference on Multimedia, Interaction, Design and Innovation, Warsaw, Poland. ACM, New York (2013)
3. Milgram, P., Kishino, F.: A taxonomy of mixed reality visual displays. IEICE Transactions on Information Systems 77(12) (1994)
4. Azuma, R.T.: A survey of augmented reality. Presence: Teleoperators and Virtual Environments 6(4), 355–385 (1997)
5. Kaufmann, H.: Collaborative Augmented Reality in Education. In: Imagina Conference 2003, Monaco Mediax, Monaco (2003)
6. Lazoudis, A., Salmi, H., Sotiriou, S. (eds.): Augmented Reality in Education: EDEN - 2011 Open Classroom Conference, Proceedings of the "Science Center To Go" Workshops. Ellinogermaniki Agogi, Athcns (2011)
7. Yuen, S., Yaoyuneyong, G., Johnson, E.: Augmented reality: An overview and five directions for AR in education. Journal of Educational Technology Development and Exchange 4(1) (2011)

Games and Entertainment

Serious Games as Positive Technologies

Luca Argenton, Esther Schek, and Fabrizia Mantovani

Centre for Studies in Communication Sciences – CESCOM, University of Milan-Bicocca,
Building U16, Via Giolli, angolo Via Thomas Mann, 20162, Milan, Italy
{l.argenton,e.schek}@campus.unimib.it,
fabrizia.mantovani@unimib.it

Abstract. Serious games are emerging as innovative tools to promote opportunities for human psychological growth and well-being. The aim of the present paper is to introduce them as Positive Technologies. Positive Technology is an emergent field based on both theoretical and applied research, whose goal is to investigate how Information and Communication Technologies (ICTs) can be used to empower the quality of personal experience at three levels: hedonic well-being, eudaimonic well-being and social well-being. As Positive Technologies, serious games can influence both individual and interpersonal experiences by nurturing positive emotions, promoting engagement, as well as enhancing social integration and connectedness. An in-depth analysis of each of these aspects will be presented in the chapter, with the support of concrete examples.

Keywords: Positive psychology, positive technology, serious games, well-being.

1 Introduction

Serious applications for computer game technologies have become important resources for the actual knowledge society. Their use and effectiveness have been broadly acknowledged in different sectors, such as education, health, and business [1]. By fostering continuous learning experiences blended with entertaining affordances, serious games have the potential to shape new opportunities for human psychological development and growth. They have in fact supported the creation of socio-technical environments [2], where the interconnection between humans and technology encourages the emergence of innovative ways of thinking, creative practices, and networking opportunities. Further, serious games have been capable of supporting wellness and promoting happiness. That is why they can be considered as "positive technologies". Based on the Positive Psychology [3] theoretical framework, the Positive Technology approach claims that technology can increase emotional, psychological and social well-being [4].

Seligman and Csikszentmihalyi identified Positive Psychology as the scientific study of "positive personal experience, positive individual traits, and positive institutions" [5,6]. By focusing on human strengths, healthy processes, and fulfillment, Positive Psychology aims to improve the quality of life, as well as to increase wellness, and resilience in individuals, organizations, and societies.

R. Shumaker and S. Lackey (Eds.): VAMR 2014, Part II, LNCS 8526, pp. 169–177, 2014.

The link with accurate and scientific methodological practices [7] has become the engine of interventions to study and promote the optimal expression of thought, emotions and behaviors. In particular, Keyes and Lopez [8] argued that positive functioning is a combination of three types of well-being: (i) high emotional well-being (hedonic level), (ii) high psychological well-being (eudaimonic level), and (iii) high social well-being (social level). This means that Positive Psychology identifies three characteristics of our personal experience – affective quality, engagement/ actualization, and connectedness – that serve to promote personal well-being.

Similarly, the Positive Technology approach claims that technology can influence both individual and interpersonal experiences by fostering positive emotions, promoting engagement, and enhancing social integration and connectedness. Positive Technology is an emergent field based on both theoretical and applied research, whose goal is to investigate how Information and Communication Technologies (ICTs) can be used to empower the quality of personal experience.

Starting from an introductory analysis of the concept of well-being as it has been framed by Positive Psychology research, this paper will reflect on the nature and the role of serious games as positive technologies. In particular, it will discuss how they can support, and train the optimal functioning of both individuals and groups, by contributing to their well-being.

2   Fostering Emotional Well-Being: The Hedonic Perspective

Kahneman, Diener, & Shwarz [9] conceptualized the idea of emotional well-being within the hedonic perspective. They in fact defined hedonic psychology as the study of "what makes the experience pleasant or unpleasant". Among the different ways to evaluate pleasure in human life, a large number of studies have focused on the concept of subjective well-being (SWB), "a person's cognitive and affective evaluation of his or her life as a whole" [10,11]. At the cognitive level, opinions expressed by individuals about their life as a whole, and the level of satisfaction with specific life-domains, such as family or work, becomes fundamental. At the emotional level, SWB is indeed related to the presence of positive emotional states and the absence of negative moods.

This point is of particular interest to the hedonic perspective. Unlike negative emotions, that are essential to provide a rapid response to perceived threats, positive emotions can expand cognitive-behavioral repertoires and help to build resources that contribute to future success [12,13].

2.1   How Can Technology and Serious Game Foster Hedonic Well-Being?

The hedonic side of Positive Technology analyzes the ways technologies can be used to produce positive emotional states. For example, Riva and colleagues tested the potentiality of Virtual Reality (VR) in inducing specific emotional responses, including positive moods [16] and relaxing states [17,18]. More recently, other studies explored the potentiality of emerging mobile devices to exploit the potential of positive emotions.

Serious Games and games in general are strictly connected to positive emotions, and to a wide variety of pleasant situational responses that make gameplay the direct emotional opposite of depression [19].

At first, serious games can evoke a *sensorial pleasure* throughout graphics, usability, game aesthetic, visual and narrative stimuli. This point has been analyzed by emerging trends, such as engineering aesthetics 2.0 [20] and hedonic computing [21], whose results will be able to significantly influence game design.

Secondly, serious games foster an *epistemophilic pleasure* by bridging curiosity with the desire of novelty within a protected environment where individuals can experience the complexity of their self, and developing mastery and control. Empowered by new media affordances and possibilities, serious games can promote a dynamic equilibrium between excitement and security.

Thirdly, serious games promote the *pleasure for victory* and, by supporting virtual interactions with real people, they nurture a *social pleasure*, promoting collaborative and competitive dynamics, communication and sharing opportunities, even outside the context of the game [22].

Games have also been traditionally recognized as marked by a *cathartic pleasure* as they represent a relief valve for emotional tensions, anger and aggressiveness.

Finally, pleasure has a *neural* counterpart. An interesting example is that of dopamine, a neurotransmitter that affects the flow of information in the brain and that is often involved in pleasant experiences, as well as in different forms of addiction and learning. In a classic study made by Koepp and colleagues to monitor the effects of video games on brain activity, a significant increase of dopamine (found in a quantity comparable only to that determined by taking amphetamines) was measured [23].

Good examples of Serious Games explicitly designed to foster positive emotion are *The Journey to Wild Divine"* (http://www.shokos.com/The_Journey_to_Wild_Divine.html) and *Eye Spy: the Matrix, Wham!,* and *Grow your Chi!,* developed in Dr Baldwin's Lab at McGill University (http://selfesteemgames.mcgill.ca). In *The Journey to Wild Divine* the integration between usable biofeedback sensors and a computer software allows individuals to enhance their subjective wellbeing throughout a 3D graphic adventure. Here, wise mentors teach the skills to reduce stress, and increase physical and mental health.

Eye Spy: the Matrix, Wham!, and *Grow your Chi!* are indeed projects whose goal is to empower people with low self-esteem respectively by working on ignoring rejection information, throughout positive conditioning, or by focusing on positive social connections [24,25].

3   Promoting Psychological Well-Being: The Eudaimonic Perspective

This perspective is associated with the possibility to fully realize human potential through the exercise of personal virtues in pursuit of goals that are meaningful to the individual and society [4,9]. In this case, happiness no longer coincides with a subjective form of well-being, but with a psychological one. Psychological well-being is based on 6 elements [26]: *self-acceptance, positive relationships with others, autonomy, environmental mastery, purpose in life,* and *personal growth.* An author that has fully interpreted the complexity of the eudaimonic perspective is Mihaly Csikszentmihalyi who formalized the concept of flow [27,28], a positive, complex and highly structured state of deep involvement, absorption, and enjoyment [28]. The basic feature of this experience is a dynamic equilibrium perceived between high environmental action opportunities (challenges) and adequate personal resources in facing them (skills). Additional characteristics are deep concentration, clear rules and unambiguous feedback from the task at hand, loss of reflective self-consciousness, control of one's actions and environment, alteration of temporal experience, and intrinsic motivation.

3.1   How Can Technology and Serious Game Promote Eudaimonic Well-Being?

Scholars in the field of human–computer interaction are starting to recognize and address the eudaimonic challenge. For example, Rogers calls for a shift from "proactive computing" to "proactive people," where "technologies are designed not to do things for people but to engage them more actively in what they currently do"[29].

Further, the theory of flow has been extensively used to study user experience with Information and Communication Technologies. It is the case of internet [30], virtual reality [31,32] social networks [33], video-games [34], and serious games [35].

Bergeron [35] defined serious games as interactive computer applications, with or without a significant hardware component, that (i) have challenging goals, (ii) are fun to play with and/or engaging, (iii) incorporate some concepts of scoring, (iv) impart to the user skills, knowledge, or attitude that can be applied in the real world.

Interestingly, all of these aspects can be easily overlapped to Csikszentmihalyi's theory of flow. Games are in fact "flow activities" [27, 28] as they are intrinsically able to provide enjoyable experiences [22], creating rules that require the learning of skills, defining goals, giving feedback, making control possible, and fostering a sense of curiosity and discovery.

In addition, the intrinsic potential of flow that characterizes serious games can be even empowered by (i) identifying an information-rich environment that contains functional real world demands; (ii) using the technology to enhance the level of presence of subjects in the environment, and (iii) allowing the cultivation, by linking this optimal experience to the actual experience of the subject [3]. To achieve the first two steps, it is fundamental to look at the following game design elements [36]:

- *Concentration.* Serious games should stimulate a mental focus on in-game dynamics, by providing a set of engaging, differentiated and worth-attending stimuli that limit the influence of external variables. Along with other aspects, concentration can result in hyperlearning processes that consist of the mental ability to totally focus on the task by using effective strategies aligned with personal traits [50];

- *Challenge.* As noted by Gee [37], who claims that the game experience should be "pleasantly frustrating", challenges have to match players' skills/level and to support their improvement throughout the game. During specific stages of the game, "Fish tanks" (stripped down versions of the real game, where gameplay mechanisms are simplified) and "Sand boxes" (versions of the game where there is less likelihood for things to go wrong) can support this dynamism;
- *Player Skills.* Games must support player skills and mastery throughout game usability, and specific support systems and rewards;
- *Control.* It is fundamental for players to experience a sense of control over what they are doing, as well as over the game interface, and input devices;
- *Clear goals.* Games should provide players with specific, measurable, achievable, responsible and time-bounded goals;
- *Feedback.* Players have to be supported by feedback on the progress they are making, on their action, and the ongoing situations represented in the virtual environment;
- *Immersion.* Players should become less aware of their surroundings and emotionally involved in the game dynamics;
- *Social Interaction.* Games should create opportunities for social interaction by supporting competition, collaboration, and sharing among players.

An interesting example of an eudaimonic serious game is *Superbetter,* developed by Jane McGonigal (https://www.superbetter.com/). SuperBetter helps people their life goals by working on personal resilience. The application of the aforementioned elements supports people being curious, optimistic and motivated and promotes high levels of user engagement.

4   Working on Social Well-Being: The Social Perspective

Social well-being indicates the extent to which individuals are functioning well in their social system and it is defined on five dimensions [39]:

- *Social integration*, conceptualized as the evaluation of the quality of personal relationships with a community or a society;
- *Social contribution*, evidenced by the perception of having something important to offer to society and the world at large;
- *Social coherence*, determined by the meaning given to the quality, organization, and operations that make up the social sphere;
- *Social acceptance*, based on the belief that people proactivity and agency can foster the development of societies and culture;
- *Social actualization*, determined by the evaluation of the potential and the trajectory of society.

4.1   How Can Technology and Serious Game Promote Social Well-Being?

At this level, the challenge for Positive Technology is concerned with the use of new media to support and improve the connectedness between individuals, groups, and organizations, and to create a mutual sense of awareness. This is essential to the feeling that other participants are there, and to create a strong sense of community at a distance.

Short and colleagues [40] introduce the term "social presence" to indicate the degree of salience of the other person in a mediated environment and the consequent salience of their interpersonal interaction. On this point, Riva and colleagues [41] argued that an individual is present within a group if he/she is able to put his/her own intentions (presence) into practice and to understand the intentions of the other group members (social presence). Nowadays, social presence has been empowered by advanced ICT systems. All these technologies can promote the development of a peak collaborative state experienced by the group as a whole and known as "networked flow" [42]. Sawyer [43,44], who referred to this state with the term of "group flow", identified several conditions that facilitate its occurrence: the presence of a common goal, close listening, complete concentration, control, blending egos, equal participation, familiarity, communication and the potential for failure. As noted by Gaggioli and colleagues [42], networked flow occurs when high levels of presence and social presence are matched with a state of "liminality". In particular, three pre-conditions have to be satisfied:

- group members share common goals and emotional experiences so that individual intentionality becomes a *we-intention* [45] able to inspire and guide the whole group;
- group members experience a state liminality, a state of "being about" that breaks the homeostatic equilibrium previously defined;
- group members identify in the ongoing activity the best affordances to overcome the situation of liminality.

Social presence and networked flow can be fostered by serious games as well. An interesting study realized by Cantamesse, Galimberti, & Giacoma [46], for example, examined the effect of playing the online game World of Warcraft (WoW), both on adolescents' social interaction and on the competence they developed on it. The in-game interactions, and in particular conversational exchanges, turn out to be a collaborative path of the joint definition of identities and social ties, with reflection on in-game processes and out-game relationships. Another interesting example is *Mind the Game*™, developed by our research group [47] to enhance the optimal functioning of groups. The serious game does not only promote cooperation and competitive processes, but also stimulates a proactive co-construction of knowledge that foster the emergence of we intentions, networking opportunities and in-group dynamics.

5   Conclusion

In this paper we discussed the role of serious games as positive technologies. According to Positive Psychology theoretical framework and Positive Technology approach, we demonstrated that these applications are able to promote hedonic well-being, eudaimonic well-being and social well-being,

First of all, serious games can foster positive emotional states by enhancing the different forms of pleasure they are intrinsically made of. In particular, we discussed the importance of sensorial, epistemophilic, social, cathartic and neural pleasure.

Secondly, serious applications for computer game technologies can be associated with flow experiences and, thus, with psychological well-being. Throughout high level of presence and flow, technologies can, in fact, promote optimal experiences marked by absorption, engagement, and enjoyment.

Finally, serious games are able to increase connectedness and integration. To achieve such a complex goal they have to work on a mutual sense of awareness, as well as social presence and situations of liminality. In this way, groups can access peak creative states, known as networked flow optimal experiences, that are based on shared goals and emotions, collective intentions, and proactive behaviours.

References

1. Fisher, G., Giaccardi, E., Eden, H., Sugimoto, M., Ye, Y.: Beyond binary choices: Integrating individual and social creativity. International Journal of Human-Computer Studies 12, 428–512 (2005)
2. Botella, C., Riva, G., Gaggioli, A., Wiederhold, B.K., Alcaniz, M., Banos, R.M.: The present and future of positive technologies. Cyberpsychology, Behavior and Social Networking 15, 78–84 (2012)
3. Riva, G., Banos, R.M., Botella, C., Wiederhold, B.K., Gaggioli, A.: Positive technology: Using interactive technologies to promote positive functioning. Cyberpsychology, Behavior and Social Networking 15, 69–77 (2012)
4. Serino, S., Cipresso, P., Gaggioli, A., Riva, G.: The potential of pervasive sensors and computing for Positive Technology. In: Mukhopadhyay, S.C., Postolache, O.A. (eds.) Pervasive and Mobile Sensing and Omputing for Healthcare, Smart Sensors, Measurement and Instrumentation. Springer, New York (2013)
5. Seligman, M.E.P.: Positive Psychology: Fundamental Assumptions. The Psychologist 16, 26–27 (2003)
6. Seligman, M.E.P., Csikszentmihalyi, M.: Positive psychology: An introduction. The American Psychologist 55, 5–14 (2000)
7. Seligman, M.E.P., Steen, T.A., Park, N., Peterson, C.: Positive psychology progress: Empirical validation of interventions. The American Psychologist 60, 410–421 (2005)
8. Keyes, C.L.M., Lopez, S.J.: Toward a science of mental health: Positive direction in diagnosis and interventions. In: Snyder, C.R., Lopez, S.J. (eds.) Handbook of Positive Psychology. Oxford University Press, New York (2002)
9. Kahneman, D., Diener, E., Schwarz, N.: Well-Being: The Foundations of Hedonic Psychology. Sage, New York (2004)

10. Diener, E.: Subjective well-being: The science of happiness and a proposal for a national index. American Psychologist 55, 34–43 (2000)
11. Diener, E., Diener, M., Diener, C.: Factors predicting the subjective well-being of nations. Journal of Personality and Social Psychology 69, 851–864 (1995)
12. Fredrickson, B.L.: What good are positive emotions? Review of General Psychology 2, 3000–3019 (1998)
13. Fredrickson, B.L.: The role of positive emotions in positive psychology: The broaden-and-build theory of positive emotions. American Psychologist 56, 222–252 (2001)
14. Riva, G., Mantovani, F., Capideville, C.S., Preziosa, A., Morganti, F., Villani, D., Gaggioli, A., Botella, C., Alcaniz, M.: Affective interactions using virtual reality: The link between presence and emotions. Cyberpsychology & Behavior 10, 45–56 (2007)
15. Villani, D., Lucchetta, M., Preziosa, A., Riva, G.: The role of interactive media features on the affective response: A virtual reality study. International Journal on Human Computer Interaction 1, 1–21 (2009)
16. Villani, D., Riva, F., Riva, G.: New technologies for relaxation: The role of presence. International Journal of Stress Management 14, 260–274 (2007)
17. Grassi, A., Gaggioli, A., Riva, G.: The green valley: the use of mobile narratives for reducing stress in commuters. Cyberpsychology & Behavior 12, 155–161 (2009)
18. McGonigal, J.: Reality is broken. The Penguin Press, New York (2010)
19. Liu, Y.: Engineering aesthetics and aesthetic ergonomics: Theoretical foundations and a dual-process research methodology. Ergonomics 46, 1273–1292 (2003)
20. Wakefield, R.L., Whitten, D.: Mobile computing: A user study on hedonic/utilitarian mobile device usage. European Journal of Information Systems 15, 292–300 (2002)
21. Reeves, B., Read, J.L.: Total Engagement: How Games and Virtual Worlds Are Changing the Way People Work and Businesses Compete. Harvard Business School Publishing, Boston (2009)
22. Bruner, J.S.: On knowing: Essays for the left hand. Belknap, Cambridge (1964)
23. Koepp, M.J., Gunn, R.N., Lawrence, A.D., Cunningham, V.J., Dagher, A., Jones, T., Brooks, D.J., Bench, C.J., Grasby, P.M.: Evidence for striatal dopamine release during a video game. Nature 393, 266–268 (1998)
24. Baccus, J.R., Baldwin, M.W., Packer, D.J.: Increasing Implicit Self-Esteem through Classical Conditioning. Psychological Science 15, 498–502 (2004)
25. Dandeneau, S.D., Baldwin, M.W.: The Inhibition of Socially Rejecting Information Among People with High versus Low Self-Esteem: The Role of Attentional Bias and the Effects of Bias Reduction Training. Journal of Social and Clinical Psychology 23, 560–584 (2004)
26. Ryff, C.D.: Happiness is everything, or is it? Explorations on the meaning of psychological well-being. Journal of Personality and Social Psychology 57, 1069–1081 (1989)
27. Csikszentmihalyi, M.: Beyond boredom and anxiety. Jossey-Bass, San Francisco (1975)
28. Csikszentmihalyi, M.: Flow: The psychology of optimal experience. Harper & Row, New York (1990)
29. Rogers, Y.: Moving on from Weiser's vision of calm computing: Engaging UbiComp experiences. In: Dourish, P., Friday, A. (eds.) UbiComp 2006. LNCS, vol. 4206, pp. 404–421. Springer, Heidelberg (2006)
30. Chen, H.: Exploring Web users' on-line optimal flow experiences. Syracuse University, New York (2000)
31. Gaggioli, A., Bassi, M., Delle Fave, A.: Quality of experience in virtual environments. In: Riva, G., Ijsselsteijn, W., Davide, F. (eds.) Being There: Concepts, Effects and Measuerement of User Presence in Syntetic Environments. IOS Press, Amsterdam (2003)

32. Riva, G., Castelnuovo, G., Mantovani, F.: Transformation of flow in rehabilitation: the role of advanced communication technologies. Behavioural Research Methods 38, 237–244 (2006)
33. Mauri, M., Cipresso, P., Balgera, A., Villamira, M., Riva, G.: Why Is Facebook So Successful? Psychophysiological Measures Describe a Core Flow State While Using Facebook. Cyberpsychology, Behavior, and Social Networking 14, 723–731 (2011)
34. Jegers, K.: Pervasive game flow: understanding player enjoyment in pervasive gaming. Computer in Entertainment 5, 9 (2007)
35. Bergeron, B.P.: Developing serious games. Charles River Media, Hingham (2006)
36. Sweetser, P., Wyeth, P.: GameFlow: A model for evaluating player enjoyment in games. ACM Computers in Entertainmet 3, 1–24 (2005)
37. Gee, J.P.: What video games have to teach us about learning and literacy. Palgrave MacMillan, New York (2004)
38. Shandley, K., Austin, D., Klein, B., Kyrios, M.: An evaluation of Reach Out Central: An online therapeutic gaming program for supporting the mental health of young people. Health Education Research 15, 563–574 (2010)
39. Keyes, C.L.M.: Social Well-being. Social Psychology Quarterly 61, 121–140 (1998)
40. Short, J., Williams, E., Christie, B.: The social psychology of telecommunications. Wiley, New York (1976)
41. Riva, G., Waterworth, J.A., Waterworth, E.L.: The layers of presence: A bio-cultural approach to understanding presence in natural and mediated environments. Cyberpsychology & Behavior 7, 402–416 (2004)
42. Gaggioli, A., Riva, G., Milani, L., Mazzoni, E.: Networked Flow: Towards an understanding of creative networks. Springer, New York (2013)
43. Sawyer, K.R.: Group creativity: Music, theatre, collaboration. Basic Books, New York (2003)
44. Sawyer, K.R.: Group genius: The creative power of collaboration. Oxford University Press, New York (2008)
45. Searle, J.: Intentionality. Cambridge University Press, Cambridge (1983)
46. Cantamesse, M., Galimberti, C., Giacoma, G.: Interweaving interactions in virtual worlds: A case study. Stud. Health. Technol. Inform. 167, 189–193 (2011)
47. Argenton, L., Triberti, S., Serino, S., Muzio, M., Riva, G.: Serious Games as positive technologies for individual and group flourishing. In: Brooks, A.L., Braham, S., Jain, L.C. (eds.) SEI 1991. LNCS, vol. 536, pp. 221–244. Springer, Heidelberg (2014)

An Experience-Based Chinese Opera Using Live Video Mapping

Xiang-Dan Huang[1], Byung-Gook Lee[1], Hyung-Woo Kim[2], and Joon-Jae Lee[3]

[1] Department of Visual Contents, Dongseo University, Busan, South Korea
[2] Department of Design, Dongseo University, Busan, South Korea
[3] Department of Game Mobil Contents, Keimyung University, Daegu, South Korea
{cileen0801me,leebyunggook,multikimmail}@gmail.com,
joonlee@kmu.ac.kr

Abstract. In this work, we choose Chinese Opera as research material, hoping to increase people's acceptance and intimate to the performance. The theme is "Havoc the Dragon Palace", one chapter of the sixteenth century Chinese novel "Journey to the West" by Wu Cheng'en. We developed the rendering technique and named "Live Video Mapping". It focuses on both the movement of human detection and the interaction with background video real-time. The virtual images on the stage not only generate good of view but also make audience experience the illusion of space in which the space is expanding and enhancing. Taking into account the above factors, this study explore the possibility of interactive video mapping, as well as understanding and increasing the affinity of Chinese Opera to promote the value of the Chinese Opera.

Keywords: Journey to the West, Chinese Opera, real-time interactive experience, live video mapping.

1 Introduction

The new experimental interactive art has been integrated with various fields of arts such as digital art, sound, lighting, photo, game, virtual reality. Work of art has remained in molting from the fact that obtains the life force while vibration. Since the digital age beginning, the heart of the media area has broken away from the fixed, deny the remained, influx the new in the works. The principle of new art creation is the participation of the audience as this work is completed through the audiences" active participation. It is also the new standard of art and fundamental principle of the structure of the media artwork [1]. If you briefly analysis form from the viewpoint of visual media, the trend from static media through dynamic media to experiential media. From that standpoint, there are various types of art in video mapping such as media facade, stage of performance art, object mapping in the exhibition and others. Therefore, it is considered to be a proper subject for this paper. With the spreading and effective using of video mapping and the video media, we believe it is necessary to figure out the current condition of the usage in the area of performing arts.

In this work, we choose the Chinese Opera as research material to recommend an experience-based culture content by "Live video mapping". Chinese Opera is one of

R. Shumaker and S. Lackey (Eds.): VAMR 2014, Part II, LNCS 8526, pp. 178–189, 2014.
© Springer International Publishing Switzerland 2014

the best ethnic arts to express and represent the symbolism of Chinese characteristics, ethnic, and personality. This traditional performance has gone through many changes such as the social changing. Globalization and the modernization of the media area become the biggest challenge for Chinese Opera as well. The culture demand expands Chinese Opera market that is considerably shrinks. When foreigners and even some Chinese new generations watch the Chinese opera for the first time, they may feel strange and distant, it is hard to recognize the content of the play and the actor's line. This fact makes people difficult to get close to Chinese Opera. Monkey King (Sun Wu Kong in Chinese) is famous for the Chinese novel "Journey to the West". There are several plays derived from the story, we choose one chapter which is called "Havoc the Dragon Palace" to help people experience it. The purpose of this work is to guide the people act performance and make them feel themselves became one part of the animation, by using the live video mapping system to increase the affinity of Chinese Opera.

This paper is organized as follows: Chapter 2 explains the system of "Live Video Mapping", and shows some examples of similar contents. Chapter 3 describes the Chinese Opera and its limitations, and discusses the plays of the Monkey King. Chapter 4 presents the interactive Chinese Opera contents "Havoc the Dragon Palace". Defining the concept of content based on the scenario, making the visual contents, setting the location of the display to implement the final work. Finally, the conclusions are presented in chapter 5.

2   Live Video Mapping and Precedent

2.1   Live Video Mapping

Projection mapping, also known as video mapping and spatial augmented reality, is a projection technology used to turn objects, often irregularly shaped, into a display surface for video projection[2]. It is using the optical illusion, projection an overlay videos to provide high immersive experience through the expansion of a real world space. The representation of the contents is diversified with the development of related technologies. Nowadays, allowing projection mapping to a moving object such as calibrate the distortion, real-tome tracking object has beyond the limits of the existences. So we developed the technology and used in the performance or exhibition to projection on the body of human. The live video mapping provides the interface between audiences and interactive contents, to make a story and communication. In order to make Chinese Opera content experience-based, we use the human body or performer's costumes as screen to make a creative stage [3]. The live video mapping is named by us, so there is no dictionary definition about it. This work needs to make visual contents and programming. To preset the guide animation for expecting behavior of the audience, within a certain range, free actions of the audience are reflected in the work. The audience comes to appreciate the art and has an extraordinary experience.

2.2   System

In this work, we uses PC, projector, Kinect and speakers (Fig. 1). Kinect is a line of motion sensing input device, which enables users to control and to make interactions. The device features an RGB camera, depth sensor and multi-array microphone running proprietary software, which provides full-body 3D motion capture, facial recognition and voice recognition capabilities [4]. The depth sensor is consists of an infrared laser projector combined with a monochrome CMOS sensor, which captures video data in 3D under any ambient light conditions [5]. The device can determine the value of depth and receive the 3-dimentional coordinates X, Y, Z. The default RGB video stream uses 8-bit VGA resolution (640 x 480 pixels), and output 30 frames per second. The kinect not only can control the Xbox game, but also possible via connect with the PC which has USB interface. There are diverse of methods to develop the interactive contents by kinect. In this work, I use the Simple-OpenNI library for Pro cessing. Processing is an open source programming language which has promoted software literacy within the visual arts and visual literacy within technology. Simple-OpenNI uses the Skeleton API to track the joints and enable auto-calibration. Besides, I use a 2d physics library for simulating rigid bodies called Pbox2d. I program the particle system interact with people. For the background visual contents I used Autodesk Maya (3D animation, modeling, simulation, rendering software); and for the post-production process I used Adobe After Effects (Motion graphics, visual effects and compositing software). The tracking data in the Processing were transferred to Resolume arena by Syphon library, and the visual sources produced in After Effects are directly imported into the Resolume (Fig. 2). Each of the images projected on the subject can be controlled manually or automatically. Detailed account of the process is given in chapter 4.

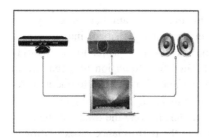

Fig. 1. Hardware system

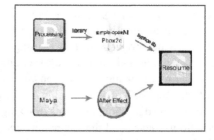

Fig. 2. Software system

2.3   Precedent of Similar Contents

Since using Kinect, the media artworks become rich. Especially in the performing arts, it can project performer's body or costumes as a screen, it is possible to reduce the constraints of the representation and to improve the effect force. The shape of the screen is unfixed, sometimes cause optical illusion. The following are some precedent of similar contents.

"Kinect Illusion" (Fig. 3) uses the motion tracking and the functions of RGB camera, depth camera. It is a multimedia music work that combined the elements of sound and video with the movement of the actors. The kinect in front of the screen is connected with a Mac Pro, and the kinect behind the screen is connected with a MacBook Pro; All videos are produced in Quartz Composer. Two performers perform interactive dance.

Fig. 3. Kinect Illusion [6]

"Puppet Parade" (Fig. 4) is an interactive installation that allows children to act as puppeteer and use their arm to simulate the larger-than-normal sized puppet creatures projected on the wall in front of them. Children can also step in to the environment and interact with the puppets directly, for example by petting them or creating food for them to eat. This dual interactive setup allows children to perform alongside the puppets, blurring the line between the "audience" and the puppeteers and creating an endlessly playful dialogue between the children in the space and the children manipulate the puppet creatures.

Fig. 4. Puppet Parade [7]

What interest people most in the above performances are that they both contained the interactive-based and communicative-based contents (real-time people track). This form of performance presents a new way of video mapping where audience can participate into the show, the visual source can be reused, and audience can easily accept the performance. In the same space and the same background video, the audience can experience the real-time image processing interaction. The performers can experience the real-time image processing interaction to deploy scenario at the same time.

3   Chinese Opera and Plays of the Monkey King

3.1   Chinese Opera

According to the statistics of the China National Academy of Arts in 1986, there are 374 kinds of traditional operas performing in China. The most popular one is "Peking Opera" (Fig. 4), and this is also that I will present in this paper [8]. Peking Opera is a form of Chinese traditional opera, which is also called Chinese Opera in western countries, for the better understanding, we use Chinese Opera instead in the following paper. Chinese Opera are famous in Beijing and Tianjin in the north of China, and Shanghai in the south [9]. In the past, it is also called Jingxi, Pingxi or Guoju, depending on the original of the region. Chinese Opera was born when "Four Great Anhui Troupes"(Sanqing Troupe, Sixi Troupe, Chuntai Troupe, Hechun Troupe) brought Anhui opera, or what is now called Huiju, in 1790 to Beijing, for the celebration of the eightieth birthday of the Qianlong Emperor [10] on 25 September[11]. Therefore, Chinese opera is generally believed to originate from southern Anhui and eastern Hubei, and to be fully formed by 1845[12]. The main body of the melodies originated from Xipi and Erhuang. The melodies that accompany each play were also simplified, and played with more different traditional instruments than in earlier forms.

Fig. 5. The Chinese Opera [13]

Chinese Opera is a traditional theatre which combines music, vocal performance, mime, dance, and acrobatics [14]. Although it is a product of traditional culture, it is the fact that there exists huge distance between this form of art and the audiences of today. The Chinese government has been attaching great efforts to advocate, protect and succeed the traditional culture. For example, they have participated in special Chinese Opera performances many times, and organized the Chinese Opera groups to perform abroad. It is truth that Chinese Opera plays an important role in the international cultural exchange. The country is making considerable efforts to train the actors and encourage the growth of successions [10]. Qi Xiaoyun one of the famous Jing (One of the role) performers, acted the "Othello" by William Shakespeare in Chinese Opera in 1982. As the first woman performed Chinese Opera in English, her performance become a hot issue at that time. Besides, she also performed an Ancient Greece Tragedy "Bakchai", "ChiSangZhen (Red Mulberry Town)", "ZhaMeiAn (Judge Bao and the Qin Xiang)" and "ChuSanHai (In addition to tree evils)" in English [10]. Chinese Opera is a substantial channel for social education and entertainment, so it is one of the tools for increasing awareness of the Chinese culture. It also plays an important role in the development of national economy and civilization.

3.2   The Limitation of Chinese Opera

Chinese Opera presents dramatic plays and figures by infusing artistic methods: sing-ing, dialogue, dancing and martial art. Singing is utilized to intensify the appeal of the art by all kinds of tones. China has different dialects in each region, it is hard to un-derstand without subtitles. Dialogue is the complement of singing which is full of musical and rhythm sensation. Dancing refers to the body movements requiring high performing skills. For example, circling with whip in hand, means riding a horse; simply walking around means a long journey; Waving a cloud patterned flag means the character is in the wind or under the sea. Martial art is the combination and trans-formation of traditional Chinese with combating exercises with dances [15].

There are four main roles in Chinese Opera: Sheng, Dan, Jing, Chou. Sheng is the main role. Dan refers female role, there are four famous roles of Dan, such as Mei Lanfang, Cheng Yanqiu, Shang Xiaoyun, and Xun Huisheng. Jing is a painted face male role and Chou is a male clown role [16]. Although four roles are sub-divided, all of them should perform professionally. The acting skills are intimately connected with their costume, facial painting and props. Costumes and the facial painting (Lian-pu) take on added importance. Costumes help to clarify the rank of the characters in the Chinese Opera. Lianpu is formed through dramatic artists" long-term practice and their awareness and judgment of the roles in the plays. The colors used in costumes and Lianpu are the Chinese traditional five elements colors, and the patterns are also the traditional ones. Besides, many contents contain in the Chinese Opera. In such a volume as this, only a bare general sketch can be given of the Chinese Opera. If people want to appreciate or even fall into love it, they need to understand about the story, subtitles, roles, the meaning of their gestures and more importantly, the know-ledge about traditional Chinese culture. This is the reason why more and more young people don't like Chinese Opera. There is little person knows well about the Chinese Opera even doesn't like to watch. It is a limitation of them to have opportunities to get close to the performance. They think the traditional opera is reflecting the life of an-cient that is far from them, so that Chinese Opera is considered difficult to compre-hend [10].

3.3   The Plays of Monky King

The titles of the Chinese Opera are more than 5800 kinds [17]. There are more than 300 episodes performed many times and got a high volume of audiences. For exam-ple, "Jiang Xiang He", "Yu Zhou Feng", "Zhui Han Xin", "Ba Wang Bie Ji", "Gu Cheng Hui" and so on [18]. The story in Chinese Opera are normally from the classic novels. There are 36 episodes derived from the famous Chinese classic novel "Jour-ney to the west" in Ming Dynasty. Sun Wukong also known as the Monkey King that is a main character around the world. Chinese like him due to his manhood and bravery. In the Chinese Opera, the performer make-up as a monkey and dazzles the audiences with agile movements. It is the glory days of the Monkey King's perfor-mance during 1937 to 1942, and people call it "play of the Monkey King" instead of "play of Journey to the west".

With the development of computer technology and means of communication, as well as improvement of the economic, internationalization and globalization are accelerating further from the end of the 20th century. Especially China has abundant culture resources and wide market, the speed to the globalization is very fast. Chinese also try hard to the revitalize of the culture contents. In the following part of the paper, I will give an example of the play: The Monkey King's "Havoc in Heaven" in Fig. 6 is a performance which using the projection mapping technique. The original play of the Monkey King is needed audience to imagine the story and the space of heaven, but the performers here use brilliant graphics and varieties of spaces to give the audiences. In addition, they make virtual characters to fight with the Monkey King, which enhances the braveness of the main character. The content is very suitable for the digital media performance. No translation is needed, and people who don't have any background in Chinese opera can also easily experience the performance.

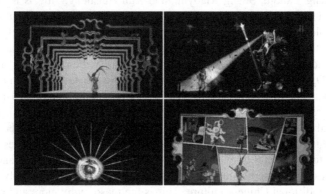

Fig. 6. Digital media performance "Havoc in Heaven" [19]

4   An Experience-Based Chinese Opera "Havoc the Dragon Palace"

4.1   The Production of the "Havoc the Dragon Palace"

The story of "Havoc the Dragon Palace" is the first havoc of the Monkey King. There are three times havocs in the novel, and the location is mainly under the sea, so it is different with the "Havoc in Heaven". After Monkey King has finished the magical and martial skills learning and returned to the Huaguo Mountain where he gathered fellows and proclaimed himself as the king. He visited the Dragon Palace under the East Sea to ask for a weapon from Dragon king. He inadvertently discovered the "Ocean-Pacifying Needle" (Golden Cudgel), a treasure of the Dragon Palace. He asked the Dragon King to present it to him as a gift, but the Dragon King refused. So Monkey King Havoc the Dragon Palace. In the end, the Monkey King got the treasure and he desired and returned to the Huaguo Mountain. For using in the experience-based Chinese Opera, there is a need adaption of the story in Table 1.

Table 1. Story table

Introduction
Monkey King visited the Dragon Palace and asked for a weapon from Dragon king
Development
Monkey King inadvertently discovered the "Ocean-Pacifying Needle".
Turn
The Dragon King refused to gift it. So Monkey King Havoc the Dragon Palace.
Conclusion
The Monkey King got the treasure and went a ceremony of victory.

There are three main characters: Monkey King, Dragon King and Conductor in this work (Fig. 7). The Monkey King can do martial arts and know 72 transformations, he is also the symbol of passion, freedom, braveness, optimism and luckiness. He takes pheasant tail crown on head, and his face is painted in red and white. The color of his eyes is yellow because he ate a bolus before. He performs Sheng and his costumes use warm colors which combines the red and the yellow, the purpose of giving audiences an impression of justice. The Dragon King is a dignity but brutal, hypocritical and stubborn character. He act as Jing and use the black and white as the main color of his Lianpu, two arms and lower body of his costume are decorated using smoke tails of dragon. Conductor is a 2D shadow with golden line who guides audiences what to do next. He induces the gestures to people when needed and disappears after work. If the performer deletes the animation part of the Conductor, the content would be used in a real performance of the Chinese Opera.

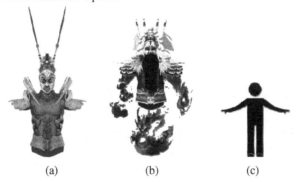

(a)   (b)   (c)

Fig. 7. (a) The 3D Monkey King. (b) The 3D Dragon King. (c) The 2D Conductor

Chinese Shadow play is known as a similar traditional performance with Chinese Opera, except the fact that they use the puppets to play. It is possible to show anytime and anywhere only if the environment is dark. Audiences can experience the puppetry freely after the show. I believe the experience-based content is designed for removability and convenience, so the audiences go approach easily. It seems to watch animation during the experience time and the visual contents are as below (Fig. 8).

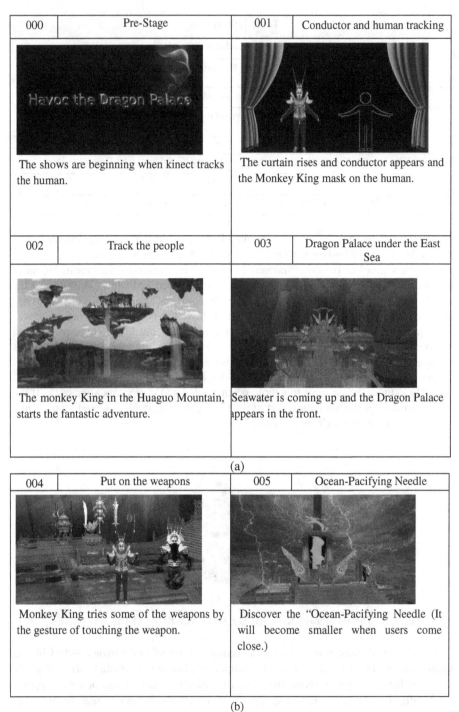

000	Pre-Stage	001	Conductor and human tracking

The shows are beginning when kinect tracks the human.

The curtain rises and conductor appears and the Monkey King mask on the human.

002	Track the people	003	Dragon Palace under the East Sea

The monkey King in the Huaguo Mountain, starts the fantastic adventure.

Seawater is coming up and the Dragon Palace appears in the front.

(a)

004	Put on the weapons	005	Ocean-Pacifying Needle

Monkey King tries some of the weapons by the gesture of touching the weapon.

Discover the "Ocean-Pacifying Needle (It will become smaller when users come close.)

(b)

Fig. 8. (a) Introduction. (b) Development. (c) Turn. (d) Conclusion

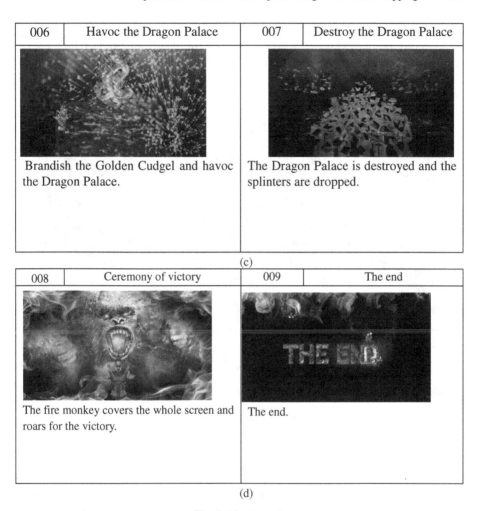

006	Havoc the Dragon Palace	007	Destroy the Dragon Palace
Brandish the Golden Cudgel and havoc the Dragon Palace.		The Dragon Palace is destroyed and the splinters are dropped.	

(c)

008	Ceremony of victory	009	The end
The fire monkey covers the whole screen and roars for the victory.		The end.	

(d)

Fig. 8. (*Continued*)

4.2   The Realization

There are 1 PC, 1 projector, 1 kinect and speakers used in the exhibition. "Havoc the Dragon Palace" is divided two parts, the visual production and image processing. The visual production part includes background images and two characters of the Dragon King and Conductor. Nobody likes to be a supporting role and wants to be a loser, so the Dragon King is produced in the background. The Monkey King masking on the audience is included in the image processing. For normal behaviors of modeling data, Monkey King just make upper body, the other part of body show real people which casts in the RGB camera. Actually, Monkey King wears dragon robe in the Chinese Opera, I design armor for the fantastic and fashionable. Besides, Monkey King chooses weapons in the Dragon Palace by the gesture of touch the weapon, the "Ocean-Pacifying Needle" becomes smaller when users come close, the particle effects come out when brandish the Golden Cudgel, Dragon Palace is destroyed and the splinters are dropped on the Monkey King's body, all of them are produced in image processing. The Monkey King transforms to various things and himself, it is logical that several audiences experience at the same time. The following images in Fig. 9 are photos of real shot.

Fig. 9. Real shot of the exhibition

5   Conclusion

This paper has interest that communication between audiences and the cultural assets, increasing the awareness of the intimate but unfamiliar Chinese Opera to people. The result of the experience is that the interactive video mapping system demarcates the subject and the object of arts to suggest the future of the digital media contents. This content make a strong satisfaction of people to appreciate and experience at the same time, visual contents also are focused on storytelling, not the list of graphic, it absolutely differentiated from the one off the experiential contents.

The media art content can easily depend on the technology so that ignore the artistic creativity. It is a suggestion that select traditional materials which have the value of the story to overcome the limitation of areas and ages to create successful contents. The method of developing a better content is to find cherished stories inside the culture then reconstruct the sources combination with the new technology. Also an experienced-based content must be delivered via experience such as a real-time interactive projection mapping. Many culture contents end in failure because their standard of culture and specialized knowledge are superficial.

The experience-based Chinese Opera explored the possibility of one of the Chinese traditional cultures to promote the value of the Chinese Opera to help for understanding and increasing the affinity. After experience, I hope to have a chance to perform with a real performer and audiences will get familiar with the Chinese Opera and get followers in the worldwide. Besides, sincerely hope this work is able to recognize by the world as an artistry culture contents. Furthermore, the communication between culture assets and the public by exploring the possibility of the sustainability that generate the potential of this content, which expend the scope of the study.

Acknowledgement. This research was supported by Basic Science Research Program through the National Research Foundation of Korea (NRF) funded by the Ministry of Education, Science and Technology (2010-0023438).

References

1. Eungyung, O.: New Media Art. Yonsei University Publishing House, Soul (2008)
2. Wikipedia, http://en.wikipedia.org/wiki/Projection_mapping
3. Kim, M.: A study on space and object expression using projection mapping, Riss Trans. Master these, Video Contents, p. 5 (2011)
4. Wikipedia, http://en.wikipedia.org/wiki/Kinect
5. The seattlepi, http://blog.seattlepi.com/digitaljoystick/2009/06/01/e3-2009-microsoft at e3 several-metric-tons-of-press-releaseapalloza/
6. Yoon, K.: Research on interactive multimedia productions with Kinect, Riss Trans. Master these, Multimedia Design. p. 32 (2012)
7. Interactive installations, environments and R&D, http://design-io.com/projects/PuppetParadeCinekid/
8. Zhang, G.: The contemporary Chinese Opera. Theatre in China, Beijing (2010)
9. Wichmann, E.: Tradition and Innovation in Contemporary Beijing Opera Performance. The MIT Press, Cambridge (1990)
10. Xu, C.: Peking Opera. Cambridge University Press, Cambridge (2012)
11. Elliott, M.C.: Emperor Qianlong: Son of Heaven, Man of the World. Longman Publishing Group, Beijing (2009)
12. Goldstein, J.S.: International Relations. Longman Publishing Group, Beijing (2003)
13. Ni Picture of China, http://www.nipic.com
14. Wikipedia, http://en.wikipedia.org/wiki/Peking_opera#cite_note-13
15. Travel China Guide, http://www.travelchinaguide.com/intro/arts/beijing_opera/
16. Hu, Q.: Encyclopedia of China. Encyclopedia of China Publishing House, Beijing (1993)
17. The art of Beijing Opera, http://www.jingju.com/zhishi/index.html
18. Zhang, X., Sheng, X.: The Art of Beijing Opera facial makeup. World Publishing Cooperation, Beijing (2002)
19. Vimeo, https://vimeo.com/43467406

Serious Games:
Customizing the Audio-Visual Interface

Bill Kapralos, Robert Shewaga, and Gary Ng

Faculty of Business and Information Technology,
University of Ontario Institute of Technology,
Oshawa, Ontario, Canada L1H 7K4
bill.kapralos@uoit.ca

Abstract. Serious games are gaining in popularity within a wide range
of educational and training applications given their ability to engage
and motivate learners in the educational process. Recent hardware and
computational advancements are providing developers the opportunity
to develop applications that employ a high level of fidelity (realism)
and novel interaction techniques. However, despite these great advances
in hardware and computational power, real-time high fidelity rendering
of complex virtual environments (found in many serious games) across
all modalities is still not feasible. Perceptual-based rendering exploits
various aspects of the multi-modal perceptual system to reduce computational requirements without any resulting perceptual effects on the
resulting scene. A series of human-based experiments demonstrated a
potentially strong effect of sound on visual fidelity perception, and task
performance. However, the resulting effects were subjective whereby the
influence of sound was dependent on various individual factors including
musical listening preferences. This suggests the importance of customizing (individualizing) a serious game's virtual environment with respect
to audio-visual fidelity, background sounds, etc. In this paper details regarding this series of audio-visual experiments will be provided followed
by a description of current work that is examining the customization of
a serious game's virtual environment by each user through the use of a
game-based calibration method.

Keywords: Serious games, virtual simulation, audio-visual interaction,
audio-visual fidelity, calibration.

1 Introduction

The use of serious games within a wide range of educational and training applications, from military, health professions education, patient education, and
business/corporate, amongst others, is becoming widespread particularly given
the ubiquity of video game play by the current tech-savvy generation of learners.
Recent hardware and computational advancements are providing designers and
developers of serious games the opportunity to develop applications that employ

R. Shumaker and S. Lackey (Eds.): VAMR 2014, Part II, LNCS 8526, pp. 190–199, 2014.
© Springer International Publishing Switzerland 2014

a high level of fidelity/realism and novel interaction techniques using off-the-shelf consumer level hardware and devices. Devices such as the Microsoft Kinect motion sensing vision-based sensor allows users to interact with their application using a natural user interface that employs gestures thus eliminating the game controller and the typically non-natural and potentially limiting interaction it affords. For example, using the Kinect within a virtual operating room, surgery trainees are able to perform their required tasks in a more intuitive manner that is better representative of the real world (see [1]).

With respect to a simulation (including serious games), fidelity denotes the extent to which the appearance and/or the behavior of the simulation matches the appearance and behavior of the real system [2]. Despite the great computing hardware and computational advances we have experienced, real-time high fidelity rendering of complex environments (found in many serious games) across all modalities is still not feasible [3]. Designers and developers of serious games, and virtual simulations in general, typically strive for high fidelity environments, particularly with respect to the visual (graphical) scene. However, evidence suggests high fidelity simulation does not always lead to greater learning [4]), and striving for high fidelity can burden our computational resources (particularly when the simulation is intended to be used on portable computing devices), increase the probability of lag and subsequent discomfort and simulator sickness [5], and lead to increased development costs. Previous work has examined the perceptual aspects of multi-modal effects (including audio-visual), and numerous studies have demonstrated that multi-modal effects can be considerable, to the extent that large amounts of detail of one sense may be ignored in the presence of other sensory inputs. Perceptual-based rendering, whereby the rendering parameters are adjusted based on the perceptual system (typically vision), is often employed to limit computational processing. For example, it has been shown that sound can potentially attract part of the user's attention away from the visual stimuli and lead to a reduced cognitive processing of the visual cues [6]. Therefore, if the enhancement of visuals within a virtual environment is economically or technically limited, one may consider increasing the quality of the audio channels instead [7].

Motivated by these studies and the general lack of emphasis on audition in virtual environments and games (where historically the emphasis has been placed on the visual scene [8]), we have begun investigating multi-modal (audio-visual) interactions within virtual environments (serious games, virtual simulations, and games). So far, a series of experiments that examined the direct effect of sound on engagement, the perception of visual fidelity (the degree to which visual features in the virtual environment conform to visual features in the real environment [9]), and task performance (the time required to complete a task within a virtual environment), of both static and dynamic 3D rendered (virtual) scenes in both stereoscopic 3D (S3D) and non-S3D viewing were conducted. Although this series of experiments have shown a strong influence of sound on visual fidelity, engagement, and task performance, results have also shown strong subjective effects whereby the influence of sound is dependent on various individual factors including musical listening preferences. This suggests the importance of individualizing (customizing) audio-visual fidelity, and the sounds employed within a virtual environment to take advantage of perceptual-based rendering. Building upon the results of these experiments, we are examining the customization of the serious game's virtual environment to each user via a novel game-based calibration technique that will allow users to customize the virtual environment before they begin using the serious game. The calibration process will be used to tailor the settings of various simulation parameters including S3D settings (interaxial settings), audio and visual fidelity, background sounds/sound effects, spatial sound settings (choosing head-related transfer functions from a pre-defined set, etc.), amongst others, to each user's preferences. Such customization provides the opportunity to increase user engagement and ultimately learning.

1.1 Paper Organization

The remainder of this paper is organized as follows. In Section 2 a brief discussion of previous work (with an emphasis on the series of our own previously conducted experiments), is provided. Details regarding the calibration game are provided in Section 3 while a discussion, concluding remarks, and plans for future research are provided in Section 4.

2 Background

Various studies have examined the perceptual aspects of audio-visual cue interaction, and it has been shown that the perception of visual fidelity can affect the perception of sound quality and vice versa [10]. For example, Mastoropoulou et al. [6] examined the influence of sound effects on the perception of motion smoothness within an animation and more specifically, on the perception of frame-rate, and infer that sound can attract part of the viewer's attention away from any visual defects inherent in low frame-rates [6]. Similarly, Hulusic et al. [11] showed that sound effects allowed slow animations to be perceived as smoother than fast animations and that the addition of footstep sound effects to walking (visual) animations increased the animation smoothness perception. Bonneel et al. [12] examined the influence of the level of detail of auditory and visual stimuli on the perception of audio-visual material rendering quality and observed that the visual level of detail was perceived to be higher as the auditory level of detail was increased. Although there are various other relevant studies, for the remainder of this section, emphasis will be placed on our own previous work that has examined visual fidelity perception in the presence of various auditory conditions. Greater details regarding the influence of sound over visual rendering and task performance is provided by Hulusic et al. [3] while an overview of "crossmodal influences on visual perception" is provided by Shams and Kim [13].

Our studies began with simple static environments that consisted of a single 2D image of a surgeon's head (a rendered 3D model). In the first study, visual fidelity was defined with respect to the 3D model's polygon count [14] while in the second study, polygon count was kept constant and visual fidelity was defined with respect to the 3D model's texture resolution [15]. A sample of the visual stimuli is provided in Fig. 1 where three renderings of the surgeon's head, each one with a constant polygon count but differing with respect to texture resolution, are shown. In both studies, participants were presented with the static visual (a total of six visuals were considered, each differing with respect to polygon count or texture resolution depending on the experiment), in conjunction with one of four auditory conditions: i) no sound at all (silence), ii) white noise, iii) classical music (Mozart), and iv) heavy metal music (Megadeth). For each of the visuals, their task was to rate its fidelity on a scale from 1 to 7. With respect to polygon count, visual fidelity perception increased in the presence of classical music, particularly when considering images corresponding to higher polygon count. When considering texture resolution, sound consisting of white noise had very specific and detrimental effects on the perception of the quality of high-resolution images (i.e., the perception of visual quality of high fidelity visuals decreased in the presence of white noise). In contrast to the study that considered polygon count, sound consisting of music (classical or heavy metal) did not have any effect on the perception of visual quality when visual quality was defined with respect to texture resolution.

Fig. 1. Sample of the visual stimuli used in a previous experiment that examined the effect of sound visual fidelity perception [15]. Here, each model of the surgeon's head contained the same polygon count but the texture resolution differed.

These two experiments were repeated but now the visuals were presented in stereoscopic 3D [16]. When visual fidelity was defined with respect to polygon count, "classical music" led to an increase in visual fidelity perception while "white noise" had an attenuating effect on the perception of visual fidelity. However, both of these effects were evident for only the visual models whose polygon count was greater than 678 (i.e., auditory condition had no effect on the two smallest polygon count models), indicating that there is a polygon count threshold after which the visual distinction is not great enough to be negatively influenced by white noise. With visual fidelity defined with respect to texture resolution, both "classical music" and "heavy metal music" led to an increase in visual fidelity perception while "white noise" led to a decrease in visual fidelity perception.

Although the results of these four studies show that sound can affect our perception of visual fidelity, it is not known if this influence of sound is affected by the introduction of contextually specific sounds. The auditory conditions considered in our previous studies have been completely disjoint from the visuals. That is, there was no (direct) relationship between the auditory and visual cues (they were non-contextual). Two experiments were thus conducted to examine visual fidelity perception, defined with respect to texture resolution, in the presence of contextual sounds, that is, sounds that had a causal relationship to the visual cues [16, 17]. The visual stimuli consisted of six images of a surgeon holding a surgical drill, against a black background (similar to the visuals employed in the previous experiment shown in Fig. 1 but with the addition of the surgeon's upper body). The polygon count of the 3D model was kept constant but as with the previous experiment, the texture resolution of the surgeon and the drill was varied. The auditory conditions included the four non-contextual auditory conditions considered in the previous experiments in addition to the following three contextual sounds: i) operating room ambiance which included machines beeping, doctors and nurses talking, ii) drill sound, and iii) hospital operating room ambiance coupled (mixed) with the drill sound. The visuals remained static in both experiments but in the second experiment, stereoscopic 3D viewing was employed. With non-S3D viewing, results suggest that contextual auditory cues increase the perception of visual fidelity while non-contextual cues in the form of white noise leads to a decrease in visual fidelity perception particularly when considering the lower fidelity visuals [17]. However, the increase in visual fidelity perception was observed for only two of the three contextual auditory conditions and more specifically, for the operating room ambiance, and operating room ambiance + drill auditory conditions and not for the drill auditory condition despite the fact that the surgeon within the visual scene was holding a surgical drill. With respect to S3D viewing, "white noise" led to a decrease in visual fidelity perception across all of the visuals considered. However, none of the auditory conditions led to a statistically significant increase in visual fidelity perception [16]. That being said, none of the participants were surgeons or medical practitioners and may not have been familiar with an operating room and the sounds contained within an operating room. The notion of contextual auditory cues may also be subjective and may depend on prior experience and musical listening preferences.

The experiments described so far considered static visual environments where the visual scene (the 3D models presented to the participants), remained static. Two additional experiments were conducted to examine the effect of sound on visual fidelity perception, and task performance in dynamic virtual environments were the participants had to interact with the environment while completing a simple task. In both experiments, participants were presented with a virtual operating room and their task was to navigate through the virtual operating room from their starting position to a point in the room which contained a tray with surgical instruments (see Fig. 2). Once they reached the tray, they were required to pick up a surgical drill (they had to navigate around a bed and a non-player character nurse to reach the tray that contained the surgical instruments). In one of the experiments, visual fidelity was defined with respect to the level of (consistent) blurring of the entire screen (level of blurring of the scene was used to approximate varying texture resolution), and the auditory cues consisted of the three contextual cues considered in the previous experiments in addition to white-noise and no sound. Sound (contextual and non-contextual), did not influence the perception of visual fidelity irrespective of the level of blurring. However, sound did impact task performance (defined as the time to required to complete the task). More specifically, white noise led to a large decrease in performance (increase in task completion time) while contextual sound improved performance (decrease in task performance time), across all levels of visual fidelity considered. In the second experiment [18], visual cues consisted of: i) original (no effect), ii) cel-shading with three levels (i.e., color is divided into three discrete levels), and iii) cel-shading with six levels (i.e., color is divided into six discrete levels). The contextual auditory conditions consisted of: i) no sound (visuals only), ii) monaural (non-spatial) surgical drill sound, and iii) spatialized surgical drill sound. In contrast to the last study, in this experiment, spatial sound (acoustical occlusion and reverberation) was considered. Contrary to our previous work, the presence of sound (spatial and non-spatial) did not have any effect on either visual fidelity perception or task completion time. That being said, only six participants took part in the experiment (in contrast to 18 for each of our previous experiments), thus the results are preliminary.

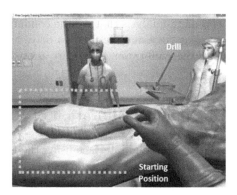

Fig. 2. View of the virtual operating room environment used in two previous experiments [18, 19]. The task of each participant was to navigate the environment from the starting position to the position of the surgical drill and then "choose" the drill.

2.1   Summary of Our Experimental Results

A total of eight experiments were conducted that examined the effect of sound on visual fidelity perception under a variety of conditions including static and dynamic environments, and stereoscopic 3D viewing. Results varied significantly across each of the experiments making it difficult to reach any firm consensus.

However, it is clear that white noise generally led to a decrease in the perception of visual fidelity and task performance, classical music led to an increase in visual fidelity perception (the majority of the time), and that the influence of sound on visual fidelity perception is very subjective. The visuals and many of the sounds considered in these experiments were medical in nature (e.g., surgeon, operating room, operating room ambiance sounds, drill sounds), yet many of the participants were students and although some were enrolled in Health Sciences-related programs, they had limited (if any), operating room exposure.

We hypothesize that the variation seen across the results of these experiments is due to subjective factors. Prior to the start of each experiment, participants were asked to complete a brief questionnaire regarding their video game play habits and game and musical preferences. A detailed analysis of the questionnaire that will examine whether any correlations exist between game/musical preferences and the experimental results is currently underway to confirm our hypothesis. However, informally, there does appear to be a relationship between musical genre preference and the influence of music on visual fidelity perception.

The variation observed across the results of all experiments and the potential consequences this variation may have on perceptual-based rendering and ultimately learning when considering serious games, motivated our work in the customization of audio-visual fidelity through a user-calibration method. This involves the use of a brief questionnaire that users complete prior to beginning the serious game followed by an interactive "calibration game" whereby the optimal audio-visual fidelity settings are determined dynamically by the player in the process of playing a game. How the questionnaire responses will be used will depend on the results of a meta-analysis that will be conducted on the results of our previous experiments but they may be used to drive the calibration game. Greater details regarding the calibration game are provided in the following section.

3   The Calibration Game: Calibration of Visual Fidelity

Although customizing the audio-visual interface using the results of a questionnaire presented to each user that may include visuals and audio clips, here, customization of the audio-visual interface is accomplished using a simple game-based approach, making the process interactive and far more engaging. Our approach is inspired by standard testing methodologies employed by optometrists to determine the optimum properties of corrective lenses in order to overcome a variety of visual deficiencies [20].

The calibration game presents the user with a split screen with the same game running in each window but under different fidelity/realism settings (see Fig. 3 for an example), with a single background sound. The player chooses the screen they prefer by clicking a button just above the corresponding window. Their choice will be registered and the audio-visual fidelity of the game running in the other window will change (increase or decrease). This process will be repeated over a number of cycles (the total number of cycles can be easily modified), until

Window selection buttons

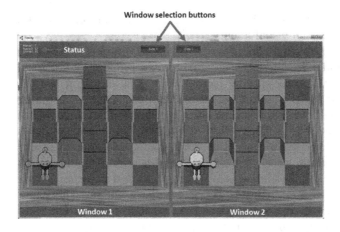

Fig. 3. Visual calibration game sample. Two versions of a game running in each window, each differing with respect to visual fidelity. The user then chooses which they prefer using one of the two selection buttons.

the optimal fidelity level is reached. Currently, the game used is a Bomberman strategic, maze-based video game where the player completes levels of the game by strategically placing bombs in order to kill enemies and destroy obstacles. The game is controlled using the 'W', 'A', 'S', 'D' keys to move the character (bomber), and bombs are placed by pressing the space bar. Both windows represent the same game-play (i.e., any actions to move the character or place a bomb will happen simultaneously in both windows). The calibration game was implemented using the Unity Game Engine and currently fidelity is defined by levels of cel-shading performed dynamically using a Unity shader. Although formal testing will follow, an informal test conducted with three participants revealed that the calibration game is easy to use and fun/enjoyable.

4 Discussion and Concluding Remarks

Prior work has demonstrated that the influence of sound on the perception of visual fidelity, and task performance within a virtual environment is complex and subjective, depending on a user's prior experience, and musical preference. However, this is rarely exploited as the vast majority of serious games take a "one-size-fits-all" approach with respect to audio-visual fidelity and the choice of background sounds and sound effects. Here, preliminary details of a novel "calibration game" being developed to custom-tailor the fidelity of the visuals within a serious game were provided. The game itself was inspired by standard optometrist testing and prior work that used a similar approach to determine the optimal interaxial distance of a stereoscopic S3D game and found the method to be effective [21]. Currently, fidelity was defined with respect to cel-shading implemented using the Unity Game Engine; this was done as a proof-of-concept to demonstrate the feasibility of such an approach and future work will examine other definitions of visual fidelity.

The work presented here is part of a larger initiative whose goal is to develop a greater understanding of visual fidelity, multi-modal interactions, perceptual-based rendering, user-specific factors, and their effect on learning. Although greater work remains, providing users the opportunity to customize the virtual environment of their serious game prior to using it will ultimately help us develop more effective serious games. Future work will see continued development and refinement of the calibration game. This will include experimenting with various other games aside from what was included here and conducting further experiments that examine audio-visual interactions and perceptual-based rendering. Furthermore, a meta analysis on the results of our previous experiments that examined audio visual interactions (in addition to any subsequent experiments that will follow), will be conducted to identify any patterns or relationships among the study results and determine the most favorable fidelity settings that can be included in the calibration game. Future work will also further develop the calibration game to allow for additional definitions of visual fidelity, including polygon count and texture resolution, followed by a usability study to examine the effectiveness of the calibration game.

Acknowledgments. The financial support of the *Social Sciences and Humanities Research Council of Canada* (SSHRC), in support of the *Interactive and Multi-Modal Experience Research Syndicate* (IMMERSe) project, and the *Canadian Network of Centres of Excellence* (NCE) in support of the *Graphics, Animation, and New Media* (GRAND) initiative is gratefully acknowledged.

References

[1] Robison, R.A., Liu, C.Y., Apuzzo, M.L.J.: Man, mind, and machine: The past and future of virtual reality simulation in neurologic surgery. World Nuerosurgery 76(5), 419–430 (2011)

[2] Farmer, E., von Rooij, J., Riemersma, J., Joma, P., Morall, J.: Handbook of simulator based training. Ashgate Publishing Limited, Surrey (1999)

[3] Hulusic, V., Harvey, C., Debattista, K., Tsingos, N., Walker, S., Howard, D., Chalmers, A.: Acoustic rendering and auditory-visual cross-modal perception and interaction. Computer Graphics Forum 31(1), 102–131 (2012)

[4] Norman, G., Dore, K., Grierson, L.: The minimal relationship between simulation fidelity and transfer of learning. Medical Education 46(7), 636–647 (2012)

[5] Blascovich, J., Bailenson, J.: Infinite Reality. Harper Collins, New York (2011)

[6] Mastoropoulou, G., Debattista, K., Chalmers, A., Troscianco, T.: The influence of sound effects on the perceived smoothness of rendered animations. In: Proceedings of the Symposium on Applied Perception in Graphics and Visualization 2005, La Coruna, Spain, August 26-28, pp. 9–15 (2005)

[7] Larsson, P., Vstjll, D., Kleiner, M.: On the quality of experience: A multi-modal approach to perceptual ego-motion and sensed presence in virtual environments. In: Proceedings of the First International Speech Communications Association Tutorial and Research Workshop on Auditory Quality of Systems, Akademie Mont-Cenis, Germany (2003)

[8] Carlile, S.: Virtual auditory space: Generation and application. R. G. Landes, Austin TX (1996)

[9] Mania, K., Wooldridge, D., Coxon, M., Robinson, A.: The effect of visual and interaction fidelity on spatial cognition in immersive virtual environments? IEEE Transactions on Visualization and Computer Graphics 12(3), 396–404 (2006)

[10] Storms, S.L., Zyda, M.J.: Interactions in perceived quality of auditory-visual displays. Presence: Teleoperators and Virtual Environments 9(6), 557–580 (2000)

[11] Hulusic, V., Debattista, K., Aggarwal, V., Chalmers, A.: Maintaining frame rate perception in interactive environments by exploiting audio-visual cross-modal interaction. The Visual Computer 27(1), 57–66 (2011)

[12] Bonneel, N., Suied, C., Viaud-Delmon, I., Drettakis, G.: Bimodal perception of audio-visual material properties for virtual environments. ACM Transactions on Applied Perception 7(1), 1–16 (2010)

[13] Shams, L., Kim, R.: Crossmodal influences on visual perception. Physics of Life Reviews 7(3), 295–298 (2010)

[14] Rojas, D., Kapralos, B., Cristancho, S., Collins, K., Conati, C., Dubrowski, A.: The effect of background sound on visual fidelity perception. In: Proceedings of ACM Audio Mostly 2011 (Extended Abstracts), Coimbra, Portugal, September 7-9, pp. 1–7 (2011)

[15] Rojas, D., Kapralos, B., Cristancho, S., Collins, K., Hogue, A., Conati, C., Dubrowski, A.: Developing effective serious games: The effect of background sound on visual fidelity perception with varying texture resolution. Studies in Health Technology and Informatics 173, 386–392 (2013)

[16] Rojas, D., Kapralos, B., Hogue, A., Collins, K., Nacke, L., Cristancho, S., Conati, C., Dubrowski, A.: The effect of sound on visual fidelity perception in stereoscopic 3-d. IEEE Transactions on System Man and Cybernetics Part B 43(6), 1572–1583 (2013)

[17] Rojas, D., Kapralos, B., Collins, K., Dubrowski, A.: The effect of contextual sound cues on visual fidelity perception. Studies in Health Technology and Informatics (to appear, 2014)

[18] Cowan, B., Rojas, D., Kapralos, B., Collins, K., Dubrowski, A.: Spatial sound and its effect on visual quality perception and task performance within a virtual environment. In: Proceedings of the 21st International Congress on Acoustics, Montreal, Canada, June 2-7, pp. 1–7 (2013)

[19] Kapralos, B., Moussa, F., Dubrowski, A.: An overview of virtual simulations and serious games for surgical education and training. In: Brooks, A.L., Braham, S., Jain, L.C. (eds.) Technologies of Inclusive Well-Being. SCI, vol. 536, pp. 289–306. Springer, Heidelberg (2014)

[20] Kerr, D.S.: The refractor/phoropter an important tool in vision correction (December 7, 2010), http://dougkerr.net/pumpkin/articles/Refractor.pdf

[21] Tawadrous, M., Hogue, A., Kapralos, B., Collins, K.: An interactive in-game approach to user adjustment of stereoscopic 3D settings. In: Proceedings of Stereoscopic Displays and Applications XXIV, San Francisco, CA, USA, February 3-7, pp. 1–7 (2007)

Designing AR Game Enhancing Interactivity between Virtual Objects and Hand for Overcoming Space Limit

Kyungyeon Moon, Jonghee Sang, and Woontack Woo

KAIST Graduate school of Culture Technology, Daejeon 305-701, S. Korea
{moonjeje,jhsang21,wwoo}@kaist.ac.kr

Abstract. We propose real-time interactive game that is based on Augmented Reality (AR). It is composed of AR marker, Head Mounted Display and depth camera. By using marker, the proposed system augments game space, fishing place. And player can interact virtual game object such as bait or fish with bare hands based on computer vision. The rapid development of AR technologies has raised profound interests in the design of AR games, but the existing games have not provided realistically felt game environments because the way to play games remains the same when the platform is changed. In addition, studies in this field did not fully utilize AR technologies, so that inherent characteristics of AR game do not impact user experience and draw attention explicitly on design concepts. Our system gives the experience that is grasping the virtual objects. Also, it can be applied to various game contents that are actually felt as real.

Keywords: entertainment, augmented reality, 3D interaction, HMD, hand-tracking.

1 Introduction

1.1 Background

User interface design environment has been known to be a part of significant elements in game system.[1] Nowadays, traditional game interfaces such as joysticks, mouse and keyboards are shrinking every year[2] and game system starts to build AR based-interface.[3] These new streams of game interface design have brought some changes which are spatial transformation. For example, people can play the game while they are walking. And game environments escape from 2D into 3D. It means that game space expands out of monitors. Also, players expect to get a new experience they cannot get from other existing or similar form of games.[4]

1.2 Problem-Posing

With respect to players' demand, game console makers have made effort to mix the reality and virtual reality. So Nintendo 'Wii', Sony 'Move' and Microsoft 'Kinect' are developed.[5] Developed AR games were based on motion recognition technologies.[6]

R. Shumaker and S. Lackey (Eds.): VAMR 2014, Part II, LNCS 8526, pp. 200–209, 2014.

However, there are some problems. First, these devices can recognize big motions like dancing or boxing. Thus, in small residential space or public place such as apartment and café, people have trouble with using it. Also, people who are wearing heavy clothes or skirts that hide body parts cannot use it because the devices cannot recognize gamers.[7] Therefore, small motion or elaborate control has difficulty handling the system embedded in these devices. Third problem is game controllers. Existing system needs to have traditional game controllers, which means that if people sit far from game devices, they cannot play with it. In addition, if users want to play tennis or guitar game, they should buy tennis racket controller or guitar controller that is suitable for specific device.[8] Finally, gamers cannot interact with game objects in 3D space. The game objects remain to be still locked in the monitor.

1.3   System Overview

Our system provides players with distinguished experience that users can get into game space. We made fishing game and developed all the components needed to play the game in AR.   A player can fish by virtual baits and virtual hook that are controlled by player's hands and motion.[9] It means that they can touch and interact with augmented objects using bare hands. Fig.1 shows the game space which is built by our system.

Fig. 1. Scene of our system, AR fishing game scene that user saw through a HMD. We developed the game environment and all objects by Unity.

2   System Design

2.1   Game Scenario

Fishing in real world is an outdoor activity. For giving users realistic-looking fishing place, we made game space in 3D not 2D which is shown as Fig.1. If users have

HMD and the marker, they can face the virtual fishing place anywhere. Fig.2 shows summary of the system scenario.

We replicated similar interactions, which existed in real fishing techniques. These interactions are controlling the system. For example, the motion of harpooning is used to catch fish in our system. There are some techniques for catching fish; hand gathering, spearing, netting, angling and trapping. Among these techniques, we focused on implementing spear fishing, which is an ancient method of fishing that has been used throughout the world. So, it is intuitive for playing and user can catch how to play more quickly.[10]

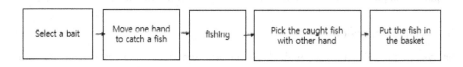

Fig. 2. The game scenario. These steps progress with a user wearing a HMD.

2.2   Game Flow

As we designed the following interactions, our system aims to provide a user with immersion. (a) When user sees the marker, the game space that is virtual fishing hole is augmented on real space. And then (b) user opens his/her palm in front of HMD, system is ready to start the AR fishing game. After that, fishing tool like rod or spear is also augmented at user's fingertip. According to [11], it is possible to recognize hand tracking in real time. So, (c) user can catch fish directly with bare hands where the virtual fishing tool hung, and put it in the basket.

We put some entertaining and sport fishing elements. For pleasure and competition, we add recreational element, which is a time limit. Player should catch fish as many as possible within limited time.

Fig. 3(a). See the marker through HMD. Left is the scene of seeing the marker. Right is the scene of game space. All objects were augmented.

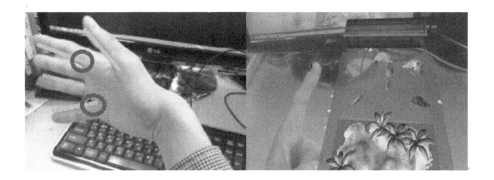

Fig. 3(b). Recognize the hands. The camera recognizes the position of tip of fingers.

Fig. 3(c). Play the game. User can play the system anywhere.

3   Implementation

3.1   Hardware

Our augmented reality system is based on a window7. We required RGB-D camera and HMD. HMD is Accupix Mybud with 852 × 480 pixel high resolution in each eye and a horizontal field of view of approximately 35° and Intel creative gesture camera as RGB-D camera which is 1280 × 720 pixel high resolution and depth resolution is QVGA(320 × 240). The software was written in a C# using Vuforia SDK in Unity3D.

3.2   Flow of System

The proposed system is divided into four procedures, capturing RGB-D image, setting the environment, hand gesture recognition, and rendering as seen from Fig.4.

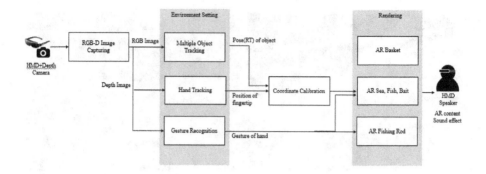

Fig. 4. System Flow chart

3.3   Interaction Techniques

Targeting. Vuforia supports sophisticated algorithms to detect and track the features. Vuforia SDK recognizes the image target by comparing these natural features against a known target resource database.[12] When the image is detected, the environment of the simulation is appeared onto the image.

The overall pattern of data flow within the software is shown in Fig.4. Recall that Intel creative gesture camera as RGB-D camera. From the data from RGB-D camera, we can exploit various kinds of interaction.[13] First, we can use the image targeting to create a coordinate frame for the image, and then we make the fish environment for the user. Second, we can use the hand tracking data to create a coordinate frame for the hand, and track the hand point direction. We can orient both of these coordinate frame in to the same sense(Y is up, X to the right, -Z in to the screen or away from the user and roll is rotation around Z, pitch around X, yaw around Y).

Tracking. The hand is recognized through camera. The user can move freely inside the interaction area in front of the Creative Interactive Gesture Camera. The tracking itself is accomplished by one camera system attached on the HMD. The visualizations is based on the camera system and rendered in HD quality on a HMD. The following paragraphs explain the components:

Tracking of the hand was only needed for viewpoint. We selected a pragmatic and inexpensive solution with a Creative Interactive Gesture Camera that detects the nearest hand in front of camera. The viewpoint (the virtual camera in the 3D world) is moved accordingly to provide an immersive depth cue. Additionally, for selected levels the user is moved to another position in the 3D world. [14]

For more natural motion, we removed controller which is disturbing immersion for the sense of realism. Without additional cumbersome supplementary devices, users can gain the use of naturalness while they enjoyed the game.

4   Evaluation

4.1   Objective

The objective of this study was to build system that users would interact with virtual objects in 3D space using bare hands. For testing effectiveness and usefulness of our system, which estimates how comfortable users use and how easy users play, we should measure what users feel by qualitative and quantitative methods. Then, we analyze the result and adjust the system for maximize user satisfaction and immersion.

4.2   Procedure

24 colleagues (12f + 12m, aged 22 – 28, students of graduate school of cultural and technology) evaluated our system. No one had previously experience with fish game with HMD. Thus, we gave a short introduction (3min) for all participants. This includes watching the video (1min) and trying one practice game for each participant.

Qualitative Measure. We collected participant comments in a post-experiment interview to gain further information. Also, making a questionnaire, we hand out a questionnaire to 24 subjects. The questionnaire is in Fig.5. The odd number of question is about ease of playing and even is about difficulty of playing. If subjects agree strongly, scoring 5 points, or else scoring 0 point.

Quantitative Measure. The quantitative measures were experiments consisted of estimating the number of fish users caught during the tests in limited time, which is in 2 minutes. This experiment was used to adjust system composition. For example, it would help us determine the most suitable size of augmented objects.

Fig. 5. The questionnaire and result

4.3   Result and Analysis

The results of the questionnaire are summarized in Fig.5. As result shows, most people strongly agreed that people understand how to use it easily (95.8%). The question that gains the lowest point is about people can acquire something before using this system. It means that people think almost nothing to be learned such as tutorial or mechanisms of some controllers when playing our system. However, 22 subjects responded to the question 'is it easy?' with strongly agreement.

Results of experiments show in Fig.6.   Subjects fished 4.8 fish averagely within 2 minutes. All subjects caught at least 3 fish. 25% of subjects clear the game. So the degree of difficulty in system needed to be modified.

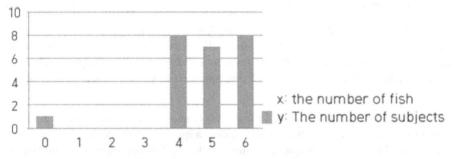

Fig. 6. Result of experiment. Limit time is 2 minutes.

4.4   Refinements of System

Color Notification. We collected qualitative data form questionnaire, comments and observations. During semi-constructed interviews, we could get some comments. Some subjects said visual superimposing of real and virtual content in 3D space creates confusion about distinction. They cannot recognize where to interact. So, we made the guidance that presented information about whether user interacts or not. For this purpose, we considered a possible solution by providing color change of augmented objects. As Fig.7 shows, if user catch augmented fish, fish color is changed.

Fig. 7. Color is changed if a fish is caught

Reducing Size. For tuning the degree of difficulty, we shortened the length, height and width of augmented fish by 0.18 times. After lessening the size of fish, people tend to take longer time to catch a fish. The result is shown in Fig. 8. Subjects caught 2.3 fish averagely.

Table 1. Change the size of fish and result of experiment. We scaled down the game object, fish. Modified fish size is one fifth than original one. Subjects try to catch the fish averagely 3 times. It is longer than before by 3times.

	Before	After
Fish scale	x=0.2 y=0.4 z=1	x=0.05 y=0.05 z=0.2
the number of times trying	1.1	3

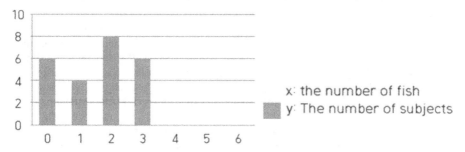

Fig. 8. After scale down, result of experiment

5   Conclusion and Discussion

In this paper, we introduce AR fishing game for enhancing user immersion and overcoming space limit. Interacting augmented objects with human hands in our system will strength the basis of how to control games. Our method is more powerful than the conventional immovable-video game using cumbersome equipment and mobile game. Our AR fishing game method can be applicable to many AR applications (i.e., future experimental education, urban planning, military simulation, collaborative surgery, etc.).

The techniques we described could be applied to other sports simulation. In order to apply the techniques to other sports simulation, different and sophisticated interaction techniques should be explored and studied in more detail.   The project also shows how interaction techniques in 3D environment can be used to create an entertainment.

6   Future Work

For refining our design environment, different interaction techniques would be explored and studied in more detail. For example, if user takes a natural posture of throwing a fishing rod to catch fish, this gesture will be implemented as direct input on the system. Also, waving hand controls how far the fishing rod casts.

For future work, we plan to use RGB-D Image capturing including color and depth information together for modeling and tracking. It makes players more focus on game with their bodies than playing traditional game. Moreover, we make augmented fish movement more realistic in specific situation and develop tracking to enable users to have a continuous experience whether or not the target remains visible in the HMD field of view. We investigate the applicability of the developmental concepts to other sports simulation or game.

References

1. Kim, N., Yoo, W., Lee, Y., Chung, S., Han, M., Yeo, W.: Designing Intuitive Spatial Game using Brain Computer Interface. In: KHCI 2009, p. 1160 (2009)
2. Ionescu, D., Ionescu, B., Gadea, C., Islam, S.: A Multimodal Interaction Method that Combines Gestures and Physical Game Controllers. In: 2011 Proceedings of 20th International Conference on Computer Communications and Networks (ICCCN), pp. 1–6 (2011)
3. Koh, R.K.C., Duh, H.B.-L.: An integrated design flow in user interface and interaction for enhancing mobile AR gaming experiences. In: 2010 IEEE International Symposium on Mixed and Augmented Reality - Arts, Media, and Humanities (ISMAR-AMH), pp. 47,52 (2010)
4. Noh, K.: A Structural Equation Modelling of the Relationship between User Experience. Self-Efficacy and Game Performance in Healthcare Serious Game, Korea Game Society 12, 15–20 (2012)
5. Lou, Y., Wu, W., Zhang, H., Zhang, H., Chen, Y.: A Multi-User Interaction System Based on Kinect and Wii Remote. In: 2012 IEEE International Conference on Multimedia and Expo Workshops (ICMEW), pp. 667,667 (2012)
6. Shires, L., Battersby, S., Lewis, J., Brown, D., Sherkat, N., Standen, P.: Enhancing the tracking capabilities of the Microsoft Kinect for stroke rehabilitation. In: 2013 IEEE 2nd International Conference on Serious Games and Applications for Health (SeGAH), pp. 1,8 (2013)
7. Zeng, M., Liu, Z., Meng, Q., Bai, Z., Jia, H.: Motion capture and reconstruction based on depth information using Kinect. In: 2012 5th International Congress Image and Signal Processing (CISP), pp. 1381,1385 (2012)
8. Kronrod, A., Danziger, S.: "Wii Will Rock You!" The Use and Effect of Figurative Language in Consumer Reviews of Hedonic and Utilitarian Consumption. Journal of Consumer Research 40(4), 726–739 (2013)
9. Foxlin, E., Harrington, M., Pfeifer, G.: Constellation: A wide range wireless motion tracking system for augmented Reality and Virtual set application. In: Studies in Proceedings of Siggraph 1998 Computer Graphics Proceedings. ACM SIGGRAPH Conference Series (1998)
10. Vasiljevic, T.P.: Fishing spear gun with dual spear projecting means. U.S. Patent (3), 340,642 (1967)
11. Chen, F.-S., Fu, C.-M., Huang, C.-L.: Hand gesture recognition using a real-time tracking method and hidden Markov models. Image and Vision Computing 21(8), 745–758 (2003)

12. Qualcomm Vuforia, `https://developer.vuforia.com/resources/dev-guide/image-targets`
13. Black, J., Ellis, T.: Multi camera image tracking. Image and Vision Computing 24(11), 1256–1267 (2006)
14. Rehg, J.M., Kanade, T.: Visual tracking of high DOF articulated structures: An application to human hand tracking. In: Eklundh, J.-O. (ed.) ECCV 1994. LNCS, vol. 801, pp. 35–46. Springer, Heidelberg (1994)

THE GROWTH: An Environmental Game Focusing on Overpopulation Issues

Charn Pisithpunth, Panagiotis Petridis, Petros Lameras, and Ian Dunwell

Coventry University, Serious Games Institute, Coventry, United Kingdom
pisithp2@uni.coventry.ac.uk,
{PPetridis,PLameras,IDunwell}@cad.coventry.ac.uk

Abstract. THE GROWTH is an environmental game aiming to tackle growing population issues and its impact on natural environment. The game also extends to cover social issues and unsustainable resources consumption caused by rapid population growth. Unlike many environmental games, THE GROWTH demonstrates that financial, social and health factors can be improved simply by committing to sustainable consumption patterns. The game aims to investigate the possibility of using serious games to promote players' environmental awareness and ultimately, the possibility of using serious games to modify players' consumption patterns. This game is designed for a specific target group of male population between 20-30 years of age in Bangkok (Thailand) and is focused on environmental issues raising the residential accommodation. Early experimental sessions were conducted with 17 participants and this paper presents the preliminary results of the study.

Keywords: Applications: Education, Applications: Entertainment, Applications: Virtual worlds and social computing, Interaction and navigation in VR and MR: Immersion, serious games.

1 Introduction

Global human population exceeded 7.1 billion by the end of 2013 [1]. The trend of rapid population growth is projected to continue at a rapid pace, with one study estimates global population to exceed 8 billion by 2030 [2]. From an environmental point of view, the growing human population imposes pressures on the natural environment through increased resources extraction and consumption rates [2]. For example, the expansion of the agriculture sector is one of the main drivers for deforestation [3]. At the same time, man-made hazardous wastes and pollutants are spreading into the environment, impacting natural habitats and wildlife [4]. The effects of pollution also reflect back on human habitats and contribute to health problems [5].

Apart from this environmental perspective, unsustainable population growth also poses social and well-being risks as well. Globally, about 1.2 billion live in extreme poverty [6]. Also, a number of populations worldwide are living in vulnerable and diminished conditions [7].

Seeking to address these issues, THE GROWTH is an environmental game which aims to highlight the interrelationship between natural environment, economic,

R. Shumaker and S. Lackey (Eds.): VAMR 2014, Part II, LNCS 8526, pp. 210–221, 2014.

population, and human community. Unlike many environmental games which use an "environmental-only" model, THE GROWTH uses financial incentives, health improvements and social well-being as key messages to reach out to non-environmentally conscious players.

2   Serious and Commercial Games with Environmental Characteristics

Researchers have highlighted the possibilities of using games and simulations to motivate the public (especially children and teenagers) in order to help them understand the importance of environmental conservation. Games and simulations can be used as supplemental material to allow learners to gain knowledge in "a more interactive way" [8]. Players can also find games to be motivating [9]. Researchers have suggested that computer games can be used to promote awareness [8] and even alter behaviors [10].

Currently, many computer games are designed to address and tackle environmental issues. For example, The CUSTOMER project (Coventry University Students' Optimization and Management of Energy Resources) is an energy awareness game developed at Coventry University [11]. The focus group of this game is students living in university accommodation or apartment complexes. The game is set in a standard student room, wherein players assume the role of a student in university accommodation. Players have to take key actions in order to minimize energy and water consumption without compromising their own health and safety issues. For example, players can put a laptop computer in stand-by mode or turn it off in order to save electricity. Players can turn-off the lights in bathroom and living room or close the window in order to prevent heat loss. Another serious game seeking to tackle environmental issues is the BBC CLIMATE CHALLENGE game [12]. The game aims to tackle global warming issue among other environmental and societal issues. The goal of this game is to set a target for CO2 reduction, and devise policies in order to achieve the target. Some policies can benefit the environment but also cause a negative impact on economy. Thus, players have to balance multiple game factors. Another serious game in this genre is ENERGYVILLE [13]. In this turn-based game, players are given a pre-defined budget and must initiate the construction of power stations in order to satisfy energy demands of the city. There are several types of power stations available to players (e.g. nuclear, coal, natural gas or wind power). Alternatively, players can invest in energy conservation policy which helps reduce some energy demands. The game also includes random events. For example, random events such as oil conflict and coal shortage can have a consequence on the energy future of the city.

Several studies have obtained interesting information and positive outcomes from serious games [14], [15]. While many games (both commercial and serious games) are now based in ICT, a study has shown that a tradition paper-based game can be used as an effective tool to address environmental issues as well [14]. Commercial games have also been designed to target environmental issues, for example ANNO2070, a game published by Ubisoft in 2011 [16] envisages a future scenario where the world has been largely affected by global warming, causing the rise of sea level and separated landscapes into chains of small islands. Environmental factor plays a prominent role in this game. Positive environmental condition improves agricultural production, and reduces health problems and disasters. Concordantly, critical environmental condition in this game inflicts negative impacts on agricultural production, magnifying health problems and disasters.

Some commercial games also highlight constraints between population size, natural resources and the environment. Examples of these games include FATE OF THE DRAGON [17] and STRONGHOLD: CRUSADER [18]. In FATE OF THE DRAGON, food supplies play a prominent role where players must maintain food stock for the army. Large armies will deplete food stock rapidly and food shortage leads to severe reduction in combat performances. The game also includes unpredictable natural disasters such as a locust swarm (affecting agricultural output severely), fires, earthquakes, and disease outbreaks, which can affect an unprepared army.

In STRONGHOLD: CRUSADER, players must maintain food supplies similar to FATE OF THE DRAGON. Population morale in STRONGHOLD: CRUSADER can be increased by providing multiple food types and issuing large food rations. The game also demonstrates the effects of disease, with a densely populated town is at higher risk from disease outbreak.

3   CASE STUDY: THE GROWTH Serious Game: A SG Aiming to Increase the Environmental Awareness of the Players

THE GROWTH is a single-player, role-playing serious game seeking to promote environmental awareness amongst players. The game is currently being developed at Coventry University, United Kingdom. This game is based on the current global trend of rapid human expansion, ecological degradation and exhaustive resources consumption, as the key issue for environmental degradation. Apart from environmental aspect, this game also attempts to demonstrate to players that unsustainable population growth causes a negative impact on society and economy as well.

This game is designed to target the Thai population specifically. The final game version will be delivered in Thai language, with an English version also available. About 50% of content in this game is based upon local issues in Thailand. The decision of creating a 'game designed for a specific group' is borrowed from Coyle (2005), who notes that the public are generally more attracted and motivated to issues in their immediate surroundings [19]. However, because environmental problems can spread from one region to another, it is necessary for the public to recognize and become aware of global environmental problems as well. Hence, around 50% of issues in this game are based on global themes.

THE GROWTH suggests that other strategies should be used in order to convey messages to players. For example, Rose (2009) suggests that environmental messages should inform the public of rewards that can be gained from environmental conservation [20]. To this end, a range of content in the game seeks to demonstrate to players that sustainable consumption can help save household expenditure as well (e.g. invest in water efficient products in order to save the environment and water bills at the same time and unplug electronic appliances after use to prevent cost associated with phantom load).

The game design approach was based on the Four-Dimensional-Framework [21]. The four dimensional framework (4DF) has been developed to aid evaluation, validation and development of serious games. The framework outlines four dimensions: the learner dimension (user modeling and profiling, specified needs and requirements of learners), the pedagogic dimension (using associative, cognitive and situative models), the representation of the game (differing levels of interactivity, fidelity and immersion required to support the learning objectives) and the context within which learning takes place (including disciplinary context, place of learning and resources available). The author decided to use this framework because the 4DF mapping allows for end-to-end development, validation and evaluation of the game, using a participatory design approach model. Furthermore, the ARCS Model of Motivational Design [22] was used as a guideline during game concept development. The setting of THE GROWTH provides a background story that shares many similarities to Earth; the world is experiencing a rapid ecological degradation situation caused by rapid human expansion, deforestation, land transformation, resources extraction and pollution. In THE GROWTH, humans have already appropriated about 78% of planetary resources. The remaining plants and animal species are being challenged by man-made pollution as well as global warming and climate change. Five years ago, a major industrial explosion (known as "The Event") occurred which collapsed an entire district and released a massive amount of pollution into the air. This causes major impacts on remaining natural environment as well as coating most buildings and landscapes with orangish polluted particles. The background story is presented to players by slides of static images and accessible to players at the main menu.

Fig. 1. Game environment

3.1 Role-Playing

The game puts players in the role of a newly elected president of a giant environmental group called 'The Environmental Consortium' or TEC. TEC is in fact, a front (covert) organization of the government, that exists to combat environmental problems and conserve the region's remaining natural resources. Apart from affiliation with the government, TEC is working closely with other major environmental organizations in the region.

3.2   Key Factors (resources)

There are four key factors in this game. These being: Population, Environment, Emergency Supply, and Wealth. Players lose the game if environmental factor is depleted. Key characteristics for each factor are the following:

- Population factor: represents total population in this region. Large population size causes environmental factor to deteriorate at faster rate. However, the region will experience economic collapse if the population size is lower than 30% of total capacity. Economic collapse will reduce players' income greatly. This means players will have to balance population size in order to maintain healthy natural environment and economy at the same time.
- Environmental factor: represents environmental situation in the city. By default, the environmental factor slowly decreases to reflect degradation caused by human activities. However, environmental factor can decrease at various speeds. For example, at 35% of total capacity, environmental factor will decrease faster by 15% (this represents the scenario where environmental condition starts to deteriorate beyond recovery). Also, natural disasters are likely to occur much more frequently when environmental factor is running low.
- Emergency Supply factor: represents supplies that players will need to spend on special missions (e.g. in the events of famine or armed conflicts).
- Wealth factor: represents accumulated wealth that players can spend on certain improvements and investments (discuss below). Also, certain amount of wealth will be automatically withdrawn from players' treasury to be spent as humanitarian aids in case of disasters.

3.3   Player Actions: Overview

There are several actions that players can perform in this game. For example, players can setup a campaign to promote sustainability which improves environmental condition and decrease population growth rate. Players can order a large amount of emergency supplies to be produced (but this also comes at the cost of the environment). Also, players can accumulate wealth which can be used to invest in certain improvements.

3.4   Player Actions: Upgrade and Improvements

Upgrades represent technologies and policies that players can research and implement in order to provide certain benefits for the region. For example, an 'advanced public transportation network' encourages the population to use the public transport which improves environmental condition as well as generate small amount of wealth (from reduced energy imports). Another example is 'family planning upgrade' which encourages parents to plan for optimum family size (slowing population growth). Each upgrade requires investment of resources from players (chiefly wealth among others). Upgrade and improvements can fail to be implemented. In this case, players will lose their investment in the process. Also, all upgrades provide temporary benefits for the region which means they need to be re-invested after certain period of time. The majority of upgrades in this game are based on existing and emerging technologies and policies. Upgrades can be further categorized into three types based on their characteristics. These being: technology, policy and propaganda. Technology represents highly advanced devices that can be used to help mitigate environmental and social problems (e.g. automation). Upgrades that fall under this category are generally very expensive to develop. They also have a low to moderate chance of successful implementation. However, successful implementation of technology can provide significant beneficial effects to the region for a very long period of time. Policies, on the other hand, represent the law imposed in the region. Upgrades that fall under this category are generally moderately expensive to initiate. A number of them have a relatively low chance of successful implementation, but can provide tremendous amount of beneficial effects to the region for a long period of time. For example, 'Carbon tax policy' can greatly improve environmental condition since it influences public's consumption patterns in many ways. However, this has a relatively low chance of successful implementation, owing to a perceived public rejection. Lastly, propaganda represents players' attempts to communicate with the public and request for their cooperation. Upgrades that fall under this category are generally inexpensive to initiate. A number of them have a relatively low to moderate chance of implementation, but can provide significant amount of beneficial effects to the region for a moderate duration. Some examples of upgrades from this category include: recycle programs, car pooling, and energy conservation program. Apart from beneficial effects, upgrades and improvements can trigger or prevent the occurrence of certain game events. For example, investing in 'Marine Conservation Program' can trigger the public to donate certain amount of wealth to support players' environmental causes. Another example can be seen in 'Disease Control Program' which reduces occurrence of disease outbreak in the region by 50%.

3.5 Real Property

Players can purchase real properties in order to gain long-term benefits. Similar to 'Upgrade & Improvements' function, players must first pay capital investment (i.e. wealth). However, unlike 'Upgrade and Improvements', real properties provide constant investment return for player permanently. Players can also further efficiencies of buildings by 'equip' them with certain improvements.

For example, players have recently purchased a high-rise apartment. This apartment now generates 300 points of wealth per second for players. Player can impose restriction on elevator usage for this building which results in players gaining 1 environmental point per second in return (for energy conservation).

3.6   Player Actions: Campaigning (quiz)

Campaigning represents players' attempts to promote environmental and social awareness to the public. This is represented by series of quiz where players have to read a random article and match them with a corresponding category. Successful matching reflects the fact that players have successfully implant awareness into the public. This provides players either population reduction, environmental or wealth bonus. For example, a random article describes recent issues on high rate of un-planned pregnancies and venereal diseases infection in Thai teenagers. A player now marks this article as 'social issue'. By solving this quiz, population growth in the city will be decreased for a short period. All articles in this game are collections of real-world events (from both local and global perspective).

3.7   Player Actions: Special Actions

Special actions represent emergency edicts that can be issues by players. There are three types of special actions in this game. These are: Emergency Supplies, Environmental and Population Special Actions. All special actions need to be 'recharged' once used.

Emergency Supplies Special Action is characterized as mass and rapid production of supplies. Once selected, it adds certain amount of Emergency Supplies to players. However, this special action costs players in wealth and also contributes some damages to natural environment. Environmental Special Action is characterized as an emergency land reclamation project. This special action helps improve overall environmental condition in the region, but costs players in wealth. Lastly, Population Special Action is characterized as the government' effort to decrease population growth rate. This function also costs players in wealth.

3.8   Random Events

The aim of random event system is to promote players' awareness on unpredictable nature of environmental and social situations. In THE GROWTH, events such as contamination, disease outbreaks and natural disaster may occur as the game progresses. For example, the game informs players of toxic waste being leaked from a landfill as a result of landslide. The resulting event causes 1,000 points of environmental damage. Also, 3,000 wealth and 100 supplies are withdrawn from player's treasury to fund a recovery project. As mentioned above, occurrences of some events are depended on players' performances. For example, a random event informs players that the public has donated 80,000 wealth for players as a reward for safeguarding their natural environment (this event has a higher probability to make appearance if environmental condition in the region is high).

4   Preliminary Sessions

Preliminary sessions were conducted between early 2012 to August 2013. The objective of preliminary sessions was to investigate key areas such as participants' overall satisfaction with the game, motivation and basic learning outcomes. Purposive sampling method was used to recruit participants. This method was selected because the game will be focus on a specific population group (Thai). Also, the method was convenient for recruiting a limited number of participants in a limited timeframe. The total of seventeen (17) male participants of Thai nationality between 22-29 years old voluntarily participated in preliminary sessions. These were: 11 post-graduate students based at Coventry University, 3 undergraduate students (based in Thailand) and 3 office employees with post-graduate degree (also based in Thailand). All 11 post-graduate students from Coventry University were contacted directly (face-to-face) by a researcher in the UK. This is the first group to participate in preliminary test sessions. The other six participants were first contacted by researcher's agent in Thailand and, after receiving participants' confirmation, the researcher contacted them again via both telephone and e-mails in order to arrange for date and time. All six participants in this group did not have any contact with the researcher prior to their recruitment. Preliminary sessions with this second group were conducted in Bangkok (Thailand).

All participants reported they had used computer games and paperboard games beforehand. In regards to computer games, five participants have identified themselves as avid gamers, while another 12 identified themselves as casual gamers. As this project aims to deliver a game from single-player perspective, all sessions were conducted with one participant at the time. All sessions have been conducted at participants' private space.

Preliminary sessions were heavily relied on physical equipments such as paper cards which were used as a 'mock-up' to represent concepts of the digital version. A laptop computer was used to assist the gameplay as well as record players' progress. A dice was used to produce randomness and uncertainty during the session. Each session was completed within approximately 90 minutes.

A Likert-style rating scale was employed to obtain players' level of satisfaction with the game (e.g. learning curve, theme, graphical representation and game mechanism). Semi-structured interview was employed to establish participants demographic, investigate players' game experiences and knowledge gains. Follow-up questions were used where necessary in order to gain additional information from players. Transcripts were analyzed using thematic analysis. Thematic analysis was selected for its flexibility, opportunity to gain insights from the information, and relatively quick in term of execution [23]. All preliminary sessions were conducted in the Thai language (participants' native language).

Each session started with the researcher welcoming a participant to the study, followed by approximately five minutes of informal discussion in order to establish an acquaintance with the participant. The researcher then opened with a formal introduction of the project. Participants were told that they were recruited to help evaluate a game project and that their opinions would contribute to future development. In all sessions, participants were encouraged by the researcher to produce comments and criticize the project freely.

4.1   Results and Discussion

The majority of participants did not experience difficulties with the learning game mechanism. However, several participants reported a degree of distraction because multiple pieces of physical equipment were utilized during preliminary sessions, due to the mock-up stage of development. A majority of participants also commented on the graphics and visual aesthetics of the game positively. Also, degree of freedom and neutral representation in THE GROWTH were appreciated by participants. One participant noted that: "I like the way there are many things you can do to help the planet". In another account, a participant noted that "The content is rich .. I also like the way [the game is] more about science, saving money and quality of life .. less about just save cute animals".

In term of motivation, 16/17 participants have reported that their main motivation was to learn about new technologies and actions that can be taken to reduce personal energy consumption. 10/17 participants have shown their strong interests in social issues highlighted in THE GROWTH. Many participants have expressed their interests to review all the cards even after game sessions in order to learn more about contents that they might have missed during the sessions. In one account, a participant noted that "I know about solar panels, but I've never imagined using the sun [solar energy] for cooking! In another account, a participant noted about solar tower technology as followings: "That's nice, so even the desert can be used to produce energy"

Cutting personal spending seems to be the top priority for almost all participants while co-benefits on the environment seem to be acknowledged to a lesser degree. This holds true for both UK and Thailand-based participants. Energy (gas and electricity) seems to be a popular topic amongst participants, possibly due to much higher electrical consumption (and cost) when compared to water. The transportation topic received good attention from participants as well. Already, public transportation is the primary choice of travel for 12 participants. 15/17 participants admitted that they are unlikely to pay premium price for environmental-friendly products such as food, but are more likely to invest on energy and water efficient products in order to save energy bills in the long run. Interestingly, 8 participants reported that they would welcome tax imposed on unsustainable products (e.g. carbon tax), but only in the form of policy (i.e. applied to all consumers). According to several participants, real-world factors also play an important role in participants' commitments to environmental causes. One participant noted that "I've been separating recyclable from [municipal] waste for many years, but garbage collectors seem to mix and crush everything altogether in the truck so I'm not sure if the government is still working on this [recycling] or not". Another participant cited the lack of recycle bins in his area as the reason to stop recycling. On another account, a participant noted that "I separate my wastes so I can give them [recyclable waste] to [a] waste buyer[1] for free as a good gesture".

In term of learning outcomes, Knowledge gains were measured by participants' ability to recall and describe articles from the game. All participants were able to recall and discuss articles from the cards (highest = 8/10, mean = 5.7/10, lowest =2/10). Energy saving and emerging technologies were most recalled topics. Deforestation and illegal

---

[1]   Waste buyers are common sight in many areas of Bangkok. These merchants visit houses in a hope to buy any recyclable wastes.

encroachment were also topics of interest to them (possibly due to recent reports of government's mass prosecution of illegal loggers and encroachment on natural habitats earlier this year). Unplanned pregnancies and crimes were topics most recalled by participants in social category.

There was no noticeable difference in knowledge gains between avid-gaming and casual-gaming participants. However, office workers and UK-based students have demonstrated greater ability to recall articles from the game. This is possibly due to an increased awareness through their responsibility over utility bills.

4.2 Limitations and Conclusion

THE GROWTH is an environmental game with a special focus on rapid population growth. Unlike many environmental games, THE GROWTH highlights interrelationship between natural environment, economy and society. THE GROWTH offers over 60 methods that players can take in order to tackle environmental and social problems. Similar to the real world, each solution has its own advantages and limitations. Some of these solutions are burrowed from experimental practices and can be considered as 'unconventional' by the standard of many environmental games. This provides players with a degree of freedom (and sometime exposes them to negative consequences should players fail to consider them carefully). Unlike many environmental games, some factors in THE GROWTH can be adapted to players' progresses (dynamic game world). The game's theme emphasizes that environmental conservation efforts are highly dependent on public support (both physical contribution and funding).

This project is still in development stage and contains many limitations. Results from preliminary sessions were obtained by post-test only method. This means the researcher is unable to establish whether the positive learning outcomes were resulted from participants' previous exposure to other environmental information or the game itself. According to participants, the game was described as simple to understand, engaging and educating. Future development aims to expand game contents based on players and experts' comments, develop a systematic evaluation framework to explore users-game interactions such as usability, level of engagement, knowledge gain, retention, and knowledge transfer.

References

1. United States Census Bureau, U.S. and World Population Clock (2013), http://www.census.gov/popclock/
2. Ferrara, I., Serret, Y.: Introduction. In: Household Behaviour and the Environment. Reviewing the Evidence (2008), http://www.oecd.org/dataoecd/19/22/42183878.pdf
3. Grau, R., Aide, M.: Globalization and Land-Use Transitions in Latin America. Ecology and Society 13(2) (2008), http://www.ecologyandsociety.org/vol13/iss2/art16/

4. Marine Debris Program, Marine debris info (2012),
   http://marinedebris.noaa.gov/info/faqs.html
5. Xing, G., Chan, J., Leung, A., Wu, S., Wong, M.H.: Environmental impact and human exposure to PCBs in Guiyu, an electronic waste recycling site in China. Environment International 35(1), 76–82 (2009), http://www.sciencedirect.com/
6. United Nations Millennium development goals and beyond 2015 (2013),
   http://www.un.org/millenniumgoals/poverty.shtml
7. Discovery News, Top 10 Most Polluted Places on the Planet (2013a),
   http://news.discovery.com/earth/top-10-most-polluted-places-on-the-planet-131105.htm
8. Diah, N., Ismail, M., Ahmad, S., Mahmud, M.: Adaptation of Environmental Anticipation in Educational Computer Game. Procedia - Social and Behavioral Sciences 42, 74–81 (2012), http://www.sciencedirect.com
9. Ozcelik, E., Cagiltay, N., Ozcelik, N.: The effect of uncertainty on learning in game-like environments. Computers & Education 67, 12–20 (2013),
   http://www.sciencedirect.com
10. Baranowski, T., Buday, R., Thompson, D., Baranowski, J.: Playing for Real: Video Games and Stories for Health-Related Behavior Change. American Journal of Preventive Medicine 34(1), 74–82 (2008), http://www.sciencedirect.com
11. Jisc, Coventry University STudents' Optimisation and Management of Energy Resources (2013), http://www.jisc.ac.uk/whatwedo/programmes/greeningict/organisational/customer.aspx
12. BBC – Climate Challenge (n.d.) Climate Challenge, http://www.bbc.co.uk/sn/hottopics/climatechange/climate_challenge/
13. Chevron-Energyville, Energyville (2011), http://www.energyville.com/
14. Arslan, H., Moseley, C., Cigdemoglu, C.: Taking attention on environmental issues by an attractive educational game: Enviropoly. Social and Behavioral Science 28, 801–806 (2011), http://www.sciencedirect.com/
15. Ruiz-Pérez, M., Franco-Múgica, F., González, J., Gómez-Baggethun, E., Alberruche-Rico, M.: An institutional analysis of the sustainability of fisheries: Insights from FishBanks simulation game. Ocean & Coastal Management 54(8), 585–592 (2011), http://www.sciencedirect.com
16. Ubisoft, Anno (2070) (2011), http://anno-game.ubi.com/anno-2070/en-gb/home/index.aspx
17. SQUARE ENIX, Three Kingdoms: Fate of the Dragon (2012), https://store.eu.square-enix.com/emea_uk/pc-windows-download/Fate-of-the-Dragon.php?nocookies=1
18. Firefly Studios, STRONGHOLD CRUSADER (2012),
   http://www.fireflyworlds.com/index.php?option=com_content&task=blogcategory&id=128&Itemid=320
19. Coyle, K.: The National Environmental Education & Training Foundation. Environmental Literacy in America (2005), http://www.peecworks.org/PEEC/PEEC_Research/01795C21-001D0211.0/NEETF%202005%20ELR%20Full%20Report.pdf (July 1, 2012)
20. Rose, C.: Climate Change, Warnings and the Car Alarm Problem. The Campaign Strategy Newsletter 55 (2009), http://www.campaignstrategy.org/newsletters/campaignstrategy_newsletter_55.pdf

21. de Freitas, S., Jarvis, S.: A Framework for Developing Serious Games to meet Learner Needs. In: Interservice/Industry Training, Simulation, and Education Conference (I/ITSEC), vol. (2742), pp. 1–11 (2006), http://trusim.biz/resources/AFrameworkForDev.pdf
22. Keller, J.: Development and use of the ARCS model of motivational design. Journal of Instructional Development 10(3), 2–10 (1987),
http://ocw.metu.edu.tr/pluginfile.php/8620/mod_resource/content/1/Keller%20Development%20%20Use%20of%20ARCS.pdf
23. Braun, V., Clarke, V.: Using thematic analysis in psychology. Qualitative Research in Psychology 3(2), 77–101 (2006), http://eprints.uwe.ac.uk/11735/2/thematic_analysis_revised..%E5%AF%86

Medical, Health and Rehabilitation Applications

Responses during Facial Emotional Expression Recognition Tasks Using Virtual Reality and Static IAPS Pictures for Adults with Schizophrenia

Esubalew Bekele[1,*], Dayi Bian[1], Zhi Zheng[1], Joel Peterman[2],
Sohee Park[2], and Nilanjan Sarkar[1,3*], IEEE

[1] Electrical Engineering and Computer Science Department
[2] Psychology Department
[3] Mechanical Engineering Department, Vanderbilt University, Nashville, TN, USA
(esubalew.bekele,nilanjan.sarkar)@vanderbilt.edu

Abstract. Technology-assisted intervention has the potential to adaptively individualize and improve outcomes of traditional schizophrenia (SZ) intervention. Virtual reality (VR) technology, in particular, has the potential to simulate real world social and communication interactions and hence could be useful as a therapeutic platform for SZ. Emotional face recognition is considered among the core building blocks of social communication. Studies have shown that emotional face processing and understanding is impaired in patients with SZ. The current study develops a novel VR-based system that presents avatars that can change their facial emotion dynamically for emotion recognition tasks. Additionally, this system allows real-time measurement of physiological signals and eye gaze during the emotion recognition tasks, which can be used to gain insight about the emotion recognition process in SZ population. This study further compares VR-based facial emotion recognition with that of the more traditional emotion recognition from static faces using a small usability study. Results from the usability study suggest that VR could be a viable platform for SZ intervention and implicit signals such as physiological signals and eye gaze can be utilized to better understand the underlying pattern that is not available from user reports and performance alone.

Keywords: facial expression, emotion recognition, virtual reality, IAPS, adaptive interaction, eye tracking, physiological processing, schizophrenia intervention.

1 Introduction

Schizophrenia (SZ) is a debilitating psychotic disorder that affects about 1% of the population, costing more than $100 billion annually in the USA. It causes emotional and cognitive impairments [1] and is defined as a splitting of thoughts from feelings [2]. Some of the psychotic symptoms such as hallucinations and delusions are partly

---

* Corresponding author.

R. Shumaker and S. Lackey (Eds.): VAMR 2014, Part II, LNCS 8526, pp. 225–235, 2014.

ameliorated by antipsychotic drugs, but the route to recovery is hampered by social impairments [3]. Currently available social interventions can be helpful but low compliance rates and lack of access to such programs for most patients can be problematic.

Deficits in social cognition, including emotion processing, social cue perception, empathy, mental state attributions, and theory of mind lead to poor functional outcome in SZ even after improvement in psychotic symptoms [3,4]. Thus, there is a need for efficacious cost-effective, low-burden and high-compliance interventions for social deficits in SZ, which would likely increase positive outcome. Improvement in emotion processing, a core deficit, and social understanding would be crucial for improved social outcomes. SZ patients appear to have impairments in recognizing faces and emotional expressions and disturbances in emotional functioning are major disability in SZ [5,6]. Traditional static emotional pictures, more specifically the International Affective Picture System (IAPS), were used to elicit emotional experience in SZ [1]. The apparent disconnect between outward display of emotion by SZ patients and the actual internal feeling could be studied by understanding the involuntary peripheral physiological responses of the sympathetic central nervous system (CNS).

In the context of technology-based SZ intervention, Virtual Reality (VR) systems have been investigated with SZ for symptom assessment [7], training of medication management skills [8], hallucinations training [9], social perception [10], role play [11], and improving the diagnosis of SZ [12]. However there are limited applications of VR in emotion processing and identification for SZ. Moreover, these VR systems solely rely on user reporting and outward measures of performance. To mitigate these limitations, one should combine dynamic presentation of emotional expressions together with implicit physiological response and eye gaze processing. Implicit cues can be useful to understand the underlying psychological states that are not possible using performance-based systems or simple user reporting.

In this work, we present a novel VR-based system that incorporates implicit cues from peripheral physiological signals [13,14] and eye tracking [15] for the understanding of facial emotional expression. We compare how a SZ group and a matched group of healthy non-psychiatric adults performed emotion recognition tasks when presented in the form of static IAPS slides and when presented in a VR environment with the avatars expressing emotions dynamically.

The remainder of the paper is organized as follows. Section 2 describes the details of the two systems (i.e., the static IAPS pictures presentation system and the VR system). Section 3 details the methods and procedures followed in the usability study. Section 4 presents the results and highlights their implications. Finally, Section 5 discusses the conclusions and future extensions of this preliminary work.

2   Systems Overview

Both the IAPS presentation system and the VR system were composed of three major components: the presentation environment, the eye tracking component, and the peripheral physiology monitoring component. The presentation environments were based on Unity3D game engine by Unity Technologies (http://unity3d.com).

A remote desktop eye tracker by Tobii Technologies (www.tobii.com) called Tobii X120 was employed for gaze tracking. A wireless physiological signals acquisition device called BioNomadix by Biopac Inc. (www.biopac.com) with 8 channels was used to record the physiological signals. Each component ran separately while communicating via a network interface.

2.1   The Static IAPS Presentation

We developed a picture presentation system using Unity3D that displayed the full screen images on a 24" flat screen monitor at 1024x768 resolution. The pictures were preselected from the pool of about 600 IAPS pictures [16]. They were categorized into 6 major groups, namely, social positive (pictures of erotica), social negative (violence pictures), social neutral (people in normal scenery), non-social positive (pictures of food), non-social negative (pictures of dirty and unpleasant scenery), and non-social neutral (normal pictures of objects). The emotional pictures were broadly divided into social and non-social and within each broad category, they were further categorized into positive, negative and neutral. All the 6 categories consisted of 4 pictures each. The erotica pictures were selected appropriately for men and women subjects. After a 10 second presentation of the picture, the subjects were presented with choices to rate their emotional experience on how aroused the pictures in the preceding category made them feel (in a pictorial scale of 1-9, see Fig. 1), the valence of the emotion they felt (in a pictorial scale of 1-9) and the actual emotion they felt (out of 5 emotions and neutral). The subjects were seated around 70-80 cm from the computer screen during the whole IAPS pictures presentation session.

Fig. 1. IAPS pictures presentation system with the arousal rating

2.2   VR Emotion Presentation

The VR environment was originally developed for emotion recognition for adolescents with autism spectrum disorders (ASD) [17]. Due to the similarity of emotion recognition impairment in ASD and SZ, we customized the system to suit the new target group with 5 emotions (joy, surprise, fear, anger, and sadness). The avatars were customized and rigged using an online animation service, mixamo (www.mixamo.com) together with Autodesk Maya. All the facial expressions and lip-syncing for contextual stories narrated by the avatars were animated in Maya. A total of seven avatars including 4 boys and 3 girls were selected. Close to 20 facial bone rigs were controlled by set driven key controllers for realistic facial expressions and phonetic visemes for lip-sync. Each facial expression had four arousal levels (i.e., low, medium, high, and extreme, see Fig. 2). A total of 315 (16 lip-synced stories + 28 emotion expression plus neutral for each character) animations were developed and imported to Unity3D game engine for task presentation.

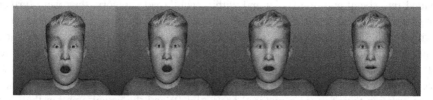

Fig. 2. Example surprise emotion with its four degrees of arousal

The logged data was analyzed offline to illustrate differences in physiological and gaze responses between the patient and the control groups.

2.3   Eye Tracking and Physiological Monitoring Components

The eye tracker recorded at 120 Hz frame rate allowing a free head movement of 30 x 22 x 30 cm (width x height x depth) at an approximately 70 cm distance. We used two applications connected to the eye tracker: one for diagnostic visualization as the experiment progressed and another one to record, pre-process and log the eye tracking data. The main eye tracker application computed eye physiological indices (PI) such as pupil diameter (PD) and blink rate (BR) and behavioral indices (BI) [18] such as fixation duration (FD) from the raw gaze data.

The wireless Bionomadix physiological monitoring system with a total of 8 channels of physiological signals was running at 1000 Hz. The physiological signals monitored were: pulse plethesymogram (PPG), skin temperature (SKT), galvanic skin response (GSR), 3 electromyograms (EMG), and respiration (RSP). Due to the apparent disconnect between what patients with SZ feel and their outward expressions, they are not usually expressive of their internal affective states and these states often are not visible externally [2]. Physiological signals are, however, relatively less affected by these impairments and can be useful in understanding the internal psychological states and pattern [1]. Among the signals we monitored, GSR and PPG are directly related to the sympathetic response of the autonomous nervous system (ANS) [19].

2.4 Physiological and Gaze Data Analysis

The collected physiological data were processed to extract useful features and decipher any differences between two subject groups for conditions of selected emotional expressions presentation and neutral baseline condition.   We specifically chose features from PPG, GSR, RSP and SKT for this analysis. These features were chosen because of their correlation with engagement and emotion recognition process as noted in psychophysiology literature [14,19,20,1]. The PPG were used to extract heart rate (HR), which is a cardiac index used to measure stress and certain emotions [21]. The GSR is decomposed into two major components, i.e., phasic and tonic components, and from them features such as skin conductance response rate (SCRrate) and mean skin conductance level (SCL) were extracted. The RSP signal was used to extract the breathing rate (BR). The mean skin temperature (SKT) was obtained from the SKT signal. For the eye tracking data, we extracted the following features: pupil diameter (PD), fixation duration (FD), sum of fixation counts (SFC), saccade path length (SPL), and blink rate (BR). Statistical two sample unequal variance t-test was used to quantify the significance of the differences.

3   Methods and Procedure

3.1   Experimental Setup

The presentation engine ran on Unity while eye tracking and peripheral physiological monitoring were performed in parallel using separate applications on separate machines that communicated with the Unity-based presentation engine via a network interface. The VR task was presented using a 24'' flat LCD panel monitor (at resolution 1980 x 1080) while the IAPS picture was presented on the same monitor with a resolution of 1024 x 768 in order to preserve the original resolution of the images. The experiment was performed in a laboratory with two rooms separated by one-way glass windows for observation. The researchers sat in the outside room. In the inner room, the subject sat in front of the task computer. The task computer display was also routed to the outer room for observation by the researchers. The session was video recorded for the whole duration of the participation. The study was approved by the Institutional Review Board of Vanderbilt University.

3.2   Subjects

A total of 6 patients with SZ (Male: n=3, Female: n=3) of ages (M=45.67, SD=9.09) and an age and IQ matched 6 healthy non-psychiatric subjects (Male: n=5, Female: n=1) controls of ages (M=42.5, SD=8.21) were recruited and participated in the usability study. All patient subjects were recruited through existing clinical research programs and had established clinical diagnosis (Table 1).

Table 1. Profile of subjects in the patient group and the control group

Demographic Information	Groups	
	Healthy Controls (1F, 5M)	Schizophrenia (3F, 3M)
Age	42.5 (8.21)	45.67 (9.09)
IQ[a]	109.5 (8.86)	106.5 (4.09)
Years of Education	16.5 (2.34)	13.33 (1.97)
Age of Illness Onset		20.83 (4.07)
Medication Dose[b]		386.89 (194.65)
Current Symptoms[c]		
BPRS		10.83 (2.56)
SAPS		13 (5.66)
SANS		21.83 (9.06)

[a]Premorbid intelligence was assessed using the North American Adult Reading Test [22]. [b]Chlorpromazine equivalent (mg/day; [23]). [c]Semi-structured clinical interviews assessing symptoms over the past month. Brief Psychiatric Rating Scale (BPRS; [24]); Scale for the Assessment of Positive Symptoms (SAPS; [15]); and the Scale for the Assessment of Negative Symptoms (SANS; [3]).

The control group was recruited from the local community. The IQ measures were used to potentially screen for intellectual competency to complete the tasks.

3.3   Tasks

The VR-based system presented a total of 20 trials corresponding to the 5 emotional expressions with each expression having 4 levels. Each trial was 12-15 s long. In each trial, first, the character narrated a context story that was linked to the emotional expression that followed for the next 5 seconds. The avatar exhibited a neutral emotional face during story telling. The IAPS picture was presented in such a way that each category was presented as a block and rating was performed after each category resulting in a total of 6 trials of 10 s for each picture in the category whereas ratings in the VR systems was after each trial of emotion expressions. Therefore, each IAPS trial consisted of four pictures from the same category. It has to be noted that all the four pictures in a category were selected carefully for equivalence as far as eliciting equivalent emotional responses were concerned. A typical laboratory visit was approximately one hour and 30 minutes long. During the first 15 minutes, a trained therapist prepared the subject for the experiment by placing the physiological sensors on the participant. Before the task began, the eye tracker was calibrated. The calibration was a fast 9 points calibration that took about 10-15 s. At the start of each task, a welcome screen greeted the subject and described what was about to happen and how the subject was to interact with the system. Immediately after the welcome screen, the trials started. At the end of each trial, questionnaires popped up asking the subject what emotion he/she thought the avatar displayed and how confident he/she was in his/her choice in the VR system. The questionnaires for the IAPS pictures asked the level of arousal and valence of the emotion they felt together with the emotion they felt by watching the pictures. The emotional expression presentations were randomized for each subject across trials to avoid ordering effects. To avoid other confounding factors arising from the context stories, the stories were recorded with a monotonous tone and there was no specific facial expression displayed by the avatars during that context period.

4   Results and Discussions

We have compared similarities and differences of physiological and eye behavioral responses using physiological and eye behavioral and physiological features. The physiological and eye tracking data were processed to extract five features each to compare elicited responses during the facial emotional recognition tasks in the dynamic virtual environment as compared to the static IAPS presentation system. Results indicate that there are differences in both physiological and eye tracking indices between the patient and the control group. We categorized the trials into three groups: negative, positive, and neutral in the IAPS study and into two groups: positive and negative in the VR study for both physiological and eye tracking data. In the IAPS pictures presentation, the 6 trials were categorized into three groups by combining the social and non-social stimuli together whereas in the VR presentation, the prominent positive (joy and surprise) and negative emotions (anger and disgust) were combined with high and extreme levels of arousal. We also extracted baseline features for the physiological data to compare the responses in these categories to note whether they were above or below the baseline values.

4.1   Physiological Features Comparison

Table 2. IAPS Pictures Session Physiological Features

| | Positive Category | | | | Negative Category | | | |
| | Patients | | Controls | | Patients | | Controls | |
	Mean	SD	Mean	SD	Mean	SD	Mean	SD
HR (bpm)	85.24	9.27	82.92	10.76	84.30	15.75	86.15	11.33
SKT (F)	85.44	11.72	93.09	3.05	85.70	11.84	93.11	3.14
BR (bpm)	16.60	6.11	16.62	3.13	18.28	9.01	15.31	4.56
SCL (µS)*	5.21	3.33	8.84	4.21	5.19	3.17	8.79	4.30
SCRrate	2.61	1.38	2.12	0.96	2.13	1.29	2.38	1.14

*$p<0.05$

As shown in Table 2, the patient group had higher emotional response indicators including higher heart and skin conductance response rates and comparable breathing rate when presented with positive emotional pictures than negative emotional pictures. However, only the tonic skin conductance rate was statistically significantly different in both the positive and negative emotional categories.

Table 3. VR Session Physiological Features

| | Positive Category | | | | Negative Category | | | |
| | Patients | | Controls | | Patients | | Controls | |
	Mean	SD	Mean	SD	Mean	SD	Mean	SD
HR (bpm)	85.53	13.23	80.80	15.04	83.27	10.39	83.10	14.36
SKT (^{0}F)*	86.84	11.28	94.29	2.35	86.78	11.15	94.22	2.43
BR (bpm)	17.25	12.77	17.65	7.04	23.18	15.95	21.35	15.07
SCL (µS)*	4.76	2.84	7.94	4.05	4.81	2.91	7.75	4.02
SCRrate	2.65	2.89	3.18	2.73	2.72	2.73	2.68	2.70

*$p<0.05$

Table 3 shows that the patient group showed similar differences from the control group as in the case of the IAPS static pictures presentation. However, in the VR case, both SKT and SCL were statistically significantly different in both the positive and negative emotion categories.

The baseline conditions were: 1) for the patient group: mean (SD), HR: 82.24 (10.76) bpm, SKT: 86.59 (10.93) ^{0}F, BR: 28.87 (16.66) bpm, SCL: 4.23 (2.41) µS, and SCRrate: 2 (0.61); and 2) for the control group: HR: 79.18 (11.72) bpm, SKT: 94.64 (1.55) ^{0}F, BR: 16.56 (3.53) bpm, SCL: 7.79 (3.55) µS, and SCRrate: 2.1 (0.65). Note that BR for the patient group decreased from the baseline case in almost all conditions whereas it increased for the control group. Another observation is that the patient group had more responses in the positive category than the negative ones, which agrees with the existing literature that people with schizophrenia report increased response to positive emotional facial pictures than negative emotional facial pictures as compared to control non-psychotic people.

4.2   Eye Tracking Indices Comparison

Most of the eye gaze indices showed statistically significant differences between the two groups (Table 4). The patient group showed more saccadic eye movement as indicated by higher SFC, lower FD and shorter SPL. These indices are known to correlate with one's engagement. Therefore, the patients were less engaged than the control group.

Table 4. IAPS Pictures Session Eye Features

| | Positive Category | | | | Negative Category | | | |
| | Patients | | Controls | | Patients | | Controls | |
	Mean	SD	Mean	SD	Mean	SD	Mean	SD
PD (mm)	2.66	0.37	2.91	0.24	2.68	0.36	2.91	0.19
FD (ms)*	203.91	177.04	453.72	176.03	170.91	103.27	371.00	146.84
SFC*	150.67	56.56	92.00	35.41	172.58	69.86	101.67	41.99
SPL (pix)*	67.24	24.56	139.00	46.73	92.16	32.35	147.63	54.69
BR (bpm)	11.25	3.51	10.83	5.00	10.58	4.70	10.08	4.94

*$p<0.05$

Similar pattern of less engagement was observed in the patient group than the control group during the VR presentation (Table 5). Only exception in this case was pupil diameter, which was statistically significantly different with the patient group having lower PD. Pupil constriction was associated with engagement. The blink rate was statistically different for the negative category of emotions.

Table 5. VR Pictures Session Eye Features

| | Positive Category | | | | Negative Category | | | |
| | Patients | | Controls | | Patients | | Controls | |
	Mean	SD	Mean	SD	Mean	SD	Mean	SD
PD (mm)*	2.61	0.39	2.91	0.20	2.62	0.40	2.95	0.18
FD (ms)*	123.38	125.71	439.67	345.32	134.00	118.98	450.78	333.50
SFC*	56.65	28.08	35.75	28.36	57.35	24.98	37.20	30.04
SPL (pix)*	48.43	30.12	101.04	43.29	52.48	35.14	88.74	38.93
BR (bpm)	2.10	1.09	3.10	1.55	2.70	1.65	2.70	1.45

*$p<0.05$

5   Conclusion and Future Works

Both the IAPS and the VR systems were able to present the facial emotional expression trials successfully. Eye tracking and various physiological signals were collected and analyzed offline. The results from gaze and physiological feature level analysis show that they are viable indicators of internal emotional states of patients with SZ although their self-reporting can be biased by their emotion processing and understanding impairments. The patient group overall responded slightly stronger in the positive emotion presentations than both the negative and neutral (baseline, in the case of VR) emotion conditions for almost all the features. This preliminary study could inform future adaptive VR applications for SZ therapy that could harness the inherent processing pattern of patients with SZ as captured from their gaze and body physiological signals. Such implicit mode of interaction is advantageous over performance-only interactions for objective, extensive, and natural interaction with the virtual social avatars. Despite several limitations related to the design of the emotional expressions in the VR system and limited interactivity in the current system, this initial study demonstrates the value of future adaptive VR-based SZ intervention systems. For example, the ability to subtly adjusting emotional expressions of the avatars, integrating this platform into more relevant social paradigms, and embedding online physiological and gaze data to guide interactions to understand psychological states of patients with SZ could be quite useful tools. We believe such capabilities will enable more adaptive, individualized and autonomic therapeutic systems in the long run.

Acknowledgement. This work was supported in part by the National Science Foundation Grant 0967170, National Institute of Health Grant 1R01MH091102-01A1, and NARSAD Distinguished Investigator Grant 19825 from the Brain & Behavior Research Foundation.

References

1. Hempel, R.J., Tulen, J.H., van Beveren, N.J., van Steenis, H.G., Mulder, P.G., Hengeveld, M.W.: Physiological responsivity to emotional pictures in schizophrenia. Journal of Psychiatric Research 39(5), 509–518 (2005)
2. Bleuler, E.: Dementia praecox or the group of schizophrenias. International University Press, New York (1911)
3. Andreasen, N.C.: Scale for the assessment of negative symptoms. University of Iowa, Iowa City (1983)
4. Couture, S.M., Granholm, E.L., Fish, S.C.: A path model investigation of neurocognition, theory of mind, social competence, negative symptoms and real-world functioning in schizophrenia. Schizophrenia Research 125(2), 152–160 (2011)
5. Herbener, E.S., Song, W., Khine, T.T., Sweeney, J.A.: What aspects of emotional functioning are impaired in schizophrenia? Schizophrenia Research 98(1), 239–246 (2008)
6. Kring, A.M., Moran, E.K.: Emotional response deficits in schizophrenia: Insights from affective science. Schizophrenia Bulletin 34(5), 819–834 (2008)
7. Freeman, D.: Studying and treating schizophrenia using virtual reality: A new paradigm. Schizophrenia Bulletin 34(4), 605–610 (2008)
8. Kurtz, M.M., Baker, E., Pearlson, G.D., Astur, R.S.: A virtual reality apartment as a measure of medication management skills in patients with schizophrenia: A pilot study. Schizophrenia Bulletin 33(5), 1162–1170 (2007)
9. Yellowlees, P., Cook, J.: Education about hallucinations using an internet virtual reality system: A qualitative survey. Academic Psychiatry 30(6), 534–539 (2006)
10. Kim, K., Kim, J.-J., Kim, J., Park, D.-E., Jang, H.J., Ku, J., Kim, C.-H., Kim, I.Y., Kim, S.I.: Characteristics of social perception assessed in schizophrenia using virtual reality. Cyberpsychology & Behavior 10(2), 215–219 (2006)
11. Park, K.-M., Ku, J., Choi, S.-H., Jang, H.-J., Park, J.-Y., Kim, S.I., Kim, J.-J.: A virtual reality application in role-plays of social skills training for schizophrenia: A randomized, controlled trial. Psychiatry Research 189(2), 166–172 (2011)
12. Sorkin, A., Weinshall, D., Modai, I., Peled, A.: Improving the accuracy of the diagnosis of schizophrenia by means of virtual reality. American Journal of Psychiatry 163(3), 512–520 (2006)
13. Liu, C., Conn, K., Sarkar, N., Stone, W.: Physiology-based affect recognition for computer-assisted intervention of children with Autism Spectrum Disorder. International Journal of Human-Computer Studies 66(9), 662–677 (2008)
14. Liu, C., Conn, K., Sarkar, N., Stone, W.: Online affect detection and robot behavior adaptation for intervention of children with autism. IEEE Transactions on Robotics 24(4), 883–896 (2008)
15. Andreasen, N.C.: Scale for the assessment of positive symptoms. University of Iowa, Iowa City (1984)
16. Lang, P.J., Bradley, M.M., Cuthbert, B.N.: International affective picture system (IAPS): Technical manual and affective ratings. Gainesville, FL: The Center for Research in Psychophysiology, University of Florida (1999)
17. Bekele, E., Zheng, Z., Swanson, A., Crittendon, J., Warren, Z., Sarkar, N.: Understanding How Adolescents with Autism Respond to Facial Expressions in Virtual Reality Environments. IEEE Transactions on Visualization and Computer Graphics 19(4), 711–720 (2013)
18. Lahiri, U., Warren, Z., Sarkar, N.: Design of a Gaze-Sensitive Virtual Social Interactive System for Children With Autism. IEEE Transactions on Neural Systems and Rehabilitation Engineering (99), 1 (2012)

19. Cacioppo, J.T., Tassinary, L.G., Berntson, G.G.: Handbook of psychophysiology. Cambridge Univ. Pr. (2007)
20. Welch, K., Lahiri, U., Liu, C., Weller, R., Sarkar, N., Warren, Z.: An Affect-Sensitive Social Interaction Paradigm Utilizing Virtual Reality Environments for Autism Intervention. Paper presented at the Human-Computer Interaction. Ambient, Ubiquitous and Intelligent Interaction (2009)
21. Bekele, E., Zheng, Z., Swanson, A., Crittendon, J., Warren, Z., Sarkar, N.: Understanding How Adolescents with Autism Respond to Facial Expressions in Virtual Reality Environments. IEEE Transactions on Visualizations and Computer Graphics (2013) (to appear) (special issue)
22. Blair, J.R., Spreen, O.: Predicting premorbid IQ: A revision of the National Adult Reading Test. The Clinical Neuropsychologist 3(2), 129–136 (1989)
23. Andreasen, N.C., Pressler, M., Nopoulos, P., Miller, D., Ho, B.-C.: Antipsychotic dose equivalents and dose-years: A standardized method for comparing exposure to different drugs. Biological Psychiatry 67(3), 255–262 (2010)
24. Overall, J.E., Gorham, D.R.: The brief psychiatric rating scale. Psychological Reports 10(3), 799–812 (1962)

Attention Training with an Easy–to–Use Brain Computer Interface

Filippo Benedetti[1], Nicola Catenacci Volpi[2],
Leonardo Parisi[3,4], and Giuseppe Sartori[1]

[1] Department of General Psychology. Padova University, 35131 Padova, Italy
[2] Computer Science Department, Univ. of Hertfordshire, AL109AB Hatfield, UK
[3] Istituto Sistemi Complessi, CNR, UOS Sapienza, 00185 Rome, Italy
[4] Dipartimento di Informatica, Università La Sapienza, 00198 Rome, Italy

Abstract. This paper presents a cognitive training based on a brain–computer interface (BCI) that was developed for an adult subject with an attention disorder. According to the neurofeedback methodology, the user processes in real time his own electrical brain activity, which is detected through a non-invasive EEG device. The subject was trained in actively self modulating his own electrical patterns within a play therapy by using a reward–based virtual environment. Moreover, a consumer easy–to–use EEG headset was used, in order to assess its suitability for a concrete clinical application. At the end of the training, the patient obtained a significant improvement in attention.

Keywords: Play therapy, Attention training, Rehabilitation, Brain–computer interface (BCI), Neurofeedback.

1 Introduction

In the last decades the development of new human–computer interaction technologies made possible to directly interface the human brain with digital devices in order to control them just using our thoughts. The brain–computer interface (BCI) through electroencephalography (EEG) arouse the attention of the scientific community thanks to its last improvements in terms of performance and applications [21] [7]. These cover a wide range of areas such as entertainment (e.g. video games) [18], military enhancement [13] and assistive technologies [15].

One of the most interesting area of investigation concerns clinical rehabilitation of physical and cognitive deficits. On one hand it is possible to enhance physical capabilities of disable patients with methodologies such as silent speech interfaces [17], thought–driven wheelchairs [9] and prosthetic devices [16]. On the other hand BCI can be exploited to rehabilitate patients with cognitive deficit. Within the neuropsychology field, one of the most successful application deals with attention disorders (as for ADHD syndrome [10][14][3]).

This paper presents an innovative and user–friendly way to apply consumer BCI technologies and play therapy with virtual reality in the neuropsychological research on attention disorders. Immersive virtual reality (VR) cognitive

R. Shumaker and S. Lackey (Eds.): VAMR 2014, Part II, LNCS 8526, pp. 236–247, 2014.

training has been already confirmed to be effective with behavioural and attention problems [25]. In the neuropsychological rehabilitation field, previous research has generally used game–like training environments in order to increase motivation and participation in the patient [23][24]. In that regard, a good virtual reality–based rehabilitation has to deal with the usability of the employed human–computer interaction technologies. Therefore, within the BCI community, one of the challenges of the last years is to develop more advanced devices and experimental methodologies in term of cost for costumers and usability. This becomes further important in the rehabilitation field with cognitive or physical disabled patients, who typically have more difficulties to be comfortable with normal EEGs.

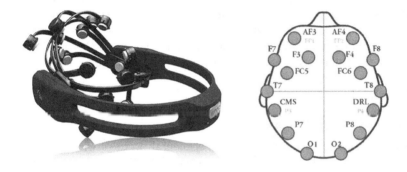

Fig. 1. The *Emotiv* EPOC and the electrodes location

In recent times, simplified consumer BCI EEG headsets were introduced, such as *Emotiv* EPOC [26] and *NeuroSky* [27]. So far, the research community still wonders about the accuracy and suitability of consumer BCI electronics in clinical environments [1]. However, although less clear and strong, *Emotiv* EPOC's recording accuracy has been already assessed within the literature as having reasonable quality compared to a medical grade device [8]. The *Emotiv* EPOC device, makes possible to simplify the equipment set up, avoiding the practical difficulties related to the EEG operations, such as skin abrasion or the application of conductive gel on the subject, which represents a particularly valuable advantage in attention disorder rehabilitation with restless patients. Our study confirm that is possible to use this type of headset in a clinical context, where the usability of the device (i.e. wireless connectivity, saline solution instead of gel, fixed arrangement of electrodes) can positively influence the compliance of the subject.

Based on neurofeedback methodology, we performed a cognitive training on an adult subject suffering from a frontal syndrome. In line with this approach, the user was confronted in real time with his own electrical brain activity: by using a reward–based virtual environment, we trained the subject with a video game to actively self modulate his own electrical patterns. In line with this approach, this study aims at further reduce problems of compliance and familiarity also with clinical equipments. Moreover the procedure has been embedded within a game–like environment to challenge the patient. Such a methodology aims to develop a training in which the subject is more motivated and involved than in a typical clinical context.

The first step of the cognitive training was to record specific electrical patterns with the *Emotiv* EPOC. These were used as input commands in the video game. The participant was then asked by the game to repeatedly recall various and specific patterns corresponding to different movements of an object in a 3D space with levels of increasing difficulty. Each correct move leads to a positive reinforcement stimulus appearance. In this case a slightly erotic kind of reward was chosen, since the frontal syndrome of the patient was characterized by a sexual disinhibition. During and after the training the subject's attention deficit has been assessed with three different neuropsychological tests (i.e. Posner, CPT–II, d2). It will be shown that with this combination of new BCI technology and play therapy one can obtain significant results: at the end of the training of this case study the subject was able to improve his attention skills.

2   Methods

2.1   Experimental Design

The method used in this study is an experimental protocol within the subject, a manipulated variable on and off. The experiment is in the alternation of two types of phases: a training phase with neurofeedback (A) and a resting phase (B) not subjected to any kind of experimental stimulus. These two phases are repeated twice in alternation and each have the duration of one month. The two training phases (A) are composed of five meetings of one–hour training. The cognitive performance of the subject is assessed at the beginning and the end of each phase, through the same neuropsychological tests. We expect to find significant performance improvements at the end of each experimental phase and no significant changes at the end of each resting phase.

2.2   Subject

The participant of this single case study is G.F. (male, age 36). In October 2003, due to a car accident, suffers a head injury. As a result he suffers from a frontal syndrome with character of medium–high severity, with outcome of cognitive and behavioural disorders: regarding to the cognitive profile, the previous neuropsychological assessments identify a "damage to the frontal lobes with impairments charged to attention and concentration, the ability to support a cognitive activity over time and switch from one line of thought to another ". On the behavioural level the loss of spontaneous initiative (apathy), a depressive mood with a tendency to restlessness, irritability and aggression, and also the lack of awareness of his own cognitive disorders and sexual disinhibition were diagnosed as the symptom of his syndrome.

The subject has no prior experience with BCI and neurofeedback.

2.3   BCI Device and Software

For the signal acqusition an EEG recording device produced by Emotiv Systems is used: *Emotiv* EPOC.The device uses a set of electrodes placed with a fixed arrangement and localized on the International 10-20 System [12], with 14 channels (with CMS/DRL references in P3/P4 locations, see Figure 1). The sampling frequency is 128Hz. The EPOC filter is set from 0.2Hz to 43Hz. The application of the sensors is easy and requires few minutes: it is sufficient to wet with a saline solution small sponges that allow the passage of the electric signal on the scalp to the EEG electrodes (without any use of electro–conductive paste or abrasion of the scalp).

The computer acquires the EEG signal directly via wireless from the EPOC device. Processing occurs online through the Software Development Kit (SDK) of EPOC and is communicated to a graphic user interface developed for the experiment. This interface was develop by using the OpenGL library and the C++ language on a Windows XP machine with Visual Studio 2010 Express and displayed during the training on a 21-inch LCD monitor.

2.4   Task Structure

During the training the participant is requested to repeatedly recall and produce various and specific electrical patterns. These are used as input commands for the task. The feedback consists of two components: the corresponding movement of a cube in a 3D space and the appearance of a positive reinforcement stimulus.

The first step is the Recording of the EEG patterns. The subject begins by defining a baseline, through a 30 seconds EEG recording in a neutral state. Then, for every possible cube's movements, the corresponding patterns are recorded for 8 seconds each (e.g., one for UP, one for DOWN, one for LEFT and so on). Once these recordings are concluded the participant has organised the commands to meet the request of the Test phase.

The Test is composed by a block of 40 consecutive trials, 15 seconds each (Figure 2a). At the beginning of each trial a word at the centre of the screen indicates the direction to which the cube has to be moved within the next 15 seconds interval (Figure 2b I). The subject must recall from time to time the pre–recorded pattern associated with the requested movement. The different directions requests are randomized and equally distributed within the 40 trials block.

In each trial a red bar on the left side of the screen indicates the power of the recalled pattern (Figure 2b II). Upon exceeding the 65% intensity of production, the appearance of a positive reinforcement visual stimulus fades in (a slightly erotic image) progressively sharper until the 100% intensity (Figure 2b III). On the contrary, if the player moves towards the wrong direction, the reinforcement will not be shown (Figure 2b IV). This type of stimulus was chosen considering the sexual disinhibition of the subject.

a)

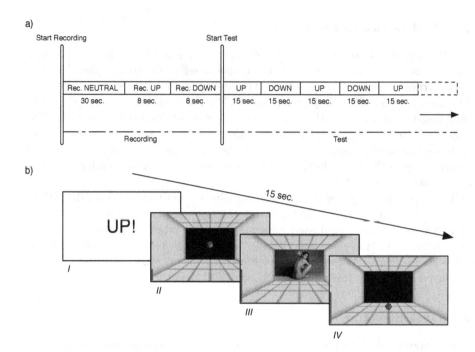

Fig. 2. a) Task structure. b) Single trial.

2.5 Training Procedure

The two experimental phases (A) consist of five training meetings distributed with rate of once or twice a week during a month in a laboratory of the Department of General Psychology, Padua, Italy.

At the beginning of the whole training GF was told to think of distinct mental states, easy to recall, and that these thoughts would have been translated into electrical patterns detected by the EEG headset as commands for the cube movement in the game.

During each meeting, after 10 minutes of practice to become familiar with the task, the participant begins the training: two sessions composed each by a Recording and a Test phase. A short break separates the two equal sessions to give to the subject a time of recovery after the attention effort. The entire cognitive training is characterised by an increasing difficulty in the requests asked to the participant and the game is organised and divided into different levels. In the first level the player has to perform actively one movement with the cube in all the trials (e.g. UP); in the second level two movements are requested (e.g. UP and DOWN) randomly distributed in the trials block, and so on for the next levels increasing the number of movements.

To unlock the access to the next level, the player must reach the 95% accuracy rate of the requested movements, crossing the threshold of 65% of intensity indicated by the reward stimulus fading in, in both Test sessions of a meeting. This criterion was set in order to be sure that once the level has been completed, the movement–skill was learned completely before adding another one to the next level. With this procedure the participant faces a sustained attention task from the very first level. In the later levels of the training the selective component of attention is also requested by switching between two or more movements. After the resting phase (B) of the entire cognitive training, in the subsequent training phase (A), the subject will start the game again from level 1.

2.6 Neuropsychological Tests

For the attention assessment an adaptation of the Posner's spatial cueing task [19], the d2 test [2] and the CPT–II [5] are used.

In this study, a computerized test on Posner's paradigm was chosen to assess mainly the intensive component of attention through the precise detection of the parameters of response accuracy (ACC) and reaction times (RT). The trials, divided into 8 blocks of 48 trials each, follow one another with a variable time between 50 ms and 150 ms and the time between the cue and the target (Stimulus Onset Asynchrony, SOA) can be 200 ms or 800 ms. The test has a total duration of 30 minutes.

The Continuous Performance Test consists of a visual test performed on the computer with an odd–ball paradigm. This test is used for the assessment of attention and vigilance, detection of the signal and the automatic response inhibition ability [4]. On this occasion Conners' version of this test is used (CCPT–II).

The d2 test is a barrage test characterized by the simultaneous presentation of visually similar stimuli. This test is presented as a standardized measurement method particularly accurate to detect individual abilities of selective attention and concentration [2].

The tests were administered at the beginning and end of every Training (A) and Rest (B) phases, at a distance of one month, for a total of five measurements taken at time $t1$, $t2$, $t3$, $t4$, $t5$, corresponding to the start of the experiment, the first training's end, the first rest's end, the second training's end and the second rest's end respectively.

3   Results

3.1   Posner

In the results analysis of the test, the values of Accuracy (Acc) and Reaction Time (RT) are considered. The obtained values were analyzed using a paired samples t–test, comparing the performances recorded after the different phases (Figure 3). As a result of the training sessions (A) significant improvements were found. Regarding the Accuracy parameter, the t–test shows a significant difference between the beginning and the end of the first phase (A) of cognitive training ($t(6) = -9128, p < 0.001$); the analysis shows also a significant reduction of Reaction Times (RT) as a result of the first experimental session ($t(6) = 42.965$, $p < 0.001$) and the second one ($t(6) = 8.916$, $p < 0.001$). Following the first rest phase (B), the t–test shows no significant differences compared to previous assessments in both parameters Accuracy and Reaction Times, while following the second rest phase the t–test presents a significant difference for both parameters (Acc: $t4 - t5$: $t(6) = 2.661$, $p =< 0.05$; TR: $t4 - t5$: $t(6) = -4,676$, $p =< 0.05$).

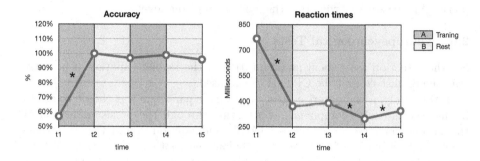

Fig. 3. Posner test results

3.2 CPT–II

The five assessments reveal a trend similar to the one detected by the Posner's test. The performance progression is analyzed looking at different parameters that are indicative of attention capacity and control of impulsivity: Confidence Index, Omissions, Commissions, Reaction Time, Variability of reaction times and capacity of Detectability. Except for the Confidence Index, the scores are converted to *T–scores* and the significance of the changes between the different performances in each parameter is calculated with the Reliable Change Index [11]. Clinically significant changes has been detected in the following parameters (see Figure 4).

Confidence Index: the percentage chance to present an attention disorder, if more than 50% is defined clinically at risk. The values show improvements after both the training sessions. A significant change after the second training phase in comparison with the first assessment has been recorded ($t1$: 52.4%; $t4$: 42.3%). It starts with a clinical classification of attention deficit in $t1$ (52.4%) to a non–clinical in $t2$ (49.9%) stable until the end of the study ($t5$: 45.5%).

Regarding the parameters of *Commissions* (the subject responds to the non–target stimulus or responds too slowly); *Variability* (the degree of constancy of the speed of response); *Discrimination* (the value related to the ability to correctly identify the target stimuli): significant improvements are recorded after the first training phase, the performance is also assessed as "mildly atypical" (i.e. T–score > 60) in $t1$ and within the average in $t2$. This significant change, as a result of the first training, remains stable and within the average until the end of the study.

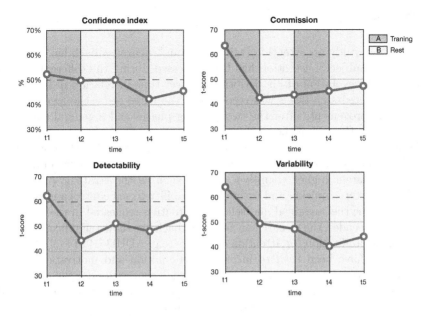

Fig. 4. CPT–II results

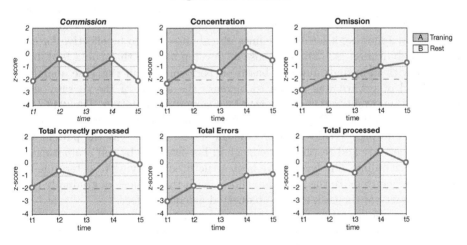

Fig. 5. d2 test results

3.3   d2

The raw scores obtained in the different categories were converted to *z–score*, showing an increase of the values as a result of both the training phases in every parameters. Furthermore, the first assessment is almost globally out of average (*z–score*> 2), excluding the parameter of Total characters processed, while the last one is characterized by data within the average, with the exception of errors of Commission (see Figure 5).

4 Discussion

In the present study an attention training through neurofeedback has been developed. The subject's attention has been assessed during the different phases to measure the evolution of his performance over time in relation to the training. The expected *step trend* was recorded in the three tests: the results show significant improvements after the two training phases and a general enhanced performance at the end of the study.

The attention improvements are the results of the effort in self modulating the EEG patterns requested within the structured neurofeedback training. This subtended different higher cognitive abilities such as the strategic process to recall these patterns quickly and precisely; the ability to self control and regulate one's behaviour; the sustained and selective attention requested in the training.

In the last decades, the research on neurofeedback has shown significant results in terms of rehabilitation for attention disorders (e.g. ADHD [10][14][3]). Game–like trainings have been used to increase participation and motivation in the subjects. The key of the training was in fact to elicit motivation for the patient to stay focused and challenge himself further, since attention deficit and behavioural issues can be considerable opponents in a cognitive training.

Virtual reality–based play therapy appeared to provide a solution to this challenge [24][28][29]. By choosing a VR game, we aimed to develop an intervention tool that would have been challenging and appealing for the user. The game was designed by following a set of guidelines already assessed to be effective for cognitive rehabilitation [23][30]. We chose to develop a game that could feed–back the user with immediate rewards based on performance, in this case a slightly erotic kind of reward was chosen to increase the appeal of the therapy since the frontal syndrome was characterized by a sexual disinhibition. The game also provided the patient with quantitative performance data: a gauge representing his ability and precise rules to overcome the levels. In this way the patient was leaded to actively and responsibly engage in his own cure by self evaluating his performance online. The levels have been structured by trying to determine the right challenge to make the game fun (flow), with the purpose of gradually raise the complexity of the task and the requested attention effort.

Moreover, the evolution towards economical and easy–to–use headsets can be considered an essential step to achieve a new generation of user–friendly BCI training equipment [20]. In this study, with the use of the *Emotiv* EPOC device, was possible to simplify the equipment set up, avoiding the practical difficulties related to the EEG operations such as skin abrasion and adding conductive gel, especially with our type of restless patient. The simple usability of this headset (i.e. wireless connectivity, saline solution instead of gel, fixed arrangement of electrodes, etc.) influenced positively the compliance of the subject. So if on one hand the *Emotiv's* recording accuracy has been already assessed within the literature as having "reasonable quality compared to a medical grade device" [8][22], on the other, regarding its suitability in clinical environments, the results of this study show the important potential of using this kind of device for concrete clinical applications. Not only significant positive results were obtained regarding the subject's attention deficit, but we could also confirm that similar technologies facilitate the creation of user–friendly training environments, and hence can improve the compliance rate of subjects. In our opinion, similar devices enable to develop a training and a play therapy in which the subject is more motivated and involved than in a typical clinical context.

5 Conclusion

In this paper a virtual reality–based play therapy with neurofeedback was used for a patient with an attention disorder. As seen in previous experiments and assessed in this single case study, the effort in self modulating one's electric patterns into a BCI has significant positive implications for attention disorder. In a clinical setting, create a user–centered training with an easy–fitting procedure for the patient can also be crucial. When opting for the experimental procedure, the right EEG device and reinforcements, our challenge was to find a trade–off between user's motivation and goals, and his health–mental state. Due to the patient's attention deficit and restlessness, we shifted the focus of our training on usability and appeal, in order to let the patient concentrate on the task without any environmental or technical distractions related to the EEG device, and trying at the same time to make his effort as pleasant as possible. A non invasive EEG device was used, since our priority was to develop a comfortable training system. Our experiment allowed us to eliminate complex procedures, which were deemed not feasible for this kind of patient. Moreover, play therapy has been an effective answer for the patient's motivation problem. Starting from the results of this case study, our aim is to extend the same procedure to a higher number of subjects, in order to confirm further our results.

In recent years the effectiveness of BCI therapy has been confirmed and the related technologies have become more commercially accessible and usable. However, it is impossible until now to carry out the neurofeedback training without the assistance of a therapist. The innovative aspect of this new kind of consumer equipment (provided with a well designed training and an adequate reinforcements) is that the patient should be able to eventually undertake his training independently. One could also think to promote a domestic therapy with home exercises and training programs (telerehabilitation), easy–to–use for the patient or for his caregiver. Therefore, the challenge for us is to further develop EEG devices enhanced in lightness and precision; create appealing and adequate training software; deepen the study of BCI and neurofeedback method for a more effective learning of the interface from the user. In order to achieve this much, a partnership is needed between engineering, computer science, neuroscience and psychology, through which virtual realities and related technologies can be better applied to healthcare and rehabilitation.

References

1. Ang, C.S., Sakel, M., Pepper, M., Phillips, M.: Use of brain–computer interfaces in neurological rehabilitation. British Journal of Neuroscience Nursing 7(3), 523–528 (2011)
2. Brickenkamp, R., Zillmer, E.: The D2 test of attention. Hogrefe & Huber Pub. (1998)
3. Butnik, S.M.: Neurofeedback in adolescents and adults with attention deficit hyperactivity disorder. Journal of Clinical Psychology 61(5), 621–625 (2005)
4. Conners, C.K., Epstein, J.N., Angold, A., Klaric, J.: Continuous performance test performance in a normative epidemiological sample. Journal of Abnormal Child Psychology 31(5), 555–562 (2003)
5. Conners, C.K., Staff, M.H.S.: Conners' continuous performance Test II (CPT II v. 5). Multi-Health Systems Inc., North Tonawanda (2000)
6. Davison, G.C., Neale, J.M.: Abnormal Psychology, Study Guide. Wiley Online Library, 117–119 (2000)
7. Dornhege, G.: Toward brain–computer interfacing. MIT press (2007)
8. Duvinage, M., Castermans, T., Dutoit, T., Petieau, M., Hoellinger, T., Saedeleer, C., Seetharaman, K., Cheron, G.: A P300-based quantitative comparison between the Emotiv Epoc headset and a medical EEG device. In: Proceedings of the IASTED International Conference Biomedical Engineering (2012)
9. Galán, F., Nuttin, M., Lew, E., Ferrez, P.W., Vanacker, G., Philips, J., del Millán, J.R.: A brain–actuated wheelchair: Asynchronous and non–invasive brain–computer interfaces for continuous control of robots. Clinical Neurophysiology 119(9), 2159–2169 (2008)
10. Gevensleben, H., Holl, B., Albrecht, B., Schlamp, D., Kratz, O., Studer, P., Wangler, S., Rothenberger, A., Moll, G.H., Heinrich, H.: Distinct EEG effects related to neurofeedback training in children with ADHD: A randomized controlled trial. International Journal of Psychophysiology 74(2), 149–157 (2009)
11. Jacobson, N.S., Truax, P.: Clinical significance: A statistical approach to defining meaningful change in psychotherapy research. Journal of Consulting and Clinical Psychology 59(1), 12 (1991)
12. Jasper, H.H.: The ten twenty electrode system of the international federation. Electroencephalography and Clinical Neurophysiology 10, 371–375 (1958)
13. Kotchetkov, I.S., Hwang, B.Y., Appelboom, G., Kellner, C.P., Connolly Jr., E.S.: Brain–computer interfaces: Military, neurosurgical, and ethical perspective. Neurosurgical Focus 28(5), E25 (2010)
14. Lévesque, J., Beauregard, M., Mensour, B.: Effect of neurofeedback training on the neural substrates of selective attention in children with attention–deficit/hyperactivity disorder: A functional magnetic resonance imaging study. Neuroscience Letters 394(3), 216–221 (2006)
15. del Millán, J.R., Rupp, R., Müller–Putz, G.R., Murray–Smith, R., Giugliemma, C., Tangermann, M., Vidaurre, C., Cincotti, F., Kübler, A., Leeb, R., et al.: Combining brain–computer interfaces and assistive technologies: State–of–the–art and challenges. Frontiers in Neuroscience 4 (2010)
16. Müller-Putz, G.R., Scherer, R., Pfurtscheller, G., Rupp, R.: Brain–computer interfaces for control of neuroprostheses: From synchronous to asynchronous mode of operation / Brain–computer interfaces zur steuerung von neuroprothesen: von der synchronen zur asynchronen funktionsweise. Biomedizinische Technik 51(2), 57–63 (2006)

17. Neumann, N., Kuübler, A., Kaiser, J., Hinterberger, T., Birbaumer, N.: Conscious perception of brain states: Mental strategies for brain–computer communication. Neuropsychologia 41(8), 1028–1036 (2003)
18. Nijholt, A., Bos, D.P.O., Reuderink, B.: Turning shortcomings into challenges: Brain–computer interfaces for games. Entertainment Computing 1(2), 85–94 (2009)
19. Posner, M.I.: Orienting of attention. Quarterly Journal of Experimental Psychology 32(1), 3–25 (1980)
20. Van Aart, J., Klaver, E.R., Bartneck, C., Feijs, L.M., Peters, P.J.: EEG headset for neurofeedback therapy enabling easy use in the home environment. Citeseer (2008)
21. Wolpaw, J.R., Birbaumer, N., Heetderks, W.J., McFarland, D.J., Peckham, P.H., Schalk, G., Donchin, E., Quatrano, L.A., Robinson, C.J., Vaughan, T.M., et al.: Brain–computer interface technology: A review of the first international meeting. IEEE Transactions on Rehabilitation Engineering 8(2), 164–173 (2000)
22. Yaomanee, K., Pan-ngum, S., Ayuthaya, P.I.N.: Brain signal detection methodology for attention training using minimal EEG channels. In: 2012 10th International Conference on ICT and Knowledge Engineering (ICT & Knowledge Engineering), pp. 84–89. IEEE (2012)
23. Bondoc, S., Powers, C., Herz, N., Hermann, V.: Virtual Reality-Based Rehabilitation. OT Practice 15(11) (2010)
24. Harris, K., Reid, D.: The influence of virtual reality play on children's motivation. Canadian Journal of Occupational Therapy 72(1), 21–29 (2005)
25. Cho, B., Ku, J., Pyojung, D., Kim, S., Lee, Y.H., Kim, I.Y., et al.: The effect of virtual reality cognitive training for attention enhancement. CyberPsychology and Behaviour 5(2), 129–137 (2002)
26. Emotiv EPOC Research Edition SDK, https://emotiv.com/store/sdk/eeg-bci/research-edition-sdk/ (accessed October 2, 2014)
27. NeuroSky, http://neurosky.com (accessed October 2, 2014)
28. Rand, D., Kizony, R., Weiss, P.L.: Virtual reality rehabilitation for all: Vivid GX versus Sony PlayStation II EyeToy. In: 5th Intl. Conf. On Disability, Virtual Environments and Assoc. Technologies, pp. 87–94 (2004)
29. Halton, J.: Virtual rehabilitation with video games: A new frontier for occupational therapy. Occupational Therapy Now 9(6), 12–14 (2008)
30. Aart, J.V., Klaver, E., Bartneck, C., Feijs, L., Peters, P.: EEG Headset For Neurofeedback Therapy - Enabling Easy Use in the Home Environment. In: Proceedings of the Biosignals -. International Conference on Bio-inspired Signals and Systems, Funchal, pp. 23–30 (2008)

Augmented Reality Treatment for Phantom Limb Pain

Francesco Carrino[1], Didier Rizzotti[1], Claudia Gheorghe[1], Patrick Kabasu Bakajika[2],
Frédérique Francescotti-Paquier[2], and Elena Mugellini[1]

[1] University of Applied Sciences and Arts Western Switzerland, Switzerland
{francesco.carrino,elena.mugellini}@hes-so.ch,
{Didier.Rizzotti,claudia.gheorghe}@he-arc.ch
[2] CHUV – Centre Hospitalier Universitaire Vaudois, Lausanne, Switzerland
{Patrick.Bakajika-Kabasu,Frederique.francescotti}@chuv.ch

Abstract. Mirror therapy is used from many years to treat phantom limb pain in amputees. However, this approach presents several limitations that could be overcome using the possibilities of new technologies. In this paper we present a novel approach based on augmented reality, 3D tracking and 3D modeling to enhance the capabilities of the classic mirror therapy. The system was conceived to be integrated in a three steps treatment called "Graded motor imagery" that includes: limb laterality recognition, motor imagery and, finally, mirror therapy. Aiming at a future home care therapy, we chose to work with low-cost technologies studying their advantages and drawbacks.

In this paper, we present the conception and a first qualitative evaluation of the developed system.

Keywords: Augmented Reality, 3D tracking, 3D modeling, phantom limb pain treatment, mirror therapy.

1 Introduction

In this paper we introduce a system based on augmented reality for the treatment of the phantom limb pain. The expression "phantom limb" describes the sensation of abnormal persistence of a member after an amputation or after that it became unresponsive due to some others reasons (as a stroke). Even if people suffering from this phenomenon are aware that this feeling is not real, usually they experience painful sensations in their amputated limb known as "phantom limb pain". The reason for these symptoms is not entirely clear and several theories coexist trying to explain the mechanisms underlying this syndrome [1].

To appreciate the importance of the phenomenon, in statistical terms 90-98% of people after an amputation report experiencing a sensation of phantom limb, about 85% of cases are accompanied by uncomfortable or painful sensations, physical limitation and disability. In 70% of cases, the phantom sensation is painful even 25 years after the loss of a limb [2].

The main treatment methods described in the literature for phantom limb pain are mirror therapy, motor imagery and graded motor imagery. All these treatments would recreate a correct cerebral representation of the missing limb for reducing phantom

R. Shumaker and S. Lackey (Eds.): VAMR 2014, Part II, LNCS 8526, pp. 248–257, 2014.
© Springer International Publishing Switzerland 2014

limb pain. In this paper, we focus on the mirror therapy. The mirror therapy was invented by V. S. Vilayanur Ramachandran [3] to help relieve phantom limb pain, in which patients can "feel" they still have the lost limb. In particular, the patient hides the stump behind a mirror (see Fig. 1) and, using the reflection of the good limb, the mirror creates the illusion that both limbs are present. The illusion persists while the patient tries to perform symmetric movements. Several experiments [4, 5] have shown that the mirror approach contributed to reduce the phantom limb pain, even if, currently, there is no general consensus regarding the real effectiveness of the mirror therapy [6].

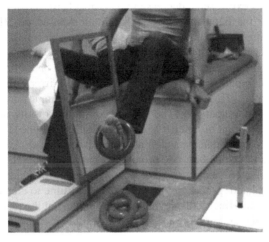

Fig. 1. Example of use of the mirror box by a healthy person. We tested the mirror therapy in order to get a better understanding of its limitations.

Starting from these assumptions, the goal of this project is to exploit the capabilities of the new technologies to develop an "augmented reality mirror therapy" capable of increasing the *immersion* and the engagement of the patient while removing some constraints related to the classic mirror therapy (i.e., restrained patient's movements, limited number of exercises, etc.). We want to study the feasibility of integrating an "augmented reality mirror therapy" within a treatment of occupational therapy for patients that suffered a lower limb amputation.

Using augmented reality (AR) to improve the classic mirror offers several advantages. First of all, AR makes possible for the patient to make more varied movements or even actions impossible to perform with a simple mirror such as movements that pass the center of the body (otherwise limited by the mirror), interaction with virtual objects to play games or perform more or less complex exercises. These new possibilities could allow enhancing the participation of the patient to the therapy presenting more entertaining scenarios. Then, the scenarios can be adapted to the different patients' needs or interest, for instance going in the direction of *gamification* for younger patients or providing more guidance to patients that need it. Furthermore, the therapist will be able to choose the more appropriate exercise scenario in relation to the physical possibilities of the patient, which can be extremely different from person to person, depending on various factors such as age, amputation type, etc.

2   Background and Related Work

Many works tried to improve the classic mirror therapy using approaches based on virtual reality (VR) or AR aiming at providing a more immersive and interactive experience for the patient.

Murray et al. [7, 8] analyzed the use of VR as a treatment for the phantom limb pain. The authors presented a test protocol focused on the quantification of the pain perceived by the participants before and after the sessions with the mirror box in VR. Three actual cases were analyzed for a period of three weeks and several sessions. The three participants expressed a decrease in pain in at least one of the sessions.

Two systems for the hand movement rehabilitation based on VR and AR were compared in [9]. The study showed that the AR approach provided better results, especially in terms of realism of the simulation.

Desmond et al. [10] presented a mirror therapy approach based on AR and tested it with three patients comparing the results with the classic mirror box. Instead of using a head-mounted display (HMD) for the AR, they used a simple screen with a consequent loss in terms of immersion. They observed similar results from the two approaches with the exception of a rather vivid sensations experienced by patients when the AR was used to display unexpected or abnormal movements.

In [11], the authors developed an AR prototype consisting of a Head-Mounted Display (HMD) and a stereo camera system. This system allowed recording images of the healthy patient's hand, processing the images in real-time to create a reproduction of the missing hand, and finally displaying the virtual hand at the place of the missing one. Unfortunately, the authors did not present any study concerning the use of their system with patients.

3   Methods

Similarly to [11], our work aims to develop an AR system using a HMD to improve the immersion of the classic mirror therapy. However, our approach aims to extend previous works under several aspects that will be highlighted in this section. First of all, we focused on the treatment of patients with amputations in the lower limbs. We chose to move in this direction because of the high incidence of patients with an amputation at a lower limb (that statistically represents the great majority [12]) and also because most of the previous works focused only on the upper limbs. However, our approach can be easily extended to track and modeling the patient's arms.

Due to the growth of the life expectancy, in the next years the need of medical attention will be larger and larger putting "Home Care" in a role of primary importance. For this reason we chose to adopt low-cost technologies available on the market following the idea of possibly bringing in the future the therapy directly in the patients' homes. However, this first study will be held in a hospital, directly under the supervision of occupational therapists. After analyzing several options, we chose the following devices (Fig. 2):

- Microsoft Kinect for the tracking of the present limb and to animate the 3D model of the missing limb.
- NaturalPoint TrackIR 5 with TrackClip PRO for the head-tracking.
- Vuzix Warp 920AR for the visualization.

Fig. 2. The devices used in the system: (from left) Microsoft Kinect, Vuzix Warp 920AR and NaturalPoint TrackIR 5

In order to conceive exercises as useful as possible for the patient, we designed the exercises with the aid of occupational therapists taking inspiration from the exercises that they usually perform with amputated patients.

Finally, our system will be used and evaluated within a medical research project with amputated patients, as part of a therapy including also limb laterality recognition tasks and motor imagery ("Graded motor imagery").

From a technical point of view, our approach is based on three main pillars:

Augmented Reality. Aiming at improving the immersivity, the realism and the interactivity of the mirror therapy, we chose to create a system in mixed reality in which the patient has the possibility to watch his real, healthy leg together with a virtual model of the missing leg replacing the stump. Moreover, augmented realty provides the possibility of integrate exercises with virtual objects that would be impossible with the classic system and that could help to motivate the patient to practice rehabilitation exercises.

3D Tracking. The present limb is continuously tracked in real time, in order to animate de virtual model of the missing limb, in particular we use information about hips, knees and ankles movements and rotations. Moreover, we track the patient head orientation to know continuously the patient point of view and therefore mix consistently virtual objects and real objects (for instance, to place the virtual limb in the right spot in relationship to the amputation and the patient's point of view).

3D Modeling. A virtual model of the missing limb is reconstructed using information of the present limb. For instance, we used parameter such as calf diameter, leg length and skin color to create a realistic 3D model of the missing leg. In our case, the skin color assumes a particular relevance since the exercises are often performed with a naked leg. Moreover, we added physical constraints to avoid abnormal movements of the model when the tracking data are noisy or imprecise. We developed four legs models to take into account amputations at the hips or knees level (see Fig. 3).

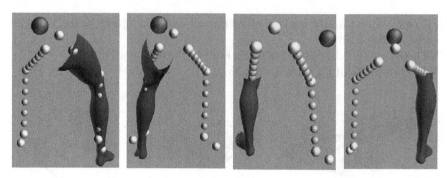

Fig. 3. The four leg models (without the skin texture)

The next section will present the use case of the application.

4   Use Case Scenario

The research project that included the development of the prototype presented in this paper proposes an occupational therapy session composed of three steps ("Graded motor imagery"): limb laterality recognition tasks, motor imagery and, finally, mirror therapy with augmented reality.

The first step "Limb laterality recognition" involves having the patient correctly identify pictures of right and left hands/legs in various positions. The second step, "Motor imagery", involves asking the patient to mentally represent movement with amputated leg. The **whole** process is important for the patient's rehabilitation; however, since this paper focuses mainly on the conception and development of a prototype for an AR mirror therapy, the scenario presented in this section will focus on this latter step.

The therapy will takes place over several sessions. The first session requires an additional step to getting started with the system so, also in the home care scenario, the first session will be held in a hospital under the supervision of occupational therapist. During the first session the system will record the patient data: the patient sits in front of a camera in a well-defined position, in a controlled environment (i.e., determined room illumination, uniform background color). Given the distance of the patient from the camera and the camera parameters, we are able to automatically measure the leg's parameters such as the legs' dimensions (e.g., calf diameter, length of the thigh, etc.) and the skin color (Fig. 4).

These parameters are stored along other patient's personal information (such as age, type of amputation, etc.) and then assigned to the 3D leg model in order to match the characteristics of the present limb and the amputation level. This setup phase is needed only the first time for a new patient. Starting from the second session, the data related to a particular patient can be simply reloaded into the system. In the case of an important change on the color of the patient skin (for instance due to a new, intense tanning) a new model can be created.

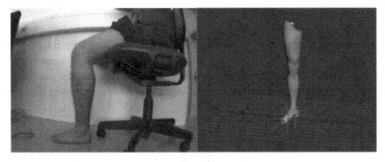

Fig. 4. Example of picture used to calculate the leg's parameters (left) to assign to the 3D leg model (right)

The following steps are common to every session, while the first session will be directed by the therapist, from the second session on the patient will be able to follow the therapy autonomously in her/his home.

Once the leg model is ready (recorded or reloaded), the occupational therapy session can begin: the patient takes place into the exercise area (i.e., inside the Kinect and Track IR field of view). The setup is depicted in Fig. 5.

Initially, a short phase of automatic calibration detects the body position and the head orientation. The leg's 3D model is then visualized attached to the patient body in the correct position accordingly with the tracking information provided by Kinect and the stored information about the patient's amputation level. The model is then animated accordingly with the movement of the healthy leg.

Depending on the exercise chosen by the therapist, the virtual limb can perform either symmetric movements or replicate the same movements of the healthy limb.

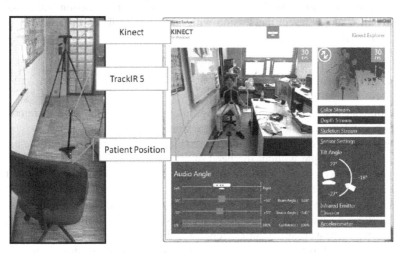

Fig. 5. Example of the setup of the exercise region

Finally, the patient can interact with virtual objects present on the scene using the virtual limb as well as the real limb (see Fig. 6). The coherence between the user perspective and the virtual objects on the scene (virtual leg, objects for the exercise, etc.) are constantly assured by tracking the user's head position and orientation.

In this first prototype we developed a simple game in which the patient can use conjointly the healthy leg and the virtual leg to pick and move a virtual ball (see [13] for a complete video demonstration).

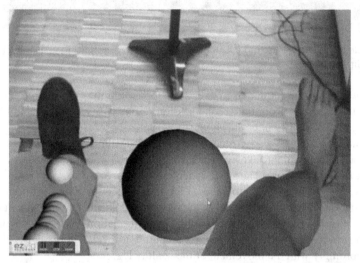

Fig. 6. Screenshot of a healthy user testing the application (from the user point-of-view)

During this preliminary study, once completed the therapy session, we asked the patient to fill a survey about the session with particular focus on the usability of the system and the realism of the simulation.

5   Discussion

The preliminary tests we performed during this study showed a series of interesting points to be analyzed and developed in future works.

Using commercial device helped us to create an application that would be easy to deploy in a user's home without the need of a long training. The Kinect is basically *plug and play* as well as the Vuzix Warp 920AR. The only problem we encountered was the setup of the Track IR for the head tracking. In fact, this device works well just in a range going from 61 cm to 152 cm from the user's head. This obliged us to put the Track IR on a support in front of the user, causing a small occlusion on the Kinect field of view. Moreover, since our exercises required the user to keep the head tilted far forward, we had to put the sensor at the knees level while setting accurately the inclination of the Track IR camera in order to detect the head movements in this very particular position. The mentioned occlusion issue did not cause many troubles. The Kinect tracking algorithm has proven to be robust enough to manage small occlusions in space and time.

Finally, Kinect and Track IR are sensible to infrared light (both technologies are based on emitters and infrared cameras); however, just avoiding placing the patient in front of a window prevented any issue related to infrared noise.

If, on the on hand, using commercial devices allowed us to build a system fairly easy to set up, on the other hand, the limitations imposed by these devices are numerous and need to be discussed.

Kinect's precision is good enough to provide a good tracking of the human body and the leg movements. However, the tracking of the ankle movements is already less precise: the *abduction/adduction*[1] movements are fairly tracked, while *plantar flexion/dorsiflexion*[2] movements are, basically, ignored. In a future application aiming at tracking more subtle movements (for instance fingers movements) another sensor or technique should be considered.

The used AR glasses have 31-degree diagonal field of view. This means that the user see in front of him a sort of "window on the real world" inside a black frame. The field of view offered to the user is good enough to perform mostly of the occupational therapy exercises involving legs (as you can see in Fig. 6), the legs are visible from the top of the knees). However, a wider field of view could facilitate the immersion for the user.

The system provides a fairly realistic representation of the missing limb adapting the 3D model to match color and size of the healthy leg. The resolution of the adopted HMD (two 640 x 480 LCD displays, 60 Hz progressive scan update rate, 24-bit true color) does not allow seeing much more details; for this reason, in this first prototype, we ignored important leg's characteristics like hairiness and muscle mass that probably should be taken into account for the higher resolution future versions.

Finally, there is a short delay between the movement of the present limb and the visualization of the movement of the virtual limb due to tracking and image processing time. In order to evaluate the impact of the lag on the therapy and how the user perceives it, deeper analyses are needed.

Talking about future possible ameliorations to improve the immersion provided by the system several options are open:

- Adding 3D vision. The HDM used, such as others, has two cameras and two screens (one per eye) making possible to provide a 3D vision of the real and virtual world.
- Adding shadows generated by the 3D models.
- Using sensors detecting muscular activity (such as electromyography) to trigger designated animations of the virtual limb overcoming the limit of parallel movements.

6   Conclusion

In this work we developed a system for the treatment of phantom limb pain based on augmented reality, 3D modeling and 3D tracking. We chose to work with commercial

---

[1]   During the *abduction/adduction* movement the tip of the foot goes left or right.

[2]   During the *plantar flexion* movement the tip of the foot goes down, while the dorsiflexion involves a movement of the toes upward.

devices, aiming to study the limitations of current technologies for a worth considering home care treatment of the phantom limb pain.

Despite the limitations discussed in the previous section, most of them resulting by the use of commercial devices, *entertaining* exercises should help to provide enough immersion to compensate some of the previous restrictions. Furthermore, the quick evolution of new sensors available on the market might soon close the gap with more expensive devices allowing a more accurate tracking of the body/head movements as well as a better visualization of augmented reality.

In this paper we provided also a first qualitative discussion about the capabilities and the limitations of such a system. Test with a first limited number of amputee patients will be performed in the next months.

References

1. Ehde, D.M., Czerniecki, J.M., Smith, D.G., Campbell, K.M., Edwards, W.T., Jensen, M.P., Robinson, L.R.: Chronic phantom sensations, phantom pain, residual limb pain, and other regional pain after lower limb amputation. Archives of Physical Medicine and Rehabilitation 81(8), 1039–1044 (2000), doi:10.1053/apmr.2000.7583
2. Hill, A.: Phantom Limb Pain: A Review of the Literature on Attributes and Potential Mechanisms. Journal of Pain and Symptom Management 17(2), 125–142 (1999)
3. Ramachandran, V.S., Rogers-Ramachandran, D.: Synaesthesia in phantom limbs induced with mirrors. Proceedings: Biological Sciences, JSTOR 263(1369), 377–386 (1996), doi:10.1098/rspb.1996.0058
4. Roches, S., Jucker, J., Bertrand Leiser, M.: Efficiency of mirror therapy for alleviating phantom sensations and pain: A systematic review. Ergoscience 4, 134–138 (2011)
5. Sumitani, M., Miyauchi, S., McCabe, C.S., Shibata, M., Maeda, L., Saitoh, Y., Mashimo, T.: Mirror visual feedback alleviates deafferentation pain, depending on qualitative aspects of the pain: A preliminary report. Rheumatology 47(7), 1038–1043 (2008), doi:10.1093/rheumatology/ken170
6. Moseley, G.L., Gallace, A., Spence, C.: Is mirror therapy all it is cracked up to be? Current evidence and future directions. Pain 138(1), 7–10 (2008), doi:10.1016/j.pain.2008.06.026; PMID 18621484
7. Murray, C.D., Patchick, E., Pettifer, S., Caillette, F., Howard, T.: Immersive virtual reality as a rehabilitative technology for phantom limb experience: A protocol. CyberPsychology & Behavior 9(2), 167–170 (2006), doi:10.1089/cpb.2006.9.167
8. Murray, C.D., Pettifer, S., Howard, T., Patchick, E.L., Caillette, F., Kulkarni, J., Bamford, C.: The treatment of phantom limb pain using immersive virtual reality: Three case studies. Disability & Rehabilitation 29(18), 1465–1469 (2007), doi:10.1080/09638280601107385
9. Shen, Y., Ong, S., Nee, A.: An augmented reality system for hand movement rehabilitation. In: Proceedings of the 2nd International Convention on Rehabilitation Engineering & Assistive Technology, pp. 189–192. Singapore Therapeutic, Assistive & Rehabilitative Technologies (START) Centre (2008)
10. Desmond, D.M., O'Neill, K., De Paor, A., McDarby, G., MacLachlan, M.: Augmenting the Reality of Phantom Limbs: Three Case Studies Using an Augmented Mirror Box Procedure. JPO: Journal of Prosthetics and Orthotics 18(3), 74 (2006), doi:10.1097/00008526-200607000-00005

11. Bach, F., Schmitz, B., Maaß, H., Çakmak, H., Diers, M., et al.: Using interactive immersive VR/AR for the therapy of phantom limb pain. In: Proceedings of the 13th International Conference on Humans and Computers, pp. 183–187. University of Aizu Press (2010)
12. Gregory-Dean, A.: Amputations: Statistics and trends. Annals of the Royal College of Surgeons of England 73(3), 137 (1991)
13. Project website and demonstrators, https://project.eia-fr.ch/plupart/Pages/Demos.aspx

Comparing Data from a Computer Based Intervention Program for Patients with Alzheimer's Disease

Agisilaos Chaldogeridis[1], Thrasyvoulos Tsiatsos[1],
Moses Gialaouzidis[2], and Magdalini Tsolaki[2,3]

[1] Department of Informatics, Aristotle University of Thessaloniki, Thessaloniki, Greece
{achaldog,tsiatsos}@csd.auth.gr
[2] Greek Association of Alzheimer Disease and Relative Disorders, Thessaloniki, Greece
moses_gf@hotmail.com
[3] Medical School, Aristotle University of Thessaloniki, GR-54124, Thessaloniki, Greece
tsolakim1@gmail.com

Abstract. Nowadays, dealing with Alzheimer's disease (AD) includes a combination of pharmaceutical and non-pharmaceutical treatment. But, current drugs do not, and potential future drugs might not, improve quality of life. Evidence suggests psychosocial interventions, like educational and arts programs, do in fact have such a benefit. Supportive and enriching information technology may be more important than biotechnology (Whitehouse, 2013). So non-pharmaceutical treatment including physical and mental exercising as well seem to perform better. There are many forms of mental exercising from simple crosswords puzzles to sophisticated video games that exercise different cognitive skills. Main object of this report is to present the results of a computer-based intervention program for people with AD that take place in two Day Care Centers of Greek Association of Alzheimer's Disease and Related Disorders in Thessaloniki, Greece. There is a significant amount of data that include patients, who have taken part in interventions programs since 2009. For the purpose of this study we included data for a period of one year only. These patients have been tested before and after each intervention program (pre-test and post-test). Our work was to compare these data to examine how the program performs and which cognitive skills seem to have better improvement. The results showed that patients' overall scores were preserved for this period of time and had a slightly improvement which is a promising result indicating that this intervention program has positive effects.

Keywords: computerized cognitive training, Alzheimer's disease, cognitive rehabilitation.

1   Introduction

According to recent data, it is expected that the number of elderly people will increase dramatically. Indeed, it has been suggested that the advancements in the medical sciences, in combination with the adoption of a healthy lifestyle can help us live longer than before and improve our quality of life. As the human population ages, it is more than a necessity to make elderly peoples' life easier, so that they would be able

R. Shumaker and S. Lackey (Eds.): VAMR 2014, Part II, LNCS 8526, pp. 258–266, 2014.
© Springer International Publishing Switzerland 2014

to live on their own, without depending on someone else that would help them perform their everyday activities. However, it is commonly accepted that as an adult getting old, his/her brain is also getting old in a way that it gets more and more weakened as the years go by. A weakened brain could result to reduced cognitive ability and performance, and, consequently, the individual might not be able to perform daily activities. Even worse still, s/he might not be able to take care him/herself. This is a basic factor that characterizes dementia and its most common form, Alzheimer's disease (AD).

AD is a neurodegenerative disease that progressively destroys brain cells and the interconnections between them. As a result, the patient who suffers from this disease loses core functions and abilities day by day, presenting symptoms like reduced memory capacity, disorientation, and judgment and reasoning declines. Furthermore, s/he may also exhibit less self-control, and listening and speaking disorders, such as problems in naming objects or other people, text and speech understanding, and reduced visual-spatial perception. During the later stages of the disease the patient may lose core abilities and functions and he cannot even live by himself, as he may not be able to move, walk, feed, and get dressed.

Unfortunately, the attempts to find a pharmaceutical treatment of AD have come to a dead end, as there is no medicine that can heal the patients and bring them to their prior condition. Although, there are some treatment methods that can deal with the disease's symptoms that are available and already implemented and research is ongoing. The best way to deal with AD is to provide each patient with the appropriate medication in order to improve specific biological indexes. However, these medicines cannot prevent AD from progressing, but they can decrease the symptoms and slow the progression temporarily, improving patients' quality of life and fostering their caregivers.

Nowadays, there is a tendency all over the world by health associations focusing on research for better ways of treatment, which will try to delay AD's onset and development. It is proven that the best way so far, to treat the disease is the implementation of a combination of pharmaceutical treatment and cognitive training (CT), which may be remarkably useful and improve mental abilities and brain functionality. Cognitive training is a term which is described as an intervention that uses properly structured exercises to improve, maintain or restore mental function (Valenzuela, 2008.). CT can be used in order to limit and offset the cognitive abilities that have been affected. Another term for CT is "brain fitness" because it is possible to create new brain cells and train the brain in order to discover alternative ways to perform functions that controlled by brain regions which have been damaged. A characteristic advantage of CT is that does not demand large amounts of effort from the patients, as they are not involved in complex activities, but in contrast, they take part in simple, everyday activities familiar to those which already perform.

The implication of CT can be done in a variety of ways with different tools and stimuli but there are specific processes that are fundamental and consist of repeating actions that are common in a person's life and providing appropriate guidance, support and help to the patient. Suitable tools which can foster a CT program are electronic cognitive exercises or in general computer based CT that can use different modalities for such kind of activities. Electronic exercises can be implied usually by a PC or a portable device (smartphones, tablets) which are appropriate tools for repeating procedures and organize activities, according to each person's needs. A core principle is the potentiality to provide adapted content, according to each person's mental status, needs, targets and expectations. Also, a CT program should motivate and stimulate the user in order to be regularly engaged in realistic situations and activities so that he can transfer the acquired knowledge in his real life scenarios.

An individual, through CT intervention programs, could improve existing core functionalities or even develop new, alternative ones which will allow him/her to have, if possible, a normal life and a better quality of living. Also, the ability to adapt the content according to cultural characteristics or each user's cognitive status and the ease of customization in general is an important and helpful prospect in order to create personalized activities. Moreover, computer based applications offer instant monitoring and control of every user as well as data collections and metrics of each action in the electronic environment, in a way that let us monitor the performance and the overall progress, which is also useful for the user to be informed and have the right feedback. Feedback is an important aspect because it enhances user's performance, leads to better results and motivates him to perform better, so that strengthens his participation and reduces his disorientation. Finally, electronic applications for CT can include enriched multimedia elements such as images, audio and video to make more attractive activities that are more pleasant and enjoyable for the users.

Greek Association of Alzheimer's Disease and Related Disorders (GAADRD) offers a variety of services for patients and their caregivers including cognitive therapies for memory, attention and language enhancement. Besides traditional forms of therapies, such as cognitive tasks and exercises, cognitive music- therapy there are also computerized cognitive exercises for attention and language practice through personal computers (PC)s. The main intervention program consists of exercises that focus on memory and attention enhancement, each patient works on his own PC and deals with several exercises which are specifically designed for memory, logic, verbal, numeric and visual-space training that improve the patient's corresponding cognitive functions. These exercises demand an important amount of attention, processing speed and memory effort and the difficulty is escalading as the patient improves his cognitive status. This is a two times per week program.

In addition to that, there is also a training program that allows patients to exercise and familiarize with computers and technology. This program includes educational exercises for learning how to operate a PC and the acquisition of basic skills such as working on Windows based platforms, using Office's suite applications (MS Word, Excel), surfing on the internet and using e-mail services. This program usually happens also two times per week. The main target is to familiarize with a PC, for people with no previous experience and to learn new skills using the current technology.

Each exercise has five levels of difficulty, according to each patient's mental status, so they are suitable for both low-level and high-level patients and additionally, they do not require any previous knowledge of computers or technological education. Furthermore, the program takes place in a room with eight PCs, so that every patient sits on his own, and all of them have a touchscreen, a feature that lets patients to use the computer just by touching in specific spots on the screen.

Every patient has a record in GAADRD's database, which uses the OpenClinica's format configured especially for the needs of GAADRD. The database holds records about patient's personal information, demographic characteristics, medical and psychological tests and other important information. We have gathered data from 41 patients who attended a specific computer-based intervention program which was designed according to each patient's mental status. Some patients started in 2008 and still continue to participate in non-pharmaceutical intervention programs. Thus, our data are for a period of nearly five years, by we selected data form only a specific period of twelve months, in order to have more homogeneous sample.

In the next sections we present the sample's profile and patients' characteristics, we describe the method that followed and the intervention program, then the results that we gathered and finally, a discussion with comments and conclusions on the study.

2   Method

Participants. The patients who were selected fulfilled some specific criteria. First of all, they were aware of their memory deficits, they didn't suffer from depression or any other psychiatric or neurological disorder and their Mini Mental State Examination was equal or above 24. All of them, preserved satisfactory sensory abilities, lucked of any speech and language disorders and weren't on cholinesterase exhibitors. It is important to mention that patients' diagnosis was "Mild Cognitive Impairment" (MCI). MCI is a medium condition between normal senescence and dementia. As there is normal cognitive functionality decay through the years, it is possible that this decay may lead to dementia and MCI is the stage just before dementia appears.

Each patient was evaluated before and after his participation in the intervention program and each program lasted at least for one year. It is mentioned that some of the patients were already participated in these interventions, or they are still continue to take part. Both pre and post-tests include the same measurements for the following neuropsychological tests:

- Mini-Mental State Examination (MMSE), a short group of tests that used for detection of possible mental decline.
- Clinical Dementia Rating (CDR), a scale used to distinct different phases of dementia.
- Functional-Cognitive Assessment Scale (FUCAS), a scale based on personal interviews with the patient.
- Functional Rating Scale for Symptoms of Dementia (FRSSD), a scale for symptoms of dementia based on interviews with caregivers.
- Test of Everyday Attention (TEA), which tests the level of attention through three different activities. It consists of six individual tests which are TEA 1-A, TEA1-B, TEA4-A, TEA4-B and TEA6.
- Trail Making Test (TMT) Part B, for testing working memory and executive functionality.
- Rey-Osterrieth Complex Figure Test (ROCF), which tests visual-spatial memory by two individual tests ROCFT1 and ROCFT3.
- Rey Auditory Verbal Learning Test (RAVLT), which tests verbal learning and memory and consists of two tests RAVLT1 and RAVLT2.
- Rivermead Behavioural Memory Test (RBMT), a scale which tests episodic memory by two tests RBMT1 and RBMT2.
- Verbal Fluency Task, a test for detecting the ease of a patient to produce semantic or/and phonological words.

Intervention Program. The main intervention program includes a number of memory exercises with the use of computers. It takes place in a room with eight Pc's, where each patient has in front of him a touchscreen and performs the exercises. It aims at both low-level and high-level patients. It doesn't require knowledge of computers. There are 5 levels of difficulty in each exercise and the following categories:

1. visual - spatial exercises
2. speech exercises
3. numerical exercises
4. reasonable exercises
5. memory exercises

The training program is aimed mainly at high-level patients or caregivers. The team is a group 6-8 people and it takes place in a class. It is desirable for students to possess a PC in order to run the exercises that are given. The modules are:

1. Usability and familiarity with a PC - Microsoft Windows XP
2. Word Processor - Microsoft Office Word 2007
3. Internet use - Internet Explorer
4. Using accounts - Microsoft Office Excel 2007

The software used for the interventions is the "Complete Brain Workout" which is a commercial product. It has forty cognitive training activities districted in the five categories that mentioned before and it can stimulate the brain by exercising the mind, improve concentration and memory. Some of the exercises that includes are: Number Recall, Stepping Stones, What's in the Box, Boxes, Linker, Path Finder and other. You can find further information in the following link: http://www.oak-systems.co.uk/index.php?option=com_content&task=view&id=51&Itemid=9 .

3   Results

For the statistical analysis we used IBM's SPSS 19. We performed descriptive analysis and paired T-tests for each variable in Table 2. In Table 1 there are statistics about the age and the years of education of our sample. As we see, the average age is 66 years (Std. Dev.=8 years) and the average years of education is 11 years (Std. Dev.=4.5 years). So we have a well-educated sample and not quite old enough. In Table 2 we see the average and Std. Dev. for every test that took a subject before and after the intervention program. And in Table 3 there are the Paired Sample Statistics that indicate which pairs of tests present significant differences in their scores. Overall, we can see that there is improvement in all scores of all post-tests. As we can see, according to Sig. (2-tailed) index, there are four tests that have significant differences before and after the intervention program. These are the RAVLT2, TEA1-A, TEA1-B and VFT.

Table 1. Descriptive Statistics

Descriptive Statistics		
N=41	**Age**	**Education**
Mean	66,8049	11,4146
Std. Deviation	8,24384	4,59334

Table 2. Means and Std. Dev. for all the tests that performed

Test	Mean	Std. Dev.
preMMSE	28,3171	1,73838
postMMSE	28,1463	1,65168
preFRSSD	2,7073	2,27205
postFRSSD	3,0000	1,34164
preRAVLT1	4,7317	1,89769
postRAVLT1	5,1707	1,43008
preRAVLT2	7,7317	4,12931
postRAVLT2	6,2195	3,11859
preTEA1-A	26,3415	8,66490
postTEA1-A	30,0000	9,84886
preTEA1-B	44,5854	10,94069
postTEA1-B	48,6341	8,56959
preTEA4-A	7,1573	2,93934
postTEA-A	7,5122	2,35714
preTEA4-B	6,41	4,567
postTEA4-B	7,64	4,520
preTEA6	4,52	1,907
postTEA6	4,13	1,494
preRBMT1	12,8293	3,49930
postRBMT1	12,5366	3,43946
preRBMT2	11,4268	3,73591
postRBMT2	10,9756	4,18621
preROCFT1	31,8902	4,21235
postROCFT1	32,2683	5,45103
preROCFT3	16,5122	7,35568
postROCFT3	17,5976	7,28974
preTRAILB	208,2000	109,74871
postTRAILB	208,7250	103,66069
preVFT	11,11	4,237
postVFT	11,96	4,762
preFUCAS	43,1707	1,73064
postFUCAS	42,9756	1,66565

Table 3. Paired Samples Test which indicate significant statististical differences

Test	Paired Differences				p
	Mean	Std. Dev.	Lower	Upper	
preMMSE - postMMSE	,17073	1,59534	-,33282	,67428	,497
preFRSSD - postFRSSD	-,29268	2,15921	-,97421	,38885	,391
preRAVLT1 - postRAVLT1	-,43902	1,78954	-1,00387	,12582	,124
preRAVLT2 - postRAVLT2	1,51220	4,03189	,23958	2,78482	**,021**
preTEA1-A - postTEA1-A	-3,65854	8,15049	-6,23115	-1,08592	**,006**
preTEA1-B - postTEA1-B	-4,04878	8,95531	-6,87542	-1,22214	**,006**
preTEA4-A – postTEA-A	-,35488	2,78271	-1,23321	,52345	,419
preTEA4-B - postTEA4-B	-1,233	6,633	-3,327	,860	,241
preTEA6 - postTEA6	,391	1,402	-,051	,834	,081
preRBMT1 - postRBMT1	,29268	2,71794	-,56520	1,15057	,494
preRBMT2 - postRBMT2	,45122	3,69257	-,71430	1,61674	,439
preROCFT1 - postROCFT1	-,37805	6,17230	-2,32627	1,57017	,697
preROCFT3 - postROCFT3	-1,08537	5,53613	-2,83279	,66205	,217
preTRAILB - postTRAILB	-,52500	108,70638	-35,2909	34,2409	,976
preVFT - postVFT	-,850	2,612	-1,675	-,025	**,044**
preFUCAS - postFUCAS	,19512	1,22922	-,19287	,58311	,316

4   Discussion and Conclusions

Results showed significant statistical differences in four psychometric tests (namely RAVLT2, TEA1-A, TEA1-B and VFT) according to pre and post scores. Concerning RAVLT2 test we can see that there is a reduction between the pre and post scores. RAVLT2 test examines learning skills, thus we can conclude that after a year of intervention patients have less learning abilities. Further research has to be done in the future, in order to compare this result with a controlled group that will not participate in an intervention program. It is important to examine if this reduction is the same and/or has the same rate between these groups. The next two tests that have significant statistical differences belong to Test of Everyday Attention (TEA1-A & TEA1-B). Both tests examine the level of attention. In this case, the subjects presented better scores in both tests after the intervention. This means that the program improves selective attention and patient's ability to stay focused. Considering that the intervention program aims to foster attention, we can say that it fulfills this purpose. The last test that has significant statistical difference is VFT which examines verbal fluency and executive functions. We can conclude that there is improvement in verbal fluency and related language functions. This is a very important improvement due to the fact that this has also effect on high-level attention abilities.

Concerning the rest of tests we can conclude that even if there is no significant statistical difference, the findings are very encouraging concerning the mental status of the subjects. More specifically, it is important to mention that the scores in three tests (namely TEA6, FUCAS and TRAILB) have been slightly reduced or they have been remain almost the same (namely TRAILB). This is a positive finding, considering that a lower the score is, as better performance is. Furthermore, we can observe that there is a reduction in RBMT and RAVLT tests, probably because the intervention program is mainly targeted on exercising attention, but further research has to be conducted to investigate this fact deeper.

In conclusion, the majority of tests has been improved after a year of intervention and this is a promising result as there was no further progression of impairment. It is expected that an MCI patient gets worse as years go by, but results indicate stability or improvement, thus we can say that this intervention program has produced positive effects in general.

Acknowledgements. This work is partly supported by the project "Augmentation of the Support of Patients suffering from Alzheimer's Disease and their caregivers (ASPAD/2875)", which is materialized by the Special Account of the Research Committee at Aristotle University of Thessaloniki. The project is funded by the European Union (European Social Fund) and the Ministry of Education, Lifelong Learning and Religious Affairs in the context of the National Strategic Reference Framework (NSRF, 2007-2013).

References

1. Ball, K., Berch, D.B., Helmers, K.F., et al.: Effects of cognitive training interventions with older adults: A randomized controlled trial (2002)
2. Barnes, et al.: Computer-Based Cognitive Training for Mild-Cognitive Impairment: Results from a Pilot Randomized, Controlled trial. Alzheimer Dis. Assoc. Disord. 23(3), 205–210 (2009)
3. Bayles, K.A., Boone, D.R., Kaszniak, A.W., Stem, L.Z.: Language impairment in dementia. Arizona Medicine 39(5), 308–311 (1982)
4. Christodoulakis, T., Petsanis, K.: Cognitive rehabilitation in the early stages of Alzheimer's Disease (2010), http://www.iatronet.gr/article.asp?art_id=12690 (retrieved at December 6, 2013)
5. Cipriani, G., Bianchetti, A., Trabucchi, M.: Outcomes of a computer-based cognitive rehabilitation program on Alzheimer's disease patients compared with those on patients affected by mild cognitive impairment. Archives of Gerontology and Geriatrics 43(3), 327–335 (2006)
6. Emery, V.O.B.: Language impairment in dementia of the Alzheimer type: A hierarchical decline? International Journal of Psychiatry 30(2), 145–164 (2000)
7. Gates, J.N., Sachdev, S.P., Fiatarone Singh, A.M., Valenzuela, M.: Cognitive and memory training in adults at risk of dementia: A Systematic Review (2011), http://www.biomedcentral.com/1471-2318/11/55 (retrieved at December 6, 2013)
8. Gunther, V.K., Schafer, P., Holzner, B.J., Kemmler, G.W.: Long-term Improvements in Cognitive Performance through Computer-assisted Cognitive Training: A Pilot Study in a Residential Home for Older People. Aging and Mental Health 7(3), 200–206 (2003)
9. Hutton, J.T.: Alzheimer's disease. In: Rakel, R.E. (ed.) Conn's Current Therapy, pp. 778–781. Philadelphia, W. B. Saunders (1990)

10. Kosmidis, M.H., Bozikas, V.P., Vlahou, C.H., Kiosseoglou, G., Giaglis, G., Karavatos, A.: Verbal fluency in institutionalized patients with schizophrenia: Age-related performance decline. Psychiatry Research 134(3), 233–240 (2005)
11. Kounti, F., Tsolaki, M., Kiosseoglou, G.: Functional cognitive assessment scale (FUCAS): A new scale to assess executive cognitive function in daily life activities in patients with dementia and mild cognitive impairment. Human Psychopharmacology: Clinical and Experimental 21(5), 305–311 (2006)
12. Linda, C., Woods, B.: Cognitive rehabilitation and cognitive training for early-stage Alzheimer's disease and vascular dementia. Cochrane Database of Systematic Reviews (2003)
13. Malegiannaki, A.: Investigation of the relationship between the performance in experimental projects and aspects of meta-attention. M.Sc., Department of Psychology, Aristotle University of Thessaloniki (2009)
14. Mentenopoulos, G.: Aphasias, agnosias, inactivities and their association with memory, pp. 21,39. University Studio Press (2003)
15. Sitzer, D.I., Twamley, E.W., Jeste, D.V.: Cognitive training in Alzheimer's disease: A meta-analysis of the literature. Acta Psychiatr Scand 2006 114, 75–90 (2006)
16. Smith, et al.: A Cognitive Training Program Designed Based on Principles of Brain Plasticity: Results from the Improvement in Memory with Plasticity-based Adaptive Cognitive Training Study. Journal of the American Geriatrics Society (2009)
17. Tsantali, E.: Cognitive Rehabilitation in the first stages of Alzheimer's disease through verbal tasks, PhD in School of Psychology of the Aristotle University of Thessaloniki, Greece (2006)
18. Tsolaki, M., Fountoulakis, C., Chantzi, E., Kazis, A.: The Cambridge cognitive examination for the elderly: A validation study in demented patients from the elderly Greek population. American Journal of Alzheimer's Disease 15, 269–278 (2000)
19. Valenzuela, M.: How Mental Exercise and Cognitive Training can modify Brain Reserve and so Reduce Dementia Risk. School of Psychiatry, University of New South Wales (2008),
    http://www.scitopics.com/How_Mental_Exercise_and_Cognitive_T
    raining_can_modify_Brain_Reserve_and_so_Reduce_Dementia_
    Risk.html (retrieved at December 6, 2013)
20. Whitehouse, P.: The end of Alzheimer's disease – from biochemical pharmacology to ecopsychosociology: A personal perspective. Biochemical Pharmacology (2013)
21. Willis, L.S., Tennstedt, S.L., Marsiske, M., Ball, K., Elias, J., Koepke, K.M., Morris, J.N., Rebok, G.W., Unverzagt, F.W., Stoddard, A.M., Wright, E.: Long-term Effects of Cognitive Training on Everyday Functional Outcomes in Older Adults (2006),
    http://jama.ama-assn.org/content/296/23/2805.full (retrieved at December 6, 2013)
22. Wilson, B.A., Cockburn, J., Baddeley, A., Hiorns, R.: The Rivermead Behavioural Memory Test: Supplement Two. Thames Valley Test Co., Reading (1991)

Virtual Reality-Based System for Training in Dental Anesthesia

Cléber G. Corrêa[1], Fátima de Lourdes dos Santos Nunes[2], and Romero Tori[1]

[1] Escola Politécnica da Universidade de São Paulo, Interactive Technologies
Laboratory, Sao Paulo, Brazil
`cleber.gimenez@usp.br`
[2] School of Arts, Science and Humanities, University of Sao Paulo, Laboratory of
Computer Application for Health Care, Sao Paulo, Brazil

Abstract. This paper presents the development and preliminary evaluation of a Virtual Reality-based system for training in dental anesthesia. The development focused the simulation of an anesthesia procedure task. The evaluation involved graphic and haptic issues and had the presence of experts in the dentistry area. The assessment aimed at attributes that may influence the human-computer interaction, hindering realism, an important challenge in systems of this type. The attributes selected were: the update rate, the appearance of the virtual models and the number of viewpoints of the virtual environment, as well as the characteristics of the haptic device. Despite constraints were found, in the perception of the experts, the system may provide realism and help with the training of certain tasks.

Keywords: dental anesthesia, human-computer interaction, Virtual Reality.

1 Introduction

Systems based on Virtual Reality (VR) are widely used in the health area, especially in the training context, for acquiring of knowledge and sensorimotor skills.

This may be related to the benefits provided by VR, such as: reducing risks to patients due to unsuccessful procedures, avoiding damage to health [1]; increasing the safety of novices, who can practice several times before dealing with real patients [2] [3] [4]; automatic evaluations of performance [5] and repeated training.

Moreover, benefits also include levels of training, situations and degrees of difficulty [6]; VR may minimize or eliminate costs involved in maintaining physical laboratories, which can count on cadavers or animals. Although cadavers and animals provide the physical presence, cadavers present physiological differences and animals have divergences in anatomy when compared to human beings. Additionally, their use involves ethical issues [1].

R. Shumaker and S. Lackey (Eds.): VAMR 2014, Part II, LNCS 8526, pp. 267–276, 2014.

Another benefit of VR is flexibility, because mannequins, for example, allow physical presence; however, they include limitations in the physiological replication and anatomical variation [1].

A procedure that does not enjoy such benefits yet is the training for dental anesthesia administration, especially the procedure to block the inferior alveolar nerve [7]. This procedure presents a high number of failures and the novices commonly train in their colleagues [8].

Therefore, this paper presents the development and preliminary experiments of a VR system for training in dental anesthesia. An important challenge in VR systems is the degree of realism, commonly defined by subjective tests with experts [9]. The realism in this context is directly influenced by the human-computer interaction, including the haptic approach, which plays an important role in applications of this type.

The paper is organized as follows: in Section 2, the main related works are described; Sections 3 and 4 present the implementation of the system and the experiments, respectively; in Section 5 the results, and finally, the conclusions in Section 6.

2   Related Work

There are a number of simulators for dental procedures [10] [11] [12] [13] [14] [15] [16] [17], but just one virtual training system for the purpose related to this work, which was not formally assessed [18].

However, as the procedure to be simulated involves needle insertion, a set of similar training systems can be mentioned. Table 1 presents the main works, including the procedure, the region of the body and whether the procedure is

Table 1. Needle insertion procedures [8]

Number	Procedure	Target region	MI
1	Anesthesia [19] [20]	Spin	No
2	Biopsy [21]	-	Yes
3	Biopsy [22]	-	No
4	Biopsy [23]	Lumbar	No
5	Biopsy [24]	Prostate	Yes
6	Biopsy [25]	Thyroid	Yes
7	Brachytherapy [26]	Prostate	Yes
8	Catheter [27]	-	Yes
9	Chinese acupuncture [28]	-	No
10	Epidural anesthesia [29] [30]	Spinal	No
11	General [31] [32]	-	Yes
12	Regional anesthesia [33]	Inguinal	No
13	Regional anesthesia [34]	-	No
14	Suturing [35]	-	No
15	Vertebroplasty [36]	Spinal	No

aided by Medical Images (MI). The term *General* in the field *Procedure* means that the needle insertion is not restricted to a specific procedure. The hyphen (-) indicates that the paper does not present the information or it may be employed in several regions.

Line 8 in Table 1 lists the insertion of catheters, which are procedures initiated for the insertion of a kind of needle. Moreover, it is worth noting that there are other more complex minimally invasive procedures that start with the insertion of certain instruments, as laparoscopy, endoscopy, arthroscopy and endovascular procedures [1].

3   Development of the System

The development of the system started with a requirements elicitation conducted in collaboration with an dentistry learning institution (School of Dentistry of Bauru - University of Sao Paulo). Students and professors of the institution provided videos and details about the dental anesthesia procedure, and also allowed us to watch real procedures [8].

Considering that the simulator is based on VR, the human-computer interaction is a fundamental characteristic. According to [37], the human-computer interaction in virtual environment may be classified into the following categories: navigation, selection and manipulation, control system and symbolic input.

Our system considered two categories:

- Navigation - visualization of the models from several viewpoints using the keyboard, allowing the study of the anatomy of the head (bones, blood vessels, gums, muscles, tongue, teeth and nerves) in various angles of vision;
- Manipulation - effected through a device, typically a specific device[1], which offers a haptic sensation and captures movements of position and rotation [38], being used to modify synthetic models that represent instruments (syringes or needles).

There are several types of haptic feedback, such as [39]: force, tactile, kinesthetic and proprioceptive. In this context, the force feedback was adopted due the task and characteristics of the device. The force feedback was defined as a constant value to the anatomical structures.

In the second step, the system was implemented using a VR framework [40] which allows: (1) - loading 3D (three-dimensional) synthetic models to represent anatomical structures and instruments; (2) - specifying properties of the models (elasticity, viscosity and thickness); (3) - detecting collision among models; (4) - deforming models, modifying their shapes; and (5) - supporting devices for interaction, including haptic device and dataglove. Figure 1 allows observing the screen of the training system, containing anatomical structures and syringe.

Due to the complexity of its development, in the third step, the procedure was segmented into tasks. The target task is the correct manipulation of the syringe,

---

[1] http://www.dentsable.com/haptic-phantom-omni.htm

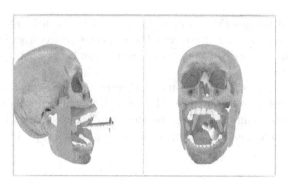

Fig. 1. Screen of the training system

encompassing certain parameters: velocity of manipulation, regions reached by the needle, movements of translation and rotation of the syringe and duration of the injection.

During the insertion, the needle must be in an angle of about 45 degrees; the motions of the syringe must be slow; the needle cannot reach nerves, bones, blood vessels and skin; and it must remain in the tissues some minutes before extracting, simulating the time for anesthetic injection. Thereby, the user could manipulate the syringe using the haptic device and could navigate in the environment using the keyboard.

In this step, an adaptation of the haptic device also was made. The adaptation consisted in replacing the pen with Carpule syringe (Figure 2) [8]. The Carpule syringe is the instrument used by dentists in the anesthesia procedure. For the tests, different versions of the same system were generated, considering several attributes.

4 Experiments Description

As the degree of realism is usually defined by experts in the area, to evaluate the system, experiments were made with a group of experts of the dentistry institution mentioned, comprising 2 teachers and 2 students who had already accomplished the procedure. The experiments considered two issues: graphic and haptic, which directly influence the human-computer interaction.

Considering the experts as system users, the hypotheses to be corroborated were: (1) users prefer the models with textures; (2) users prefer two viewpoints to determine the position and rotation of the syringe, as well as the distance between it and anatomical structures; (3) the maximum force provided by device is not enough to simulate the needle insertion; (4) the workspace of the device is not enough to capture all movements of the insertion task and (5) users prefer the device adapted with the real syringe.

The graphic issue aimed at certain attributes, such as: the appearance of the models (wire, color and texture - Figures 3, 4 and 5), and the number of viewpoints (Figures 6 and 5).

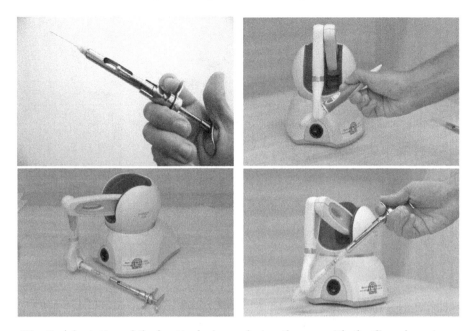

Fig. 2. Adaptation of the haptic device replacing the pen with the Carpule syringe

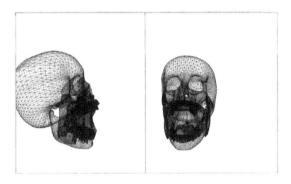

Fig. 3. Virtual models in wire mode

The haptic issue dealt with examining the ergonomic attributes of the device (shape of the manipulation "pen", workspace and maximum force). The update rate during the human-computer interaction was analyzed with several values to verify the minimum value required for the task, being a critical point in the haptic issue. The frequency values were decreased according to users' perception, identifying suitable delays in the haptic human-computer interaction.

In order to collect the users' preferences questionnaires were used after experiments. The task to be performed was detailed before experiments, including the presentation of the training system.

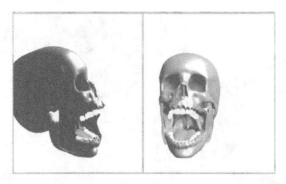

Fig. 4. Virtual models in colors

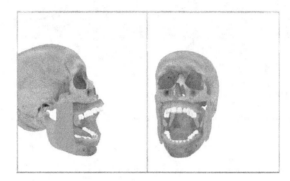

Fig. 5. Virtual environment with textures and presented in two viewpoints

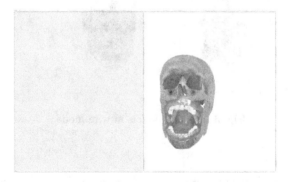

Fig. 6. Virtual environment presented in one viewpoint

5   Results

After analyzing the answers, in the graphic issue the experts preferred the models
with textures and two viewpoints. The two viewpoints improved the orientation

in the virtual environment; however, the textures were not considered correlated to reality.

In the haptic issue, the adaptation of the device was considered a positive point because the pen of the device differs from the syringe, which compromises realism. The experts highlighted the importance of the force feedback, and the maximum force provided by the device (3.3 Newtons) was considered enough to simulate the contacts with the anatomical structures, including bones, which must offer the higher stiffness during the contact with the needle.

The capture and reproduction of the movements between the device and the syringe in the virtual environment were considered suitable. The workspace of the device (170 millimeters, 120 millimeters and 70 millimeters in the axes x, y and z, respectively) was not considered enough, specially in the z axis.

A constraint identified was the direction of the force feedback because the device provides three degrees of freedom for force feedback (axes x, y and z) and the syringe must be inserted diagonally, making the force feedback impossible in this position.

The experts did not want to use the navigation in the virtual environment, opting for mere manipulation. Finally, it is worth noting that in the evaluation of the update rate, the value of **40 Hertz** did not affect the human-computer interaction, generating acceptable delays.

6   Conclusion

Considering the results, hypotheses 1, 2, 4 and 5 were confirmed, because the experts who participated in the experiment preferred the models with textures (hypothesis 1), however, the textures should be improved; the experts preferred two viewpoints to determine the position of the syringe and to orientate the actions inside the virtual environment (hypothesis 2); the workspace of the device was not enough, which was only observed in movements in the z axes (hypothesis 4), being resolved for reducing the distance between the syringe and the anatomical structures; and the experts preferred the device adapted with the real syringe (hypothesis 5).

According to the experts, the adaptation of the device provided a way to hold the instrument as in the real world. Figure 2 shows how people usually manipulate the device with and without the syringe.

Hypothesis 3 was rejected because the maximum force provided by the device was considered enough; yet, as the device does not offer six degrees of freedom of force feedback, considering the position of the models and the orientation of the syringe, the direction of the feedback cannot be simulated. One possible solution would be acquire a device that offers six degrees of freedom of force feedback.

Regarding to update rate, the haptic update rate is recommended to be about **1.000** Hertz, with some different cases, for instance, **300** Hertz and **550** to **600** Hertz [1]; nevertheless, the value of **40** Hertz was considered acceptable.

In summary, the degree of realism was considered satisfactory, showing that, despite constraints were found, the system may currently contribute to training of an anesthesia procedure task. Future works include an analysis of the low update rate and the perception of the experts; force feedback values according to properties of each anatomical model, including sets of models; tests with the participation of more experts and more realistic textures for the models.

Acknowledgements. The authors would like to thank CAPES (National Council for the Improvement of Higher Education Personnel) for the scholarship to Cléber Gimenez Corrêa, INCT-MACC (National Institute of Science and Technology - Medicine Assisted by Scientific Computing) and Design Group in Health Care - Pediatric Dentistry (School of Dentistry of Bauru - University of Sao Paulo).

References

1. Coles, T.R., Meglan, D., John, N.W.: The role of haptics in medical training simulators: A survey of the state of the art. IEEE Transactions on Haptics 4(1), 51–66 (2011)
2. Shakil, O., Mahmood, F., Matyal, R.: Simulation in echocardiography: An ever-expanding frontier. Journal of Cardiothoracic and Vascular Anesthesia 26(3), 476–485 (2012)
3. O'Neill, M.J., Milano, M.T., Schell, M.C.: Simulation training in health care: A role in radiation oncology? International Journal of Radiation Oncology Biology Physics 81(2), 697–698 (2011)
4. Lambden, S., Martin, B.: The use of computers for perioperative simulation in anesthesia, critical care, and pain medicine. Anesthesiology Clinics 29(3), 521–531 (2011)
5. Anjos, A.M., Nunes, F.L.S., Tori, R.: Avaliação de habilidades sensório-motoras em ambientes de realidade virtual para treinamento médico: uma revisão sistemática. Journal of Health Informatics 4(1), 28–34 (2012)
6. Ullrich, S., Kuhlen, T.: Haptic palpation for medical simulation in virtual environments. IEEE Transactions on Visualization and Computer Graphics 18(4), 617–625 (2012)
7. Malamed, S.: Handbook of local anesthesia, 5th edn., Mosby, St. Louis, MO, USA (2004)
8. Corrêa, C.G., Tori, R., Nunes, F.L.S.: Haptic simulation for virtual training in application of dental anesthesia. In: Proceedings of the 2013 XV Symposium on Virtual and Augmented Reality, pp. 63–72 (2013)
9. Steinbach, E., Hirche, S., Ernst, M., Brandi, F., Chaudhari, R., Kammerl, J., Vittorias, I.: Haptic communications. Proceedings of the IEEE 100(4), 937–956 (2012)
10. Bogoni, T.N., Pinho, M.S.: Haptic rendering techniques supporting material removal. In: Proceedings of the 2013 XV Symposium on Virtual and Augmented Reality, SVR 2013, pp. 36–45. IEEE Computer Society, Washington, DC (2013)
11. Moog Inc.: Medical and dental simulation (2013)
12. Wang, D., Zhang, Y., Hou, J., Wang, Y., Lu, P., Chen, Y., Zhao, H.: Idental: A haptic-based dental simulator and its preliminary user evaluation. IEEE Transactions on Haptics 5(4), 332–343 (2012)
13. Ullah, F., Park, K.: Visual, haptic, and auditory realities based dental training simulator. In: International Conference on Information Science and Applications (ICISA), pp. 1–6 (2012)

14. Tse, B., Harwin, W., Barrow, A., Quinn, B., San Diego, J., Cox, M.: Design and development of a haptic dental training system: Haptel. In: Kappers, A.M.L., van Erp, J.B.F., Bergmann Tiest, W.M., van der Helm, F.C.T. (eds.) EuroHaptics 2010, Part II. LNCS, vol. 6192, pp. 101–108. Springer, Heidelberg (2010)
15. Kolesnikov, M., Zefran, M., Steinberg, A.D., Bashook, P.G.: Periosim: Haptic virtual reality simulator for sensorimotor skill acquisition in dentistry. In: International Conference on Robotics and Automation, pp. 689–694. IEEE Computer Society (2009)
16. Forsslund, J., Sallnas, E.L., Palmerius, K.J.: A user-centered designed foss implementation of bone surgery simulations. In: World Haptics 2009 - Third Joint EuroHaptics Conference and Symposium on Haptic Interfaces for Virtual Environment and Teleoperator Systems, pp. 391–392. IEEE Computer Society, Salt Lake City (2009)
17. Ranta, J.F., Aviles, W.A.: The virtual reality dental training system-simulating dental procedures for the purpose of training dental students using haptics. In: Proceedings of the Fourth PHANTOM Users Group Workshop, vol. 4, pp. 67–71 (1999)
18. The Glasgow School of Art Media Centre: Ground-breaking 3d visualisation set to revolutionise medical and dental training (April 2013)
19. Zhang, D., Albert, D., Hockemeyer, C., Breen, D., Kulcsár, Z., Shorten, G., Aboulafia, A., Lövquist, E.: Developing competence assessment procedure for spinal anaesthesia. In: Proceedings of the 21st IEEE International Symposium on Computer-Based Medical Systems, pp. 397–402. IEEE Press (June 2008)
20. Albert, D., Hockemeyer, C., Kulcsar, Z., Shorten, G.: Competence assessment for spinal anaesthesia. In: Holzinger, A. (ed.) USAB 2007. LNCS, vol. 4799, pp. 165–170. Springer, Heidelberg (2007)
21. Vidal, F.P., John, N.W., Healey, A.E., Gould, D.A.: Simulation of ultrasound guided needle puncture using patient specific data with 3D textures and volume haptics. Computer Animation and Virtual Worlds 19(2), 111–127 (2008)
22. Ra, J.B., Kwon, S.M., Kim, J.K., Yi, J., Kim, K.H., Park, H.W., Kyung, K.U., Kwon, D.S., Kang, H.S., Kwon, S.T., Jiang, L., Zeng, J., Geary, K., Mun, S.K.: Spine needle biopsy simulator using visual and force feedback. Computer Aided Surgery 7(6), 353–363 (2002)
23. Gorman, P., Krummel, T., Webster, R., Smith, M., Hutchens, D.: A prototype haptic lumbar puncture simulator. Studies in Health Technology and Informatics 70, 106–109 (2000)
24. Matsumoto, E.D.: Development and validation of a virtual reality transrectal ultrasound guided prostatic biopsy simulator. Canadian Urological Association Journal 5(1) (February 2011)
25. de Almeida Souza, I., Sanches Jr., C., Kondo, M.N.S., Zuffo, M.K.: Development and evaluation of a virtual reality simulator for training of thyroid gland nodules needle biopsy. In: Proceedings of the ACM Symposium on Virtual Reality Software and Technology (VRST 2008), pp. 245–246. ACM Press (2008)
26. Goksel, O., Sapchuk, K., Morris, W.J., Salcudean, S.E.: Prostate brachytherapy training with simulated ultrasound and fluoroscopy images. IEEE Transactions on Biomedical Engineering 60(4), 1002–1012 (2012)
27. Zorcolo, A., Gobbetti, E., Pili, P., Tuveri, M.: Catheter insertion simulation with combined visual and haptic feedback. In: Proceedings of the First PHANToM Users Research Symposium (PURS 1999), Heidelberg, Alemanha (1999)

28. Heng, P.A., Wong, T.T., Leung, K.M., Chui, Y.P., Sun, H.: A haptic needle manipulation simulator for chinese acupuncture learning and training. In: Proceedings of the ACM SIGGRAPH International Conference on Virtual Reality Continuum and its Applications in Industry (VRCAI 2004), pp. 57–64. ACM Press (2004)
29. Kagalwala, D.Z., Adhikary, S., Murray, W.B., Webster, R.: The use of a computerized haptic simulation model to track angles of epidural needle insertion by anesthesiology residents. British Journal of Anaesthesia 108, 179–180 (2012)
30. Mayooran, Z., Watterson, L., Withers, P., Line, J., Arnett, W., Horley, R.: Mediseus epidural: Full-procedure training simulatorfor epidural analgesia in labour. In: Proceedings of the SimTecT Healthcare Simulation Conference, Brisbane, Austrália, pp. 11–14 (September 2006)
31. Chan, W., Qin, J., Chui, Y., Heng, P.: A serious game for learning ultrasound-guided needle placement skills. IEEE Transactions on Information Technology in Biomedicine, 1–11 (June 2012)
32. Bello, F., Bulpitt, A., Gould, D.A., Holbrey, R., Hunt, C., How, T., John, N.W., Johnson, S., Phillips, R., Sinha, A., Vidal, F.P., Villard, P.F., Woolnough, H., Zhang, Y.: Imagine-S: Imaging guided interventional needle simulation. In: Proceedings of Eurographics, Munique, Alemanha, pp. 5–8 (March-April 2009)
33. Grottke, O., Ntouba, A., Ntouba, S., Liao, W., Fried, E., Prescher, A., Deserno, T.M., Kuhlen, T., Rossaint, R.: Virtual reality-based simulator for training in regional anaesthesia. British Journal of Anaesthesia 103(4), 594–600 (2009)
34. Hu, J., Lim, Y.J., Tardella, N., Chang, C., Warren, L.: Localized virtual patient model for regional anesthesia simulation training system. Studies in Health Technology and Informatics 125, 185–190 (2007)
35. Webster, R.W., Zimmerman, D.I., Mohler, B.J., Melkonian, M.G., Haluck, R.S.: A prototype haptic suturing simulator. Studies in Health Technology and Informatics 81, 567–569 (2001)
36. Chui, C.K., Ong, J.S.K., Lian, Z.Y., Wang, Z., Teo, J., Zhang, J., Yan, C.H., Ong, S.H., Wang, S.C., Wong, H.K., Teo, C.L., Teoh, S.H.: Haptics in computer-mediated simulation: Training in vertebroplasty surgery. Simulation and Gaming 37(4), 438–451 (2006)
37. Bowman, D.A., Kruijff, E., Joseph, J., Laviola, J., Poupyrev, I.: 3D User Interfaces: Theory and Practice. Addison Wesley Longman Publishing Co., Inc., Redwood City (2005)
38. Salisbury, J.K.: Making graphics physically tangible. Communications of the ACM 42(8), 74–81 (1999)
39. Burdea, G.C.: Virtual reality and robotics in medicine. In: Proceedings of the 5th IEEE International Workshop Robot and Human Communication, pp. 16–25. IEEE Press (1996)
40. Oliveira, A.C.M.T.G., Nunes, F.L.S.: Building an open source framework for virtual medical training. Journal of Digital Imaging: The Official Journal of the Society for Computer Applications in Radiology 23(06), 706–720 (2010)

Adaptive Architecture to Support Context-Aware Collaborative Networked Virtual Surgical Simulators (CNVSS)

Christian Diaz[1], Helmuth Trefftz[1], Lucia Quintero[2],
Diego Acosta[3], and Sakti Srivastava[4]

[1] Grupo de I+D+I en TIC
Universidad EAFIT, Medellin, Colombia
[2] Grupo de Investigacion de Modelado Matematico
Universidad EAFIT, Medellin, Colombia
[3] Grupo de Investigacion DDP
Universidad EAFIT, Medellin, Colombia
[4] Department of Surgery
Stanford University, Palo Alto, USA

Abstract. Stand-alone and networked surgical virtual reality based simulators have been proposed as means to train surgical skills with or without a supervisor nearby the student or trainee. However, surgical skills teaching in medicine schools and hospitals is changing, requiring the development of new tools to focus on: (i) importance of mentors role, (ii) teamwork skills and (iii) remote training support. For these reasons a surgical simulator should not only allow the training involving a student and an instructor that are located remotely, but also the collaborative training session involving a group of several students adopting different medical roles during the training session.

Collaborative Networked Virtual Surgical Simulators (CNVSS) allow collaborative training of surgical procedures where remotely located users with different surgical roles can take part in a training session. Several works have addressed the issues related to the development of CNVSS using various strategies. To the best of our knowledge no one has focused on handling heterogeneity in collaborative surgical virtual environments. Handling heterogeneity in this type of collaborative sessions is important because not all remotely located users have homogeneous Internet connections, nor the same interaction devices and displays, nor the same computational resources, among other factors. Additionally, if heterogeneity is not handled properly, it will have an adverse impact on the performance of each user during the collaborative session. In this paper we describe the development of an adaptive architecture with the purpose of implementing a context-aware model for collaborative virtual surgical simulation in order to handle the heterogeneity involved in the collaboration session.

Keywords: Context Aware, Collaborative Networked Surgical Simulators, Remote Medical Training.

R. Shumaker and S. Lackey (Eds.): VAMR 2014, Part II, LNCS 8526, pp. 277–286, 2014.
© Springer International Publishing Switzerland 2014

1   Introduction

Over the last few years how a surgeon is trained has changed considerably. Nowadays, new tools allowing the surgeon train and validate your skills, before going a real operating room with a real patient are in common use. Moreover, the role of the mentor during surgical training is of great importance, since he guides the learner not only considering technical aspects of the surgical procedure but also supporting the professional vocation of the surgeon. Nonetheless, issues such as the low number of expert surgeons located in distant regions or with enough time to provide face-to-face training in surgical centers have made difficult to apply the learning model mentor-apprentice in this context.

Networked virtual surgical simulators (NVSS) have been proposed to overcome these issues. NVSS has been created to allow a student to be trained remotely by an instructor. In such a system, the instructor can perform the procedure remotely while the student not only watches, but also feels (haptic feedback provided) what the instructor is touching without actually participating in the execution of the surgical procedure. Nevertheless, a surgical procedure usually requires several medicine specialists playing a specific role and collaborating each other, with the purpose of saving the patient's life. Additionally, hand eye coordination skills are as important as communication and collaboration skills during a procedure. Considering this goal, CNVSS have been proposed to allow for the collaborative training of users located remotely with each member playing a role during the training session.

However, differences in users' machine capabilities and network conditions, called heterogeneity factors, may affect the level of collaboration achieved by the users in a CNVSS, which directly affects the purpose of surgical training as a team. As far as we know no one has proposed a strategy in order to handle the heterogeneity in CNVSS and thus mitigate the impact that these factors have over collaboration.

In this paper we describe the development of an adaptive architecture, extending the SOFA framework developed in [1], with the purpose of implementing a context-aware model for collaborative virtual surgical simulation in order to handle the heterogeneity involved in the collaboration session. The proposed architecture allows the modification in real time of simulation variables such as: (i) mesh resolution, (ii) collision, visual rendering and deformation algorithms, (iii) local and remote computation in order to adapt the CNVSS to the context of the system (i.e. user preferences and roles, network conditions and machine capabilities) and optimize the collaboration of the users.

The paper is structured as follows: Section 2 describes similar projects and opportunities of research. Section 3 describes an adaptive architecture proposed to mitigate heterogeneity issues raised in CNVSS. Section 4 shows the results and section 5 conclusions and future work.

2   Related Works

Collaborative Networked Virtual Surgical Simulators (CNVSS) allow collaborative training of surgical procedures where remotely located users with different surgical roles can take part in a training session. Several works have addressed the issues related to the development of CNVSS using various strategies. In [2] and [3], two specific middleware systems for CNVSS are proposed. These middleware systems use specific protocols, different architectures, compensation mechanism, among other strategies to address network impairments such as jitter, delay and packet loss, in order to maintain adequate collaboration and shared state consistency of the virtual environment.

In [4], [5] and [6] a middleware is proposed to handle network connection issues while maintaining the consistency of the collaborative surgical virtual environment. The proposed middleware is composed by: network management approaches (including services management), collaboration mechanisms, adaptive protocols, various deformation models, 3D to 2D synchronization and flexible computation policies. They try to manage the heterogeneity of the network connection and machine capabilities of the user, implementing two computation policies to handle the deformation: (i) local computation policy, where deformation computation is off-loaded to individual participants; and (ii) the global computation policy, where a participants hardware with powerful computational capability is assigned as the server in the system. The bandwidth requirement for the former is low since the data transfer only involves the parameters of the computation.

A high-performance, network-aware, collaborative learning environment is developed in [7]. A middleware system that monitors and reports network conditions to network-aware applications that can self-scale and self-optimize based on network weather reports is described. The core system and applications have been developed within the context of a clinical anatomy testbed. A review about CNVSS is presented in [8]. Challenges characterizing these CVE (Collaborative Virtual Environments) are identified, and a detailed explanation of the techniques used to address these issues are provided. Finally, some collaborative surgical environments developed for different medical applications are described. In this review, strategies to handle heterogeneity in CNVSS are not reported.

Yet, to the best of our knowledge, no one has proposed an arquiture and an adaptive model to handle heterogeneity in CNVSS. This paper describes the development and implementation of an adaptive architecture that provides the sotware structure and functionality required to apply an adaptive mathematical model.

3   Description of CNVSS Network Architecture

The network architecture describes the functional relationship existing between network elements that compose a CNVSS. Client-server and peer-to-peer are the most commonly implemented network architectures, each one providing different advantages and disadvantages for the development of CNVSS. Peer-to-peer architecture computes the simulation on each client machine providing low response time but making difficult to guarantee shared state consistency of the simulation for each user. By contrast, client-server architecture centralize the computation of the simulation in a machine called server and transmits the result to each one of the clients, so shared state consistency is guaranteed but increasing response time of actions performed by each user. Additionally, the server can become a bottleneck for the computing load and data that needs to be communicated through server [9].

To avoid some disadvantages of client-server and peer-to-peer architectures, a hybrid client-server architecture is implemented in our CNVSS, based on the one proposed by [10]. This architecture allows to maintain the consistency of the collaborative virtual surgical environment, centralizing the computing of the surgical simulation on a server, and also preventing the server from becoming a bottleneck by distributing the computation load of collision, visual and haptic rendering algorithms among each client.

In hybrid client-server architecture the server role consists of computing the deformation of anatomical structures and the client role consists of running, locally, the visual rendering, collision detection and haptic rendering algorithms. Whenever a collision between an anatomical structure and a client surgical instrument (local user input) arises, the client sends the primitives of the anatomical structures which are colliding with the surgical instrument, as well as the instrument position and orientation data to the server. Then, considering the collision primitives of all clients, the server calculates the deformation of the anatomical structures and sends the simulation data, mostly composed by the deformed state of organs and tissues, to each client. This process is involved in all of the operations supported by our CNVSS such as probing, attaching, carving, cutting and attaching of clips.

Figure 1 shows an example scheme of the architecture where two users are collaborating.

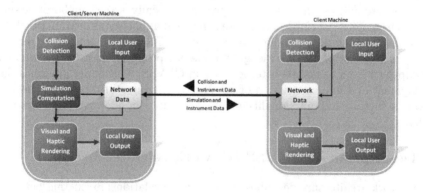

Fig. 1. Network elements and the funtional relationships that compose the architecture implemented by our CNVSS. Right one plays server role and left one plays client role.

4 Description of Adaptive System

An adaptive architecture allows modifying its parameters or structure using different mechanisms, in order to maximize the objective for which it was developed [11]. Considering CNVSS its main objective is to guarantee collaboration between users, performing a surgical training session as a team, despite different conditions that system could face. This collaboration must only be affected by the level of expertise of users performing surgical training, and not by system conditions such as machine capabilities or network conditions.

The process of adapting an application is composed by two important concepts: context and adaptive mechanisms [12]. The first refers to everything that surrounds the application and can affect their status or behavior. The second is the mechanisms used by the application to adapt to the current context. For example, considering CNVSS context refers to network conditions (i.e. bandwidth, jitter, latency and packet loss rate), computing capabilities of user machines and preferences, and role of users. On the other side, adaptive mechanisms are the size of data transmitted between user computers (i.e. resolution of anatomical structures simulated in the training session), visualization quality of anatomical structures, deformation algorithms, among others.

An adaptive architecture consists of three components. (i) The monitoring component, (ii) the inference or adaptation machine, and (iii) the reconfiguration system component (Figure 2). Each one of these components and their implementation in SOFA framework will be described in the next.

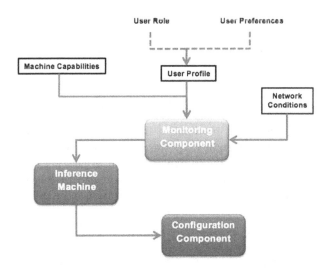

Fig. 2. Components taking part of the adaptive architecture proposed

4.1   Monitoring Component

This component gathers all the information related with the context of the system. Table 1 summarizes variables that are part of the context of the CNVSS developed.

Table 1. CNVSS Context Variables

Variable	Measurment Method
Jitter and packet loss	Iperf application was implemented (Milliseconds / Percentage) [13].
Delay	Ping service was used, which returns the round-trip time of a data packet transmitted between two nodes in the network (Milliseconds).
Bandwidth	Pathload application was implemented (Mbits/s) [14].
Frames per second	This value is calculated by the framework SOFA for each of the machines.
User role and preferences	The role options in the CNVSS are attaching anatomical structures, handling the camera, cutting, applying clips and cauterizing. Considering user preferences, the user chooses between display and interactions preferences. The scale range is from 0 to 1, where 0 was a low preference and 1 was a high preference.

Furthermore, this component defines the time interval for updating the context.

4.2   Inference or Adaptation Machine Component

This component infers which mechanism is required to adapt the simulation considering the context determined by the monitoring component. So far, the inference component is based on an expert system, consisting of a set of rules, which compare variables of the context with predefined thresholds, and determines the best options available for each of adaptation mechanisms.

4.3   Reconfiguration System Component

This subcomponent applies the mechanisms and actions required by the system and determined by the inference machine. Our system basically has three different mechanisms that vary the parameters of the simulation, and allow the system to adapt to the conditions of context maximizing collaboration among users:

- Changing resolutions and algorithms: This mechanism allows to interactively change the resolution and the algorithms used to simulate the anatomical structures, in each of the user machines taking part of the collaborative training session. Using this strategy is possible to vary the computing capacity required by each machine to run the simulation.
- Quality of data transmission: Using this mechanism the amount of data being transmitted per unit time over the network, from the server role machine to the client role machines, can be changed. This change in the quality of data transmitted is performed using two methods: (i) the mapping method, which allows decreasing the resolution of the mesh transmitted from server to client, and (ii) varying the transmission frequency of the data.
- Local and remote computation: By default the system performs the computation of the deformation in a centralized manner and the result is transmitted to clients which update their simulation state. However, when it is required this mechanism allows clients to change between the centralized manner to calculate the deformation locally and then update it with the computation performed by the server. In this way, response time of the simulator is decreased for deformations performed locally and mitigates the possible effects of latency on collaboration of the users.

5   Implementation of the Network Architecture and Adaptive System

The SOFA framework allows the development and integration of new components in order to extend the basic functionality it provides. This framework provides all the elements to develop a surgical scenario such as: collision, visual and haptic rendering, deformation and topological changes algorithms, and data structures for loading and storing the geometry of the anatomical structures that will be simulated. However, the framework lacks of capabilities to develop CNVSS and adaptive components. In this section we describe each of the components developed for this purpose:

- CNVSS-MW is a middleware layer which provides three main networking capabilities to our CNVSS; (i) organize the event data in messages that can be transmitted using an specific application level communication protocol developed, (ii) defines, depending on the type of message, whether it needs to be sent using UDP (User Datagram Protocol) or TCP (Transmission Control Protocol), (iii) controls the connection state and manages the session between clients and server.
- MultilevelThetrahedralHybridForceField allows to switch between two algorithms with different complexity to computes the deformation of the anatomical structures.
- MultiResolutionMeshLoader and MultilevelMesh: These components are responsible for loading and storing data structures at different resolutions for each of the anatomical structures simulated in the surgical scenario.

- MultilevelFixedConstraint is a component that allows applying fixed mechanical constraints in multiresolution meshes.
- MultilevelBarycentricMapping applies the barycentric mapping method in data estructures with different resolutions.
- AttachingController, CarvingController and AttachingClipController receive all the collision and basic surgical operation data sent by each client and apply them modifying the simulation state at the server side. Additionally, determine whether a local surgical instrument is colliding with an anatomical structure and if it is, all the information related with the col- lision and the basic surgical operation performed (attaching, carving, clip attaching, among others) are stored to be send to server by CNVSS-MW component.
- OmniDriver and RemoteOmniDriver functionality is described in [15].
- NetworkController is a very important component in our architecture that runs at the client and server side as an independent thread. Its function is to read the state of the components described above and determines whether there is an event to be transmitted by CNVSS-MW to the clients or to the server.

6   Results

A preliminary test was performed in order to evaluate the CNVSS developed, and determines if it is possible to maintain collaboration of users conducting a training session as a team while context is changed to deteriorate conditions. Ten users grouped as team of two members performed the experiment. The surgical procedure trained was cholecystectomy and users were expert in the surgical task trained (Figure 3). Each team performed the procedure twice: (i) using the CN-VSS described in this work and (ii) using a non-adaptive version of CNVSS. The order of the experiments was determined randomly. Network conditions and machine capabilities were varied at the beginning of the experiments so that they were not suitable to guarantee good collaboration. Task completion time and number of errors were measured.

Table 2 and 3 shows the results obtained in the experiment described.

Table 2. Preliminary results for the task completion time (seconds)

Experiment	Adaptive CNVSS	NonAdaptive CNVSS
1	132	164
2	124	156
3	131	155
4	129	160
5	118	158

Fig. 3. Two users performing a Cholecystectomy using the CNVSS developed. Each instrument is controlled by one user.

Table 3. Preliminary results for the number of errors

Experiment	Adaptive CNVSS	NonAdaptive CNVSS
1	4	10
2	2	11
3	6	15
4	4	9
5	3	20

From the results obtained it can be observed that when users performed the experiment using the adaptive CNVSS had a shorter task completion time and fewest errors. Considering users were expert in the execution of the task, it can be determined that metrics are affected only by system conditions (i.e. machine capabilities or network conditions).

7   Conclusions and Future Work

The conceptual development of a CNVSS able to adapt to the current context, and maintain the collaboration of users when the machine capabilities and network conditions are not the best is described. Three important components are part of the system: the monitoring component, the inference machine and configuration component. Additionally, CNVSS implementation using the SOFA framework is described, and its integration with hybrid client-server architecture is presented. Finally, an experiment to evaluate the developed CNVSS is performed. From the results obtained it can be concluded that the adaptive CNVSS allows users collaboration to be more effective, and task completion time and number of errors are decreased.

As future work the development of an inference machine based on robust mathematical models is proposed including the dynamic adaptation of the CNVSS.

References

1. Allard, J., Cotin, S., Faure, F., Bensoussan, P.J., Poyer, F., Duriez, C., Delingette, H., Grisoni, L.: Sofa: An open source framework for medical simulation. In: Medicine Meets Virtual Reality, MMVR (2007)
2. Montgomery, K., Bruyns, C., Brown, J., Sorkin, S., Mazzella, F., Thonier, G., Tellier, A., Lerman, B., Menon, A.: Spring: A general framework for collaborative, real-time surgical simulation. In: Medicine Meets Virtual Reality (MMVR 2002), pp. 23–26. IOS Press (2002)
3. Liberatore, V., Cavusoglu, M.C., Cai, Q.: Gipsinet: An open source/open architecture network middleware for surgical simulations. In: Surgical Simulations, Medicine Meets Virtual Reality 14, MMVR (2003)
4. Tang, S.W., Chong, K.L., Qin, J., Chui, Y.P., Ho, S.M., Heng, P.A.: Eciss: A middleware based development framework for enhancing collaboration in surgical simulation. In: IEEE International Conference on Integration Technology, ICIT 2007 (2007)
5. Qin, J., Choi, K.S., Poon, W.S., Heng, P.A.: A framework using cluster-based hybrid network architecture for collaborative virtual surgery. Computer Methods and Programs in Biomedicine 96(3), 205–216 (2009)
6. Qin, J., Choi, K.S., Heng, P.A.: Collaborative simulation of soft-tissue deformation for virtual surgery applications. Journal of Medical Systems 34, 367–378 (2010), doi:10.1007/s10916-008-9249-2
7. Dev, P., Heinrichs, W.: Learning medicine through collaboration and action: collaborative, experiential, networked learning environments. Virtual Reality 12, 215–234 (2008), doi:10.1007/s10055-008-0099-5
8. Qin, J., Choi, K.S., Pang, W.M., Yi, Z., Heng, P.A.: Collaborative virtual surgery: Techniques, applications and challenges. The International Journal of Virtual Reality 9, 1–7 (2010)
9. Marsh, J., Glencross, M., Pettifer, S., Hubbold, R.: A network architecture supporting consistent rich behavior in collaborative interactive applications. IEEE Transactions on Visualization and Computer Graphics 12, 405–416 (2006)
10. Lin, S., Narayan, R.J., Lee, Y.S.: Hybrid client-server architecture and control techniques for collaborative product development using haptic interfaces. Computers in Industry 61(1), 83–96 (2010)
11. Salehie, M., Tahvildari, L.: Self-adaptive software: Landscape and research challenges. ACM Transactions on Autonomous and Adaptive Systems 4(2), 14:1–14:42 (2009)
12. Hong, J.-Y., Suh, E.-H., Kim, S.-J.: Context-aware systems: A literature review and classification. Expert Systems with Applications 36(4), 8509–8522 (2009)
13. Russel, J., Cohn, R.: Iperf. Book on Demand (2012)
14. Jain, M., Dovrolis, C.: Pathload: A measurement tool for end-to-end available bandwidth. In: Proceedings of Passive and Active Measurements (PAM) Workshop, pp. 14–25 (2002)
15. Diaz, C., Trefftz, H., Quintero, L., Acosta, D., Srivastava, S.: Collaborative networked virtual surgical simulators (CNVSS): Factors affecting collaborative performance. Presence: Teleoperators and Virtual Environments 22(1), 1–29 (2013)

Three-Dimensional Fitt's Law Model Used to Predict Movement Time in Serious Games for Rehabilitation

Sergio García-Vergara and Ayanna M. Howard

Georgia Institute of Technology, Electrical and Computer Engineering Department,
85 5th Street NW, Atlanta, GA 30332
sergio.garcia@gatech.edu, ayanna.howard@ece.gatech.edu

Abstract. Virtual reality serious game platforms have been developed to enhance the effectiveness of rehabilitation protocols for those with motor skill disorders. Such systems increase the user's motivation to perform the recommended in-home therapy exercises, but typically don't incorporate an objective method for assessing the user's outcome metrics. We expand on the commonly used human modeling method, Fitt's law, used to predict the amount of time needed to complete a task, and apply it as an assessment method for virtual environments. During game-play, we compare the user's movement time to the predicted value as a means for assessing the individual's kinematic performance. Taking into consideration the structure of virtual gaming environments, we expand the nominal Fitt's model to one that makes accurate time predictions for three-dimensional movements. Results show that the three-dimensional refinement made to the Fitt's model makes better predictions when interacting with virtual gaming platforms than its two-dimensional counterpart.

Keywords: Fitt's law, virtual reality games, physical therapy and rehabilitation, linear modeling.

1 Introduction

Gaming platforms for serious games play an important role in the rehabilitation field [1]. Such systems have been developed to increase the motivation of users to perform their in-home recommended exercises [2], [3]. Moreover, previous research has shown these systems can be used to calculate kinematic metrics associated with an individual's movement profile. In [4], a prototype rehabilitation game was presented that used the Kinect system to analyze biomechanical movements of the upper extremities represented as range of motion and posture data. In [5], an augmented reality system that enabled 3D-reaching movements within the environment was presented. They derived a set of kinematic data represented as movement time and end-effector curvature values. Finally, [6] evaluated the probability of recognizing six different movement gestures, useful for rehabilitation, when using a virtual gaming system. Although virtual systems such as these show the viability of collecting kinematic movement data, they do not provide a quantifiable means of determining the quality of that movement. As such, we focus on incorporating a methodology within

R. Shumaker and S. Lackey (Eds.): VAMR 2014, Part II, LNCS 8526, pp. 287–297, 2014.

existing virtual reality (VR) gaming platforms that objectively evaluates the outcome metrics of an individual during game play.

A common symptom experienced by individuals who have a motor skill disorder is slow movements [7]. As such, movement time (MT) – defined as the time needed to complete a given task – is a kinematic parameter of interest in rehabilitation interventions because it directly correlates with the speed of the individual's movements. In this paper, we focus on predicting the MT needed to complete a task in any VR gaming platform. We use the prediction as the ground truth value for quantitatively comparing the user's nominal MT as a means for assessing their kinematic performance. Because of its wide adoption, we make use of the model of human movement, Fitt's law [8]. This law predicts the amount of time a user needs to reach a given target in a virtual environment. Even though refinements to improve the accuracy of Fitt's law have been made to the original model, to the best of our knowledge, there has not been any directly derived for time prediction for three-dimensional (3D) movements; which are inevitable when interacting with a VR system or a serious gaming platform.

As such, we propose a new variation on the Fitt's law model that takes into consideration 3D spatial movements. Section 2 presents a short literary review on previous variations and modifications made to the original model. Section 3 discusses in detail the procedure taken to create our final model. Section 4 presents the results obtained in testing sessions with human participants. Finally, we analyze the results in Section 5, and make our concluding remarks in Section 6.

2   Background

Fitt's law was initially designed to predict the amount of time a user needs to complete a task in order to design better human-computer interaction (HCI) interfaces or to determine the best input method for a digital system. Card et al. [9] used Fitt's law to evaluate four devices with respect to how rapidly they can be used to select text on a CRT display. Walker et al. [10] compared selection times between walking menus and pull-down menus. Gillian et al. [11] used Fitt's law to examine the needed time to select a text using a movement sequence of pointing and dragging.

Even in these applications for Fitt's law, HCI researchers have developed several refinements to improve the accuracy of the model. MacKenzie [12] summarized some refinements that deal with the definition of the difficulty of a task. In the original model, the difficulty of a movement task (*DI* for "difficulty index"), was quantified by (1).

$$DI = \log_2(2 * A/W) \tag{1}$$

where A is the distance to move, and W is the width of the target to reach. Welford [13] proposed a new formulation for DI (2) after noting a consistent departure of data points above the regression line for 'easy' tasks (i.e. DI < 3 bits).

$$DI = \log_2(A/W + 0.5) \tag{2}$$

Moreover, a preferred formulation (3), known as the Shannon formulation [14], is commonly used because it provides a better fit with observations, mimics the information theorem underlying Fitt's law, and provides a positive rating for the DI.

$$DI = \log_2(A/W + 1) \tag{3}$$

To the best of our knowledge, none of the previous studies have used Fitt's law for human movement assessment purposes, and the supporting literature for the theory behind Fitt's law is limited to two-dimensional (2D) movements. In this paper we discuss a methodology for building a model that: 1) predicts movement time for three-dimensional movements, and 2) is used as a tool for quantitatively assessing an individual's kinematic performance.

3   Methodology

3.1   Serious Game Platforms

In this paper we focus on expanding the functionality of serious game platforms used for rehabilitation by incorporating an objective kinematic assessment methodology. We make use of the developed platform called *Super Pop VR^{TM}* [15], [16]. It combines interactive game play for evoking user movement with an objective and quantifiable kinematic algorithm to analyze the user's upper-arm movements in real-time. While engaged with the game, users are asked to move their arms to 'pop' virtual bubbles of various sizes, which appear at various locations in the virtual environment. As the bubbles appear on screen, a 3D depth camera maps the user's movements into the virtual environment. These movements map into movement tasks that require reaching a target from a specified initial position; which are evaluated by Fitt's law. Figure 1 shows a comparison between a reaching task evaluated by Fitt's law (Figure 1a), and an example of a reaching exercise in the *Super Pop VR^{TM}* platform (Figure 1b). The ability to reach is critical for most, if not all, activities of daily living such as feeding, grooming, and dressing [17]. Failure to recover upper-extremity function can lead to depression [18]. As such, reaching movements, correlated to reaching exercises, are of interest in various rehabilitation scenarios.

(a)   (b)

Fig. 1. Comparison between a common movement task evaluated by Fitt's law (where A is the distance traveled, and W is the width of the target) (a), and a reaching exercise in the Super Pop VR^{TM} platform (b). Figure (a) adapted from [12].

Applying Fitt's law to the Super Pop game, we focus on predicting the amount of time a user needs to move between two displayed 'bubbles' as a function of the distance between the virtual objects and the width (diameter) of the target 'bubble'. Given the nature of the described platform, users move their arms in the 3D space in order to interact with the virtual objects on the screen. As such, we first need to build an appropriate model (i.e. define a DI), that is able to make accurate time predictions for 3D movements.

3.2   Linear Models

Fitt's law predicts movement time as a linear function of the difficulty index (DI) of a task (4). Because of its wide adoption and popularity, we adhere to the DI definition of the Shannon formulation as seen in (3), resulting in a model of the form (5).

$$MT = a + b * DI \tag{4}$$

$$MT = a + b * \log_2(A/W + 1) \tag{5}$$

where MT is the predicted movement time (in milliseconds), A is the distance to move, W is the width of the target to reach, and a and b are the intercept and the slope of the model respectively. Building a Fitt's model refers to training the slope and intercept to fit MT data collected from users interacting with the system. In general, a number of movement tasks are defined by selecting different combinations of traveled distances and widths of targets, and then by calculating the corresponding DI. Human MT data are collected for each defined task, and a linear regression between the MT averages per task and their corresponding DIs is performed to compute the slope and intercept of the model.

Since we are interested in building a model that is appropriate for 3D movements, the distance travelled is now the 3D Euclidean distance between the initial position of the user's hand, and the target. However, a complication arises because the positions of the 'bubbles' in the virtual platforms are defined in a 2D space. This means that the movement tasks are selected based on 2D data. As such, we built two linear models. The first model correlates the 2D pixel distance between the virtual objects to the user's 3D path length (PL). We then use this model to calculate the distance travelled parameter in (5) and create our second model: the correlation between the DI of a movement task and the time needed to complete it.

For collecting human MT data needed to develop the model, we recruited seven able-bodied adults to interact with the *Super Pop VR*[TM] game. Sixteen tasks were empirically selected; each participant was assigned to repeatedly complete eight of them. We collected, on average, 24 ± 5 PL and MT points for each task. To increase the correlation factor between variables for both models, we assume that both datasets follow a Gaussian distribution, and thus only considered data points that were within one standard deviation of the mean of the complete dataset. Moreover, taking into consideration the learning curve of the platform, the

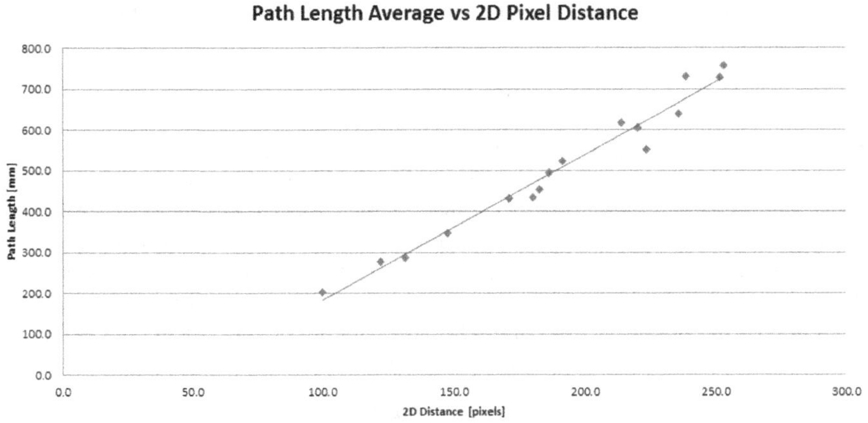

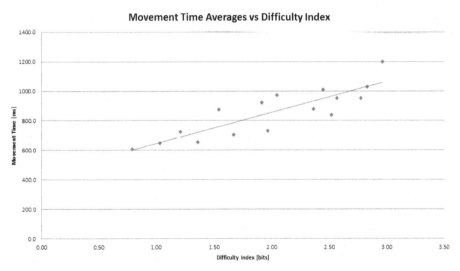

Fig. 2. 3D path length averages of collected human data versus 2D pixel distance between virtual objects. Figure also shows the final linear correlation (continuous line) between the two variables.

Fig. 3. Movement time averages collected from human data versus the corresponding DIs for each task. Figure also shows the final linear correlation (continuous line) between the two variables.

participants were required to interact with the system twice before starting the actual collection of the data. This practice eliminates the possible errors due to unfamiliarity with the game.

A linear regression was performed on the collected path length data to correlate the participants' 3D PL to the selected 3D pixel distance between 'bubbles' (Figure 2); which yielded (6) with a correlation factor of $\mathbf{R^2=0.9703}$. MacKenzie [12] argues that correlations above 0.900 are considered to be very high for any experiment involving measurements on human subjects. Thus, we can conclude that the PL model provides a good description of the observed behavior.

$$PL = 3.5651 * D_p - 174.3 \tag{6}$$

where D_p is the 2D distance between the two virtual targets, and PL is the 3D path length travelled by the user for the corresponding D_p in mm.

A second linear regression was performed on the collected MT data to correlate the participants' MT to the DI of the corresponding tasks (Figure 3); which yielded (7) with a correlation of $\mathbf{R^2=0.7428}$. Although the resulting correlation factor is not considered to be 'very high', it still suggests that the MT model also provides a good description of the observed behavior. The DI of the tasks was calculating using (5), making use of the built PL model (6) to substitute for the travelled distance.

$$MT = 208.97 * DI + 435.02 \tag{7}$$

where DI is the difficulty index of a given task, and MT is the movement time prediction made for the task (in milliseconds). It's important to mention that (7) is limited to the selected definition of DI. If a different definition were to be used, the MT model would have to be retrained.

Combining equations (5), (6), and (7), we obtain the final MT model (8) as a linear function of the 2D pixel distance between two virtual objects by making use of a second linear model of human PL data.

$$MT = 208.97 * \log_2 \left(\frac{3.5651*D_p-174.3}{W} + 1 \right) + 435.02 \tag{8}$$

where D_p is the 2D pixel distance between two virtual objects of the given task, W is the width of the second virtual object, and MT is the movement time prediction made for the given task (in milliseconds). Since the argument of the logarithm has to be unit less and since the PL model computes values in millimeters, the width of the target has to also be in millimeters.

In order to better determine the accuracy of the 3D Fitt's model, we also created a common 2D Fitt's model and compared the prediction results to the nominal MT values collected from the participants. The 2D model was built in a similar fashion than the 3D model. The selected tasks were the same as those for the 3D model. The difference relies on the fact that the DIs for the tasks were computed using the 2D pixel distance directly, instead of applying the PL model. A linear regression was applied to the collected MT data to correlate the participants' MTs to the DIs of the corresponding tasks; which yielded (9) with a correlation factor of $\mathbf{R^2=0.7346}$.

$$MT = 245.2 * DI + 377.42 \tag{9}$$

4   Experimental Results

The final model was tested with seventeen able-bodied high school students. Seven females and ten males ranging in age between 15 and 16 years (mean age = 15.5 years, standard deviation = 0.5 years) were recruited to interact with the *Super Pop*

VR^{TM} game in order to validate that the proposed methodology for creating a Fitt's law model is appropriate for 3D movements. The participants interacted in an office setting, which was maintained constant in order to maintain consistency. The virtual reality game screen was projected onto a large screen via a projector connected to a PC laptop. The chair height upon which the participants sat was 41cm tall, the distance between the user's chair and the depth camera was 190cm, and the distance between the projector and the screen was 170cm. Each participant was asked to play four games (two per arm), and PL and MT was collected for a total of six trials per arm.

Taking into consideration the learning curve of the used platform, we evaluate the last trial of the participants' dominant hand. Table 1 summarizes a comparison between the participants' nominal MT for the selected trial and the movement time predictions made by the 2D and 3D models. The error of the prediction is defined as the absolute difference between the participant's MT and the prediction made. The table also shows which model made the best prediction for each case; the model that best fits the given scenario is the model with the smallest difference between the actual MT and prediction. Figure 4 expands on Table 1 by organizing the results in a graphical medium.

Table 2 shows the progression of MT values over the six trials of Participant 2's dominant hand. Similar to Table 1, Table 2 shows a comparison between Participant 2's nominal MT and the predictions made by the 2D and 3D models. The table also includes the decision of the model that makes the most accurate prediction based on the absolute difference between the actual MT value and the predictions made.

Table 3 shows a summary of how the models behave for clear 2D and 3D movements. The data collected from the last trial of Participant 7's dominant hand are considered as 3D movements, while the data collected from the last trial of Participant 16's dominant hand are considered as 2D movements. The table shows the MT predictions made by both models on the two described scenarios, and the participants' actual MT for both scenarios.

5   Analysis

It's important to keep in mind that the linear models were built with data collected from adults. This allows for the possibility of over (or under) predicting path length (PL) and movement time (MT) values given that they were tested with data collected from high-school teenagers. Previous research has been shown that kinematic capabilities, among other parameters, are a nonlinear function of the age of the individual [19]. As such, there are some scenarios where neither the 2D nor 3D models make accurate MT predictions. For example, Participant 5 moved in almost double the time than what both models predicted (Table 1). Moreover, we only collected 24 ± 5 data points per task, while studies similar to [20] collected 470 trials per task. More data would results in a higher correlation and, thus, more stable models.

Another important observation is that our 3D Fitt's model falls into the known two-dimensional model when the movements are (almost) planar. Table 1 shows that both models make very similar predictions in these scenarios, suggesting that there is no deterioration when applying the 3D model to 2D movements. More importantly, in scenarios where the individual makes 3D movements, the 3D model makes more accurate predictions than the 2D model. Table 3 shows an example of such scenarios. The table shows that the predictions made by both models for a case where the movements were in the 2D space (participant 16), are relatively similar to each other. The difference between the predictions is **5.22 ms**, the difference between the prediction of the 3D model and the actual MT is **208.28 ms**, and the difference between the prediction of the 2D model and the actual MT is **213.51 ms**.

Similarly, Table 3 shows that the prediction made by the 3D model is more accurate than the prediction made by the 2D model for a case where the movements where in the 3D space. The difference between the two predictions is **411.41 ms** (which is considerably of greater value than that of the 2D movements), the difference between the prediction made by the 3D model and the actual MT is **35.96 ms**, and the difference between the prediction made by the 2D model and the actual MT is **375.45 ms**. These results show that, for 3D movements, the proposed Fitt's model with a PL model included makes more accurate MT predictions than the original Fitt's model.

Table 1. Comparison between the participants' MT nominal values and the predictions made by the 2D and 3D models to determine the best predictor for each scenario

Participants	MT_U [ms]	2D DI [bits]	2D MT_p [ms]	Difference [ms]	3D DI [bits]	3D MT_p [ms]	Difference [ms]	Best Predictor
1	1129.69	1.44	731.67	398.02	1.33	713.42	416.27	2
2	901.69	1.46	735.63	166.05	1.54	757.77	143.92	3
3	1180.66	1.01	624.60	556.07	2.73	1005.02	175.64	3
4	980.43	1.27	689.89	290.54	1.48	743.60	236.83	3
5	1413.22	1.68	789.09	624.13	1.48	745.13	668.09	2
6	1283.64	1.54	754.32	529.32	1.60	770.16	513.48	3
7	958.87	0.84	583.42	375.45	2.68	994.83	35.96	3
8	1071.39	1.46	734.25	337.14	1.99	850.30	221.09	3
9	978.12	1.17	665.26	312.85	1.10	664.87	313.25	2
10	913.74	1.80	819.61	94.13	1.64	777.94	135.80	2
11	1167.51	1.50	745.69	421.83	1.34	715.61	451.91	2
12	943.35	1.50	745.43	197.92	1.81	812.25	131.10	3
13	926.22	1.86	834.28	91.93	1.76	802.81	123.41	2
14	949.05	1.31	699.43	249.62	2.40	935.79	13.26	3
15	1352.22	1.59	767.88	584.34	1.56	760.11	592.11	2
16	934.13	1.40	720.62	213.51	1.39	725.84	208.28	3
17	1046.67	1.55	756.61	290.05	1.46	739.80	306.86	2

Table 2. Progression of MT values over the six trials of participant 2's dominant hand

Trials	MT_U [ms]	2D DI [bits]	2D MT_p [ms]	Difference [ms]	3D DI [bits]	3D MT_p [ms]	Difference [ms]	Difference [ms]	Best Predictor
1	1055.81	1.38	716.67	339.13	1.59	768.14	287.66	51.47	3
2	1352.83	1.31	697.57	655.26	1.32	711.19	641.64	13.62	3
3	1010.50	1.76	808.77	201.73	1.89	830.98	179.52	22.21	3
4	972.78	1.51	748.32	224.45	1.50	748.91	223.87	0.59	3
5	898.18	1.43	727.28	170.89	1.87	824.94	73.23	97.66	3
6	901.69	1.46	735.63	166.05	1.54	757.77	143.92	22.14	3

Table 3. Predictions made by both models when applied to clear 2D and 3D movements

	2D Movement (Participant 16)	3D Movement (Participant 7)
Prediction from 2D Model [ms]	720.62	583.42
Prediction from 3D Model [ms]	725.84	994.83
Participant's Actual MT [ms]	934.13	958.87
Difference between predictions [ms]	5.22	411.41
Difference between 2D prediction and actual MT [ms]	213.51	375.45
Difference between 3D prediction and actual MT [ms]	208.28	35.96

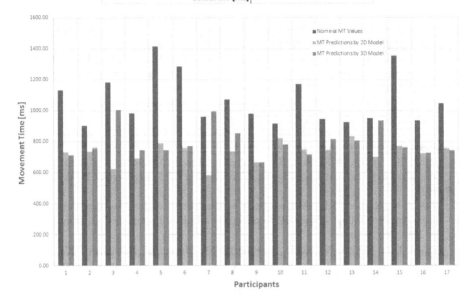

Fig. 4. Comparison between the participants' nominal MT and the predictions made by the 2D and 3D models

6   Conclusion and Future Work

The proposed methodology for developing a 3D Fitt's law model has the potential to be incorporated into existing serious game platforms as an effective means of rehabilitation. Results show that the final 3D model can better predict human MT for different reaching tasks when compared to its 2D counterpart. For future consideration, in order to have a fully robust methodology for 3D time prediction model, data from different age demographics must also be collected and added to the model.

Acknowledgements. This work was supported in part by the NSF Graduate Research Fellowship under Grant No. DGE-1148903, and NSF Grant 1208287. Any opinions, findings, and conclusions or recommendations expressed in this material are those of the author's and do not necessarily reflect the views of the National Science Foundation.

References

1. Taria, S., Johanneson, M., Backlund, P.: Serious Games: An overview (2007)
2. Harris, K., Reid, D.: The influence of virtual reality on children's motivation. Canadian Journal of Occupational Therapy 72(1), 21–29 (2005)
3. Reid, D.: The influence of virtual reality on playfulness in children with cerebral palsy: A pilot study. Occupational Therapy International 11(3), 131–144 (2004)
4. Freitas, D.Q., Da Gama, A., Figueiredo, L., Chaves, T.M., Marques-Oliveira, D., Teichrieb, V., Araújo, C.: Development and Evaluation of a Kinect Based Motor Rehabilitation Game. In: Brazilian Symposium on Computer. Games and Digital Entertainment (SBGames 2012), Brazil, pp. 144–153 (2012)
5. Goffredo, M., Schmid, M., Conforto, S., D'Alessio, T.: 3D reaching in Visual Augmented Reality using Kinect™: The Perception of Virtual Target. In: Proc. International Conference on NeuroRehabilitation ICNR, vol. 2, pp. 711–715 (2012)
6. Davaasambuu, E., Chiang, C.C., Chiang, J.Y., Chen, Y.F., Bilgee, S.: A Microsoft Kinect based virtual rehabilitation system. In: Proceedings of the 5th International Conference (FITAT 2012), pp. 44–50 (2012)
7. Morris, M.E.: Movement disorders in people with Parkinson Disease: A model for physical therapy. Physical Therapy 80(6), 578–597 (2000)
8. Fitts, P.M.: Perceptual-motor skill learning. Categories of Human Learning 47, 381–391 (1964)
9. Card, S.K., English, W.K., Burr, B.J.: Evaluation of mouse, rate-controlled isometric joystick, step keys, and text keys for text selection on a CRT. Ergonomics 21(8), 601–613 (1978)
10. Walker, N., Smelcer, J.B.: A comparison of selection times from walking to pull-down menus. In: Proceedings of the CHI Conference on Human Factors in Computing Science, pp. 221–225 (1990)
11. Gillian, D.J., Holden, K., Adam, S., Rudisill, M., Magee, L.: How does Fitt's Law fit pointing and dragging? In: Proceedins of the CHI Conference on Human Factors in Computing Systems, pp. 227–234 (1990)
12. MacKenzie, I.S.: Movement time prediction in human-computer interfaces: A brief tour on Fitt's Law. Proceedings Graphics Interface 92, 140–150 (1992)
13. Welford, A.T.: The measurement of sensory-motor performance: Surbey and reappraisal of twelve years' progress. Ergonomics 3, 189–230 (1960)
14. Shannon, C.E., Weaver, W.: The mathematical theory of communication. ILL University of Illinois Press, Urbana
15. García-Vergara, S., Chen, Y.-P., Howard, A.M.: Super Pop VR™: An adaptable virtual reality game for upper-body rehabilitation. In: Shumaker, R. (ed.) VAMR 2013, Part II. LNCS, vol. 8022, pp. 40–49. Springer, Heidelberg (2013)
16. García-Vergara, S., Brown, L., Park, H.W.: Engaging children in play therapy: The coupling of virtual reality games with social robotics. In: Brooks, A.L., Brahnam, S., Jain, L.C. (eds.) SEI 1991. SCI, vol. 536, pp. 139–163. Springer, Heidelberg (2014)
17. Granger, C.V., Hamilton, B.B., Sherwin, F.S.: Guide for the user of the uniform data set for medical rehabilitation. Uniform Data System for Medical Rehabilitation Project, Buffalo General Hospital, New York (1986)
18. McCrea, P.H., Eng, J.J., Hodgson, A.J.: Biomechanics of reaching: Clinical implications for individuals with acquired brain injury. Disability & Rehabilitation 24(10), 534–541 (2002)

19. Ketcham, C.J., Stelmach, G.E.: Age-related declines in motor control. In: Handbook of the Psychology of Aging, vol. 5, pp. 313–348 (2001)
20. MacKenzie, I.S., Sellen, A., Buxton, W.: A comparison of input devices in elemental pointing and dragging tasks. In: Proceedings of the CHI Conference of Human Factors in Computing Systems, pp. 161–166 (1991)

Multi-users Real-Time Interaction with Bacterial Biofilm Images Using Augmented Reality

Mohammadreza Hosseini[1], Tomasz Bednarz[2], and Arcot Sowmya[1]

[1] UNSW, Sydney NSW, Australia
{Mhosseini,Sowmya}@Cse.unsw.edu.au
2 CSIRO, Brisbane QLD, Australia
Tomasz.Bednarz@Csiro.au

Abstract. Augmented Reality (AR) applications may be used to enhance understanding of physical objects by addition of digital information to captured video streams. We propose new bio-secure system for interactions with bacterium biofilm images using the AR technology to improve safety in experimental lab. In proposed application we used state-of-the-art real-time features detection and matching methods. Also, various methods of feature detection and matching were compared with each other for real-time interaction and accuracy. The implementation of an app on a tablet device (Apple iPad) makes it useable by multi users in parallel.

Keywords: Multi-user, Real-time, biofilm, Augmented reality.

1 Introduction

Bacteria can reproduce simply and rapidly by doubling their contents and splitting in two. A colony of bacteria that sticks to a surface forms a biofilm. Furthermore, information such as the biofilm diffusion coefficient, bacterium dimension and trajectory are among quantities that scientists are interested in to understand and possibly explain the effect of new drugs on single species of bacteria. Computer vision and imaging techniques could be utilised to support better understanding of those mechanisms by helping to localize, track and measure bacteria features. Also, use of interactive visualisation techniques could enhance users' understanding; for instance, the user could explore naturally complex interior structures and morphology of bacteria during the course of biofilm formation. User interactions with visualization systems may be carried out using either a touch-based interface such as a keyboard and mouse, or a touchless interface such as gesture recognition cameras.

In the bio-imaging space, the user has the ability to pause a biofilm evolution movie and call up data annotations extracted from the database by selecting a bacterium. Based on an earlier study [1], users are more willing to use touch-based interfaces compared to a touchless ones. In most situations only one person interacts with the system. Additionally, users could use mobile handheld devices to capture biofilm fragments and call up augmented information on the top of it.

R. Shumaker and S. Lackey (Eds.): VAMR 2014, Part II, LNCS 8526, pp. 298–308, 2014.
© Springer International Publishing Switzerland 2014

In visualisation setup, any number of users could interact with the system at a time, without interfering with other users or even collaborating with them. For instance, tapping on a bacterium in the biofilm evolution movie watched through a tablet camera, could display related information on the tablet display held in the user's hand. The same augmented data displayed on a dynamic moving bacterium, must also be available to the user in following frames until the user selects another bacterium.

Bacterium morphological properties may vary from frame to frame. Therefore, determining a specific bacterium in the biofilm on tap commands, from an underlying moving image taken by a tablet camera in real time, is the major challenge of this research. The initial prototype will assume that tablet devices are aware of the frame number currently displayed on a large screen or hemispherical dome. Image cross-correlation techniques will allow detection of the biofilm sub image that will be further used to find a corresponding bacterium automatically.

Displaying a 3D object on the surface of a marker (a point of reference) and estimating camera position to stabilise the object is not a new concept [18]. Many algorithms have implemented and are available in various SDKs [16-18]. The API function allows displaying the virtual information over a predefined visual marker. Interaction using AR without a predefined marker is classified as marker-less AR, where any part of the real environment may be used as a target to be tracked in order to place a virtual object on. Marker-less augmented reality relies heavily on natural feature detection in images received through the camera. As soon as a known physical object is detected, the appropriate virtual object may be displayed over it. The detection of a known objects require that the features in an unknown image watched through a camera are matched with feature from a known object. Features are parts of an image that can be used for image matching or object detection and can usually be classified into three categories: regions, special segments and interest points [4]. Interests points such as corners are usually faster to detect in images and more suitable for real-time applications. Scale-invariant feature transform [5], Speeded Up Robust Features [6] and Harris [7] corner detector methods have been used widely in the literature to detect features but heavy mathematical computation involved in any of these methods may slow down an application significantly. SCARF [8] and ORB [9] are the recent attempts to improve the speed of feature detection.

Feature descriptors are used to describe image structure in the neighbourhood of a feature point. Using the descriptors, a feature points in an image can be matched with features in other images. SIFT, SURF and ORB are among feature descriptor methods that are rotation and scale invariant. Other feature descriptors such as BRIEF [10] and Daisy [11] are designed to be fast by sacrificing the rotation and scale-invariant properties. Similar feature points (i.e. points with similar feature descriptors) in source and destination images may represent the same point on single object in separate views. Matching features using brute force search (search among all features in the destination image)[12] is very time consuming and has little use in real-time applications. FLANN [15] is a library for performing fast approximate nearest neighbour searches in high dimensional spaces. The library includes a collection of algorithms for performing the nearest neighbour hood search and a system for automatically picking the best algorithm based on the data characteristic. Based on a survey [13] the Vantage-Point tree is a good method for estimating the nearest neighbour for matching feature descriptors. The vantage-point tree has the best overall construction and search performance and is used in this work.

2   System Implementation

The system for interacting with biofilm images through an AR application is configured as shown in Figure 1.

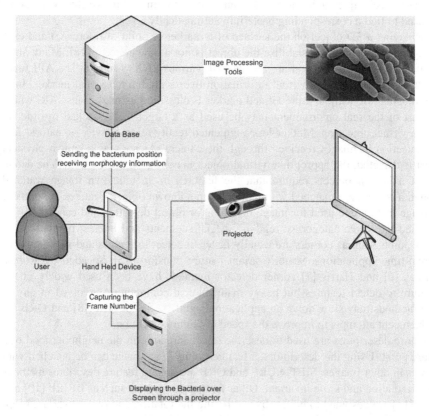

Fig. 1. Overall System Configuration

A bacterium tracking method [2] is used to extract morphological properties of each bacterium in every frame. The information is stored in a database, which can be accessed individually based on the bacterium position in the biofilm.

The biofilm evolution movie, which is displayed over a wall surface by a projector, is viewed through the camera of a handheld device (tablet). Interaction with images displayed on the wall is by an augmented reality application.

The following tasks are to be performed in order to add virtual information archived for every bacterium in the database through an AR application:

1. A server displays the biofilm movie on the large screen and continuously updates a variable used to keep track of the frame number.
2. Users watch the movie through the camera of handheld device (tablet). The video filmed by the camera is displayed on the handheld device.
3. Tapping on a single bacterium in the live video watched on a handheld device triggers the information retrieval process.
4. The frame number is fetched from the server.
5. The bacterium position in the biofilm image that is matched with frame number is calculated.
6. Bacterium position is used to extract the required information from database.
7. Bacterium is highlighted and information is displayed back (augmented) on the handheld device.
8. Until the next tapping, the previously detected bacteria position will be used to update the location of the bacterium virtual information in subsequent image. This is more explained in section 2.5.

The major concern as discussed before is the ability to locate the position of a tapped bacterium in the biofilm sub image on the handheld device. The methods used and the reasons for selecting them will be described in the following sections.

2.1   Feature Detector

Detection of the features and matching descriptors around a tapped bacterium is used to retrieve bacterium position in the original biofilm image. FAST is one of the fastest corner detection methods suitable for real-time applications [3]. It is based on the pixel intensity comparison around a circular neighbourhood of a query point. Each pixel in the circle is labeled from 1 to 16 clockwise. If *a set of N contiguous pixels in the circle is all brighter than the intensity of candidate pixel p plus a threshold value t or all darker than the intensity of candidate pixel p minus threshold value t, then p is classified as a corner.*

2.2   Feature Descriptor

We used BRIEF as the feature descriptor. The formulation of the BRIEF descriptor as follows:

1. Select a series of N, (X, Y) where $X=(x_1,y_1)$, $Y=(x_2,y_2)$ are location pairs around the feature point.

$$2.\ T(X,Y,P)=\begin{cases}1, & p(X)<p(Y)\\0, & p(X)\geq p(Y)\end{cases} \qquad \text{for every selected (X,Y)} \qquad (1)$$

Here *P represents a patch around a feature point, T represents a test on patch P and p(X) is pixel intensity at pixel X.* Performing the above operation on *N* pairs creates a binary string as a feature descriptor. Selecting the size of the patch around the feature point and selection of *N* pairs can affect the accuracy of the method. A study [10] shows that selection of the pairs from a double Gaussian distribution or selecting randomly around the feature points can produce better results. The advantage of the binary string as a descriptor is the ability to calculate the distance between every pair (e.g. Hamming distance) very quickly on many processors [10]. Our experiments show that the major bottleneck of marker-less AR is the feature matching part (section 2.3). So selecting a not very sophisticated descriptor that is fast to calculate is the only way to achieve near real-time AR. This is discussed more in section 3.

2.3   Feature Matching

We use Vantage-Point as the feature matching method. The matching method itself and a technique to improve the search speed are discussed in the following section.

Vantage-Point (VP) Search Tree Construction. The idea of constructing a binary search tree is to divide the search space recursively based on a similarity measurement in order to increase search speed, which is possible by pruning nodes that cannot be better than the best answer already found. Rather than partitioning points on the basis of relative distance from multiple centres (as is the case with k-means), VP-tree splits points using the absolute distance from a single centre. Tree construction begins by assigning all points to the root node, and then recursively partitioning the points into one of several children of the node. This process continues until some termination criteria are met. Two common criteria are the maximum leaf size (the leaf contains fewer than a given number of points) and the maximum leaf boundary [12].

The algorithm for constructing the Vantage-point tree with hamming distance as a measure of similarity between two bit strings is summarized in Algorithm Vantage-PointTree.

```
VantagePointTree (lower, upper)

If Termination condition is met, return
Create a node
Select a random bit string in the search space as the
vantage point and place it in the node
Sort the other bit string in ascending order based on
their distance to the Vantage-Point
Select the median bit strings
Keep the distance between the vantage-Point and the me-
dian as the vantage-point boundary in the tree node
Node leftchild =VanatagePointTree(lower+1,median)
Node right child=VanatagePointTree(median,upper)
```

In this algorithm, lower and upper are the indices of an array used to store the binary strings. The search algorithm is shown in Algorithm VantagePoinTree-Search.

```
VantagePoinTreeSearch (target, node, σ)

If node=Null return
dist= distance(node , target)
If dist < σ
  Keep tree root
  keep σ
if leftchild(node) =empty and rightChild(node)=empty re-
turn
if dist < node threshold
  if dist- σ <= node threshold
    VantagePoinTreeSearch(taget,node left child, σ)
  if dist+ σ >= node threshold
    VantagePoinTreeSearch(taget,nde right child, σ)
else
  if dist+ σ >= node threshold
    VantagePoinTreeSearch(taget,tree right child, σ)
  if dist- σ <= node threshold
    VantagePoinTreeSearch(taget,node left child, σ)
```

In this algorithm σ is the smallest distance that has been found so far. The target binary string is a descriptor of a feature in the source image.

The tree construction is performed for every frame in the original biofilm evolution movie beforehand, so that the tree construction phase does not have any effect on application processing speed.

Increasing Search Speed Using Triangle Inequality. The search algorithm may not need to process all the points in a leaf if the distance between every point in a leaf and the leaf node is calculated during tree construction. Let $\{b_1, b_2 \ldots b_n\}$ be the points in the leaf, B the leaf node and $d(b_1, B) > d(b_2, B) > \ldots > d(b_n, B)$ where d is the Hamming distance. Based on triangle inequality we have

$$d(target, B) < d(target, b_i) + d(B, b_i) \text{ for } i=1,2,\ldots,n \tag{2}$$

$$d(target, B) - d(B, b_i) < d(target, b_i) \text{ for } i=1,2,\ldots,n \tag{3}$$

So $d(target, B) - d(B, b_i)$ is the lower bound for the $d(target, b_i)$. If at any stage of searching a leaf point we find $j \in \{1 \ldots n\}$ where $d(target, B) - d(B, b_j) > \sigma$, the algorithm will stop searching the other points, as the distance between the target and remaining leaf points will be higher that σ since $d(b_i,B)$ $i \in \{1,...,n\}$ are sorted in descending order.

2.4   Matching and Outliers Removal

In Fig. 2, pairs of feature matching of the source image (images on left are viewed through handheld device camera) and destination image (biofilm images stored in a database) are displayed. As the images show although there are some correct matches there are also many mismatches that must be removed before further processing. Estimating homography using RANSAC [14] can be used to remove the outliers. The result after removing the outliers is shown in Fig. 3.

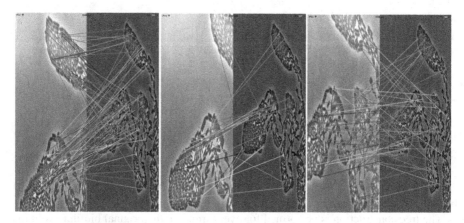

Fig. 2. Matching feature based on similarity of feature descriptor

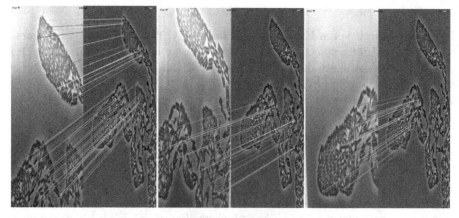

Fig. 3. Removing outliers

2.5   Bacteria Position Retrieval and Displaying Information

Homography matrix is used to translate the tapped position in held device coordinates to image coordinates. A search inside the database is carried out to find the closest bacterium. The information for this bacterium will then be displayed on handheld device. The inverse of the homography matrix and the bacterium position in image coordinates is also used to track the position of the last tapped bacterium in subsequent frames before any new tapping. This can be used to display the virtual information at the right position even if the handheld device moves in a different direction (Fig. 4).

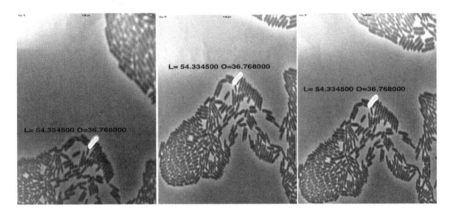

Fig. 4. Displaying the information in right position in different device orientation

3   Experimental Results

The application frame rates when implemented using different combination of feature detector and descriptor methods is calculated. The application runs for 30 seconds and frame rate was recorded prior to feature matching. As Fig. 5 shows, the combination of FAST feature detector and BRIEF feature descriptor method (Fig. 5 c) is the best choice for a real-time application. It is necessary to mention that this result is valid for high-density biofilm image sets and may not be valid for other image sets.

The accuracy of application was also evaluated and compared with other implementation of the application using different feature detection and matching methods. The application accuracy is estimated by measuring the acceptable range of device rotation. The acceptable range is the maximum rotation in every direction before the application loses the bacterium position between two consecutive taps (refer to section 2.5). This is carried out by comparing the positions extracted from inverse homography of different matching methods with results from SURF matching inverse homography method in different device orientations. The reason for selecting SURF as the base model is because of its rotation and scale invariant properties. The results are shown in Fig. 6. These images are produced when the device rotated around the vertical axis. Fig. 6 shows that FAST/BRIEF feature matching acceptable device rotation range is limited to [-5.05, 25.80] (Fig. 6 b) which is shorter that other rotation and scale invariant feature detector and descriptor. This means that the user can only use the application in situation where there are no significant changes in handheld vertical device orientation.

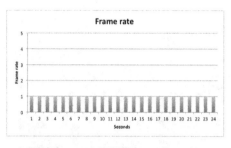

a) SIFT Detector, SIFT Feature Descriptor

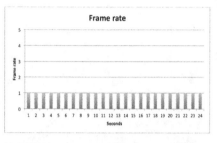

b) SURF Detector, SURF Feature Descriptor

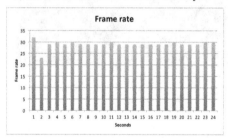

c) FAST Feature Detector, BRIEF Feature Descriptor

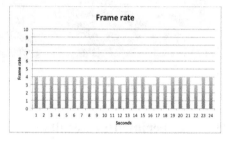

d) FAST Feature Detector, SURF Feature Descriptor

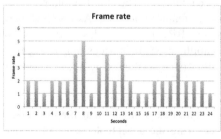

e) FAST Feature Detector, SIFT Feature Descriptor

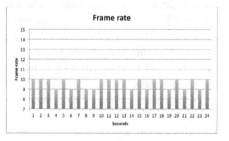

f) ORB Feature Detector, ORB Feature Descriptor

Fig. 5. Frame rate achieve during 30 seconds experiments using different method

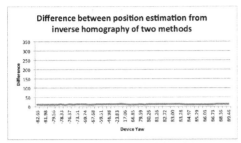

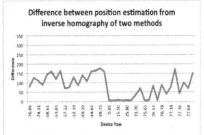

a) FAST Feature Detector, SURF Feature Descriptor

b) FAST Feature Detector, BRIEF Feature Descriptor

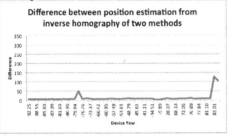

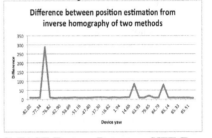

c) ORB Feature Detector, ORB Feature Descriptor

d) FAST Feature Detector, SIFT Feature Descriptor

Fig. 6. Difference between estimated positions using inverse homography of various methods and SURF feature and descriptor matching

4   Conclusions

Lower processing power of handheld devices in comparison with desktop computers raise the necessity of developing a low-computational approach for real-time application. Employing a feature descriptor method, which is not scaled and rotation invariant was an approach used in this paper. The application lets the user experience a real-time AR but limited device acceptable rotation, drop usability of the application. The whole experiments reveal that a real-time and a rotation and scale invariant feature detector and descriptor in high-dense environment are still an ongoing research.

References

1. Hosseini, M., Vallotton, P., Bednarz, T., Sowmya, A.: A Study of Touchless Versus Touch-based Interactions with Bacterial Biofilm Images. In: 12th ACM International Conference on Virtual Reality Continuum and Its Applications in Industry (VRCAI 2013). The Chinese University of Hong Kong, Hong Kong (2013)

2. Vallotton, P., Sun, C., Wang, D., Ranganathan, P., Turnbull, L., Whitchurch, C.: Segmentation and tracking of individual Pseudomonas aeruginosa bacteria in dense populations of motile cells. In: Image and Vision Computing New Zealand (IVCNZ), Wellington, New Zealand (2009)

3. Rosten, E., Drummond, T.: Machine learning for high-speed corner detection. In: Leonardis, A., Bischof, H., Pinz, A. (eds.) ECCV 2006, Part I. LNCS, vol. 3951, pp. 430–443. Springer, Heidelberg (2006)

4. Gundogdu, E., Alatan, A.A.: Feature detection and matching towards augmented reality applications on mobile devices. In: 3DTV-Conference: The True Vision - Capture, Transmission and Display of 3D Video (3DTV-CON) 2012, October 15-17, pp. 1,4 (2012)

5. Lowe, D.G.: Distinctive image features from scale-invariant key points. IJCV 60(2), 91–110 (2004)

6. Bay, H., Tuytelaars, T., Van Gool, L.: SURF: Speeded up robust features. In: Leonardis, A., Bischof, H., Pinz, A. (eds.) ECCV 2006, Part I. LNCS, vol. 3951, pp. 404–417. Springer, Heidelberg (2006)

7. Harris, C., Stephens, M.: A combined corner and edge detector. In: Proceedings of the 4th Alvey Vision Conference (1988)

8. Thomas, S.J., MacDonald, B.A., Stol, K.A.: Real-time robust image feature description and matching. In: Kimmel, R., Klette, R., Sugimoto, A. (eds.) ACCV 2010, Part II. LNCS, vol. 6493, pp. 334–345. Springer, Heidelberg (2011)

9. Rublee, R., Rabaud, V., Konolige, K., Bradski, G.: ORB: An efficient alternative to SIFT or SURF. In: Proceedings of the IEEE International Conference on Computer Vision (ICCV), p. 13 (2011)

10. Calonder, M., Lepetit, V., Strecha, C., Fua, P.: Brief: Binary robust independent elementary features. In: Daniilidis, K., Maragos, P., Paragios, N. (eds.) ECCV 2010, Part IV. LNCS, vol. 6314, pp. 778–792. Springer, Heidelberg (2010)

11. Tola, E., Lepetit, V., Fua, P.: A Fast Local Descriptor for Dense Matching. In: Proceedings of IEEE Conference on Computer Vision and Pattern Recognition (2008)

12. Nielsen, F., Piro, P., Barlaud, M.: Bregman Vantage Point Trees for Efficient Nearest Neighbor Queries. In: Proceedings of IEEE International Conference on Multimedia and Expo, pp. 878–881 (2009)

13. Kumar, N., Zhang, L., Nayar, S.: What Is a Good Nearest Neighbors Algorithm for Finding Similar Patches in Images? In: Forsyth, D., Torr, P., Zisserman, A. (eds.) ECCV 2008, Part II. LNCS, vol. 5303, pp. 364–378. Springer, Heidelberg (2008)

14. Fischler, M., Bolles, R.: Random sample consensus: A paradigm for model fitting with application to image analysis and automated cartography. Commun. Assoc. Comp. Mach. 24, 381–395 (1981)

15. Muja, M., Lowe, D.G.: FLANN – Fast Library for Approximate Nearest Neighbors, http://people.cs.ubc.ca/~mariusm/index.php/FLANN/FLANN

16. Metaio Augmented Solutions, http://www.metaio.com

17. Qualcomm Vuforia, https://www.vuforia.com

18. ARLab, http://www.arlab.com

Attention Control and Eyesight Focus for Senior Citizens

Miikka Lääkkö[1], Aryan Firouzian[1], Jari Tervonen[1],
Goshiro Yamamoto[2], and Petri Pulli[1]

[1] University Of Oulu, Department of Information Processing Science, Oulu, Finland
{miikka.laakko,aryan.firouzian,jari.tervonen,
petri.pulli}@oulu.fi
[2] Nara Institute of Science and Technology, Nara, Japan
goshiro@is.naist.jp

Abstract. The population is aging fast and with aging come cognitive impairments that often require costly facility care. This paper proposes Smart Glasses that can help alleviate these impairments at their early stages and thus allow senior citizens stay away from facility care longer. The Smart Glasses produce exogenous cues to attract user attention. Four usability experiments are described to evaluate the utility of the cues and other usability factors of the proposed system. We expect the results will give us valuable information on how to improve the design of the system based on senior citizens' needs.

Keywords: smart glasses, aging in-place, assistive technology, attention control, cognitive impairment.

1 Introduction

Ferri et al. estimated that 24.3 million people suffered from dementia in the year 2005 and 4.6 million people are added to this number every year. It is predicted that number of people suffering from dementia will be about 81.1 in the year 2040. Unobservable cases of dementia should also be added to the estimation. [4]

Abovementioned statistics and estimations have led numerous researchers developing tools and systems to support health care of senior citizen in their home. This concept is known as aging-in-place. Supporting senior citizens' independent daily life and monitoring health, safety, physical and cognitive functionalities are the main purposes to develop new tools and systems. [2]

Common problems for the senior citizens are memory related issues, and range from simple age-related problems to Alzheimer's Disease. A collaborative study in Nordic countries [5] was conducted on individuals with dementia and the goal was to find out what kinds of aid devices are used for assistance, how suitable they were for the users, and to gather improvement feedback for the aid device researchers [8]. Conclusions indicated that introducing aid devices for the caretakers and people suffering from dementia has improved management of daily activities; it helped caretakers and patients to maintain skills and made people socially more active. Prior researches have also suggested that navigation technology has the potential to provide

R. Shumaker and S. Lackey (Eds.): VAMR 2014, Part II, LNCS 8526, pp. 309–315, 2014.

important support for the elderly by similarly motivating and empowering them to perform their daily activities. [7]

The ability to achieve and maintain focus of cognitive activity on a given task is a fundamental component of the cognitive capacities of humans. Researches on visual capabilities of the elderly have concluded that aging itself brings along decline in both cognitive abilities and the capabilities of the visual system, added with constraints brought by dementia. [9], [12]

Research on attentional capacity of the elderly [1] suggests that both normal aging and Alzheimer's Disease (AD) impair people's performance in reaction tests but continue to conclude that people in the earlier phases of AD were not significantly more impaired by the increase in difficulty of a given task than the normal elderly. AD patients may have more problems in filtering interference from similar background material. The paper concludes there was no apparent decline in the capacity to divide attention with age, whereas there was a clear impairment in the dual-task performance of AD patients.

Visual performance of humans depends on both operational variables and physical variables. The operational variables include age, visual capabilities (contrast and light sensitivity, color and depth perception) and the characteristics of the task. The physical variables consist of lighting conditions, disability or discomfort glare, and colors in the vicinity, among others. In addition, several cognitive processes affect how information is filtered for processing through the general physical features. Attention has been described as limited by the mental effort available, and the limited cognitive capacity of attention can be actively spread over several cognitive demands at a time. How much attentional capacity and finite processing resources are allocated and needed for each task is determined by a combination of factors. [9]

There is also evidence that endogenous and exogenous cues have separate and additive effects. Endogenous cues allow the participant direct their attention to the indicated location at will, which also implies the symbology of the cues must be understood and their meaning remembered throughout the task. Exogenous cues, such as a flash of light, attract attention automatically. Such a cue is still effective even if the participant's cognitive resources are occupied elsewhere. [13]

We have founded our approach for the Smart Glasses on the premises set by the referenced literature. Section 2 describes the system setup, section 3 explains the test setup and the usability tests we have planned, and Section 4 concludes the paper.

2   Smart Glasses System

The first version of Smart Glasses prototype contains 12 red LEDs and 12 green LEDs as presented in Figure 1, and the second prototype version contains 6 red LEDs and 6 green LEDs as presented in Figure 2. The LEDs are positioned on the frames of Smart Glasses and are controlled by TLC5940 drivers. The drivers are connected to a micro-controller (low-power ATMega168V) via serial communication bus. The commands for different LED patterns are received through the wireless communication module. A Li-ion battery supplies power for the micro-controller. The micro-controller is connected to a Bluetooth Serial Port Profile (SPP) module. SPP module is the communication gateway of the micro-controller and an Android application. SPP is used to send 32-bit control messages from the remote controlling device (Android tablet) to the Smart Glasses. Remote controlling device translates 32-bit control messages to voice commands, and sends them to an audio device via Bluetooth.

Fig. 1. First prototype version of smart glasses having 12 green LEDs and 12 red LEDs positioned on the frames

Fig. 2. Second prototype version of smart glasses having 6 green LEDs and 6 red LEDs positioned on the frames

3   Usability Test for Smart Glasses

The main objective of conducting usability experiment is to remove blocking and problematic issues from user's path through the application. Problematic issues mostly cause failure in achieving maximum desired application's usability. Analyzing tasks of usability test facilitates designing user interface and application concept more accurately. There should be four to six participants in usability testing to rely on results; a final report should outline findings and provide developers with recommendations to redesign the system. [3], [10]

Usability experiment setting is defined as specific number of participants, a moderator and a set of tasks to test the system. It identifies problems, which have been hidden through the development process from developer's point of view. In order to organize usability testing before conducting it, a set of assumptions should be predefined, and then assumption should be evaluated after the usability testing. [6], [11]

In order to measure usability in experiment, it is necessary to define following factors:

- Effectiveness means user's ability to accomplish tasks.
- Efficacy means user's ability to accomplish tasks quickly without difficulty and frustration.

- Satisfaction means how much user is enjoying doing tasks.
- Error frequency and severity means how often user makes errors and how serious are the errors.
- Learnability means how much user could learn to use the application after doing the first task.
- Memorability means how much user could remember from one task during next tasks.

Separate tasks could be designed to evaluate different usability factors. [6], [11]

3.1   Test Setting

Subjects in all the experiments will be senior citizens suffering from dementia, and people suffering from other illnesses like color-blindness, tinnitus or Parkinson's Disease potentially affecting their performance in the tests will be excluded. The minimum number of participants in each experiment will be four. An observer representing the medical center will be present in all the experiments.

In order to evaluate satisfaction properly, the observer will be advised to encourage participants to think aloud during the experiment and give feedback to observer at the end of each experiment. Qualitative questionnaires will be presented after each experiment to collect participants' satisfaction and preferences.

One video camera will be used to record participants' actions and another video camera will be used to record their eye movements during the tests. The recordings will be synchronized and time-stamped, which will help to investigate the sequence of events properly.

Different kinds of test applications on an Android tablet will be used to record the results and log other necessary information on the experiments. These tools accompanied with the qualitative questionnaires will help us to investigate effectiveness, efficacy, satisfaction and learnability of the system.

3.2   Test Scenarios

We have defined four usability tests to evaluate usability factors of Smart Glasses system. The foremost purpose will be to establish the feasibility of the designed Smart Glasses for the indoor and outdoor navigation scenarios. The second objective will be to measure usability factors that can have either strengthening or weakening effect on the design. Salient factors are effectiveness, efficacy, satisfaction and learnability of the system.

The first test will focus on finding the best way the system can attract participant's attention. In the second test we will be asking the participants' opinion of the best pattern for indicating all possible directions. The third test will tell us how well the navigation instructions given by the Smart Glasses can be followed by the participant by moving their finger on a tablet PC to the direction indicated. Finally, the fourth set of tests will be first conducted in open space indoors where the participant is walking through a predefined route with the help of the Smart Glasses. This test will also be repeated in open space outdoors to capture how the changes in ambient light and sounds will affect the usability of the Smart Glasses.

The first test is designed to identify how accurately senior citizens can recognize precisely which LED on Smart Glasses is lit or blinking. At the same time, this test aims to identify how accurately senior citizens can recognize the general direction in which the LED on Smart Glasses is lit or blinking. The directions are defined as lighting up a single LED or a combination of LEDs depending on the Smart Glasses prototype version. A test application for the tablet PC will be developed to store participants' responses. Participants will be divided into two groups, one having the prototype version with six LEDs per lens and the other having three LEDs per lens. A number of sequences for lighting up the LEDs will be defined beforehand and the sequences are used in tests randomly in order to avoid any learning effect from one test to another. By comparing the results obtained from tests with different LED configurations we hope to be able to define the specific number and configuration of LEDs per lens that yields the best results. After identifying the most suitable pattern of LEDs per lens on the Smart Glasses, two further experiments will be conducted.

In the second test, we will present the participants with all feasible LED combinations for a given direction. We will then ask their opinion on which particular pattern they would associate the best with the specific direction in question.

The third test will incorporate a Bluetooth headset to accompany the Smart Glasses. In addition, a tablet PC with a stylus and two cameras will be utilized. An application running on the tablet PC will communicate with the Smart Glasses and headset via Bluetooth. The application user interface is designed as a grid layout with invisible lines and it will include a specific number of cells. The operator selects a route from predefined set of routes to follow. A route is a set of adjacent cells (Figure 3), having a starting point and an endpoint. When participant moves the pen on the screen from a cell to another cell, the application recognizes if the pen is moving along the route or not. The application calculates the next movement direction based on the current position of the pen and its relation to the next cell in the route. After a specific time delay, a new direction indication is sent to Smart Glasses and headset. If participant makes an error and moves the pen to a cell outside the route, the application will provide a direction indication towards the nearest cell in the route. The application will guide the participant periodically to reduce the amount of errors during the usability testing. To evaluate intuitiveness and learnability of the system, this test will be conducted in three different variations. The guidance can be audio only, LEDs and audio or LEDs only. By evaluating the results, we will also be able to determine whether the modalities support or hinder each other with participants being cognitively impaired.

The fourth and last test is a navigation experiment to guide the users through a specific route in both an indoor and an outdoor environment. The routes will be predefined and contain a fixed number of turns to each direction and predetermined length. Participants will be randomly assigned a route from the set. These navigation tests will not only evaluate usability of the system under more realistic conditions, but also evaluate the influence of ambient light on visibility of the LEDs and the effect of ambient sounds from the environment to the audio-cues.

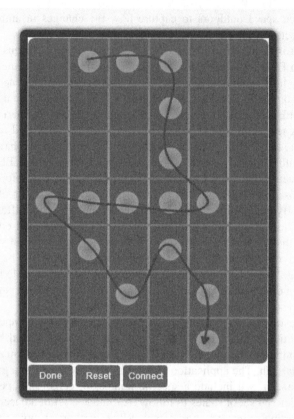

Fig. 3. A predefined route in the third test contains a sequence of cells (gridlines are not visible for the participants)

4   Conclusion

In this paper, we have described our Smart Glasses approach to assist senior citizens in their daily activities. Four usability tests have been defined to evaluate usability factors of the system. We will be conducting the tests in the next few months and report the results on HCII 2014. During the testing, we will iterate over the design for the Smart Glasses based on test results and participant feedback.

Acknowledgments. This paper has been written as part of ASTS project funded by Academy of Finland and Japan Science technology Agency (JST). We want to thank Timo Jämsä, Maarit Kangas, Niina Keränen, Jaakko Hyry, Eeva Leinonen, Zeeshan Asghar, Mika Naukkarinen, Tomi Sarni and Pekka Räsänen for contribution, co-operation and fresh ideas.

References

1. Baddeley, A.D., Baddeley, H.A., Bucks, R.S., et al.: Attentional Control in Alzheimer's Disease. Brain 124, 1492–1508 (2001)
2. Bharucha, A.J., Anand, V., Forlizzi, J., et al.: Intelligent Assistive Technology Applications to Dementia Care: Current Capabilities, Limitations, and Future Challenges. The American Journal of Geriatric Psychiatry: Official Journal of the American Association for Geriatric Psychiatry 17, 88 (2009)
3. Donahue, G.M., Weinschenk, S., Nowicki, J.: Usability is Good Business. Verfügbar unter (1999) (April 24, 2003), http://www.yucentrik.ca/usability.pdf
4. Ferri, C.P., Prince, M., Brayne, C., et al.: Global Prevalence of Dementia: A Delphi Consensus Study. The Lancet 366, 2112–2117 (2006)
5. Hyry, J., Yamamoto, G., Pulli, P.: Requirements Guideline of Assistive Technology for People Suffering from Dementia, 39 (2011)
6. Jeng, J.: Usability Assessment of Academic Digital Libraries: Effectiveness, Efficiency, Satisfaction, and Learnability. Libri. 55, 96–121 (2005)
7. Kangas, M., Konttila, A., Lindgren, P., et al.: Comparison of Low-Complexity Fall Detection Algorithms for Body Attached Accelerometers. Gait Posture 28, 285–291 (2008)
8. Kangas, M., Vikman, I., Wiklander, J., et al.: Sensitivity and Specificity of Fall Detection in People Aged 40 Years and Over. Gait Posture 29, 571–574 (2009)
9. Kretschmer, V., Griefahn, B., Schmidt, K.-H.: Bright Light and Night Work. Effects on Selective and Divided Attention in Elderly Persons. Light Res. Technol. 43, 473–486 (2011)
10. Nielsen, J.: Usability Inspection Methods, 413-414 (1994)
11. Sauro, J., Kindlund, E.: A Method to Standardize Usability Metrics into a Single Score, 401-409 (2005)
12. Staub, B., Doignon-Camus, N., Després, O., et al.: Sustained Attention in the Elderly: What do we Know and what does it Tell Us about Cognitive Aging? Ageing Res. Rev. 12, 459–468 (2013)
13. Tales, A., Muir, J.L., Bayer, A., et al.: Spatial Shifts in Visual Attention in Normal Ageing and Dementia of the Alzheimer Type. Neuropsychologia 40, 2000–2012 (2002)

Sense of Presence and Metacognition Enhancement in Virtual Reality Exposure Therapy in the Treatment of Social Phobias and the Fear of Flying

Ioannis Paliokas[1], Athanasios Tsakiris[1], Athanasios Vidalis[2],
and Dimitrios Tzovaras[1]

[1] Centre for Research and Technology Hellas-CERTH, Information Technologies Institute-ITI,
P.O. Box 60361, 6th km Xarilaou-Thermi, 57001, Thessaloniki, Greece
{ipaliokas,atsakir,tzovaras}@iti.gr
[2] Pan-Hellenic General Hospital Psychiatric Society
D. Gounari 32, 54621, Thessaloniki, Greece
athvidalis@gmail.com

Abstract. The aim of this research effort is to identify feeling-of-presence and metacognitive amplifiers over existing well-established VRET treatment methods. Patient real time projection in virtual environments during stimuli exposure and electroencephalography (EEG) report sharing are among the techniques, which have been used to achieve the desired result. Initialized from theoretical inferences, is moving towards a proof-of-concept prototype, which has been developed as a realization of the proposed method. The evaluation of the prototype made possible with an expert team of 28 therapists testing the fear of public speaking and fear of flying case studies.

Keywords: Virtual Reality Exposure Therapy, Anxiety Disorders, Sense of Presence, Metacognition, Fear of Public Speech, Fear of Flying.

1   Introduction

Virtual Reality Exposure Therapy (VRET) is a technique that uses Virtual Reality technology in behavioral therapy for anxiety disorders treatment. Having many people suffering from disorders, as such as social phobia, etc., VRET therapies that rely on Computer Based Treatment (CBT) principles for a diagnosis and evaluation establishment of the patient's progress, constitute a promising method. VR interfaces enable the development of real world models to interact with. In other than phobia therapy application areas, like cultural and scientific visualization, education and infotainment, this aims at altering the model in such ways that the user can navigate in the artificially created environment in an immersive manner. Using VR environments, people can immerse themselves in models ranging from microscopic to universal scale, e.g. from molecules to planets. In phobias treatment there is an antistrophe to this rule and the concept is to change the behavior of the user after exposure to visual and auditory stimuli in a simulated experience.

R. Shumaker and S. Lackey (Eds.): VAMR 2014, Part II, LNCS 8526, pp. 316–328, 2014.
© Springer International Publishing Switzerland 2014

1.1   Past Projects and Short History of VRET

VR in service of cognitive-behavior therapies (CBT) has offered a lot over the past decades projecting several advantages including the generation of stimuli on multiple senses, active participation and applicability to most frequent phobias. Today, it is considered very effective from a psychotherapeutic standpoint, especially in carefully selected patients [23]. For example, Social Anxiety Disorder, the most common anxiety disorder [28], can be treated using VRET systems [17] [13] [4]. There is a great variety of VRET systems related to a specific phobias, like fear of flying [2] [19], cockroach phobia [3] and dog-phobia [9], to name a few. More information can be found on the extensive list (300 studies) of the meta-analysis of Parson & Rizzo [23].

1.2   Facts about Phobias

Over 2.2% of the adult populations of European citizens suffer from Social Phobias [31]. Although anxiety disorders can be treated in most cases, only one third of the sufferers receives treatment and even the specific phobia is not the primary reason to seek treatment [14] [5]. Actually, only the 26% of mental disorder sufferers have made a contact with formal health services [1]. Similarly, the US National Institute of Mental Health (NIMH) indicates that 6.8% of the US adult population suffer from 12-month prevalence Social Phobia, while the 29.9% of those (e.g. 2.0% of adult population) suffer from lifetime prevalence Social Phobia [16]. The rates for teenagers (13 to 18 years old) include 5.5% of the population, with a lifetime prevalence of severe disorder affecting 1.3% of the population [21]. On the other hand, in Greece, the prevalence of all Phobias is 2.79% (2.33 M, 3.26 F) [25].

1.3   Structure of the Paper

This paper is organized as follows: After the introduction, Section 2 (Requirements of a new approach) identifies main areas of VRET adaptation on exposure therapies. The therapeutic aims and the functional requirements of the new approach are presented in section 3 (A more flexible approach). The use cases of the pilot studies and the content development are discussed on Section 4 (Performance situations and content development). The evaluation section (Section 5) presents the results of the prototype evaluation by a group of experts. Finally, an overview of the novel approach as well as future plans are discussed in the last section (Section 6: Conclusions).

2   Requirements of a New Approach

The lack of widely accepted standards for the use of VR to treat specific phobias forces research and clinical use in vertical solutions in most cases. What if a new approach could load new content on demand and be programmable by the therapist to adapt to specific cases and parameters of each patient?

In order to design a VRET system to help therapists achieve a permanent change in patient's behavior, contemporary efforts should take into account current technological trends, updated psychological research results and certain limitations. For example, haptics are not required in social phobias, and/or fear of internal states (e.g. fear of vomit) against stimuli is difficult to be replicated in VR.

After a thorough research on existing solutions, we identified three main areas of adaptation: A) adaptation to the requirements of the therapists, including special conditions of the clinical use and the trends of exposure therapy (e.g. portability, reusability, reliability, effectiveness) and B) adaptation to the specific phobia or anxiety disorder as a matter of content and functional automation (virtual world, scenarios, avatars, stimuli) and C) adaptation to the needs of individuals (phobia history, level of anxiety, human factors). The following sections discuss certain aspects of adaptation.

2.1   Adaptability in Performance Situations

Social anxiety disorder refers to a wide range of social situations, so adaptability of a VRET system can be extremely difficult. Instead of creating and using a highly adaptive VRET system with moderate or poor quality of immersion and presence, a targeted solution would be more appropriate, especially in performance situations.

2.2   Self-awareness

As Hood and Antony note, phobia sufferers 'exhibit biased information processing related to specific threads, while their attention and interpretation are biased' [14]. The mechanism behind that, as well as the result itself stays invisible to the sufferer even if most individuals understand that they overreact. The difficult point seems to be around error estimation, because patients are not able to see themselves and the outcome of their overreaction during stimuli.

2.3   Feeling of Presence

According to Eichenberg [10], VR is experienced as realistic under the conditions of *'immersion'* (virtual world perceived as objective and stimulating) and *'presence'* (the subjective experience of 'being there'). The feeling of presence, or Sense of Presence (SoP), and the Immersion are logically separable, with the former considered as 'a response to a system of a certain level of immersion' [26]. It is believed that, in order a projected word model to be therapeutically useful, it requires a strong SoP [18] [6].

2.4   User Profiling and Monitoring

Not all people respond in the same way given the same stimuli [20] and thus, some patients do not respond to typical cognitive-behavior therapy in VR. Regarding human responses, Behavioral Activation System (BAS) activity is reflected to changes in heart rate, while electrodermal responses resound the behavioral inhibition system

(BIS) activity [11]. Having a reliable activation of BAS and BIS on a real world exposure with the fear-provoking stimulus [29], phobic individuals have a weak BAS activity in contrast to overactive BIS [15]. Similarly, it was found that VR exposure activates the BIS alone [30]. Thus, heart rate and EEG data could be collected by the VRET system to fulfil the patient's profile and monitor the progress achieved in a systematic way. Served with a detailed, after-VRET-session reports could offer an objective variable quantification basis for discussion and trigger metacognition.

2.5   Customization and Personalization

It is not uncommon that therapists would like to change the VRET scenario according to their personal intuition about the problem and the needs of their patients. VRET is by no means a one-size-fits-all tool to treat all phobic populations in a uniform way, because such an assumption could cancel its fundamental psychotherapeutic principles. Therapists need full control over the stimuli, the duration of the exposure and the simulated world itself. Moreover, variations of the same virtual environment could serve in avoiding the memorization of the simulated world and the way stimuli are affecting patient's responses (memory effect). Thus, adaptation tools should be made available to therapist's rather than VRET developers.

3   A More Flexible Approach

The proposed approach is a set of extensions to be applied over the well-established VRET methods and practices to maximize benefits. Figure 1 presents in a flowchart the main components of the proposed VRET system and the way patient's response regulation is achieved, as an evolution to the schema used by Moussaoui et al. [22].

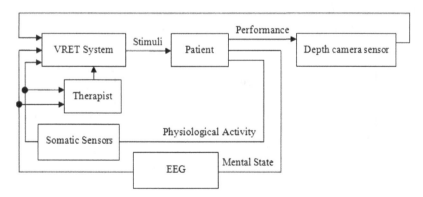

Fig. 1. A basic schema of the proposed treatment rule

The sufferer performs in front of a depth camera which previously had taken a picture of the room (background) as a reference of non-moving objects. Keeping the rule of not moving the depth camera during a session, the system can isolate the figure of the moving actor (patient) from the static background and transfer that figure to the virtual world. At the same time, the patient can navigate in a small area around initial position. Full body movements are transferred in real time (~20fps) in the virtual world to let the body language be directly observed (usually being seen from the back).

Therapists use the keyboard to control the VR, the quality and intensity of the stimulus, like a film director. In the *fear of flying* scenario for example, the therapist can create turbulence to trigger the patient's catastrophic thoughts and the overreaction. The VRET alarm subsystem is flashing when somatic sensors exceed predefined thresholds based on the patient's profile. Those are used to monitor the flow of emotional responses during a session. Currently, there are sockets for heart rate sensors and Electroencephalography (EEG), transmitted wirelessly to PC (via Bluetooth).

3.1 Therapeutic Aims and Functional Requirements

The extension key-points of the therapeutic aims and the functional requirements of the prototype can be summarized as follows: A) To truly disconnect the VRET supportive system from the performed scenarios and the kind of phobia (highly structured), B) Extensive reporting and monitoring of somatic symptoms via physical sensors (feedback), C) Enhance the feeling of presence and metacognition having in mind its importance on the treatment success, D) Be adaptable to the needs of specific scenarios to treat heterogeneous set of phobias in individuals (personalization).

3.2 Feeling of Presence and Metacognition Amplifiers

After a period of practical experimentation (Nov. 2012-May 2013), we finally achieved VRET-scenario disconnection, sensor data reporting and personalization using client profiles. Table 1 briefly presents the followed approach for each encountered challenge, based on the factors influencing the SoP as Bouchard [7] adapted from Sadowski & Stanney [24] together with which, novel methods were used to achieve scenario-specific or mode-specific adaptation.

Table 1. Factors and methods used in the prototype

Factors	Challenge	Approach	Limitations
System related factors	Large field of view to make the system transparent Convincing level of realism	Head movement tracking when HMD is in use. Stereoscopic display in 3DTV when Kinect is used Build-in virtual laptop presentations	LCD Screen sizes Delays in HMD fast movements The virtual laptop plugin is capable of loading ppt files only
Ease of interaction	Highly synchronous Interactions	Self-video VR projection in LCD mode using Kinect Intuitive orientation and short distance navigation	Narrow area navigation when use Kinect Self-projection in VR not appropriate for body shape concerns

Table 1. (*Continued*)

Factors	Challenge	Approach	Limitations
User initiated control	Direct user initiated control Indirect by the therapist initiated control	The system responses to sensor's input, based on zones of accepted values Interruptions allowed by the therapist (having the highest priority)	Lack of previously captured physical and EEG input during the first session
Objective Realism	High quality of stimuli	Immersive prioritized stimuli (continuity, consistency, connectedness and meaningfulness)	Known VR technology limitations
Social factors	Interaction with other avatars Observation of other's reactions when exposed to the same stimuli	Acknowledge the existence of other passengers / audience Restrained reaction of passengers and crew during turbulence in flight scenarios Crowd reactions as a result of the collective identity	Limited artificial intelligence
Duration of immersion	Avoid unnecessarily prolonged immersion Familiarization with the system	Time slots with quantized duration depending on the performed scenario Demo or introduction mode which implements VR exposure without the stimuli (easy flight or idle audience)	Lack of familiarization [or] Too much familiarization with the system
Internal factors	Individuals' characteristics	Create user profiles for accepted ranges of sensor (physical and EEG data) input based on the first session	Noisy user profiles (low accuracy, narrow testing periods, human factors)
Side effects	Eliminate motion sickness, to avoid dizziness on returning participants	Immobilized virtual camera for the public speaking scenario Eliminate motion sickness by eliminating camera rotations during flight scenario	If the fear is caused by the fear of dizziness (not the turbulence), then the stimuli cannot be realistically reproduced

4   Performance Situations and Content Development

Using VRET to treat phobias is a stepped procedure regarding elimination of the distance between the desired sufferer's response and the actual one. The concept is partially programed *a priori* by the therapist during the scenario preparation. This is made possible through a simple additional software tool, which generates scenario files to be used later by the VRET. Scenario files follow a simple XML schema to describe elements and attributes of the VRET execution over specific virtual scenes.

4.1   Scenario Preparation and Execution

In Figure 2, the interface of the scenario preparation tool is demonstrated. The therapist can chain a series of short independent incidents to create a whole session. The therapist can modify the session duration and level of difficulty, while he/she can also intervene during the session's execution and modify the computer-controlled avatars and certain parameters in real-time. The following two scenario-chains were initiated as working demonstration content, while in later phases they were used as case studies in pilot tests. Both were carefully designed by experienced psychiatric staff with long route in Clinical Psychiatry (members of the General Hospital Psychiatric Society, Greece). The model development was based on the detailed scenarios provided by the psychiatric staff and was performed by experienced computer scientists/artists.

Fig. 2. The VRET scenario maker, used by therapists to prepare automated scenario sessions

4.2   The Fear of Public Speaking Scenario

Figure 3 is a view of the virtual conference room used in the *fear of public speech*. A virtual laptop is available for running the client's custom presentation (especially useful when HMD is in use) and to strengthen the feeling of presence by providing enhanced presentation-flow realism. The computer-controlled avatars behavior is defined by the scenario, but affected to some degree by their position (distance to the speaker). Virtual characters sitting in front of the speaker exhibit more detailed behavior and appearance. As one moves towards the far end of the conference room, there are three zones: A) 3D models with skeletal animation, bone facial expressions and lip synchronization, B) virtual persons who participate as 2D animations and C) in the far away, there were only static figures who can perform idle or imperceptible horizontal movements. The intelligence of the avatars follows the axis of detailed visual representation having the front seated ones to be more smartly interactive than ones seating further back. Currently the idle, silent, normal, look bored, noisy and aggressive modes are available for the audience.

4.3   The Fear of Flying (Turbulence) Scenario

Figure 4 depicts what the patient is viewing from own perspective (in stereo mode). This scenario was created for people who fear flights and believe in catastrophic consequences of turbulence. During the flight, other passengers look and behave naturally, while the crew is offering beverages. The therapist can select whether to create discomfort at any time. In auto-mode, the intensity and quality of the stimuli can be raised or lowered by the artificial intelligence of the VRET system.

Fig. 3. The conference room captured at a time audience express disapproval (aggressive mode)

Fig. 4. The flight scenario viewed in stereo from patient's perspective

4.4   Tools Used for Content Development, Rendering and Projection

The content development of the supported case studies, mainly 3D objects and avatars, was made with SketchUp 8.0 and iClone 5.0. Scenes were imported into Unity Game Engine (version 4) in order to be projected through the HMD (Virtual Research v.8) in a very good realistic representation. The depth camera used in pilot studies was Microsoft Kinect and the OpenNI SDK was used for the 3D sensing middleware interface development. The patient's body moves sensing functionality, engineered in Visual Studio, was exported as a dynamic link library (dll file) to the front-end application. The scenario development tool and the front-end application for stereoscopic projection on 3DTVs were developed with Delphi.

5   The Evaluation

Given the feature and functionality extension to existing VRET approaches, the evaluation of the first working demonstrator aims at evaluating the proposed approach. The prototype was evaluated by a body of twenty eight professionals (N=28) from which 18 of which were women and 10 men. Their mean age was 47.73 (SD=13.16). Eleven of them were Psychiatrists (medical doctors) while the rest were clinical and counseling psychologists, including a 14.28% of students. The prototype used in the pilot study was a mature version which supported the two scenarios descried earlier, the depth camera and both the 3DTV and HMD versions in a dual graphics output. The output was rendered in full HD, in 16:9 aspect ratio. In the 3DTV version, it was viewed by a distance of 1.5 m (indicated by a colored area in the demo room floor).

Table 2. Responses on the elements of the questionnaire (Likert scale: 1-5)

#	Question	Mean	SD
B1	How familiar are you with Virtual Reality technology?	2,25	1.11
B2	How often have you used similar applications in the context of your professional obligations, research or your studies?	1,57	0.92
Q1	Are the stated aims and goals of the modules obvious and intuitive?	3,85	0.77
Q2	Is the workflow of loading and control of new modules intuitional and without problems?	3,13	1.45
Q3	Did the modules you have tested so far covered your expectations on Virtual Reality Exposure Therapies?	3,48	1.92
Q4	Did the overall system worked as expected?	3,6	1.10
Q5	Are you satisfied from the quality of content (graphics, realism)?	3,85	1.24
Q6	Using the VR tools, do you think your effectiveness as a therapist will be increased?	3,79	1.94

After 5-10 minutes experimentation with the VRET system, participants were asked to fill up a questionnaire, the results of which are presented in Table 2. Responders were familiar with the VRET, but the lack of personal experience gave a 2.25 mean to the B1 question (SD=1.11) and 1.57 in B2 (SD=0.92). From Q1 it was made clear that of the VRET prototype was perceived as obvious and intuitive. The means of 3.85 (SD=0.77) was the highest in the questionnaire. In Q2, participants found the workflow of loading and using modules to be intuitive and free of problems (M=3.13, SD=1.45). Also, in Q3, good expectations from the system was reported (M=3.48, SD=1.92). The prototype worked as expected (Q4, M=3.6, SD=1.10) and the level of satisfaction was very encouraging (M=3.85, SD=1.24). Based on their demonstration experience, testers believe that the proposed VRET system could increase their effectiveness as therapists (Q6, M=3.79, SD=1.94).

The last open-questions aimed to capture missing functionality (Q7: In your opinion, what features or functionality are missing from the system or its modules?) and take feedback on the time and effort it would be necessary to learn how to use the system (Q8: Make a comment on the time & effort needed to learn the tools). Apart from the fact that the head tracking mechanism of the HMD was not available during the demonstration, most therapists did not find missing features. Two therapists mentioned that using VRET systems cannot reveal much about the etiology of a specific phobia. However, some believe that knowing the reasons behind the onset of the phobia is not necessary to complete the treatment [14]. In Q8, most therapists implied that the VRET prototype was rather easy or very easy to learn (80%). A good learning curve and the low price -they said-would be necessary for a future investment.

6   Conclusions

VRET is used in phobias treatment as a tool to treat anxiety disorders which cause great impairment of patient's socialization, professional activity and quality of life. Given the long distance VRET has covered during the last decades, an extension to well-known approaches is proposed in order to enhance the Sense of Presence (SoP), disconnect content from VRET functionality by adopting the idea of scenario preparation by therapists themselves and support multiple sensors to serve as objective measures of anxiety levels. It is not a therapist-free solution like Virtually Free developed by Green, Flower and Fonseca [12] which uses mobile technology.

A novel addition to the overall architecture is personalization (user profiles) and depth camera sensors which can project in real time the patient into the simulated world and leverage higher mental processes like social self-awareness and metacognition to amplify VR benefits as a therapeutic modality. Realism was given attention, but not to the extreme that could raise the development cost, as a VRET system can be effective even at low representational level [27]. It is expected that therapists will use such VRET sessions before real life situation exposure.

It is believed that the proposed approach is suitable for certain types of specific phobias, standardized over existing Diagnostic Classification systems like the Diagnostic & Statistical Manual of Mental Disorders of the American Psychiatric

Association [8]. Although the target audience of this study was the therapists, as users of the VRET system, a future clinical use with people who suffer from phobias would be necessary to confirm the usability of the prototype and the findings of the literature regarding the therapeutic use of the VRET.

Acknowledgement. This work is supported by the EU funded project VERITAS (FP7 247765).

References

1. Alonso, J., Angermeyer, M., Bernert, S., Bruffaerts, R., Brugha, T.S., Bryson, H., de Girolamo, G., de Graaf, R., Demyttenaere, K., Gasquet, I., Haro, J.M., Katz, S., Kessler, R.C., Kovess, V., Lépine, J.P., Ormel, J., Polidori, G., Vilagut, G.: Use of mental health services in Europe: Results from the European Study on Epidemiology of Mental Disorders (ESEMeD) Project. Acta Psychiatrica Scandinavica 109(suppl. 420), 47–54 (2004)
2. Botella, C., Osma, J., Farcia-Palacios, A., Quero, S., Banos, R.M.: Treatment of Flying Phobia using Virtual Reality: Data from a 1-Year Follow-up using a Multiple Baseline Design. Clinical Psychology and Psychotherapy 11, 311–323 (2004)
3. Botella, C.M., Juan, M.C., Baños, R.M., Alcañiz, M., Guillén, V., Rey, B.: Mixing realities? An application of augmented reality for the treatment of cockroach phobia. Cyber-Psychology & Behavior 8(2), 162–171 (2005)
4. Brinkman, W.P., Vliegher, D.: Virtual reality exposure therapy for social phobia: A pilot study in evoking fear in a virtual world. In: HCI 2008 Proceedings, pp. 85–88 (2008)
5. Brown, T.A., Campbell, L.A., Lehman, C.L., Grisham, J.R., Mancill, R.B.: Current and lifetime comorbidity of the DSM-IV anxiety and mood disorders in a large clinical sample. Journal of Abnormal Psychology 110, 585–599 (2001)
6. Busscher, B., de Vlieger, D., Ling, Y., Brinkman, W.P.: Analysis of Physiological Response to Neutral Virtual Reality Worlds. In: ECCE 2010 Workshop on Cognitive Engineering for Technology in Mental Health Care and Rehabilitation, pp. 59–71 (2011)
7. Bouchard, S., Robillard, G., Larouche, S., Loranger, C.: Description of a Treatment Manual for in virtuo Exposure with Specific Phobia. In: Virtual Reality in Psychological, Medical and Pedagogical Applications, pp. 81–108 (2012)
8. DSM-5 (2013). Diagnostic and Statistical Manual of Mental Disorders. American Psychiatric Association's Annual Meeting, http://www.dsm5.org/Pages/Default.asp (retrieved from October 11, 2013)
9. Delmon-Viaud, I., Znaidi, F., Bonneel, N., Doukhan, D., Suied, C., Warusfel, O., Guyen, K.N.N., Frettakis, G.: Auditory-Visual Virtual Environments to Treat Dog Phobia. In: Proc. of 7th ICDVRAT with ArtAbilitation, Portugal (2008)
10. Eichenberg, C.: Application of Virtual Realities in Psychotherapy: Possibilities, Limitations and Effectiveness. In: Kim, J.-J, ed. (2011), doi:10.5772/12914
11. Fowles, D.C.: The three arousal model: Implications of Gray's two-factor learning theory for heart rate, electrodermal activity, and psychopathy. Psychophysiology 17(2), 87–104 (1980)
12. Green, R., Flower, R., Fonseca, A.: Virtualy-Free project (2012), http://virtually-free.com

13. Grillon, H., Riquier, F., Herbelin, B., Thalmann, D.: Use of virtual reality as therapeutic tool for behavioural exposure in the ambit of social anxiety disorder treatment. In: Proccedngs of the 6th International Conference on Disability, Virtual Reality and Associated Technologies, Denmark, pp. 105–112 (2006)
14. Hood, H.K., Antony, M.M.: Evidence-Based Assessment and Treatment of Specific Phobias in Adults. In: Intensive One-Session Treatment of Specific Phobias, pp. 19–42. Springer, New York (2012)
15. Kasch, K.L., Rottenberg, J., Arnow, B.A., Gotlib, I.H.: Behavioral Activation and Inhibition Systems and the Severity and Course of Depression. Journal of Abnormal Psychology 111(4), 589–597 (2002)
16. Kessler, R.C., Chiu, W.T., Demler, O., Walters, E.E.: Prevalence, severity, and comorbidity of twelve-month DSM-IV disorders, in the National Comorbidity Survey Replication (NCS-R). Archives of General Psychiatry 62(6), 617–627 (2005)
17. Klinger, E., Légeron, P., Roy, S., Chemin, I., Lauer, F., Nugues, P.: Virtual reality exposure in the treatment of social phobia, Cybertherapy: Internet and Virtual Reality as Assessment and Rehabilitation Tools for Clinical Psychology and Neuroscience. Stud. Health Technol. Inform. 99, 91–119 (2004)
18. Krijn, M., Emmelkamp, P.M., Olafsson, R.P., Biemond, R.: Virtual reality exposure therapy of anxiety disorders: A review. Clinical Psychology Rev. 24(3), 259–281 (2004)
19. Krijn, M., Emmelkamp, P., Ólafsson, R., Bouwman, M., van Gerwen, M.L., Spinhoven, P., Schuemie, M.J., van der Mast, C.A.: Fear of flying treatment methods: Virtual reality exposure vs. cognitive behavioral therapy. Aviation, Space and Environmental Medicine 78(2), 121–128 (2007)
20. Matu, S.A., David, O., David, D.: Virtual Reality Technology Applications in Clinical Field. Journal for Neurology and Psychiatry of Child and Adolescent in Romania, RJCANP 15(1), 23–30 (2012)
21. Merikangas, K.R., He, J., Burstein, M., Swanson, S.A., Avenevoli, S., Cui, L., Benjet, C., Georgiades, K., Swendsen, J.: Lifetime prevalence of mental disorders in U.S. adolescents: Results from the National Comorbidity Study-Adolescent Supplement (NCS-A). J. Am. Acad. Child Adolesc Psychiatry 49(10), 980–989 (2010)
22. Moussaoui, A., Pruski, A., Cherki, B.: Emotion regulation for social phobia treatment using virtual reality. In: HuMaN 2007 Proceedings, Timimoun (2007), http://dspace.univ-tlemcen.dz/handle/112/891 (retrieved from December 11, 2013)
23. Parson, T.D., Rizzo, A.A.: Affective outcomes of virtual reality exposure therapy for anxiety and specific phobias: A meta-analysis. Journal of Behavior Therapy and Experimental Psychiatry 39, 250–261 (2008)
24. Sadowski, W., Stanney, K.M.: Presence in Virtual Environments. In: Stanney, K.M. (ed.) Handbook of Virtual Environments: Design, Implementation and Applications, pp. 791–806. IEA, Mahwah (2002)
25. Skapinakis, P., Mavreas, V.: Prevalence and sociodemographic associations of common mental disorders in a nationally representative sample of the general population of Greece. BMC Psychiatry 13, 163 (2013), doi:10.1186/1471-244X-13-163
26. Slater, M.: A note on presence terminology (2003), http://www0.cs.ucl.ac.uk/research/vr/Projects/Presencia/ConsortiumPublications/ucl_cs_papers/presence-terminology.htm (retrieved from November 14, 2013)

27. Slater, M., Pertaub, D.P., Barker, C., Clark, D.: An Experimental Study on Fear of Public Speaking Using a Virtual Environment. CyberPsychology & Behavior 9(5), 627–633 (2006)
28. Stein, M.B., Stein, D.J.: Social anxiety disorder. The Lancet 371, 1115–1125 (2008)
29. Wilhelm, F.H., Roth, W.T.: Taking the laboratory to the skies: Ambulatory assessment of self- report, autonomic, and respiratory responses in flying phobia. Psychophysiology 35(5), 596–606 (1998)
30. Wilhelm, F.H., Pfaltz, M.C., Gross, J.J., Mauss, I.B., Kim, S.I., Wiederhold, B.K.: Mechanisms of Virtual Reality Exposure Therapy: The Role of the Behavioral Activation and Behavioral Inhibition Systems. Applied Psychophysiology and Biofeedback 30(3), 271–284 (2005)
31. Wittchen, H.U., Jacobi, F., Rehm, J., Gustavsson, A., Svensson, M., Jonsson, B., Olesen, J., Allgulander, C., Alonso, J., Faravelli, C., Fratiglioni, L., Jennum, P., Lieb, R., Maercker, A., van Os, J., Preisig, M., Salvador-Carulla, L., Simon, R., Steinhausen, H.C.: The size and burden of mental disorders and other disorders of the brain in Europe 2010. European Neuropsychopharmacology 21, 655–679 (2011)

Severe Neglect and Computer-Based Home Training
A Case Study

Inge Linda Wilms

Dept. of Psychology. University of Copenhagen, Denmark
Inge.wilms@psy.ku.dk

Abstract. Cognitive rehabilitation from a functional perspective often requires intensive training over a longer period of time. In the case of rehabilitation of unilateral neglect, the frequency and intensity needed is expensive and difficult to implement both for the therapists and the patients. For this reason, this case study tests the possibility of using computer-based training in the rehabilitation efforts for a patient with severe neglect who had no previous skills in computer usage. The article describes the results of the training both in terms of neuropsychological tests and the reading ability of the patient.

Keywords: optokinetic training, home training, computer-based training, unilateral neglect, prism adaptation training, bottom-up.

1   Introduction

"All I want is to be able to read again". These were the first words from the patient PK, when I met him in July 2013. PK had fallen down a flight of stairs in March the same year and had been committed to care and rehabilitation for almost 4 months prior to this meeting. Although his behavior expressed textbook neglect to a degree you rarely see 4 months after injury, he also demonstrated an impressive ability to maintain an artistic composition in memory and the will to fight his way back to life.

The MRI and CT scans showed no apparent, recent injury. However, PK had a severe and maltreated renal condition and also a previous history of infarcts. From the MRI and CT scans it was imminently clear that PK had shown an extraordinary ability to overcome the effects of the previous injuries, despite the apparent extent of physical damage.

In this paper, I will try to illustrate how computer-based training was used in the patient's home to accommodate the intensity needed to get effects from bottom-up cognitive training. I will go into details about injury, the assessment, the training and the results so far. I will outline the tools used for assessment as well as the computer-based training and also show how the reading ability of PK changed over time as the speed of visual perception improved. The paper will demonstrate how cognitive rehabilitation of neglect may benefit from intensive home training using computer-based prism training, optokinetic training and scanning training but also how much is required by the patient and the therapist.

R. Shumaker and S. Lackey (Eds.): VAMR 2014, Part II, LNCS 8526, pp. 329–339, 2014.
© Springer International Publishing Switzerland 2014

2   Etiology

PK is a 75 year old male, with an academic education as a geologist. PK is a renowned artist, painter, sculptor and essayist and has travelled extensively around the world completing the latest of 16 polar expeditions to the arctic areas of Greenland in 2011.

In 2000, PK suffers from a sudden, large intracerebral hemorrhage in the right parietal lobe. A four centimeter hematoma is formed in deep tissue and an emergency evacuation had to be performed. Although subsequent CT scans reveals extensive damage to the right parietal and temporal lobe, PK recovers fully over time and is able to return to work after a brief period of recovery.

In 2009, PK has another cardiovascular incident on a trip to Greece. Subsequent CT scans reveal ischemic changes in the left temporal-occipital lope. The neuropsychological test confirms that PK has lost color vision, the ability to recognize faces, has an upper right quadranopia, unilateral neglect and reduced reading ability.

The hospital records indicate that PK demonstrates symptoms of neglect both after the first incident in 2000 and the second in 2009. PK is offered assistance and rehabilitation in 2009, but he declines and after some months of recovery, he is able to resume his artistic work both as a painter, sculptor and essayist. According to him and his wife, he never recovers from prosopagnosia but color vision returned to normal after a while.

In early spring 2013, PK accidentally falls down a flight of stairs in his home suffering a contusion. CT and MRI scan reveals only small superficial injuries and no new major incidents but PK is severely disoriented and the old neglect symptoms return in full force. Prolonged hospitalization is required due to a severe inflammatory, renal condition and the treatment seems to further aggravate the neuropsychological deficits. In July 2013, PK is released from hospital with severe neglect, and left sided hemiparesis rendering him tied to a wheelchair.

3   Unilateral Neglect

Neglect is a cognitive attention deficit that is defined as a failure to respond to, attend to, report, or orient toward stimuli presented in the contralesional side of space, which cannot be attributed to primary motor or sensory dysfunction [1, 2]. Space, in this context, should be understood in the broadest sense of the word. It includes occurrences in the physical environment outside an arm's reach of the patients (extrapersonal space), the immediate surroundings (peripersonal space) and even the body (personal space)[3] and internal representations of body (the proprioceptive model) [4]. In addition to a particular spatial domain, neglect may be observed from different midline-frames of reference, one being viewer-centered in which the neglected area is positioned relative to a midline projection from the retina, the head or the torso; the other being an allocentric reference frame where the neglected area is positioned relative to the stimulus or object [5].

3.1   Symptoms of Neglect

Neglect is a challenging syndrome in that it leaves the patient unaware of the consequences and effects of the impairment [6]. Patients, however, will often complain about bumping into things, not being able to locate objects in their homes or bruising the contralesional side of the body because of the inattention. The ability to read may also influenced in various ways either at word or sentence level [7]. The most common behavior of neglect patients is extinction, which is the inability to detect stimuli presented to the contralesional side, if stimuli are presented simultaneously to the ipsileasonal side [8]. Extinction has been demonstrated in different modalities with visual, auditive or somatosensory stimuli, either individually or in combination [e.g. 2, 9, 10].

3.2   Neural Correlation of Neglect

The diversity in neglect symptoms reflects the degree to which attention depends on different neural mechanisms [11] and as a consequence different types of lesions may trigger one or more neglect behaviors. Neglect is often characterized as being a contralesional impairment and it is more frequently observed with right hemisphere damage than left hemisphere damage [12-14].

The most common cause of neglect are lesions to the right posterior parietal cortex [15-17] but also damage to the inferior temporal region and the superior/middle temporal gyri have been found to correlate with neglect [18]. In a recent study, Verdon et al. [19] found that damage to the right inferior parietal lobe was correlated with perceptive and visuo-spatial components of neglect. They also found that damage to the right dorsolateral prefrontal cortex was correlated to impairments in exploratory/visuomotor components and, finally, that damage to deep temporal lobe regions was a component of allocentric/object-oriented neglect.

3.3   Prevalence

Neglect is a fairly common, cognitive impairment in patients with brain injury. Across studies, there seem to be amble agreement that neglect behavior fades rapidly, and after 3-4 weeks only approx. 8-10 % of patients will test positive for neglect [20]. Long-term chronicity of neglect does not seem to correlate with sex, handedness or lesion volume but both the severity and persistence of neglect do increase with age [13, 21]. Right hemisphere lesions have been measured to cause neglect symptoms that are more persistent and less responsive to spontaneous remission [18] and therapy [22]. The severity of the neglect behavior in the acute stages of injury has been found to be a strong predictor for the subsequent severity of symptoms a year post onset [23]. Finally, the presence of visual field disturbances and defects has been shown to be more prevalent amongst patients with chronic neglect [23].

4   Assessment of PK

It is always a challenge to assess all aspects of a multifaceted syndrome like neglect. The cause as well as the expression of neglect may vary from patient to patient and symptoms fade and change over time as patients acquire some compensatory techniques such as positioning their body or head differently when solving tasks. In the case of PK, assessments from previous incidents had established that neglect was present. The current task was to ascertain the current level and to choose tests that would assist in the choice of training and be sufficiently sensitive to measure progress. For this reason, a combination of tests was used to determine the type, extent and severity of the neglect and to distinguish perceptual from spatial neglect as the literature indicates a difference in effect from training depending on the type [24]. The choices also took into consideration that we wanted to avoid fatigue in the patient when administering the tests.

Schenkenberg's line bisection [25] was chosen to assess both perceptive and visuomotor neglect. In this test, 17 horizontal lines of various lengths have to be divided at the middle. In the visuomotor task, the patient is asked to divide the lines by setting a mark. In the perceptual task, the therapist moves a pencil along each line from left to right and the patient indicates orally when the middle of the line is reached. Next used was the Mesulam cancellation tasks [26] including both the letter and the object cancellation tasks to assess neglect behavior. The baking tray test [27, 28] was used to assess spatial neglect and the computer-based Test of Attentional Performance (TAP) (subtests visual field test and neglect test) was used to assess visual field and extinction and the processing speed of the perceptual system. Due to PK's initial reduced performance, a special version of the TAP test was used in which the detection period was extended to 10 seconds per trial for the first two tests. A simple estimation test was used to confirm perceptual neglect [24]. Finally, picture copying of a star, a flower and a cube was used to test visuospatial difficulties.

These tests have been used to assess progress throughout the training period and have been administered when major changes to training were instigated. The scores from the tests can be found in chapter 6.

All tests indicated severe egocentric visuo-motor and perceptual neglect along with highly reduced processing speed and difficulties in combining visual stimuli to a usable percept.

5   Training of PK

Almost immediately upon arrival at the Center for Rehabilitation of Brain Injury, PK was subjected to intensive physiotherapy training at least 1.5 hours a day for 4 days a week. He still maintains this practice 6 months later. He was mobile and out of the wheelchair after 3 months and is now able to walk about without support. Due to the intensity of the physical training, PK needed a long daily break before starting any other training. We discussed the requirement for intensity and daily cognitive training and together with PK we decided that training at home would offer the best flexibility for PK.

Apart from the neglect, the most severe problem observed in PK was the reduced processing speed of the perceptual system (fig. 2). We therefore chose to a bottom-up strategy in training to try to ameliorate as much of the basic problems as possible. No single treatment has been demonstrated effective for all types of neglect [29], in the latest report on rehabilitation from brain injury from the Danish Board of Health [30], an analysis based on 17 papers concludes that best effect of treatment of neglect is achieved through a combination of therapies.

In 1998, Rossetti et al. published a seminal study which demonstrated that exposure to prism adaptation might alleviate some of the symptoms related to egocentric visual neglect in patients, regardless of the severity of neglect [31]. Internal data used to interpret sensory feedback from different modalities must be kept in alignment to ensure that action and attention are directed towards the same location [32]. Rossetti et al. hypothesized that the visuomotor realignment of the internal representation of the personal midline observed in standard prism exposure studies might alleviate symptoms of neglect. Prism Adaptation Therapy (PAT) has since become one of the most promising therapies in the treatment of egocentric visual neglect [33-36].

Since PK had shown visuomotor problems, we decided to start up with PAT twice a day for two weeks. The author provided a computer-based prism adaptation system for the purpose of training and follow-up. In this version of computerized PAT, the patient performs three training sets at each of the two daily sessions. In the first set, the patient performs 30 pointing trials on a touch monitor, 10 trials at each of three locations with no visual feedback. This set measures baseline performance at the session. In the second set, the patient performs 90 pointing trials, 30 at each of three locations this time wearing prism goggles. The goggles cause a deviation of visual input 10 degrees to the right. At the end of each trial, the patient receives terminal feedback (seeing his fingertip when touching the monitor) and is asked to attempt to adjust to the deviation. In the final set, the patient removes the prism goggles and performs an additional 60 pointing trials, 20 at each of the three locations again without feedback. The aftereffect from the prism exposure is measured to determine if adaptation is taking place. Data is collected and stores at the computer for each trial, set and session for further and later processing. PK could not administer PAT training on his own so helpers and the spouse were trained by the author to assist PK during the two weeks of training.

As PK had also demonstrated perceptual neglect problems and reading difficulties, it seemed appropriate to try computer-based optokinetic stimulation, in which patients are asked to attend to targets on a background moving towards left [37-39]. The system EyeMove from www.medicalcomputing.de was chosen based on the documented results [40, 41]. Rather than using the preset versions for training, we started out with a single dot moving towards the left at three preset speeds. After a week, the speed and size and number of moving objects were adjusted to ensure that PK was practicing at the limit of his ability. PK trained once a day for 45 minutes for three weeks and after 6 weeks, PK managed to train at the highest level of difficulty. After the first three weeks, we added a picture naming task using the computer-based system

"Afasi-assistant" from www.afasi-assistent.dk where the task was to read a word and find the matching object amongst first 2 and later 4 pictures. In November, we added cancellation training using the iPad APP "Visual Attention" from the suite TherAppy from the company www.tactustherapy.com. Table 1 summarizes the training schedule.

Once a week, the training regimen was adjusted by the therapist. On a daily basis the spouse or hired helpers would assist PK in the starting the appropriate application.

Table 1. Training regimen at home. Training was adjusted weekly to constantly challenge the ability of the patient.

Type	Period	Intensity
Test 1		
Prism Adaptation Training	2 weeks	2 x 30 minutes, daily
Test 2		
Prism adaptation Training	1 week	1 x 30 minutes, daily
Optokinetic training 1	3 weeks	45 minutes, daily
Test 3		
Optokinetic training 2	Ongoing	45 minutes, daily
Therappy Visual Perception	4 weeks	15 minutes, daily
Afasi-assistent, object determination	4 weeks	20 minutes, daily
Test 4		

PK has since continued to practice with the optokinetic system every morning as he feels that it "warms" up his perceptual system and further reduce the perceptual effects of neglect for a period of 30-60 minutes after practice.

6   The Result so Far

As can be seen in table 1, PK was tested before and after each major change in training. The results from the line bisection tests before and after the training have been listed in figure 1. PK's scores are vastly different in the two tests, which is indicative of separate systems being activated in the bisection task[42]. PK improved on both tests after PAT (test 2) and on the perceptual part after the optokinetic training (test 3). However, test 4 indicates that the effect has not been stable although PK is still improving but at a slower rate.

The cancellation tasks (table 2) show some improvement at Test 3 but at Test 4 the effect to the left has disappeared.

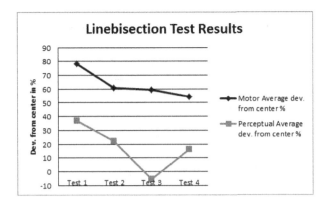

Fig. 1. The results from the line bisection tasks. "Motor" indicates the result where PK set the mark with a pencil and "Perceptual" is where the therapist sets the mark on PK's request.

Table 2. Results from the Cancellation tasks over time

	Figure				Letter			
	Upper left	Lower left	Upper right	Lower right	Upper left	Lower left	Upper right	Lower right
Test 1	N/F	N/F	N/F	N/F	N/F	N/F	N/F	N/F
Test 2	N/F	N/F	N/F	N/F	0	0	1	5
Test 3	2	1	6	4	1	0	5	8
Test 4	0	0	7	7	0	3	7	7

The baking tray test improved dramatically after the PAT (table 3) and at the most recent test, all 16 "buns" were spread out equally across the "tray".

Table 3. The results from the baking tray test

	Left	Right	Comment
Test 1	0	16	
Test 2	8,5	7,5	Skewed right
Test 3	7	9	Still skewed towards right
Test 4	8	8	Spread all over the plate

The TAP test was used in an attempt to establish whether the visual field was intact. It also provides data on processing speed by measuring the time from stimuli onset until button activation by the patient. Albeit a rough estimate, it is still a good indicator for overall processing speed of the perceptual system. The results over the training period are shown in figure 2.

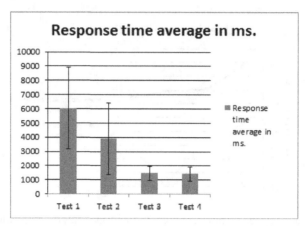

Fig. 2. The change in response time to stimuli presented during the TAP test. Changes between Test 1, Test 2 and Test 3 were tested highly significant ($F_{3,60}$=35.1, p < 0.005).

Reading ability was monitored by administering reading tests. At Test 1, PK was not even able to read two letter words. At Test 2, PK still had trouble even reading single words. After the optokinetic training, PK was able to read poetry again and shorter pieces of prose (Test 3). However, he still has some problems keeping track of the lines losing the position in the text lines and has to use his finger or a ruler to keep track.

PK's ability to draw from memory has been intact for almost the entire training period. The performance on copying of drawings has improved so PK is able to copy a star, a cube and a flower. Introduction of new drawings in test 4 did, however, show a bias to the right in one out of three drawings.

The most encouraging improvements so far has been in relation to PK's work as an artist. He has been able to resume his work as an artist and the most recent improvement has been intermittent periods of resumed color vision and absence of neglect when painting. Previously, he was unable to leave his work for just a little as he was unable to recognize his work from visual input alone. Although he still cannot recognize older pieces of work as his own, he is able to return to current work in progress and recapture how far he is using visual cues from the painting. We will keep monitoring overall progress for the next 6 months.

7   Discussion and Conclusion

In this study, we tested if training of severe neglect could be accomplished by setting up training systems at the home of a patient with no previous experience in the use of computers.

The first obstacle was the need for assistance in initiating the daily training of PAT. Although the program could be started with one click, moving boxes back and forth and putting on prism goggles required assistance from the spouse and local helpers who had to be trained in the execution of PAT. It was fairly expensive, but it did allow PK to train as intensive as required. The optokinetic training was much easier to use although it was impossible to start the program without having to go through several menus. Being unable to read, PK was unable to start the program by himself for many weeks and had to have assistance from helpers. The Afasi-assistant could be setup to start with only one click and so could the TherAppy APP on the iPad.

PK was and still is extremely motivated for training. He has meticulously trained almost every day and been good at stating when training became too easy or required adjustments. Adjustments to the programs were done at a weekly basis by a visiting therapist (the author) and this worked well for all parties. The visit at home provided an opportunity to observe and respond to changes and improvements in activities of daily life. When asked about the advantages of being able to train at home, both PK and his wife stated that above all, the flexibility of being able to train when time and strength allowed it was very important for keeping up motivation to train. The disadvantage was the requirement for hired help. Using the spouse as assistant trainer was not a success and created marital conflicts and aggravation to the disappointment of both parties. The reason for this is currently being investigated and be dealt with in a subsequent paper.

Often, patients have to practice once or twice daily for 2-5 weeks and the training needs to be adjusted frequently as the function and processing speed improves. It has been pointed out many times that computer-based training offer solutions to these challenges and the advance of AI algorithms and online profiling will eventually alleviate adjustment challenges. However, even fairly simple computer-based training like PAT and optokinetic training will require assistance to start up the programs, adjust the equipment and monitor the progress of the patient.

Acknowledgement. I wish to thank Doctor Georg Kerkhoff for valuable advice and recommendations in the setup and execution of the EyeMove system.

References

1. Heilman, K.M., Valenstein, E., Watson, R.T.: Neglect and related disorders. Seminars in Neurology 20(4), 463–470 (2000)
2. Heilman, K.M., Valenstein, E.: Auditory Neglect in Man. Archives of Neurology 26(1), 32–35 (1972)
3. Halligan, P.W., et al.: Spatial cognition: Evidence from visual neglect. Trends in Cognitive Sciences 7(3), 125–133 (2003)
4. Redding, G.M., Wallace, B.: Prism adaptation and unilateral neglect: Review and analysis. Neuropsychologia 44(1), 1–20 (2006)
5. Medina, J., et al.: Neural Substrates of Visuospatial Processing in Distinct Reference Frames: Evidence from Unilateral Spatial Neglect. Journal of Cognitive Neuroscience 21(11), 2073–2084 (2009)
6. Bisiach, E., et al.: Unawareness of Disease following Lesions of the Right-Hemisphere-Anosognosia for Hemplegia and Anosognosia for Hemianopia. Neuropsychologia 24(4), 471–482 (1986)
7. Leff, A., Starrfelt, R.: Pure Alexia. In: Alexia, pp. 71–115. Springer, London (2014)

8. Kinsbourne, M.: Mechanisms of unilateral neglect. In: Jeannerod, M. (ed.) Neurophysiological and Neuropsychological Aspects of Spatial Neglect, pp. 69–86. Elsevier Science Publishers B.V., Amsterdam (1987)

9. Karnath, H.O., Zimmer, U., Lewald, J.: Impaired perception of temporal order in auditory extinction. Neuropsychologia 40(12), 1977–1982 (2002)

10. Vallar, G., et al.: Exploring somatosensory hemineglect by vestibular stimulation. Brain 116(1), 71–86 (1993)

11. Szczepanski, S.M., Konen, C.S., Kastner, S.: Mechanisms of Spatial Attention Control in Frontal and Parietal Cortex. Journal of Neuroscience 30(1), 148–160 (2010)

12. Pedersen, P.M., et al.: Hemineglect in acute stroke - Incidence and prognostic implications - The Copenhagen Stroke Study. American Journal of Physical Medicine & Rehabilitation 76(2), 122–127 (1997)

13. Ringman, J.M., et al.: Frequency, risk factors, anatomy, and course of unilateral neglect in an acute stroke cohort. Neurology 63(3), 468–474 (2004)

14. Stone, S.P., Halligan, P.W., Greenwood, R.J.: The Incidence of Neglect Phenomena and Related Disorders in Patients with an Acute Right or Left-Hemisphere Stroke. Age and Ageing 22(1), 46–52 (1993)

15. Mishkin, M., Ungerleider, L.G., Macko, K.A.: Object vision and spatial vision: Two cortical pathways. Trends in Neurosciences 6, 414–417 (1983)

16. Newport, R., Jackson, S.R.: Posterior parietal cortex and the dissociable components of prism adaptation. Neuropsychologia 44(13), 2757–2765 (2006)

17. Corbetta, M., et al.: Neural basis and recovery of spatial attention deficits in spatial neglect. Nature Neuroscience 8(11), 1603–1610 (2005)

18. Buxbaum, L.J., et al.: Hemispatial neglect - Subtypes, neuroanatomy, and disability. Neurology 62(5), 749–756 (2004)

19. Verdon, V., et al.: Neuroanatomy of hemispatial neglect and its functional components: A study using voxel-based lesion-symptom mapping. Brain 133, 880–894 (2010)

20. Sunderland, A., Wade, D.T., Hewer, R.L.: The natural history of visual neglect after stroke Indications from two methods of assessment. Disability & Rehabilitation 9(2), 55–59 (1987)

21. Gottesman, R.F., et al.: Unilateral neglect is more severe and common in older patients with right hemispheric stroke. Neurology 71(18), 1439–1444 (2008)

22. Appelros, P., et al.: Prognosis for patients with neglect and anosognosia with special reference to cognitive impairment. Journal of Rehabilitation Medicine 35(6), 254–258 (2003)

23. Karnath, H.O., et al.: The anatomy underlying acute versus chronic spatial neglect: A longitudinal study. Brain 134, 903–912 (2011)

24. Striemer, C.L., Danckert, J.A.: Through a prism darkly: Re-evaluating prisms and neglect. Trends in Cognitive Sciences 14(7), 308–316 (2010)

25. Schenkenberg, T., Bradford, D.C., Ajax, E.T.: Line bisection and unilateral visual neglect in patients with neurologic impairment. Neurology 30(5), 509–517 (1980)

26. Mesulam, M.M.: A Cortical Network for Directed Attention and Unilateral Neglect. Annals of Neurology 10(4), 309–325 (1981)

27. Appelros, P., et al.: Unilateral neglect: Further validation of the baking tray task. Journal of Rehabilitation Medicine 36(6), 258–261 (2004)

28. Tham, K., Tegner, R.: The baking tray task: A test of spatial neglect. Neuropsychological Rehabilitation 6(1), 19–25 (1996)

29. Ting, D.S.J., et al.: Visual Neglect Following Stroke: Current Concepts and Future Focus. Survey of Ophthalmology 56(2), 114–134 (2011)

30. Sundhedsstyrelsen: Hjerneskaderehabilitering - en medicinsk teknologivurdering. In: Hørder, M., Beck, M., Andersen, S.E. (eds.) Medicinsk Teknologivurdering. København, Sundhedsstyrelsen (2011)

31. Rossetti, Y., et al.: Prism adaptation to a rightward optical deviation rehabilitates left hemispatial neglect. Nature 395(6698), 166–169 (1998)

32. Bedford, F.L.: Perceptual and Cognitive Spatial Learning. Journal of Experimental Psychology: Human Perception and Performance 19(3), 517–530 (1993)

33. Frassinetti, F., et al.: Long-lasting amelioration of visuospatial neglect by prism adaptation. Brain 125, 608–623 (2002)

34. Serino, A., et al.: Effectiveness of Prism Adaptation in Neglect Rehabilitation A Controlled Trial Study. Stroke 40(4), 1392–1398 (2009)

35. Serino, A., et al.: Neglect treatment by prism adaptation: What recovers and for how long. Neuropsychological Rehabilitation 17(6), 657–687 (2007)

36. Vangkilde, S., Habekost, T.: Finding Wally: Prism adaptation improves visual search in chronic neglect. Neuropsychologia 48(7), 1994–2004 (2010)

37. Pizzamiglio, L., et al.: The use of optokinetic stimulation in rehabilitation of the hemineglect disorder. Cortex 40(3), 441–450 (2004)

38. Kerkhoff, G., et al.: Repetitive optokinetic stimulation induces lasting recovery from visual neglect. Restorative Neurology and Neuroscience 24(4-6), 357–369 (2006)

39. Schroder, A., Wist, E.R., Homberg, V.: TENS and optokinetic stimulation in neglect therapy after cerebrovascular accident: A randomized controlled study. European Journal of Neurology 15(9), 922–927 (2008)

40. Kerkhoff, G., Schenk, T.: Rehabilitation of neglect: An update. Neuropsychologia 50(6), 1072–1079 (2012)

41. Kerkhoff, G., et al.: Smooth pursuit eye movement training accelerates recovery from auditory/visual neglect and reduces disability and unawareness: 2 randomized controlled trials. Journal of the Neurological Sciences 333, e570 (2013)

42. Halligan, P.W., Marshall, J.C.: Two techniques for the assessment of line bisection in visuo-spatial neglect: A single case study. Journal of Neurology, Neurosurgery & Psychiatry 52(11), 1300–1302 (1989)

Industrial, Safety and Military Applications

Spatial Augmented Reality in Collaborative Design Training: Articulation between I-Space, We-Space and Space-Between

Samia Ben Rajeb and Pierre Leclercq

LUCID Lab for User Cognition & Innovative Design - University of Liège , Belgium
{samia.benrajeb,pierre.leclercq}@ulg.ac.be

Abstract. This paper analyses the use of augmented reality in advanced project-based training in design. Our study considers how augmented environments can contribute to this type of group training: what types of interaction spaces constitute these new learning environments and how are these spaces constructed so as to promote collective reflection ?

Keywords: Project based learning, collaborative design, augmented reality.

1   Context and Hypotheses

We propose to study the use of Augmented Reality (AR) in advanced project-based training. Following the taxonomy proposed by Dubois [1], AR is considered here to be the interactive and non-immersive real-time superposition of virtual information in a real environment. The aim of project-based training in this context is to develop the learners' general and specific skills to devise complex projects in design, architecture and engineering [2]. In the present study, this type of training will be implemented through group activities based on group dynamics.

Indeed, the contemporary designer no longer works alone on projects; rather, he or she collaborates with other experts because projects must evolve in a regulatory framework, integrating progressively more coercive qualitative demands with shorter and shorter deadlines [3]. It is therefore impossible today to speak of initiation at the origin of complex projects in design, architecture and town planning without training students in collective activities. This is why we hypothesise that group activities promote learning through collective reflection on a concrete project, as such activities are well-adapted to the integration of the knowledge and skills required to master complex design.

2   Research Question

The aim of this paper is to understand how augmented reality supports group dynamics in project-based training. In other words, what types of interaction spaces constitute

R. Shumaker and S. Lackey (Eds.): VAMR 2014, Part II, LNCS 8526, pp. 343–353, 2014.

these new augmented learning environments and how are these interaction spaces constructed so as to promote collective reflection?

3   Scope: Instrumenting Collaborative Practices

Our teaching approach is to develop specific skills in collaborative practices, which are clearly distinguishable from so-called cooperative activities. We consider this distinction to be important because it implies the establishment of a specific pedagogical framework, and it already exists in the definition of collective activities in general (without mentioning the notion of design [3, 4, 5]). Despite the diversity of definitions, all agree on one major characterization: the differences between the tasks assigned to the project participants. As the common goal is the project, the designers are only required to work together because of the need to access shared resources held by individual parties. Bearing these definitions in mind, it is our opinion that design as an activity includes solitary work as much as it includes cooperation or collaboration. The present article will only tackle the moments in which students, teachers and experts work together and share the real-time annotations and graphic documents necessary for design.

4   Integration of Augmented Reality in Training Students in Collaborative Design

The application of augmented reality as it is understood in the present study therefore concerns the real-time projection of virtual documents onto actual work surfaces (tables and boards) and the creation, manipulation and annotation of those documents using electronic pens. Such an application is here linked to how work can be shared via a network and it involves students, trainers and experts working together - remotely and/or in co-presence - on an (architectural) project. It is implemented in specific spatial configurations and the whole is therefore covered under the title SAR - Spatial Augmented Reality.

4.1   Presentation of the Tool used in Collaboration

Our study concerns four different SAR. All four are based on a software solution called SketSha - for "sketch sharing" - developed by LUCID, University of Liège [6]. SketSha is based on the metaphor of a meeting whereby several people are gathered around the same document. In addition to the social exchange between collaborators via videoconferencing, SketSha enables the participants to share annotations and graphical documents both in real-time and remotely. Concretely, this involves the connection, via internet, of several digital surfaces on which users interact graphically with an electronic pen.

Fig. 1. Collaborative system SketSha

4.2   Introduction to the SAR and their Usages

Four SAR were installed as part of the training in collaborative design for students of architectural engineering at the University of Liège. The workshop was attended by about fifteen students and lasted three months during which time the students collaborated in real-time with students from the School of Architecture of Nancy. In these workshops, the students were also able to benefit from consultation and advice from remote experts (architecture, structure, building engineering, fire safety, etc.) thanks to the various SAR which had been installed as part of the course.

SAR 1 Consultation. The first SAR allows individual students to consult various remote experts for help in developing their own project. At this meeting, students are asked to prepare documents and hierarchize the information that they would like to communicate to the expert relative to any questions they have. The pedagogical aim of this SAR is to prepare the students to deal with other expertise and skills while also providing access to other knowledge, references and experiences.

SAR1 Consultation   SAR2 Collaboration

SAR3 Project Review   SAR4 Evaluation

Fig. 2. 4 SAR for collective work

SAR 2 Collaboration. The second SAR brings together two geographically separate groups of students for weekly sessions to work on the same project. At these sessions, two or three students seated around a large graphic table collaborate remotely and in real-time with two or three students from the School of Architecture of Nancy. The pedagogical objective of this SAR is to initiate students in co-ordination (as regards public speaking and joint production of annotations and graphic documents) and in sharing their own opinions in which they explain, negotiate and justify their choices so as to encourage new collective ideas.

SAR 3 Project Review. The third SAR is used to review the project in co-presence between students, trainers and experts. At these meetings, the students are asked to display their project on an interactive board and interact with the rest of the class throughout the presentation. The expert and the teacher share the same annotated document, but theirs is projected onto a graphic table. The aim of this SAR is for the teachers, experts and students to share opinions in real-time and to enable each party to interact either orally or through drawing. Each individual's project thereby evolves through collective reflection which, in our opinion, helps to reduce competition between students.

SAR 4 Evaluation. The fourth SAR enables collective evaluation of student projects by various co-present and remote experts interacting in real-time. Here, the student is asked to present his or her project to the class but also to the remote experts whom they have already met on two previous occasions in the context of SAR 1. SAR 4 enables all participants to intervene on the final graphic documents of the student's project. The major objective of this SAR is to transform the documents presented – supposedly frozen images at a final jury – into working documents to stimulate collective reflection and the emergence of new ideas.

5   Methodology

5.1   Collection of Data

Longitudinal observations were conducted for each SAR; in other words, observations made over the course of several sessions on how students appropriate the tool and prepare the design project. Only the teachers were aware of the objectives of the observations: to define the involvement and contributions of the various SAR in the student's learning process in design collaboration.

In the definition of our protocol, we considered it vital to vary the parameter of number of actors as several publications focusing on collective activities (like [7]) show that the performances of the interactions between the designers as well as the decisions made can be influenced by the number of actors taking part (directly or indirectly) in the design. This is why the experimental protocol was defined in such a way as to use the same augmented system in the same class of students for collaboration over the same lapse of time while varying spatial configuration and the number of participants. All our observations were recorded using an audio/video recording device.

Table 1. Total of data accumulated in the four SAR

	SAR 1	SAR 2	SAR 3	SAR 4
Configuration	Remote	Remote	Co-presence	Remote
Participants	1 student 1 teacher 4 experts - Alès	3 students 3 remote students 2 experts/teachers	1 student 3 experts/teacher 16 students (public)	1 student 7 experts/teachers 16 students (public)
Students	17	5 groups x 6	17	17
Sessions	2 x 0:30	7 x 0:30	2 x 0:30	1 x 0:30
Durations	17:00	17:30	17:00	8:30

5.2 Data Analysis

Collaborative design can be analyzed from various points of view: (1) physical working conditions, (2) the emotional or psychological aspect and (3) cognitive. This final point of view - analysis of the design process relative to the situation, actors and the subject being dealt with - is the one we will be focusing on in this study by considering group awareness, intermediary objects and the common referential used to study these situations.

This is why the discussions, annotations, imported documents, use of the tool and use of the different SAR by all participants are observed and analysed qualitatively using a specific coding scheme (fig. 3). This scheme distinguishes between three types of interaction spaces according to how the actors use them:

1. We-Space: in which remote participants annotate and modify a shared real-time document using the electronic pen;
2. I-Space: in which the actor works on his or her document alone;
3. Space-between: a private conversation in which certain members of the group isolate themselves to work together independently of the We-Space in which they are participating.

These spatial interactions are first of all described as actions relative to various parameters which are mainly:

— active actors: this group is made up of all the participants of the SAR under analysis and they are coded as being active when they explicitly intervene in the observed situation;
— documents: these are categorized according to how they are shared. If it is shared, is it with the participants as a whole or solely with one collaborator in a private conversation?
— action typology: these define the objective of actions such as isolating oneself, pooling information, challenging, acting on a decision or giving instructions, evaluating, producing together, negotiating or formulating group's rules, and so on.

These spatial interactions are then studied and analyzed by regrouping them into sequences to illustrate conversational dynamic between collaborators. We believe that the sequence designates a series of successive choices which form a narrative unit in

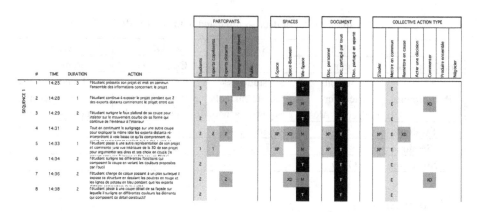

Fig. 3. Example of the coding used to analyze the data: SAR 4 "Evaluation".

response to general questions (and/or proposals) raised by the actors during the design process. This sequential empirical division refers to logic behind the actions shown by the transition from one problem to the next and/or by the transformation from one state to another – a process in perpetual movement [8]. Stating a new problem (and/or a proposal, and/or a question) is what marks the end of one sequence and the beginning of the next.

6   Results: Towards a New Classification of Intermediary Spaces

Based on Johansen's proposed spatiotemporal matrix in the domain of CSCW for groupware classification [9], the observation of the SAR implemented in our training environment requires a review of the "co-presence/remote" dichotomy in synchronous collaboration.

Even if the tool used in these SAR was originally designed to support remote collaboration between the various protagonists involved in the project, in presence public evaluation (SAR 3) actually revealed itself to be the most interesting application. Indeed, we noticed the emergence of "augmented presence" between the student using the board (explaining his or her project) and those using the digital table (the expert and the teacher discussing the project with the class). Interaction was established between the actors as a whole, based both upon a direct and in presence modality (a conversation within the same physical space) and remote indirect modality (the annotation of a virtually shared document on physical supports situated in the same room but distinct from one another). This SAR therefore involves new intermediary spaces and also nuances Johansen's notion of spatiality, distinguishing between real presence and augmented presence as well as virtual co-presence, in the synchronous activity of collaboration [10].

And so, as regards spatial configuration, these SAR influence the relationship the actors have with these intermediary work spaces which are of a short duration, and which are created as a function of the needs, aims, negotiation process, justification and consensus building in project design. These co-spaces vary, change and evolve between the actors' personal spaces (I-Space), co-work spaces which bring the actors together (We-Space) and the junction between the two (Space-Between). These changes enable students, teachers and experts to participate in building joint reflections so that all the actors may evolve together towards the same objective.

The collaborators/learners who are working together on the same project and sharing a We-Space (SAR 2) show a tendency towards working as a unit to assure coherent choices and interdependence between the different elements making up each individual's reflections. The learner, showing his or her project to the other students, experts and teachers and thereby making the transition from I-Space to We-Space (SAR 3), has a new perspective on his or her own production while benefiting from the collective reflections of the other participants. Learners, in appealing to experts from other domains to nurture and answer their queries (SAR 1), enrich the pool with opinions, knowledge and references linked to the project. At the final jury (SAR 4), private conversations develop between the learner and the students, and occasionally even the expert in co-presence (Space-Between), thereby creating a situation where the project as an end-product is discussed and challenged.

All these intermediary spaces therefore involve the mechanisms implicit in mutualizing knowledge, sharing comprehension and the cognitive synchronization relative to building mutual awareness of the working environment (social awareness), the design (activity awareness) and the tasks and contributions of each person within a group (action awareness) [11]. These mechanisms and their links to the intermediary spaces - We-Space, I-Space and Space-Between - are detailed in the following paragraphs.

6.1   We-Space

The SAR as a whole principally encourage this intermediary space: the co-work space. This space was analyzed using the coding table and more specifically, the actions, the documents brought into play, and the relationships maintained between the actors. It is nevertheless important to highlight the fact that the project evolves principally through speech, even though these words are often put into drawings to explain and justify these choices and find a consensus between the actors as a whole. These drawings are collectively manipulated in presence and remotely. They constitute a shared interactive boundary object that evolves from a negotiation process and consensus building between students (SAR 2), experts (SAR 1) and trainers (SAR 3&4). These artefacts promote collective reflection on the productions which generate new shared representations (especially in SAR 2). Moreover, they translate the student's individual design project, thereby enabling him or her to view the project from a different perspective (I-Space) and construct his or her own speech as well as new interpretations and reflections between the other learners (Space-Between) who are present at the public evaluation (SAR 3) and the jury (SAR 4). The SAR in which these interactive intermediary objects are manipulated therefore reduce the spatiotemporal gaps brought into play because the interval of time between the action made on the document and the information feedback to the various users is immediate.

The We-Space is particularly encouraged because it does not involve any loss in the causality links between what is said and the annotations created by the actor – in either augmented presence or virtual co-presence – and what the other actors receive as regards information.

Consider the case of remote collaboration between ULg students and students from the School of Architecture of Nancy (SAR 2). New modes of exchange were observed in this scenario: one which brings out the need to create one's own I-Space from a We-Space and one which shows the possibility of creating a joint drawing with two people, thereby emphasizing the We-Space. In both situations, graphic representations created by two people were brought into play to work on the object being designed. In the first case, the students individually propose different points of view of the project under discussion by dividing the We-Space into two and thereby creating two I-Spaces. One student draws an interior view of the project while the second draws a cross-section; both are able to see the plan they have previously discussed. As all participants see what the others are doing, the student drawing the interior view can, without speaking, readjust his or her sketch while looking at the cross-section being simultaneously constructed by the remote collaborator. This juxtaposition of representations developing on the same shared digital interface encourages cross-interpretation from both actors, even if their initial intention was for each to have his or her personal working space. In the second scenario, the students both draw the same perspective of the plan that has been discussed and collaboratively worked on beforehand. In this way, they pool the choices previously made without even having to speak to one another.

6.2   I-Space

The SAR were implemented so as to promote the We-Space. They were not particularly designed so as to enable independence. Independent work is synonymous with isolating oneself and designing independently while taking into account the work done by the others [9]. Visser also introduces this notion when she speaks about "parallel activities" and their importance in collective work. In her opinion, these parallel activities are marked by interruptions and recoveries throughout the process. They "constitute an indication of the place 'individual conception' can occupy in a co-design meeting between architects" [2, p.152].

In our opinion, independence marks the time spent working in isolation; these are the moments when the project is thought out independently while still taking the opinions of the others into account. Thus, the need to "create one's own I-Space" emerges, because work involving several people does not systematically lead to continuous interaction. Even if the students, trainers and experts tend to reflect together on how the project will evolve, our analyses show that each individual thinks independently and constructs their own isolated reflection at given moments. Even the students/audience take note during the presentation at the jury because they are strategically readjusting what they are planning to say and their answers relative to the remarks made by the experts and teachers. Often, this I-Space is marked by:

- moments of silence during which the actors isolate themselves, either to produce notes and/or personal graphic sketches, or simply to read data or look for a reference to illustrate an idea. In this situation, certain I-Spaces enable continued joint reflection while others interrupt it so as to enable the actors to reflect upon a new point of view;
- personal spoken comments, made in an undertone and not intended to be shared but which result nevertheless from collaborative situations. The I-Space becomes, in this case, a Space-Between which allows certain actors to create private conversations in a collaborative activity (*cf.* 6.3).

Yet this I-Space is not supported by the SAR installed in our training programs. Here, participants in the various sessions do not have the possibility to create their own individual graphic space (I-Space) unless they use the tool differently, or create a personal space which is independent of the SAR concerned, by use of a personal notebook, for example. As previously seen in the SAR 2 We-Space, certain collaborators find a solution by geometrically dividing the space into two parts. This juxtaposition of I-Space within a We-Space encourages cross-interpretation followed by a pooling of this information and the confrontation of the two proposals, thus leading to new cross-interpretations. Once these independent actions are completed, new reflections emerge which are often then pooled to be shared with other participants. An example of this is when an expert takes notes during a student's presentation and then shares the comments with said student so that they may work together to develop a joint reflection on the project.

Today, we believe that it is important to develop the SAR so that I-Spaces can be formed. Indeed, even if the SAR do not prevent the participant from creating his or her own private notebook by using a pen and paper outside the shared interface for example, the SAR nevertheless oblige said participant to change the tool's function by installing a private work methodology so as to construct a personal work space. This I-Space is all the more important in collaboration because it allows the participant, the student in particular, to refocus on his or her own perceptions and individual interpretations. These choices and personal interests are more often than not defined by dividing the tasks according to the needs and/or interests of each individual in the group (particularly in the case of SAR 2).

6.3   Space-Between

The Space-Between is a private conversation that is created between two or several participants independently from the rest of the group. Like the I-Space, the Space-Between is not managed by the SAR, especially not between remote actors. It is all the more problematic because the Space-Between is principally based on oral exchange. In SAR 2 and SAR 4, the creation of a Space-Between actually disturbs the collaborative process rather than nurturing it, as in group communications and via video-conferencing, all sounds emitted from one place (near, far, low voice, high voice) are heard with the same tonality by the geographically remote participants.

Yet collective activities develop from social interactions, amongst other things, whether they are collective or private. Private interactions gain particular importance in the case of collective activities which present a well-identified hierarchical relationship between actors. As the tool enables the participant to draw synchronously and remotely, remote actors can intervene peer-to-peer (SAR 1&2). All other players attending the project review may also modify their drawings on the basis of the examiner's corrections (be the examiner an expert or a teacher).

In giving this possibility to all participants to make adjustments to the document, the modifications made by the teacher become less sacrosanct, and this encourages the challenging of choices made, regardless of the participant involved. Where a classic review of a project places learners alone with the teacher with no possible interaction with their classmates, the SAR encourages exchange between students and limits competition. Sharing points of view, building common operative referentials, finding common ground and cognitive synchronization are thereby encouraged by the SAR, enabling the We-Space, but also managing the Space-Between. These SAR contribute to building common ground relative to the project, and perfectly managing activity awareness. In contrast, they do not allow social awareness (because it is difficult to know what is happening behind the screen and where such and such a background noise is coming from) and action awareness (because the SAR do not hint at the specific characteristics of each participant and their tasks in the collaborative activity). This is principally due to the impossibility of creating a Space-Between, particularly in the case of SAR 2 and 4.

7   Conclusion : Towards Articulation between Intermediary Spaces

As observed in the previous paragraphs, it is impossible to separate the intermediary spaces. The We-Space, I-Space and Space-Between as a whole define the co-work space between the actors. Nevertheless, adjusting between these diverse intermediary spaces involves flexibility that should be provided by the tool, so that each individual may easily manipulate and structure his or her interface. This flexibility is currently only partially managed by the system used in the SAR presented here. SketSha, a piece of software enabling synchronous sharing of graphic annotations, was initially designed for the pooling of synchronous work on documents, but video-conferencing does not enable the actors either side of the screen to isolate themselves and create their own private conversations. Our qualitative analysis also confirms our former results [10] : the SAR participate perfectly in group cohesion by creating intermediary spatialities between augmented presence and virtual co-presence. They aid and equip the student in learning how to collaborate. They encourage peer-to-peer sharing between learners, trainers and experts, but at the expense of independent work and the creation of private conversations. Moments of isolation enable interlocutors to express their ideas using their own knowledge, references and contexts and they tend to bring together a certain number of singularities, those of: the student, the other participants, the project to be designed and the tool being used. The designer/student must therefore juggle between these singularities by personal interpretations constructed in the I-Space and the Space-Between that he or she gradually appropriates as the collaboration process progresses.

In this way, the next generation SAR will also have to enable users to easily move between the shared work space (the We-Space as it stands today) and a personal or private space according to the needs and contexts of the collaborators. Articulation of these intermediary spaces within the SAR is currently at the pre-test stage, using technical solutions based on the use of individual graphics tablets placed upon the shared table. This will better support cognitive synchronization in the co-actors as it will be promoted by the flexibility of access to the other intermediary augmented spaces. In turn, this will promote comprehension of the complex activity that is design.

References

1. Dubois, E., Bortolaso, C., Bach, C., Duranthon, F., Blanquer-Maumont, A.: Design and Evaluation of Mixed Interactive Museographic Exhibits. International Journal of Arts and Technology, Inderscience Publishers, Numéro Spécial Interactive Experiences in Multimedia and Augmented Environments 4(4), 408–441 (2011)
2. Hmelo-Silver, C.E.: Problem-Based Learning: What and How Do Students Learn? Educational Psychology 16(3), 235–266 (2004)
3. Visser, W.: Co-élaboration de solutions en conception architecturale et rôle du graphico-gestuel: Point de vue de la psychologie ergonomique. In: Détienne, F., Traverso, V. (eds.) Méthodologies d'analyse de Situations CoopéRatives de Conception, pp. 129–167. Presses Universitaires de Nancy, Corpus MOSAIC (2009)
4. Allwood, J., Traum, D., Jokinen, K.: Cooperation, Dialogue and Ethics. International Journal of Human-Computer Studies 53, 871–914 (2000)
5. Boujut, J.-F., Roulland, F., Castellani, S., Willamowski, F., Martin, D.: The mediation role of shared representations in cooperative activities: New challenges. In: Stevens, G. (ed.) Workshop Proceedings of 9th International Conference on the Design of Cooperative Systems, International Reports on Socio-Informatics, vol. 7 (1), pp. 170–320 (2010)
6. Safin, S., Juchmes, R., Leclercq, P.: Use of graphical modality in a collaborative design distant setting. In J., Dugdale, C., Masclet, M. A., Grasso, J.-F., Boujut, & P., Hassanaly (eds.) Proceedings of COOP 2012 : 10th International Conference on the Design of Cooperative Systems. Springer (2012)
7. Fay, D., Frese, M.: Self-starting behavior at work: Toward a theory of personal initiative. In: Heckhausen, J. (ed.) Motivational Psychology of Human Development: Developing Motivation and Motivating Development, pp. 307–337. Elservier, Amsterdam (2000)
8. Ben Rajeb, S.: Conception collaborative distante : étude architecturologique pour la caractérisation des opérations cognitives. In: Agnenot, V., Safin, S., Dondelero, M.G., Leclecq, P. (eds.) Interfaces Numériques : Collaborer à Distance, Enjeux et Impacts des Interfaces Numériques dans les Pratiques Collaboratives Synchrone, Lavoisier, vol. 2(3), pp. 509–530 (2013)
9. Ellis, C.A., Gibbs, S.J., Rein, G.: Groupware: Some issues and experiences. Communications of the ACM 34(1), 39–58 (1991)
10. Ben Rajeb, S., Leclercq, P.: Using Spatial Augmented Reality in Synchronous Collaborative Design. In: Luo, Y. (ed.) CDVE 2013. LNCS, vol. 8091, pp. 1–10. Springer, Heidelberg (2013)
11. Carroll, J.M., Neale, D.C., Isenhour, P.L., Rosson, M.B., McCrickard, D.S.: Notification and awareness: Synchronizing task-oriented collaborative activity. International Journal of Human-Computer Studies 58, 605–632 (2003)

Passenger Ship Evacuation – Design and Verification

Luis Guarin[1], Yasmine Hifi[1], and Dracos Vassalos[2]

[1] Brookes Bell – Safety at Sea, United Kingdom
{luis.guarin,yasmine.hifi}@brookesbell.com
[2] University of Strathclyde, Glasgow, United Kingdom
d.vassalos@strath.ac.uk

Abstract. This paper introduces the concept of escape and evacuation from passenger ships from a perspective of ship design and risk management. As part of that process, the use of computer simulation tools for analysing the evacuation performance of ships carrying large numbers of persons on board is becoming more relevant and useful. The objective of this paper is to present the pedestrian dynamics simulation tool EVI, developed to undertake advanced escape and evacuation analysis in the design verification of cruise vessels, passenger ferries and large offshore construction vessels, among others.

Keywords: Evacuation analysis, passenger ships, offshore vessels.

1 Introduction

Innovation in ship design has traditionally been a feature of the cruise and ferry sectors of the maritime industry. The design of passenger ships has evolved dramatically during the past 30 years, driven among others, by increasing customer expectations, business opportunities, technological progress and societal demands for increased safety and environmental greenness. The single most significant trend is the growth in ship size, with the largest cruise vessel today being able to carry more than 5000 passengers on-board (some 8,400 people including the crew), and measuring more than 350m in length.

Another trend in the industry has been fuelled by the emergence of offshore construction, which has led to the development of a new type of working vessels with the capacity to carry and accommodate large number of special personnel (workers) on board. These vessels, referred to as Special Purpose Ships (SPS), may be subject to the same rigorous design verification as large passenger ships when the numbers of persons on board exceed 240.

Safety is arguably the single most significant design driver for passenger ships today with safety requirements now driven by explicit safety goals and include quantitative verification of residual capabilities in case of accidental events. Those capabilities relate to stability after flooding extensive fire protection, redundancy of essential ship systems (in line with the 'safe return to port' philosophy) and ultimately escape and evacuation arrangements – the last safety barrier if everything else fails.

R. Shumaker and S. Lackey (Eds.): VAMR 2014, Part II, LNCS 8526, pp. 354–365, 2014.

Given this level of significance, validation of escape and evacuation arrangements is gradually taking a more prominent place in the conceptual ship design iteration and verification process. To this end, following initial developments at the University of Strathclyde in the late-1990s to support the rule-making process, the focus at Safety at Sea since 2001 has been clearly on ship design/operation support. Initially, the software was designed to undertake advanced evacuation analysis for Ro-Ro passenger vessels in accordance with the guidelines developed by the International Maritime Organization [1]. More recently, the software has been used as a consequence analysis tool during the conceptual design risk analysis of large passenger vessels, offshore platforms and special purpose ships (pipe layers, drilling ships, crane vessels, among others).

A brief overview of the ship-evacuation problem is presented in Section 2 with emphasis on the many factors that influence the process of ship evacuation. In Section 3, a general description of the key features of the EVI simulation model is presented. These key features represent the concept and implementation of the solution to the problem defined in Section 2.

The paper concludes in Section 4 with some practical observations based on the experience gained from the use of the tool in a number of commercial applications and design projects.

2   Ship-Based Evacuation Problem

The ship evacuation process has a number of aspects which influence the outcome of a ship evacuation and therefore have to be taken into account when trying to simulate and analyse the process. A brief overview of these factors is given in the following.

2.1   Emergency Scenarios

A ship may need to be evacuated in an emergency if the risk to the persons on-board is deemed to be unacceptable. For the majority of ships, emergency scenarios requiring ship abandonment may be associated with shipping accidents, such as collision/grounding leading to flooding, fire or explosions. A generic procedure, referred to as 'muster list', for dealing with an incident is illustrated in **Table 1**. As it can be noted, the process of evacuation is normally carried out in stages. In each stage, there might be different activities occurring concurrently but having different objectives.

Table 1. Generic (typical) muster list for a passenger ship

STAGE 1	STAGE 2	STAGE 3
INCIDENT (1) Detection & Alarm	(2) Damage control (3) Muster of Pax (4) Preparation of LSA	(5) Abandon Ship (6) Rescue

The incident itself (e.g. fire, flooding) might physically impact on the evacuation arrangements. This impact can include the following:

- Impairment/inaccessibility of escape routes, muster areas or evacuation systems (e.g. due to damage, heat, smoke or floodwater);
- Heel and/or trim of the ship (due to flooding), leading to inclination of the surfaces used as escape routes; these may slow down the movement of evacuees or stop them altogether. Severe inclinations (more than 20 degrees) can prevent the occupants from deploying evacuation systems.

2.2   The Ship Environment

The ship purpose determines the internal layout of the ship. The layout is a complex collection of spaces of different use, distributed along horizontal decks and vertical fire zones. The function of the spaces varies greatly from ship to ship:

- **Passenger Vessels:** Layout includes a variety of public spaces (such as restaurants, theatres, shopping malls, lobbies, sun decks, bars, discos, casinos and many others), cabins and crew service spaces (machinery, galleys, hotel services, etc.)
- **Offshore Vessels:** Layout includes a variety of spaces in the living quarters (cabins, recreation spaces, meeting rooms, offices, control rooms, etc.), working stations for special personnel (pipe manufacturing stations, crane workstations, working decks, etc.) and marine crew service spaces (machinery, workshops, stores, etc.).

The geometrical and topological features as well as the different functions of spaces within a ship will greatly influence the location of the evacuees at the moment of the incident and in some cases, the awareness and/or the response time of the occupants. For example, people in cabins may be asleep, people in working stations (e.g. welding, heavy lift cranes) may be subject to a delay due to safe termination of work requirements.

2.3   Escape and Evacuation Arrangements

Escape and evacuation arrangements can be considered as risk control measures or barriers aimed at mitigating the severity of the consequences of an accidental event. These measures are mainly of passive nature and include the following:

Alarm Systems. Public address and alarm systems are the means of communicating an emergency signal to all persons on-board. This will influence the time for people to become aware of and respond to the incident. The General Alarm signalling the order to muster is typically activated by the crew once the incident is validated;

Escape Routes. These comprise hatches, doors, corridors, stairs, walkways, ladders and other spaces, connecting all spaces on-board to a muster area or a safe refuge. Most spaces on-board ships are fitted with at least two emergency exits. All exits lead to a primary and a secondary escape route to a muster point. The capacity of the escape routes is generally driven by the width of the escapes and the redundancy of the routes from different areas of the layout.

Muster Areas. These are spaces that can be located internally (public areas) or externally (near embarkation stations). The capacity and specification of muster areas varies significantly from passenger ships to offshore units/vessels. For passenger ships, at least 0.35 m^2 per person has to be provided (e.g. 500 persons, a minimum of 175 m^2 of deck space has to be provided in the muster area).

Lifesaving Systems. These comprise survival craft (e.g. lifeboats) and other systems to assist in the abandonment of the ship. These systems have to be prepared before use (if not stowed in the embarkation position) and are usually located near or by the muster areas. The capacities of these systems vary from ship to ship. Typically, lifeboats for up to 150 persons are fitted to most passenger ships. Recently lifeboats with capacities up to 370 persons have been developed. The arrangement of survival craft can significantly influence the procedures and time of ship abandonment.

2.4   Human and Organisational Factors

Number of Persons on Board (POB). The number of POB depends on the purpose of the vessel/offshore unit and the operational mode. A typical cruise vessel carries about 4000 persons (including crew). Offshore construction vessels may carry up to 600 persons.

Demographics. The demographic characteristics (age, gender, etc.) of the evacuees would greatly influence the walking speed and the reaction time to an alarm. The demographics differ greatly between passenger ships and offshore working vessels. Whilst on passenger vessels the sample of people is representative of the normal population demographics (including children and people with mobility impairments), on offshore working vessels, the population sample corresponds to personnel specifically trained to work in offshore conditions (the level of fitness, familiarity with the layout, emergency preparedness and competence is significantly higher than that of the typical passengers population).

Crew Emergency Tasks. As indicated in **Table 1**, in most situations, crew are expected to undertake active damage control and assist passengers during the muster and ship abandonment process. Crew emergency tasks involve directing passengers to the correct muster point or to alternative routes if the primary escapes are impaired and reduce the awareness time (active search of people in cabins), among others. This requires active internal communication among crew and between crew and passengers, which in essence amounts to giving and updating the objectives of individual evacuees.

2.5   External Factors

Sea State. The direct impact of wind and waves is on the ship behaviour, which in turn, translates into ship motions. Ship motions-induced accelerations may affect the walking speed of evacuees and even their decision making.

Time of Day. In passenger vessels, the time of day determines the initial location of persons on-board at the moment of an incident. During the night, persons are more likely to be located in cabins and asleep, which decreases their awareness and increases reaction time. During the day, the range of activities on-board and the location of the spaces will determine the choice of muster areas (usually the nearest possible) are the routes they would eventually take to reach the muster points (usually the most familiar). In working ships, the impact of the time of day is lower as these ships usually work in shifts i.e. they have the same persons load during the day and at night.

3   Evacuation Simulation

The software EVI, in its current form, was conceived in 2001 [2]. The first concept of the simulation tool was first presented in 2001 [3]. Since then, the code has undergone further development driven mainly by commercial applications. The key design principles and assumptions are outlined below.

3.1   Multi-agent Simulation

The EVI simulation is an implementation of multi-agent modelling, which is a further generalisation of process-based modelling methods where the environment is very well defined and the agents may communicate in a fairly versatile manner. In natural systems, all component parts "live" in some sort of topological space (predators and prey may live on a two dimensional forest floor, data packages traverse a network graph and the evacuees move around on a 2D deck). An environment is defined to be an artificial representation of this space. Autonomous agents can perform the activities defined by a computer program in this environment. This strong sense of environment does not exist in a process-based simulation. Processes are only aware of themselves and the resources they wish to acquire. Communication in multi-agent simulation describes all interaction between real life entities. This makes multi-agent simulation an extremely powerful tool but also one, which is hard to verify in the context of known mathematical theory. The essence of using agents requires a rigorous definition and full implementation of the environment and its interfaces with the agents as well as an inter-agent communication protocol.

3.2   The Environment

Definition of the environment is one of the most important aspects of multi-agent modelling. This consists of three aspects: (i) geometry, (ii) topology and (iii) domain semantics. The whole ship layout is segmented into Euclidean convex *regions* with a structure of a linear space, directly connected if they have a common gate. This connectivity topology, for all computation and analysis purposes can be represented by a graph.

In ship layout terms, regions correspond to spaces and gates correspond to doors. Regions can be defined as rectangular or convex polygons with attributes that control initial conditions and semantic information that agents may query when traversing through (such as initial number of persons, fire zone, destination, etc.). Regions can be located at different level entities, called decks, defined by the height above a reference level or baseline. The problem of finding the path of an agent to a muster point becomes reduced to searching the topology graph.

3.3   The Agents

The lowest common denominator of the many definitions of "agent" is an encapsulation of code and data, which has its own thread of control and is capable of executing independently the appropriate piece of code depending on its own state (the encapsulated data), the observables (the environment) and the stimuli (messages from other parts of the system or interactively provided). The agent-action model is essentially a 'sense-decide-act' loop. The sense and decide steps may be coalesced, as the sensing is nothing more than the interface of the agent with the data structures representing the environment. The decision process requires access to the perceived information, thus perception is not a complex process but rather a simple access interface between the environment and the agents. Notably, the actions of agents may also change the environment, giving rise to what is called interactive fiction. To address the modelling of human behaviour at the microscopic and macroscopic level, the agent model itself can be seen as being composed of a number of levels, see **Fig. 1**.

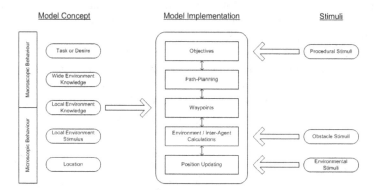

Fig. 1. The agent model in EVI

At the highest level, an Objective defines agent task or desire, for example, go to a cabin and wait for 60 seconds, search all the cabins on deck 7, fire zone 3, port side or evacuate to the nearest assembly station. In order to fulfil this desire, the Objective requests a path plan (routing) to be calculated, which defines what door and the order of the doors the agent should go through to advance from the current location to the destination. Once this data structure is in place, the agent will select a waypoint, an intermediate location to travel to, usually in direct line-of-sight from the agent (i.e. within a convex region), from the first door in the path plan route. With a defined direction to travel to, defined by the waypoint, the agent will move towards that location using position updating. In doing so, the agent will avoid the boundaries of spaces and other agents in the locality by taking account of environment and inter-agent conflicts.

3.4   Mesoscopic Modelling

Ship arrangements are large with many routes from one location to another and endless choices along the way. As a person traverses a route he/she will have to interact with other people along the route and react to the surrounding environment. This gives rise to a need to have two main methods of considering the problem: (i) Macroscopic modelling: addressing the problem of how passengers may find their way from one part of the ship environment to another (high-level planning), and (ii) Microscopic modelling: considering how individuals interact with the environment within close proximity (low-level planning).

Microscopic Behaviour. The microscopic model covers the behaviour of movement of agents within spaces. It dictates the way agents avoid boundaries of spaces and how it should avoid other agents. Given these constraints, the objective is to steer the agent towards a local destination (waypoint) in an optimal manner without being uncooperative towards the other agents in the space.

Environment discretisation and the agents. Given that the environment is discretised into convex *regions*, the process of moving from one door (gate) to another becomes a process of pursuit of a static target. However, with additional complexities such as other agents and obstacles, the process of steering becomes significantly more complex. The decision of how to approach this specific problem is one that determines the entire design of the simulation architecture. In this respect, two general approaches can be identified: (i) grid-based techniques and (ii) social forces models. Both approaches have their merits and constrains. However, EVI combines the effectiveness of grid-based technique with the flexibility of social force methods, see **Fig 2**.

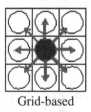
Grid-based

Hybrid (EVI)

Social forces

Fig. 2. Agents in the environment

In order to simplify calculation, a range of discrete decisions are established around the agent with the objective of identifying the one which will allow the agent to travel the greatest distance toward the local target. In addition, a continuous local (social/personal) space is established around each agent, which other agents will aim to avoid. This space is used to prevent a deadlock situation when the number of agents in an area becomes high. The agent makes a decision of the best use of its personal space to resolve any conflicts that may arise. As a result, this approach allows the evacuation process to be modelled in sufficient detail and still run in real time or faster. In order to move, each agent needs to be aware of the local surrounding environment and draw conclusions on how to move. This update procedure is defined in terms of three steps: perception, decision and action.

Perception. Agents use their update vector to check their personal space for boundaries (containment) and other agents (collision avoidance and lane formation). This takes place in the form of discrete directions. The magnitude of the vector corresponds to the distance that can be travelled over the time step for a given nominal walking speed.

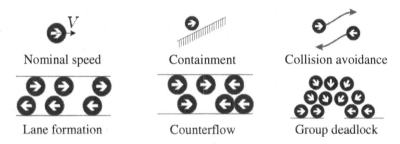

| Nominal speed | Containment | Collision avoidance |

| Lane formation | Counterflow | Group deadlock |

Fig. 3. Agent microscopic behaviour

Decision. A rational rule-based process is used to select the action to take for the current time step. The decision process makes use of information on the previous time step combined with information acquired from the Perception algorithm. The algorithm also gathers state information from the current environment and considers a number of discrete possibilities for updating the agent status:

- Update: The agent should update as normal moving as far along the update vector as possible.
- Wait: The agent does not move.
- Swap with Agent: The agent in collaboration with another on-coming agent has decided to swap positions to resolve deadlock.
- Squeeze through: The agent is congested but perception has indicated that if the agent disregards its personal space it can progress
- Step back: An agent who is squeezing through has violated the   personal space of another agent. The direction of update is reversed to allow the squeezing agent through.

Action. This consists of careful updating of the status of all agents based on updating the decisions made. Due to the nature of software programming, this is, of necessity, a sequential activity to avoid loss of synchronisation. To ensure that agents update properly, order is introduced into the system whereby each agent requests those in front, travelling in the same direction, to update first before updating itself.

Macroscopic Behaviour. The macroscopic behaviour defines the way an agent will travel from one location to another on board the ship layout. Building on the graph structure defined within the model, the process of identifying the shortest route to a destination is achieved using Dijkstra's classic shortest path algorithm with the weighting taken as the distance between doors. This concept is very similar to the Potential methods used in other evacuation simulation models except that distance is only considered along the links of the graph rather than throughout space. Once route information has been generated for each node, the process of travelling from one point in the environment to another is just a case of following the sequence of information laid down by the search; this is referred to as the path plan.

Path-plan information is generated on demand when required by agents, and except for cases where the path plan refers to an assembly station, route information is deleted when no longer required. To ensure that the path-planner will respect the signage within the ship arrangement regions and doors attributes include definitions of primary exits and primary routes, which can force agents to use specific routes.

3.5   Modelling Uncertainty

The psychological and physiological attributes of humans are non-deterministic quantities. Even in a contrived experiment one can hardly reproduce human actions/reactions even if all of the conditions remained the same. This inherent unpredictability of human behaviour, especially under unusual and stressful circumstances, requires that human behaviour be modelled with some built-in uncertainty.

Demographics. All parameters related to human decision or action, are modelled as random variables with user-defined probability distributions. This information, referred to as demographics includes variables such as awareness/response time, gender and walking speed, among others, is almost exclusively collected through observational research using experiments that measure the response of people in controlled and uncontrolled environments. Typical demographic information is available from full scale trials in the form of basic statistics; see for example [1] and [5]. This information in conjunction with the probabilistic assumptions is used to carry out Monte-Carlo sampling to derive the values of response time and walking speed for each agent taking part in the simulation.

EVacuability Index (EVI). For the purpose of undertaking evacuation analysis, a number of performance measures can be evaluated, such as time for a group of persons to clear a particular area (ESCAPE), time for all agents to complete assembly after a signal (MUSTER), time for a group or agents to complete escape, muster and ship abandon if these were carried out in sequence (EVACUATION). The choice of performance measure will depend on the specific scenario being evaluated.

Considering the above, the term Evacuability is defined as the probability of the given objective (Escape, Muster, Evacuation, etc.) being achieved within a time t from the moment the corresponding signal is given, for a given state of the ship environment (env) and for a given state of initial distribution (dist) of people in the environment. Thus, results from a number of simulation runs (given that the environment and the distribution remain the same) as a multi-set {t1, t2, t3, t4,... , tn} then by the law of large numbers Evacuability may be determined with an accuracy directly dependent on the number of runs. For practical applications, at least 50 individual simulations of the same evacuation scenario are required, and from these results, the 95 percentile values are used for verification in accordance with IMO guidelines [1].

3.6   Scenario Modelling

Based on the general aspects presented in Section 2, escape and evacuation scenarios may range from local escape from an individual zone of the ship (e.g. due to fire) to a complete ship evacuation (muster and abandon, e.g. due to a flooding incident).

The impact of hazards associated with flooding and fire can be incorporated in EVI in time and space. The software is capable of reading time histories of ship motions and flood water in the ship compartmentation from time-domain flooding simulation tools such as PROTEUS-3.1 [7]. The impact of ship motions and floodwater on the agents is modelled by applying walking speed reduction coefficients that are functions of the inclination of the escape routes due to heel and/or trim of the ship, generated by the damage [5] [6]. The impact on the environment is modelled by way of treating regions directly affected by floodwater as inaccessible.

In terms of fire hazards, the software is capable of importing fire hazards information from fire analysis tools such as FDS [8]. Fire hazards are described in the form of parameters such as temperature, heat fluxes, concentrations of toxic gases (such as CO, CO_2) and oxygen, smoke density, visibility, etc. The impact of these hazards on the agents is modelled by comparing against human tolerability criteria [6].

4   Conclusions

This paper presents a high level description of the concept and implementation of the multi-agent simulation tool EVI – a pedestrian dynamics simulation environment developed with the aim of undertaking escape and evacuation analysis of passenger vessels in accordance with IMO guidelines [1].

Multi-agent simulations are computationally intensive; however for practical engineering applications, they have become viable with the advent of cheap and high computing power.

The particular implementation of EVI combines a number of concepts and approaches which make EVI a versatile tool suitable for efficient and practical design verification.

Due to the implicit level of uncertainty in the process, driven by human behaviour, verification of the tool has been successfully achieved in terms of component testing, functional and qualitative verification [4][5]. Data for quantitative verification is still lacking.

Over the past 5 years, EVI has evolved into a consequence analysis tool for design verification of passenger ships and SPS (offshore construction vessels, pipe-laying, large crane vessels) subject to design risk analysis. Among this type of applications, the following can be highlighted:

- Verification of escape arrangements for alternative design & arrangements: this is part of the engineering analysis required in accordance with IMO MSC\Circ.1002, see **Fig. 4**;
- Escape, evacuation and rescue assessment for SPS (offshore construction vessels carrying more than 240 personnel onboard) – see **Fig. 5**.
- Analysis of turnaround time in passenger ship terminals – see **Fig. 6**.

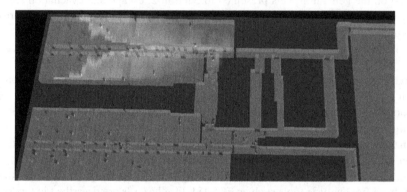

Fig. 4. Verification of human tenability criteria for a layout fire zone

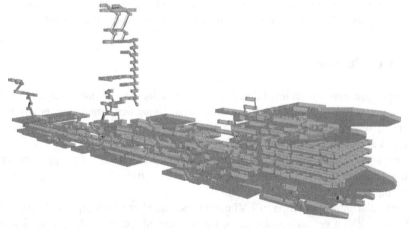

Fig. 5. EVI model of a pipe-laying vessel (LQs with accommodation for 350 POB) for evacuation analysis

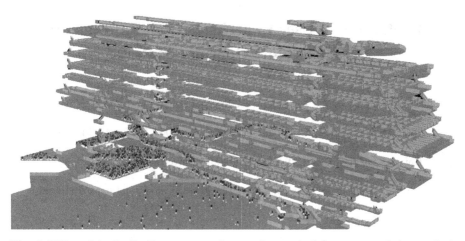

Fig. 6. EVI model of a Ro-Ro passenger ferry at the terminal for turnaround time analysis (2700 passengers disembarking)

References

1. IMO (2007), MSC 1\Circ.1238, Guidelines for evacuation analysis for new and existing passenger ships (October 30, 2007)
2. Majumder, et al: Evacuation Simulation Report – Voyager of the Seas, Deltamarin, SSRC internal report (January 2001)
3. Vassalos, et al.: A mesoscopic model for passenger evacuation in a virtual ship-sea environment and performance-based evaluation. In: PED Conference, Duisburg (April 2001)
4. SAS (2009), EVI Component testing, Functional and Qualitative Verification in accordance with Annex 3 of the IMO Guidelines, MSC\Circ.1239. Safety at Sea Ltd report (September 2009)
5. SAFEGUARD, EC-funded project under FP 7 (2013)
6. Guarin, et al.: Fire and flooding risk assessment in ship design for ease of evacuation. In: Design for Safety Conference, Osaka, Japan (2004)
7. Jasionowski, A.: An integrated approach to damage ship survivability assessment, University of Strathclyde, Ph.D dissertation, 1997-2001 (2001)
8. NIST, Fire Dynamics Simulator software
9. SAFENVSHIPS, EUREKA R&D project (2005)

Evaluation of User Experience Goal Fulfillment: Case Remote Operator Station

Hannu Karvonen[1], Hanna Koskinen[1], Helena Tokkonen[2], and Jaakko Hakulinen[3]

[1] VTT Technical Research Centre of Finland, P.O.Box 1000, FI-02044 VTT, Finland
{hannu.karvonen,hanna.koskinen}@vtt.fi
[2] University of Jyväskylä, P.O. Box 35, FI-40014 University of Jyväskylä, Finland
helena.tokkonen@gmail.com
[3] University of Tampere, Kanslerinrinne 1, FI-33014 University of Tampere, Finland
jaakko.hakulinen@sis.uta.fi

Abstract. In this paper, the results of a user experience (UX) goal evaluation study are reported. The study was carried out as a part of a research and development project of a novel remote operator station (ROS) for container gantry crane operation in port yards. The objectives of the study were both to compare the UXs of two different user interface concepts and to give feedback on how well the UX goals experience of safe operation, sense of control, and feeling of presence are fulfilled with the developed ROS prototype. According to the results, the experience of safe operation and feeling of presence were not supported with the current version of the system. However, there was much better support for the fulfilment of the sense of control UX goal in the results. Methodologically, further work is needed in adapting the utilized Usability Case method to suit UX goal evaluation better.

Keywords: remote operation, user experience, user experience goal, evaluation.

1 Introduction

Setting user experience (UX) goals, which are sometimes also referred to as UX targets, is a recently developed approach for designing products and services for certain kinds of experiences. While traditional usability goals focus on assessing how useful or productive a system is from product perspective, UX goals are concerned with how users experience a product from their own viewpoint [1]. Therefore, UX goals describe what kind of positive experiences the product should evoke in the user [2].

In product development, UX goals define the experiential qualities to which the design process should aim at [2,3]. In our view, the goals should guide experience-driven product development [4] in its different phases. The goals should be defined in the early stages of design and the aim should be that in later product development phases the goals are considered when designing and implementing the solutions of the product. In addition, when evaluating the designed product with users, it should be assessed whether the originally defined UX goals are achieved with it.

R. Shumaker and S. Lackey (Eds.): VAMR 2014, Part II, LNCS 8526, pp. 366–377, 2014.

In the evaluation of UX goals in the case study reported in this paper, we have utilized a case-based reasoning method called Usability Case (UC). For details about the UC method, see for example [5]. In order to test empirically how the method suits the evaluation of UX goals, we used it to conduct an evaluation of UX goals of a remote operator station (ROS) user interface (UI) for container crane operation. Next, the details of the evaluation study case and the utilized UC method are described.

2   The Evaluation Study Case

Our case study was carried out as a part of a research and development project of a novel ROS for container gantry crane operation in port yards. These kinds of remote operation systems exist already in some ports of the world and are used for example for the landside road truck loading zone operation of semi-automated stacking cranes.

Both safety and UX aspects motivated the case study. Firstly, taking safety aspects into account is naturally important in traditional on-the-spot port crane operation as people's lives can be in danger. However, it becomes even more important when operating the crane remotely, because the operator is not physically present in the operation area and for example, visual, auditory, and haptic information from the object environment is mediated through a technical system. Secondly, although UX has traditionally not been in the focus of complex work systems development, it has recently been discussed as a factor to be taken into account in this domain also (e.g., [6]).

Hence, the aim of our project was to explore ways to enhance the UX of the remote crane operators by developing a novel ROS operation concept, which also takes into account the required safety aspects. To achieve this aim, we defined UX goals and user requirements based on an earlier field study by us. The field study (for details, see [7]) was conducted in two international ports and included operator interviews and field observations of their work. The UX goals were created in the beginning of the project and then utilized in guiding the design work throughout the development of the new ROS. In addition, altogether 72 user requirements (when counting both main and sub requirements) were defined and connected to the created UX goals.

The overall UX theme for the new ROS was defined to be 'hands-on remote operation experience'. The four UX goals to realize this theme were chosen after a deliberate process to be 'experience of safe operation', 'sense of control', 'feeling of presence', and 'experience of fluent co-operation'. Details about how these goals were chosen and what they mean in practice regarding the developed system can be found in [2] and [3]. In the evaluation study of the ROS reported in this paper, the experience of fluent co-operation goal could not be included as the functionalities supporting co-operation between different actors in operations were not yet implemented to the ROS prototype and the participants conducted the operations individually.

The main objectives of the conducted evaluations were twofold. Firstly, we wanted to compare the user experience of two optional ROS user interface concepts, which were developed during the project. Secondly, we strived to receive data from the evaluations on how well the UX goals experience of safe operation, sense of control, and feeling of presence are fulfilled with the current ROS prototype system.

2.1   The Study Setting

The evaluations were conducted with a simulator version of the ROS system, which was operated with two industrial joysticks and a tablet computer (see Fig. 1 for a concept illustration). A 32-inch display placed on the operator's desk provided the main operating view, which included virtual reality (VR) camera views and simulated, but realistic operational data (e.g., parameters related to the weight of a container).

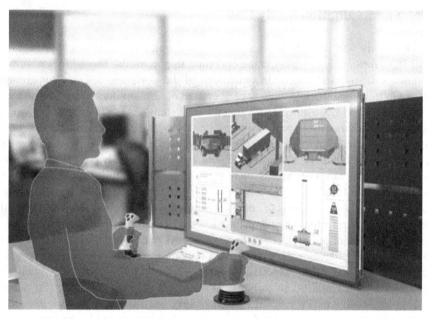

Fig. 1. Concept illustration of the ROS system with the four-view setup in the main display

The main display's user interface consisted of camera views and operational data provided by the system. In this display, two different user interface setups were implemented to the virtual prototype: a four-view (see Fig. 1 for a simplified concept illustration version) and a two-view setup. Wireframe versions of the layouts of these two user interface setups for the main operating display can be seen in Fig. 2.

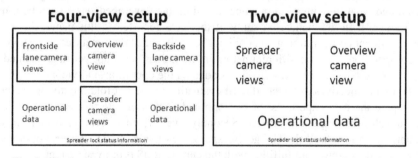

Fig. 2. Wireframe versions of the two alternative main display setups of the concepts

Operation Tasks in Remote Container Crane Operation. Semi-automated gantry cranes in ports are operated manually for example when lifting or lowering containers from and to road trucks, which are visiting the port. These operations happen physically in a specific area called the loading zone. The cranes are operated manually from an ROS after the spreader (device in the cranes used for lifting and lowering the containers) reaches a certain height in the loading zone during the otherwise automated operation. The remote operator utilizes real-time data and loading zone cameras to ensure that the operation goes safely and smoothly.

User Interface of the Four-view Setup. The user interface of the four-view setup (Fig. 1) included four distinct camera views: 1) overview camera view (top-middle), 2) spreader camera view (bottom-middle) that combined pictures of the four cameras attached to the corners of the spreader, 3) frontside lane camera views (top-left), and 4) backside lane camera views (top-right). Both of the lane camera views combined two video feeds from the corners of the truck into one unified view. Three separate camera views could be changed to the overview camera view: an area view (seen in the top-middle view of Fig. 1), a trolley view (a camera shooting downwards from the trolley), and a booth view (a camera showing the truck driver's booth in the loading zone). On the left and right side of the spreader camera view, different types of operational data were displayed.

User Interface of the Two-View Setup. The user interface of the two-view setup (see Fig. 2) consisted of only two, but larger camera views than in the four-view setup: the spreader camera view on the top-left side and the overview camera view on the top-right side. Both of these views could be easily changed to show the relevant camera view at each phase of the task. To the left-side view, also the lane camera views could be chosen. To the right-side view, the aforementioned area, trolley and booth views could be chosen. Under the camera views, there were several crane parameters and different status information displayed in a slightly different order than in the four-view setup.

Control Devices of the Concepts. The joystick functions of the two- and the four-view concepts varied. In the joystick functions of the four-view concept, the left joystick's functions were related to the overview camera (e.g., zoom, pan, and tilt) and for moving the trolley or the gantry. The right joystick was used for special spreader functions such as trim, skew, opening/closing the twist locks (that keep the container attached from its top corners to the spreader), and moving the spreader up- and downwards.

In the two-view concept, the joystick functions were optimized for the operation of the two camera views: the left joystick had controls related to the spreader view (e.g., skew and moving the spreader) and the right joystick to the overview view (e.g., the aforementioned camera operations).

On the tablet, located between the joysticks, there were functions for example for changing the different camera views: in the four-view concept there was only a possibility to change the top-middle overview view while in the two-view concept it was possible to change both the left and right side camera views. In addition, the received task could be canceled during operation or finalized after operation from the tablet.

2.2   Participants

In total, six work-domain experts were recruited as participants for the evaluation study. Three of them had previous experience in remote crane operation. All subjects were familiar with the operation of different traditional container cranes: two of them had over ten years of experience of operating different types of industrial cranes, three of them had 1-5 years of experience, and one of them had 6-10 years of experience.

2.3   Test Methods

In order to evaluate how the originally defined UX goals and user requirements are fulfilled with the evaluated prototype, we used a combination of different methods. During a one evaluation session, the participant was first interviewed about his experience and opinions regarding crane operation. Then, the participant was introduced to the developed prototype system and asked to conduct different operational tasks with the two alternative concepts of the system.

The test tasks included container lifting and landing operations to and from road trucks in varying simulated conditions. The first task was for training purposes and included a very basic pick-up operation; its aim was to learn to use the controls and the simulator after a short introduction to them. To support the joystick operation, the participants received a piece of paper describing the function layouts of the joysticks.

The other operation tasks were more challenging than the first one, and included different disruptive factors, such as for example strong wind, nearly similarly colored container chassis as the container to be landed, other containers in the surrounding lanes, a truck driver walking in the loading zone, and a locked chassis pin. These tasks were conducted with both of the concepts, but not in the same order.

The two different concepts (the four- and the two-view concepts) were tested one at a time. The order of starting with the two-view or with the four-view concept was counterbalanced. Therefore, every other user started first with the two-view concept and every other with the four-view concept.

A short semi-structured interview was conducted after each operational task. In addition, two separate questionnaires were used to gather information: the first one about the user experience and the second one about the systems usability [8] of the concepts. The UX questionnaire consisted of twelve user experience statements that were scaled with a 5-point Likert scale. The UX questionnaire was filled in when the test participants had completed all the tasks with either of the concepts. Ultimately, the UX questionnaire was filled in regarding both of the concepts.

In the end of the test session, some general questions related to the concepts were asked before the participants were requested to select the concept that they preferred and that in their opinion had a better user experience. Finally, a customized systems usability (see e.g., [8]) questionnaire was filled in for the selected concept. The systems usability questionnaire included thirty-one statements that were also scaled with a five-point Likert scale. Due to space restrictions, neither of the abovementioned questionnaires is presented in detail in this paper.

The test leader asked the participants to think-aloud [9], if possible, while executing the operation tasks. The think-aloud protocol was utilized to make it easier for the researchers to understand how the participants actually experience the developed concept solutions. The evaluation sessions were video recorded to aid data analysis.

2.4   Analysis

The ultimate aim of the evaluations was to assess whether the chosen UX goals were fulfilled with the VR prototype version of the system. To do this, we utilized the Usability Case method, because we wanted to explore the suitability of the method for this kind of research. UC provides a systematic reasoning tool and reference for gathering data of the technology under design and for testing its usability in the targeted work [10]. The method applies a case-based reasoning approach, similar to the Safety Case method [11]. Throughout the development process, the UC method creates an accumulated and documented body of evidence that provides convincing and valid arguments of the degree of usability of a system for a given application in a given environment [5]. The main elements of UC are: 1) *claim(s)* (nine main claims of systems usability [8], of which three are related particularly to UX) that describe an attribute of the system in terms of usability (e.g., "User interface X is appropriate for task Y"), 2) *subclaim(s)* describing a subattribute of the system that contributes to the main claim (e.g., "X should work efficiently), 3) *argument(s)* that provides ground for analyzing the (sub)claims (e.g., "It is possible to quickly reach the desired result with X"), and 4) *evidence*, which is the data that provides either positive or negative proof for the argument(s) (e.g., task completion times in usability tests) [5].

In line with the UC method, the data gathered from our studies was carefully analyzed regarding each defined user requirement (i.e., a subclaim in UC) on whether positive or negative cumulative evidence was found about the fulfillment of each requirement. This fulfilment was based on the arguments derived from the evidence. On the basis of the fulfilment of different user requirements, it was possible to determine whether a certain UX goal (i.e., a claim in UC) is fulfilled or not. If most of the user requirements connected to a certain goal were met, then also the UX goal could be said to have been fulfilled. In addition to this kind of evidence-based reasoning, the UC method also provided us with data on the usability and UX of the concepts under evaluation. These results support the design work by providing feedback for future development.

3   Results

The results of our studies are presented in the following order: First, we present general user experience and usability related results that affected the chosen UX goals regarding both the four- and the two-view concepts. Then, we discuss which of the concepts the participants chose in the end of the test sessions and why. Finally, we discuss whether the defined UX goals were fulfilled and make hypotheses on what were the underlying reasons for these results.

3.1   Notes on General UX and Usability of the Concepts

Four-view Concept. In general, the participants felt that the information provided by the main display's four-view setup was appropriate and understandable: for example, the participants commented that the amount of presented camera views at once was suitable and most of the necessary information was available for the basic crane operations. However, some of the participants felt that for example information about possible fault conditions concerning the crane were missing from the current solution.

While performing the test tasks, the participants utilized most frequently the area and the spreader camera views. The spreader camera view was experienced to be useful especially at the beginning of a lifting task. However, when the spreader approached the container, it became more difficult to understand the position of the spreader in relation to the container in detail. In addition, the participants thought that the provided lane camera views did not support the beginning phase of the container pick-up operations, because the participants could not clearly comprehend the orientation of the provided views until the spreader was seen moving in the views.

Regarding the joystick functions in the four-view concept, the placement of some functions was not reported to support the operations very well. For example, the positions of the skew and trim functions were not optimal, since participants made frequent mistakes with them and reported to get emotionally frustrated with them. In addition, the position of the zoom was proposed to be placed together with the steering functions, i.e., to be designed into the right-hand joystick.

The overall nature of the results of the UX questionnaire statements related to sense of control with the four-view concept was positive. The participants felt that they were able to start, conduct, and stop the operations at their own pace. In addition, according to the interviews, the provided joysticks were experienced to be suitable for the remote operation of cranes and the feel of the joysticks to be robust enough. Also, the crane's reactions to the joystick movements was experienced to be appropriate.

Nevertheless, the UX goal feeling of presence did not get as much supportive results as sense of control. This was mostly due to the problems identified with the solutions aimed to fulfil requirements concerning the operation view. For example, the four-view concept's camera views were experienced to be too small for the participants to easily see everything that was necessary. In addition, combining two camera views together (in the lane cameras) received negative evidence; the participants had difficulties to orientate themselves with the combined camera views and perceive to which direction each of the cameras was shooting at.

The experience of safe operation with the four-view setup was reported to be negatively affected by the presentation layout of the operational parameters. For example, the grouping of the information was not experienced to be in line with a typical task flow of one operation.

Two-view Concept. The two-view setup in the main display was generally experienced to be clearer than the four-view concept according to the participants' thinking-out-loud comments and interviews. For example, the camera views were found to be big enough to spot relevant things from the object environment. Especially the area view was utilized a lot during the operations, because it offered a possibility to see better the spreader in relation to the container.

With the two-view concept the users felt that all the needed operational information was available and in a logical order (i.e., in line with a typical task flow of one operation). The participants for example mentioned that it was possible to perceive easily the status of the operation with one glance from this information.

The UX questionnaire results concerning statements related to sense of control with the two-view concept were positive, mostly due to the same reasons as they were with the four-view concept. In addition, these results showed that the participants felt that they were able to concentrate on a sufficient level on performing their operations with the two-view concept.

However, the UX goal feeling of presence received somewhat negative results from the tests. For example, the participants had difficulties to perceive the operation view provided through the different combined camera views. As with the four-view setup, especially the views of the combined camera views of spreader and lane cameras were experienced to be hard to understand what is seen from them. In addition, the camera views were not reported to support the comprehension of depth and different distances between objects in the loading zone very well.

Furthermore, the results regarding requirements connected to the provided camera views were fairly negative. Some of the participants commented that due to the placement of the camera views they were not able to see critical objects related to the task at hand through the camera views in the outmost truck lanes; for example, it was not possible to see easily all corners of the container and the truck's position. These results had a significant effect to the experience of safe operation UX goal.

3.2 Concept Selection

When asked at the end of the test session that which of the two concepts the participant preferred, four of the participants selected the two-view concept and two of them chose the four-view concept. Based on the participants' experience, the two-view concept was easier to understand: it was reported to be effortless to observe the loading zone through the big camera views and the provided operational information was said to be placed in a logical order. However, according to the participants, some of the joystick functionalities were placed better in the four-view concept than in the two-view concept.

In general, it can also be said that the results of the systems usability questionnaire were fairly positive regarding the both concepts. These results were further utilized in the analysis of fulfillment of the defined user requirements and UX goals described in the next section.

3.3   Fulfilment of User Requirements and UX Goals

Most of the user requirements were not fulfilled on a comprehensive level with neither the four- nor the two-view setups of the current prototype system. Especially the evidence related to the user requirements that were connected to the UX goals experience of safe operation and feeling of presence was mostly negative. Therefore, it can be said that these two goals were not fulfilled with the current versions of the ROS's two- and four-view concepts.

The experience of safe operation was affected for example by the fact that the participants were not able to form a clear picture of the situation in the loading zone when handling the container in the outmost truck lanes. Therefore, they needed to manually adjust the cameras a lot in order to gain a better view to the position of the truck and corners of the container. In addition to the aforementioned factors, the overview camera was not experienced to be sharp enough (when zoomed in) for the participants to be able to see whether the truck's chassis' pins are locked or unlocked when starting a lifting operation. An obvious danger to safety from this problem is that if the pins are locked when starting a container lifting operation, also the truck will be lifted to the air with the container.

The feeling of presence UX goal was negatively affected for example by the fact that some of the camera views (e.g., lane cameras) were difficult for the participants to understand and orientate themselves into. Furthermore, understanding distances between different objects in the loading zone was not experienced to be sufficient with the current camera views. In addition, some of the default zooming levels of the cameras were not very optimal for the conducted task in question and the participants had to do a lot of manual zooming. In Fig. 3, we provide an example of the used Usability Case-based reasoning regarding negative evidence for one requirement connected to the UX goal feeling of presence.

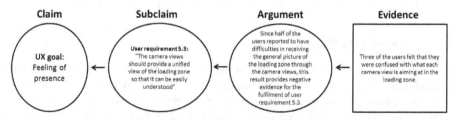

Fig. 3. Example of Usability Case based reasoning in our analysis.

The example of evidence in Fig. 3 was negative comments from three different participants while conducting the tasks with the ROS. In general, other than verbal evidence (the thinking-out-loud comments or the interview answers) provided by the participants were for example the results of the (UX and systems usability) questionnaires and task performance indicators. All this data was considered when creating the final Usability Case, which cannot be described here entirely due to its large size.

Regarding the sense of control UX goal, there was clear positive evidence in the end results from both of the concepts. For example, the utilized joysticks were felt to be robust enough and to control the crane with an appropriate feel of operation. Overall, the participants felt that they were able to master the crane's operations and concentrate on the task at hand. In addition, the possibilities to freely decide when to start and stop operating and to easily adjust the speed of operation with the joysticks were felt to be positive features. Therefore, it can be said that sense of control was achieved with both of the evaluated concepts.

4   Discussion

The results indicate that the evaluated concepts had both positive and negative aspects. The design of the final concept solution should be based on the positive aspects taken from both of the evaluated concepts. From the two-view concept, especially the placement of the operational data and size of the camera views should be adopted to the final concept. From the four-view concept, for example the layout of the joystick functions regarding the basic crane movements should be utilized.

In general, the results confirmed that providing real-time camera feeds for this kind of remote operation is essential. Visual validation of the situation in the object environment allows taking into consideration possible extra variables affecting the operation, such as weather conditions or debris on top of the container to be lifted up. Therefore, good quality camera views could support the experience of safe operation and feeling of presence goals with the final system.

The ecological validity of the prototype system also needs to be discussed as it may have had an effect to the UX goals. First, the fact that the operations with the system were not happening in reality, had an obvious effect on the participants' user experience and attitude towards the operations; if for example the people seen in the object environment would have been real human beings instead of virtual ones, the participants could have been more cautious with the operations. This fact had an obvious effect especially to the experience of safe operation UX goal.

Second, the virtual camera views cannot of course correspond to real camera views from the object environment. This had an obvious effect on the feeling of presence UX goal. However, it must be noted that some of the test participants thought that the virtual simulator was near equal to a real remote crane operation system, since the provided virtual camera views were implemented with such a good resolution. The simulator was also reported to provide a relatively precise feel of the operation, but did not for example have as much swaying of the container as it would have in real operations.

Third, the fact that in real life there are truck drivers with whom the operators communicate through the phone in case of problems affected the ecological validity of the conducted tasks. In addition, the participants conducted the tasks individually in a small room, which is not the case in real remote crane operation work. Therefore, as in real conditions the work is actually much more social than in our evaluation study, this had an obvious effect on the validity of the results of the studies.

5   Conclusions

The conducted study did not give an exact answer to the question, which one of the concepts should be selected for future development. Both concepts had positive factors that should be taken into account when designing the final system.

Different camera views provided essential information from the operating area. A decision concerning the amount of cameras in the loading zone and the camera views provided in the ROS needs to be made for the final concept to support safe crane operation. Another important factor is the size of the camera views in the main display. The two-view setup was experienced to have large enough views for the operation. A balance between the amount and size of the views presented in the user interface needs to be found. If the display space of a one monitor does not allow to present big enough camera views, then the possibility of two monitors needs to be considered.

To some extent, it was possible to evaluate the user experience of remotely operated crane operations with our virtual simulator even though the camera views were not real. However, the user experience of the system was not the same as if it was when operating in a real work environment. For example, the sounds, tones, or noises from the operating environment were not in the focus of the concept development or this evaluation study. In the final system's development, careful attention should be paid to the auditory information provided by the system from the object environment.

In general, as most of the user requirements related to the UX goals feeling of presence and experience of safe operation were not supported by the evidence from the evaluation studies, it can also be said that the originally defined main UX theme of 'hands-on remote operation experience' was not yet fulfilled with the current prototype system. In the future development, the requirements that were not met should be taken under careful investigation and answered with sufficient solutions. In this way, also the defined UX goals could be met better with the final system.

Nevertheless, the evidence from our study results supported the fulfillment of the UX goal sense of control for both of the concepts. Especially the feeling of the joystick operation and reactions of the crane were experienced to be appropriate and realistic. Support for aiming the spreader and the container to the correct position could enhance the sense of control even more in the future versions of the UI.

In the future development of the ROS, special attention should also be paid to the experience of fluent co-operation UX goal and different aspects related to it (e.g., the interaction between the co-workers and the truck drivers) as in the present study it was not possible to address this goal appropriately. Therefore, future studies with the system should include for example several test participants operating simultaneously with the system in order for the operational setting to be more realistic. To increase the ecological validity of the results, a more comprehensive study with a wider range of data inquiry methods could be carried out in a real control room setting with actual operators. This kind of a study could be conducted by adding some features of the proposed concept to the current, already implemented ROS solutions at some port and then evaluating whether the new features are useful and make the work more pleasant.

Methodologically, this paper has contributed to the discussion on how UX goals can be evaluated. According to the results, although the evaluated concepts were still in quite early stages of their design, the Usability Case method seemed to suit to this kind of UX goal evaluation with some modifications. Firstly, further work is needed especially on linking the arguments regarding the user requirements to the detailed design implications (for details see e.g., [3]) of the UX goals. Secondly, a scoring method for the evidence provided by study data should be implemented to the UC method in general, so that more emphasis could be placed on the data concerning the most critical parts of the evaluated product. Finally, it should be experimented whether other than the utilized data gathering methods could provide relevant data in constructing the Usability Case and studied how the method supports also later phases (than just the early-stage evaluation) of UX goal driven product development.

Acknowledgements. This research was carried out as part of the Finnish Metals and Engineering Competence Cluster (FIMECC)'s UXUS program. We would like to thank the participants of the evaluation sessions and our partners for the possibility to organize the evaluations.

References

1. Rogers, Y., Sharp, H., Preece, J.: Interaction Design: Beyond Human-Computer Interaction. John Wiley & Sons, Chichester (2011)
2. Karvonen, H., Koskinen, H., Haggrén, J.: Defining User Experience Goals for Future Concepts. A Case Study. In: Proc. NordiCHI2012 UX Goals Workshop, pp. 14–19 (2012)
3. Koskinen, H., Karvonen, H., Tokkonen, H.: User Experience Targets as Design Drivers: A Case Study on the Development of a Remote Crane Operation Station. In: Proc. ECCE 2013, article no. 25 (2013)
4. Hassenzahl, M.: Experience Design – Technology for All the Right Reasons. Morgan & Claypool (2010)
5. Liinasuo, M., Norros, L.: Usability Case - Integrating Usability Evaluations in Design. In: COST294-MAUSE Workshop, pp. 11–13 (2007)
6. Savioja, P., Liinasuo, M., Koskinen, H.: User experience: Does it matter in complex systems? Cognition, Technology & Work (2013) (online first)
7. Karvonen, H., Koskinen, H., Haggrén, J.: Enhancing the User Experience of the Crane Operator: Comparing Work Demands in Two Operational Settings. In: Proc. ECCE 2012, pp. 37–44 (2012)
8. Savioja, P., Norros, L.: Systems Usability Framework for Evaluating Tools in Safety-Critical Work. Cognition, Technology and Work 15(3), 1–21 (2013)
9. Bainbridge, L., Sanderson, P.: Verbal Protocol Analysis. In: Wilson, J., Corlett, E.N. (eds.) Evaluation of Human Work: A Practical Ergonomics Methodology, pp. 159–184. Taylor & Francis (1995)
10. Norros, L., Liinasuo, M., Savioja, P., Aaltonen, I.: Cope Technology enabled capacity for first responder. COPE project deliverable D2.3 (2010)
11. Bishop, P., Bloomfield, R.: A Methodology for Safety Case Development. In: Redmill, F., Anderson, T. (eds.) Industrial Perspectives of Safety-Critical Systems, pp. 194–203. Springer, London (1998)

Increasing the Transparency of Unmanned Systems: Applications of Ecological Interface Design

Ryan Kilgore and Martin Voshell

Charles River Analytics, Inc., Cambridge, MA, United States
{rkilgore,mvoshell}@cra.com

Abstract. This paper describes ongoing efforts to address the challenges of supervising teams of heterogeneous unmanned vehicles through the use of demonstrated Ecological Interface Design (EID) principles. We first review the EID framework and discuss how we have applied it to the unmanned systems domain. Then, drawing from specific interface examples, we present several generalizable design strategies for improved supervisory control displays. We discuss how ecological display techniques can be used to increase the transparency and observability of highly automated unmanned systems by enabling operators to efficiently perceive and reason about automated support outcomes and purposefully direct system behavior.

Keywords: Ecological Interface Design (EID), automation transparency, unmanned systems, supervisory control, displays.

1 Introduction

Unmanned systems play a critical and growing role in the maritime domain, with coordinated air and water vehicle teams supporting an increasing range of complex operations, ranging from military missions to disaster response and recovery. Traditionally, unmanned vehicle operators have served as teleoperators, monitoring video or other sensor feeds and controlling vehicle behaviors through continuous "stick-and-rudder"-type piloting commands. However, significant advances in platform and sensor automation (e.g., flight control systems; onboard navigation; hazard detection; wayfinding capabilities) have increasingly offloaded these lower-level control tasks. This has allowed operators to instead focus on higher-order supervisory control activities, paving the way for a single operator or small team of operators to simultaneously manage multiple vehicles.

Despite advances in autonomy, unmanned system operators are still faced with significant challenges. As in other domains where operators supervise highly complex and automated systems (e.g., nuclear power, air traffic control), the introduction of support automation does not allow operators to simply shed control tasks and their associated workload. Rather, this automation shifts the emphasis of operator tasks from continuous display tracking and physical control inputs to activities that focus on system monitoring and understanding, coordination, and troubleshooting. In the

R. Shumaker and S. Lackey (Eds.): VAMR 2014, Part II, LNCS 8526, pp. 378–389, 2014.

case of managing autonomous vehicle teams, this supervisory role involves high cognitive workload, both in monitoring system performance and in supporting frequent re-planning and re-tasking in response to evolving mission needs and changes to the operational environment. These activities place significant demands on operators' taxed attentional resources and require operators to maintain detailed situation awareness to successfully detect and appropriately respond to changing conditions. Workload and potential for error is further increased when "strong and silent" automation support is not designed from inception to be observable by human users, making it difficult for operators to understand, predict, or control automated system behavior [1]. This typically results in users turning off or disregarding automated support tools or, paradoxically, completely trusting and over-relying upon automation even when it is insufficient [2].

The inherent challenges of supervisory control are further exacerbated by the growing size and heterogeneity of the unmanned vehicle teams themselves [3,4]. While automation provides significant support, operators of mixed-vehicle teams must still carefully consider and reason about the consequences of individual vehicle capabilities and performance parameters (e.g., platform speed, agility, fuel consumption and range; available onboard sensor and automation systems), as well as safety-critical differences (e.g., a specific vehicle's need to maintain a larger separation from other traffic due to its lack of onboard sense-and-avoid autonomy; the expected communication intermittencies and latencies for a long-duration underwater vehicle). Currently, much of these between-vehicle differences, and their associated mission impacts, are masked by opaque automation systems. This limits operators' ability to reason about platform differences and predict how these will uniquely affect mission performance. When such information is made available through operator interfaces, it is typically buried within individual vehicle specifications, accessible only through serial, "drill-down" exploration methods. More critically, this vehicle-specific information is rarely related to higher-order mission goals, nor is it presented in way that enables operators to anticipate or understand the behaviors of lower-level system automation. In this paper, we describe ongoing efforts to address these challenges by applying demonstrated principles of Ecological Interface Design [5,6].

2   Background

The effective supervision of complex and highly automated sociotechnical systems—of which unmanned vehicle teams are but one timely example—presents unique challenges to human operators. In light of this, highly specialized interfaces are required that enable operators to both: (1) readily perceive and reason about the critical functional connections across myriad system components; and then (2) expertly identify and execute strategies purposefully driving system behaviors. These interfaces must serve, in effect, to increase the transparency of otherwise opaque system automation and processes, providing operators with intuitive mechanisms for high-level understanding of, and interaction with, complex systems. Ecological Interface Design (EID) represents a promising and powerful approach to develop such interfaces.

The practice of EID stems from decades of applied research focused on understanding how expert knowledge workers monitor, identify problems, and select and execute response strategies in complex systems. While early applications typically focused on physical process systems, such as nuclear power generation and petrochemical refinement [9,10], the EID approach has been extended to settings as diverse as anesthesiology [11], military command and control [12], and the supervisory control of unmanned vehicles and robot teams [13,14]. The EID approach derives its name and underlying philosophy from theories of ecological visual perception [15], which propose that organisms in the natural world are able to directly perceive opportunities for action afforded by elements of their surrounding environment ("affordances") without the need for higher-order cognitive processing. Unlike cognitive, inferential activities—which are slow and error-prone—control actions or responses based on direct visual perception are effortless and can be performed rapidly without significant cognitive overhead.

EID techniques strive to capture similar intuitive affordances for control actions within highly automated and display-mediated systems, whose inner workings are otherwise fully removed and hidden from the operator. Within such complex technological systems, decision-critical attributes of the operational domain are typically described by abstract properties, such as procedural doctrine, physical laws, mathematical state equations, or meta-information attributes (e.g., uncertainty, pedigree, recency of available information), in addition to traditional data resources. In contrast to natural ecologies, these critical properties cannot be directly perceived and acted upon by human operators. For this reason, EID attempts to increase system transparency and observability to "make visible the invisible" [5], using graphical figures to explicitly map such abstract properties—and their tightly coupled relationships across system components, processes, and operational goals—to readily perceived visual characteristics of interface display elements (e.g., the thickness, angular orientation, or color of a line; the size or transparency of an icon).

Various tools and methodologies have been proposed to generate such visual mappings from underlying analyses of the cognitive work domain [6,16,17] and interface designers may also able to incorporate or otherwise adapt a wide variety of demonstrated, reusable ecological interface display components [6]. Purposefully designed arrangements of these simple display elements can facilitate direct perception of system state and support the rapid invocation of operator's highly automatic, skill- and rule-based control responses during normal operations. Also, because these graphics provide veridical, visual models of system dynamics across multiple levels of abstraction, they provide a useful scaffold for supporting deep, knowledge-based reasoning over system behavior during novel situations or fault response [8,18].

Our own work builds upon and extends previous applications of EID to the unmanned systems domain, focusing specifically on the challenges of enabling operators to supervise teams of heterogeneous unmanned vehicles. In these situations, differences in the operating characteristics of individual vehicles (e.g., platform capabilities and handling, available sensor systems, extent of onboard autonomy) can have a profound impact on how the operator must interpret system information and interact with individual team components. In the remainder of this paper, we describe our ongoing applications of the EID approach to the unmanned systems domain and discuss several exemplar design outcomes from this process.

3   Approach

The development of EID displays begins with a structured analysis of the work domain the interfaces are intended to support. Although specific approaches differ across the practitioner community, these underlying work domain analyses typically involve the development of an abstraction hierarchy model (AH) [18], often as part of a broader Cognitive Work Analysis (CWA) effort [5]. The AH structure provides a scaffold for representing the physical and intentional constraints that define what work can be accomplished within a technical system. An AH model describes these constraints across multiple levels of aggregation (e.g., system, subsystem, component) and functional abstraction. Connections between elements and across levels of abstraction in the model represent "means/ends" relationships, describing how individual, low-level system components relate to complex physical processes and the achievement of higher-order system goals. These maps closely correspond to the problem-solving strategies of system experts [18] and they are used to directly inform the underlying informational content and organizing structure of EID displays [6].

To ground our own design efforts, we have developed multiple models across the naval unmanned systems domain, including abstraction hierarchies that focus on teams of heterogeneous vehicles operating collaboratively within a single mission context. These models have explored a number of operational scenarios built upon emerging concepts of operations for collaborative vehicle teaming. As such, they feature a number of elements relevant to challenging supervisory control, including large numbers of mixed military and civilian vehicle types in a constrained physical space, manned/unmanned traffic mixing, and communication intermittency. In developing our domain models, we have collaborated extensively with subject matter experts, building upon an extensive foundation of prior knowledge elicitation efforts, cognitive task analyses, and simulation-based modeling efforts that our team has conducted within the heterogeneous unmanned systems domain (see [3,4]). Throughout these efforts, we have considered how the constraints imposed by complex, dynamic operational environments affect the ability of a team of vehicles with varying capabilities to support mission goals. We have also explored operators' need to understand and purposefully direct automation, particularly when interacting with vehicle tasking and route planning tools in dynamic operating environments with significant and shifting operational hazards, including weather and traffic.

Building upon these AH models, we have applied EID techniques to identify and explore methods to integrate displays of relevant system information (e.g., airspace, bathymetry, and terrain maps; sensor data; vehicle health and status; weather reports; threat conditions; target locations), and automated planning products (e.g., vehicle routing and task assignments; alternative plan options; safety alerts) in ways that facilitate operators' awareness and deep understanding of critical system interactions, as well as constraints and affordances for control. The outputs of these analytical efforts led to descriptions of key cognitive tasks and interaction requirements. These products drove multiple loops of design, prototyping, and evaluation activities, which allowed us to rapidly assess the technical risk and feasibility of emerging design concepts, while simultaneously gaining feedback from domain experts and potential users. Key findings from these design efforts are described below.

4   Ecological Design Strategies for Automation Transparency

Based on the modeling activities described above, we designed and prototyped a series of ecological mission display concepts for supervising heterogeneous unmanned vehicle teams in a variety of operational contexts. These concepts ranged from individual, task-specific display forms (e.g., a widget optimized for managing available fuel considerations when addressing pop-up tasking; a multi-vehicle mission timeline) to full workspaces that incorporate and coordinate such display components within navigable views that can be tailored to address specific mission configurations and operator roles. Across these efforts, we have applied general EID design heuristics (see [6] for a comprehensive primer) to address the specific operator support needs, information requirements, and underlying functional structures gleaned from our domain analyses. The resultant interface solutions have been tailored to particular missions, vehicle configurations, and operator tasks. However, they also highlight a number of generalizable design strategies for increasing the transparency of unmanned systems, much as prior EID literature has provided similar exemplars for the process control and medical domains [6]. A subset of these applied EID strategies is discussed here.

4.1   Increasing the Perceptual Availability of Task-Critical Information

One of the key challenges facing supervisory controllers is that of understanding and confirming (or recognizing the need to intervene and adapt) automated decision outcomes, such as vehicle tasking or path planning. To do this effectively—and avoid automation evaluation errors that can lead to surprise or disuse [7]—operators must recognize and efficiently access the key system variables that affect automated outcomes. Unfortunately, geospatial (map) displays, which are the dominant frame of reference for most supervisory control interfaces, do not comprehensively support this need. Geospatial displays excel at conveying spatial constraints, as seen in Figure 1(a), where an automated path plan (blue line) can be intuitively perceived as avoiding a navigational threat (red circle) on its way to a target. However, when automation outcomes are driven by constraints that are not directly spatial in nature (such as the time it would take for a vehicle to reach a location, or the ability of a vehicle's onboard hardware to support a specific sensing task), typical geospatial display approaches are insufficient to support operator understanding. As seen in Figure 1(b), it may not be readily apparent why an automated planner has chosen to route a particular vehicle to a target when other vehicles are physically much closer.

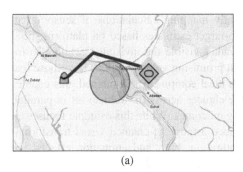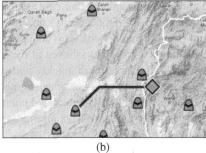

(a)   (b)

Fig. 1. (a) When key planning constraints are spatial in nature, automated planner outputs may be intuitively presented in a map display; (b) However, when key constraints are not directly spatial (e.g., the travelling speed of a vehicle; the efficacy of onboard sensor payloads), map-based displays of automated outcomes are much less intuitive

In geospatial displays that use standard military symbology (MIL-STD-2525C; [19]) vehicle icons typically encode only spatial locations and gross platform differences (e.g., whether a vehicle is friendly or foe, ground or air-based, fixed-wing or rotary). In this case, to understand how individual vehicle differences have affected an automated tasking response, the operator must perform multiple drill-down searches through vehicle details, for example clicking on individual vehicles to identify their sensor payloads and travel speeds, as in Figure 2(a). With this approach, the operator must mentally consider and compare other vehicles to the one selected by the automation, using a serial exploration process that is time consuming and places a significant load on working memory.

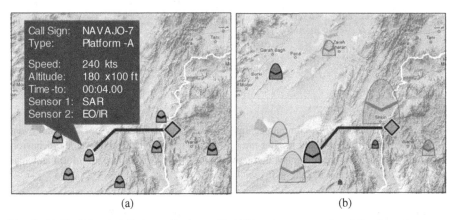

(a)   (b)

Fig. 2. (a) Traditional drill-down display, with hidden data accessed serially through pop-up windows; (b) An example of an ecological display alternative, with data provided in parallel through explicit visual cues—in this case *time-to-location* coded as icon size, and *sensor efficacy* coded as icon opacity

In contrast, ecological display approaches, such as Figure 2(b), can support operators' direct perception of the non-spatial considerations that led to an automated planner's decision—in this case, by visually mapping calculations of sensor/target pairing efficacy (icon opacity) and time-to-target estimates based on platform speed and distance (icon size). This mapping "makes visible the invisible," while also increasing the perceptual salience of the most promising vehicle options (i.e., those that can get to the target both quickly *and* with ideal equipment). Combined, this enables the operator to rapidly consider alternative choices across the vehicle set in parallel, and intuitively interpret automated planning outcomes. While this example focuses on geospatial displays, we have similarly applied a range of chained visual transformations (including manipulations of hue, saturation, blur, and animation effects; see [20]) across mission timelines, asset/task link diagrams, and health and status views.

Beyond visually encoding the key system and environmental attributes that drive automation outcomes, we have also explored methods to visually represent automated behaviors themselves, and particularly the ways in which these may differ across heterogeneous vehicle teams. For example, differences in platform type and onboard sensing and processing capabilities may have profound impact on how different vehicles within a team may respond to abnormal events, such as a lost communications link. While better-equipped vehicles may be able to continue autonomously for some time on a pre-filed course in the absence of communications, it is also typical for many vehicles to continue at their current heading and altitude indefinitely, or to abandon an established flight plan after only a short period time and proceed directly to a pre-configured emergency landing location.

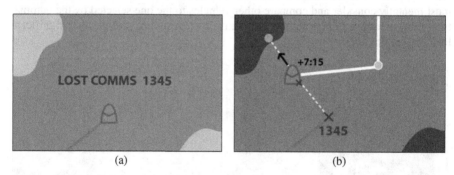

(a)   (b)

Fig. 3. (a) A typical display, communicating only the location (and time) of a critical event (e.g., lost communications), and forcing the operator to reason about future vehicle behavior; (b) Example of an ecological display alternative, using explicit visual cues to inform and augment the operator's mental modeling of vehicle state

Unfortunately, if they show anything at all, supervisory control displays often simply reflect the location, and possibly time, of a system state change (e.g., a comms link switching from "active" to "lost"), and not the *impact* of this event, as in Figure 3(a). This forces the operator to anticipate how the particular vehicle will respond to this new situation and invites significant opportunity for operator surprise in the event of an incorrect or misapplied mental model [1]. In contrast, an ecological approach such as that shown in Figure 3(b) increases system transparency by explicitly representing the processes governing system behavior. In this particular example, the display not only indicates the lost communications event time and location, but also explicitly represents anticipated behavior based on the vehicle's loaded operating protocol (proceeding directly to a an emergency landing site), the estimated progress against that plan in the time since the event, *and* the expected behavior should communications be regained (an immediate redirection to the next waypoint).

4.2   Presenting Information in Context

Beyond simply increasing the perceptual availability of task-critical information, ecological design techniques emphasize situating this information in context. As with more traditional process control systems [9,10], unmanned system displays benefit when health-and-status and automated planning outcomes (e.g., available pounds of fuel; engine speed; altitude; time-on-station) are provided against the framing of expected values, nominal minimum/maximum ranges, and critical limits (e.g., total fuel capacity and minimum-remaining fuel requirements; normal and red-line RPM levels; aircraft flight performance envelopes). Additionally, useful temporal context can be provided by showing changes in data values over time (e.g., a trailing graph of engine pressure) or calculating and then graphically representing instantaneous rates of change ("engine temperature is 280 degrees, but RISING RAPIDLY") Such visual depictions of range and temporal context aid the operator in interpreting how current system operations compare to expected behaviors and critical safety boundaries, and support timely perception of when such boundaries may be breached.

Supervisory control displays can also be improved by presenting information attributes not only within the context of their own expected limits, but also within the context of other information that pertains to related system functions (with the structure of these relationships identified through the previously described AH modeling process [5,6]). Unfortunately, many supervisory control displays artificially disperse related system information over discrete, stovepiped views (e.g., maps, timelines, health-and-status dashboards), both as a matter of convention and convenience. This approach inadvertently serves to mask critical relationships that occur across view boundaries—for example, relationships such as those between engine RPM, altitude, wind speed, and the aeronautical distance of a mission leg, all of which directly impact fuel consumption and, with it, available time on station.

In contrast, EID methods purposefully seek to integrate these diverse representation modalities within coordinated display perspectives that explicitly reflect these complex relationships. Figure 4(b) shows how such an approach could support common fuel or power management tasks (which are often performed in-the-head during re-plan, relying on heuristics and estimations that are subject to calculation error). The left-most image depicts estimated fuel to be consumed by each leg of the mission flight (green shaded segments) against the context of overall fuel capacity (full set of squares), the amount of fuel that is currently available (sum of all shaded squares), anticipated fuel reserves (dark grey), and the minimum amount remaining reserve fuel that is required by mission safety doctrine (red line). If this particular vehicle is allocated to a pop-up task (center image), the fuel cost of this activity is added to the display (indicated by light blue squares) and the total fuel consumption is visibly pushed beyond the minimum safe reserve amount required (indicated by red squares). As the operator directly manipulates elements of a coordinated mission plan display (not shown here, but see Figure 6 for an example)—perhaps by increasing the altitude of the first mission leg and reducing the travel speed of the third—the efficiency gains anticipated by these changes are represented directly within the context of the fuel display. The coordinated behaviors enable the operator to intuitively sense of the maximum gains to be had in manipulating attributes of a particular mission leg, as well as when the combined impact of some set of changes is sufficient to overcome the negative impact of the pop-up task on the fuel safety margin.

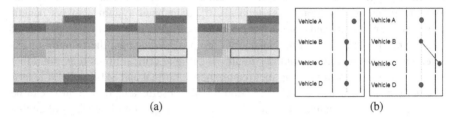

(a)   (b)

Fig. 4. (a) Example of an ecological fuel management display (left), showing the relative impact of a pop-up tasks on available fuel reserves (center), as well as efficiency gains as altitude and time-on-station variables are manipulated in a coordinated flight plan display (not pictured); (b) Example of an ecological mission coordination display, showing the relative impact of two different vehicle retasking options on overall team and mission efficacy as these plan alternatives are selected on a map (not pictured)

In a similar example of context, Figure 4(b) shows a mission coordination display that presents the relative timing vehicle activities with respect to established goals and windows of opportunity. Continuing the example of the pop-up task, automated recommendations for vehicle-retasking strategies (and their resultant path plan modifications) may be depicted in a map view (not shown here). As the operator explores alternative retasking plans by selecting them in the map view, this coordinated display provides a depiction of the relative impact on current vehicle tasking, against the temporal context of acceptable servicing windows (e.g., the time during which the current tasks must be completed for the mission to be of value). In this example, assigning Vehicle A to the new pop-up (left) results in a delay to the primary mission, but one that is within acceptable bound. In contrast, assigning vehicle C not only pushes that vehicle's primary task out of the acceptable window, it *also* negatively impacts vehicle B, which must perform a coordinated task within a similar period of time). Such explicit context enables the operator to readily assess automated behaviors.

4.3   Managing Operator Attention

One of the central design strategies of EID is to create display figures whose emergent visual behaviors—driven by mapping graphical sub-elements of the figures to specific low-level attributes of the dynamic work-domain—reflect higher-order system properties [5,6]. When designed well, these mappings (which can be as simple as the scale and opacity icon transformation strategies shown in Figure 2b) modulate the perceptual salience of elements across the display, automatically directing the operator's attention towards critical system process information and causing less critical information to recede into the background.

An example of this salience mapping approach can be seen in Figure 5 (a), where a vehicle is traveling out of the range of its primary emergency landing site, at which point the operator must confirm a secondary site. When this transition point is far in the future, the boundary is flagged as a simple stroke across the planned path. As the vehicle approaches this point, however, the stroke gradually grows in size and salience, and additional cues (all of which would otherwise clutter up the display) are incrementally added to increase the salience of the pending alert, clarify the specific nature of the alert type, and recommend a secondary sight for selection, as in Figure 5(b).

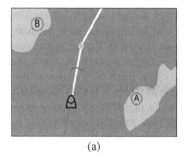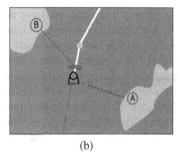

| (a) | (b) |

Fig. 5. Example of an ecological display using variable perceptual salience cues to direct operator attention while managing clutter; (a) a simple marker (green arc) flags an upcoming event boundary; (b) as the vehicle approaches the marker (both in space, and in time) the cue becomes more salient and additional information regarding the anticipated automation behavior is provided—in this case signaling that the aircraft is about to head out of range of the primary emergency landing location and the operator must confirm a secondary location

Unfortunately, it is impractical to support all management of operator attention through emergent display features—both because display designs would quickly become overwhelmingly complex, and because not all requirements for directing operator attention can be known *a priori*. Through our interactions with operators—both during our analyses of the work domain and in our subsequent walkthroughs of our design prototypes—we learned that it is often the relative amount of time until key events (e.g., "check the available fuel and confirm the emergency landing site location *when we are five minutes outside of the search area*") that is more critical to cueing and directing operator attention than absolute timing (e.g., "check the fuel *at 1345*"), particularly when the future time in question is not easily calculated from available display information. This is particularly true in directing operators' prospective memory, or the memory to recall and perform a task in the future. Unfortunately, supervisory control displays rarely capture and manage such relative times explicitly. Instead, they must be calculated and then later recalled by the operator, often via physical reminders, such as Post-it Notes. In addition to being error prone under high-workload settings, these methods are divorced from the actual supervisory control information system and thus become inaccurate (or irrelevant) when changes occur to vehicle plans or in the environment (e.g., an unanticipated headwind aloft adds 30 minutes of travel time to the search area).

Fig. 6. Example of a prospective memory aid in the context of a mission timeline/altitude display; the operator has chosen to pin a notification not to a specific mission time, but rather a relative one—in this case the traversal of a marked airspace (purple shading)

To address this need, we have designed a number of light-weight interaction methods that enable operators to readily establish and manipulate such relative-time reminders within the display itself. For example, as shown in Figure 6, the operator can select an element within a timeline display—such as a waypoint, or a marked airspace that is being traversed—and with a single click, pin a notification to the start of that event, regardless of the absolute mission time at which it occurs. Similarly, the operator can leave reminders by interacting with route plans, waypoints, or other objects across the display (e.g., selecting a distance or time range from a location pin on a map), aiding their future recall to perform critical control tasks.

5   Conclusions

This paper has presented the results of several recent and ongoing efforts to improve the transparency of unmanned system automation through the design of ecological supervisory control displays. Although this work has focused on supporting specific missions, vehicle teams, and operator tasks within the maritime domain, we believe that many of the display concepts described may be generally applied to the design of supervisory control tools for heterogeneous unmanned systems. As such, we hope these concepts provide useful resources for other developers of unmanned systems. We are currently undertaking an effort to further refine these and other related design concepts, as well as to formally evaluate their utility in enabling operators to more efficiently and effectively supervise heterogeneous teams of unmanned vehicles. Based on the outcomes of these evaluations, we hope to leverage our efforts to guide capabilities requirements and design guidelines for new and emerging unmanned vehicle control systems, such as the Navy's Common Control Station.

Acknowledgements. This material is based upon work supported by the NAVAIR under Contract No. N68335-13-C-0408 and by the ONR under Contract No. N00014-10-C-0289. Any opinions, findings and conclusions or recommendations expressed in this material are those of the author(s) and do not necessarily reflect the views of NAVAIR or ONR.

References

1. Sarter, N.B., Woods, D.D.: How in the world did we ever get into that mode? Mode error and awareness in supervisory control. Human Factors 37(1), 5–19 (1995)
2. Parasuraman, R., Riley, V.: Humans and automation: Use, misuse, disuse, abuse. Human Factors 39(2), 230–253 (1997)
3. Kilgore, R.M., Harper, K.A., Nehme, C., Cummings, M.L.: Mission planning and monitoring for heterogeneous unmanned vehicle teams: A human-centered perspective. In: AIAA Infotech@ Aerospace Conference in Sonoma, CA (2007)
4. Nehme, C.E., Kilgore, R.M., Cummings, M.L.: Predicting the impact of heterogeneity on unmanned-vehicle team performance. In: Proceedings of the Human Factors and Ergonomics Society Annual Meeting, vol. 52(13). SAGE Publications (2008)
5. Vicente, K.J., Rasmussen, J.: The ecology of human-machine systems II: Mediating 'direct perception' in complex work domains. Ecological Psychology 2, 207–250 (1990)
6. Burns, C.M., Hajdukiewicz, J.: Ecological interface design. CRC Press (2004)
7. Dzindolet, M.T., Peterson, S.A., Pomranky, R.A., Pierce, L.G., Beck, H.P.: The role of trust in automation reliance. Int. J. of Human-Compt. Studies 58(6), 697–718 (2004)
8. Vicente, K.J.: Cognitive work analysis: Toward safe, productive, and healthy computer-based work. CRC Press (1999)
9. Itoh, J., Sakuma, A., Monta, K.: An ecological interface for supervisory control of BWR nuclear power plants. Control Engineering Practice 3(2), 231–239 (1995)
10. Jamieson, G.A., Vicente, K.J.: Ecological interface design for petrochemical applications: Supporting operator adaptation, continuous learning, and distributed, collaborative work. Computers & Chemical Engineering 25(7), 1055–1074 (2001)
11. Watson, M., Russell, W.J.: Sanderson, P.: Anesthesia monitoring, alarm proliferation, and ecological interface design. Australian J. of Info. Systms 7(2), 109–114 (2000)
12. Hall, D.S., Shattuck, L.G., Bennett, K.B.: Evaluation of an Ecological Interface Design for Military Command and Control. J. of Cognitive Engineering and Decision Making 6(2), 165–193 (2012)
13. Linegang, M.P., Stoner, H.A., Patterson, M.J., Seppelt, B.D., Hoffman, J.D., Crittendon, Z.B., Lee, J.D.: Human-automation collaboration in dynamic mission planning: A challenge requiring an ecological approach. In: Proceedings of the Human Factors and Ergonomics Society Annual Meeting, vol. 50(23), pp. 2482–2486 (2006)
14. Furukawa, H.: An ecological interface design approach to human supervision of a robot team. In: Autonomous Robots and Agents, pp. 163–170. Springer, Berlin (2007)
15. Gibson, J.J.: The ecological approach to visual perception. Routledge (1986)
16. Reising, D.V.C., Sanderson, P.M.: Designing displays under ecological interface design: Towards operationalizing semantic mapping. In: Proceedings of the Human Factors and Ergonomics Society Annual Meeting, vol. 42(3), pp. 372–376. SAGE Publications (1998)
17. Kilgore, R., St-Cyr, O.: The SRK inventory: A tool for structuring and capturing a worker competencies analysis. In: Proceedings of the Human Factors and Ergonomics Society Annual Meeting, vol. 50(3), pp. 506–509. SAGE Publications (2006)
18. Rasmussen, J.: The role of hierarchical knowledge representation in decision making and system management. IEEE Transactions on Systems, Man and Cybernetics (2), 234–243 (1985)
19. Department of Defense: MIL-STD-2525C: Common Warfighting Symbology (2008)
20. Bisantz, A.M., Pfautz, J., Stone, R., Roth, E.M., Thomas-Meyers, G., Fouse, A.: Assessment of Display Attributes for Displaying Meta-information on Maps. In: Proceedings of the Human Factors & Ergonomics Society Annual Meeting, vol. 50(3), pp. 289–293 (2006)

Collaborative Visualization of a Warfare Simulation Using a Commercial Game Engine

Hyungki Kim[1], Yuna Kang[1], Suchul Shin[1], Imkyu Kim[2], and Soonhung Han[2]

[1] Department of Mechanical Engineering, KAIST, Korea
{diskhkme,balbal86,eva317}@kaist.ac.kr
[2] Department of Ocean Systems Engineering, KAIST, Korea
{kimimgoo,shhan}@kaist.ac.kr

Abstract. The requirement about reusable 3D visualization tool was continuously raised in various industries. Especially in the defense modeling and simulation field, there are abundant researches about reusable and interoperable visualization system, since it has a critical role to the efficient decision making by offering diverse validation and analyzing process. Also to facilitate the effectiveness, many current operating systems are applying VR(Virtual Reality) and AR(Augmented Reality) technologies aggressively. In this background, we conducted the research about the design for the collaborative visualization environment for the warfare simulation through commercial game engine. We define the requirements by analyzing advantages and disadvantages of existing tools or engines like SIMDIS or Vega, and propose the methods how to utilize the functionalities of commercial game engine to satisfy the requirements. The implemented prototype offers collaborative visualization environment inside the CAVE environment, which is the facility for immersive virtual environment, by cooperating with handheld devices.

Keywords: 3D Visualization, Game Engine, Warfare Simulation, Collaborative Visualization Environment.

1 Introduction

At present, 3D visualization tools are employed both directly and indirectly in research fields that require intuitive analysis and accurate data validation. A well-known application can be found in the product design field, which moved on to the 3D CAD (computer-aided design) system from paper drawings. Moreover, in the pre-manufacturing stage, the manufacturing process can now be simulated and analyzed based on the 3D visualization environment. The process based on this type of 3D-visualization-oriented analysis and validation has better effects compared to the use of traditional values or parameter-based reports of the result [1]. The requirements of 3D visualization techniques in the defense modeling and simulation field also can be estimated, as current commercial battle lab systems actively include 3D visualization functions, as do training simulators, which inherently require 3D visualization capabilities.

R. Shumaker and S. Lackey (Eds.): VAMR 2014, Part II, LNCS 8526, pp. 390–401, 2014.

However, there are several issues that require attention when adopting 3D visualization in the defense modeling and simulation fields. The main obstacle is related to the time and cost required for development. The characteristics of defense modeling and simulation systems are such that interoperability is mandatory, as new systems are frequently developed at relatively high costs. Interoperability can suppress the duplicated costs incurred during the development, interoperation and maintenance of the system. On the other hand, interoperability is closely related to reusability, as reusability is ensured if the interoperability requirement is satisfied to a certain level.

In this research, our goal is to develop an efficient decision-making environment between experts by providing the 3D visualization result of a warfare simulation. This is termed here a collaborative visualization environment. The proposed collaborative visualization environment is a limited concept stemming from the CVE (collaborative virtual environment) in its physical space as a CAVE (cave automatic virtual environment). Because the CAVE is intended to provide an immersive environment through a high-resolution multi-channel visualization system, it provides a satisfactory user experience. However, the system is usually designed for a single user with one shared screen. Therefore, we provide a collaborative visualization environment by adopting already widespread personal devices, in this case the smartphone and tablet. The interoperability and reusability problem is addressed simultaneously with the visualization quality and collaborative issues.

2   Related Research

The related researches and cases can be divided into three categories based on the interoperability level. The researches for the first category are the system dependent development cases which is widespread method in the current operating simulators. The researches belonging to the second categories are the works based on the HLA(High Level Architecture)/RTI(Run-Time Infrastructure), which is IEEE 1516 standard. The researches for the third categories are proposing the custom data structure considering the reusability issue with performance improvement.

At first, the common approach in the various systems is developing the integrated structure with simulator and visualization module. In [2], the large scale visualization system is adopted for the digital mock-up and driving simulation of the evaluation process in the maglev business. The Ogre3D engine was used for 3D visualization in this research, based on the classification and comparison between diverse graphics engines and toolkits. In [3], the simulation architecture was proposed based on the visualization engine for the real-time visualization of the defense simulation system. Also by providing the plug-in functions to manipulate the visualization algorithm, user can customize their visualization results. In [4], the objective was similar with the [3], but they focused on the representation of the synthetic environments that can be used in defense modeling and simulation systems. In [5-7] researches, the ground and aerial warfare simulation system was developed in the integrated structure with simulator and visualization module. In [5], the XNA, which is commercial game engine, was used and in [7], X-Plane was used for the visualization. In [6], authors pointed out the problem of cost-effectiveness with the commercial visualization tools. So they developed the novel LOD controlling algorithm which was described as a key problem in the visualization of the aerial warfare simulation.

In the previous researches the visualization function was developed as a part of supporting tool. And since the visualization module was integrated with the system, it is system dependent and the redundant cost for development is unavoidable as we described in the background section.

Typically in the defense modeling and simulation field, using HLA/RTI is considered as an efficient way of solving this problem [8]. HLA/RTI is the methodology to guarantee the interoperability and improving the reusability by standardizing the configuration method of the middleware. In [9], authors pointed out the interoperability problem from using the various 3D models in the single simulation system. So the proposed the Scene Simulation Platform based on the HLA/RTI. In [10], X-Plane and Google Earth was designed to interoperate based on the HLA/RTI to enable the geospatial information on the simulator. Furthermore, the simulation result was visualized on the Google Earth environment by logging the result in KML(Keyhole Markup Language) file.   In [11] and [12], HLA/RTI was aggressively adopted to enable the real-time monitoring and visualization by constructing the visualization module as a separate federate. Since all the systems mentioned above are constructed as HLA-compliant, the efficient interoperation is possible by facilitating the standard-based interoperation.

However, the discussion about the semantic interoperability is not fully investigated in the previous researches. To satisfy the semantic interoperability, the data should be exchanged in unambiguous and shared manner which can be supported by the analysis and capability of the data in the individual system. HLA/RTI can guarantee the syntactic interoperability between the systems while we can point out the lack of consideration about the semantic interoperability. For instance, Vega[13] and MeraVR[14] provides the user interface, API(Application Programming Interface) and additional package to extend the visualization system as semantic interoperable. It can be a solution of efficient visualization if there is no restriction about the target simulator/federator. However, the cost and time consumption is still considerably high for the extension of semantic interoperability.

Another way to get the semantic interoperability is giving the limitation about the data that system can handle. In [15], author proposed the Universal Heterogeneous Database Metadata Description, which enables the integrated description about the battlefield by designing the data structure which has capability of heterogeneous simulation result. In [16], XML(Extensible Markup Language schema) schema was proposed to represent the state of the object in web-based battlefield visualization. In [17], the data model for construction simulation was proposed and the result was visualized. At last, SIMDIS[18] proposed the ASI format for similar objective and developed the visualization tool for defense modeling and simulation systems.

In summary, the visualization tool which depends on the simulation system suffers from redundant cost consumption for development. There are researches based on the HAL/RTI to attempt to solve the problem but still remain the requirements about the researches considering the semantic interoperability. For now, the semantic interoperability can be achieved by limiting the capable data of system.

3   Proposed Method

3.1   Overview

In this research, we adopt an approach that limits the capable data of a system in an effort to develop a collaborative visualization environment. This approach allows the efficient development of a reusable visualization tool at the level of current technology. The data is intended to represent the result of a warfare simulation. Also, to provide an efficient collaborative visualization environment for decision-making processes between experts in a 3D visualization environment, we develop a system that is based on the CAVE system, which works with state-of-the-art visualization techniques coupled with ubiquitous devices.

To address these issues, we define two underlying currently available technologies.

1. SIMDIS data file structure
2. 3D visualization and networking technologies in commercial game engine

First, SIMDIS is a well-known analysis and display tool developed by NRL (Naval Research Laboratory). SIMDIS can be utilized for result analyses in the defense modeling and simulation field. One of its advantages is that the implementation process is not necessarily for the visualization session. The ASI data file structure is well defined and has large coverage of warfare related simulation results; therefore, simply logging or parsing the simulation result allows instant visualization. Various use cases and related research show the semantic interoperability of SIMDIS in defense modeling and simulation fields. Our research allows the data file structure of SIMDIS to achieve a certain level of semantic interoperability of the tool as well as the syntactic interoperability of existing simulators with functions that log the results with a SIMDIS data file.

On the other hand, SIMDIS lacks functions for game-like scene generation, unlike other visualization toolkits such as Vega or MetaVR, as SIMDIS focuses more on objective analysis. In our research to meet the needs of game-like scene generation efficiently, we decided to use a commercial game engine. Current commercial game engines are capable of relatively high performance for 3D visualization, and the networking functions of a game engine can be employed to construct a collaborative environment.

3.2   Hardware Configuration

The collaborative visualization environment proposed in our research is based on the CAVE facility. The iCAVE facility at KAIST was built to provide an immersive virtual environment with a resolution of 6400x1920 pixels in a field-of-view angle of 120 using a seven-channel display on a cylindrical screen. The scene for each channel is controlled by single multi-channel client run on a desktop PC, and the main controller PC is set to manipulate the entire visualization system. Furthermore, personal handheld devices cooperate with the main controller to provide domain-specific data to individual users. The overall hardware configuration is illustrated in Fig. 1. The main controller PC and multi-channel clients generate the scene by means of distributed visualization with the master-slave concept. Handheld devices are connected to the main controller PC to synchronize the visualization time with the generated scene on the shared screen.

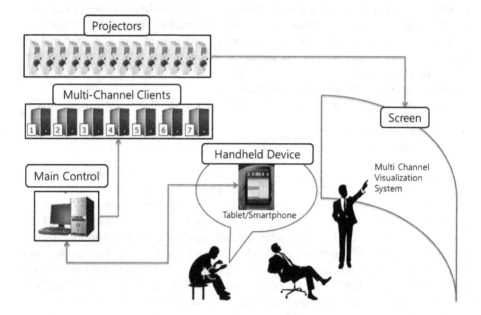

Fig. 1. Overall hardware configuration

3.3   Module Design

The entire system is designed to have a modularized structure for easy maintenance. Each module performs independent functions, and the data exchanges are accomplished through an interface that is de-signed specifically for this research. Therefore, if an update is required in the future, there is an advantage to using this type of modular design, as easily changing an individual module is all that is required.

The modules are divided into the data processing module, the weapon system visualization module, the terrain/environment visualization module, the animation module, the graph plot module, the user inter-face module and the multi-channel module. The weapon system visualization module and the terrain/environment visualization model also have an interface between their own 3D model databases. The layer structured module is illustrated in Fig.2. As noted in section 3.1, the component functions in a commercial game engine consist of upper-level visualization modules designed as part of this research. These modules run on each hardware platform to offer collaborative visualization

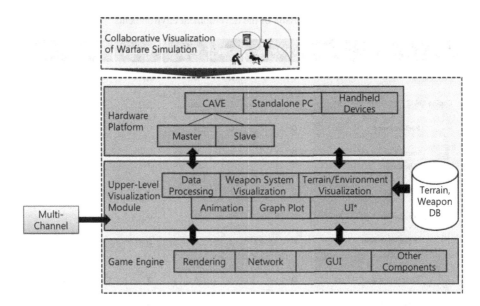

Fig. 2. Layer structure of the system and modules

3.4   Development Environment

With the designed module, a comparative study was carried out to determine the best possible development environment to use. The comparison factors are divided depending on the visualization, user interface, and networking aspects, and the compatibility. Each factor is compared in terms of its performance and efficiency during the development process. Compatibility pertains to the handheld devices, which are based on the Android OS for smartphones. Finally, the cost is also an important factor for development, as our system is based on the CAVE environment, which in some cases requires a separate license for each client PC. The result is illustrated in Table 1.

First, SIMDIS is a complete tool package which lacks extensibility compared to visualization engines, thus making multi-channel visualization difficult to achieve. OSG (OpenSceneGraph), Ogre3D and Delta3D are open-source rendering/game engines which have similar characteristics apart from their detailed features, such that Ogre3D is weaker at geospatial data handling and Delta3D supports HLA/RTI related features. Vega and Unity3D are high-level engines which have greater functionality than others. Vega offers various functions in the form of plug-in packages, but the cost is not negligible. On the other hand, Unity3D is one of the most actively applied engines in the current game market, and the range of application is expanding to the engineering and science fields. In particular, extensibility and compatibility to diverse platforms is considered to be a major advantage of this engine despite its relatively low cost. This advantage can lower the cost and shorten the time of development. In our research, the Unity3D engine was utilized for good cooperation with handheld devices in a collaborative visualization environment given its sufficient 3D visualization quality.

Table 1. Comparison of the development environments

		SIMDIS	VR-Vantage	OSG	Ogre3D	Delta3D	Vega	Unity 3D
Commercial		N	Y	N	N	N	Y	Y
Engine Level		X*	X*	△	△	△O	O	O
Visualization	Performance	△	O	O	O	O	O	O
	Implementation Efficiency	△	O	X	X	△	O	O
	GIS Support	△	O	△	X	△	△	X
UI	Scalability	X	△	O	O	O	△	O
	Implementation Efficiency	X	O	△	△	△	O	O
Network	Performance	△	O	△	△	O	O	O
	Implementation Efficiency	O	O	△	△	△	O	O
Compatibility	Coverage	X	△	△	△	△	△	O

4 Module Development

In Unity3D, the application is constructed by setting the component functions in the scene graph nodes, known as GameObject. The components, including the rendering, networking and particle effects and the encapsulating scripts, readily enable efficient development. Thus, the upper-level module consists of the set of scripts, and the scripts control component functions and external libraries simultaneously.

4.1 Data Processing Module

The data processing module passes the data through the interface to the other modules after processing the result of the simulation data and stores it in the defined data model. In this research, we utilize the data format of SIMDIS to define the data model for defense modeling and for the simulations. The data model is a class of model which includes the overall scenario information (reference coordinates, reference time), the platform information (platform ID, classification and the name of the 3D model), the platform data (position, velocity and orientation along the simulation time), among other data. The core function of the data processing module is the parsing of the data from the result of the simulation into the class to hand over the data to other modules if the proper requirements are detected.

4.2   Weapon System Visualization Module

The weapon system visualization module manages a range of saved data in the data processing module, such as scenarios, platform information and the weapon model database. It also loads 3D model data for visualization depending on the scenario. To generate game-like scene, the visualization module can generate particle effects such as smoke and flames on the 3D model. In Fig. 3, left side figure shows a visualization result on Unity3D through the weapon system visualization module.

4.3   Terrain/Environment visualization Module

The terrain visualization module performs the loading of the terrain model near the referenced coordinate system of the scenario from the terrain database. In addition, this module performs the rendering of the sea and atmospheric environment to construct the overall environment corresponding to the scenario. The terrain database includes significant geographic information because the 3D terrain polygon models created through the pre-processing of a DEM (digital elevation map) and satellite images contain latitude and longitude information. An ocean surface model is also generated according to the camera projection matrix to create an un-bounded ocean surface, and the clouds are created using a volume model to create a realistic and atmospheric scene. Additionally the underwater effect using particles and the terrain using observed bathymetry data is implemented to render the underwater view. In Fig. 3, right side figure shows a visualized environment which encompasses the use of terrain near Ulleung Island of Korea.

Fig. 3. Weapon system and environments around Ulleung Island visualized with Unity3D

4.4   Animation Module

The animation module manages changes of the position and orientation of the weapon system in the scenario according to the simulation time. The execution mode of the application can be divided into the real-time visualization and the after-action review steps. In the after-action review mode, visualization is performed after the parsing of the simulation log saved in the ASI file format from the completed simulation in the data processing module, making the visualization time independent on the simulation time. However, in the real-time visualization mode, the visualization time is dependent on the simulation time given that the simulation and the visualization are performed at the same time. The visualization time proceeds according to the frame update at a certain interval internally, and the position and orientation of the platform are updated with the most current data at that time. Additionally, because the data update rate should be held at 60Hz to ensure the production of smooth animations in applications such as a game, the position and orientation of the platform are updated using linear interpolation even if the simulation data does not exist at some times in the after-action review mode. This module allows the creation of smooth animations from simulation data which has irregular time intervals generated by discrete event simulations.

4.5 Multi-channel Module

The multi-channel module is developed using a type of master-slave model to visualize the entire scene in the iCAVE facility. The master-slave model is one way to realize distributed visualization, as it only transfers the data for state synchronization and runs the same applications on all node PCs. This model has advantages when used for large-scale visualization, as the network bandwidth requirement is relatively low [18].

Each multi-channel module recognizes the role of the master or the slave relative to themselves from the external initialization file at the very beginning. If the node is a slave, the view frustum of the camera of the master node is divided by seven and only renders the scene for each respective assigned camera region. The transferred data can be divided into the command information that is the one-time events, and streaming information which needs continuous transfer. The streaming information is transferred at 60Hz from master to slave and the command information is transferred immediately if the command occurs in the master. According to the information transfer, the same scene can be visualized in a multi-channel environment with the scene generated in the master. The visualized result in the iCAVE environment is illustrated in Fig. 4.

4.6 UI Module

The UI module enables the user to control and manipulate the visualization system using GUIs such as buttons or scroll bars. For instance, the input of a scenario file, termination of the application, and environment control and manipulation of the camera position are processed by means of user input commands. The UI module then transfers this information to the appropriate module through the interface.

4.7 Graph Plot Module

The graph plot module is a separate module which represents detailed values of the data of the position and orientation of individual platforms in the scenario. The graph

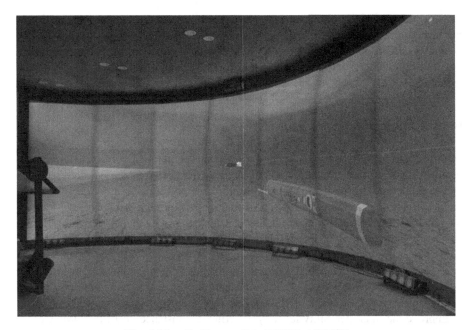

Fig. 4. Visualization result in iCAVE at KAIST

plot module is developed based on handheld devices, as the interests of individual experts can differ. Thus, to realize an immersive multi-channel environment and provide expert-specific information simultaneously, we provide detailed information with personal devices. In a situation in which divers (the experts in this case) are in the decision-making process, displaying the detailed values of each platform on a single screen is not efficient. In our study, handheld devices run the graph plot module, the data processing module, the simplified UI module and the multichannel modules for the synchronization of the visualization times so that detailed values can be observed on a smartphone.

5   Result

The entire system is implemented with the designed modules and operated with one master PC, seven slave PCs and two handheld devices, which are both smartphones running the Android OS. For the test scenario, a decoy operation scenario which includes the maneuvering of a submarine and a decoy and a battleship with the movement of its torpedoes is included. A surface-to-air and surface-to-surface missile operation scenario based on an engineering-level model was also tested. Each scenario includes three to six weapon systems and, for the decoy operation scenario, two additional 3D models were visualized to represent the detection range of the torpedoes.

The visualization was successfully done for run-time visualization and after an action review. However, in the orbit camera mode, there were shaking effects in the scene. The orbit camera mode keeps the observed platform always at the center of the camera such that if the position of the platform is updated frequently, any small synchronization difference between the animation module and the multi-channel module generates defects. This problem can be solved if the slave itself calculates the camera position by changing its updating method for the camera position as the command information.

6   Conclusion

In this research, we proposed a method to develop a collaborative visualization environment for a warfare simulation which involves the design of the required modules and the functions of the modules, and we implemented it using a commercial game engine. Regarding the interoperability of the visualization environment, we focused on semantic interoperability with the use of an existing data model stemming from a frequently utilized tool in the defense modeling and simulation field. In addition, game-like scene generation is achieved at a relatively low cost via an appropriate commercial game engine. Finally, the utility of the system is enhanced using handheld devices to provide expert-specific information.

For future works, the issue of HLA/RTI compliancy can be considered in an effort to improve the interoperability level by referring, for instance, to RPR-FOM. Moreover, the functionality of the handheld devices can be expanded to provide a more efficient collaborative environment for the decision-making process of the experts.

Acknowledgements. This work was supported by the Human Resources Development program(No. 20134030200300) of the Korea Institute of Energy Technology Evaluation and Planning(KETEP) grant funded by the Korea government Ministry of Trade, Industry and Energy and Development of Integration and Automation Technology for Nuclear Plant Life-cycle Management grant funded by the Korea government Ministry of Knowledge Economy (2011T100200145).

References

1. Delmia, http://www.3ds.com/ko/products-services/delmia/
2. Cha, M., Lee, J., Park, S., Park, D., Shin, B.: A development of maglev design review system using real-time visualization technology. In: Proceedings of the Society of CAD/CAM Conference (2010)
3. Hang, Q., Leiting, C.: Real-Time Virtual Military Simulation System. In: Proceedings of the 2009 First IEEE International Conference on Information Science and Engineering, pp. 1391–1394 (2009)
4. Hong, J., Park, Y., Park, S.C., Kwon, Y.: A Technology on the Framework Design of Virtual based on the Synthetic Environment Test for Analyzing Effectiveness of the Weapon Sys-tems of Underwater Engagement Model. Journal of the Korea Society for Simulation 19(4), 291–299 (2010)

5. Baki, K., Erkan, B.: Using Lanchester combat models to aid battlefield visualization. In: Internaltional Conference on Computer Science and Information Technology, pp. 290–292 (2009)
6. Kim, C., Park, Y., Lee, J., Kim, M., Reu, T.: A Study of the UML modeling and simulation for an analysis and design of the reconnaissance UAV system. J. of the Korean Society for Aeronautical and Space Sciences 36(11), 1112–1120 (2008)
7. Kim, S., Choi, J., Kim, C., Lim, C.: 3D Visualization for Situational Awareness of Air Force Operations. Jounal of KIISE 32(5,6), 314–323 (2005)
8. IEEE.: IEEE standard for modeling and simulation (M&S) high level architecture (HLA) - federate interface specification. Std. 1516.1 (2000)
9. Gang, C., Shang, X., Guan, Q.J., Quan, D.: Scene Simulation Platform Based on Data Fusion of Multiple Format 3D Models. In: International Conference on Computer Modeling and Simulation, pp. 342–346 (2009)
10. Martin, A.: Using the HLA, Physical Modeling and Google Earth for Simulating Air Transport Systems Environmental Impact. In: Simulation Interoperability Workshop (2009)
11. Hwam, W.K., Chung, Y., Choi, J., Park, S.C.: A Study on Implementation of Monitoring Sys-tem of Distributed Simulation for Underwater Warfare. Journal of the Korea Society for Simulation 22(2), 73–83 (2013)
12. Hur, P., Han, S.: Internet-Based Visualization of Underwater Vehicle Simulation using X3D. In: Proceedings of the 2006 Korea Society for Simulation Conference, pp. 48–58 (2006)
13. Vega, http://www.presagis.com/products_services/products/modeling-simulation/visualization/vega_prime/
14. MetaVR., http://www.metavr.com/
15. Wu, S.: Generic Battlefield Situation Dynamic Visualization Solution Based on Distributed Heterogeneous Database. In: 2012 Fourth International Conference on Computational and Information Sciences (ICCIS), August 17-19, pp. 1364–1367 (2012)
16. Koyuncu, B., Bostanci, E.: Using Web Services to Support Battlefield Visualization and Tactical Decision Making. In: International Conference on Computational Intelligence, Modelling and Simulation, CSSim 2009, September 7-9, pp. 138–141 (2009)
17. Kamat, V.R., Martinez, J.C.: 3D visualization of simulated construction operations. In: Proceedings of the Simulation Conference, vol. 2, pp. 1933–1937 (Winter 2000)
18. SIMDIS, https://simdis.nrl.navy.mil/

VELOS: Crowd Modeling for Enhanced Ship Evacuation Analysis

Konstantinos V. Kostas[1], Alexandros-Alvertos Ginnis[2],
Constantinos G. Politis[1], and Panagiotis D. Kaklis[2,3]

[1] Dept. of Naval Architecture (NA),
Technological Educational Institute of Athens (TEI-A)
[2] School of Naval Architecture & Marine Engineering (NAME)
National Technical University of Athens (NTUA)
[3] Department of Naval Architecture, Ocean and Marine Engineering (NAOME)
University of Strathclyde

Abstract. *Virtual Environment for Life On Ships* (VELOS) is a multi-user Virtual Reality (VR) system that supports designers to assess (early in the design process) passenger and crew activities on a ship for both normal and hectic conditions of operations and to improve the ship design accordingly [1]. Realistic simulations of behavioral aspects of crowd in emergency conditions require modeling of panic aspects and social conventions of inter-relations. The present paper provides a description of the enhanced crowd modeling approach employed in VELOS for the performance of ship evacuation assessment and analysis based on the guidelines provided by IMO's Circular MSC 1238/2007 [2].

1 Introduction

Under the impact of a series of events involving large number of fatalities on passenger ships [3], the International Maritime Organization (IMO) has developed regulations for RO-RO passenger ships, requiring escape routes to be evaluated by an evacuation analysis described in IMO's Circular MSC 1238/2007, entitled Guidelines for evacuation analysis for new and existing passenger ships [2]. It is worth mentioning that, although the evacuation scenarios in [2] address issues related to the layout of the ship and passenger demographics, they do not address issues arising in real emergency conditions, such as unavailability of escape arrangements (due to flooding or fire), crew assistance in the evacuation process, family-group behavior, ship motions, etc. To heal such deficiencies, [2] adopts the mechanism of safety factors.

Crowd simulation is a complex task with issues related to collision avoidance, considering a large number of individuals, path planning, trajectories and so forth. Depending on the application, other requirements such as real-time simulation is needed to populate virtual environments in VR systems. Moreover, in order to provide a tool to simulate behavioral aspects of crowd in emergency conditions, panic aspects and social conventions of inter-relations are needed, [4, 5]. In general, three approaches are used to model crowd motion. The *Fluid* model, where fluid equations, such as Navier Stokes equations, are used to model crowd

R. Shumaker and S. Lackey (Eds.): VAMR 2014, Part II, LNCS 8526, pp. 402–413, 2014.

flow [6–8]. The *Cellular Automata* (CA) model, which are discrete dynamic systems whose behavior is characterized by local interactions. Each CA is made up of a regular lattice of cells and at each unit of time the state of each cell is recalculated by the application of a set of rules to neighboring cells [9, 10]. The majority of crowd simulation uses the *Particulate* approach, which is also called the *atomic* approach. This is also the approach for crowd modeling used in VELOS and it is briefly presented in §2.1. The first pioneer work on this area was that of Reynolds [11] who worked on simulations of flocks of birds, herds of land animals and schools of fish. A later work of the same author [12] extends these concepts to the general idea of *autonomous characters* with an emphasis on animation and games applications. A *Social force model* for crowd simulation was introduced by Helbing and Molnár in [13]. They suggest that the motion of pedestrians can be described as if they are subject to social forces - Acceleration, Repulsion and Attraction- which measure the internal motivation of individuals to perform certain actions. By combining these three forces they produce an equation for pedestrian's *total motivation* and finally the *social force model*. In [5] the social force model was applied to the simulation of building escape panic, with satisfactory results.

The paper is structured as follows: Section 2 presents VELOS's base: VRsystem, along with its major components and functionalities including a brief description of the employed crowd modeling approach for the performance of ship evacuation assessment & analysis, while §3 is devoted to our proposed additions in steering behaviors and crowd modeling allowing their usage in ship evacuation analysis. Our last section includes the presentation of ship evacuation test cases investigating the effects of crew assistance, passenger grouping and fire incidents. Furthermore, an additional test case demonstrating the effects of ship motions on passengers movement is also included.

2   The VELOS System

VELOS is based on *VRsystem* [1], a generic multi-user virtual environment, that consists of mainly two modules, the server and client modules connected through a network layer. Figure 1 provides a schematic overview of the VRsystem architecture. As depicted in this figure, users' participation in the virtual environment is carried out through the CLIENT module in the form of AVATARS enabling them to be immersed in the virtual world and actively participate in the evacuation process by interacting with agents and other avatars. On the other hand, system administrator utilizes the SERVER module for creating the virtual environment, setting all properties and rules for the scenario under consideration, e.g., scheduling of fire/flooding events, and awaits participants to connect to the system. Administrator's interaction may also take place during simulation phase.

The server module comprises two major components, namely the VRkernel and the User-Interface, while the client module has a similar structure and comprises customized versions of them, referred to as VRkernelLT and User-InterfaceLT; see again Fig. 1. VRkernel is the core component of VRsystem

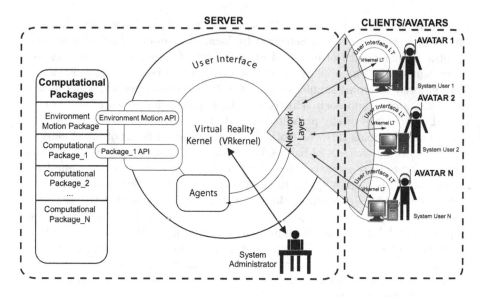

Fig. 1. The VRsystem Architecture

platform in the server module. It can be thought of as a library of objects and functions suitable for materializing the synthetic world with respect to geometric representations, collision detection, crowd modeling, motion control and simulation, event handling and all other tasks related to visualization and scene organization. The core functionalities of VRkernel are provided by Open Inventor, an OpenGL based library of objects and methods used to create interactive 3D graphics applications.

2.1   Crowd Modeling for Ship Evacuation

Crowd Modeling is a major part of VRkernel and, in view of VELOS areas of interest (evacuation, ergonomics, comfortability), it could be considered as the most significant of its components. It is based on agents, avatars, scene objects (such as obstacles) and steering behaviors technology. The term agent in VRkernel is used to describe autonomous characters, defined as *autonomous robots with some skills of a human actor in improvisational theater*; see [12]. Avatars are the system users' *incarnation* within the virtual environment and their major difference from agents is their *controlling entity*: humans for avatars vs. computer for agents. Steering behaviors technology is the core of VRkernel's crowd modeling and is presented in the following paragraphs while enhanced crowd modeling features for ship evacuation are presented in section 3.

The motion behavior of an agent is better understood by splitting it into three separate levels, namely action selection, steering and locomotion. In the first level, goals are set and plans are devised for the action materialization. The steering level determines the actual movement path, while locomotion provides the articulation and animation details.

Agents' autonomy is materialized within the steering level, where the steering behaviors technology is applied. Specifically, agents' autonomy is powered by an artificial intelligence structure, referred to in the pertinent literature as mind; see, e.g., [12, 14]. The mind utilizes a collection of simple kinematic behaviors, called steering behaviors, to ultimately compose agent's motion. Specifically, for each time frame, agent's velocity vector is computed by adding the previous velocity vector to the mind-calculated steering vector. This vector is a combination of the individual steering vectors provided by each associated steering behavior in agent's mind. In mind modeling we employ two different approaches for the steering vector calculation. The first and rather obvious one, used in simple mind, produces the steering vector as a weighted average of the individual ones. The second approach that takes into account priorities, called priority blending, is an enhanced version of the simple priority mind proposed in [12]. Agent's velocity at each time frame is calculated as follows:

1. Compute steering vector $f = \sum w_i f_i$, where w_i are weights and f_i are the individual steering vectors from each simple behavior included in agent's mind.
2. New velocity is computed as:

$$v_{new} = c \cdot (v_{prev} + f), \text{ where } c = \min\left\{\frac{v_m}{\|v_{prev} + f\|}, 1\right\}, \qquad (1)$$

where, v_m is the agent's maximum allowable velocity.

Nearly twenty steering behaviors have been so far implemented within VRkernel. These behaviors, based on the works by C.W. Reynolds [12] and R. Green [14], include: *Seek, Arrive, Wander, Separation, Cohere, Leader Follow, Obstacle Avoidance & Containment, Path-following, Pursuit, Flee, Evade, offset-{Seek, Flee, Pursuit, Evade, Arrive}*.

3   Enhanced Features of Crowd Modeling

Crowd modeling, as described in [1] can be used to materialize a ship evacuation scenario adopting the advanced method of analysis proposed by IMO in circulars [2, 15]. Although this advanced method is more realistic than the simplified approach proposed in the same circulars, it is still subject to some restrictive assumptions and omissions as, e.g., ship motions, fire/smoke, crew assistance and passenger grouping effects which are collectively accounted via corrective safety factors. Aiming in the elimination of these restrictions, we herein enrich crowd modeling in VELOS with appropriate features, which are described in detail in the following sub-sections. These features include the introduction of new behaviors, as the *Inclination behavior*, modeling the effect of ship motions, the *Enhanced Cohere* behavior applied in passenger grouping, and the adoption of behavioral models and aids, such as the *Triggers* supporting crew assistance modeling. Finally, passenger's *health index* and ship's *space availability* are introduced for modeling smoke and/or fire influence on the evacuation process.

3.1 Modeling Ship Motions and Accelerations

VELOS provides several interfaces for the consideration of ship motions and accelerations. Specifically, there are modules that allow importing of precomputed ship responses either in the frequency or time domain. Furthermore, there is also functionality for importing time histories of linear velocities and accelerations for selected points aboard a ship that are recorded with the aid of accelerometers. Thus, ship accelerations can be either estimated via numerical differentiation of ship motions or acquired from the experimental measurements. Generally, ship motions comprise time histories of the displacements of a specific point P of ship (usually ship's center of flotation) as well as time histories of ship rotational motions (pitch, roll and yaw). Using numerical differentiation we can calculate linear velocity (v_p) and acceleration ($\dot{v}_p$) of point P and angular velocity (ω_B) and acceleration ($\dot{\omega}_B$) of the ship. Then, using the following well-known relations from rigid-body kinematics we can calculate velocity and acceleration at every point Q on ship: $q = p + \omega_B \times r_{pq}$, $\dot{v}_q = \dot{v}_p + \omega_B \times (\omega_B \times r_{pq}) + \dot{\omega}_B \times r_{pq}$, where, r_{pq} is the vector formed by P and Q.

The effects of ship motions on passengers and crew aboard are modeled in two ways as it is presented in detail in the sequel. The first simplified approach is based on a kinematic modeling that utilizes the ship motions while the second approach takes into account the dynamic nature of the phenomenon and relies on the availability of ship accelerations.

Inclination Behavior. Advanced evacuation analysis in VELOS is combining the availability of ship motion data with the so-called *Inclination* behavior that has been introduced, as a first layer, for considering the effect of ship motion on agent's movement. Precomputed ship-motion history is imported in VELOS through a suitable series of interfaces. Inclination behavior resembles in definition and effect the influence of a gravity field that would hinder agent motion accordingly. Specifically, we consider a static global force-vector g normal to deck's plane in the upright position of the ship. If the deck deviates from its upright position (i.e., non zero heel, and/or trim, angles), the projection of g on it will obviously acquire a non-zero value g_p, which forms Inclination's steering vector as follows: $f_i = \lambda(\phi)g_p$, where $\lambda(\phi)$ is an appropriate weight function depending on the angle ϕ formed between g and the normal to the deck plane. Inclination behavior is active when ϕ lies between two threshold angles: the lower threshold is used to discard plane motions with negligible effect on agent's motion, while values above the upper threshold lead to movement inability, as the limit of agent's balancing capabilities is surpassed. Threshold angles and the weight function $\lambda(\phi)$ are defined via experimental data; see, e.g., [16, 17].

Motion Induced Interruptions (MII). During certain weather conditions, i.e., rough weather, walking and even more working in the ship becomes difficult and even the most experienced sailors will experience events where they must stop their activity, be it a specific task or merely standing, and take suitable measures to minimize the risk of injury, or more generally change their stance so that balance can be retained; these events are called, in pertinent literature, *Motion-Induced Interruptions (MIIs)*. MIIs can be identified by considering the dynamic equations of motions of the person due to ship motion leading to the onset of loss-of-balance due to tipping or sliding. Baitis et al [18] and Graham et al [19, 20] have proposed the following relations for the consideration of tips to port or starboard. Specifically, a tip to port will occur if: $T_{LATp} = \frac{1}{g}\left(\frac{1}{3}h\ddot{\eta}_4 - \ddot{D}_2 - g\eta_4 - \frac{l}{h}\ddot{D}_3\right) > \frac{l}{h}$, and analogously for tip to starboard. Similarly, the following tipping coefficients can be derived when considering tips to the aft or fore part of the ship: $T_{LONa} = \frac{1}{g}\left(\ddot{D}_1 + \frac{1}{3}h\ddot{\eta}_5 - \frac{d}{h}\ddot{D}_3\right) > \frac{d}{h}$ and analogously for tip to fore.

In the above equations, η_1 (surge), η_2 (sway), and η_3 (heave) stand for the translational while η_4 (roll), η_5 (pitch) and η_6 (yaw) stand for the rotational components of ship motion along the $x-$, $y-$ and $z-$ axis of the ship-coordinate system, respectively. Furthermore, $\mathbf{D} = (D_1, D_2, D_3) = (\eta_1, \eta_2, \eta_3) + (\eta_4, \eta_5, \eta_6) \times (x, y, z)$ denotes the displacement of point $\mathbf{P}(x, y, z)$. Finally, symbols l, h and d denote the half-stance length, the vertical distance to person's center of gravity and half-shoe width respectively. Typical values for $\frac{l}{h}$ lie in the interval $(0.20, 0.25)$ while for $\frac{d}{h}$ lie in $(0.15, 0.17)$.

Taking into account the above discussion concerning tipping coefficients, the effect of ship motions on passenger movement is implemented in the following way:

1. Adjustment $\tilde{v}_m$ of the maximum allowable velocity v_m according to the following rule: $\tilde{v}_m = k \cdot v_m$, where

$$k = \begin{cases} 1, & \text{if } T_{LAT} < 0.20 \wedge T_{LON} < 0.15 \\ (-20T_{LAT} + 5), & \text{if } 0.20 < T_{LAT} < 0.25 \wedge T_{LON} < 0.15 \\ (-20T_{LAT} + 5)(-50T_{LON} + 8.5), & \text{if } 0.20 < T_{LAT} < 0.25 \wedge 0.15 < T_{LON} < 0.17 \\ (-50T_{LON} + 8.5), & \text{if } T_{LAT} < 0.20 \wedge 0.15 < T_{LON} < 0.17 \\ 0, & \text{if } T_{LAT} > 0.25 \wedge T_{LON} > 0.17 \end{cases}$$

$$(2)$$

2. Adjustment of w_i weight values in computation of the steering vector. A typical scenario would include an increase of the wander behavior contribution and a decrease in Obstacle Avoidance and Separation contribution.
3. Adjustment of the parameters of each individual steering behavior.

3.2 Passenger Grouping

Passenger grouping in VELOS, as presented in [21], is based on the *Enhanced-Cohere* behavior which constitutes an enhancement of the standard *Cohere* behavior. *Enhanced-Cohere* behavior is responsible for keeping together agents that are not only geometrically close to each other (as in the standard *Cohere* behavior), but also belong to the same group, e.g., a family, a crew guided group, etc. For this purpose, each agent is endowed with an ID in the form of a common length binary representation and the new velocity vector of every agent is obtained by applying the standard *Cohere* calculations on the subset of the neighboring agents that belong to the same group.

In this way, by blending properly the *Cohere* behavior we can produce different grouping levels which can be categorized as follows:

Grouping Level 0: In this level, grouping is formed indirectly, via a common short-term target for the *group* members, as, e.g., followers of the same leader, or through the usage of the standard *Cohere* behavior.

Grouping Level 1: The members of the group are endowed with an *ID* and the *Enhanced-Cohere* behavior described above. Group cohesion is maintained only among nearby agents (within Cohere's neighborhood) sharing a common ID. However, if a member of the group gets out of the *Cohere* behavior's neighborhood, the remaining members will take no action.

Grouping Level 2: The members of the group are endowed with the same properties as in Level 1 and moreover at least one member (e.g., the group leader) has the responsibility of checking group's integrity. In this way, cohesion of the group is maintained, since if a member of the group is lost the responsible agent will take some corrective action, as to wait for the lost member to join the group or to search for finding the lost member.

3.3   Crew Assistance

Crew-Assistance behavior [21] is offered by affecting the *simple-* or *priority-mind mechanism* in two ways, either by using *Triggers* or via the *Guide Operation*.

A *Trigger* attached to a crew agent is a scene object and at the same time a scene area *(Neighborhood or TN)* that, when visited by a passenger agent, a prescribed list of actions or property changes, the so called *Trigger Actions or TAs*, are applied to the agent. A TA example could be the following: if passenger density at the chosen TN exceeds a prescribed limit, the TA enables the crew agent to redirect passengers towards the closest muster station along a path different from the main escape route; see scenario 3 in §4.1.

Guide Operation is materialized through the *Enhanced-Cohere* behavior and the basic *Leader-Follow* behavior. A *Guide-Operation* example could involve a crew member that is ordered by the officer in charge to guide a group of passengers from a specific site to the closest muster station along a path different from that provided by the evacuation plan; see see scenario 2 in §4.1.

Furthermore improvement of *Crew Assistance* services could be provided by properly combining *Triggers* with *Guide Operation*. An example of this combined operation could involve a crew member that is charged to guide a group of passengers blocked at a space where a fire event is evolved.

3.4   Influence of Smoke, Heat and Toxic Fire Products

VELOS offers the possibility to model a fire event during evacuation process by permitting passengers/crew to be influenced by smoke, heat and toxic fire products that are present in fire effluent. This is achieved by:

- importing precomputed time-series of fire products, according to different methods for calculating fire growth and smoke spread in multiple compartments; see, e.g., [22, 23],
- setting the time of fire explosion (before, simultaneously or after the evacuation starting time),
- modeling the influence of fire products on the behavioral model of agents with the aid of the Function *Health_ Index* presented below,
- visualizing the fire products in the synthetic world.

Function Health_ Index: In order to model the influence of fire products on agents we introduce the Health Reduction Rate function as follows:

$$HRR(t) = F(aT(t) + bC_{CO}(t)), \qquad (Health\_units/sec) \qquad (3)$$

where, F describes the used functional model, T is the temperature ($^\circ C$) and C_{CO} the carbon monoxide concentration (ppm) of the space where the agent is at the time t (see §4.2). We introduce now the *Health Index* function as follows

$$HI(t) = 1 - \int_0^t F(aT(t) + bC_{CO}(t))dt \qquad (4)$$

where, we have assumed that the initial Health Index of all agents is 1. When the Health Index of an agent becomes zero the agent is considered dead. Moreover, when the Health Index of an agent deteriorates this also affects, by a suitable law, its maximum speed (ability of walking).

Function Space_Availability: In a typical ship evacuation simulation, the path-finding module of VELOS computes the required path for each passenger to reach their designated muster station from their initial position. The employed algorithm is Dijsktra's shortest path algorithm [24] and is applied on ships topological graph where nodes correspond to ship spaces and edges to doors and/or passageways. Edge weighting between two connected nodes, in the simplest case, corresponds to the walking-distance between the two spaces' center points while this weighting scheme becomes more complex when space availability is considered. Specifically, ship spaces availability is connected and contribute to the edges' weighting implemented on the topology graph of ship spaces. For example, an increase of ambient temperature or CO concentration, or a visibility decrease in a certain space results in an increase of the weighting factors of the edges connected to the graph node representing this space. Consequently, paths passing through this particular space is less possible to be chosen by the path planning algorithm. Furthermore, when going beyond certain temperature, CO concentration and visibility thresholds, the corresponding space(s) is(are) rendered unavailable, i.e. removed from the topological graph.

4   Test Cases

In this section we use VELOS for performing evacuation analysis for a RO-RO passenger ship: 1. with and without crew assistance and grouping behaviors, and 2. with and without a concurrent fire event. Furthermore, we also examine the effect of ship motions on passengers' movement in the test case described in §4.3.

4.1   Crew Assistance and Grouping

It the first test case examined, one hundred passengers are located in the cabins of Deck 5 (see Fig. 2) of the aft. vertical zone of a ship, while Muster Station is located on Deck 7. Population demographics are as proposed in [2]. For every simulation run we distribute randomly the population in the aforementioned areas. Three variations of the above scenario are simulated 3000 times each. For each variation, we compute the *travel time* required for all passengers to reach Muster Station as well as *cumulative arrival time* corresponding to the percentage of passengers reaching Muster Station for each time unit.

In the first variation (Scenario 1), passengers follow the designated escape route without crew assistance; Fig. 3 provides a snapshot of the evacuation process. The other two variations involve crew assistance. In Scenario 2 passengers are directed by two crew members to follow two distinct routes (see Fig 4), while in Scenario 3 a crew member monitors passengers' density at a specified place and, whenever congestion is likely to arise, he/she redirects a group of passengers towards a secondary escape route; see Fig. 5. In both cases, crew assistance is materialized through *Triggers*, which in Scenario 2 involves TAs applied to all passengers passing through the corresponding TN, while in Scenario 3 TAs are of dynamic character as a result of the attached density sensor.

Figure 6 depicts the average of the cumulative arrival time for each scenario. As it can easily be seen from this figure, Scenarios 2 and 3, based on crew-assistance & grouping, achieve a considerably better performance compared to Scenario 1. Among Scenarios 2 and 3, the latter is marginally better as a result of the dynamic crew-assistance policy adopted. Analogous conclusions can be drawn from Fig. 7, where the distributions of travel-time of the three scenarios are depicted. Average travel time for Scenarios 1, 2 and 3 are equal to 147 s, 112 s and 113 s, respectively. Moreover, in Scenarios 2 and 3 travel-time distribution is narrow-banded, which reflects the effectiveness of the adopted evacuation processes versus that of Scenario 1.

4.2   Fire Event

In this test case, we have the same arrangement and passenger distribution with the first test case; see Fig. 2. Population demographics are as proposed in [2]. A fire event occurs simultaneously with the beginning of the evacuation process. The initial fire site is located on deck 5 and depicted in Fig. 2. The fire propagation, along with temperature distribution, Carbon Monoxide (CO) concentration and visibility due to smoke has been precomputed [23] for all affected spaces on deck 5 and the time history of all corresponding quantities has been imported to VELOS. Fire and its products (temperature, CO concentration and visibility-degradation due to smoke) affect both the availability of ship spaces and the movement capabilities of passengers and their health. Space availability changes are implemented via the edge weighting mechanism described in §3.4

For every simulation run we distribute randomly the population in the aforementioned areas. The fire scenario under consideration is simulated 360 times

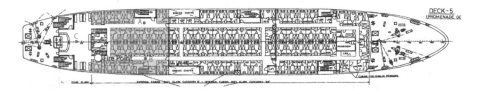

Fig. 2. General Arrangement and passengers distribution at the aft. vertical zone

Fig. 3. Scenario 1	**Fig. 4.** Scenario 2	**Fig. 5.** Scenario 3

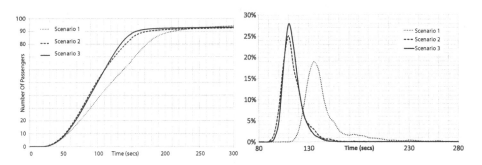

Fig. 6. Average cumulative arrival time for Scenarios 1, 2 and 3

Fig. 7. Travel time distribution for Scenarios 1, 2 and 3

and for each run, we record the *travel time* required for all passengers to reach Muster Station and compute the *cumulative arrival time* corresponding to the percentage of passengers reaching Muster Station for each time unit. As illustrated in Fig. 8 the passengers reaching muster station are around 30% less when compared to the evacuation without the fire event. This is caused by the fire-blockage of passage ways and the resulting fatalities. Furthermore, the slight acceleration of the evacuation process depicted in the same figure for the fire-event example case is due to the fact that the effective evacuation population has been reduced due to the effects of the fire incident and thus the available spaces and pathways are used by less evacuating passengers.

4.3 Ship Motions' Effect

This last test case examines passengers' movement on Deck 5 of a RO-RO passenger ship with and without ship motions' effect consideration. Specifically, we simulate the movement of two groups of passengers (20 persons) from points A and B respectively, to point C (see Fig. 2) in still water, and at a sea state described by a wave spectrum with 4m significant wave height, 11 sec. peak period and 90^0ship heading (beam seas). Ship responses were pre-computed and imported into VELOS using the SWAN seakeeping software package. The cases examined have as follows: 1. Still water (No Waves), 2. (Sea state as described above): Kinematic modeling of motion effects through inclination behavior, 3. (Same sea state): Dynamic modeling using tipping coefficients implementation.

Figure 9 depicts the average cumulative arrival time to point C for each of the three example cases. Each of the test cases has been simulated 500 times and the average travel times and arrival rates at point C have been collected. As it can easily be seen from this figure the time required for the prescribed passengers movement is the least when we are in still water. The effect of the wavy sea state, which induces ship motions and hinders passengers movement is illustrated with the right-shifting of the remaining two curves. The total travel time needed for both inclination behavior and tipping coefficient modeling is about the same ($\approx$70secs) and considerably higher than the still water case ($\approx$50secs), where, obviously, no motion effect is considered. However the arrival rate (slope) for the tipping coefficient modeling is steeper than the slope of the curve corresponding to the kinematic approach.

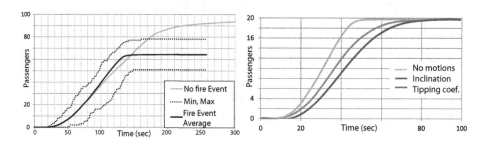

Fig. 8. Ship evacuation with and without a fire event

Fig. 9. Average cumulative arrival time for test cases 1, 2 and 3

References

1. Ginnis, A.A.I., Kostas, K.V., Politis, C.G., Kaklis, P.D.: VELOS: A VR platform for ship-evacuation analysis. CAD, Special Issue on Computer Aided Ship Design 42(11), 1045–1058 (2010)
2. I.M.O.: Guidelines for evacuation analyses for new and existing passenger ships. Msc.1/circ, 1238 edn. (October 30, 2007)
3. Vanem, E., Skjong, R.: Designing for safety in passenger ships utilizing advanced evacuation analyses - A risk based approach. Safety Science 44, 11–35 (2006)
4. Thalmann, D., Musse, S.: Crowd Simulation. Springer (2007)
5. Helbing, D., Farkas, I., Viscek, T.: Simulating dynamical feaatures of escape panic. Nature 407, 487–490 (2000)

6. Henderson, L.: The statistics of crowd fluids. Nature 229, 381–383 (1971)
7. Helbing, D., Molnar, P., Farkas, I., Bolay, K.: Self-organizing pedestrian movement. Environment and Planning B: Planning and Design 28, 361–383 (2001)
8. Hughes, R.: The flow of human crowds. Annual Review of Fluid Mechanics 224, 120–123 (1970)
9. Gardner, M.: Mathematical games: Conway's game of life. Scientific American 407, 487–490 (2000)
10. Blue, V., Adler, J.: Cellular automata microsimulation of bi-directional pedestrian flows. Transportation Research Board 1678, 135–141 (2000)
11. Reynolds, C.: Flocks, herds and schools: A distributed behavioral model. Computer Graphics 21(4), 25–34 (1987)
12. Reynolds, C.W.: Steering behaviors for autonomous characters. In: GDC 1999 (Game Developers Conference) (1999)
13. Helbing, D., Molnár, P.: Social force model for pedestrian dynamics. Phys. Rev. E 51, 4282–4286 (1995)
14. Green, R.: Steering behaviors. In: SIGGRAPH 2000 Conference Proceedings (2000)
15. I.M.O.: Interim Guidelines for evacuation analyses for new and existing passenger ships, MSC/Circ. 1033 (June 2002)
16. Bles, W., Nooy, S., Boer, L.: Influence of ship listing and ship motion on walking speed. In: Proceedings of Conference on Pedestrian and Evacuation Dynamics (2001)
17. Crossland, P.: The influence of ship motion induced lateral acceleration on walking speed. In: Proceedings of the 2nd International Conference on Pedestrian and Evacuation Dynamics, Greenwich (2003)
18. Baitis, A.E., Holcombe, F.D., Conwell, S.L., Crossland, P., Colwell, J., Pattison, J.H.: 1991-1992 motion induced interruptions (mii) and motion induced fatigue (mif) experiments at the naval biodynamics laboratory. Technical Report CRDKNSWC-HD-1423-01, Bethesda, MD: Naval Surface Warfare Center, Carderock Division (1995)
19. Graham, R.: Motion-induced interruptions as ship operability criteria. Journal of Naval Engineers 102(2), 65–71 (1990)
20. Graham, R., Baitis, A.E., Meyers, W.: On the development of seakeeping criteria. Journal of Naval Engineers 104(3), 259–275 (1992)
21. Kostas, K., Ginnis, A.I., Politis, C., Kaklis, P.: Use of VELOS platform for modelling and accessing crew assistance and passenger grouping in ship-evacuation analysis. In: Rizzuto, E., Guedes Soares, C. (eds.) Sustainable Maritime Transportation and Exploitation of Sea Resources, vol. 2, pp. 729–736 (2011)
22. Rein, G., Barllan, A., Fernandez-Pell, C., Alvares, N.: A comparison of three models for the simulation of accidental fires. Fire Protection Engineering 1, 183–209 (2006)
23. McGrattan, K., Klein, B., Hostika, S.: Fire Dynamics Simulator. NIST. NIST Special Publication 1019-5, Maryland (2007)
24. Dijkstra, E.W.: A note on two problems in connexion with graphs. Numerische Mathematik 1, 269–271 (1959)

Applying Augmented Reality to the Concept Development Stage of the Total Design Methodology

Gordon M. Mair, Andrew Robinson, and John Storr

Department of Design, Manufacture, and Engineering Management, University of Strathclyde,
75 Montrose Street, Glasgow, G1 1XJ, Scotland, UK
g.m.mair@strath.ac.uk

Abstract. This paper suggests an approach to assist the identification of suitable areas of application of AR within the product design process. The approach utilizes an established methodology for product design development that allows each stage in the design process to be identified and considered in a logical and structured manner. By doing this we can consider the suitability for AR at each stage as opposed to the use of hand drawings, basic computer aided design, virtual reality, or rapid prototyping techniques and suchlike to produce physical models. As an example of this we consider the concept design stage of the product design process and conduct some preliminary experiments in the use of AR to facilitate the activity.

Keywords: Augmented reality, product design, total design, concept design, industrial design.

1 Introduction

It is apparent that within the realm of product design and manufacture there is an ongoing need to reduce the time from the identification of a market need for a product and the satisfaction of that need in the form of a finished product that meets the customer's requirements. Over the past few decades an important method of meeting this need has been the implementation of the concept of Concurrent Engineering - this is an attempt to consider in an integrated and parallel manner, product design, development, manufacture, delivery, maintenance, and end of product life considerations. This approach has been employed by many major manufacturing companies and utilizes multidisciplinary teams comprised of, for example, component suppliers, product design and manufacturing engineers, purchasing personnel, and customers. Efficient and unambiguous communication of ideas is essential throughout this activity and we consider here how this can be facilitated by the use of Augmented Reality.

As an essential part of this process it is clearly necessary to design the product in a rational manner and a number of methodologies have been developed in order to achieve this. One of these is 'Total Design' developed by Pugh [1] and defined as "The systematic activity necessary, from the identification of the market /user need, to the selling of the successful product to satisfy that need – an activity that encompasses product, process, people and organization." The elements of this methodology are summarized here and used as a vehicle for identifying specific aspects of the design

R. Shumaker and S. Lackey (Eds.): VAMR 2014, Part II, LNCS 8526, pp. 414–425, 2014.

process where AR could be usefully employed. We show that not only is the use of AR beneficial for the product designer but also for improving communication with the final customer and others involved in the integrated concurrent engineering exercise of new product innovation.

2   Total Design

Total Design is a methodology that allows a rational and detailed approach to product design from identification of a market need through to satisfaction of that need by the provision of a desired product. The main stages involved include the following.

1. Based on the market need a Product Design Specification (PDS) is produced. This is a comprehensive document that forms the basis of all the work that follows. It does not state what the final design should be but it sets the criteria the design must satisfy. As this stage does not require any graphical images AR is not relevant here.
2. Once the PDS has been completed the 'concept design' stage is implemented to create and critically assess potential designs that can satisfy the PDS. Various techniques, such as brainstorming, are employed to generate the concepts which are then compared and evaluated using decision matrices in order to select a final concept. This paper will show that AR is potentially very useful at this stage.
3. 'Detail design' is now carried out to develop the concept design into a practical form. Here the individual components and sub-assemblies are designed and accompanying detailed calculations for mechanical, thermodynamic, electrical, electronic and other aspects are carried out. Within this process other 'design for X' considerations will be considered. For example; design for manufacture and assembly, design for ergonomics, design for maintenance, design for the environment, and design for remanufacturing are among a number aspects that are important. While AR could be used at this stage there is much more scope for application of established computer aided design and simulation methods to develop and examine the design. Of course larger products such as ships and aircraft will also benefit from the use of virtual reality at this stage.
4. Manufacturing the product, at this stage simulation packages for factory layout are used coupled with computer aided process planning and other computer based tools to optimize the work flow, material control, and final dispatch. However there is also the opportunity here to utilize AR when considering the positioning of production machinery such as industrial robots, CNC machines, conveyors, etc.
5. Finally, at the stage where the product is being delivered to, and used by, the customer there are already applications in commercial use for AR in product advertising and as an aid for product maintenance and repair.

2.1   Concept Design

This paper is focused on the potential use of AR in stage 2, the concept design stage. It is worth noting that some studies have noted the fact that CAD modelling can be harmful to the early stages of the design process, the representation of a component in this form is deemed to be too detailed and overbearing when concepts should be considering innovation and development [2,3]. Specifically results of a study by Benami and Jin [4] state that "The essential finding from the experiment was that ambiguous entities stimulate behaviours more than non-ambiguous entities". Based on these observations, it is apparent that the use of basic CAD modelling at this stage of the design process can potentially stunt a designer's ability for creativity in a design. However we consider that it may be possible for the use of Augmented Reality to increase levels of creativity for conceptual design, whilst allowing appropriate interaction and detail for the designer.

Two systems presented by Fuge et al. [5] and Fiorentino et al. [6] have looked at the use of AR in conceptual design and product realisation. The system presented by Fuge et al. focused on the construction of freeform surfaces. The role of multiple shape representation was addressed and the user was required to interact using a data glove and a head-mounted display in order to create an immersive style environment. The system was successful in that it allowed rapid creation of freeform surfaces without the need for constraints generally required in CAD modelling. A similar system was presented by Fiorentino et al. [6] where semi-transparent glasses were used instead of an HMD.. Again the system allowed a designer to create freeform curves and surfaces in an AR environment. Although the objective of the system was to assist in product realisation, the use of AR to assist in Rapid Prototyping technologies was suggested. They observe that the method of using trial-and-error to evaluate design iterations is "one of the biggest bottlenecks in the industrialisation process." This observation was also acknowledged by Verlinden and Horváth in two separate publications [7, 8], where the idea that the use of AR to assist in concept generation and the reduction of design iteration was introduced. However it appears a knowledge gap is present here as the use of AR to support concept realisation is not yet fully investigated. Ong et al [9] also applied AR in the early design stages during the product development process. This was done by introducing a spatial AR (SAR) configuration where real world images or textures are projected onto a physical shape model to give the impression of the final design which can then be inspected. This is a very basic use of augmented reality as an image is simply projected using a projector. Another study looked at the use of augmented reality to aid the visualisation of Computer-Aided Design (CAD) parts [10]. It was found that certain students had difficulty with the spatial cognition of the multi-view projections of a CAD model they had created. To resolve this, a quick response (QR) code was placed onto the drawing. AR software was then used to view the specific 3D model, aiding the spatial cognition of the students.

The multiple systems and applications presented show that AR has the potential to replace traditional methods of design evaluation. When introducing the research, Park [11] discusses use of CAD modelling, giving pros and cons of the use within the design process. Although it is noted that CAD is a key component for conceptualisation and product realisation, it is apparent that CAD has a "fundamental problem of intangibility". It is thought that the use of AR applications within product development can be utilised to overcome these issues.

2.2   Collaborative Design

It is not uncommon for design teams in the current design climate to be working in separate countries or even continents; synchronous and a-synchronous working has become a vital component in the design process and this must be facilitated with collaborative design applications. Even if the situation arises where a design team are all working together in one place, it is likely that the group will consist of members from many backgrounds and disciplines. In order to facilitate these members, design techniques which easily represent a product concept or component for design evaluation must be utilised. AR technologies have been implemented extensively for collaborative design applications [12–16] allowing for representation, evaluation and modification of a design in a group environment.

It has been recurrently observed that although CAD systems are a vital component in the current product development process, they lack the "natural feel" that is provided with traditional methods of product realization. The result of this is a lack of tactile feedback provided to the user regarding their design.

Collaboration with users, clients and other stakeholders throughout the design process is vital as it allows for the development of usable and useful products [17]. It allows for a "human-centric" approach within the design process creating solutions that are directly influenced by the user and other stakeholders.

One of the main issues when designing products for clients is the fragmentation in the client-designer relationship. This can be related to the relationship between the designer and a senior manager or CEO of a company who may not be familiar with the design process. Schumann et al noted that "Nowadays the convincing presentation of new products is a lengthy and often very expensive task" [18]. This is due to the different experience levels of stakeholders which can make the communication of ideas very difficult for the designer. Wang explained that while the designer is working at a conceptual level, they will tend to "interpret client needs and desires into artistic form" [19]. However, this can create issues as the client may be unfamiliar with the "language of design" at this very early stage of the process.

3   Augmented Reality and Mobile Technology

The main problem with using mobile devices for AR has been their computational power however recently this is being being largely ameliorated. Nee et al argued that "higher processing power and hardware, such as high resolution camera, touch screen and gyroscope etc. have already been embedded in these mobile devices" [20]. A number of relatively advanced mobile AR systems were released in 2013. These include Aurasma [21] Metaio Junaio [22] and Layer – Augmented Reality [23]. These apps are readily available on modern smartphones and other mobile devices. It is therefore now evident that modern mobile devices are ideal for augmented reality applications.

Therefore, the question we pose is - does the use of a mobile device to facilitate an augmented reality application, adds value to the concept design process?

4   Design of the Experiment

The experiment involved two parts. Firstly, the participants were asked to undergo multiple scenarios using augmented reality to analyse concepts. A mobile application that allows custom AR environments to be created using a mobile device was utilised alongside two basic mock-ups made from simple materials. The type of augmented reality is video-see-through which can be implemented by modern mobile devices. CAD models will be projected onto the two basic physical mock-ups to imitate the viewing of models in real life. The user was able to hold and touch the mock-ups and through the mobile device, it will appear as if they are handling the CAD model. This is a form of passive haptic feedback. The user was asked to analyse the con-cepts against basic criteria. During this first part, an informal interview was taken during the experiment where questions relating to the topic and the experience were asked. Responses were noted and any common answers analysed to reach a conclusion. The second part of the experiment was a questionnaire. Within this, questions were asked that relate to the experimental technique's usability, practicality and how it compared to other techniques that the user has experienced

4.1   Software

After analysis of various options software chosen was 'Metaio'[24] an AR program in which custom computer generated models can be integrated into an environment cho-sen by the user. To do this, any 3d model can be imported into the Metaio Creator where the model's dimensions and position can be altered. A target is then used for tracking and allows the chosen model to appear in the real world. Once this position of the model over the target is decided, it is fixed and the only way that the user can manipulate it is to handle the object that the tracker is attached to. This is important as it replicates the viewing of a model in real life. The program links directly to the Me-taio Cloud and every user can create a 'channel' that contains their custom augmented reality developments. These channels are held in the Cloud and can be viewed through mobile devices using the 'Junaio' application developed by 'Metaio' in which anyone can view your models using specific targets. The type of 3D model used was an OBJ file, an object file.

The CAD models used were sourced from TurboSquid.com an online source for professional 3D models. OBJ files can be downloaded from this source which is well suited for the 'Metaio' software. The models chosen were similar to allow for more focussed evaluation similar to that of concepts created within the same project. Two mobile phones were used, a model of the Nokia N82 Mobile Phone and the Sony Ericsson W960i Mobile Phone.

The aim was to make the prototypes very simple. They were created out of white foam card that was cut and shaped to the size of the CAD model. No detail was in-cluded in the mock-up as it was the CAD model that was intended to show detail. The participant was to understand that the simplest model could be created to then project over a CAD model as this would take minimal time in a design process.

Fig. 1. AR displays of hand-held mobile phone model

4.2   Basic Scenarios

Certain scenarios will be developed to replicate how a designer may examine a proto-type during the evaluation stage of the design process. Klinker et al (2002) pro-duced a set of scenarios that exemplify how a car designer would use their developed aug-mented reality system. These scenarios are different from that of a basic prototype analysis that may be completed for a consumer product. The set of scenarios have been developed from those used when testing augmented reality from car design.

1. Handling – The designer views the product holding the prototype in one hand and the mobile device in the other. They will rotate the product as if they were analys-ing its form.
2. Overview – The designer will place the product on a surface and hold the device to view it. The position of the device will be changed to evaluate the prototype at various angles.
3. Detail viewing – The designer will view a specific detail of the model by han-dling the product and the mobile device. This could be a specific component or mate-rial within the model.
4. Compare – The user will be asked to compare the model to another that they have not viewed yet. It will be recorded how the user chooses to view the other proto-type.

During each of these scenarios, recordings of comments and visual impressions will be taken. The experiments will focus on the evaluation of concepts by a single designer. Each designer will be asked to undertake these scenarios to evaluate two given augmented reality concepts using a provided mobile device that has the AR app installed.

The criteria used for evaluation were as follows: Quality – Which model appears to be of a higher quality? (build quality, material etc.) Robust - Which model appears to be more robust in that it can resist impact from dropping? Aesthetic Appeal – Which model is more aesthetically pleasing? Usability – Which model appears to be more user-friendly i.e. simple and easy to use? Purchasing – Which product would you purchase on first impressions?

4.3   Informal Questions

The set questions for during the experiment are simply guidelines and are subject to change depending on the participant. These questions are as follows: How do you find the Augmented Reality System? Do you feel you can visualise the model clearly? Does the technique work as you had first imagined? How does this compare to other techniques for model viewing you have used? Is this a technique that you can see using in the future? If not, do you see it being used in the future when the technology advances? What are the advantages and hindrances, if any, brought with this technique? Participants

The experiments included participants of varying age and experience in the design process. Participants were sourced from the Design, Manufacture and Engineering Management Department of the University of Strathclyde. Students in their fourth and fifth year were included in experimentation as they had accumulated reasonable experience in the field.

5   Experiment Results and Discussion

In this section the statement provided to the participants is shown followed by the response in graphical and textual form.

Statement - *'The use of augmented reality to view and evaluate a model is more intuitive than when viewing a model within a 3D CAD program.'*

From the Graph below it can be seen that these results are very conclusive as no participants stated that they disagree with the statement. This shows that the vast majority of participants agree that augmented reality is a much more intuitive tool for viewing concepts than viewing on a screen in a CAD program. However, three participants stated that they neither agree nor disagree and so the comments have been analysed to further investigate the comparison of techniques.

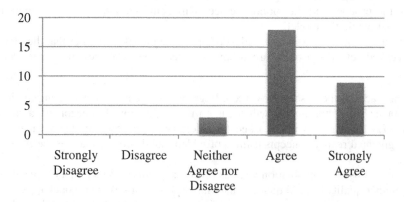

The majority of participant comments are pro Augmented Reality when compared to CAD but for a variety of reasons. Several participants noted the novelty of AR over CAD in that it is 'fun and interactive' and therefore would be beneficial to promote

concepts to others or to involve others in the evaluation process. Others appreciated the ability to fully control the model intuitively and they naturally like the control when handling a final product. One participant stated that customers 'may look at a CAD model and think "very good, but how does that affect me'. When compared to CAD, the user found that they were able to 'minutely adjust the view easily' and that 'user adjustments become instinctive'. One participant noted that this may only be true of hand held products. A larger product may be more difficult to assess if it cannot be handled. It is suggested that for future work, a variety of models of different sizes are used to explore the application further. It is clear from these responses that the use of augmented reality adds value to the concept design stage of the product design process.

Statement - *'The use of augmented reality to view and evaluate a model is more intuitive than viewing a model on an engineering drawing.'*

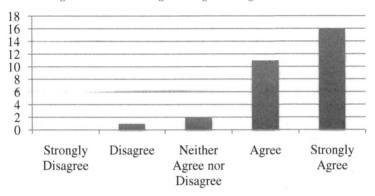

It is evident that the technique is much more accessible to those who may not be familiar with the format of engineering drawings i.e. those with little manufacturing or product design background. One participant noted that 'drawings give no sense of scale and struggle to convey emotive shades.' Another stated that '2D shapes on engineering drawings provide little user feedback.' This was a common thought during the experiments. There were several participants that saw benefits in both techniques. One participant noted that there is more detail on an engineering drawing as it provides details on dimensions, materials, assembly, bill of materials etc. whereas all that can be seen in the augmented reality model is the outer aesthetics which are put in the context of the surrounding environment. For those who may require details for manufacture or higher amounts of detail of the product, the use of augmented reality may not be beneficial. Participants agreed with this, one of which stated that augmented reality is more beneficial 'in some aesthetic aspects though it lacks obvious information on construction, fit, materials, etc.'

One definite benefit would be in the collaborative design and evaluation of products with clients, customers and those who may not be familiar with the design process. This is due to the overall intuitiveness of the AR technique which allows people to hold and view product as if it were there in front of them. This technique is natural much like viewing and handling a finished product.

Statement - *'You would use augmented reality in future work for concept design.'*

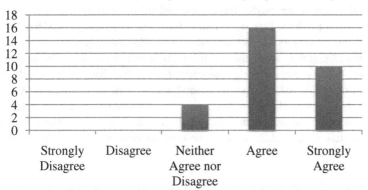

It was found in these results, as well as discussions with the participant, that they would use this technique for a variety of applications in concept design. They could see real benefit in the use of AR in this context but could also see where the technology could be developed to increase the number of possible applications.

The main application was that it would be used to present ideas to others who may not be familiar with CAD e.g. customers or clients. The reasons for this were that ideas could be shown to anyone at any time. All that is needed is a rough model and a mobile device e.g. a smartphone or tablet. In doing so, quick and early feedback could be gained from customers or clients but also, they could be involved in the development of the early concepts. This is due to the accessibility and intuitiveness of the technology. One participant mentioned that it would be beneficial to show to clients as it is similar to the empathetic modelling technique for early design. Also, multiple concepts could be shown to different user groups very early on without the need to create physical detailed prototypes. This would give an early insight into necessary design changes which would save time and money during the process. One participant also stated that it is a very cost effective method of 'prototyping' and that they would use this to develop designs quickly and efficiently.

Multiple participants noted that one of the main benefits of the technology was the ability to see the product in the context of the real world. It is very intuitive when viewing the model as the user gets an instant impression of the scale and dimensions of the product which is unlike other techniques such as viewing a CAD model on a screen or on an engineering drawing. One participant stated that it is a 'dynamic form of product evaluation'. Despite the real benefits of augmented reality in this context, it was noted that it may only be beneficial for hand held devices that users can interact with. With larger models, it may not be as beneficial as the use of a small screen to view a model of 1:1 scale may not be practical and the convenience of taking small rough hand held models to meetings and clients is lost.

Statement   - *AR technology is beneficial for presenting concepts to managers, CEO's, customers, clients or anyone who may not be as familiar with CAD but it is necessary for them to view and understand the design.*

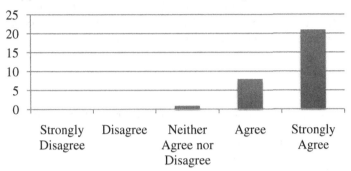

Of all the questions within the questionnaire, this can be seen as the most conclusive in terms of results. With 29 of 30 participants selecting either agree or strongly agree, it is clear that there is a real benefit of using AR in this context. Many agreed that the benefits lay in the intuitiveness of the technology for those who may not be familiar with other techniques such as CAD or 2D drawings. One participant stated that 'for those not used to CAD, it would provide an easy hands-on method of viewing concepts.' Many agreed that the ability to gain tactile feedback from a model aids the understanding of it in terms of design, feel, weight, how it is used etc. The results from this question showed that there are two main applications, the presentation of designs and the collaborative design of products with those unfamiliar with design processes. One participant noted the benefit of AR in the early concept design stages where prototypes may not be available or financially viable at the time. AR can provide designers a tool for presenting models and a technique for evaluating them. One participant noted that AR is an 'interesting and captivating form of presentation.' Designers who want to push for an idea may wish to use this tool to enhance the design.

From these results it is clear that AR adds value not only to the evaluation of design, but the concept design stage as a whole. It allows for collaborative design as well as creating an exciting and appealing form of presenting.

6   Conclusions

The review of literature identified that there was no previous research on the application of mobile augmented reality in the concept design stage of product design. It is this identification of a gap in knowledge that formed the research focus.

The empirical study involved the contribution of participant knowledge in the field of product design. The research concluded that augmented reality does add value to the concept design process. It does so by allowing for the collaborative evaluation between those with experience in product design i.e. designers, and those who may not be familiar with the processes i.e. customers, clients etc. It was found that the system was highly intuitive and allowed for early evaluation of concepts without the need to build prototypes. This, in turn, saves time and money, further adding value for the designer.

The implementation of augmented reality in this context will add great value. As the technology advances in augmented reality and the capability of mobile devices increases, the value can only increase in the oncoming years.

References

1. Pugh, S.: Total Design: Integrated Methods for Successful Product Engineering. Addison-Wesley Publishing Company, Glasgow (1991)
2. Chrysikou, E., Weisberg, R.: Following the wrong footsteps: Fixation effects of pictorial examples in a design problem solving task. Journal of Experimental Pyschology 31(5), 1134–1148 (2005)
3. Pertulla, M., Liikkanen, L.: Structural tendencies and exposure effects in design idea generation. In: ASME 2006 (2006)
4. Benami, O., Jin, Y.: Creative stimulation in conceptual design. In: ASME 2002, Montreal (2002)
5. Fuge, M., Yumer, M., Orbay, G., Kara, L.: Conceptual design and modification of freeform surfaces using dual shape representations in augmented reality environments. Computer-Aided Design 5(9), 1020–1032 (2011)
6. Fiorentino, M., de Amicis, R., Monno, G., Stork, A.: Spacedesign: A mixed Reailty Workspace for Aesthetic Industrial Design. In: International Symposium on Mixed and Augmented Reality (2002)
7. Verlinden, J., Horváth, I.: A Critical Systems Position on Augmented Prototyping Systems for Industrial Design. In: Proceedings of the ASME 2007 International Design Engineering Technical Conferences & Computers and Information in Engineering Conference IDETC/CIE (2007)
8. Verlinden, J., Horváth, I.: Framework for testing and validating Interactive Augmented Prototyping as a Design Means in Industrial Practice. In: Virtual Concept 2006, Playa Del Carmen (2006)
9. Ong, S.K., Pang, Y., Nee, A.Y.C.: Augmented Reality Aided Assembly Design and Planning. CIRP Annals - Manufacturing Technology 56(1), 49–52 (2007)
10. Serdar, T., Aziz, E.-S.S., Esche, S., Chassapis, C.: Integration of Augmented Reality into the CAD Process (2007)
11. Park, J.: Augmented Reality Based Re-Formable Mock-Up for Design Evaluation. In: Proceedings of the 2008 International Symposium on Ubiquitos Virtual Reality, pp. 17–20. IEEE Computer Society, Washington DC (2008)
12. Sidharta, R., Oliver, J., Sannier, A.: Augmented Reality Tangible Interface for Distributed Design Review. In: International Conference on Computer Graphics, Imaging and Visualisation, CGIV 2006 (2006)
13. Regenbrecht, H., Wagner, M., Baratoff, G.: MagicMeeting - A Collaborative Tangible Augmented Reality System. Virtual Reality - Systems, Development and Applications 6(3), 151–166 (2002)
14. Smparounis, K., Alexopoulos, K., Xanthakis, V., Pappas, M., Mavrikios, D., Chryssolouris, G.: A Web-based platform for Collaborative Product Design and Evaluation. Digital Factory for Human-Oriented Production Systems (2011)

15. Schumann, H., Burtescu, S., Siering, F.: Applying Augmented Reality Techniques in the Field of Interactive Collaborative Design, Darmstadt, Germany
16. Shen, Y., Ong, S., Nee, A.: Augmented reality for collaborative product design anf development. Design Studies 31, 118–145 (2010)
17. Kujala, S.: User involvement: A review of the benefits and challenges. Behaviour & Information Technology 22(1), 1–16 (2003)
18. Schumann, H., Silviu, B., Frank, S.: Applying Augmented Reality Techniques in the Field of Interactive Collaborative Design (1998)
19. Wang, X.: Exploring augmented reality benefits in collaborative conceptualization. In: 2008 12th International Conference on Computer Supported Cooperative Work in Design, pp. 699–704 (2008)
20. Nee, A.Y.C., Ong, S.K., Chryssolouris, G., Mourtzis, D.: Augmented reality applications in design and manufacturing. CIRP Annals - Manufacturing Technology 61(2), 657–679 (2012)
21. Aurasma (2014), http://www.aurasma.com
22. Metaio (2014), http://www.metaio.com
23. Layar - Augmented Reality (2014), http://www.layar.com

Authoring of Automatic Data Preparation and Scene Enrichment for Maritime Virtual Reality Applications

Benjamin Mesing and Uwe von Lukas

Fraunhofer Institute for Computer Graphics Research IGD, 18059 Rostock, Germany

Abstract. When realizing virtual reality scenarios for the maritime sector a key challenge is dealing with the huge amount of data.

Adding interactive behaviour for providing a rich interactive experience manually requires a lot of time and effort. Additionally, even though shipyards today often use PDM or PLM systems to manage and aggregate the data, the export to a visualisation format is not without problems and often needs some post procession to take place. We present a framework, that combines the capabilities of processing large amounts of data for preparing virtual reality scenarios and enriching it with dynamic aspects like interactive door opening capabilities. An authoring interface allows orchestrating the data preparation chain by non-expert users to realise individual scenarios easily.

1 Introduction

At our institute we have done research within the field of virtual reality in maritime sector for more than ten years. During this time, we have identified two key factors that need to be addressed when developing virtual reality applications:

1. The amount of data is huge and, when exported, often comes divided into a large number of files. For example a ship of middle complexity consists of one million individual parts, often split in tens of thousands of files. This data needs to be converted and optimised for visualisation.
2. The enrichment of scenes with dynamic aspects, e.g. for more realistic design reviews or training scenarios, requires large numbers of objects to be handled in a similar way. For example for realistic lighting conditions, each lamp designed within CAD, must be assigned a light source within the visualisation. Manual processing is time-consuming and expensive, being a show-stopper for many VR applications in the maritime industry.

We address those issues with an extensible data processing framework capable of processing 3D geometry and performing geometry specific operations like the calculation of bounding boxes. The framework supports the notion of modules performing the actual processing and offers a selection of predefined modules for basic operations. Additionally, an authoring interface is provided allowing the orchestration of the modules

R. Shumaker and S. Lackey (Eds.): VAMR 2014, Part II, LNCS 8526, pp. 426–434, 2014.
© Springer International Publishing Switzerland 2014

2   Related Work

Authoring of dynamic virtual reality scenarios has received increased attention during the last fifteen years. Specific authoring application exist for a number of application domains with a tight focus on the specific domain. Examples are the "High-Level Tool for Curators of 3D Virtual Visits" of Chitarro et al. [3] or the authoring approach for "mixed reality assembly instructor for hierarchical structures" of Zauner et al. [11] as well as commercial software products like the Unity editor environment.

Generic authoring approaches are much harder to design and often provide more generic building blocks. Kapadia et al. introduce an approach how to author behaviour in a simple behaviour description language [6]. To this end, various constraints and settings can be specified. The focus is laid on the authoring of the behaviour itself.

Many approaches ground on the idea of object based behaviour [2,5,4]. Here an object consists of geometry and behaviour, i.e. both form a unit. When authoring virtual worlds based on those approaches, the workflow is usually to create at least the interactive objects of the world within an authoring environment. The authoring environment is specific to the creation of behaviour objects and provides often only limited geometric modelling capabilities. Backman suggests a slightly different approach [1]. His authoring framwork for virtual environments is also based on the notion of objects, where the link between physical behaviour and geometry is maintained through a link definition. For visual authoring however, he utilizes an existing 3D modelling tool, and the object properties responsible for the behaviour are defined as annotations to the 3D-objects.

A comprehensive approach on the authoring of "Compelling Scenarios in Virtual Reality" is presented by Springer et al. [10]. The authors describe a system, consisting of several stages. The system addresses automatic scenario generation by creating objects in a predefined way based on e.g. 2D-terrain images. Further, scenario editing is provided, supporting the creation of additional objects. The geometry is loaded from external files, while the object behaviour must be implemented in the presented application. Finally, an immersive viewer displays the scenario and can be coupled with the scenario editor supporting a live editing of the scenarios. The idea of a tight coupling between scenario editor and immersive environment is also pursued by Lee et al. [7]. The authors describe an authoring system for VR-scenarios, that allows doing the authoring within VR. The approach is named "immersive authoring and testing" and, according to the authors, avoids frequent changes from desktop to VR system.

A step further in automatic scenario generation is done by Zook et al. [12]. They propose the creation of training scenarios based on computer stored world knowledge, learning objectives and learners attributes. For a specific domain, the approach allows to generate a large amount of different training scenarios for training different objectives in various combinations. The approach requires a high initial effort to store the world knowledge and learning objectives in a computer processable way.

3   Data Processing and Enrichment Framework

Current state of the art authoring approaches provide means to either create dynamic scenes from ground up or to manually enrich existing geometric models with behaviour. In the latter case, the geometry usually gets exported from a CAD system or a 3D modelling tool. This approach works well, when only a limited set of objects needs to be interactive and when the basic 3D geometry does not change over times. In 2006 we have presented a first approach for defining an automatic enrichment process for enriching geometry with behaviour to address this issue [8]. However, this approach was limited in a way, that it allowed addressing geometric objects solely by name and was closely tied to the VRML programming language.

We present a framework, that allows applying specific behaviour to a large number of objects based on custom selection mechanism. The work presented in this paper is based on our previous work but features an open architecture and additionally incorporates flexible mechanisms for data processing. Apart from the addition of geometric behaviour the framework also supports the pre-processing of geometric data like data conversion or geometry cleanup. It can be used to define a fully automated data processing chain from CAD-model to interactive virtual reality scenario.

The new architecture consists of a generic data processing platform which can basically handle any kind of data. The data processing flow can be defined using a graphical authoring environment, enabling non-IT experts to set up the data conversion chain for a VR session. The platform has a strong focus on 3D content and behaviour enrichment.

3.1   Data Processing Framework

In this section we will discuss the data processing framework in more detail. The basic components of the framework are:

Modules perform the actual data processing, they receive data and operate on the data, usually transforming it in a way. Each module contains a set of typed in-slots for they data that gets processed, a set of typed out-slots for the data generated by the module and a set of attribute to configure various parameters of the module.

Components are a special form of modules. They can also perform data processing and, additionally, can contain other modules or components, called inner modules. In addition to the normal in- and out-slots, they can also contain internal in- and out-slots. Internal slots are utilised to release data available to the component to its inner modules, and to receive data generated by the inner modules to the surrounding component.

Routes describe the data flow between modules and components, i.e. they connect the out-slots of one module with the in-slot of another module.

Figure 1 illustrates the usage of modules and routes. The *Creator* module creates an X3D scene based on the X3D code specified in the attribute and

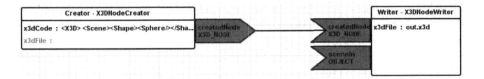

Fig. 1. A simple data processing chain, the module *Creator* creates an X3D scene and the module *Writer* writes the scene to the hard drive

sends the scene to its out slot. The *Writer* module receives the scene and writes it to an X3D file.

An example for a component is given in Fig. 2. The *ForEachComponent* receives a list of objects at its *objectsIn* slot. When executed, it creates instances of its inner modules for each element of the list, and sends the object to be processed through its inner out-slot *listObject*. In the example, a list of X3D objects is processed and a transform node is inserted around each of the nodes. The resulting objects are collected by the foreach component and released via its out-slot *objectsOut* once all objects have been processed.

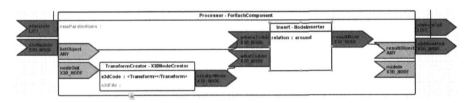

Fig. 2. The component *Processor* receives the list of objects and for each of those objects runs its inner modules. The resulting objects are collected by the component and released via the out-slot *objectsOut* once all objects have been processed.

The platform offers an authoring environment which allows to visually combine the data processing modules, define the attributes and connect the modules via routes. The illustrations of data processing modules throughout this paper have been exported from the authoring environment. With the predefined modules provided by the framework common data processing tasks for preparation of geometry can be realised. This includes the iteration over a collection of objects, the selection of specific items and the processing of files with external tools like geometry converter or optimiser.

3.2 Creating Custom Modules

The open architecture of the data processing framework allows users to develop modules and components for their specific application domains. When developing a new module or component, its interface must be described within an XML definition and the behaviour must be implemented in the Java programming language. This includes the information about attributes, in- and out-slots supported by new modules, its name and the Java-classes implementing the data processing. This task is suitable for IT-experts only.

Once the custom modules have been developed, the end user can utilise them in the same way as the modules predefined by the framework. In fact, the predefined modules are in no way different from custom modules. For example the *ForEach*-component given in Fig. 2 is just an ordinary component. The functionality to iterate over the list of objects and send it to the in-slots is implemented within the component-implementation. A module-designer could decide to remove the available *ForEach*-component and provide its own implementation. Figure 3 gives an overview over the roles involved.

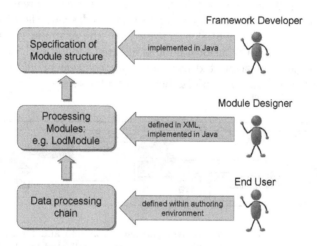

Fig. 3. The structure of the modules, and components as well as the type system is defined by the framework developer. The module designer can define custom modules for their specific application domain which can be used by the end user.

3.3   Geometry Modification and Behaviour Enrichment

The main focus of the platform is the preparation of geometry for interactive virtual reality scenarios. This is reflected by special support for the X3D language. In particular, a special type for X3D-data and a set of modules specific for processing X3D geometry is provided.

The most important modules are presented hereafter. The *X3DCreator* module allows to read whole X3D files as well as fragment X3D code. The code can consist of any possible top level node and thus be used to create e.g. Touch-Sensors, Script nodes, or additional geometry as required for the realisation of arbitrary behaviour. The *X3DWriter* module can write out X3D code to a file. The *X3DNodeSelector* supports selection of specific nodes from a X3D scene. Selection can happen either based on the node names using wildcard expressions, or using XPath expressions. Using XPath as selection criteria is very flexible and can e.g. be utilised to select nodes based on associated meta information, which is stored in separate Metadata nodes in X3D. Finally the *NodeInserter* can insert one node inside or around another one. This can be required, e.g. if a *Transform* node must be added to allow the movement of an object or if a *TouchSensor* should be added to allow interaction with the object. Fig. 4 shows, how different modules are combined to add a *Transform* node around all doors within a scene.

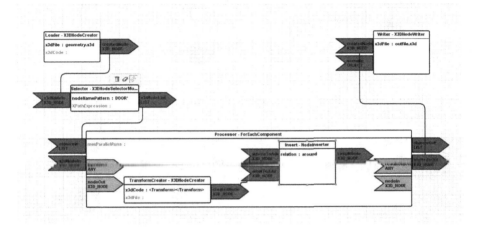

Fig. 4.

3.4   Maritime Enrichment Scenario

We have used the platform to realise data processing for different maritime application scenario. This section describes the realisation of one such scenario.

In this scenario we got a ship model consisting of approximately 20.000 geometry files and more then 100.000 objects from the shipyard Flensburger Schiffbau Gesellschaft. To allow for an interactive walk-through we needed to add the functionality to open and close the doors within the model. We have set up the data processing chain shown in Fig. 5. The chain sets up a VR scene and automatically enriches it with the interactive behaviour. It first scans the content of the directories where the geometry files are located and then creates and X3D-Group node containing and Inline-Node for each of the files. A filter then selects all nodes where the name matches the string *216** (indicating a door). The list of nodes is passed to the *ForEachComponent*, where one module calculates the bounding box for each of the doors and a second module inserts the behaviour to open and close the doors. The route from the *Inline* module to the *ForEach* component is merely to make the grouping node available to the *ForEach* component. The resulting file is then written to the specified X3D file

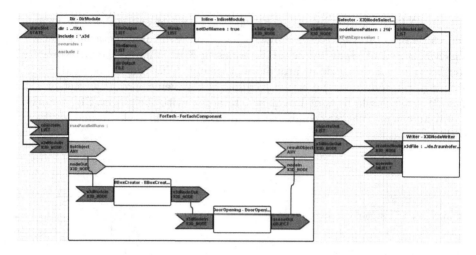

Fig. 5. Data processing chain to enrich a ship scene with the behaviour to allow opening and closing of doors

Fig. 6. Walk through an enriched 3D scene, when the user approaches the door opens automatically

by the *X3DNodeWriter*. Figure 6 illustrates how a walk through looks like, when approaching a door it opens automatically.

Since the model was to large to be displayed fluently as a whole, we have set up additional data processing steps to implement on demand loading of objects. When the users approaches the object the objects are shown only up to a certain distance and when the user moves away, the object are hidden again. The modules for the data processing consist of the *BoundingBox* creator module to calculate the bounding boxes of the individual objects and a *OnDemandLoader* module which inserts a *ProxyimitySensor* node for each object and shows or hides the object as appropriate. More information on this industry scenario can be found in our paper [9].

The implementation of the behaviour enrichment with our data processing framework has two major advantages. First, it allows to be executed multiple times, being applicable to new versions of the CAD geometry or, with usually only a few adjustments like the name pattern, to totally new ships. Second, it allows to apply the behaviour to large numbers of object in very little time.

4 Summary and Outlook

In industry virtual reality scenarios, the geometry for the scenario is usually provided by CAD or modelling tools. In this paper we have presented our approach for authoring the data preparation chain for geometry processing and behaviour enrichment. The behaviour enrichment of large amounts of objects is handled through a general object selection mechanism and an iteration mechanism allowing processing of homogeneous objects. The framework enables users to quickly set up interactive virtual reality scenarios. Once a processing chain is set up, it can be applied to updated versions of the geometry and to other base geometries with little effort.

In future we plan to extend our approach in different directions. One direction is, to allow summarizing components with integrated modules to high level building blocks, providing a higher level of abstraction to the user, while still supporting fine-grained data processing modules. Another direction is to ease the authoring process by increasing the graphical capabilities. Currently selecting objects from an X3D scene must be done manually, e.g. by name. Graphically presenting a loaded X3D-scene and allowing selection to happen through the visual representation would further ease the authoring process.

References

1. Backman, A.: Colosseum3d – authoring framework for virtual environments. In: Proceedings of EUROGRAPHICS Workshop IPT & EGVE Workshop, pp. 225–226 (2005)
2. Beeson, C.: An object-oriented approach to vrml development. In: Proceedings of the Second Symposium on Virtual Reality Modeling Language, VRML 1997, pp. 17–24. ACM, New York (1997)
3. Chittaro, L., Ieronutti, L., Ranon, R., Visintini, D., Siotto, E.: A high-level tool for curators of 3d virtual visits and its application to a virtual exhibition of renaissance frescoes. In: Artusi, A. (ed.) VAST 2010, pp. 147–154. Eurographics Association, Goslar (2010)
4. Dachselt, R., Rukzio, E.: Behavior3d: An xml-based framework for 3d graphics behavior. In: Proceedings of the Eighth International Conference on 3D Web Technology, p. 101. ACM, Saint Malo (2003)
5. Dachselt, R., Hinz, M., Meissner, K.: Contigra: An xml-based architecture for component-oriented 3d applications. In: Proceedings of the Seventh International Conference on 3D Web Technology, Web3D 2002, pp. 155–163. ACM, New York (2002)
6. Kapadia, M., Singh, S., Reinman, G., Faloutsos, P.: A behavior-authoring framework for multiactor simulations. IEEE Computer Graphics and Applications 31(6), 45–55 (2011)
7. Lee, G.A., Kim, G.J., Billinghurst, M.: Directing virtual worlds: Authoring and testing for/within virtual reality based contents. In: Proceeding of the 14th International Conferent on Artifical Reality and Teleexistence (ICAT), Seoul, Korea (2004)

8. Mesing, B., Hellmich, C.: Using aspect oriented methods to add behaviour to x3d documents. In: Web3D 2006: Proceedings of the Eleventh International Conference on 3D Web Technology, pp. 97–107. ACM, New York (2006)
9. Mesing, B., Kluwe, F., von Lukas, U.: Evaluating evacuation simulation results in a virtual reality environment. In: Bertram, V. (ed.) 10th International Conference on Computer and IT Applications in the Maritime Industries (COMPIT 2011), Hamburg, pp. 326–334 (2011)
10. Springer, J.P., Neumann, C., Reiners, D., Cruz-Neira, C.: An integrated pipeline to create and experience compelling scenarios in virtual reality. In: Beraldin, J.A., Cheok, G.S., McCarthy, M.B., Neuschaefer-Rube, U., Am Baskurt, McDowall, I.E., Dolinsky, M. (eds.) Three-Dimensional Imaging, Interaction, and Measurement. Proceedings of SPIE-The International Society for Optical Engineering. SPIE-INT SOC Optical Engineering, 1000 20TH ST and PO BOX 10 and Bellingham and WA 98227-0010 USA, vol. 7864 (2011)
11. Zauner, J., Haller, M., Brandl, A., Hartman, W.: Authoring of a mixed reality assembly instructor for hierarchical structures. In: Proceedings of the Second IEEE and ACM International Symposium on Mixed and Augmented Reality 2003, pp. 237–246 (2003)
12. Zook, A., Lee-Urban, S., Riedl, M.O., Holden, H.K., Sottilare, R.A., Brawner, K.W.: Automated scenario generation. In: El-Nasr, M.S. (ed.) Proceedings of the International Conference on the Foundations of Digital Games, p. 164. ACM, S.l. (2012)

AR-Based Vehicular Safety Information System for Forward Collision Warning

Hye Sun Park and Kyong-Ho Kim

Human-Vehicle Interaction Research Center, ETRI, Daejeon, Korea
hspark78@etri.re.kr

Abstract. This paper proposes an AR (augmented reality) based vehicular safety information system that provides warning information allowing drivers to easily avoid obstacles without being visually distracted. The proposed system consists of four stages: fusion data based object tracking, collision threat assessment, AR-registration, and a warning display strategy. It is shown experimentally that the proposed system can predict the threat of a collision from a tracked forward obstacle even during the nighttime and under bad weather conditions. The system can provide safety information for avoiding collisions by projecting information directly into the driver's field of view. The proposed system is expected to help drivers by conveniently providing safety information and allowing them to safely avoid forward obstacles.

Keywords: AR (augmented reality), vehicular safety information, forward collision, warning system, data fusion, object tracking, threat assessment, warning strategy.

1   Introduction

To avoid collisions with stationary obstacles, other moving vehicles, or pedestrians, drivers have to be aware of the possibility of a collision and be ready to start braking early enough. In addition, when following other vehicles, drivers need to keep a safe distance to allow for proper braking. An understanding of how drivers maintain such a safe distance, the type of visual information they use, and what visual factors affect their performance is clearly important for improving road safety. A driver has to rely on direct visual information to know how rapidly they are closing in on a forward vehicle. Therefore, if this information is poor, there is a danger of the driver not sufficiently braking in time. In addition, a system for the rapid detection of neighboring objects such as vehicles and pedestrians, a quick estimation of the threat of an obstacle, and a convenient way to avoid predicted collisions is needed. Automobile manufactures are highly concerned about problems related to motor vehicle safety, and are making greater effort to solve them, for example, adaptive cruise control (ACC) [1], antilock brake systems (ABSs) [2, 3], collision-warning systems (CWSs) [4], and emergency automatic brakes (EABs). AR-based driving support systems (AR-DSSs) have also been recently developed [5, 6]. These developed AR-DSSs differ from traditional in-vehicle collision avoidance systems (CASs) in that they provide warning signals overlapping with real physical objects. Compared to a

R. Shumaker and S. Lackey (Eds.): VAMR 2014, Part II, LNCS 8526, pp. 435–442, 2014.

traditional CAS, an AR-DSS attempts to support the direct perception of merging traffic rather than the generation of a warning signal. Therefore, an AR-DSS can lower the switching costs associated with a traditional CAS by providing signals that align with a driver's perceptual awareness [5]. Accordingly, an active visual-based safety information system for preventing collisions has become one of the major research topics in the field of safe driving. Thus, this paper proposes an AR-based vehicular safety information system that provides visual-based collision warning information to match the driver's viewpoint. We expect that the proposed system will contribute significantly to a reduction in the number of driving accidents and their severity.

2   AR-Based Vehicular Safety Information System

The proposed system consists of four stages: fusion data based object tracking, collision threat assessment, AR-registration, and a warning display strategy. An I/O flowchart of the proposed system is presented in Fig. 1. Once a driver starts driving, the system continuously detects and tracks forward objects and classifies the collision threat level. Simultaneously, the system tracks the driver's eye movement and presents potential collision threats on a see-through display; the results are then matched with the driver's visual viewpoint to help the driver identify and avoid obstacles. Unlike conventional ABS, the goal in this paper is to provide forward-object location based on the driver's viewpoint through an interactive AR-design for maintaining a safe distance from forward objects and preventing collisions. Thus, two modules, i.e., collision threat assessment and a warning display strategy, will be described in detail.

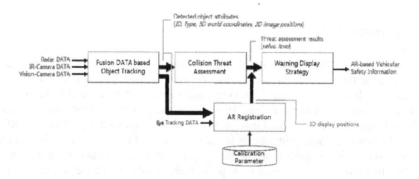

Fig. 1. The proposed system configuration

2.1   Fusion Data Based Object Tracking

To track forward objects accurately and robustly, the proposed system uses both video and radar information, which provide important clues regarding the ongoing traffic activity in the driver's path. Fig. 2 shows how to track based on fusion data.

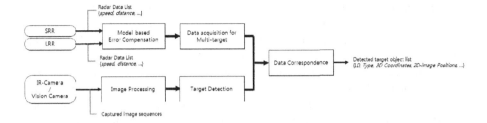

Fig. 2. Sensor Data Fusion for object tracking

In vision-based object tracking, all objects on a road can be deemed potential obstacles. In this system, we first extract all obstacles using their geometric properties. We also classify them into *significant* and *less significant* objects, which are triggered under certain circumstances. Significant objects are obtained using specialized detectors (i.e., vehicle and pedestrian detectors) [7, 8]. In an invisible environment, the proposed system detects multiple forward obstacles using three radar systems, and then recognizes and classifies them based on fusion with a night-vision camera through a processing shown in the flowchart in Fig. 2.

2.2 Collision Threat Assessment

The threat assessment measure of the proposed system is defined in Eq. (1). This measure is based on the basic assumption that a threatening object is in the same lane as the host vehicle, and is the closest object ahead. The proposed system estimates the collision possibility using the velocity and distance between the host vehicle and obstacle, which is referred to as TTC (time to collision) in this paper. To measure the TTC, an experimental DB is first generated, and the optimal threshold value is then extracted using this DB.

$$TTC = \frac{D_{c2o}}{V_c},$$ (1)

where D_{c2o} is defined as the distance between the host car and obstacle, and V_c is the velocity of the host car in Eq. (1).

Table 1. The complied DB under various conditions

Type	Driving Condition		The compiled DB
Vehicle	Velocity (V)	≤60 km/h	Acquired images including more than 500 vehicles, which were taken during an 18-hour period
	Distance (D)	<100 m	
	Road Type	· Highway · Public road	
Pedestrian	Velocity (V)	≤40 km/h	Acquired images including more than 800 pedestrians, which were taken during a 12-hour period
	Distance (D)	<15 m	
	Road Type	· Crossway · Residential street	

The proposed system divides a threat into three levels according to the TTC value. To measure the TTC value of each of the three levels, an experimental DB of various driving conditions is first generated, as shown in Table 1. Next, the optimal threshold value is extracted using the DB, as shown in Table 2. In general, a TTC is defined as the time remaining until a collision between two vehicles that will occur if the collision course and difference speeds are maintained [9]. A TTC has been one of the well-recognized safety indicators for traffic conflicts on highways [10–12]. However, the proposed system provides warning information for safety fitting the driver's viewpoint through an interactive AR-design, and is applied to public road environments for both vehicles and pedestrians. Therefore, the TTC values used by the proposed system are extracted through various experiments.

Table 2. TTC threshold value of each of the three levels (*m/s*)

Type / Level	Vehicle	Pedestrian
1 (Danger)	$0.0 \leq threshold < 0.3$	$0.0 \leq threshold < 1.1$
2 (Warning)	$0.3 \leq threshold < 0.7$	$1.1 \leq threshold < 6.0$
3 (Attention)	$0.7 \leq threshold < 5.0$	$6.0 \leq threshold < 10.0$

2.3 AR Registration

For the registration, the calibration parameters are generated offline through an expression of the relations among the three coordinates of the vehicle, driver, and display. The system then detects and tracks the driver's head and eyes in real time. The coordinates of the target objects transform into display coordinates matching the driver's viewpoint. A flowchart of this AR registration module is shown in Fig. 3.

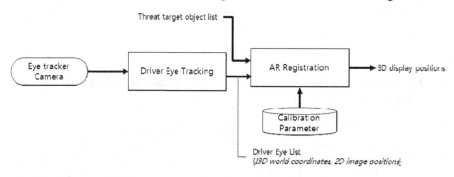

Fig. 3. AR registration module

2.4 Warning Display Strategy

To improve the driver's cognition of the displayed information, an interactive UX design is needed. For this, the information provided should not only be easier to understand, but also more intuitively acceptable by considering the driver's characteristics, the type of information provided, and the driving conditions. The system expresses information differently depending on both the threat level in the previous module and the study results from [13]. Table 3 shows the AR-display design and a representative scene on the see-through display according to the three levels of obstacle type. In the AR-display design, the color and line thickness are set based on the ISO rules [14]. In addition, the design type was determined through the study results of [13] and the HUD concept design in [15].

Table 3. AR-display design for three levels of obstacle type

Obstacle Type	Design Type	Level			Real Display Scene
		1	2	3	
Vehicle	Type 1	5ₘ	13ₘ	36ₘ	
	Type 2	5ₘ	13ₘ	36ₘ	
Pedestrian	Type 1	STOP	4ₘ	12ₘ	
	Type 2	STOP	4ₘ	12ₘ	
	Type 3	STOP	4ₘ	12ₘ	

3   Experiment Results

To provide driving-safety information using the proposed AR-HUD, various sensors and devices were attached to the experimental test vehicle, as shown in Fig. 4. The two cameras used for the forward obstacle recognition are *GS2-FW-14S5* models from Point Grey Research Co., which are 12 *mm* cameras with a resolution of *1384 x 1036*, and can obtain an image at a speed of 30 *fps*. In addition, we used *IEEE 1394b* for the interface. To cover multi-target tracking, two SRRs (short range radar) and one LRR (long range radar) are used in environments with poor visibility such as under rainy conditions and at night. Both radar models are a *Delphi ESR* at 77*GHz* with a CAN interface. The IR-camera is a *PathfindIR* model from FLIR Co., and has a resolution of *320 x 240* with a speed of 30 *fps* using an RCA interface.

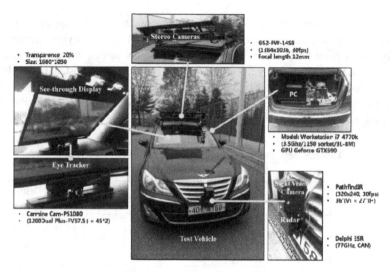

Fig. 4. Experimental test vehicle

To show our AR-based vehicle safety information system, we used a 22-*inch*, transparent Samsung LCD display with a transparency of 20%. This LCD display has low transparency, and thus cannot allow AR-based vehicle safety information to be seen very well at nighttime. To solve this problem, it is necessary to develop a large-area transparent OLED based display. Fig. 5 shows images of pedestrians detected by the proposed system based on the estimated optimal TTC value shown on the display.

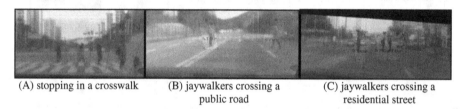

| (A) stopping in a crosswalk | (B) jaywalkers crossing a public road | (C) jaywalkers crossing a residential street |

Fig. 5. Experiment results

To evaluate each module, the experimental DB was generated from various driving environments, including a simulated road environment and actual roads (a highway, public roads, and residential streets). For vehicle recognition in the daytime, a total of 10,320 frames were obtained from the experimental stereo camera. For pedestrian recognition, a total of 3,270 frames were acquired. Furthermore, a total of 5,400 frames were obtained from the IR-camera for recognition of both vehicles and pedestrians during the nighttime. Fig. 6 shows the real road test region. As indicated in Fig. 6, the test region includes public roads, residential streets, and crossways for recognition of both vehicles and pedestrians in the daytime. In contrast, Fig. 7 shows the test-bed used for obstacle recognition during the nighttime.

Fig. 6. Experiment test region on real roads

Fig. 7. Experiment test-bed for nighttime recognition

The recognition rate of the driving-safety information obtained by the proposed system during the daytime is 85.01%, and the system has a recognition speed of 15 *fps* for both vehicles and pedestrians. The recognition rate of the driving-safety information and recognition speed of the proposed system during the nighttime are 77% and 10 *fps* for both vehicles and pedestrians.

4   Conclusions

This paper proposed an AR-based vehicular safety information system for forward collision warning. This paper showed that 1) a forward obstacle can be successfully detected and tracked by fusing radar and two types of vision data, 2) fusion based forward obstacle tracking is robust compared to single sensor based obstacle detection, and objects can be reliably be detected, 3) collision threat assessments can be efficiently classified into threat levels by measuring the collision possibility of each obstacle, 4) AR-registration can provide warning information without visual distraction by matching the driver's viewpoint, and 5) a warning strategy can conveniently provide safety information considering both the obstacle and human-vision attributes. The experiment results show that the proposed system achieves an 81.01% recognition rate. We expect that the proposed system will provide suitable information according to the driver's viewpoint as a way to reduce traffic accidents.

Acknowledgement. This work was supported by the Industrial Strategic technology development program, Development of Driver-View based in-Vehicle AR Display System Technology Development (10040927), funded by the Ministry of Knowledge Economy (MKE, Korea). The first author would like to thank the institutes that participated in this study for their helpful experiments.

References

1. Ganci, P., Potts, S., Okurowski, F.: A forward looking automotive radar sensor. In: IEEE Intelligent Vehicles Symposium, Detroit, USA, pp. 321–325 (September 1995)
2. Lin, C.M., Hsu, C.F.: Neural-network hybrid control for antilock braking systems. IEEE Transactions on Neural Networks 14(2), 351–359 (2003)
3. Mirzaei, A., Moallem, M., Mirzaeian, B.: Optimal Design of a hybrid controller for anti-lock braking systems. In: IEEE/ASME International Conference on Advanced Intelligent Mechatronics, Monterey, CA, USA, pp. 905–910 (July2005)
4. Dagan, E., Mano, O., Stein, G.P., Shashua, A.: Forward Collision Warning with a Single Camera. In: IEEE Intelligent Vehicles Symposium, Parma, Italy, pp. 37–42 (June 2004)
5. Fu, W.T., Gasper, J., Kim, S.W.: Effects of an In-Car Augmented Reality System on Improving Safety of Younger and Older Drivers. In: International Symposium on Mixed and Augmented Reality, Adelaide, Australia, pp. 59–66 (October 2013)
6. Ferreira, M., Gomes, P., Silveria, M.K., Vieira, F.: Augmented Reality Driving Supported by Vehicular Ad Hoc Networking. In: International Symposium on Mixed and Augmented Reality, Adelaide, Australia, pp. 253–254 (October 2013)
7. Park, H.S., Park, M.W., Won, K.H., Kim, K.H., Jung, S.K.: In-Vehicle AR-HUD System to Provide Driving-Safety Information. ETRI Journal 35(6), 1038–1047 (2013)
8. Won, K.H., Jung, S.K.: Billboard sweep stereo for obstacle detection in road scenes. Electronics Letters 48(24), 1528–1530 (2012)
9. Hayward, J.C.: Near miss determination through use of a scale of danger. Highway Research Board (384), 24–34 (1972)
10. Farah, H., Bekhor, S., Polus, A.: Risk evaluation by modeling of passing behavior on two-lane rural highways. Accident Analysis and Prevention 41(4), 887–894 (2009)
11. Svensson, A.: A method for analyzing the traffic process in a safety perspective. Doctoral Dissertation, University of Lund, Lund, Sweden, vol. 166, pp. 1–174 (October 1998)
12. Vogel, K.: A comparison of headway and time to collision as safety indicators. Accident Analysis and Prevention 35(3), 427–433 (2003)
13. Park, H., Kim, K.-h.: Efficient Information Representation Method for Driver-centered AR-HUD system. In: Marcus, A. (ed.) DUXU 2013, Part III. LNCS, vol. 8014, pp. 393–400. Springer, Heidelberg (2013)
14. ISO International Standards, ISO 15008: Road vehicles - Ergonomic aspects of transport information and control systems - Specifications and compliance procedures for in-vehicle visual presentation (February 11, 2009)
15. BMW Concept Video, BMW Head Up Display HUD - Simulation Augmented Reality, Webpage: http://www.youtube.com/watch?feature=player_detailpage&v=33D ME4SHTSI

An Augmented Reality Framework for Supporting and Monitoring Operators during Maintenance Tasks

Guido Maria Re and Monica Bordegoni

Politecnico di Milano, Dipartimento di Meccanica,
Via La Masa, 1, 20156 Milano, Italy
{guidomaria.re,monica.bordegoni}@polimi.it

Abstract. The paper proposes a framework for supporting maintenance services in industrial environments through the use of a mobile device and Augmented Reality (AR) technologies. 3D visual instructions about the task to carry out are represented in the real world by means of AR and they are visible through the mobile device. In addition to the solutions proposed so far, the framework introduces the possibility to monitor the operator's work from a remote location. The mobile device stores information for each maintenance step that has been completed and it makes them available on a remote database. Supervisors can consequently check the maintenance activity from a remote PC at any time. The paper presents also a prototype system, developed according to the framework, and an initial case study in the field of food industry.

Keywords: Augmented Reality, Framework, Maintenance tasks, Remote Supervision.

1 Introduction

Maintenance operations in a factory are necessary duties in order to provide a continuous functioning of the machineries and of the production. In several cases, operators are trained in order to acquire skills necessary to intervene on the machines on a scheduled time and to operate by following proper procedures. However, the outcome and the time planned to achieve these maintenance operations are always uncertain. The uncertainties are due to difficulties that the operator must face to complete the maintenance task, such as the functional and mechanical complexity of the machine.

The level of uncertainty increases when the maintenance operation is not a routine work because it is a fortuitous or compelling event that the operator is not used to carry out. In other cases, instead, an operator carries out a maintenance task even though his background is not sufficient to accomplish it autonomously or accurately, such as when the operator gets confused because he deals with several similar machines or when an unskilled operator performs the task. This case usually happens to avoid the intervention of an expert operator, which could be costly and require a long waiting. Thus, an instruction manual traditionally supports the operator to accomplish the maintenance activity.

However, maintenance operations accomplished with lack of depth or without complying with the protocols could lead to functioning problems of the machine.

R. Shumaker and S. Lackey (Eds.): VAMR 2014, Part II, LNCS 8526, pp. 443–454, 2014.

A malfunctioning can be dangerous to the people working in the factory or it can lead up to additional maintenance, due to unexpected machine fails. From these considerations it turns out that the complexity of the machine, inexperience, negligence and the human predisposition to errors affect the maintenance effectiveness. Consequently, these issues negatively influence a machine, by affecting its production in a plant, its working life and, in a long-term perspective, it leads to the increase of the industrial costs.

According to the above-mentioned considerations, current research trends are oriented to reduce maintenance costs by improving the operator's performances at work. In particular, one of the main trends aims at reducing time and money for the training, by providing supports for instructions that are more accessible and easy to understand also for unskilled operator.

A great advantage in the field of maintenance is offered by Augmented Reality (AR), which is an emerging technology coming from Computer Science. AR enables the user to see and interact with virtual contents seamlessly integrated in the real environment [1, 2]. In case of maintenance operations, the virtual contents are the instructions to perform, which can be represented as text or as three-dimensional objects. Hence, the instructions are provided in a way that it is more direct, accessible and easy to understand than the approach based on a traditional paper manual.

In this research work, the authors describe a framework that aims at extending the AR solutions for supporting maintenance tasks so far proposed. The framework combines a method to provide maintenance instructions to the operator by means of a mobile device and a solution to record and monitor the performed tasks in a remote location. The mobile device shows the instructions to the operator by using AR and, at the same time, sends data and pictures regarding the on-going maintenance task to a remote PC through a wireless network. The advantage of this framework is twofold. Operators have an intuitive support to achieve maintenance at their disposal, while supervisors can visualize the maintenance history of a machine and check the operators' work from remote. In particular, the remote PC can be used to evaluate if the tasks have been carried out in accordance with the protocols, if the operator did a mistake and if the maintenance has been accomplished on schedule.

The paper is divided as follows. The most relevant research works carried out in the field of AR for maintenance are reported in Section 2. Then, the developed framework is described in Section 3, while an initial case study is presented in Section 4. The paper ends with a discussion and an outlook on future developments.

2   Background

AR technology has been successfully experimented in the field of maintenance [3] and nowadays first industrial cases and applications are coming out [4]. The advantage of applying AR in this field is the reduction of the operator's abstraction process to understand the instructions. In fact, the instructions are represented by means of virtual objects directly within the real world so that paper manuals are no longer required. Comparative tests demonstrated the improvement of operator's work in some manual activities by using AR in comparison with other supports to provide instructions. Tang et Al. demonstrated how AR reduces the user errors during manual operations and the mental workload to understand a given task [5]. Henderson and Feiner showed that AR reduces the time to understand, localize and focus on a task during a maintenance phase [6]. In summary, AR increases the effectiveness of the operator activity and it consequently speeds up the whole workflow.

Many AR applications conceived for conducting maintenance operations are based on immersive visualization devices, as for instance the Head Mounted Displays (HMD). The first research focused on maintenance using AR was carried out within the context of the KARMA project [7], in which they provided maintenance instructions on a laser printer through an HMD tracked by an ultrasonic system. A case study in the automotive domain has been described in [8] for the doorlock assembly into a car door, while an immersive AR support is proposed for a military vehicle in [9]. Lastly, the immersive AR solution presented in [10] enables the operator to manipulate maintenance information by means of an on-site authoring interface. In this way, it is possible to record and share knowledge and experience on equipment maintenance with other operators and technicians.

However, HMDs have ergonomic and economic issues that impede their wide deployment in industry, even though they are an effective means to give AR instructions. It is a relatively expensive technology that does not provide a good compromise between graphic quality and comfort for the user [11]. Moreover, its use is unsuitable for a long period, as for an entire working day [12].

Mobile devices are currently the most interesting support for AR applications. Billinghurst et Al. evaluated the use of mobiles as AR support for assembly purposes [13]. Klinger et Al. created a versatile Mobile AR solution for maintenance in various scenarios and they tested it in a nuclear power plant [14]. Also Ishii et Al. tackled maintenance and inspection tasks in this very delicate environment in [15]. As negative aspect, mobile AR has the disadvantage of reducing the manual ability of the operator during its use, if compared with the HMD case. In the first case, in fact, he has to hold the device. For this reason, Goose et Al. proposed the use of vocal commands in order to obtain location-based AR information during the maintenance of a plant [16]. Nevertheless, from an industrial point of view, mobile devices are currently the most attractive and promising solution for supporting maintenance tasks by means of AR. They are powerful enough to provide augmentation and they are cheap and highly available on the market, due to their high volume production for the mass market. In addition, since these devices are easy to handle, to carry and they are currently present in the everyday life, they are considered more socially acceptable than the HMDs.

This work aims at extending the use of AR in maintenance by monitoring the operator's activity from a remote location. Some research works partially dealt with this idea by integrating AR in tele-assistance. Boulanger demonstrated it by developing an immersive system for collaborative tele-training on how to repair an ATM machine [17]. Reitmayr et Al., instead, integrated a simultaneous localization and mapping system (SLAM) in an online solution of annotations in unknown environment [18]. The integration of mobile devices into maintenance activities increases the effectiveness of remote assistance by experts because it makes as if the expert was collaborating on-site.

The research described in this paper distinguishes itself from the others because it presents a framework to record the work done for future monitoring. Actually, the cited works focus only on the support and supervision of the operator in real-time and they do not allow recording his work in order to check it afterwards. By the time this paper has been written, only Fite-Georgel et Al. have proposed a research with a similar approach to monitor the accomplished work [19]. Their solution is a system to check undocumented discrepancies between the designed model of a plant and the final object. However, it works only offline and it has not been conceived for maintenance purposes.

3   Framework Description

The developed framework enables the visualization of maintenance instructions through a mobile device and the remote monitoring of the accomplished work. In this section, an overview of the framework is firstly depicted and subsequently the two main modules, of which the system is made up, are described in detail.

3.1   Overview

Figure 1 provides a schematic representation of the framework and shows its two modules. The first one is the Maintenance Module and it is based on an AR solution to display instructions to accomplish on a mobile device. Thus, the instructions, which are traditionally provided by a paper manual, are stored in a database as digital information and loaded automatically by the AR solution when they are required. For each maintenance step, the module saves data about how the maintenance operation is going and, if the device is connected to a Wi-Fi network, it sends them to a remote storage server.

The data stored into the server are visible at any time by means of the Monitoring module. In this way, a supervisor can check the entire maintenance history carried out on a specific machine.

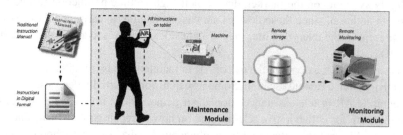

Fig. 1. Schematic representation of the framework

3.2   Maintenance

The Maintenance module is basically an application that provides a mobile AR visualization of the instructions. Besides this, a Wi-Fi client is integrated in the application and it sends the data about the accomplished step to the remote server.

Figure 2 shows the tasks of Maintenance Module. The camera, embedded in the mobile device, frames the machine that requires maintenance service and provides video stream to the AR application. Specific algorithms estimate the position of the camera with respect to the mechanical component by the video stream. This task, also referred to as tracking, allows the module to represent precisely the virtual contents in the real world, with a proper perspective and spatial coherency.

The instructions of the tasks to carry out are stored in configurations files and they are loaded during the initialization of the AR application. They are textual information about how to perform the task and the spatial position of the machine components on which the operator should intervene. The instructions are rendered in a graphic manner, by using also the tracking data. The graphic result is superimposed onto the video stream and shown through the video display of the device.

Once a step is finished, the module automatically saves the maintenance information and makes them available to the remote PC through the Wi-Fi client.

Data Communication. Every time the operator presses the button to move to the next maintenance task, the application saves the data of the last operation concluded and sends them to the remote server. This approach, if scaled with several AR mobile maintenance devices, is a cloud-computing network, which is referred to as *cloud* in

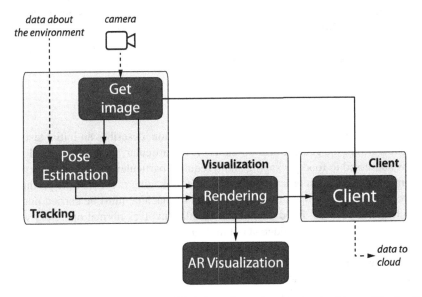

Fig. 2. The tasks that the Maintenance Module performs in order to provide an AR visualization and the data to the remote database

this work. These data are two pictures of the machine at the end of the task and additional textual information. The pictures are the same one and they distinguished between each other because one shows also the augmented content. In this way, the supervisor can check the correctness of the operation by comparing it also by the AR instructions.

The other pieces of information are complementary data to complete the description of the operation and they are the following:

- Operator's name
- Data
- Time
- Machine ID number
- Typology of maintenance (ordinary, extraordinary, intervention for breakdown/error)
- Name of the maintenance operation
- Step Number
- Step description
- Time taken to execute the task

These data are saved in a file and organized according to a simple XML-like structure so as to have an effective communication protocol to exchange information between Maintenance and Monitoring Modules.

3.3   Monitoring

Monitoring Module is constituted by a software application that allows the supervisor to check the maintenance data stored in the Cloud. A parser retrieves the maintenance data saved in the XML files and makes them available to the module. Then, a GUI collects all the data and enables the supervisor to visualize and navigate through the pictures and the maintenance information of each task.

4   Case Study

The case study, which will be presented in this section, describes an initial test of the framework within the context of food industry. In particular, the machine used for the study is addressed to food packaging and it requires particular attentions and a periodic maintenance service in order to provide a safe packaging process of the product.

Several maintenance operations on this kind of machine must be carried out daily, due to hygienic reasons. Food Companies usually involves normal operators without any particular skills or knowledge about the machine to take care of it. The reason lies in the necessity to avoid the constant need of a skilled operator, but it involves a higher risk of uncertainty on the outcome of the operation.

The system developed according to the framework is described in the following. Then, the case study is presented.

4.1   System Description

The system used for the case study is here described according to the two modules of the framework. This section takes into account both hardware and software components.

Maintenance. The Maintenance Module used by the operator is an AR application, constituted by a GUI designed for maintenance purposes, which runs on a mobile device. The mobile device used for this case study is a Windows-based tablet PC. The tablet is equipped with a 1.80 GHz processor, 2 GB RAM, 10.1in color touch screen display and a 640x480 camera working at 30Hz.

Once the operator has selected the right maintenance service to perform on the machine through the GUI, the application provides him with the AR instructions. All the tasks have been taken directly from the paper manual, while the machine components, which are visible as augmented contents in the scene, have been exported from the CAD model of the machine. Each set of instruction for a specific maintenance service is saved in a separated file.

A very stable marker-based tracking solution has been chosen to detect the camera pose and subsequently to properly represent the virtual content in the real environment. Thus, tracking is performed by placing squared, black and white markers on the machine. The tracking algorithms are from the library called ARToolkit Plus [20]. These algorithms detect the markers placed in the environment and they retrieve the camera pose by means of mathematical considerations on the four corners of each marker in the scene.

The visualization of the AR contents in the real world is a merging process between the video stream of the camera on the tablet and the virtual objects, which are rendered with the right perspective according to the tracking data. OpenSceneGraph[1] is the Computer Graphics library used for this purpose and it updates the visualization at every new camera frame.

The interface has been specifically designed for the AR use on a mobile device. Thus, some considerations regarding how to represent and manage the AR content for the operator in the best manner have been taken into account. Actually, the instructions to execute a task have to be provided by the system in a way that is simple to understand and interact. The guidelines presented in [21] have been used as starting point. Figure 3 shows the achieved result of the following considerations.

The first consideration regards the visibility of the virtual objects in the working environment. The objects are 3D or 2D elements and each of them has a precise purpose, such as indicating the point on which the user has to work or showing the action to perform. For this reason, animations applied to them in order to show how to deal with a component can increase the understanding of the user. In addition, these virtual elements must be easy to be recognized into the scene by the operator.

---

[1] OpenSceneGraph library: http://www.openscenegraph.org/

2D textual   3D virtual   3D textual   virtual
instruction   objects   instruction   buttons

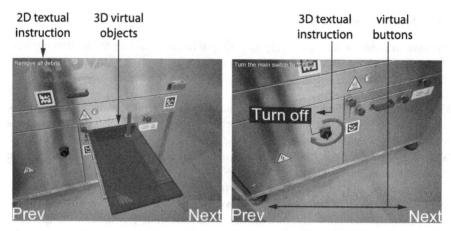

Fig. 3. The virtual objects present in the augmented visualization

Second, the instruction has to be also complemented by some textual information. The purpose of the text is to give additional information, which cannot be provided by other graphical representations. The text is represented as a 2D element on the Graphic User Interface (GUI) and also as a 3D element, which is in a fixed position on the machine. The text should be short, clear and direct, so as to enlighten the operator about the task to accomplish.

Finally, a way to manage the instructions has to be taken into account, since they are represented as a sequence of tasks. By means of a step-by-step instruction approach, the user focuses only on one operation at a time. Therefore, two virtual buttons are present on the GUI and they enable the operator to switch from one instruction to the next one.

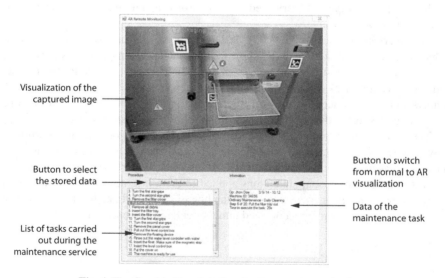

Visualization of the
captured image

Button to switch
from normal to AR
visualization

Button to select
the stored data

Data of the
maintenance task

List of tasks carried
out during the
maintenance service

Fig. 4. The Graphic User Interface for the remote monitoring

Monitoring. The Monitoring Module is a Windows application that runs on a desktop PC. As shown in Figure 4, the application provides a GUI to visualize the pictures, which were automatically taken by the Maintenance Module, and to show all the complementary maintenance data in a textbox. Finally, a button enables the supervisor to switch from the normal to the AR visualization of the picture.

Fig. 5. Maintenance of the machine. The user frames the machine with the tablet (left) and looks at the instruction by means of the tablet (center and right).

4.2 Maintenance Service on a Machine

The case study is a simulation of maintenance service on a machine from food industry. For safety reason, the machine was not installed and operative; all the required utilities (water and electricity) were not plugged. The study regards an ordinary and extra-ordinary maintenance service. As depicted in Figure 5, the user was asked to select the proper operation through the GUI on the tablet and to accomplish it by following the AR instructions. The user involved did not have any experience with the machine.

Figure 6 shows some screenshots during the maintenance simulation. The markers placed on the machine allow the user to move in the environment and to experience

Fig. 6. On the left, the remote user checks the work of the operator. On the right, a screenshot of the interface.

the AR visualization from both a close and a far distance. At the same time, a supervisor, who knows the maintenance tasks of the machine, sits in front of the remote PC and visualizes the user's work. This interface turns out to be a very effective means to check the work and find possible mistakes.

5   Discussion

The case study shows the benefit of the framework to support and monitor maintenance operations. Actually, AR allows avoiding the use of traditional instruction manual and the training of operator on how to perform a correct maintenance. The visualization of the instructions contextualized on the machine makes the operator's work easy, potentially faster and more precise than the one carried out with traditional means. Thus, experts are less required. In addition, the use of AR in maintenance tasks introduces the mobile devices in industrial fields, which can be used also for other purposes. In this case, the mobile device has been used to send information to a remote PC about how the maintenance process is going. Therefore, a company can increase its control on the operator's work and collect the maintenance history of its machines in the factory. For these reasons, the proposed framework meets the expectations about the increase of the effectiveness of maintenance tasks through AR and remote supervision.

The only drawback noticed during the case study is related to the tracking technology used in the AR application. Markers allow having a very stable and precise tracking, but they have to be placed onto the machine and its components. Thus, a time-consuming procedure for fixing and calibrating the markers is required. In addition, the camera must always frame at least one marker to estimate the camera pose. The use of different camera tracking methods, which are not based on markers, can be used in order to overcome the problem. Currently, some methods are able to estimate the pose by means of distinguishable geometrical features that are already present on the mechanical component and the environment without placing any marker. These methods are usually called marker-less or natural features tracking. Examples of the use of these tracking technologies can be found in the automotive field [22] and in the aeronautic maintenance [23].

6   Conclusion

This paper presents a framework for supporting maintenance tasks in industrial environments. The framework provides a method to represent instructions through mobile AR that eases the operator's work. In addition, the framework introduces a new way to monitor the worker. The mobile device, which provides the AR instructions, records information about the performed maintenance steps and it makes them available on a remote PC. Thus, a supervisor can check the maintenance activity from the remote PC.

In the future, new technologies will be integrated in order to provide more advanced tracking and interaction systems. Moreover, the power offered by the cloud computing will be investigated by making the data exchange between the mobile device and the remote PC in both ways. Therefore, the supervisor will be able to collaborate with the operator by sending notes or alerts that will be automatically visible by the operator in the augmented environment.

Acknowledgments. The Authors thank Sealed Air, the Company that kindly provided the industrial machine to perform the case study. The Authors are also grateful to Serena Graziosi, Francesco Furini and Prof. Giorgio Colombo for their support and collaboration during this project.

References

1. Milgram, P., Kishino, F.: A taxonomy of mixed reality visual displays. IEICE Trans. Inf. Syst. E77-D (1994)
2. Azuma, R.: A survey of augmented reality. Presence 6, 355–385 (1997)
3. Fite-Georgel, P.: Is there a reality in Industrial Augmented Reality? In: 10th IEEE International Symposium on Mixed and Augmented Reality (ISMAR), pp. 201–210. IEEE (2011)
4. Davies, P., Sivich, L.: Augmented Reality and other Visualization Technologies for Manufacturing in Boeing. SAE Int. J. Aerosp. 4(2), 1133–1139 (2011)
5. Tang, A., Owen, C., Biocca, F., Mou, W.: Comparative effectiveness of augmented reality in object assembly. In: Proceedings of the Conference on Human Factors in Computing Systems (CHI), pp. 73–80. ACM Press, New York (2003)
6. Henderson, S.J., Feiner, S.: Exploring the benefits of augmented reality documentation for maintenance and repair. IEEE Trans. Vis. Comput. Graph. 17, 1355–1368 (2011)
7. Feiner, S., Macintyre, B., Seligmann, D.: Knowledge-based augmented reality. Commun. ACM. 36, 53–62 (1993)
8. Reiners, D., Stricker, D., Klinker, G., Stefan, M.: Augmented Reality for Construction Tasks: Doorlock Assembly. In: IEEE and ACM International Workshop on Augmented Reality (IWAR), pp. 31–46 (1998)
9. Henderson, S.J., Feiner, S.: Evaluating the benefits of augmented reality for task localization in maintenance of an armored personnel carrier turret. In: 2009 8th IEEE International Symposium on Mixed and Augmented Reality, pp. 135–144. IEEE (2009)
10. Zhu, J., Ong, S.K., Nee, A.Y.C.: An authorable context-aware augmented reality system to assist the maintenance technicians. Int. J. Adv. Manuf. Technol., 1699–1714 (2012)
11. Ong, S.K., Yuan, M.L., Nee, A.Y.C.: Augmented reality applications in manufacturing: A survey. Int. J. Prod. Res. 46, 2707–2742 (2008)
12. Didier, J.-Y., Roussel, D., Mallem, M., Otmane, S., Naudet, S., Pham, Q.-C., Bourgeois, S., Mégard, C., Leroux, C., Hocquard, A.: AMRA: Augmented Reality assistance in train maintenance tasks. In: 4th ACM/IEEE Int. Symp. Mix. Augment. Real. - Work. Ind. Augment. Real., pp. 1–10 (2005)
13. Billinghurst, M., Hakkarainen, M., Woodward, C.: Augmented assembly using a mobile phone. In: Proceedings of the 7th International Conference on Mobile and Ubiquitous Multimedia (MUM), pp. 84–87. IEEE (2008)
14. Klinker, G., Creighton, O., Dutoit, A.H., Kobylinski, R., Vilsmeier, C., Brugge, B.: Augmented maintenance of powerplants: a prototyping case study of a mobile AR system. In: Proceedings IEEE and ACM International Symposium on Augmented Reality, pp. 124–133. IEEE Comput. Soc. (2001)

15. Ishii, H., Shimoda, H., Nakai, T., Izumi, M., Bian, Z., Morishita, Y.: Proposal and Evaluation of a Supporting Method for NPP Decommissioning Work by Augmented Reality. In: 12th World Multi-Conference on Systemics, Cybernetics, pp. 157–162 (2008)
16. Goose, S., Güven, S., Zhang, X., Sudarsky, S., Navab, N.: Paris: Fusing vision-based location tracking with standards-based 3d visualization and speech interaction on a PDA. In: International Conference on Distributed Multimedia Systems, pp. 75–80 (2004)
17. Boulanger, P.: Application of augmented reality to industrial tele-training. In: Proceedings of First Canadian Conference on Computer and Robot Vision, pp. 320–328. IEEE (2004)
18. Reitmayr, G., Eade, E., Drummond, T.W.: Semi-automatic Annotations in Unknown Environments. In: 6th IEEE and ACM International Symposium on Mixed and Augmented Reality, pp. 1–4 (2007)
19. Fite-Georgel, P., Schroeder, P., Navab, N.: Navigation Tools for Viewing Augmented CAD Models. IEEE Comput. Graph. Appl. 29, 65–73 (2009)
20. Wagner, D., Schmalstieg, D.: Artoolkitplus for pose tracking on mobile devices. In: Proceedings of 12th Computer Vision Winter Workshop (CVWW), pp. 139–146 (2007)
21. Agrawala, M., Phan, D., Heiser, J., Haymaker, J., Klingner, J., Hanrahan, P., Tversky, B.: Designing effective step-by-step assembly instructions. In: ACM SIGGRAPH 2003 Papers on - SIGGRAPH 2003, p. 828. ACM Press, New York (2003)
22. Platonov, J., Heibel, H., Meier, P., Grollmann, B.: A mobile markerless AR system for maintenance and repair. In: Proceedings of the 5th IEEE and ACM International Symposium on Mixed and Augmented Reality (ISMAR), pp. 105–108 (2006)
23. De Crescenzio, F., Fantini, M., Persiani, F., Di Stefano, L., Azzari, P., Salti, S.: Augmented Reality for Aircraft Maintenance Training and Operations Support. IEEE Comput. Graph. Appl. 31, 96–101 (2011)

Using VR for Complex Product Design

Loukas Rentzos, Charalampos Vourtsis,
Dimitris Mavrikios, and George Chryssolouris

Laboratory for Manufacturing Systems and Automation,
Dept. of Mechanical Engineering and Aeronautics, University of Patras, Greece
xrisol@lms.mech.upatras.gr

Abstract. Virtual reality is a key technology for the designing of products through complex human-product interactions. This paper deals with the development of a product design method for complex human-product interactions, using the virtual reality (VR) technology. This VR method uses the graph theory in order for the complexity of the designed product to be measured on the basis of human task analysis. The latter is for the purpose of recording and analyzing the human-product interactions within an immersive simulation session. The proposed method undergoes tests in a realistic aerospace case.

Keywords: Product Design, Product Complexity, Immersive Environment, Virtual Prototyping.

1 Introduction

Modern design versions of traditional products (e.g. aircrafts) have become more and more complex due to the constantly growing demand for regulations and standards, imposed by the globalized nature of their associated markets. Most of the products that are being manufactured today have some kind of interaction with humans. It can be considered that the human is the end-user of the product (e.g. airline passenger), or the operator of the product (e.g. aircraft pilot), or the worker involved in its manufacturing (e.g. human worker in aircraft assembly line), or the technician/engineer concerned with the maintenance of the product (e.g. aircraft maintenance tasks). All different aspects of human-product interaction define a vast number of factors that need to be taken into account during product design. Furthermore, some products go through a heavy "automatization" (e.g. commercial aircraft) that further increases the complexity of human-product interaction. Virtual reality is a key enabling technology for designing products with complex human-product interactions. The study presented in this paper aims at developing a product design method for complex human-product interactions through the virtual reality (VR) technology. The latter enables the simulation of human factors during product design, in their full context, with high flexibility and reusability [1], [2]. Furthermore, it provides high levels of flexibility and cost efficiency during the early phases of product design. Since VR enables the simulation of human tasks in full context, it can provide the ideal platform for the measuring of product complexity by analyzing the human tasks, during the usage of products.

R. Shumaker and S. Lackey (Eds.): VAMR 2014, Part II, LNCS 8526, pp. 455–464, 2014.
© Springer International Publishing Switzerland 2014

Product design with the CAD systems available, offers a perception of a 3D model's parameters such as shape, color, kinematics etc., nevertheless, the need for real time human interaction is not satisfied. The VR technology allows engineers/designers to interact, to a great extent, with the 3D model in an immersive environment and enables the testing, experimentation and evaluation of the product in full context. This technology can be considered as an extension to the conventional CAD tools by means of further extending the human integration with the product in its environment. Therefore, the VR technology offers a great added value for use in the early design phases of complex products by means of testing and simulating them. However, a question that arises is whether or not besides testing and simulating a product in a virtual environment, VR can also measure its complexity and provide a useable metric that could support the engineers and designers to improve their design. According to [3], a good design is the one that satisfies all functional requirements with a minimum number of components and relations. In addition, a simple design is preferable to a complex design [4]. Therefore, there is a need that this complexity be minimized during design. A collection of different views has been made to increase the value of perception over the definition of complexity. In product design, from an assembly aspect, the predominant definition of complexity is the interconnection of parts. [5]. The information aspect of complexity suggests that complexity is a measure of the minimum amount of information required to describe the given representation [3, 6]. Complexity could also be stated as a measure of entropy randomness in a design [7] and as a measure of the number of basic operations, required for the solution of a problem [8]. A more generic perspective is that complexity can be defined as an intersection between elements and attributes that complicates the object in general [7]. In [9], a complex system is defined as that comprising a large number of parts interrelating in a non-simple manner. Approaches to reducing complexity can also be found in the literature out of methodologies for the reduction of assembly complexity [5] to approaches leading to product simplification [10].

Complexity measures could be categorized on the basis of what is evaluated, the basis of the measure, the method, as well as the type of measure. Considering the existing complexity measures, the most common types are size, coupling and solvability complexity [11]. Size complexity measures focus on several product elements, including the number of design variables, functional requirements, constraints applied and subassemblies. Size complexity measures are usually developed based on the information that primarily derives from entropic measures of a representation. . The complexity of a design could be measured as the cluster of reduced entropy at each step of the design process, thus a more complex design requires more reduction in entropy. Coupling complexity measures refer to the strength of interconnection among the elements of a design product, problem or process. The representation of the elements measured, needs to be in graph format. Coupling complexity, in most cases, is measured by the decomposability of every graph's representation. Finally, solvability complexity measures indicate whether the product design may be predicted to satisfy the design problem. It is also referred as the difficulty of the design process to result in the final design. Measuring the difficulty, could be stated as the time required for the designing of a product or the number of steps to be followed for its completion.

In [11], a comparison of the complexity measures is presented based on the existing literature. The main variables for this comparison are the focus of complexity evaluation (i.e. design process, design problem, design product), the basis (computational/algorithmic analysis, information based, and traditional design), the focus of measurement (size, coupling and solvability), the interpretation (objective, subjective) and finally, whether an absolute or relative metric has been used.

This paper presents a VR method, developed for complex product design that records and analyzes the human-product interactions within an immersive simulation session and evaluates the product's coupling complexity. The VR framework is based on graph theory methods for the measuring of a product's coupling complexity. The latter is generated automatically, whilst the function structure and bipartite graphs of human-product interactions are analyzed.

2   Complexity Evaluation Method

The coupling complexity measure of a product could be defined as the measurement of interconnections between a product's variables at any level. The coupling measure chosen to be used has been thoroughly described by [12]. The process requires that the design be represented in a graph format, where the tasks are depicted with nodes and are connected with simple lines in order to form dependencies. The method tries to decompose the product's graph representation and thus, the working principle is that any relationships be removed until the graph could be separated into other graph formats in order for the coupling in each of them to be measured. The algorithm (see Fig. 1) aims to decompose the graph to the utmost extent. The graph is being decomposed every time by questioning its connectivity feature. The algorithm for the graph analysis begins with the removal of unary relations and continues with the recording of the remaining variables. After this point, the algorithm keeps applying to all the sub graphs produced from the initial one. The arithmetic record is being kept so as for the interconnectedness of the graph to be measured and finally, conclude to an arithmetic value of the product's coupling complexity.

The current study aims at applying this algorithm inside a virtual environment. The calculation is made on the basis of graphs generated by the interactions performed with the product inside the virtual environment by the human user. The representation method chosen in this case is the function structure graph that seems to be most appropriate for the engineering systems. The function structure graph is a block based diagram, used for the analysis of engineered systems by representing the relations among the different functions of a product (see Fig. 2). The relations to be created for the representation of a problem are described by three basic types, namely Function-Function (F-F), Input-Function (I-F), Function-Output (F-O). These are also referred to as primitive relations (operators) and the building blocks of the graph primitive modules (operands). Complexity is usually correlated with the type of representation. The coupling complexity in a function structure graph is visualized by the interconnectedness of functions in a product.

Eliminate unary relations
Level = 1, **Total** = 0
FOR each (sub)-graph:
    Size = 1
    FOR all combinations of relations in **Size**
        Remove **Size** relations
        Check for separation
        IF Separation = TRUE
            THEN *Mark* relation as removed
    IF no relation removed
        THEN **Size** = **Size** +1 AND *Go* to step 3b
    FOR all relations sets marked
        Find combination of **Sets** → *Remove* "MAX(relations)" AND "Duplicate = FALSE"
    Total – **Total** ı **Level*Size*Sets**
    Level = **Level** +1

Fig. 1. Pseudo-code for bi-partite graph decomposition [11]

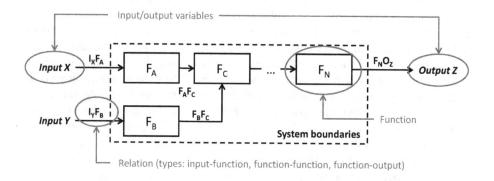

Fig. 2. Function structure example representation [12]

Following the definition of the function structure graph, a bi-partite graph (see Fig. 3) is used as the basis for decomposition. This graph is composed by left and right hand nodes, which are the entities and constraints respectively. The connection lines between them are the relations derived from the function structure graph. In order for the final coupling complexity score to be reached, the bi-partite graph is decomposed, to its fullest extent, into several sub-graphs. Record of the complexity score is kept through the iterative decomposition of equation (1). The index number of the iteration step is the level (l), the minimum number of relations to be removed for a separated sub-graph to be had is the size (s) and the actual number of removed entities is the number (b).

$$\sum_{l=1}^{n} \sum_{l=1}^{n-1} l_n * s_n * b_n \tag{1}$$

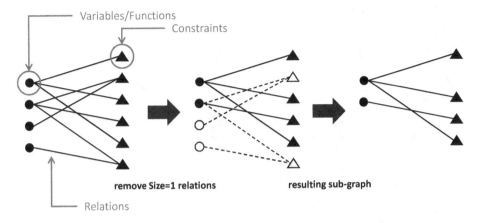

Fig. 3. Bi-partite decomposition method [12]

The coupling complexity of a product design is an aspect of complexity in a design. There are different representations available in literature, besides the various algorithms that can be used for the performance of graph analysis. The method selected for this study relies on the functions involved in the user-product interaction. Function decomposition does not take into account the relationship between the functions, through and input and output associativity, but provides a realistic evaluation of complexity, while remaining less representation-dependent, compared with other methods (e.g. size complexity).

3   VR Design Method

The VR method developed aims at measuring a product's coupling complexity by monitoring the human-product interaction within an immersive virtual environment. The main philosophy of this development in VR is to enable the human user to perform all natural operations and procedures with a product and at the same time to generate the function structure graphs to be used for the evaluation of the complexity of the product at hand. The VR method proposed uses an algorithm developed for the generation of the function structure graph, based on the human user's motion and his interactions (i.e. collisions) with several elements of the virtual product. As depicted in Fig. 4, the architecture of the proposed VR method, implemented for the use-case, described in section 4 of this paper, uses a repository of the product elements in the virtual environment and of the tasks carried out by the human. These repositories are currently used for the generation of the function structure graph and can be replaced by semantic ontologies that will allow for further reasoning to be used and more complex function structure graphs to be generated in a future study. Human motion tracking is performed with 3D objects in the user's virtual hand for the detection of collision with various elements of the product (cockpit).

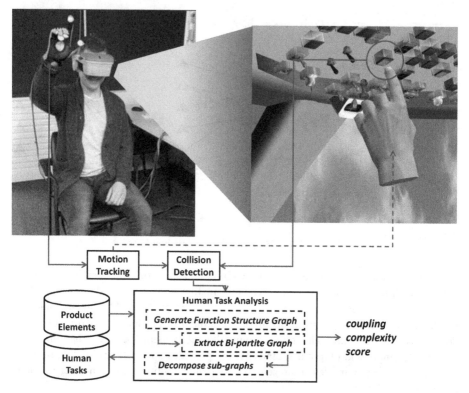

Fig. 4. Architecture of the proposed VR method

The human task analysis (HTA) capabilities are brought about primarily with the user's hierarchical categorization (pilot) inside the virtual environment (cockpit). The input is the task to be performed by the user (e.g. flight procedure performed by the pilot). The HTA module of the VR method starts by generating the function structure graph, based on the elements, which are stored in a repository in the form of an array and the user interacts with. Each component of the product corresponds to a certain functionality.

As far as the function structure graph implementation in VR is concerned, the first thing to be stated is the number and type of every variable to be included in the graph. The function structure graph has three types of variables namely, input, function, and output. Every value considering the graph generation is stored and handled in an array. The array has three corresponding rows, which the variables are stored in. Considering the interactions that the user performs with the virtual environment, the relations are stored in the array. Specifically, according to the users' type of interaction, (hand, eye, camera tracking) the algorithm stores the appropriate types in the input row. The engine recognizes the users' interaction (Boolean check, collision detection TRUE/FALSE, ray cast TRUE/FALSE) with the virtual environment and due to the fact that every element's function is stored in a product element database, the engine stores the elements outcome in the output row. The connections are stored in a similar manner. For example, after collision detection is made with an element, the engine registers the human hand in the first input cell, the human motion in the first function cell and the relation between them, in a format (cell, cell, 1) where the number 1, will be held for the relation statement. The number increases after the first element of the connection is used again. The engine's configuration is to avoid duplication of the input variable. For example, the users' hand variable and the human motion should exist only once, and only after the interaction type is stated as collision detection performed with some kind of human motion. At the same time, the HTA module updates the human tasks repository that is based on the tasks/actions performed by the user in the environment. The human tasks are stored in an array and act as the relations between the human user and the product. A key logger function is able to distinguish and keep track of the user's every element of interaction, in the virtual environment. In addition, the human task repository is also updated for further task evaluation. An array keeps the stored product elements that the user must interact with in order to perform a distinct task hierarchically. In case of error, the user is virtually notified, of the right element to interact with, or in what manner, considering the value set or the kinematic of the element.

After the function structure graph has been generated, the algorithm extracts the bipartite diagram and starts its decomposition. The function structure graph and the bipartite graph are used as the basis for the decomposition algorithm implementation. The first thing to be examined is the way that the function structure graph is generated and in what degree of detail. In order for the complexity results to be accurately compared, the function structure graphs need to be identical.. After the relations between the variables have been stored in the relation row, the next step is to translate the coupling complexity measure algorithm, proposed for graph decomposition in an array handling engine. The algorithm is transformed accordingly so as to handle the arrayed data. Firstly, the third row of the existing table should be reformed into one unique table for the better handling of its elements. The new table comprising three rows should have the address of the first cell in the first row, in the second one, that of the second cell and in the third row the connection number. The implementation described above follows the pseudo-code, presented in section 2 of this paper.

4   Aerospace Use-Case: Aircraft Cockpit

A realistic use-case aerospace industry, specifically that of an aircraft cockpit design, is used for the demonstration of the applicability and value of the VR method developed. Aircraft cockpits are highly complex products with a huge degree of human interaction during all operating conditions. The proposed VR method offers an easy to use way of evaluating the complexity of a cockpit design by performing flight procedures in a virtual environment. The use-case presented is based on a simple procedure so as to extract the necessary data for the evaluation of complexity. The user, in the virtual environment, interacts with the cockpit in order to perform the procedure set. While performing each task, the user is monitored by the VR algorithm, described in the previous section.

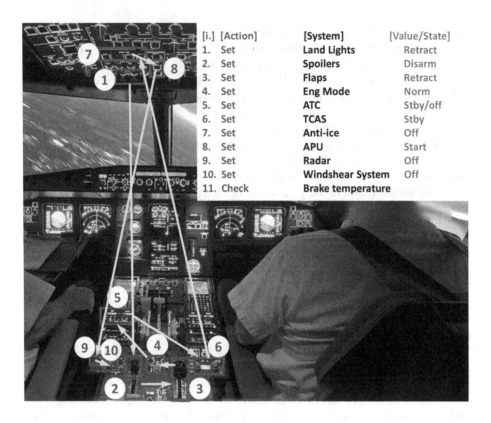

[i.]	[Action]	[System]	[Value/State]
1.	Set	Land Lights	Retract
2.	Set	Spoilers	Disarm
3.	Set	Flaps	Retract
4.	Set	Eng Mode	Norm
5.	Set	ATC	Stby/off
6.	Set	TCAS	Stby
7.	Set	Anti-ice	Off
8.	Set	APU	Start
9.	Set	Radar	Off
10.	Set	Windshear System	Off
11.	Check	Brake temperature	

Fig. 5. Actions performed in cockpit during the "After landing" procedure [13]

The procedure selected for this use-case is an "AFTER LANDING" procedure from the Flight Crew Operations Manual of a commercial airliner. The "AFTER LANDING" procedure is an eleven-task (11) procedure included in the standard operating procedures and is immediately performed after landing (see Fig. 5). It should be mentioned that the procedure was selected among others, due to the high number of the pilots' interactions with several physical objects and the low need for their communicating with air traffic control (ATC). The user during the procedure needs to interact with two levers, three toggle switches, three rotation knobs and one display. The user is expected to interact with the elements in the predefined order and set the necessary values or states. In cases indicated by the task that the user has to interact with a display or checklist, it is considered as the human user is the output variable.

After the procedure has been carried out, the VR method generates the function structure and the corresponding bipartite graph as depicted in Fig. 6. For this particular procedure, the graph consists of two input variables, twelve function variables and eleven output variables. The coupling complexity algorithm yields a score of 46 for this use-case (level=1, size=1, number=2 and level=2, size=2, number 11).

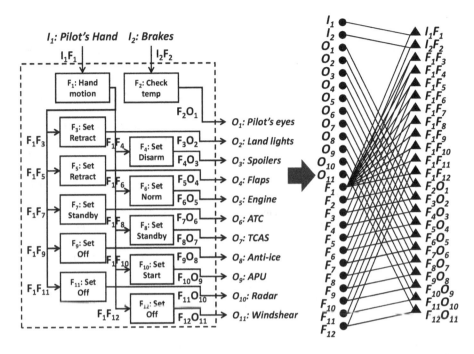

Fig. 6. Function structure graph (left) and bi-partite graph (right) for "after landing" procedure

5   Conclusions

In this paper a VR method for evaluating complex product design is proposed. It enables the evaluation of the complexity by executing the tasks in a natural way. This paper aims at discussing the development and usage of a complexity calculator, in a virtual environment, in order to support the fast and efficient development of the early design product phases. The proposed VR method is implemented on a realistic aerospace use-case. The human user performs a normal flight procedure, in the virtual environment, whilst the tool can calculate the coupling complexity of this particular procedure.

Future study and further enhancement of the VR method presented will consider any additional complexity measurement techniques, used inside a virtual environment, in order for more aspects of product complexity to be evaluated under a single metric. In addition, a semantic implementation of this VR method will allow for advanced reasoning capabilities, during the human task analysis, and will provide the means for increasing the level of detail for the evaluation of complexity.

Acknowledgements. This study was partially supported by the project i-VISION (AAT-2013-605550), funded by the European Commission under the 7th Framework Programme.

References

1. Chryssolouris, G.: Manufacturing Systems: Theory and Practice, 2nd edn., p. 606. Springer, New York (2006)
2. Makris, S., Rentzos, L., Pintzos, G., Mavrikios, D., Chryssolouris, G.: Semantic-based taxonomy for immersive product design using VR techniques. CIRP Annals - Manufacturing Technology 61(1), 147–150 (2012)
3. Suh, N.P.: Theory of complexity, periodicity and the design axioms. Research in Engineering Design - Theory, Applications, and Concurrent Engineering 11(2), 116–131 (1999)
4. Pahl, G., Beitz, W.: Engineering Design: A Systematic Approach. Springer, New York (1996)
5. Boothroyd, G., Dewhurst, P., Knight, W.: Product Design for Manufacture and Assembly. Dekker, New York (2002)
6. Braha, D., Maimon, O.: The measurement of a design structural and functional complexity. IEEE Transactions on Systems, Man, and Cybernetics Part A: Systems and Humans 28(4), 527–535 (1998)
7. El-Haik, B., Yang, K.: The components of complexity in engineering design. IIE Transactions (Institute of Industrial Engineers) 31(10), 925–934 (1999)
8. Ahn, J., Crawford, R.: Complexity analysis of computational engineering design processes. In: Proceedings of the 1994 ASME Design Technical Conferences, Minneapolis, MN, USA, vol. 68, pp. 205–220. American Society of Mechanical Engineers, Design Engineering Division (1994)
9. Simon, H.: The sciences of the artificial. MIT Press, Cambridge (1998)
10. Balazs, M.E., Brown, D.: Design Simplification by Analogical Reasoning. In: Cugini, Wozny (eds.) From Knowledge Intensive CAD to Knowledge Intensive Engineering (2002)
11. Summers, J.D., Shah, J.J.: Mechanical Engineering Design Complexity Metrics: Size, coupling, and solvability. Journal of Mechanical Design, Transactions of the ASME 132(2), 0210041–02100411 (2010)
12. Ameri, F., Summers, J.D., Mocko, G.M., Porter, M.: Engineering design complexity: An investigation of methods and measures. Research in Engineering Design 19(2-3), 161–179 (2008)
13. Airbus Flight Crew Operating Manual A319/A320/A321 Flight Operations 3

Maritime Applications of Augmented Reality – Experiences and Challenges

Uwe von Lukas[1,2], Matthias Vahl[1], and Benjamin Mesing[1]

[1] Fraunhofer Institute for Computer Graphics Research IGD, 18059 Rostock, Germany
{uwe.von.lukas,matthias.vahl,
benjamin.mesing}@igd-r.fraunhofer.de
[2] University of Rostock, Rostock, Germany

Abstract. The paper summarizes experiences from applied research in visual computing for the maritime sector. It starts with initial remarks on Augmented Reality in general and the specific boundary conditions of the maritime industry. The focus is on a presentation of various concrete AR applications that have been implemented for use cases in maritime engineering, production, operation and retrofitting. The paper closes with remarks on future research in this area.

Keywords: Augmented Reality, Mixed Reality, Applied Research, Maritime Industry, Mobile Systems.

1 Introduction and Motivation

In this first section, we will give a short overview of Augmented Reality (AR) systems as well as the maritime sector that forms the application background of our applied research work.

1.1 AR Building Blocks

Augmented Reality can be understood as the confluence of computer graphics and computer vision. Azuma characterizes an AR system by the following three aspects [1]: AR (1) combines real and virtual objects in a real environment, (2) runs interactively and in real time, and finally (3) registers/aligns real and virtual objects with each other. If we translate this characterization from an end user's view to the view of the developer of an AR system, Azuma has identified three major building blocks [2] that are based upon a selection of basic technologies:

- Sensing/Tracking: Determine the position and orientation of the head or a mobile device and follow in real time. This is often done by fusion of various sensors such as cameras, gyroscopic and/or acceleration sensors.
- Registration: Derive real world coordinates as a prerequisite to mix real and virtual objects.
- Augmentation: blending real and virtual images and graphics. This compasses the display and/or visualization techniques.

R. Shumaker and S. Lackey (Eds.): VAMR 2014, Part II, LNCS 8526, pp. 465–475, 2014.

Due to the enormous boost in (mobile) graphics and the upcoming commercial availability of ergonomic AR devices such as the Google Glass, AR has gained outstanding attention – from the research community as well as from the general public.

1.2   Maritime Context

Implementing visual computing technology in the maritime domain differs in various ways from applications in sectors such as automotive, military, medical or cultural heritage. The last mentioned sectors offer the typical application field for prototyping of new interactive IT applications. The high R&D spending of medical, automotive and military companies on the one hand and sectorial funding schemes for cultural heritage especially by the European Commission and other public funding bodies can explain this situation.

Compared to those other sectors, the maritime forms a niche market which is typically characterized by relatively low R&D intensity, many small and medium-sized companies, and a conservative attitude [3]. However, the awareness of the maritime industry as an important economy is constantly rising. Individual sectors cover a broad range from cruise tourism over offshore oil and gas to fishery and seaborne transport. This can be underpinned by the following quote from the European Commission in their Blue Growth strategy [4]: "If we count all economic activities that depend on the sea, then the EU's blue economy represents 5.4 million jobs and a gross added value of just under €500 billion per year. In all, 75% of Europe's external trade and 37% of trade within the EU is seaborne."

Beside those economical differences, there are also various technical differences we have to cope with when implementing IT solutions for the maritime sector. Those bounding conditions are incompletely described as follows:

- We typically find harsh environments where mobile applications are faced with water and pressure (in underwater settings), dust and flying sparks (shipyards), splash water, extreme temperatures and heavy movements due to waves (aboard a ship).
- For underwater applications, we need to consider the specific physical effects such as refraction, deflection and attenuation that affect optical tracking as well as the registration process and visualization [5]. Color correction and distortion correction must be integrated into the AR solutions.
- Connectivity to networks such as a global navigation satellite system (e.g. GPS) or wireless data networks (3G) is sometimes limited or completely shielded on open sea and under water. Satcom networks are much more expensive and acoustic underwater communication is offering only a quite small bandwidth and high delay.
- A ship is not fixed but will roll, pitch and yaw. So – depending on the use case – we have to determine the movement of the ship relative to the earth and the movement of a person (or device) relative to the ship.
- The dockyard hall as well as the outer hull of a ship and even internal structures such as pipes and frames are quite uniform and offer quite few characteristic visual

features. When we just see a detail of the overall structure, it is often impossible to identify the correct position of the clipping.

- Ships can be quite big – not only in terms of physical dimension but also in terms of data volume. We can roughly estimate that a large ship has 10 times more parts than a plane and 100 times more parts than a car.
- Furthermore, there are some economical or organizational specialties to mention:

  – Ships or offshore installations are not built in large volumes but as unique copies or a small series of two to five ships. The economy of scales is hard to reach here.
  – The design systems used in the maritime industry are very production-focused. There are various CAD systems that are only used in the maritime industry, maybe in plant design, but nowhere else. The native APIs and data formats demand a very specific know-how when interfacing with this IT environment.

1.3   Related Work

Plenty of work has been done in various applications fields of AR (ref. Fig. 1). Most of the publications present research in medical training or assistance [6, 7, 8], the automotive sector [9], aerospace industry [9, 10]. Not as widespread but also visible in the research community is work in ambient assisted living [11], architecture and civil engineering [12]. A new trend is AR in production in the context of Industry 4.0 and Cyber Physical Systems [13, 14].

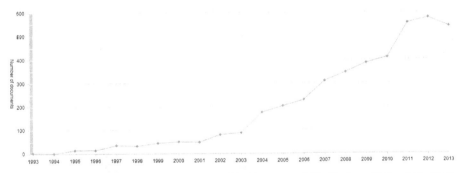

Fig. 1. Number of scientific publications with "Augmented Reality" or "Mixed Reality" in article title, abstract or keywords. (Source: Scopus; generated February 2014)

Those publications show that a large number of use cases has been addressed by (prototypic) AR systems. However, it is nearly impossible to easily transfer those systems to other sectors. All those solutions are designed to support a very limited task and do not offer the flexibility to adapt to similar settings. Most of the applications need a controlled environment in respect to lighting conditions or fast movements. And even their limited scope is the result of a time-consuming development process. So we can observe that there are just very few commercial applications of AR outside R&D.

From those findings we can argue that it is still necessary to concentrate on a particular domain to develop AR systems that fulfill the needs of a certain community with their bounding conditions.

There is a small number of publications that explicitly address maritime use cases of Augmented Reality. Among them we find navigation and watchkeeping and naval warfare [15-19], maintenance of ships [20], diver support [21], ship production [22], and two surveys [23,24].

2   Our Examples

The following Augmented Reality applications in different phases of the lifecycle have been developed by Fraunhofer IGD so far:

2.1   Sales and Marketing

Use Case. Especially in the maritime domain, AR still is an eye catcher at trade fairs or show rooms. Such an application neither has to be integrated into the existing IT environment nor does it has to support a complex process. For this reason, projects with sales and marketing often serve as a "door opener" to introduce Virtual or Augmented Reality in a company. In our project, a tablet PC is used to support the sales process for the retrofitting of ships. The tablet serves as a window to the "future" and shows the customer what his or her ship could look like with a new generation of rescue boats and davits. It is designed not for the real world, so we used large posters to visualize a cruise liner. The end user can choose between different augmentations: the new davit plus rescue boat in parking position, in swing-out position and with additional dimensions.

Fig. 2. AR application for the retrofitting of rescue boats and davits

Challenges. There have not been any specific challenges of the maritime sector due to the setting at a booth of a trade fair. The challenge here was to implement an application that is very robust, working with different lighting conditions and easy to use for the visitors without explanations.

Implementation Aspects. The application made use of Fraunhofer IGDs framework for mobile AR applications [25]. This speeds up the authoring phase and generates the content that will be read in by the player running on an iPhone or iPad and implementing markerless optical tracking – in our case with a poster tracker.

2.2   Product validation

Use Case. A kinematic simulation has been introduced in the design process to validate the model of a davit. To support confidence in the simulation, we implemented an AR application where the simulation was used as an overlay to real video of a physical acceptance trial. An animated wireframe model of the davit is rendered into the real video with the correct viewpoint [26].

Challenges. The challenging part of this project has been the poor video quality of the test trial and the fact that the small partnering company did not have much experience with 3D CAD, simulation and data exchange. These two challenges are not unique to the maritime sector but quite typical from our experience.

Implementation Aspects. We used a marker for a first pose estimation and then utilized the available CAD model for fine registration. The visualization was implemented with our VR/AR framework instantReality [27].

Fig. 3. The processing pipeline: (a) Original video frame; (b) extracted visible edges from the CAD model; (c) Extracted edges from the image; (d) Augmentation with control and corresponding hit points

2.3   Design and Production

Use Case. As already mentioned above, shipbuilding is characterized by a highly parallel process of design and production: Some parts of the ship are still in a very early design stage while other parts are already built. Similar requirements arise from late changes that can be demanded by the customer or stem from other disruptions in the process such as wrong dimension of delivered supply parts or significant deviations in production steps such as welding.

A specific use case is the design of pipes in the context of a bundle of existing pipes. Fitting pipes can be designed in physical context using an AR application where start and endpoint of the pipe can be selected [28].

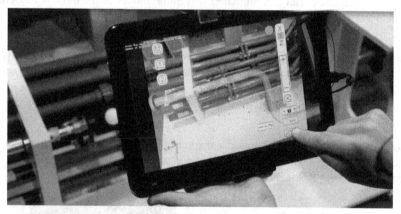

Fig. 4. Mobile design application for pipe design in the physical context

Challenges. In this production-oriented use case, we have had to fulfill very high accuracy demands of the customer. The system is intended to send the design parameters of the pipes directly to the production department without additional post-processing.

Implementation Aspects. Without additional aids, we could not reach the necessary accuracy. A measurement tool with two illuminating points was used to align virtual straight pipe segments in such a way that they fit exactly through existing bolt holes.

2.4   Harbour Surveillance

Use Case. For harbor surveillance, the operator today typically has to switch between map view with radar and AIS information of ship tracks on the one hand and different video cameras on the other hand. Our objective with introducing AR in context of the Seatrax project is to bring both worlds together: For example the operator can look at the video system to instantly get all information about a vessel by touching on the ship, or she can start a radio call instantly.

This video mode offers the classical camera view – but augmented with annotation on every vessel with its name and optional meta data from the Vessel Tracking System (VTS). Using the *follow-me* function, the operator can stick the camera to a ship, and the camera automatically follows the ship. Also buoys, lights, navigation aids and sea marks are drawn as overlay into the video stream on the right position in the right scale and correct perspective.

Besides the AR mode, the system should offer a second mode to the operator: the virtual model mode. This mode presents a nautical map and/or a static 3D harbor model augmented with dynamic ship models as representation of vessels in the real world. Parametric VR ship models for different AIS ship types (e.g. fishing, towing, tug, pilot) will be adapted in length and breadth gained from the VTS. In this mode, the *bridge view* function allows to "jump" to any ship's bridge. In this way, the operator has the same viewpoint as the captain and can check sight conditions. The other function in the virtual model mode is the *bird's view* function to get an overview.

Fig. 5. Augmented harbor scene: (left) real video mode, (right) virtual model mode

Challenges. There have been three big challenges in the project: Firstly, the camera mechanic. For controlling the surveillance camera of Funkwerk, we used the MULTISEC protocol. Whereas the pan and tilt of the camera housing of Funkwerk is very precise (tenth degree), the built-in zoom mechanic is very slippery. The lens system has a hysteresis, so that the same input value leads to a different zoom factor depending on the zooming direction. This was solved by introducing discrete zoom steps.

Secondly, the correction of the lens distortion. The radial distortion of the lens is minimal. But the optical center (also known as principal point) is not in the center of the lens as assumed by most synthetic camera models. This is a big problem because we need to precisely synchronize the real camera with a virtual one. The camera model of the VRML standard does not regard this parameter. Our AR framework instant Reality [33] allows to set this parameter and provides an extended camera model on top of the VRML standard.

Thirdly, we had to cope with the delay given by the irregularity period of the AIS signals (10 sec. up to 10 min.). Ships' AIS transmitters send AIS signals depending on different circumstances, e.g. their speed over ground, the current rate of turn, the availability of free time slots at the broadcast frequency. Assuming that a ship has a big inertia of mass, we implemented a simple linear interpolation. As an alternative position source, the system is able to connect with VTS to make use of the exact and frequently updated position derived from radar information.

Implementation Aspects. We developed a C# application connected with the AR framework instantReality via its' EAI (External Authoring Interface) and different connectors to the camera, to AIS and VTS as well as to an AIS simulation. The solution consequently uses a 3D world to correctly place and scale the sign posts with the ship name and additional information. The user can control the cameras via pan, tilt, zoom and focus, and the camera parameters of the augmentation will always mimic the current settings of the real camera. Pan, tilt, zoom and focus commands will be propagated to both the real camera and the virtual camera synchronously.

3   Discussion

Compared to AR applications in other areas, the maritime sector obviously raises some additional challenges. First of all, we have to find a solution for registration and tracking. The ship hull or the water shields GPS signals, so we have to rely on alternative technologies for an initial position. For practical reasons, optical tracking should not be based on markers but use implicit features. However, in many areas of the ship we find very similar objects such as long pipes or steel plates. So we need additional sensors and adequate sensor fusion to determine the user's pose. Outside the shipyard, we have a ship with a 6 DOF movement which makes the tracking problem even harder.

In sectors with mass products, we have high-quality 3D models from the design phase that are nearly 100% equivalent to the physical product. The digital 3D model of a ship from the engineering department will typically not cover all details or late changes due to complications in production or varying supplier parts. Furthermore, the virtual ship and the real ship will depart even more in operation with every part replaced during repair and overhaul. But without a correct 3D model, many AR applications are hard to implement in a robust way.

Mobile AR systems with integrated optical 3D reconstruction have the potential to replace the expensive process of laser scanning in some areas: e.g. they can be used to collect all the geometric information for detailed planning of a retrofit project for ballast water treatment.

Future AR applications also address underwater scenarios such as diver assistance for control and repair operations at the rudder or propeller. For those kinds of applications, we have to solve all the physical challenges of underwater settings such as optical refraction, challenging light situations and marine snow resulting in extreme noisy images.

4   Summary and Outlook

Augmented Reality is a promising approach to support users in many different situations. Specific AR applications for maritime use cases have to cope with a bunch of technical and economic challenges. Those challenges do not only affect the feasibility but also the business case for commercial usage. However, the increasing importance of the sea as the backbone of worldwide transport, the premier location for regenerative energy, a supplier of food for a growing world population, motivates (applied) research in this area.

In this article, we have presented several examples of AR applications that have been developed for end users in different sectors of the maritime industry. We have demonstrated that we can already find technical solutions for most of the difficult bounding conditions.

But there is still a long way to go: Additional research is necessary to prepare the ground for a further dispersion of AR in all sectors of maritime industry. The following topics are on our R&D roadmap:

Efficient authoring of AR content is a pre-condition for stakeholders in a market that is characterized by SME and the lack of economies of scale. Our tools that rely on available material such as manuals [25] or CAD data [29] are a first step in this direction.

Robust optical tracking – even under very poor conditions (e.g. underwater) – needs different steps of correcting the different physical effects such as color cast [30] or noise that would hinder a feature correspondence algorithm to work correctly.

Precise inship tracking is an important building block for nearly all AR use cases during operation of a ship. Here, we rely on fusion of various sensors with promising first results [31].

Cyber physical equivalence is our placeholder for a bundle of technologies that are needed within the context of Augmented Shipbuilding. It is about a continuous mutual alignment of the virtual world and the real world. A first small example of a 3D discrepancy check via AR in the outfitting phase was demonstrated successfully [32] but has to be extended to much larger volumes, must be seamlessly integrated into the environment and must be more flexible to be adaptive to similar scenarios.

Acknowledgements. Some of the work presented here has been funded by the German Federal Ministry Economics and Technology upon decision of the German Bundestag in context of the projects POWER-VR and eKon. Additional support has been given by grants of the Ministry of Economics, Construction and Tourism of the state of Mecklenburg-Vorpommern. The project Seatrax was realized on behalf of Signalis GmbH.

References

1. Azuma, R., Baillot, Y., Behringer, R., Feiner, S., Julier, S., MacIntyre, B.: Recent advances in augmented reality. IEEE Computer Graphics and Applications 21(6), 34–47 (2001)

2. Azuma, R.: A Survey of Augmented Reality. Presence: Teleoperators and Virtual Environments 6(4), 355–385 (1997)
3. Perunovic, Z., Vidic, J.: Innovation in the Maritime Industry. In: Correa, H., College, R. (eds.) Proceedings of the 22nd Anual POM Conference: Operations Management: The Enabling Link, Reno, Nevada, U.S.A, April 29-May 2 (2011)
4. Blue Growth - Opportunities for marine and maritime sustainable growth Communication from the Commission to the European Parliament, the Council, the European Economic and Social Committee and the Committee of the Regions COM(2012) 494 final. European Union (2012)
5. Dolereit, T., Kuijper, A.: Converting Underwater Imaging into Imaging in Air. In: VISAPP 2014 - Proceedings of the International Conference on Computer Vision Theory and Applications, vol. 1, pp. 96–103 (2014)
6. Abhari, K., Baxter, J.S.H., Chen, E.S., Khan, A.R., Wedlake, C., Peters, T., Eagleson, R., de Ribaupierre, S.: The role of augmented reality in training the planning of brain tumor resection. In: Liao, H., Linte, C.A., Masamune, K., Peters, T.M., Zheng, G. (eds.) MIAR/AE-CAI 2013. LNCS, vol. 8090, pp. 241–248. Springer, Heidelberg (2013)
7. Sonntag, D., Zillner, S., Schulz, C., Weber, M., Toyama, T.: Towards medical cyber-physical systems: Multimodal augmented reality for doctors and knowledge discovery about patients. In: Marcus, A. (ed.) DUXU/HCII 2013, Part III. LNCS, vol. 8014, pp. 401–410. Springer, Heidelberg (2013)
8. De Paolis, L., Pulimeno, M., Aloisio, G.: An Augmented Reality Application for Minimally Invasive Surgery. In: Katashev, A., Dekthyar, Y., Spigulis, J. (eds.) 14th Nordic-Baltic Conference on Biomedical Engineering and Medical Physics. Springer, Heidelberg (2008)
9. Regenbrecht, H., Baratoff, G., Wilke, W.: Augmented Reality Projects in the Automotive and Aerospace Industries. IEEE Computer Graphics and Applications 25(6), 48–56 (2005)
10. Crescenzio, F.D., Fantini, M., Persiani, F., Stefano, L.D., Azzari, P., Salti, S.: Augmented Reality for Aircraft Maintenance Training and Operations Support. IEEE Computer Graphics and Applications 31(1), 96–101 (2011)
11. Kaufmann, H.: From where we sit: Augmented reality for an active ageing European society. Journal of Cyber Therapy and Rehabilitation 5(1), 35–37
12. Chi, H.-L., Kang, S.-C., Wang, X.: Research trends and opportunities of augmented reality applications in architecture, engineering, and construction. Automation in Construction 33, 116–122 (2013)
13. Ong, S.K., Yuan, M.L., Nee, A.Y.C.: Augmented reality applications in manufacturing: A survey. International Journal of Production Research 46(10) (2008)
14. Nee, A.Y.C., Ong, S.K.: Virtual and Augmented Reality Applications in Manufacturing. In: Manufacturing Modelling, Management, and Control, vol. 7, Part1. IFAC PapersOnline (2013)
15. Filipkowski, D.: See More – Analysis of Possibilities of Implementation AR Solutions During Bridge Watchkeeping. In: Weintrit, A. (ed.) Marine Navigation and Safety of Sea Transportation, pp. 255–260. CRC Press (2013)
16. Hugues, O., Cieutat, J.M., Guitton, P.: An experimental augmented reality platform for assisted maritime navigation. In: Proceedings of the 1st Augmented Human International Conference (AH 2010). ACM, New York (2010)
17. Zysk, T., Luce, J., Cunningham, J.: Augmented reality precision navigation. GPS World, North Coast Media LLC (June 2012)
18. Haase, K., Koch, R.: AR Binocular - Augmented Reality System for nautical navigation. In: Workshop on Mobile and Embedded Interactive Systems. LNI, pp. 295–300. Springer, Heidelberg (2008)

19. Moulis, G., Bouchet, A.: A collaborative approach of augmented reality for maritime domain. In: Proceedings of the 2012 Virtual Reality International Conference (VRIC 2012). ACM, New York (2012)
20. Lee, J., Lee, K., Kim, K., Kim, D., Kim, J.: AR-based ship design information supporting system for pipe maintenance. Paper presented at the 11th International Symposium on Practical Design of Ships and Other Floating Structures, PRADS 2010, 1, pp. 607–612 (2010)
21. Morales-Garcia, R., Keitler, P., Maier, P., Klinker, G.: An Underwater Augmented Reality System for Commercial Diving Operations. In: OCEANS 2009, MTS/IEEE Biloxi - Marine Technology for Our Future: Global and Local Challenges (2009)
22. Matsuo, K., Rothenburg, U., Stark, R.: Application of AR Technologies to Sheet Metal Forming in Shipbuilding. In: Abramovici, M., Stark, R. (eds.) Smart Product Engineering. Proceedings of the 23rd CIRP Design Conference, pp. 937–945. Springer, Heidelberg (2013)
23. Vasiljević, A., Borović, B., Vukić, Z.: Augmented Reality in Marine Applications. In: Brodogradnja, vol. 62(2). Brodarski Institute d.o.o (2011)
24. von Lukas, U.: Virtual and augmented reality for the maritime sector – applications and requirements. In: 8th IFAC Conference on Control Applications in Marine Systems CAMS 2010, Rostock-Warnemünde, Germany, IFAC-PapersOnline (2010)
25. Engelke, T., Keil, J., Rojtberg, P., Wientapper, F., Webel, S., Bockholt, U.: Content first - A concept for industrial augmented reality maintenance applications using mobile devices. In: 2013 IEEE International Symposium on Mixed and Augmented Reality (ISMAR), October 1-4, pp. 251–252 (2013)
26. Mesing, B., König, C.R., von Lukas, U., Tietjen, T., Vinke, A.: Virtual Prototyping of Davits with Parameterized Simulation Models and Virtual Reality. In: Bertram, V. (ed.) Proceedings of the 11th International Conference on Computer and IT Applications in the Maritime Industries (COMPIT 2012), pp. 336–343. Technische Universität Hamburg-Harburg, Hamburg (2012)
27. Fellner, D., Behr, J., Bockholt, U.: Instantreality - A Framework for Industrial Augmented and Virtual Reality Applications. In: Ma, D., Fan, X., et al. (eds.) The 2nd Sino-German Workshop Virtual Reality & Augmented Reality in Industry, pp. 91–99. Springer, Heidelberg (2009)
28. Olbrich, M., Wuest, H., Riess, P., Bockholt, U.: Augmented reality pipe layout planning in the shipbuilding industry. In: 2011 10th IEEE International Symposium on Mixed and Augmented Reality (ISMAR), October 26-29, pp. 269–270 (2011)
29. Mesing, B., von Lukas, U.: Authoring of Automatic Data Preparation and Scene Enrichment for maritime Virtual Reality Applications. In: Shumaker, R. (ed.) Human-Computer Interaction, Part II, HCII 2014. LNCS, vol. 8526, pp. 426–434. Springer, Heidelberg (2014)
30. Bieber, G., Haescher, M., Vahl, M.: Sensor requirements for activity recognition on smart watches. In: ACM International Conference on Pervasive Technologies Related to Assistive Environments (PETRA). ACM, New York (2013)
31. Kahn, S., Wuest, H., Stricker, D., Fellner, D.W.: 3D discrepancy check via Augmented Reality", Mixed and Augmented Reality (ISMAR). In: 2010 9th IEEE International Symposium, October 13-16, pp. 241–242. IEEE (2010)

Author Index